ALSO BY RAYMOND ARSENAULT

The Wild Ass of the Ozarks: Jeff Davis and the Social Bases of Southern Politics

St. Petersburg and the Florida Dream, 1888–1950

Crucible of Liberty: 200 Years of the Bill of Rights (editor)

The Changing South of Gene Patterson: Journalism and Civil Rights, 1960–1968
(coeditor with Roy Peter Clark)

Paradise Lost? The Environmental History of Florida
(coeditor with Jack E. Davis)

Freedom Riders: 1961 and the Struggle for Racial Justice
(2006; abridged edition 2011)

*The Sound of Freedom: Marian Anderson, the Lincoln Memorial,
and the Concert That Awakened America*

Dixie Redux: Essays in Honor of Sheldon Hackney
(coeditor with Orville Vernon Burton)

Arthur Ashe: A Life

The Long Civil War: New Explorations of America's Enduring Conflict
(coeditor with John David Smith)

John Lewis

BLACK LIVES

———

Yale University Press's Black Lives series seeks to tell the fullest range of stories about notable and overlooked Black figures who profoundly shaped world history. Each book is intended to add a chapter to our larger understanding of the breadth of Black people's experiences as these have unfolded through time. Using a variety of approaches, the books in this series trace the indelible contributions that individuals of African descent have made to their worlds, exploring how their lives embodied and shaped the changing conditions of modernity and challenged definitions of race and practices of racism in their societies.

John Lewis

IN SEARCH OF THE BELOVED COMMUNITY

Raymond Arsenault

Black Lives

Yale University Press | New Haven and London

The Black Lives series is supported with a gift from
the Germanacos Foundation.
Published with assistance from Jonathan W. Leone, Yale '86.

Yale University Press books may be purchased in quantity
for educational, business, or promotional use. For information,
please e-mail sales.press@yale.edu (U.S. office) or
sales@yaleup.co.uk (U.K. office).

Set in Freight Text by Westchester Publishing Services, Danbury, CT.
Printed in the United States of America.

Library of Congress Control Number: 2023935308
ISBN 978-0-300-25375-7 (hardcover: alk. paper)

A catalogue record for this book is available from the British Library.

This paper meets the requirements of ANSI/NISO Z39.48-1992
(Permanence of Paper).

10 9 8 7 6 5 4 3 2

To Dr. Bernard LaFayette Jr.—

and to my beloved grandchildren,

Lincoln and Poppy Powers

CONTENTS

———

CONTENTS

PREFACE

———

THIS BOOK—the first attempt to write a comprehensive biography of John Lewis—deals primarily with his public life, though it also tries to recapture the most important elements of his private experiences. Like most biographers, I am interested not only in his public activities—his successes and failures, and his impact on the world around him—but also in the personal and interior aspects of his life story. While realizing no historian or biographer can ever know everything there is to know about a historical figure, I hope my research and writing reveal certain truths about his thoughts, feelings, and character. Lewis has long been widely acknowledged as a great man, a nonviolent warrior intent on bringing social justice and racial equality to a nation beset by prejudice and more than two centuries of broken promises to its most vulnerable citizens. But what forces and influences set him apart from the rest of us? How did he become a man capable of inspiring millions with his commitment to democracy and freedom—with his ennobling ideas about forgiveness, reconciliation, and an ideal society he called the Beloved Community?

Finding the answers to these questions must begin with gaining a historical perspective on his identity as an African American born in Alabama in the mid-twentieth century. Just below the surface of Lewis's iconic public persona was a living, breathing human being, a man descended from generations of men and women who endured the horrors of slavery and its aftermath. Both the text and context of his life, public as well as private, emerged from a litany of historical injustices born of a racial dilemma that has long lain at the heart of the American experiment. The rise of a mass movement intent on challenging this dark reality is the broad story I want to tell. But fully understanding Lewis's part in it—how he helped to create a movement that altered the trajectory of the civil rights struggle—will require many pages of exploration and careful deliberation.

Maintaining a healthy level of scholarly detachment is always a challenge when writing about an admirable figure like Lewis. But it is especially difficult when the author both knows the subject personally and shares many of his beliefs. This is the situation I faced as I strove to maintain a critical edge that fostered a balanced view of Lewis's life. My intention throughout has been to avoid hagiography and hero worship, telling Lewis's full story with all of its ups and downs intact. The result, I hope, is a realistic and nuanced interpretation of one of the most intriguing figures of our time.

I first met Lewis during the fall of 2000 in his Washington congressional office—a comfortable but cluttered room filled with books, historical photographs, and civil rights memorabilia. Though excited, I didn't know quite what to expect. As a veteran historian of the civil rights movement, I already knew about the basis of his fame—about his bravery as a Freedom Rider in 1961, his speech at the March on Washington in 1963, and his courageous march across the Edmund Pettus Bridge in Selma, Alabama, two years later. But I wondered what he would be like as a human being. Would he be gracious and generous with his time, giving me the full, hour-long interview I had requested? Or would he be cold and formal, perhaps even dismissive?

The answer came almost immediately, as the congressman smiled and extended his hand, asking me politely why I wanted to write a book about the Freedom Rides. Over the next hour his warmth and openness washed over me, putting me completely at ease. He not only answered all of my questions, many of which he had undoubtedly been asked hundreds of times in the past; he also assured me that he genuinely valued truth-telling history—that he wanted to see the true story of the Freedom Rides shared with as much of the world as possible. As he once explained, he believed it is imperative to "study and learn the lessons of history because humanity has been involved in this soul-wrenching existential struggle for a very long time." I knew, of course, that in 1998 he had published a highly acclaimed autobiography, *Walking with the Wind: A Memoir of the Movement*, for which he later received the 2006 Roosevelt-Wilson Award presented by the American Historical Association to recognize "public service to the discipline of history."[1]

The interview went well, and before we had finished he even recruited me to help him contact the hundreds of Freedom Riders he wanted to invite to an upcoming fortieth reunion, to which I was also invited. By the time I left his office we had become friends, drawn together by both emotional and intellectual ties. Thus began a twenty-year friendship, a gift that afforded me numerous opportunities to observe him "up close and personal." The more I saw of him, the more I came to appreciate his depth and character. He was, without a doubt, a man of uncommon decency and almost breathtaking moral courage. Not only did he live up to his reputation for greatness, but he did so without a hint of pretense or self-absorption. Early on, when I made the mistake of addressing him as Congressman Lewis, he waved me off with a gentle admonition: "Just call me John. Everyone does."

There was a quiet shyness about him that magnified his charm. To my surprise, he had a soft conversational voice that contrasted with the soaring oratory he often displayed in the public arena. He also had a slight but noticeable speech impediment that, combined with a thick Southern drawl, gave him an air of vulnerability. But, as he told the press on several occasions, he was primarily a man of action, not of words. While many of his admirers found him to be eloquent, he thought of himself as "a tugboat, not a showboat."[2] This unprepossessing self-image was consistent with his physical appearance: his short stature, his stocky body, and his clean-shaven head bearing the marks of beatings suffered during his movement years. Lewis's most revealing feature, however, was his dark brown, penetrating eyes; it was there that one sensed the enormous energy driving his spirit. As the journalist Milton Viorst noted after interviewing Lewis in the mid-1970s, "beneath his unassertive manner lay a fierce inner zeal, which gave him incredible courage and inflexible will."

He could be dramatic and animated, especially when talking about civil or human rights—or more mundanely when he confessed his love of simple pleasures such as freshwater fishing and sweet potato pie. Yet he never seemed flustered or diverted from what he wanted to say or do. Even in highly stressful situations, he was always calm and collected, as if guided by an inner peace grounded in faith and tolerance. This poise allowed him to make decisions, large and small, in accordance with his principles and not as reactions forged in the heat of the moment. "I learned early on to pace my-self," Lewis once remarked in an attempt to explain his personal style—his "curious mixture of manners and militancy," as the journalist John Egerton put it. He recalled: "I felt we were involved in a lifetime struggle—hard, tedious, continuous. There were disappointments, but I had faith that con-tinued pressure and pushing would pay off. . . . You have to have a sense of hope to survive. I didn't give up. I didn't become bitter or become engulfed in hatred. That's just not a part of me."

I witnessed one telling example of this in 2011, when I visited his office as part of a design team that hoped he would sponsor a multi-million-dollar earmark appropriation for an expansion of the Freedom Rides Museum in Montgomery, Alabama. Dressed in suits and ties, looking like an official dele-gation with serious matters to discuss, we arrived at the appointed time. Yet the congressman made us wait for more than an hour before escorting us into his office. The reason for the delay was his promise to help a fourteen-year-old boy from Ohio with a National History Day school project on the history of Black voting rights. The day's schedule had gotten backed up, but Lewis was not about to short-change the boy. He had promised to give him an hour of his time, and no inconvenience for a delegation of adults, no matter how important they might be, was going to prevent him from following through with his promise. In my experience, he always treated everyone—regardless of age, or race, or gender, or social status—with the same respect and consideration. Equal treatment was vitally important to him—not just under the law but in all aspects of everyday life.

Later that same year, in May 2011, I was privileged to witness a second incident that revealed the depth of Lewis's commitment to equity and fair-ness. This time the essential values expressed were forgiveness, compassion, and reconciliation. Fifty years earlier, on May 9, 1961, Lewis and the other twelve original Freedom Riders traveling from Washington to New Orleans encountered violent resistance for the first time. As soon as they arrived at the Greyhound bus terminal in the upcountry South Carolina mill town of Rock Hill, Lewis and two other Freedom Riders were assaulted by a gang of mostly young Klansmen. Lewis was punched and kicked, suffering bruised ribs and cuts around his eyes and mouth and a deep gash on the back of his head. This was his first serious beating at the hands of white supremacist vigilantes, and he never forgot it. Nor did one of his attackers, Elwin Wilson, a rough-cut twenty-four-year-old with malice and racial hatred in his heart and mind.

Years later, after witnessing profound changes in the post–civil rights South, Wilson found religion, relinquished his racial animus, and left the Klan. But even after aging into his seventies, he still felt guilty about the part he had played in the Rock Hill assault on Lewis and the Freedom Riders. He felt a strong need to apologize to Lewis in particular, and in 2009 he got his chance. After spotting Lewis on television, sitting on the 2009 inauguration grandstand in the row behind President Barack Obama, Wilson steeled his nerves and contacted Lewis by phone to offer a tearful apology for what he had done. Lewis accepted the apology, of course, and for most aggrieved individuals that would have been the end to it. But not with Lewis, now a congressional leader renowned for his belief in forgiveness, generosity, and justice. Inviting Wilson to his office in Washington, he embraced his former tormentor and adversary as a friend and wept with him as they joyously prayed for redemption.

Two years later, during the fiftieth anniversary celebration of the Freedom Rides, the two men met again, this time as guests on *The Oprah Winfrey Show*. After learning about Wilson's belated apology, the show's producers thought they had the perfect guest to represent the theme of reconciliation—if this frail and enfeebled man could hold it together long enough to tell his story in front of millions of viewers. Sitting just off camera to Lewis's right, I saw the look of fear and bewilderment on Wilson's face and worried there was no way he would make it through a stressful, live interview. After Oprah posed her first question, Wilson stammered nervously and then retreated into silence, appearing to be on the verge of fleeing the stage—until Lewis smiled and leaned toward him. Reaching out to comfort him, the seventy-one-year-old congressman gently held Wilson's right hand and declared in a voice loud enough for everyone in the studio to hear, "He's my brother." Among the nearly 180 Freedom Riders gathered in the Chicago studio audience— all of whom knew they had just witnessed a powerful expression of the compassionate, Beloved Community Lewis spoke about so often—there was not a dry eye to be seen.[3]

These two incidents—Lewis's respectful treatment of a young boy seeking information on civil rights history, and his compassionate rescue of an aging ex-Klansman—are not the most dramatic stories of Lewis's long and eventful life. Yet as micro-narratives of his approach to ethical and moral challenges, they give us glimpses of his inner self. Along with countless other human interactions between him and other individuals—some of which will be discussed in the chapters of this book—they reveal an important dimension of his psyche and moral sensibility.

Lewis was called many things during his lifetime—ranging from radical troublemaker and starry-eyed idealist to saint and civil rights icon—and there was undoubtedly a measure of truth in each of these characterizations. Yet no single label does justice to the fullness of his remarkable life. Like the rest of us, he was capable of contradiction, and of making mistakes and misjudgments. But he was by no means an ordinary person. In company with a small number of other transcendent historical figures—Martin Luther King Jr., Frederick Douglass, and Harriet Tubman, to cite three examples— Lewis became inextricably bound with the promise of freedom and democracy. The meaning of his life, rooted as it was in his passionate determination to replace the horrors of the past and present with the future blessings of a Beloved Community, is worth pondering in a nation still struggling to fulfill its professed ideal of liberty and justice for all.

ABBREVIATIONS

———

ABT	American Baptist Theological Seminary
ACAHR	Atlanta Committee on Appeal for Human Rights
ACLU	American Civil Liberties Union
ADA	Americans for Democratic Action
BLM	Black Lives Matter
CBC	Congressional Black Caucus
CORE	Congress of Racial Equality
CRDL	Civil Rights Digital Library
FOR	Fellowship of Reconciliation
FPI	Faith and Politics Institute
ICC	Interstate Commerce Commission
MFDP	Mississippi Freedom Democratic Party
NAG	Nonviolent Action Group
NCCB	National Consumer Cooperative Bank
NCLC	Nashville Christian Leadership Council
NOW	National Organization for Women
NSM	Nashville Student Movement
PCTS	Pike County Training School
PLO	Palestine Liberation Organization
SCLC	Southern Christian Leadership Conference
SNCC	Student Nonviolent Coordinating Committee
SRC	Southern Regional Council

SSOC   Southern Student Organizing Committee
VEP   Voter Education Project
VISTA   Volunteers in Service to America

Introduction

In Search of the Beloved Community

J OHN ROBERT LEWIS (1940–2020) traveled a great distance during his
eighty years, moving from poverty to protest to politics. It is little
wonder that his extraordinary journey from the cotton fields of Alabama's Black Belt to the front lines of the civil rights movement to the halls
of Congress became the stuff of legend. Considering his beginnings in a
static rural society seemingly impervious to change and mobility, the arc of
his life had an almost surreal trajectory, even though the obstacles he encountered along the way were all too real. In this regard, Lewis merits comparison with the great nineteenth-century figure Frederick Douglass, who
went from an enslaved laborer to a "radical outsider" as an abolitionist to
a near "political insider" after the Civil War. Like Douglass, he transcended
his humble origins with a fierce determination to change the world through
activism and ceaseless struggle, ultimately finding a path to greatness that
took him well beyond the limited horizons of Jim Crow culture.[1]

During his years as a protest leader, from 1960 to 1966, Lewis evolved from
student sit-in participant to Freedom Rider to one of the nation's most visible
voting rights advocates. By 1963, "the boy from Troy," as he was often called,
had become chairman of the Student Nonviolent Coordinating Committee
(SNCC) and the youngest member of the civil rights movement's so-called
Big Six, joining A. Philip Randolph of the March on Washington movement,
Roy Wilkins of the NAACP, Martin Luther King Jr. of the Southern Christian

Leadership Conference (SCLC), James Farmer of the Congress of Racial Equality (CORE), and Whitney Young of the National Urban League. Among these leaders, Lewis stood out as the one most likely to put his body on the line, to have a bandage on his head, or to find himself behind bars. Within movement circles, he earned an unrivaled reputation for physical courage, enduring more than forty arrests and nearly as many assaults. Decades later as a congressman, he would urge his followers to make what he called "good trouble," a fitting rallying cry for a leader who as a young man repeatedly demonstrated his willingness to shed "a little blood to help redeem the soul of America." That he did so without expressing a hint of self-pity and without relinquishing hope of reconciliation with those who beat or imprisoned him made him something of an "enigma," as the Nashville-based journalist John Egerton put it in 1970. "How could anybody who's been through what that guy's been through," one fellow activist marveled, "really be that free of bitterness and hate?"[2]

Lewis's status as a fearless nonviolent warrior was a major source of his fame. But he also drew considerable acclaim for his steadfast commitment to the moral elevation of humanity. Many observers, both inside and outside the movement, characterized him as "saintly," particularly during his years as a congressman, when moral and spiritual pronouncements punctuated his public speeches. His pleas for mercy, peace, love, forgiveness, and reconciliation stood out in a political system dominated by partisan rhetoric, intense competition, and interest-group politics. In Washington, where talk of civil rights was often shallow and abstract, he took full advantage of his experiences as a freedom fighter, bringing into play the spirit of a nonviolent movement enveloped in Christian and Gandhian ideals. Invoking powerful historical images of communal responsibility and common decency, he spoke with authority about rising above self-interest and doing the right thing, especially on matters of racial inequality and discrimination. Eventually, he won recognition as "the conscience of Congress," a scrupulous champion of honesty and moral rectitude.

Lewis had many things going for him, from an endearing personality and disarming modesty to a strong work ethic and an indomitable will. But if there was one element that set him apart from his peers—one indispensable secret to his success—it was his incomparably strong sense of mission. Grounded in an unshakable faith in the human potential for moral improvement and divinely inspired redemption, he focused on one overarching goal: to bring about a heavenly community on earth. He knew, of course, that the chance of even approaching this goal was slim, but that did not stop him from encouraging everyone around him to cultivate, as Abraham Lincoln once counseled, "the better angels of our nature." For Lewis, this call to action was a sacred responsibility, a cry from the heart on behalf of moral and ethical regeneration. This was a heavy burden to assume, one that would involve a lifetime of commitment and struggle as well as the mass mobilization of what Gandhi called *satyagraha,* or "soul force." But Lewis did not shrink from the task, which he identified as movement toward a "Beloved Community," a society of equity and justice freed from the deep wounds inflicted by centuries of exclusion, prejudice, and discrimination.[3]

With this in mind, Lewis devoted six decades—virtually his entire adult life—to the search for a Beloved Community. From his first encounters with formal philosophy and political activism as a seventeen-year-old student at Nashville's American Baptist Theological Seminary, he embraced this simple two-word phrase as his chosen social and moral ideal. Coined by the philosopher and theologian Josiah Royce in 1913, it later became a shorthand expression of the goals and aspirations of the Fellowship of Reconciliation (FOR), an international pacifist organization founded in England in 1914. Royce characterized the Beloved Community as "a perfectly lived unity of men joined in one divine chorus." For him, fostering this ideal was "the principle of principles," the only path to "infinite atonement" or, as one Royce scholar put it, "a human community based on love." Anticipating the theme of unmerited suffering in the thought of Gandhi and other proponents of nonviolence as a way of life, he stressed the importance of "self-sacrifice" and "union with others."

Over the next half century, a procession of FOR activists and intellectuals—including Howard Thurman, one of Martin Luther King Jr.'s theological mentors—reshaped and refined the concept to suit a variety of purposes. For Thurman, as for King and Lewis, the Beloved Community was both "a philosophical theory and a call to service." During these years, this vision of love, peace, and unity beckoned to generations of social, economic, and racial justice activists, all of whom faced the daunting challenges of world war, colonialism, and the fierce rivalry between capitalism and communism. In a number of societies, ranging from Gandhi's India to the Jim Crow South, an emerging struggle for civil and human rights took hold, and in each case some form of the Beloved Community became relevant to the aspirations of oppressed people and their champions.

Lewis was introduced to this struggle, and to the philosophy of nonviolence, by two of America's most sophisticated and eloquent proponents of the Beloved Community, King and James Lawson. Both men had deep roots in FOR, in a social gospel–inspired version of African American Protestantism, and in Gandhian philosophy, and both exerted an enormous influence on Lewis during and after his college years. Together they set his heart and mind on fire, lighting the way to a life of morality-based activism. As the noted religious scholar Charles Marsh once observed, "Beloved community gave expression to all that Lewis was longing for as a young seminarian devoted to the venture of making the teachings of Jesus come alive in the segregated South."[4]

In FOR-sponsored nonviolent workshops held in Nashville from 1958 to 1961, Lawson mentored Lewis in both the tactics of nonviolent direct action and the philosophical and spiritual foundations of the Beloved Community. This experience built on Lewis's budding discipleship to King, whom he met in 1957 after being inspired by the Montgomery Bus Boycott the previous year. At the successful conclusion of the yearlong boycott in December 1956, King quoted the book of Matthew and urged the boycotters to "inject a new dimension of love into the veins of our civilization." "Love your enemies," he recited, "bless them that curse you, pray for them who despitefully use you, that you may be the children of your Father which is in Heaven." "We must remember," King continued, ". . . that a boycott is not an end within itself; it is merely a means to awaken a sense of shame within the oppressor and challenge his false sense of superiority. But the end is reconciliation; the end is redemption; the end is the creation of the beloved community." Placing the goals of nonviolent direct action on such a high moral plain could be inspiring, drawing Lewis and many people of faith into the movement. But as the historian Mills Thornton has noted, King's frequent allusions to the "beloved community" as a reachable promised land sometimes had the opposite effect, prompting more practical listeners to "dismiss it as a pipe dream." Perhaps even more important, as Thornton points out, the claim by King, Lewis, and others that they "could by their efforts initiate the beloved community" inevitably left many of their followers with feelings of disappointment when the nonviolent movement fell "short of its promise."[5]

Unmet expectations would eventually trouble Lewis and test his fortitude, but as an impressionable sixteen-year-old, he welcomed King's statement as a new and exciting vision of Christian faith and witness. The historian Peniel Joseph recently observed that Lewis "revered King to the point of unconscious imitation," immediately embracing his search for the Beloved Community. Over the next sixty years Lewis put his own stamp on this idealized community, which he defined near the end of his life as "a society based on simple justice that values the dignity and the worth of every human being." "Consider these two words," he counseled. "*Beloved* means not hateful, not violent, not uncaring, not unkind. And *Community* means not separated, not polarized, not locked in struggle." Lewis's hopes for creating this community were rooted in his belief that "the power of faith is transformative."[6]

As he wrote in 2017, the search for the Beloved Community "can be used in your own personal life to change your individual condition, and it can be used as a lifeline of spiritual strength to change a nation. Each and every one of us is imbued with a divine spark of the Creator. That spark links us to the greatest source of power in the universe. It also unites us with one another and the infinity of the Creation. If we stand on this knowledge, even if it is in direct conflict with the greatest forces of injustice around us, a host of divine help, both seen and unseen, will come to our aid. This does not mean you will not face adversity. You can be arrested, jailed, and beaten on this quest, and sometimes you must be prepared to lose all you have, even your life. But if you do not waver, your sacrifice even in death has the power to redeem a community, a people, and a nation from the untruths of separation and division and from the lies of inferiority and superiority.

Once you realize your own true divinity, no one can imprison you, reject you, abuse you, or degrade you, and any attempt to do so will only be an aid to your own liberation."[7]

*　*　*

During a long political career, Lewis's approach to reform, like his ideology, was ecumenical and expansive. As a congressman, he became involved in the full array of causes embraced by the progressive wing of his party: the elimination of poverty and economic inequality; universal health care; opposition to war and militarism; feminism and reproductive freedom; environmentalism; immigrants' rights; multiculturalism; equity for Hispanics, Asian Americans, Native Americans, and homosexuals; the protection of civil liberties; criminal justice reform; concern for the special needs of the disabled; and expanded educational opportunities for all. Lewis addressed all of these matters on numerous occasions and took each one seriously. A strong supporter of the American Civil Liberties Union (ACLU), the National Organization for Women (NOW), and organized labor, he was also one of the leading figures in Americans for Democratic Action (ADA), the organization founded by Eleanor Roosevelt and other New Deal liberals in 1947, and even served as president of the ADA from 1993 to 1995.

Despite his eclectic reform agenda, Lewis's entry point in politics—and the core of his personal world view—were both closely tied to his passionate commitment to civil rights activism. His primary target was always the destructive and debilitating legacies of slavery and Jim Crow. Throughout his years in Washington, he viewed politics through the lens of a nonviolent movement organized to combat racial discrimination and injustice. Even after several decades in Congress, he was still the same John Lewis—an older version of the student radical who boarded a freedom bus in 1961 and the SNCC leader who bravely faced the forces of white supremacy on the Edmund Pettus Bridge in Selma four years later. While his devotion to democracy and inclusion now called for service and sacrifice on behalf of a wide range of disadvantaged or dispossessed groups, his politics still rested on a foundation of belief that the extension of America's unrealized ideal of equal justice and freedom for all to African Americans was crucial to any advancement toward the Beloved Community.

Lewis was not, however, a classic "race man." While he embraced many aspects of African American culture—from its folklore to its foodways—he exhibited little interest in Black nationalism, race-based ideologies such as Black Power, or what eventually became known as "identity politics." Among the civil rights movement's leading figures, he was, as the historian Sean Wilentz argued in a perceptive 1996 essay, "The Last integrationist."[8] Though proud of his African American heritage, Lewis never forgot his fundamental commitment to the broader interests of humanity. Most obviously, his long-standing concern for the plight of the poor of all colors tempered his racial loyalty. Acutely aware of the connections between race and class, he extended his belief in equity and even-handed treatment to all classes and races.

Indeed, in the spirit of Gandhian and Kingian nonviolence, he expressed his concern for the well-being of all human actors, including the privileged individuals whom he challenged as agents of oppression and inequality. Like Gandhi and King, he professed to love his enemies as much as he loved his friends, an expansive embrace that set him apart from the vast majority of his political colleagues as well as from much of the civil rights community. When Lewis took the high road, he was often alone. But that did not deter him from his quest or shake his faith in the transcendent power of love and forgiveness.

As a congressman, Lewis became adept at practical politics and the art of compromise. But somehow he always kept his eyes on the prize, which for him was the realization of the Beloved Community. Unlike most political leaders, he did not allow his vision of a better future to be diverted by the pursuit of competitive advantage or parochial interests. If this sometimes made it more difficult to get things done—to pass legislation or advance his constituents' interests—he accepted the trade-off because he believed he was in office to serve a higher purpose. If forced to choose, he was willing to sacrifice short-term gains for the sake of long-term objectives. As in his movement days, Lewis's determination to live up to his reputation for moral rectitude guided the logic of his politics. Through it all, his moral sensibility remained universalistic and utopian, with a steady focus on the behavior and beliefs that would elevate humankind to a higher moral plane: integrity, compassion, generosity, forgiveness, reconciliation—and above all, respect for human dignity.[9]

Despite these lofty goals, Lewis cast his lot with a highly imperfect political party that often disappointed him. Partisan politics frequently tried both his patience and his loyalty, but within the American political system his only viable option as a progressive was identification with the Democratic Party. He knew, of course, that the party harbored many white supremacists who did not share his values, that as recently as the 1930s the party's platform had unashamedly endorsed racial discrimination, and that several of the party's most powerful figures continued to represent the white South's traditional obsession with race. But he also knew that the Southern wing of the Democratic Party had come a long way since the 1960s, when racial demagogues such as Lester Maddox, George Wallace, and Ross Barnett held sway. The liberal awakening among Democratic leaders who had once supported racial segregation and discrimination—leaders such as Presidents Lyndon Johnson and Jimmy Carter—and the emergence of a new generation of liberal Southern Democrats such as Bill Clinton and Al Gore gave him hope that his party would eventually shed its Jim Crow heritage. While he had no illusion that this turn to tolerance and inclusion would meet the standards of a Beloved Community anytime soon, he was determined to do everything he could to accelerate the process of regional and national liberalization.[10]

With the election of Barack Obama in 2008, this liberalization appeared to be entering a new and more promising stage, one that would bring American democracy closer than ever to the realization of its professed ideals. But it soon became apparent that the election of an African American president had provoked a savage reaction among a distressingly large number of white citizens who felt threatened by his elevation to power. As Lewis watched in horror, racist rhetoric and extremist white nationalism reached unprecedented levels of intensity in an outpouring of contempt for an allegedly illegitimate president. Though popular enough to be reelected, Obama eventually saw many of his hopes and dreams dissolve under the pressure of Republican obstructionism and racial intolerance. For Lewis, this meant not only the likelihood of legislative failure but also a potential rollback of some of the key reforms instituted during the past half century. Undercut by several retrograde Supreme Court decisions, the future of everything from voting rights to gun control was now in jeopardy.[11]

During the final year of Obama's second term, Lewis was heartened by the prospect of former first lady and secretary of state Hillary Clinton's election as the nation's first woman president. But in November 2016 this hopeful scenario gave way to Donald Trump's stunning upset victory in the Electoral College. Once Trump actually gained control of the White House in January 2017, Lewis's worst fears were confirmed as the new president's menacing brand of right-wing populism rapidly evolved into "Trumpism," an extreme form of Republican politics based on an aggressively authoritarian cult of personality. With the political path to the Beloved Community completely blocked, Lewis feared American democracy itself was suddenly in peril.[12]

As one of the nation's leading exponents of the democratic ethos, Lewis sounded the alarm, working tirelessly to protect all Americans' rights to "Life, Liberty and the pursuit of Happiness," as articulated in the Declaration of Independence in 1776. True to form, the hero of Nashville, Montgomery, and Selma fought on valiantly against long odds, never succumbing to hopelessness or despair. For the last three and a half years of his life— until his death in July 2020—the great civil rights champion, bloodied but unbowed, continued to stand up for freedom and equality with every fiber of his being. This courageous effort put the final touches on an inspiring legacy that gave hope to the millions of Americans determined to carry on his struggle. Lewis was gone, but the spirit of "good trouble"—a phrase that had become synonymous with his style of activism—survived as a vital form of resistance and a potentially powerful force for democratic renewal.

CHAPTER 1

"The Boy from Troy"

JOHN ROBERT LEWIS was a true son of the soil, even though he spent much of his boyhood trying to escape the burdens and limitations of farm life. His friend and mentor Martin Luther King Jr. liked to call him "the boy from Troy," identifying him with the county seat of Pike County, an overwhelmingly rural backwater that straddled the southern edge of Alabama's Black Belt and the "wiregrass" area to the south. Lewis was actually born and raised in Carter's Quarters (part of which was later known as Lewis), a remote, unincorporated area eight miles northeast of Troy. Little more than a cluster of farmhouses and cotton fields situated along a dirt road, Carter's Quarters had been home to Lewis's mother's family, the Carters, since the mid-nineteenth century. Nearly everyone within a radius of two miles was related to the Carters in one way or another, and the entire local population had either black or brown skin. All were descended from enslaved Africans, and all were officially classified by the federal census as either "Negroes" or "mulattoes."

By the standards of the American mainstream, Carter's Quarters was dirt poor, and even its most prosperous residents had difficulty hanging on to the few scraps of property they managed to accumulate. Lewis's great-great-grandparents Tobias and Elizabeth Carter, who passed from slavery to freedom at the beginning of Reconstruction, were able to purchase a small farm for $125 in 1882 but were soon forced to sell their land, reportedly after being threatened by night-riding "whitecappers"—white vigilantes who used intimidation and violence to force Black farmers to abandon their farms.

Their son, Frank Carter, Lewis's great-grandfather, fared somewhat better, becoming the patriarch of the extended Carter clan by acquiring the largest house in the Quarters by the end of the nineteenth century.

Born into slavery in Pike County at the beginning of the Civil War, Frank Carter lived through several wars and depressions, attaining elevated status within his community—status based on a lifetime of hard work, a long family heritage, and his light skin color (his great-grandson, who knew him until the age of seven, reported that he could have easily passed for white). Even so, he suffered his share of sorrow, losing his first wife, Martha, after only two years of marriage and the birth of only one child, a daughter later known as Aunt Hattie to Lewis. His second wife, Bessie, whom he married in 1885, bore a large family, including her first-born son, Dink, Lewis's grandfather. A skilled midwife, Grandma Bessie oversaw scores of births in Carter's Quarters for more than half a century, including her great-grandson John Lewis's birth in 1940.

In the early decades of the twentieth century, Dink and his brothers worked in the fields alongside their father, who brokered their dealings with "Little Josh" Copeland, Pike County's largest landowner. Eventually, Frank Carter could mobilize a sizable portion of the labor force of Carter's Quarters, and he and Dink were able to farm as "standing" renters, the most desirable form of tenancy. But neither he nor any of his sons could get out from under the burdensome patronage of a powerful white employer. The monthly "draw day" visits to the Copeland building in Troy, where financial matters between owners and tenants were settled, remained an unfortunate and often exploitative fact of life. Despite all of his accomplishments, at his death in 1947 Frank Carter was still, Lewis later pointed out, "just a tenant farmer. He worked for 'The Man'"—just like several hundred other Black men scattered throughout the county.[1]

This lack of independence did not stop Frank Carter from exhibiting a measure of pride that sometimes bordered on arrogance. He was not inclined to hide his feelings of superiority over his neighbors, including the less fortunate members of his extended family. Though barely visible to white people, class distinctions within the Black community often came into play when marriages were under consideration, as in the case of Eddie Lewis's courting of Frank Carter's granddaughter, Willie Mae. Eddie's family was new to Carter's Quarters, having migrated from Rockford, Alabama, in Coosa County, in the late 1920s. The Lewis family was originally from New Albany, Georgia, in Dougherty County, where, as the descendants of slaves, they made a meager living picking cotton and working in turpentine mills. Born in Georgia in 1910, Eddie was the son of Henry and Lula Lewis, though by the time Lula arrived in Pike County in the late 1920s, she had separated from her husband. Arriving as a single parent with five children, she rented a small farmhouse in Carter's Quarters, where she and the older children worked as hired farmhands, the lowest rung of agricultural labor in the Cotton Belt.

Willie Mae Carter lived nearby with her mother and father, Frank's oldest son, Dink. One Sunday morning in 1931, she met Eddie at the Macedonia Baptist Church, and after a year of courtship they married, despite some misgivings on the part of the Carter family. Poorer and noticeably darker than Willie, Eddie was not considered to be a "catch," but his sweet manner won her heart—and ultimately the respect and affection of her imposing family. For a time they lived with his mother and worked in the fields together as hired day laborers, though sometimes Willie worked as a domestic in Troy.

Their income was meager, barely enough to keep them fed and clothed, but somehow they saved enough to rent their own house in 1934. It was little more than a shack, a classic, wood-frame shotgun house with a narrow hallway flanked by "small, square single-window rooms." The house had no electricity or running water, only a leaky roof and a privy out back. But it was their home for ten years, a modest haven for them and their children, the first of whom, Ora, was born in 1936. Two years later Ora's younger brother Edward was born, and a second brother, John Robert, was added in February 1940. Seven more children, one girl and six boys, came later, blessing a marriage that would last for forty-five years, until Eddie's death in 1977.[2]

*   *   *

During the early 1940s, the Lewises had few resources and no reason to believe they had much chance of improving their condition. Even though a world war would soon bring an end to the Great Depression, their lives did not change in any meaningful way. Despite the New Deal and the unfolding opportunities of the war economy, they remained near the proverbial "bottom rail," poor and Black in a white supremacist society that had no regard for their needs or aspirations. Looking back on his early years in Carter's Quarters, Eddie and Willie's second son, then known as Robert, conceded that his family was "dirt poor," burdened by a desperate struggle to make a living wage. He once described himself "as a child born on the dark side of the American dream."

Yet Lewis had fond memories of his boyhood home. "The world I knew as a little boy was a rich, happy one. . . . It was a small world, a safe world, filled with family and friends. There was no such thing as a stranger," he explained. "I never ventured out of the woods of Carter's Quarters—there was no reason and no means. And outsiders rarely ventured in—especially white people. I knew the man who owned our house and land was named Josh Copeland—I would hear the grownups talk now and then about Little Josh. But I didn't know what he looked like."[3]

Later in life, after encountering the insecurity and violence of Black life in inner cities, Lewis realized he had been fortunate to grow up in a close-knit, nurturing community. Despite the limited and inertial nature of rural enclaves such as Carter's Quarters, the cocoon of family and social stability gave him a grounding that served him well as an adolescent and even more as an adult. But the rest of Alabama, even the nearby communities and farms within a twenty-mile radius of Carter's Quarters, were virtually unknown to him as a young child.

For centuries, the surrounding area had been home to bands of Creek Indians, but in the decades after Alabama achieved statehood in 1819, Pike County, so named in 1821 for the noted explorer General Zebulon Pike, became cotton and slave country. By 1850, slaves accounted for one-fifth of the county's sixteen thousand residents, but only a handful of the white farmers who owned them were wealthy planters. Most were yeoman farmers who tilled small or medium-size cotton farms with fewer than ten slaves. Unlike other so-called Black Belt counties, Pike never realized a Black majority population, and since the Civil War Black people have accounted for roughly one-third of the local population, which, after two decades of sharp decline during Reconstruction, remained relatively stable for the next century. The red clay that dominates the local landscape is not as rich as the dark loamy soil found in Black Belt counties cut by wide rivers filled with silt. But by the end of the nineteenth century, Pike County's agricultural economy, based as it was on the exploitation of cheap labor, was strong enough to sustain Troy—a county-seat town and minor railroad hub with several thousand residents—and three small incorporated villages: Brundidge, Banks, and Goshen.

The dominant social institution in Pike County has always been the Protestant church, spread among several denominations but united in its focus on evangelical Christianity. This was certainly the case in Carter's Quarters when Lewis was growing up. Even though it was difficult for many rural families to attend church every Sunday, due to limitations of transport and a shortage of ministers in remote areas such as Carter's Quarters, organized religion exerted a powerful influence on everything from individual lives and marriages to race relations and politics. Historically, Pike County was part of the Bible Belt, and few people, Black or white, could escape the entreaties of local preachers and religious orthodoxy. For the Lewises, as for most of their neighbors, religious faith was a core value, the primary source of moral behavior and ultimately the glory of blessed afterlife. It was the force that bound families and communities together, that made life worth living and death less frightening. Not everyone invested their hopes and dreams in the church, but the Lewises were among those who came close to doing so.

The entire Lewis family faithfully attended church twice a month, at Macedonia Baptist on the first Sunday and Dunn's Chapel AME on the third. But John was the only member of the family who turned scriptural lessons into an all-encompassing personal quest. Early on, not long after he was given his first Bible at the age of four, he decided he wanted to become a pastor. Preaching the Gospel became his fondest wish, even though part of his motivation, he later confessed, was a desire to avoid a life of toil in the cotton fields. He also cherished church as a social institution. For him and his family, he recalled, "church was an exciting place, a colorful, vibrant place. For people whose lives were circumscribed by the rhythms and routines of hard, hard work, with relatively little time or opportunity for contact with others beyond their immediate neighbors, church was literally a time of congregation, a social event much like going into town, a chance to see and spend time with friends you might not see at all the rest of the month."

Lewis's approach to religion during his childhood presaged his later life as a moral leader. While his faith in Jesus was abiding, he kept an open mind about the relationship between scripture and Christian duty. Even as a young boy, he was not one to accept anything without first applying a measure of reason and inquisition. Though respectful toward, and sometimes even in awe of, the preachers he encountered, he was always full of questions, always trying to dig deeper into the meaning of things.[4]

*   *   *

Strangely enough, Lewis's first experience with preaching took place in a decidedly un-churchlike setting: the family chicken coop. It was a story he loved to tell later in life. At the age of five, he was given the responsibility of caring for the family's sixty-odd chickens. He quickly came to love them, regarding them as his personal wards. "I never had any feelings one way or the other about the rest of the animals that came and went on our farm—the horses, cows, mules, hogs, dogs, and cats," he explained. "But I was always drawn to the chickens. I know now that the reason was their absolute innocence. They seemed so defenseless, so simple, so pure. There was a subtle grace and dignity in every movement they made, at least through my eyes. But no one else saw them that way. To my parents and brothers and sisters, the chickens were just about the lowest form of life on the farm—stupid, smelly nuisances, awkward, comical birds good for nothing but laying eggs and providing meat for the table. Maybe it was that outcast status, the very fact that those chickens were so forsaken by everyone else that drew me to them as well."

Lewis spent a great deal of time with the chickens, feeding and leading them back and forth from the coop to a dirt yard. And that is where the preaching began. "I never took the chickens straight out to the yard to feed them," he recalled. "For some reason, I felt a need to talk to them first. And for some reason, they listened. I'd speak softly, gently, as if I were hushing a crying baby, and very quickly the cackling would subside, until finally the shed was as silent as a sanctuary. There was something magical, almost mystical, about that moment when those dozens and dozens of chickens, all wide awake, were looking straight at me, and I was looking back at them, all of us in total, utter silence. It felt very spiritual, almost religious. I could swear those chickens felt it, too."

Talking the chickens into silence soon evolved into a prelude to actual preaching: "I preached to my birds almost every night. I would get them all into the henhouse, settle them onto their roosts, and then stand in the doorway and speak to them, reciting pieces of the Bible, the same verses I memorized for Sunday school. They would sit very quietly, some slightly moving their heads back and forth, mesmerized, I guess, by the sound of my voice. I could imagine that they were my congregation. And me, I was a preacher." His family found all of this behavior curious and amusing, but they played along by calling him "Preacher." Lewis, by contrast, took his responsibilities to the chickens very seriously, speculating years later that this caregiving experience "provided an early glimpse into my future, a first indication of what would come to shape my character and eventually guide me into the heart of the civil rights movement." In a 1970 interview, he recalled his fondness for the chickens, telling the journalist John Egerton that he "refused to eat . . . whenever one of them was killed for food. . . . I guess that was my first protest demonstration."[5]

If attending church and tending chickens were the best parts of Lewis's life as a young boy, chopping cotton was surely the worst. His work in the fields began just after his sixth birthday, and from the beginning he hated the "tedious, grinding, monotonous rhythm of cotton." At twelve he learned how to use a plow, which he discovered was the only halfway tolerable chore for a cotton farmer. But he found the rest of the planting and harvesting to be pure misery. "You had to bend down to pick cotton," he explained. "Eight to ten hours of stooping like that and your back would be on fire. It would ache all night, and it would still be aching when you got up the next morning to go out and do it all over again."

The physical pain might have been more bearable if the sharecropping system had provided an avenue for upward mobility or escape. But the system required a lot of work for little or no economic gain. "I hated the work itself," Lewis insisted, "but even more than that, from a very early age I realized and resented what it represented: exploitation, hopelessness, a dead-end way of life." His father's sharecropping contract with Josh Copeland

took half of the crop off the top, and then most of the other half was de-
ducted as reimbursement for supplies fronted earlier in the year—essentials
such as seed, fertilizer, and equipment rental. "What was left after that was
ours," Lewis noted in disgust. "It was never enough. Even a six-year-old
could tell that this sharecropper's life was nothing but a bottomless pit. I
watched my father sink deeper and deeper into debt, and it broke my heart.
More than that, it made me angry. There was no way to get ahead with this
kind of farming. The best you could do was do it well enough to *keep* doing
it. That looked like no kind of life to me, and I didn't keep my opinion to
myself. Early on, to the dismay of the rest of my family, I would speak out
against what we were doing right there in the fields."[6]

Eddie Lewis fared much better than most Alabama tenant farmers,
managing to purchase a farmhouse and 110 acres of land for $300 in 1944.
Surrounded by fields of cotton, corn, and peanuts with dense woods in the
background, the house, like their previous home, had no electricity, running
water, or indoor plumbing. But with three bedrooms, a large front porch, a
small barn and a smokehouse nearby, a working well in the front yard, and a
stand of pecan trees in the back, it was definitely a step up—even though it
soon became clear that owning a small patch of land did not rescue the Lewis
family from the dictates of an agricultural system designed to keep white
people on top and Black people on the bottom. Most of their meager income
continued to come from sharecropping, and at that time there didn't seem
to be anything that young Robert or anyone else could do about it. Even so,
he began to fantasize about finding a better way of life, if not for his entire
family, then at least for himself.[7]

*   *   *

Lewis's first glimpse of liberation came during the late summer of 1946,
when he began the first grade at Dunn's Church Elementary School. Located
a half mile from his house, it wasn't much of a school, he recalled, just two
rooms in a small, ramshackle building hidden behind the church. But it gave
him a welcome respite from the drudgery of the fields and, he hoped, looking to the future, a path to a wider world. Built with money donated by the
Chicago-based Julius Rosenwald Fund, which had constructed thousands of
Black schools across the South since its inception in 1917, Lewis's first haven

from the farm accommodated three grades under the supervision of one teacher, Miss Williams. Books and other educational materials were in short supply, as the county school board provided little more than the teacher's meager salary, a fraction of a white teacher's pay. "Our desks, worktable, maps, paper and pens all had to be bought piecemeal with cash raised by community events," Lewis remembered. The county did provide a large, red-and-white Alabama state flag that was mounted next to the blackboard, but there was no American flag in sight.

This was Black education, Alabama style. Yet Lewis never complained. "I loved school, loved everything about it, no matter how good or bad I was at it," he later explained. "Most of all, though, I loved reading, especially about real people and the real world. Biographies were my favorite, stories that opened my eyes to the world beyond Carter's Quarters. By the time I was in the third grade, I had learned that there were actually black people out there who had made their mark on the world—Booker T. Washington, Joe Louis, Mary McLeod Bethune, George Washington Carver." This intellectual and cultural awakening was reinforced early on by a school field trip to the Tuskegee Institute, only fifty-five miles down the road but a world away. It was Lewis's first trip outside Pike County, and he marveled at the sprawling campus established by Washington in 1881, and at the museum exhibit that replicated the laboratory where Carver had conducted his famous experiments with peanuts.

Lewis's intoxication with education set him apart from his brothers and sisters, and from his parents, neither of whom went beyond the ninth grade. His parents never quite understood his unbridled enthusiasm for school. While they generally encouraged this enthusiasm, there were clear limits to their acceptance of education as a high priority. After he grew old enough to become a productive field hand, they sometimes asked him to help the family by skipping school. As he later acknowledged, this became a serious bone of contention between him and his parents, who suspected that at least part of his attachment to schoolwork stemmed from a desire to escape the drudgery of farm work. "I resented that," he explained. "It wasn't a question of falling behind my classmates; we were all in the same boat. But it was clear that all these days we were missing—a couple here, three or four there, sometimes an entire week—interfered with our learning. We were playing catch-up, not just with ourselves, but with children in other schools who didn't have to work in their families' fields to survive."

The stark inequality between white and Black educational opportunities became obvious to Lewis during his years at the Dunn's Church school. One clear indication was the poor condition of textbooks used in his classes: "I knew that the names written in the fronts of our raggedy secondhand textbooks were white children's names, and that these books had been new when they belonged to them." Even then, as a young boy largely unaware of the strictures imposed by Jim Crow culture, he sensed there was something wrong with a school system that treated Black students as second-class citizens. But a broader understanding of the negative implications of racial discrimination and white privilege emerged only after he left Carter's Quarters for the first time in 1946.

"Until I took my first trip into the town of Troy with my father at age six," he remembered, "I had seen just two white people in my entire life—a mailman and a traveling merchant." On that Saturday trip and others that followed, he encountered small-town Southern life with all of its structures and rules, formal and informal. He had heard his mother, who sometimes worked as a domestic in Troy, talk about the ways of white folk, "about how there were certain things you did and didn't do around white people, how there were certain things you could say and certain things you could not." But all of this became more concrete and intelligible after he actually saw a bit of Troy with his father.

There were white people on the streets and in the shops along Main Street, more people than he had ever seen at one time. And there was the town square, surrounding a tall Civil War monument with the inscription "LEST WE FORGET," an imposing structure befitting a bustling county seat of eight thousand people. Among the shoe stores and banks and hair salons was a corner drugstore, Byrd's Drugs, outside of which Black farmers like Lewis's father and grandfather would congregate on Saturday mornings. Spending much of the day with his father's friends "chewing the fat" and taking in the scene, Lewis began his initiation in racial etiquette. He found he could buy a Coca-Cola at the soda fountain counter, "just like anyone else, but I had to take it outside to drink it." "Blacks were allowed to buy anything they wanted in Byrd's—their money was as welcome as white folks'," he later explained, "but they could not sit down at those wrought-iron tables and chairs and have a sandwich or relax up at that counter with a nice, cool drink. That was simply not allowed. It was unthinkable."[8]

* * *

This and later lessons in the mores of Jim Crow, combined with the drudgery of sharecropping, left Lewis with a restless spirit of dissatisfaction and a growing urge to flee a life of severely limited possibilities. As a precocious nine-year-old, he and his cousin Della Mae concocted a plan to build a bus that would take them away to a shiny, new land. "We were going to saw down a tree," he recalled, many years after he became a Freedom Rider, "and somehow we were going to make it into a bus. And then we were going to roll right out of Alabama, leave the place behind for good and forever."

This wild scheme apparently grew out of his recent experiences with visiting relatives from Michigan, New York, and New Jersey. Two of his mother's brothers had migrated to Buffalo during World War II, and other aunts and uncles had settled in Detroit and Newark. Once a year, in late July, they would return to Carter's Quarters for a family reunion, full of stories about life in the North. As Lewis listened and asked questions, he began to understand why his uncles and aunts had resettled a thousand miles away. "The North was no longer just a foreign, faraway place to me," he explained. "Now I was sensing that it was a *different* place, different specifically in terms of race. I wondered what it would be like to live in a place like that, where the lines between whites and blacks weren't so sharply drawn as they were in Pike County. . . . All I had to do was merely look at these relatives from the North, wearing their city clothes, driving their big, shiny cars, and I could see that they lived in a different world than I did." Never short on imagination and curiosity, he, in his words, "started obsessing about it, about what it would be like to live up north. I thought about it all the time. I would be out in the field, leaning on a plow handle, picturing in my mind one of these big, bustling cities where black people were not programmed from birth to be nothing but field hands."

Lewis's fascination with the North gained new life in June 1951, when he actually visited the "promised land" as an eleven-year-old. Traveling with his uncle Otis, a schoolteacher and principal who lived in Dothan, he experienced a challenging cross-country trip to Buffalo, where he spent the remainder of the summer. "Arriving in Buffalo—seventeen hours after we'd left the front yard of my Alabama home—was like stepping into a movie, into a strange, otherworldly place," he remembered. "It was so busy, almost frantic, the avenues filled with cars, the sidewalks crowded with people, Black and white alike, mixing together as if it was the most natural thing in the world. What a contrast to sleepy, segregated little Troy. When we reached my uncle O.C.'s and Dink's house, I couldn't believe it—they had white people living next door to them. On *both* sides."

Later, he visited Niagara Falls, and even rode an escalator, a device he could not have imagined before his arrival in Buffalo. Spending time with his uncles and cousins, exploring neighborhoods with paved streets and sidewalks, and "soaking up the sights and sounds and smells" of the city transformed his view of the world. But in the end, it was all a bit too much. By the end of the summer, the mystique of the North was broken and he was ready to go home, even though he knew "home would never feel the same as it did before that trip." "I missed my brothers and sisters. I missed my parents," he explained. "When I finally arrived home, climbing out of my uncle Otis's car and giving him a hug goodbye, I was crying, it felt so good to be back."[9]

That fall he entered the sixth grade at Banks Junior High School, a much larger institution than the Dunn's Church school. Located eight miles southeast of the Lewis farm, just off Route 29, the major thoroughfare crossing Pike County from east to west, Lewis's new school had multiple classrooms, several teachers, a principal, and even a school bus. Lewis embraced the classes at Banks as a pathway to a better life, and despite severely limited resources, the education he received outstripped his expectations. Part of that education, which took place going to and from school on the bus, was exposure to parts of Pike County beyond Carter's Quarters. Riding the bus, Lewis later noted, "should have been exciting and fun." But instead he found it "sad, just another reminder of how different my life was from those of white children." "The bus itself was a rattling, rusty jalopy, an old hand-me-down, just like our schoolbooks," he recalled. "I realized how old it was when we finally climbed onto the paved highway, the main road running east from Troy, and passed the white children's buses, so new and shiny. We went past their schoolhouse as well, very sleek, very modern, with nice playground equipment outside, nothing like our cluster of cinder-buildings, with the dirt field on which we played at recess and the privies out back."

Lewis and the other Black students on the bus also frequently encountered prison work gangs along the road—always Black prisoners being supervised by armed white guards—as well as cotton fields dotted with Black workers. All of this reinforced his sense of grievance, of being held down and denigrated by white people. "Now, when I went into Troy on a Saturday afternoon, I was more acutely aware than ever of how black men and women—the grownups of my world—addressed all white people, even white *children,* as 'Mr.' or 'Mrs.' or 'Miss,' always adding 'Sir' or 'Ma'am' and never receiving any of these courtesies in return," he wrote years later. "The signs of segregation that had perplexed me up till then now outright angered me." Life was getting more complicated and frustrating as his teen years approached, and his parents began to worry that his dissatisfaction with his condition and theirs might get him into trouble.

After two years at the Banks school, Lewis moved farther afield to the county's only Black high school, Pike County Training School (PCTS), located in the Black section of Brundidge, a small town twenty miles south of Carter's Quarters. The year was 1953, and there was no hint of the social and political upheaval that would follow the U.S. Supreme Court ruling in *Brown v. Board of Education* in the spring of 1954. The dual school systems of the Jim Crow South seemed immutable, especially in remote Black Belt counties like Pike, and educational traditions that had been in place for generations—such as PCTS's focus on "vocational agriculture"—appeared secure and inviolate. This state of affairs concerned Lewis, who had decided that he wanted to become either a preacher or a lawyer, and who suspected that a liberal arts education was the best means of joining either of these two professions. PCTS, he feared, fell far short of what he needed. "Basically," he concluded, "we were being trained to go right back out into the fields from which we had come."

Fortunately, there were several teachers at PCTS who encouraged their most promising students to seek a college education that went beyond the agricultural and building trades curriculum that dominated Tuskegee Institute and many other historically Black colleges. For Lewis, the most important part of high school was the school library, where an enterprising librarian named Coreen Harvey had amassed a large collection of Black newspapers and magazines. "My dear children, read. Read *everything*," she liked to say, and that is essentially what Lewis did, making the library his "second home," as he later put it. Reading the *Chicago Defender* and the *Pittsburgh Courier*, along with popular magazines such as *Jet* and *Ebony*, he gained a richly textured knowledge of the world beyond Pike County and Alabama. It was a world he was determined to experience, though he knew the odds were against him.[10]

There was a single bright ray of hope, however, one that appeared without warning in mid-May 1954. Sitting in the school library reading a newspaper, Lewis came upon a headline that both amazed and thrilled him. In a unanimous decision, the Supreme Court in Washington had struck down the six-decade-old "separate but equal" doctrine as unconstitutional. If the ruling was enforced, Lewis reasoned, racially segregated schools would soon be a thing of the past and no longer the law of the land. His initial reaction was pure jubilation. As he later recounted his soaring expectations, "Everything was going to change now. No longer would I have to ride a broken-down bus almost forty miles each day to attend a 'training' school with hand-me-down books and supplies. Come fall I'd be riding a state-of-the-art bus to a state-of-the-art school, an *integrated* school."

As that hopeful spring turned into summer and then into fall, the reality of what would later be known as "Massive Resistance" crushed Lewis's hopes of a new day in public education and race relations. Instead of seeing compliance with the *Brown* decision, he read story after story about white supremacist defiance and the rise of the White Citizens' Councils, first in Mississippi and then all across the Deep South. Demagogic Southern politicians had turned May 17, Lewis's day of jubilee, into Black Monday, a rallying cry for resistance and repression. A resurgent Ku Klux Klan held cross burnings and hooded marches in several Alabama communities, and Lewis "heard talk that summer of black men being beaten and even castrated—not in Pike County but in places just like it."

Lewis, like virtually everyone else in the Black South, was fearful that a dark age was descending on the region. But he was also heartened by his sense that, after so many years of quiescence, there was a noticeable stirring in the social order. The situation might get better or worse, but at least there was a subtle shift in the status quo. Although only fourteen, he was ready to push hard for change, an attitude that worried his parents. While they welcomed the *Brown* decision in the abstract, they opposed any public agitation for immediate implementation or rapid change. Lewis recalled their attitude as reflexive disapproval "of people trying to push things, no matter how justified the cause. Right or wrong didn't matter to them as much as reality. We heard stories all the time about black men being arrested in Troy, for one offense or another and being physically manhandled, even beaten. As far as my parents were concerned, anyone who was arrested for any reason was 'riffraff,' and that was that. 'Decent' black folks stayed out of trouble. It was that simple."

To Lewis's dismay, this attitude was almost universal among the Black citizens of Pike County, many of whom took their cue from local religious leaders who studiously avoided any involvement in activities related to civil rights and social justice. Early on, Lewis lost all respect for the minister at Macedonia Baptist, where the Lewis family attended services once a month. "Sunday after Sunday," Lewis complained, "he'd talk about an eye for an eye, a tooth for a tooth, how the soul must be saved by and by for that pie in the sky after you die, but hardly a word about *this* life, about *this* world, about some sense of salvation and righteousness right *here*, between the cradle and the grave." At this point, Lewis had never heard of Walter Rauschenbusch or the Social Gospel movement, but he was desperate for some recognition that the church had a responsibility to advocate justice and social change—to improve people's lives in the here and now, while they were still on earth.

Lewis later remembered wondering why "there was no talk in our church" of the *Brown* decision, "or any mention of the acts of violence that followed it." And quite naturally, for a boy who took religion seriously, he "wondered if God might not be wondering why as well." A yearning for some form of divine intervention occupied his thoughts by the fall of 1954; he looked for some sign that Alabama's Black preachers were ready to acknowledge, and perhaps even challenge, the oppressive conditions in which most of their parishioners lived.[11]

*   *   *

The sign, when it appeared in the form of a radio sermon early in 1955, initiated a spiritual awakening that would change his life forever. Listening to a Sunday-morning broadcast by WRMA in Montgomery, he heard an extraordinary voice that, in his words, "held me right from the start. It was a strong voice, a deep voice, clearly well trained and well-schooled in the rhythmic, old-style tradition of black Baptist preaching we call whooping." Beyond the quality of the voice was a striking message the radio preacher called "Paul's Letter to the American Christians," based on the apostle Paul's letter to the church at Corinth, in which he took complacent and self-absorbed Christians to task. Adapting Paul's jeremiad to the current situation in Jim Crow Alabama, the preacher insisted "it wasn't enough for black people to be concerned only with getting to the Promised Land in the hereafter . . . [and] it was not enough for people to be concerned with roads that are paved with gold, and gates to the Kingdom of God." Instead, he declared, "we needed to be concerned with the gates of schools that were closed to black people and the doors of stores that refused to hire or serve us."

For Lewis this was a new and exhilarating interpretation of the Gospel. This preacher, he marveled, was not talking about the angels "over yonder": he "was talking about dealing with the problems people were facing in their lives right now, specifically black lives in the South." "I was on fire with the words I was hearing," Lewis recalled. "I felt this man—his name was Martin Luther King Jr.—was speaking directly to me. This young preacher was giving voice to everything I'd been feeling and fighting to figure out for years." He knew nothing about King before the broadcast, but a quick newspaper search at the PCTS library located a clipping revealing that the preacher was a twenty-six-year-old Morehouse College graduate from Atlanta who had come to Montgomery in September 1954 to become pastor of the Dexter Avenue Baptist Church. Lewis had been to Montgomery only once, as a seventh-grader traveling with an uncle, even though it was only fifty miles down the road. But he promised himself that he would keep tabs on his new hero and perhaps even meet him in person someday. He even began to dream about finding a way to attend King's alma mater, Morehouse, though he had no idea how to make that happen, academically or financially.[12]

In late May 1955, several months after his intellectual encounter with King and the Social Gospel, Lewis learned that the Supreme Court had stepped back from its initial ruling in the *Brown* decision with an implementation decision that allowed Southern politicians and school leaders to proceed "with all deliberate speed" toward compliance with the desegregation mandate. There would be no pressure to comply immediately, in Pike County or anywhere else. Predictably, many white Southerners interpreted *Brown II* as a sign that resistance to school desegregation might delay implementation indefinitely, a suspicion that increased such resistance exponentially in the wake of the new ruling.

Emboldened by this turn of events, white supremacists in Alabama and elsewhere became increasingly aggressive in defending what they called "the Southern way of life." Acts of violence and intimidation against Black people, especially those who dared to assert their constitutional rights, became much more common in the post–*Brown II* era. One act in particular that pushed this atmosphere of fear to new levels was the murder of fourteen-year-old Emmett Till in Money, Mississippi, in August 1955. A Black boy from Chicago visiting relatives in the Mississippi Delta, Till ran afoul of Deep South racial etiquette by allegedly flirting with a white woman working in a country store. He paid with his life, and the white men who kidnapped and murdered him, including her husband and brother-in-law, were acquitted by an all-white jury that all but mocked the sworn testimony of Till's uncle, Moses Wright, who witnessed the abduction. Before the trial, the case drew national and international attention when Till's mother insisted on an open casket at her son's Chicago funeral, revealing to the world how a Black boy's body had been mutilated by his killers.

Few racially motivated murders, before or since, had such a powerful effect on public opinion, especially among young Black people who identified with Till. "As for me," Lewis noted more than four decades later, "I was shaken to the core by the killing of Emmett Till. I was fifteen, black, at the edge of my own manhood just like him. He could have been me. That could have been me, beaten, tortured, dead at the bottom of a river. It had been only a year since I was so elated at the *Brown* decision. Now I felt like a fool. It didn't seem that the Supreme Court mattered. It didn't seem that the American principles of justice and equality I read about in my beat-up civics book at school mattered."

For a time, Lewis's disillusionment was profound and disturbing, affecting his view of his family, his neighbors, and the moral failings of the people, past and present, Black and white, who had created and sustained such a monstrous system of social injustice. "By the end of that year," he explained, "I was chewing myself up with questions and frustrations and, yes, anger—anger not at white people in particular but at the system that encouraged and allowed this kind of hatred and inhumanity to exist. I couldn't accept the way things were, I just couldn't. I loved my parents mightily, but I could not live the way they did, taking the world as it was presented to them and doing the best they could with it."

Although Lewis did not yet have all the words to describe what he wanted to do with his life, he knew he had to do something to make at least his part of the world a more just and humane place. He was ready to become an activist for social justice, even if he didn't understand all the implications of that. The watchwords of his life—seeking the Beloved Community and promoting "good trouble"—lay in his future. But he had reached a tipping point in his journey to a life devoted to purposeful action. All he needed was a role model to show him how he could draw on the wellspring of courage and commitment flowing through his heart and mind.[13]

* * *

Lewis's role model turned out to be virtually the entire Black community of Montgomery. In early December 1955, just as he was completing the first semester of his junior year at PCTS, Montgomery witnessed an unprecedented mass protest triggered by the arrest of Rosa Parks, a forty-two-year-old Black seamstress and NAACP activist who violated a local segregation ordinance by refusing to move to the back of a city bus. After years of mistreatment and discrimination on the city's buses, Black Montgomerians decided to boycott the bus line until their grievances were addressed by local officials. Led by a coalition of Black preachers, teachers, and labor leaders, they formed the Montgomery Improvement Association, with the Reverend Martin Luther King Jr., the young preacher whose radio sermon had inspired

Lewis earlier in the year, as its president and chief spokesperson. When city officials refused to negotiate in good faith, a short-term protest turned into a yearlong struggle attracting national and international attention. In the process, King, through stirring oratory and personal charisma, assumed the role of an "American Gandhi" by promoting and implementing a strategy of nonviolent direct action.

The boycott, which Lewis followed with rapt attention on radio and in the daily pages of the *Montgomery Advertiser,* stirred his soul. "This was riveting. This was real," he explained. "I'd heard firsthand accounts of what the mood was like over in Montgomery from the grownups who lived or worked there. They described buses normally full of black passengers now rolling up and down the city streets with no one inside them. This wasn't just talk. This was action. And it was a different kind of action from anything I'd heard of before. This was a fight, but it was a different way of fighting. It wasn't about confrontation or violence. Those 50,000 black men and women in Montgomery were using their will and their dignity to take a stand, to resist. They weren't responding with their fists; they were speaking with their feet."

Nothing in Lewis's life had ever affected him as much as what became known as "the miracle in Montgomery." As he explained more than forty years later, "With all that I have experienced in the past half century, I can still say without question that the Montgomery bus boycott changed my life more than any other event before or since." In addition to stoking his desire to become a social gospel–style preacher like King, the boycott reinforced his predisposition for nonviolence; he already had an aversion to guns, being the only Lewis brother with no interest in hunting. But now he had an established philosophy to justify and deepen a point of view that had been considered odd among his family, friends, and neighbors.[14]

In mid-February 1956, with the boycott entering its third month, Lewis's rapidly evolving feelings about new ways to serve the Lord became manifest in his first public sermon, a trial effort delivered at Macedonia Baptist Church. He had a lot on his mind that day, including the riots that had broken out twelve days earlier at the University of Alabama, when Autherine Lucy tried to enroll as the university's first Black student. His sermon, based on the first book of Samuel, dealt with "moral courage," a subject of increasing interest to him as the boycotters and other civil rights activists such as

Lucy steeled their courage in the face of white supremacist intimidation. The Macedonia congregation gave the sermon a rousing response. After the church's deacons promptly rewarded him with a preliminary ordination, he posed for a formal photograph dressed in his Sunday best with Bible in hand; a week later the "Negro Section" of the *Montgomery Advertiser* used the photograph in a story about Pike County's "boy preacher."

Lewis and his family were thrilled to see his name in print, but by that time they had suffered a cruel and devastating blow when Dr. Thomas Brewer, an uncle by marriage and the pride of the extended Lewis family, was murdered in Columbus, Georgia, by a white man who took exception to Brewer's recent activities on behalf of Black voting rights. A leader of the Columbus branch of the NAACP, Brewer often visited Carter's Quarters, where he was a favorite and highly esteemed uncle to the Lewis and Carter families' children. "That killing jolted me even more than the others I'd read about," Lewis remembered. "This was a man I knew. I was horrified by what happened, and I was enraged at a system that could condone and encourage such hatred."[15]

Two months after his uncle's murder, in April 1956, Lewis channeled his outrage—and his growing need to do something to register disapproval of the rising tide of racial discrimination and repression in Alabama—into an effort to desegregate the Pike County Public Library. In what he later called "the first formal protest action of my life," he directly challenged a stricture of Jim Crow culture by walking up to the library reference desk to apply for a library card. Like most Pike County Black people, young or old, he knew the public library was for white people only, so he wasn't surprised when the librarian turned him away. He was, however, determined to carry his protest forward in the same spirit of direct action being employed by King and the boycotters. Instead of retreating into resignation by telling himself there was nothing he could do to change the system that had excluded him, he organized a petition drive to open the library to all of the county's citizens regardless of race.

After circulating his petition at PCTS, he soon discovered that very few of his schoolmates were willing to sign on, and most of those who did were his cousins. Undaunted, he mailed the petition to the library anyway, hoping the white administrators would acknowledge the protest with a formal response. When no response came, he reluctantly abandoned the library campaign. But for a boy aching to become an activist, it was, in his words, "a start. It was an *act*, and that meant something, at least to me."

Later in the year, after Alabama's attorney general and future governor John Patterson convinced a state circuit judge to suspend the charter of the Alabama NAACP, effectively banning it from the state, Lewis defiantly submitted a youth membership application to the national NAACP office in New York. "It arrived in a matter of days," he recalled, "and I carried that blue and white card in my wallet for years."[16]

*　*　*

That fall, as the boycotters' legal challenge to bus segregation made its way to the U.S. Supreme Court, Lewis began his senior year at PCTS. Unlike the vast majority of his classmates, he began to formulate college plans, even though he had no notion of how he or his family could afford even a modest amount of college tuition. Although no one from the Lewis family had ever gone to college, his mother and father supported his college plans as best they could. Following his trial sermon the previous February, they harbored renewed hope that he would become an ordained minister, a profession that often involved higher education, even among Black Baptist preachers.

Lewis dreamed of following the Reverend King to Morehouse, but he soon learned that his grades, though generally good, were not high enough to warrant consideration for a scholarship, which he would need if he were to attend an expensive private school. Troy State Teachers College, the only institution of higher learning in Pike County, was more affordable, but it had never accepted applications from Black students since its founding in 1887. Alabama had several state colleges reserved for Black people—including Alabama State College (known as Alabama State College for Negroes until 1954) in Montgomery—but they, like Troy State, were well beyond the Lewis family's means. Several Black teachers at PCTS had gone to Alabama State—and a number of current Alabama State students and faculty were involved in the bus boycott—making it an attractive choice for Lewis, if he could somehow come up with enough money. Fortunately, during his final semester at PCTS, as he contemplated the virtually impossible task of acquiring the funds to attend Alabama State, an unexpected stroke of good fortune directed him elsewhere.[17]

Working as a laundress at the Alabama Baptist Children's Home, a whites-only orphanage in Troy, Lewis's mother picked up a brochure describing the American Baptist Theological Seminary (ABT) in Nashville, Tennessee. Co-owned by the all-white Southern Baptist Convention and the all-Black National Baptist Convention, ABT was a small seminary with fewer than a hundred students. As soon as Lewis read the brochure, which to his amazement said that ABT did not charge any tuition and that its students paid for their room and board through on-campus employment, he knew where he wanted to go to college. Despite having only the vaguest sense of where Nashville was, he applied for admission, receiving his acceptance letter several weeks later. He could hardly believe it. "Now it was real," he suddenly realized. "I was actually going away, leaving my family and Pike County, and leaving everything I knew. It was frightening and exhilarating and unnerving all at once."[18]

Later in the spring of 1957, he completed his studies at PCTS, becoming the first member of his family to graduate from high school. By then, the bus boycott that had inspired him to dream about a new and more just racial order was over, the buses in Montgomery were fully integrated thanks to a November 1956 Supreme Court ruling, and Dr. King had founded a new civil rights organization known as the Southern Christian Leadership Conference. The goal of the SCLC, which attracted courageous Black ministers from across the South, was to spread the spirit of Montgomery to other Southern communities, especially in Deep South states such as Alabama. All of this reinforced Lewis's desire to become a minister who could help change the world by preaching and acting on the social gospel.

After a summer of working on the farm—which served as a reminder of why he was so eager to leave the cotton rows behind—Lewis was ready to venture out beyond the circumscribed world of Carter's Quarters. In early September, his footlocker—a gift from his uncle Otis, the same uncle who had taken him to New York six years earlier—was packed with clothes, a few odds and ends, and a Bible. Just before his father drove him to the Greyhound bus station in Troy, Uncle Otis came by to wish him well—and to give him a $100 bill. "I'll never forget that as long as I live," Lewis later wrote. "A hundred dollars, *solid*. I'd never held that much money in my hand before." After a few hugs from his brothers and sisters, who must have wondered whether they would ever see him again, or what he would be like if and when he did return from such a faraway place, he embraced his mother, who tried to smile at him through her tears. The boy she called Robert had always been different from her other children, always determined to find his own way in the world. And now he was about to undertake a journey of faith and discovery that she could scarcely imagine. She could only hope that God would protect him when she could not.[19]

CHAPTER 2

―――

Nashville

JOHN LEWIS'S daylong journey from Carter's Quarters to Nashville in 1957 was, in a sense, his first ride to freedom. At the time, he would not have called himself a "freedom rider," a term that would not appear in the civil rights lexicon until the spring of 1961. But when he boarded a Greyhound bus in Troy, he carried with him an expansive dream of freedom and a new life.

As he made his way to Montgomery and Birmingham and then on into Tennessee, Lewis made sure he sat in the rear section of the bus, as all Black interstate passengers were required to do under the segregation laws of Alabama and Tennessee. In 1957, some Black passengers, inspired by Rosa Parks and other pioneering activists, were already challenging these racially restrictive laws, but at seventeen Lewis was not quite ready for anything like that. His mother's last words as he left the security of the family farm were a cryptic "Be particular," which he took to mean, "Be careful and stay out of trouble." The time would come, in the not-too-distant future, when he would embrace civil rights activism as the most important aspect of his life. But for now, he was content to focus on getting an education.[1]

Years later, Lewis recalled his inauspicious arrival in Nashville: "I was just a boy from the woods, nervous and unsure as I climbed out of the taxi-cab that had carried me from Nashville's downtown bus station out to the American Baptist campus. . . . As I hauled my trunk up to the second floor of Griggs Hall, which would become my home for the next four years, I felt very alone, very out of place." Ninety students, seventy men and twenty women, were enrolled at ABT that fall, and Lewis would eventually come to know almost all of them. Located on the north side of town, separated from the downtown business district by the Cumberland River, ABT, or "Holy Hill" as the students called it, was an isolated enclave of red-brick buildings and leafy trees.

ABT was its own world, with students and faculty immersed in the study of theology and preaching. Virtually all of the students received financial aid in the form of campus work—Lewis, for example, worked as a dishwasher in the dining hall kitchen for $42.50 a month—so there was little time for frivolities or road trips. "Three times a day—breakfast, lunch and dinner—I positioned myself at the cafeteria kitchen sink," he explained, "where my job was to scrub the biggest, heaviest pots and pans I'd ever seen." The school took $37.00 of his income for various fees, leaving him with $5.50 of disposable funds, much of which was spent on textbooks.[2]

ABT, Lewis soon discovered, was a serious place for serious students. It was not, however, a place for serious activists. Other than preparing young pastors to fill Baptist pulpits, the school had no tradition of community outreach. The intellectual and theological culture of the campus had always been inwardly directed and preoccupied with questions of scriptural ortho-doxy and heavenly salvation. To Lewis's dismay, very few of his teachers or classmates evidenced any interest in the social gospel or the need to address the inequities of the Jim Crow South. During his first semester, he searched in vain for someone who shared his passion for employing religion as an en-gine of social change as Dr. Martin Luther King Jr. had done in Montgomery. "My first semester I was in church every Sunday," he recalled in 1970, "but by the second semester I had begun to drift away. It was a period of real doubt and change for me. I started to question for the first time the ritual, the ceremony, the creeds and beliefs of the church, and I began to identify more and more with the social aspects of Jesus' life."

The closest he came to finding a kindred spirit was Professor John Lewis Powell, who introduced him to philosophers such as G. W. F. Hegel, whose ideas about thesis, antithesis, and synthesis seemed relevant to the ongoing struggle to turn the status quo—what is—into what should be. But when he tried to discuss this connection with other students, he got nowhere. "Most of my fellow students at American Baptist were at best lukewarm when it came to Martin Luther King," he discovered, and some were openly dismissive of Lewis's views. During one late-night dormitory debate, Jim Bevel, an outspoken twenty-one-year-old from Itta Bena, Mississippi, asked him, "Lewis, why you always preaching this social gospel and not the Gospel gospel?" Lewis's response was a paraphrase of King's words: "Well, I think we need to be less concerned with getting people up to those streets paved with gold and more concerned about what people are dealing with right down here on the streets of Nashville."[3]

After little more than a month at ABT, Lewis decided he had to do something about the passive, complacent spirit on campus. Just after his arrival in Nashville, he had accompanied one of his classmates, Harold Cox, to several meetings of Nashville's NAACP youth council. Excited by what he heard, he inquired about NAACP activity on campus, only to discover that ABT had never sponsored a campus branch. Surprised, he set out to remedy this situation, which seemed especially unfortunate in light of what was happening that month in Little Rock, where the NAACP was waging a valiant effort to desegregate Central High School. With Arkansas's demagogic governor Orval Faubus pulling out all stops to keep the school and the surrounding city and state segregated, it was time, Lewis reasoned, for everyone who cared about freedom and racial justice to step up and speak out. ABT needed to do its part, and the establishment of an on-campus NAACP branch would be a good start toward doing so.

When Lewis made an appointment to discuss the matter with ABT's president, Dr. Maynard P. Turner Jr., he was optimistic that Turner would approve his request to bring the NAACP on campus. But the meeting did not go well. Turner was polite but firm in his refusal to allow Lewis or anyone else to establish an on-campus branch of an organization closely associated with the civil rights movement. Turner, who had only been at ABT for three years, explained to Lewis that the seminary was in a precarious position as an institution that received most of its funding from the Southern Baptist Convention, a white organization that had long opposed racial integration. Any formal association with the NAACP or any other organization involved in the civil rights movement was out of the question, he added, since it would jeopardize the Southern Baptist Convention's patronage of the financially strapped school.

Deeply discouraged, Lewis began to look for other ways of acting on his belief in the social gospel. But he feared he was in the wrong place to do so—that even though he enjoyed his classes at ABT, the school was a poor fit for a student determined to join the struggle for civil rights. As his first semester drew to a close, he didn't know quite where to turn, though an idea that had been percolating in his head for more than a year began to occupy his thoughts. He kept returning to the disturbing image of the rioting that accompanied Autherine Lucy's unsuccessful attempt to desegregate the University of Alabama in February 1956. She was turned away, brutally and with no concern for her rights as a citizen of Alabama, or for her feelings as a human being. He just couldn't let it end that way; someone had to pick up the baton and carry on the fight. So he decided, as he later put it, "to take action, to put myself in the path of history. I wanted to be involved. I didn't want to stand on the sidelines anymore. That was when I decided to apply as a transfer student to Troy State University. I didn't particularly want to go to Troy State. . . . But I had thought of Troy a lot. Ever since I had watched Autherine Lucy attempt so courageously to integrate the University of Alabama. I had thought about the fact that Troy State, the closest college to where I was raised, where my family still lived, allowed no black students inside its doors."[4]

Convinced that this Jim Crow state of affairs "was simply, inherently wrong," he took time during his 1957 Christmas break to send in an application through registered mail. For two months, as he waited for a reply from the admissions office, he told no one, not even his parents, about what he had done. In March, while he was still waiting, he decided to write to Dr. King in Montgomery to ask for advice. A quick response from King's attorney, Fred Gray, led to a series of letters back and forth over the next few weeks. There were also several phone calls from Gray and King's close associate, the Reverend Ralph Abernathy of Montgomery's First Baptist Church (Colored), before Lewis was finally invited to meet with King himself. It was now late spring, and Lewis was about to return to Pike County for the summer. The invitation included a bus ticket from Troy to Montgomery, so he knew King was taking him seriously. But that did not relieve his nervousness. "I had only just turned eighteen. I was a boy, really," he recalled. "And now I had an appointment with destiny."[5]

Following an anxious bus ride, during which he rehearsed what he hoped to say, Lewis found his way to Gray's law office before being taken to a room in the basement of First Baptist. There were two men in the room, Abernathy and King, who greeted Lewis with a welcoming salutation. "So you're John Lewis," King said with a smile, "the boy from Troy." Then Abernathy followed up with the first of many probing questions. "Who is this young man who wants to desegregate Troy State?" he asked. At first, Lewis was too petrified to say a word. "I was mesmerized," he later explained, "just listening, just trying to take it all in." But he eventually managed a few words of explanation, relating why he wanted to attend a white university and confirming his commitment to the struggle for civil rights.

As King and Abernathy sized him up, the discussion of motivation turned to questions about his understanding of the gravity of his decision to challenge the sanctity of segregated education, one of the white South's most cherished institutions. He needed to think long and hard about whether he actually wanted to go through with his challenge, they counseled. "You know, John, if you do this, something could happen to you," King warned, adding, "It's not just you who could be hurt, John. Your parents could be harassed. They could lose work, lose their jobs. They could be assaulted. Your home could be attacked. The farm could be burned." After King assured him that the SCLC would back him to the hilt, including obtaining funds for a lawsuit if it came to that, Lewis nodded in assent.[6]

As a minor, he would need his parents' approval before becoming party to a lawsuit, so talking about his plans with them was essential. Considering what was at stake, he could not be certain they would approve, but he left Abernathy's office in a state of exhilaration. "I could have floated back to Troy," he remembered. "The bus ride home that evening was like a dream." When he sat down with his mother and father the next day to discuss the situation, they listened patiently to what he had to say. But they could not hide their fears. "They were afraid, deathly afraid, not just for me or for themselves, but for the people around us, our neighbors," he remembered. And yet, somehow they mustered the courage to give him their blessing: "They were worried, they told me, but they were willing for me to go ahead with this lawsuit if that's what I really wanted to do."

This decision did not last, however. After Lewis returned to Tennessee to begin a summer job teaching vacation Bible school in the town of Jackson, his parents began to have second thoughts. As they contemplated what might happen to their family if they lost their land, or if their furnishing contract for feed and seed was canceled, or if Eddie lost his part-time job as a school bus driver, their fears reached the breaking point. When Lewis received a letter from his mother saying she and his father had changed their minds, he was crestfallen. But he decided it was fruitless to argue with them. Besides, he understood their feelings and concerns. "It was one thing to decide that this was my fight," he acknowledged, "but I had no right to make it theirs." In late summer, just before returning to ABT, he informed Dr. King that he had no choice but to abandon his effort to enroll at Troy State.[7]

*   *   *

Though disappointed that his bold assault on segregated education at Troy had been stymied, Lewis soon found other opportunities to expand his horizons. As he began his sophomore year in the fall of 1958, he sensed a new and more vital spirit, both at ABT and in the city of Nashville. "It felt like a different place than it had been the year before," he noted. "There was a sense of urgency and awareness spreading among my classmates and friends, and indeed, among Black students throughout the city." Part of the change, he later decided, stemmed from a rising consciousness of anticolonial developments in Africa. The new independent nation of Ghana, established a year earlier, inspired thoughts of liberation, not only in Africa but also among many African Americans. "We could hardly miss the lesson for ourselves," Lewis observed. "They were getting their freedom, and we still didn't have ours in what we believed was a free country." "Black Africans on their native continent were raising their own national flags for the first time in history," he explained, "and we couldn't even get a hamburger and a coke at a soda fountain. Here we were, in the capital of the state of Tennessee, and there was only one movie theater that would allow us to enter, and *that* was by way of the balcony."

Lewis was also heartened by more mundane developments closer to home. During his second year at ABT, he interacted with a much wider assortment of acquaintances and friends, both on and off campus. As a freshman he had spent most of his time at work, in class or in the library, or in his room with his roommate, Ellis Toney, a studious, older army veteran from Illinois who did not share his enthusiasm for the social gospel. But now, feeling more secure and less obsessive about his work and his studies, he took time to explore Nashville's Black neighborhoods, churches, and crosstown schools such as Fisk University and Tennessee A&I State College. In the process, he had a wide range of experiences and met a whole new set of friends. One enterprising, worldly friend whom he had met the year before, Harold Cox, accompanied him to Fisk to attend a string of lectures by notable civil rights leaders such as Roy Wilkins and Thurgood Marshall of the NAACP, the Reverend Fred Shuttlesworth of Birmingham, and the Reverend Martin Luther King Sr. He also witnessed Coretta King's speech at an SCLC rally and even had a brief encounter with the legendary Black intellectual and Fisk alumnus W. E. B. Du Bois while walking across the Fisk campus.[8]

This was all very heady stuff for an eighteen-year-old who hoped to become a social gospel preacher involved in the civil rights struggle. But the experience that affected him the most during that fall, the one that solidified his determination to join the struggle, was listening to the weekly sermons of the Reverend Kelly Miller Smith, the pastor of the First Colored Baptist Church. Established in the 1830s, First Colored Baptist was the oldest Black church in Nashville and the church of choice for the city's most prosperous Black families. Since coming to the church in 1951, Smith had earned a reputation as the local Black community's most influential minister, partly because of his magisterial preaching. He was both a spellbinder and an eloquent proponent of civil rights, and when the Nashville affiliate of the SCLC, the Nashville Christian Leadership Council (NCLC), was formed in 1958 he became its first president. He was also an intellectual who sometimes taught classes on homiletics—the writing and preaching of sermons—at ABT, where Lewis became one of his students. In class, and every Sunday at First Colored Baptist, Lewis marveled at Smith's ability to interweave scripture with the moral and ethical dictates of the social gospel. Here, Lewis and several other ABT students decided, was an inspiring model to be emulated.

Smith alone might have changed Lewis's life forever. But there was a second figure, a visitor to Smith's church, who exerted an even greater influence on the would-be preacher from Pike County. His name was James Lawson, a thirty-year-old divinity student born in Uniontown, Pennsylvania, and raised in Massillon, Ohio. A sophisticated student of Gandhian nonviolence and pacifism, Lawson had served a year in prison as a conscientious objector during the Korean War and spent three years as a Methodist missionary in India.

Following his return from India, where he met with a number of Gandhi's disciples, Lawson had a fateful encounter with King during the bus boycott leader's visit to Oberlin College. Impressed with Lawson's grasp of Gandhian principles and strategies for liberation and social change, King urged him to postpone his divinity studies and to head south to spread the word about the power of nonviolence. Intrigued by the idea, Lawson decided to take King's advice after a subsequent meeting with A. J. Muste, the leader of FOR. In early 1958, Muste hired Lawson as FOR's roving Southern field secretary, and several months later, at the suggestion of Glenn Smiley, a white FOR activist whom he had known for years, the young Gandhian made Nashville his base of operations.

During a Sunday service in the early fall of 1958, Lewis heard Kelly Miller Smith's announcement that there would be an FOR workshop at the church that evening. Although he knew next to nothing about FOR and wasn't quite sure what a "workshop" entailed, he was intrigued and decided to return to the church to see for himself. Years later, he recalled his first and fateful encounter with Lawson. "About six-thirty that night," he wrote, "I walked into a small room at the church, took a seat along with seven or eight other young men and women, all of us college students, all of us black—I was the only one from ABT—and watched a man named James Lawson introduce himself. Even before he began speaking, I could see there was something special about this man. He just had a way about him, an aura of inner peace and wisdom that you could sense immediately upon simply seeing him."

Lawson's message that evening was that all of the world's major religions revolved around the concept of justice. This was a theme worth exploring in depth, he announced, before inviting Lewis and the others to attend a series of Tuesday-night workshops to be held at Clark Memorial United Methodist Church, located two blocks from the Fisk campus. Eager to hear more, Lewis showed up at Clark the following Tuesday—and just about every Tuesday thereafter. He was drawn in by both the style and substance of Lawson's teaching. "There was something of a mystic about him," he observed, "something holy, so gathered, about his manner, the way he had of leaning back in his chair and listening . . . taking everything in before he would respond. Very patient. Very attentive. Very calm. The man was a born teacher, in the truest sense of the word."

During those Tuesday-night workshops, Lewis encountered the words and ideas of a wide range of thinkers from Reinhold Niebuhr and Henry David Thoreau to Gandhi and the Chinese philosopher Laozi. The common thread throughout was the search for justice or, more specifically, how to bring justice into the world. Christian principles were frequently part of the discussion, but more often than not the center of attention was Gandhian nonviolence and the related themes of civil disobedience, passive resistance, pacifism, redemptive suffering, and righteous truth. The obvious subtext that Lawson revealed in carefully rendered stages was the applicability of what he called "nonviolent direct action" to the struggle for civil and human rights, not just in India or the so-called Third World but also in the United States. Pointing to the success of the Montgomery Bus Boycott and to Martin Luther King Jr.'s emergence as an American Gandhi, he laid out a plan of action for the students to follow. Like King, he fused Gandhianism with the prophetic visions of the Old and New Testaments, an almost irresistible combination for Lewis and many others enamored with the social gospel.

Emotionally and intellectually, Lewis caught fire that fall. "Those Tuesday nights in the basement of Clark became the focus of my life, more important even than my classes," he remembered. "I'd finally found the setting and the subject that spoke to everything that had been stirring in my soul for so long. This was stronger than school, stronger than church. This was the word made *real,* made whole. It was something I'd been searching for my whole life."[9]

Two of the key concepts stressed by Lawson were the power of "soul force," by which he meant the combined strength of "rightness and righteousness," and the Beloved Community. As Lewis interpreted the Beloved Community, it "was nothing less than the Christian concept of God on earth." "All human existence throughout history, from ancient Eastern and Western societies up through the present day," he learned from Lawson, "has strived toward community, toward coming together. That movement is as inexorable, as irresistible, as the flow of a river to the sea. Wherever it is interrupted or delayed by forces that would resist it—by evil or hatred, by greed, by the lust for power, by the need for revenge—believers in the Beloved Community insist that it is the moral responsibility of men and women with soul force, people of goodwill, to respond and to struggle nonviolently against the forces that stand between a society and the harmony it naturally seeks."

The cultivation of soul force and the search for the Beloved Community became the animating principles of Lewis's life as a civil rights activist. "These were incredibly powerful ideas," he observed in his 1998 memoir, "and their beauty was that they applied to real life, to the specifics of the world we walked in. They applied to Byrd's drugstore and to the Troy theater. They applied to the buses I rode to high school and to the all-black classes in which I sat. They applied to the men and women who refused to serve black people at the lunch counters of downtown Nashville. They applied to the admissions office at Troy State University."[10]

* * *

One aspect of this reality was that no one could reach the Beloved Community alone. Fighting for truth and justice was a collective enterprise requiring cooperation and mobilization. With this in mind, Lewis set out to bring other ABT students into Lawson's orbit. He began with Bernard LaFayette, an eighteen-year-old divinity student from Ybor City, the Latin section of Tampa, Florida, who left the South in the fourth grade to spend three years at an integrated elementary school in Philadelphia, Pennsylvania. Six months younger than Lewis, LaFayette had become his best friend since arriving at ABT in the fall of 1958. A high-spirited, whimsical boy of Afro-Cuban descent who, like Lewis, had long chafed at the restrictions of Jim Crow, LaFayette soon became one of Lawson's most devoted followers.

Together, Lewis and LaFayette recruited several other ABT students, including a highly skeptical Jim Bevel, who joined the workshops before the end of the school year. Along with a number of other recruits from Fisk and Tennessee A&I, the ABT contingent swelled the ranks of the workshops, creating the core of a citywide student movement. Over time, the content of the workshops became less abstract and more concerned with preparations for actual nonviolent direct action. Lewis and other would-be activists were asked to participate in role-playing, sociodramas where they were taught the art of passive resistance—how to endure racist taunts and physical blows without fighting back.

Lawson also stressed that, to be successful, the civil rights movement would have to become interracial, incorporating liberal white people as full partners in the struggle. To this end, he encouraged white students to join the workshops, and before long several, including two white exchange students from Fisk and two others from George Peabody College for Teachers, became regulars at the weekly meetings. The interracial component of Lawson's workshops took on new meaning in the late fall of 1958 after he arranged a weekend retreat at the Highlander Folk School in Monteagle, Tennessee. Labeled a "Communist training school" by white supremacists, Highlander, established in 1932 by several white Christian socialists, including Myles Horton, a former student of Reinhold Niebuhr, was a retreat center for labor organizers and civil rights advocates. In the late 1950s, it was one of the few places in the South where white and Black people could come together to discuss racial and regional issues, which is why Lawson was eager to send his workshop students there.

Both Martin Luther King Jr. and Rosa Parks had attended Highlander seminars before the bus boycott, and there was no better place to absorb the spirit of movement culture. The camaraderie of interracial cooperation, the stirring music later known as freedom songs, the liberty to speak openly and honestly about matters of race and class—it was all there for Lewis, LaFayette, and their comrades to experience and ponder. While they had heard Lawson's stories about the liberating atmosphere at Highlander, seeing it for themselves took them to a new level of movement consciousness. Lewis would never forget the thrill of hearing Myles Horton hold forth on the long struggle against racism, or the powerful voice of Septima Clark, a sixty-year-old Black woman and movement veteran from South Carolina who talked about Highlander's citizenship and literacy schools, a form of grassroots organizing designed to prepare impoverished Southern Black people to vote. Clark, Lewis recalled, was "the single person who most impressed me that weekend," in large part because "the people she aimed at were the same ones Gandhi went after, the same ones I identified with, having grown up poor and barefoot and black."

By the time Lewis returned to Nashville, he had a much greater understanding of the historical context and roots of the civil rights struggle, especially as a movement directed at and often propelled by ordinary people. "I left Highlander on fire," he remembered, and many of his workshop colleagues felt the same way. Sensing the students were nearing the point where they were ready to turn ideas into action, Lawson, with Kelly Miller Smith's help, invited several of Nashville's older civil rights advocates to participate in his workshops during the winter and spring of 1959. Drawing on ministers such as the Reverend C. T. Vivian and others associated with the NCLC, Lawson deepened the students' understanding of the problems facing the local Black community.[11]

Despite its racial hierarchy and segregationist customs, Nashville, Vivian told them, was not a Deep South city obsessed with race and crawling with Klansmen. Like several other cities in the "upper" or "rim" South, it had already experienced a measure of racial progress since World War II. Unlike hard-edged cities such as Birmingham and Montgomery, Nashville relied more on customs than local statutes to maintain racial segregation, which gave city leaders more flexibility in reacting to calls for desegregation. In response to increasing pressure from the Black community, the city had managed to desegregate its police force and city buses during the past decade. Nashville also had a fairly liberal daily newspaper, the *Tennessean*; two Black people, Z. Alexander Looby and Robert Lillard, sitting on its city council; and a self-styled moderate, Ben West, serving as mayor throughout the 1950s.

Since their initial election in 1951, Looby and Lillard had pushed hard for a series of reforms such as desegregation of restaurants, golf courses, and other public accommodations but had met with little success. Rooted in a self-congratulatory tradition of paternalism, the local white power structure's complacent self-image made it difficult to challenge racial arrangements that had been in place for generations. Nashville's political and business leaders, along with most of their white constituents and clients, were not only proud of the city's moderate image; they also took offense at any suggestion that local race relations were oppressive and in need of improvement. Nashville, they were quick to point out, was a cosmopolitan city, known as the Athens of the South for its many colleges and universities and religious publishing houses. It was also "Music City," the home of the Grand Ole Opry and commercialized country music.

Black Nashvillians, many of whom were poor and very few of whom had ever set foot in any of the city's music clubs or on its white university campuses, generally had a different take on the quality of local life. They knew the situation was far worse for most Black people living in the Deep South, but they also knew that life in Black Nashville could be much better than it was. How to work toward a more humane and equitable racial order without provoking a white backlash—that was the question that dominated the meetings and deliberations of the NCLC as the decade of the 1950s drew to a close.[12]

The NCLC planned to attack racial discrimination on three fronts—voting rights, employment opportunities, and access to public accommodations— and its first venture came in early 1959 when Kelly Miller Smith and several colleagues (including two white liberals, the Reverend Will Campbell of the National Council of Churches, and Nelson Fuson, a Fisk physics professor and devout Quaker) met with the owners of two downtown department stores, Harvey's and Cain-Sloan. Predictably, the request that the stores' lunch counters be voluntarily desegregated met with a firm no, though both owners allowed for the possibility of removing the color bar in the distant future, expressing their "willingness to desegregate after the rest of the city had changed in this direction." This vague promise sent the NCLC back to the drawing board, where it began to develop a strategy that called for mass protest. In need of volunteers to press its case through direct action, the NCLC soon turned to the students in Lawson's nonviolent workshops.

The emerging relationship between the NCLC and Lawson's workshops had few precedents. Political and social activism on college campuses was a sporadic and largely inconsequential phenomenon before the 1960s, so there was little expectation that students could be counted on to fill the ranks of a mass protest. For a time in the late 1930s, a picaresque form of student activism, the Veterans of Future Wars movement, rose in response to the perception that the current generation of college students would soon end up as cannon fodder in a second world war. But the students' pledges not to fight in any future wars proved to be a fleeting fad and had little influence on the broader pacifist movement. Among high school or college-age Black students, the NAACP Youth and College Division, founded in 1936, created local councils that occasionally became involved in direct action campaigns. But the youth councils, operating under strict adult supervision, generally focused more on membership than actual protest. Extracurricular activity at Black colleges, as at most white institutions, centered on self-indulgent activities such as participation in fraternities and sororities, sports, house parties, and road trips. For the vast majority of students, participation in sit-ins and picket lines was simply unthinkable.[13]

* * *

This was certainly true in Nashville, where in early 1959 Lawson's student followers were regarded as malcontents and oddballs by most of their class-mates. But as the number of students in the workshops grew from fewer than a dozen to scores of activists in training, the idea of enlisting students to engage in mass protest became credible. By the fall of 1959, Lewis and the original core of Lawson devotees were joined by a cadre of new volunteers who would later become prominent in the Nashville student movement, including Paul Brooks of ABT; Bill Harbour, Pauline Knight, and Lucretia Collins of Tennessee A&I; and Diane Nash and Marion Barry of Fisk.

With Lawson's and the NCLC's blessing, the group adopted a formal structure in late October, when it formed a central committee and started calling itself the Nashville Student Movement (NSM). The urge to organize and mobilize had intensified over the summer of 1959 after Lawson, Camp-bell, and several of the workshop students, including Lewis, attended a gath-ering called the Institute on Nonviolent Resistance to Segregation, held at Spelman College in Atlanta. For Lewis, this meeting was another milestone in his developing consciousness as an activist. The dazzling list of speak-ers and panelists featured the Gandhian sage Bayard Rustin, the longtime NAACP organizer and current SCLC staff member Ella Baker, and Lawson's old friend from FOR, Glenn Smiley. Lawson and Campbell also held forth on an approach to social change and direct action labeled the New Gandhianism, a mode of protest that went beyond tactics and strategy to encompass a philosophy of life based on nonviolence.[14]

Lewis returned from Atlanta with a heightened sense of purpose. There were others who felt the same way—a desire to move from theory to action, a growing impatience that soon prompted Lawson to intensify the weekly workshop lessons. The sociodramas and role-playing developed a harder edge as the students took "turns playing demonstrators and antagonists." "Several of us," Lewis recalled, "would sit in a row of folding chairs, acting out a sit-in, while the others played waitresses or angry bystanders, calling us niggers, cursing in our faces, pushing and shoving us to the floor. Always, Jim Lawson would be there, hovering over the action, pushing, prodding, teaching, cajoling. It was not enough to resist the urge to strike back at an assailant. 'That urge can't *be* there,' he would tell us, 'You have to do more than just not hit back. You have to have no *desire* to hit back. You have to *love* that person who's hitting you.'"

This was the hardest challenge of all—to render forgiveness unnecessary by embracing your attacker as part of the Beloved Community. But this spirit of love, Lawson maintained, was the essence of Gandhi's *satyagraha* that had liberated India from British colonialism, and that had the potential to liberate the American South. As difficult as this was to put into practice, the students felt ready to test Lawson's ideas in the real world. "By November," Lewis remembered, "we were itching to get started. We had our training, and toward the end of that month we established our target."[15]

Lawson's conversations with members of Nashville's Black community, especially with women, revealed that one of the most irksome and insulting aspects of local Jim Crow culture was the abusive treatment they experienced in downtown department stores and lunch counters. Barred from trying on clothes, from using whites-only restrooms, or from eating at the lunch counters, they and the children who often accompanied them suffered systemic and gratuitous discrimination that turned downtown shopping trips into humiliating experiences. Challenging this pattern of injustice, the students agreed, was the place to start their campaign to rid the city of segregation. They began with a test at Harvey's on Saturday morning, November 28. The plan called for something less than an actual sit-in; three carloads of students, including several white students, all dressed in their Sunday best, would sit down at Harvey's lunch counter and request service—and then, after the request was refused, they would leave. "No issues would be forced, no confrontations created," Lewis noted. "Our aim was simply to establish the issue, and in the process to dip our toes in the water, to get a taste of the setting in which things would soon get real—very, very real."

In comparison to what was about to unfold in Nashville and other Southern cities in early 1960, the November 28 action was obviously tame. But at the time, Lewis and his colleagues had no idea what reaction their unprecedented behavior might provoke among white people. "I was nervous. We were all nervous," Lewis remembered. "We didn't know what to expect. All my life I'd heard, seen and obeyed the rules. You can't use that library. You can't drink at that fountain. You can't go in that bathroom. You can't eat in that restaurant. I hated those rules, but I'd always obeyed them. Until now." The white waitress's and later the store manager's refusals were polite, prompting the students' spokesperson Diane Nash to inquire whether the white students could be served. After the manager said no, not as long as they were part of an interracial group, the students stood up and quietly filed out of the store. Later, back at First Colored Baptist, they told Lawson what had happened—an encounter but no harsh words and no violence. Relieved, he congratulated them and promised this was only the beginning of their activism. "I came back to my dorm that afternoon elated, just about ready to burst," Lewis remembered. "I told a few of the guys what had happened. Some seemed interested, but most really didn't care. They had sermons to work on."[16]

During the next week, Lawson and the students met each evening to plan and prepare for the campaign to follow. Hundreds of recruits beyond the trained corps of workshop participants would be needed if the sit-ins were to be successful, so Lewis and others began to spread the word that additional volunteers were welcome. Several adult leaders, including most of the NCLC and Councilman Looby, offered their support, and by the following Saturday the students were ready for a second test sit-in. This time the Cain-Sloan lunch counter, a somewhat more upscale establishment than Harvey's, was the target, and Lewis was the designated spokesperson. When the group of eight protesters, which included several white students, requested service from a white waitress, they were turned down and referred to the manager, who promptly reiterated the store's segregationist policy. Once again

Lewis and the others left quietly without incident and promptly reported to Lawson, who all but promised them that once they returned from their Christmas break, there would be no need for more tests. In the new year—the first year of a new decade—the Nashville sit-ins would be real.

No one was more excited by the prospect of actually engaging in nonviolent direct action than Lewis and his best friend, Bernard LaFayette. During the week before Christmas break, they studied for their final exams, but otherwise they talked about little else but the coming sit-ins. And they continued this conversation during the bus ride home, Lewis headed for Troy, and LaFayette bound for his more distant home in Tampa, Florida. Filled with thoughts of challenging segregation, the two young men decided on the spur of the moment to begin their challenge on the bus.

Knowing full well that they were expected to sit near the back of the bus, they dared to take seats directly behind the driver, several rows in front of the white passengers. They knew they were breaking the law, just as Rosa Parks had known four years earlier, but they were not trying to establish a constitutional test by getting arrested. They just hoped the bus driver would prove tolerant enough to overlook their breach of racial etiquette and state law. The driver, as it turned it out, was in no mood to let two Black boys challenge the law or his authority. He brusquely ordered them to move to the back, but to his surprise they held their ground in stony silence. Furious, he went into the bus station, probably, Lewis and LaFayette feared, to call the police. "When I come back, you better be out of there," he warned before stepping off the bus. He did, in fact, call the Nashville police, but they refused to intervene.

When the disappointed driver returned to the bus, the two boys were still sitting defiantly in the front. After sliding into the driver's seat, he angrily pushed the seat back as far as it would go, all but trapping their legs and crushing LaFayette's suitcase in the process. Throughout the long trip south, the two would-be "Freedom Riders" stubbornly remained in the front. At several stops, the driver left the bus to use the phone, convincing the boys that he was alerting the Klan. Mercifully, no Klansmen ever appeared, but when the two friends parted company later that night in Montgomery, they nervously joked that they might not see each other again. For LaFayette, who still had over four hundred miles to travel before reaching home, the situation seemed especially dangerous. In the end, they both arrived home safely, suffering no more than the broken suitcase and the driver's scowls.[17]

* * *

The whole experience filled Lewis and LaFayette with a strange mixture of exhilaration and outrage, and after their return to Nashville in January, a discussion of their narrow escape led to the idea of a second and more ambitious ride. At that point, neither had any inkling that eighteen months later, in the spring of 1961, they would be deeply engaged in a history-making, national movement known as the Freedom Rides. Their attention in the early weeks of 1960 was focused elsewhere—squarely on the expectation that Nashville's first real sit-in was about to unfold. Indeed, they were confident that their planned February sit-in at three downtown lunch counters—Kress's, McClellan's, and Woolworth's—would be the South's first student-led sit-in since the mid-1950s, when a series of short-term protests had erupted in Baltimore, Durham, Oklahoma City, and Wichita. None of the earlier student sit-ins garnered much organizational or popular support, or press coverage, in part because regional and national civil rights leaders either opposed them or gave only grudging and minimal support. But the reaction to the Nashville sit-ins would be different, Lawson told his followers—if they were conducted carefully according to the principles of nonviolence.

Any public protest action by the NSM required the approval of a majority of the members of the NCLC, but Lawson assured the understandably nervous ministers that the well-trained students could be trusted to carry out such a protest with discipline and solidarity. It took time, however, to convince a majority of the NCLC that the students were ready, and as January came to a close, Lewis and other NSM activists were growing increasingly impatient. Then, on February 1, they received the shocking news that four students at North Carolina A&T College had staged a sit-in at the Woolworth's lunch counter in Greensboro. Lewis and his NSM colleagues were both thrilled and deflated by the news—thrilled that there were other students like them, willing and able to engage in nonviolent direct action, but a bit saddened by the realization that they had been upstaged by student activists in another city and state. Over the next two weeks, the Greensboro sit-in spread to a number of other Southern cities, as hundreds of college students—some white but mostly Black—joined what the press was calling the "sit-in movement."[18]

Though taken by surprise, the NSM, with the NCLC's approval, wasted no time in joining the swelling wave of student sit-ins. On Wednesday, February 3, Lawson addressed a mass meeting of more than five hundred students packed into the auditorium of Fisk's chemistry building. After announcing plans for a series of sit-ins, he asked for volunteers willing to adhere to the principles of nonviolence. As Lewis recalled the scene, Lawson struck a wise balance between advancing the schedule and careful preparation: "We did not want to act impulsively. We were speeding up our schedule, yes, but we remained determined to do this right. We did not want to unleash hundreds of eager, emotional college students without properly preparing them in the ways of restraint."

Over the next week, Lawson and NSM leaders held daily clinics on the dos and don'ts of properly conducted nonviolent direct action—how to avoid unnecessary confrontation, how to control aggression, and how to accept the hardships of arrest and imprisonment. By Friday, February 12— coincidentally Abraham Lincoln's birthday—Lawson felt that his volunteers were ready to meet the challenge ahead of them. But at a mass meeting held at First Colored Baptist that night, Kelly Miller Smith and several other NCLC leaders "argued for a delay." Pointing out that the NCLC had "a mere $87.50 in its treasury," Smith pleaded for time to raise enough funds to cover the bail costs of any arrested students. Others, including Lawson, suggested there were other reasons to postpone Nashville's first sit-in; seeing that many of the older activists had decided to err on the side of caution, he admitted he wasn't sure that all of the volunteers for the first sit-in had received enough training to withstand the pressure to strike back if they were assaulted.

In the end, however, Lawson, Smith, and the others calling for postponement found that Lewis and the leaders of the NSM were unwilling to wait any longer. "There was no stopping this thing now," Lewis insisted. "The hundreds of students in that room were dead set to sit in the next day. We weren't about to wait. We were young, we were ready. We had nothing to lose. We didn't owe anybody anything. We weren't tied to the community the way Kelly Smith and the other adults were. We were young, free and burning with belief—the perfect foot soldiers for an assault like this."[19]

This was the feeling the next morning when 124 students, walking two abreast, made their way downtown from the staging area at First Colored Baptist. The three target stores were on Fifth Avenue, where the students split into three groups. Lewis, eight days shy of his twentieth birthday, was the designated leader of the Woolworth's group, which he led inside and upstairs to a second-floor lunch counter. After taking their seats, spacing themselves along the length of the counter, the students waited patiently to put in their orders. "A few people were already there eating lunch," Lewis remembered. "No one got up. No one said anything. A waitress came out from the kitchen, stopped when she saw us, then picked up a cloth and began wiping the counter. She didn't say anything, but the next waitress who came out stopped dead in her tracks. 'Oh my God,' she said to no one in particular, 'here's the niggers.'" When Lewis asked to be served, he was told flatly, "We don't serve niggers here."

Before long, the white customers filed out, a sign reading "Counter closed" was placed in front of the students, the waitresses left, and the lights were turned off. Thus began an afternoon-long standoff, with the students passing the time reading or writing in their notebooks. They could hear whispers from below, and at one point a group of tough-looking young white men came upstairs to taunt them with racial epithets. But mostly they sat in an almost eerie silence waiting for a message from the organizing committee that it was time to leave. One white witness quoted in the press likened the scene to "a science fiction movie, where a stunned city is laid siege by aliens or giant grasshoppers." At 6:00 p.m. the message came, and the students, in Lewis's words, "stood and walked out in as orderly and silent a fashion as we had arrived." "It couldn't have gone any more smoothly," he observed. "When we got back to First Baptist, it was like New Year's Eve—whooping, cheering, hugging, laughing, singing. It was sheer euphoria, like a jubilee. The other sites had gone just as well as ours."[20]

During the next three weeks, sit-ins in downtown Nashville became routine. A second round was launched on February 18, this time with nearly 200 students involved, and two days later a third round saw 340 students march downtown to the Fifth Avenue stores, including Walgreen's. The Nashville sit-in movement showed no signs of fading away, an alarming situation for a white community unaccustomed to public protests by a racial minority that until recently had seemingly accepted its inferior status. The sit-ins had begun to attract groups of angry white hecklers, prompting the affected store owners and managers to promise a compromise proposal for gradual and partial desegregation if the protesters agreed to a moratorium.

Lawson and the central committee of the NSM reluctantly agreed to a weeklong stoppage, but when no proposal materialized, the sit-ins resumed on February 27. The day before the sit-in, Nashville's chief of police Douglas Hosse threatened to invoke a city ordinance that called for the arrest of anyone "inciting others to engage in riotous, violent or disorderly conduct," and he made it clear he intended to arrest the student activists, not the white protesters itching to stop the sit-ins. There was also a disturbing rumor that Mayor Ben West, normally a moderate on racial matters, had secretly agreed to let the white protesters rough up some of the students before the police moved in to make the arrests. All of this caused serious concern among the NCLC ministers, who were virtually unanimous in their belief that the students should wait before engaging in any more sit-ins. Even some members of the NSM central committee agreed with them, but after hours of debate the committee decided to go ahead with the February 27 sit-ins by a vote of eight to five.

Late that night, in preparation for the sit-ins the next morning, Lewis and LaFayette drew up a list of instructions and ran off five hundred mimeograph copies using a machine in the ABT administration building. The list, which became an important document in local civil rights lore, was divided into two categories, "Do Not" and "Do":

DO NOT: 1. Strike back or curse if abused.

2. Laugh out.

3. Hold conversations with floor walker.

4. Leave your seat until your leader has given you permission to do so.

5. Block entrances to stores outside nor the aisles inside.

DO: 1. Show yourself friendly and courteous at all times.

2. Sit straight; always face the counter.

3. Report all serious incidents to your leader.

4. Refer information seekers to your leader in a polite manner.

5. Remember the teachings of Jesus Christ, Mahatma Gandhi and Martin Luther King. Love and nonviolence is the way.

MAY GOD BLESS EACH OF YOU.[21]

At the church staging ground in the morning, Lewis and LaFayette walked through the crowd passing out copies of the instruction sheet. But in the end they had hundreds of copies left over. Fewer than a hundred students had shown up, clear evidence of the growing fear that this time the white response to the sit-ins would be violent and bloody. Before leaving the church, Will Campbell warned the brave souls who had shown up that arrests and possibly beatings awaited them downtown. The word in the white community was that the time had come to show the Black students who had real power in Nashville.

As the marchers approached Fifth Avenue, they encountered a crowd of young white men, some in their teens, who taunted them before pushing and shoving them off the sidewalk. The police, out in full force and standing nearby, did nothing to stop the melee. The students were on their own. As Lewis entered Woolworth's, one of six targeted stores, he and the other students were surrounded by a second group of tough-looking young white men, some shouting racial epithets. "Go home, nigger," and "Get back to Africa," they screamed before jabbing at and trying to provoke a fist fight with the students who were trying to make their way up to a second-floor lunch counter. When Lewis and the others refused to fight back, the white men called them cowards and "chickens." "We weren't playing by those rules, of course," Lewis observed, "and that infuriated them even further."

As soon as the students sat down at the upstairs counter, they heard a commotion at the downstairs counter, where a second band of students was being punched and dragged off their stools. "We immediately went down to join our brothers and sisters, taking seats of our own," Lewis recalled, but within seconds a punch in the ribs knocked him off his stool. Refusing to leave, he immediately got back on the same stool and sat defiantly in silence. As the assault continued all around him, he waited for the police to arrive, hoping they would stop the violence and restore order. But when the police finally came, they all but ignored the white assailants and promptly arrested Lewis and his companions for "disorderly conduct." This was the first of dozens of arrests that Lewis would experience during his career as a civil rights activist. And it was one he would never forget. Recalling his reaction to being arrested for the first time, he wrote, "It was strange how I felt. . . . A lifetime of taboos from my parents rushed through my mind as the officer gripped me by the bicep of my left arm. *Don't get in trouble. . . . Only bad people go to jail.* I could see my mother's face now. I could hear her voice: *Shameful. Disgraceful.*" Yet, he insisted, "I felt no shame or disgrace. I didn't feel fear, either. As we were led out of the store single file singing 'We Shall Overcome,' I felt exhilarated."[22]

Eighty-two students were arrested that day, and some undoubtedly shared Lewis's feelings of release and joy. But it seems likely that his sense of what was happening carried more meaning for him than it did for many others. Deeply introspective and always on the lookout for signs of what he called "the spirit of history," Lewis interpreted his first arrest as both a pivotal life-changing experience and a spiritual rite of passage. "It was really happening, what I had imagined for so long," he later wrote, "the drama of good and evil playing itself out on the stage of the living, breathing world. It felt holy, and noble, and good. That paddy wagon—crowded, cramped, dirty, with wire cage windows and doors—seemed like a chariot to me, a freedom vehicle carrying me across a threshold. I had wondered all along, as anyone would, how I would handle the reality of what I had studied and trained and prepared for so long, what it would be like to actually face pain and rage and the power of uniformed authority. Now I knew. Now I had crossed over. I had stepped through the door into total, unquestioning commitment. This wasn't just about that moment or about that day. This was about forever. It was like deliverance."

February 27 was also a turning point for Nashville's Black community, much of which rallied behind the arrested students. Hundreds of fellow students attended gatherings to find out what they could do to help, and the adult leaders of various Black churches, the NCLC, and other community organizations raised more than $50,000 in bail money. Though appreciative, most of the students locked in the city jail had no intention of seeking to be released on bail. Following the Gandhian strategy of overwhelming the criminal justice system by filling the jails beyond capacity, they adopted "jail, no bail" as a guiding principle. Even after local officials—eager to relieve the pressure on their jail facilities—lowered the bail rate from one hundred dollars to five dollars per person, they had few takers. Stymied, the officials threw up their hands and released all of the arrested students at eleven that night, only six hours after the arrests.

Released into the custody of Fisk's president, Stephen J. Wright, the students held a massive rally at the Fisk Memorial Chapel the following morning. The NSM felt it had won a great victory, especially after Wright told the crowd that he, along with many other adult Black leaders in Nashville, was a wholehearted supporter of their cause. Their sense of accomplishment was justified, considering Wright was one of the first Black college presidents to take such a forthright stand on the controversy surrounding the sit-in movement.[23]

The next day, the students appeared in court, after walking through downtown Nashville accompanied by their attorney, Z. Alexander Looby, and more than two thousand supporters. Despite Looby's best efforts to prove the students were victims rather than perpetrators of disorder, Judge John Harris found them guilty of inciting a riot and gave them the option of paying a fifty-dollar fine or serving a month in the Davidson County workhouse. In response, Diane Nash, acting as the NSM's spokesperson, explained to the judge that the students could not, in all good conscience, pay a fine that supported "the injustice and immoral practices" inherent in convicting defendants who had exercised their constitutional right to engage in peaceful protest. With this, all eighty-two of the convicted students were taken back to jail to await a transfer to the workhouse.

Four days later, after sixty-three more students, including Bevel, were arrested at the Nashville Greyhound and Trailways bus stations, Mayor Ben West decided he had to do something dramatic to counter the escalating disorder and racial polarization. After releasing all of the arrested students, he formed a biracial committee and negotiated a two-week-long moratorium that barred further sit-ins. These actions temporarily cooled the situation down but did not prevent the arrest of Lawson on March 4, or his subsequent expulsion from Vanderbilt's School of Divinity. This attempt to figuratively cut off the movement's head—an editorial in the ultraconservative *Nashville Banner* called Lawson a "flannel-mouthed agitator"—angered

Lewis and others in the NSM and the NCLC and ultimately backfired, deepening the students' commitment to the man who had taught them how to stand up for their rights.[24]

* * *

During the moratorium, the new biracial committee met several times in an attempt to reach a settlement that would satisfy both Black and white parties and prevent a new wave of sit-ins. LaFayette, Bevel, Nash, and several other NSM representatives testified before the committee, and on March 16, the day after the moratorium was lifted, Nash and three other students were served without incident at the Greyhound bus terminal restaurant. This successful test of a long-ignored 1953 interstate transportation desegregation order issued by the Interstate Commerce Commission (ICC) offered some hope that the color bar would soon be lifted in other areas of local life. The biracial committee continued to meet, but as March drew to a close, there was no sign of any real progress toward desegregation in the downtown business district.

Tired of waiting, Lewis and more than a hundred other students drew national television coverage on CBS news when they conducted sit-ins at nine downtown stores on March 25. This time there were no arrests, but the pressure on white business owners soon intensified after the parishioners of several Black churches organized a "Don't Buy Downtown" boycott. By the end of the month, business in many downtown stores had fallen off dramatically as the number of Black customers dwindled to almost zero. Even some sympathetic white people soon joined the boycott, while others stayed away out of fear or annoyance. As the normally busy Easter season approached, some white business owners, alarmed by "empty streets and empty cash registers"—felt enough panic to beg the biracial committee to do something to end the boycott, even if the solution involved substantial desegregation.

On April 5, the committee announced a plan for "partial" desegregation, one that created "a three-month trial period" during which Black customers would be served "in designated sections of the formerly whites-only restaurants." All of the students in the NSM, and many Black adults, considered the plan to be insulting, and they were shocked that the committee's two

Black members—the presidents of Fisk and Tennessee A&I—had endorsed it. "This felt like a betrayal of sorts to us," Lewis declared many years later, "more evidence of the differences between generations."

Confirmation of this generation gap came the next night when Lewis and hundreds of others attended a lecture at Fisk's gymnasium. The speaker was Thurgood Marshall, the legendary head of the NAACP Legal Defense Fund and the man most responsible for the fund's landmark Supreme Court victories such as *Smith v. Allwright* in 1944 and *Brown v. Board of Education* a decade later. Marshall's speech essentially damned the sit-in movement with faint praise; the real battle for justice was in the courts, not in the streets, he insisted. That was the way to bring about fundamental change, through the law and not through direct action gimmicks like filling the jails. "Once you've been arrested," he declared, "you've made your point. If someone offers to get you out, man, get out." Lewis was crushed. A man who had been one of Lewis's heroes had demonstrated his ignorance of what had actually happened in Montgomery, and much earlier in India. He seemed to have no awareness of the power of nonviolence, or even the existence of movement culture. "It was clear to me that evening," Lewis later revealed, "that Thurgood Marshall, along with so many of his generation, just did not understand the essence of what we, the younger blacks of America, were doing."[25]

Despite Marshall's admonition, the sit-ins resumed five days later, on April 11. There were a few minor altercations and only one arrest on that first day, but over the following week, sit-ins at nearly a dozen downtown stores were disrupted by bomb threats, multiple arrests, and armed bystanders both white and Black. Sensing that this powder keg was about to explode, the NCLC stepped in and suspended the sit-in campaign. The suspension was also prompted by the absence of Lawson and most of the NSM's central committee, who left the city on April 15 to attend a three-day organizing conference held at Shaw University in Raleigh, North Carolina. Only a few of the NSM's most visible leaders, including Lewis, stayed behind to monitor the volatile situation in Nashville.

The brainchild of the fifty-six-year-old veteran organizer and tactician (and Shaw alumna) Ella Baker, the Raleigh conference brought together 126 student activists representing more than forty colleges and universities, nineteen of which were predominantly white institutions located in the North. More than a dozen white students attended the conference, but the vast majority of the delegates were Black Southerners who had recently participated in the sit-in movement. The NSM sent the largest delegation—sixteen activists—and Lawson delivered the keynote address at Baker's request. Dr. King, who hoped the conference would produce a youth division of the SCLC, also spoke at length. But with encouragement from both Baker and Lawson, the students voted to create an independent organization, which they initially called the Continuations Committee before changing the name to the Student Nonviolent Coordinating Committee. Marion Barry, a twenty-four-year-old chemistry graduate student at Fisk and an NSM stalwart, was elected SNCC's first president.[26]

When Barry, Nash, LaFayette, and Lawson returned to Nashville on Sunday evening, April 17, they were eager to tell Lewis and others how exhilarating it had been to share experiences and plans with so many fellow student activists from other cities. But their euphoria disappeared the next morning when they learned that white supremacists had dynamited Z. Alexander Looby's home. Although Looby and his family escaped injury, the effect on the local student movement was electric and galvanizing. With Lawson and C. T. Vivian leading the way, more than two thousand students marched several miles from the Tennessee A&I campus to city hall to express their outrage directly to Mayor West.

By the time they arrived at the city hall steps, there were well over three thousand marchers, including a number of like-minded white participants. No Southern city, not even Montgomery during the bus boycott, had ever witnessed such a scene. After West came out on the steps to address the marchers, he waited as Vivian described the Black community's anguish and indignation. West's response was a plea to the crowd to disperse. "You all have the power to destroy this city," he conceded. "So let's not have any mobs." After promising to maintain order and explaining that he did not have the power to force store owners to desegregate, he asked for forbearance. "We are all Christians together. Let us pray together," he declared, prompting one marcher to yell out, "How about eating together?"

When West offered no immediate answer, Nash walked over to the obviously flustered mayor and began reading a list of questions that Lewis and others had drawn up earlier in the day. One of the first questions was whether West was willing to use the prestige of his office to implore the city's white citizens "to stop racial discrimination." His answer was that he would "appeal to all citizens to end discrimination, to have no bigotry, no bias, no hatred." Sensing an opening, Nash cut to the chase. "Do you mean that to include lunch counters?" she asked. Lewis, standing only a few feet away, later noted that the mayor was "rankled" by Nash's assertive interrogation. "Little lady," West responded, almost snarling, "I stopped segregation seven years ago at the airport when I first took office, and there has been no trouble there since." As the crowd stirred, a cool and determined Nash rephrased her question: "Then, Mayor, do you recommend that the lunch counters be desegregated?" After a brief pause, West said "yes," the word Nash and the marchers had been waiting to hear. Although he immediately qualified his response, insisting, "That's up to the store managers, of course, what they do. I can't tell a man how to run his business," the die was cast.

West's reluctant but unmistakable rejection of the moral basis of Jim Crow, as represented in the press and as interpreted by most of the white business community, turned out to be a milestone in the ongoing struggle to desegregate the city. On at least this one issue—the desegregation of the downtown stores—the resistance to change soon lost its momentum, and within three weeks the mayor's biracial committee worked out an agreement to end the de facto color bar at the lunch counters. On the afternoon of May 10, 1960, at the same stores where the students had been assaulted and arrested earlier in the year, Black and white customers ate at the same lunch counter for the first time in living memory.[27]

CHAPTER 3

———

In the Movement

JOHN LEWIS and his fellow NSM activists felt vindicated by their limited victories in 1960 and vowed to continue their nonviolent struggle until all aspects of local life were free of racial segregation and discrimination. Many more challenges and many more protests, marches, and arrests lay ahead. But James Lawson's protégés were proud of what they had accomplished, and proud of the movement they had nurtured. Their roles in the desegregation of Nashville's lunch counters and in the founding of SNCC were major points of pride, and an additional point emerged unexpectedly the night after the mass march on city hall.

On that night, April 19, one that Lewis would never forget, Martin Luther King Jr. came to Nashville at the request of Lawson and the NCLC. Lawson hoped King's words, delivered before an overflow crowd of four thousand at Fisk's gymnasium, would counter the despair fostered by the Looby bombing and propel the local movement to new heights. King did not disappoint him. Following a bomb threat that delayed the event for nearly an hour, C. T. Vivian's brief remarks on behalf of the NCLC, and a raucous response to Looby's emotional and tearful appearance onstage, the SCLC leader delivered an eloquent tribute to the NSM.

Calling the Nashville sit-ins "the best-organized and most disciplined in our Southland today," King thrilled the crowd by paying the NSM the highest possible compliment. "I come not to bring inspiration but to gain inspiration from the great movement that has taken place in this community," he insisted, offering high praise for the brave students who had "lifted the jails from badges of dishonor to badges of honor." He went on to criticize those who were content to accommodate segregation, those who refused to use the "soul force" that God had given them. Nonviolence and "our capacity to love," the students had proved, represented the only true path for a brighter future for Black Americans, and indirectly for white Americans as well.

For Lewis, who hadn't seen King since their meeting in Montgomery two years earlier, these were words to live by. Any doubt that he had chosen the correct path—any hesitancy that he might have harbored about the social gospel, and any confusion about the true meaning of the Beloved Community—it all slipped away that night at Fisk. Now the challenge was to cultivate the seeds of freedom that King and Lawson had planted in him, to turn ideas into action and intention into reality. He knew the search for the Beloved Community would take a lifetime, that it would consume all of his spirit, but he also knew that the struggle ahead was worth any worldly burden or any sacrifice that God called on him to make. "It was an exciting time, that time of beginning," he recalled years later. "Everything was so simple, and we were so clear about where we were going. It was just right. It was nonviolent and interracial, and daring, and religious. It was like a holy war, a crusade, and we saw the movement rising across the South, we saw change coming, and we were helping to bring it about. We were volunteers committed to the philosophy of nonviolence, in keeping with the New Testament and the Christian faith. My motivation came from religious conviction—segregation was immoral, illegal, and unchristian, and it had to be destroyed."[1]

The spring of 1960 was a time of deep change for Lewis. Not quite a man but no longer in his teens, he began to think more seriously about what he wanted to do with the rest of his life. One thing was now clear: he did not want to become a preacher. This decision, separating him from most of his classmates at ABT, did not come from any loss of religious faith. On the contrary, his faith in God and Judeo-Christian ethics was stronger than ever. Yet he had come to the conclusion that his stewardship of the social gospel, his destiny as a man of faith, and his agency as an advocate for Black America could best be attained through the struggle for civil rights. He now believed that a spiritually driven movement, not the church per se, was the most appropriate institution for his quest for freedom and justice. The movement in Nashville, as in other centers of activism, was still in its infancy, and no one knew where it was headed. But he knew he wanted to be a part of this unfolding story of liberation, not just as a stage of his college-age transition to adulthood but as a lifelong commitment.

This decision did not sit well with his family back in Pike County. When he heard that his mother and father had learned of his arrest in late February, he sent them a letter explaining why this had happened and how it had grown out of both his faith and his desire for justice and racial equality. "I have acted according to my convictions and according to my Christian conscience," he explained. "My soul will not be satisfied until freedom, justice and fair play become a reality for all people." His mother's response, layered with shame and disappointment, was searing. "You went to school to get an education," she reminded him. "You should get out of this movement, just get out of that mess." Sensing there was no room for productive discussion or compromise, he decided to keep his distance from his family during the summer break before his senior year. This, on top of the arrest, opened a rift between Lewis and his parents, one that would take years to bridge. From time to time, usually on holidays, he would return to Carter's Quarters for brief visits. But the tight bond that had tied him to his parents was gone. In its place, he later explained, "the movement became my family."[2]

The biggest news story that summer was the 1960 presidential election. Much of the nation was captivated by the dramatic confrontation between the Republican candidate, Vice President Richard Nixon of California, and the Democratic candidate, Senator John F. Kennedy of Massachusetts. After eight years of the low-key presidency of Dwight Eisenhower, many voters were ready for an exciting new era of energetic and strong political leadership. Indeed, for some the national election promised to be a pivotal event that would shape the new decade and beyond.

This rising spirit of political engagement extended to certain elements of the Black community, primarily among middle-aged and older voters. But this spirit was rare among young Black citizens, many of whom had little interest in mainstream partisan politics, which they found irrelevant to their lives. Lewis and his NSM colleagues had few connections to either party; many were too young to vote, and others found it difficult or impossible to become a registered voter under the Jim Crow regime. Besides, they didn't think much of either presidential candidate. Neither had a strong civil rights record, and neither said much about race and desegregation until the last week before the election. On occasion, Nixon tried to identify with Eisenhower's intervention in Little Rock in 1957, and Kennedy made positive statements about civil rights during the first televised presidential debate and later promised to end racial discrimination in federally funded public housing, which he claimed could be accomplished by an executive order—by, as he put it, the mere "stroke of a pen." But otherwise they were silent on the issues that the student activists of the NSM regarded as crucial to the future of Black America.[3]

The candidates' lack of attention to civil rights dampened the Nashville students' interest in the presidential race, but it did not deter them from working to expand Black suffrage. Lewis and his colleagues recognized that the right to vote was an essential part of citizenship. The situation in Tennessee, as in the rest of the South, where white registrars routinely denied Black citizens access to the polls in local, state, and national elections, was seen as an intolerable barrier to true democracy and racial progress. Among Southern cities, Nashville had one of the highest rates of Black voter registration, a rate that had steadily increased since the mid-1940s. But in 1960 the proportion of Black registrants in the city remained well below that of white registrants.

In May, following their initial victory at the downtown stores, the NSM activists—with the encouragement of the NCLC—decided to do something about this gap. Turning their attention from lunch counters to ballot boxes, they launched an ambitious voter registration campaign, reaching out to Black churches and other institutions where potential voters gathered. Wearing large lapel buttons that read, "WE SAT IN FOR YOU, NOW STAND UP FOR US," they passed out leaflets explaining how to register and vote. By the end of June, when the campaign ended, the number of new Black registrants was approaching four hundred, a significant addition to the Black voting rolls and an impetus for future efforts to strengthen the Black community's political presence in the city. For Lewis, the campaign was the beginning of a long personal struggle for voting rights, a passionate concern destined to become his signature issue.[4]

While he was a college student, Lewis was also drawn into campus politics, and at the end of the 1960 spring semester he was elected student body president. He had come a long way since his arrival on campus as a shy country boy unsure of his capacity to succeed anywhere beyond the limited world of Pike County. Now he was both a campus leader and a rising star in the constellation of local civil rights activists. He even spent much of the summer traveling to college campuses in the North and West, where student groups were eager to learn about the NSM, which had garnered considerable national publicity during the sit-in campaign. Sometimes he would speak as part of a group—often with Diane Nash, Bernard LaFayette, Jim Bevel, and Marion Barry—and sometimes alone. But the agenda was always the same: to spread the word about the power of nonviolent direct action and to create a network of student groups capable of coordinating and leading a national movement.

One by-product of the summer lectures was an infusion of funds into the local movement, which began to expand its activities accordingly. The NSM also attracted a number of visiting students who gravitated to Nashville hoping to become involved in an exciting center of activism. This led to complaints by local white residents who feared that the NSM had become a haven for troublemaking "outside agitators." The realization that most of the visitors were white added to these anxieties, raising the specter of an interracial movement that might someday attract their own children. The role of white people in the movement was also a subject of controversy within the NSM, though interracial cooperation was not nearly as volatile an issue as it would become later in the decade.[5]

*　*　*

In the fall of 1960, as the presidential race drew to a close and students at ABT and other Nashville colleges returned to school for the fall semester, the NSM's central committee began to implement a new and expanded sit-in campaign aimed at segregated grocery stores, hotels, and movie theaters. The plan was to attack Jim Crow culture institution by institution until the whole system collapsed, a strategy that had emerged during lengthy discussions at the founding conference of SNCC in April. In October, when

SNCC held its first annual conference at Atlanta University, this ambitious approach to racial insurgency was a given, as was the organization's determination to remain independent of the SCLC, CORE, and other established civil rights organizations. Joining more than two hundred other delegates, mostly from the South but some from the North, Lawson, Lewis, and a dozen other NSM leaders made the journey to Atlanta to exchange ideas with activists from the civil rights world beyond Nashville.

The NSM was the best known of the groups present, and the only other delegation of comparable size was the host group, the Atlanta Committee on Appeal for Human Rights (ACAHR). Like many of the groups represented at the conference, the ACAHR was more secular than the NSM and more inclined to push SNCC toward "a greater emphasis on political issues." Within a month, Chuck McDew—an Ohio native, a converted Jew, and a student leader at South Carolina State in Orangeburg—would replace Nashville's Marion Barry as SNCC's chairman, confirming SNCC's move away from Lawson's pietistic religious emphasis.[6]

The ACAHR, which staffed SNCC's Atlanta headquarters with volunteers, had a close but uneasy relationship with King, who had moved from Montgomery to Atlanta in January and who still harbored hope that SNCC would eventually be folded into the SCLC. The most prominent member of the ACAHR was Julian Bond, a twenty-year-old student at Morehouse College and the son of the distinguished educator and college president Horace Mann Bond. Light skinned, poised, and raised in an upper-middle-class urban family, Bond appeared to be as different from Lewis as he could be. But from their first meeting at the Atlanta SNCC conference, they became fast friends. Over the next three decades, their lives and careers would be intertwined and at times almost inseparable.

The workshops that weekend in October focused on the details of conducting demonstrations—especially how to behave when arrested and incarcerated, and how to deal with the implications of "jail, no bail." The speakers included Lawson, who discussed the moral and strategic dictates of nonviolence, and Amzie Moore, a veteran Mississippi activist who hoped SNCC would send volunteers to the Delta to help him register Black voters. King also spoke, though he found the circumstances more than a bit difficult. After several months of encouraging him to join their sit-in campaign in downtown Atlanta, the leaders of the ACAHR had grown tired of waiting. At one point during the weekend, a delegation that included his younger brother, A. D. King, met with him in private to urge him to march and sit in alongside the SNCC activists before it was too late—before he lost their loyalty and respect. Martin Luther King Jr. knew, Lewis later observed, "that if he stayed on the sidelines much longer, he and the SCLC risked losing us. Basically he knew it was time for him to stick his neck out, as so many of us had been doing for months."

All of this set the stage for a drama that altered the course of the civil rights movement—and more proximately the presidential race that was in its last days. Ignoring the advice of his father, "Daddy King," as he was known, King decided to take the plunge. On Wednesday, October 19, several days after the SNCC conference had adjourned, he joined eighty other marchers in a sit-in on the sixth floor of Rich's Department Store in downtown Atlanta. All were arrested, and at the arraignment King refused Judge James Webb's offer to release him on a $500 bond. "I cannot accept bond," King declared. "I will stay in jail one year, or ten years."[7]

This was the kind of courageous leadership that the SNCC militants had been advocating, but they got more than they had bargained for when Georgia authorities dropped the charges against all of the defendants but King. The singling out of the nation's most celebrated civil rights leader raised doubts about his safety, a concern that turned into near panic after he was moved from the relative safety of his Atlanta cell first to the DeKalb County Jail and later to the maximum-security prison at Reidsville. When Lewis heard about what had happened, he was proud of King but, as he told his closest friend Bernard LaFayette, he was terrified that the movement might lose its greatest leader. Fearing that King's life was in danger, SCLC and other movement leaders urged the Justice Department to intervene but got no response—a development that led to one of the most fateful decisions in modern American political history.

Harris Wofford, a liberal campaign aide to Kennedy, had known King since 1957 and had even raised funds for the SCLC leader's trip to India, where Wofford had spent several years studying Gandhian philosophy. Frustrated by Kennedy's reluctance to take a forthright stand on civil rights, he sensed that King's endangerment provided his candidate with a golden opportunity to make up for past mistakes. After receiving a phone call from King's distraught wife, Coretta, Wofford made the political and ethical case for an expression of sympathy. "If the Senator would only call Mrs. King and wish her well," he told Sargent Shriver, his boss and Kennedy's brother-in-law, "it would reverberate all through the Negro community in the United States. All he's got to do is show a little heart." While campaigning in Chicago, Shriver relayed Wofford's suggestion, which, to the surprise of the entire campaign staff, led to an impulsive late-night phone call from Kennedy. Startled and touched by Kennedy's expression of concern, Mrs. King made it clear to the press that she appreciated the senator's gesture, which stood out in sharp contrast to Vice President Nixon's refusal to comment on her husband's situation.

Nixon's inaction widened the opening for the Kennedy campaign, allowing the Democratic candidate's younger brother Robert to refine and extend the politics of the gesture. Though initially opposed to any public association with King, and furious with Shriver and Wofford for leading his brother astray, Robert Kennedy decided to make the best of a potentially bad situation by matching his brother's impulsiveness. Calling Georgia judge Oscar Mitchell, who had jurisdiction over King's imprisonment, he demanded the civil rights leader's release from prison. Following some additional prodding from Atlanta's progressive mayor, William Hartsfield, Mitchell complied, and after eight harrowing days behind bars King was out on bail. Following a joyful reunion with his family, King expressed his gratitude to the Kennedy brothers—and his intention to vote Democratic, something he had not done in previous presidential elections. Daddy King also weighed in, announcing that he had intended to vote against Kennedy on religious grounds, but now he planned to cast his first vote for a Roman Catholic.

Coming during the final week of the campaign, this delighted Kennedy's staff. But the best was yet to come. On the Sunday before the election, more than two million copies of a pro-Kennedy pamphlet titled *The Case of Martin Luther King: "No Comment" Nixon versus a Candidate with a Heart* appeared in Black churches across the nation, thanks in part to the efforts of Gardner Taylor, a leading figure in the National Baptist Convention who also served on the national council of CORE. Later known as the "blue bomb," the brightly colored comic-book-style pamphlet produced a groundswell of support for Kennedy, who received an estimated 68 percent of the Black vote, 8 percent more than Adlai Stevenson had garnered in 1956. Some observers even went so far as to suggest that Kennedy, who defeated Nixon by a mere 114,673 votes in the closest presidential election to date, owed his victory to a late surge in Black support. In all likelihood, this surge represented the difference between victory and defeat in five swing states, including Illinois, Michigan, and New Jersey, ensuring Kennedy's comfortable margin (303 to 212) in the Electoral College.[8]

*   *   *

The day would come when Lewis looked on John Kennedy's election as an important stride toward freedom. But in November 1960 he put much more faith in what was happening in the streets of Nashville. At the time, he was too young to vote, and he did not participate in either partisan campaign. While he preferred Kennedy to Nixon, he had serious misgivings about supporting anyone allied with white Southern Democrats. He did not pay much attention to the presidential contest, but he was well aware that some of Kennedy's most vocal supporters were white segregationists, including his unofficial Southern campaign manager Governor John Patterson of Alabama.

On the other hand, he also knew that Kennedy himself claimed to be in favor of desegregation, and that his running mate, Senator Lyndon Johnson of Texas, in his capacity as Senate majority leader, had been instrumental in the passage of the 1957 Civil Rights Act, which established the U.S. Commission on Civil Rights and the Civil Rights Division of the Justice Department, and the more recent 1960 Civil Rights Act, which empowered federal officials to inspect local voter registration polls and established fines for any obstruction of voter registration.

The first civil rights acts since 1875, these measures, though saddled with weak enforcement provisions, were encouraging signs that both major parties were awakening to the need for federal civil rights laws. Unfortunately, the expectation of additional civil rights legislation plummeted when the new president made no mention of civil rights issues in his inaugural address. For Black Americans, the address and the ceremony on January 20 were disappointing on several counts. While Kennedy mentioned "human rights" and spreading freedom across the world—to Asia, Africa, Eastern Europe, and Latin America—he failed to address the absence of freedom in the Jim Crow South. The VIPs invited to attend the ceremony as the president's special guests included a long and varied list of celebrities, but Dr. King, despite the famous phone calls to Georgia before the election, was noticeably absent from the list. Indeed, the only high point of the inauguration for the civil rights community came when the great Black contralto Marian Anderson sang the national anthem, evoking memories of the groundbreaking 1939 Easter Sunday concert at the Lincoln Memorial.

In the early days of the new administration, Lewis and other civil rights advocates did not know what to expect in the months to come. Most reasoned that the young president could hardly be worse than Dwight Eisenhower. Personally conservative on matters of race and preoccupied with the Cold War and foreign affairs, Eisenhower had allowed the executive branch's commitment to lag far behind that of the federal courts. Indeed, during the last two years of his presidency, the pace of school desegregation had slowed noticeably without provoking any apparent sense of alarm among administration officials.

While Kennedy, too, was an inveterate Cold Warrior with a weak civil rights record, the soaring rhetoric of his New Frontier, first mentioned in his acceptance speech at the 1960 Democratic National Convention, suggested that he planned to pursue an ambitious agenda of domestic reform. Whether this agenda included civil rights legislation or strict enforcement of legal and constitutional protection was unclear. But this was at least a possibility, especially if pressure from civil rights groups could be brought to bear. Despite his reluctance to make specific promises related to civil rights, he often talked about the moral imperatives of a true democracy, and on one occasion during the campaign he even alluded to the need for a presidency that would "help bring equal access to public facilities from churches to lunch counters and . . . support the right of every American to stand up for his rights, even if on occasion he must sit down for them."

This implicit endorsement of the sit-ins did not go unnoticed in the civil rights community, though by the second or third month of his presidency, there were increasing suspicions that Kennedy's commitment to civil rights and social justice was more rhetorical than real. Civil rights leaders were deeply disappointed when he passed over his campaign aide, the liberal lawyer Wofford, and appointed Burke Marshall, a corporate lawyer with no track record on civil rights, as the assistant attorney general in charge of the Civil Rights Division. This decision, among other tacks to the political center, left Lewis and other activists in a state of confusion, though many remained hopeful that the arc of American politics was at least tilting toward racial justice.

In the days and weeks after the election, and even after President Kennedy assumed office, life went on pretty much as usual for Lewis and his friends. Campus life at ABT was a bit more political than in the past, but studying and working, punctuated by occasional partying, still took up most of their time. The close race between Kennedy and Nixon clearly left a residue of interest in partisan politics among some students, yet the most ideologically and emotionally charged politics on campus continued to revolve around the small minority of students actively engaged in the sit-in movement. For Lewis, the local movement remained his most passionate interest. He attended class and studied hard, but nothing excited him as much as testing and challenging the power of Jim Crow. Sometimes, of course, it was both exciting and harrowing.[9]

On November 10, 1960, for example, Lewis and Bevel were at First Colored Baptist when they got word that a sit-in had gone wrong at a Krystal fast-food hamburger restaurant four blocks from the church. LaFayette and two female students—Elmyra Gray and Maryann Morgan—had asked to be served, but the white waitress angrily "emptied a bucket of water over their heads and poured detergent powder down their backs" before turning a hose on them. Fearing the situation might lead to violence, Lewis and Bevel raced to the restaurant, told LaFayette and the women to leave, and then sat down to resume the sit-in. The manager informed them that the restaurant was closed, but they didn't budge. Running out of patience, the manager ordered his employees to leave and headed for the back door himself. But before leaving, he flipped a switch that turned on an automatic fumigator. Within seconds, the dining room filled with insecticide. The white cloud was soon "so thick," Lewis remembered, "we could not see out the front window." After discovering that both the front and back doors were locked, they began to wonder if they were going to make it out alive. Fortunately, after smelling the fumes and seeing a smoky cloud coming through the roof, a passerby called the fire department for help. Just as the two trapped students were about to give up—"We're going to suffocate. . . . We're going to die," Lewis remembered thinking—"the firemen burst through the front door." Never in his life had he been happier to see white faces.

Most of the sit-ins that fall and winter were far less dramatic than the Krystal episode. But there was almost always some form of active resistance by white people, and no one from the NSM actually received service. There were also numerous arrests, including one of Lewis during a sit-in at a Tic-Toc restaurant one week after the Krystal fumigation incident. This was his third arrest and jailing in less than a year—"the third," he later noted, "of what would eventually total forty arrests in my lifetime."[10]

*   *   *

In January 1961, Lewis entered his final semester at ABT. For him and his classmates, it was time to prepare for the future, to think about what they wanted to do after graduation, to begin the search for a job. As a young man with no financial resources, Lewis was well aware of these practical concerns. Yet he had difficulty thinking beyond the next episode of activist involvement—the next sit-in, the next march. Though only twenty years old, he had become part of a movement culture, an all-encompassing band of brothers and sisters, a collective experience that transcended individual needs or concerns. His commitment to nonviolent struggle—as he would prove time and again in the future—was complete and unreserved.

The protests that laid the foundation for this commitment became even more intense as the year progressed. After a brief hiatus in January, during which Lewis and the rest of the central committee planned the NSM's next campaign, the organization's focus shifted from sit-ins to stand-ins. The new campaign was directed at the city's segregated movie theaters, targets of a different character and scale. In the stand-ins, a number of students were needed to form a line on the sidewalk outside the theater. When one student was turned away from the box office because of his color, another would step up to try to buy a ticket in the section of the theater reserved for white patrons, and so on. The goal was to create a human barrier that prevented white patrons from buying tickets and entering the theater. That all of this took place either on a public sidewalk or in a lobby—places where a crowd of incensed white people could gather—made confrontations between Black students and white protesters almost inevitable.

For the white officials who begrudgingly learned to tolerate the lunch counter sit-ins, the stand-ins were an especially provocative and irritating public disruption. For the students, of course, they were a risky and potentially dangerous breach of civic order. Nevertheless, for the NSM's leaders—many of whom found the racial restrictions at theaters to be one of Nashville's most insulting and gratuitous racial traditions—it was a risk worth taking. Lewis, in particular, had strong feelings about his bitter boyhood experiences at the Jim Crow theater in Troy. "I remember that we had to sit upstairs, in a balcony section set aside for 'Coloreds.' We called it the Buzzard's Roost, and I hated it," he recalled. "I didn't go to too many movies before I decided I would never go again. It was an insult to have to sit up there. I felt it intensely. To this day I rarely go out to the movies. The memory of sitting up in that balcony is just too strong."

The NSM stand-ins began on February 1, 1961, as part of a regionwide commemoration of the Greensboro sit-ins that had begun one year earlier. SNCC members in cities across the South held sit-ins and marches that day, hoping to initiate a new wave of nonviolent direct action. In Nashville, the downtown theaters were all clustered along Church Street within easy walking distance of First Colored Baptist. All of the theaters were rigidly segregated, usually with whites-only seating downstairs and Black seating in an upstairs balcony, which in some cases required Black customers to "walk outside, go into a dark alley and climb an exterior fire escape" after buying their tickets.

The proximity of the theaters simplified the logistics of mobilizing the stand-ins, making it easy to put long lines of students up and down Church Street. Gathering there each night for two weeks, the students raised the ire of the theater managers and inconvenienced white patrons, and before long the scene attracted both the police and roving bands of angry and unruly young white men. Taunting soon escalated to random physical assaults that threatened to lead to serious violence. During the second week of protests, after two students, Fred Leonard and LeRoy Wright, were injured by nightstick-wielding policemen, the NCLC asked the NSM to suspend the stand-ins.

In a tense meeting at First Colored Baptist, Kelly Miller Smith, Will Campbell, and several other NCLC ministers urged the NSM's central committee to back off in the true spirit of nonviolence. But the students stood firm, with Lewis at the forefront. When Campbell asked him to express his opinion, Lewis said simply, "We're gonna march." With this, Campbell lost his temper. "There's very apt to be some serious violence if there's another demonstration," the normally calm and collected minister said with a touch of alarm. "You agree with that, and still you say, 'We're gonna march.' What it comes down to is that this is just a matter of pride with you. This is about your own stubbornness, your own sin." Stunned by Campbell's challenge, Lewis, who had long admired the city's most courageous white minister, hesitated before he responded. Gathering his words carefully, he looked Campbell straight in the eyes and said, "Okay, I am a sinner. But we're gonna march."[11]

Following the showdown at First Colored Baptist, the stand-ins resumed and continued without interruption for three weeks. Assaults and harassment by white people also continued, but the violent eruption that the NCLC had anticipated never materialized. The situation never got out of control, largely because the students participating in the stand-ins maintained a strict discipline. They followed Lawson's teachings to the letter, thanks in part to the leadership and organizing skills of Nash, who had become the chairperson of the NSM central committee earlier in the year.

Bright and beautiful, Nash enjoyed a special status within the NSM's ranks. A native of Chicago who had attended Howard University in Washington before transferring to Fisk, she was one of the few Northerners among Lawson's disciples. With a personality that somehow combined sweetness and toughness, she had an uncanny ability to bring out the best in the people around her, as she did with Mayor Ben West on the courthouse steps the previous April. Early on, Lewis developed deep respect and admiration for her, and like several other male members of the NSM, he harbored thoughts about a romantic relationship with her. "The first thing you have to say about Diane—the first thing anyone who encountered her noticed, and there was no way *not* to notice—is that she was one of God's beautiful creatures, just about the most gorgeous woman any of us had ever seen," he wrote years later. He also remembered how she came to the workshops "with a lot of doubt at first. But she quickly absorbed all that Jim Lawson had to share, and she soon emerged as the leader of our group, which was an extraordinary thing, considering the role of women in society at large at that time. . . . She was dead serious about what we were doing each week, very calm, very deliberate, always straightforward and sincere. As time passed, she came to be seen more as our sister than as an object of lust. We all became brothers and sisters, a family."

A role model for Lewis and many other NSM activists, Nash displayed an unswerving commitment to nonviolence that inspired imitation throughout the local movement's ranks, even, as it turned out, when she was absent from the scene. During the first week of the stand-ins, she, along with three other SNCC stalwarts—Charles Jones of Charlotte, Ruby Doris Smith of Atlanta, and Charles Sherrod of Richmond—volunteered to join a group known as the Rock Hill Nine in a South Carolina jail. The Rock Hill Nine included Tom Gaither, a young Black CORE field secretary from Orangeburg, who had encouraged a group of Rock Hill students to stage a sit-in at a segregated McCrory's lunch counter on February 1. The Rock Hill sit-in became a show-case for the "jail, no bail" policy that CORE's executive director Jim Farmer had been advocating. As Farmer later explained, he and his staff "felt that one of the weaknesses of the student sit-in movement of the South had been that as soon as arrested, the kids bailed out. . . . This was not quite Gandhian and not the best tactic. A better tactic would be to remain in jail and to make the maintenance of segregation so expensive for the state and the city that they would hopefully come to the conclusion that they could no longer afford it. Fill up the jails, as Gandhi did in India, fill them to bursting if we had to."

The courage of the Rock Hill Nine was a major topic of conversation when SNCC leaders from around the region met in Atlanta on February 3. Lawson had always encouraged his Nashville followers to refuse bail—both as a matter of principle and as an effective tactic—but to date virtually no SNCC arrestee outside Nashville had chosen to remain behind bars. A heated discussion of the Rock Hill situation engaged the SNCC leaders well into the night but seemed to be going nowhere until a phone call from Gaither focused their attention on a request for volunteers. After promising that the Rock Hill Nine were committed to serving out their thirty days of hard labor, he pleaded for reinforcements that would magnify the impact of the jail-in. SNCC could stage jail-ins in other cities or its members could go to Rock Hill, but the organization had to do something dramatic to sustain the movement's momentum.

Four of the SNCC leaders at the meeting, including Nash, volunteered immediately, but a SNCC press release calling for additional volunteers found no one else willing to embrace arrest in Rock Hill. The jail-in movement did, however, spread within a few days to Atlanta and Lynchburg, Virginia, raising the total number of students choosing jail over bail to nearly one hundred. Even more important was the effect of the Rock Hill crisis on the overall relationship between CORE and SNCC, which to date had seen little cooperation. As the expanded incarcerated group in South Carolina, now known as the Rock Hill Thirteen, served out their month in jail, a bond between the two civil rights organizations with the firmest commitment to nonviolent direct action began to form, establishing a core of solidarity and shared sacrifice that would inspire later activists.[12]

Nash's monthlong stint in a Rock Hill jail enhanced her growing reputation as a freedom fighter, and she enjoyed a warm homecoming reunion with Lewis and her other Nashville friends in early March. By that time the stand-in campaign was in its final stage and on the verge of a hard-won victory. In Nash's absence, the NSM had increased the pressure on the segregated theaters, especially after the central committee adopted a new tactic on February 20. Instead of simply forming a line in front of the ticket booth, Lewis, LaFayette, and Bevel directed a group of students to block the entrance to Loew's Theater. This daring confrontational move immediately drew the police, who arrested twenty-six of the students, including Lewis. The next day was Lewis's twenty-first birthday, which he spent behind bars.

Normally, Lewis would have taken his latest arrest in stride, perhaps even welcoming it in Gandhian style as beneficial unmerited suffering. But on that day, February 21, 1961, he faced the confounding complication of an afternoon appointment to deliver his senior sermon; for a theology student at ABT, this was the equivalent of a comprehensive final exam and a requirement for graduation. Now, his chosen sermon—based on the tenth chapter of Matthew, which offered words of wisdom on "discipleship, commitment, and sacrifice"—would have to be postponed for at least a week and perhaps longer. While he didn't feel burdened with shame or regret, he did not want to do anything that would interfere with his graduation, which he knew meant so much to his parents. Despite their opposition to his involvement in the movement, his mother and father planned to attend his graduation ceremony, traveling over six hundred miles roundtrip to honor the first of their ten children to receive a college degree.

Fortunately for Lewis, the ABT administration allowed him to postpone his senior sermon until early March. His performance, grounded in four years of diligent study, received a high grade, a triumph followed a week later by the successful completion of the stand-in campaign. Tired of the continuing disruption and the loss of business, several Church Street theater owners capitulated to the NSM's demands, and by mid-March a significant number of Black and white patrons were attending movies on an integrated basis. Although complete integration of the theaters would not come until early May, this sign of progress and the promise of more to come represented a great victory for Lewis and his friends. Thus they decided it was time to extend their efforts to other targets, including segregated transit facilities.[13]

* * *

In the spring of 1961, Nashville's city buses had been desegregated for several years, and during the previous summer the local bus company had even hired its first Black driver. But all of the city's major bus and rail terminals, where the facilities and vehicles often catered to interstate passengers, remained strictly segregated. In mid-February, two impromptu sit-ins—both spillovers from the stand-in campaign—had led to a brief breach of the color bar at the Trailways and Greyhound terminals' lunch counters. But these proved to be momentary lapses of racial etiquette, especially at the Greyhound lunch counter, where the management only permitted Black employees to serve the Black students and where angry whites tried to assault and evict the students.

Lewis did not take part in this particular episode, but he and LaFayette had already had several discussions about a plan to conduct a second challenge to interstate bus segregation along the same lines as their December 1959 ride from Nashville to Alabama. For more than a year, they let the idea simmer, but in March 1961 they sent a letter to the Reverend Fred Shuttlesworth, Birmingham's leading civil rights activist, proposing a test of two Supreme Court decisions mandating the desegregation of interstate bus travel.

The first decision, *Morgan v. Virginia*, had been on the books since June 1946, when the Court ruled that Irene Morgan, a young Black woman traveling from Gloucester County, Virginia, to Baltimore, Maryland, had the constitutional right to sit anywhere she wanted on an interstate bus. On paper, the ruling nullified Virginia's state law (and by implication similar laws in other states) requiring racial segregation on interstate buses, but in fact the bus companies and attorneys general across the South openly flouted the *Morgan* decision for fifteen years, all but daring the federal courts and the executive branch to enforce it.

The second decision, *Boynton v. Virginia*, was much more recent, coming in December 1960, when the Court overturned the conviction of Bruce Boynton, a Howard University law student from Selma, Alabama, arrested in 1958 for attempting to desegregate the whites-only Trailways terminal restaurant in Richmond. To the delight of Thurgood Marshall, the NAACP attorney who argued the case, the Court ruled by a vote of seven to two that state laws mandating segregated waiting rooms, lunch counters, and restroom facilities for interstate passengers were unconstitutional.

This time, unlike with the *Morgan* ruling, there was initially a widespread expectation that the Justice Department, led by the president's brother, would enforce what appeared to be a landmark decision. Yet, two months into the Kennedy era, there was no evidence that enforcement would come anytime soon. Many civil rights activists, including Lewis and LaFayette, were disappointed in the new administration's lack of action on this and a host of other civil rights matters. But the two Nashville students were among the first to decide to do something about this aggravating delay. In their letter to Shuttlesworth, they advanced the idea of having "a core group of us ride the bus down to Birmingham and test the waiting areas, rest rooms and eating facilities in the Greyhound station there—perhaps the most rigidly segregated bus terminal in the South—applying the same tactics we'd used with our sit-ins and stand-ins in Nashville."

Though appreciative of their bravery, Shuttlesworth urged the Nashville insurgents to find some other way to serve the cause. Birmingham, he warned, was a racial powder keg that would explode if local white supremacists were unduly provoked, especially by outsiders. This was not what Lewis and LaFayette expected to hear, but they had no choice but to defer to a man renowned within the movement as a fearless advocate of racial justice—a man who knew far more about the situation in Birmingham than they did. Though disappointed, they decided to shelve their plan, hoping that a test of bus desegregation could be worked out sometime in the future.[14]

At that point, April was approaching, and the spring semester was winding down. For Lewis, whose graduation was only two months away, it was time to think about the future and postgraduation plans. He thought about applying to graduate school, but he was unsure about what program of study would be best for him, or about where he had a chance of acceptance. The only certainty was that he did not want to continue his theology studies in preparation to become a preacher. He also had a strong urge to see more of the world, particularly Africa and Gandhi's India. With this in mind, he submitted an application to the American Friends Service Committee (AFSC), the secular arm of Quaker pacifism, to enter a two-year foreign service program aimed at building homes in underdeveloped, postcolonial countries. Going abroad for two years, he calculated, would give him enough time to figure out how he could best contribute to the realization of the goals of the struggle for civil and human rights. He was willing to leave Nashville but not the movement broadly conceived.

In early April, Lewis waited anxiously for the AFSC's decision about whether he had made the interview stage of the selection process. But within days of submitting his application, his wait was interrupted by an unexpected development that would divert him to another path—one that would radically alter the course of his life. While walking across the ABT campus, he ran into the Reverend J. Metz Rollins, a movement friend who had participated in the 1956 Tallahassee bus boycott and who had recently moved to Nashville to serve as the field director of the United Presbyterian Church. Holding a sheaf of papers, Rollins handed one of them to Lewis and said, "John, you might want to take a look at this." The sheet of paper, a page from SNCC's monthly newsletter, the *Student Voice,* carried a CORE recruiting advertisement headlined "Freedom Ride 1961."

This was Lewis's first encounter with the phrase "freedom ride," and it sent a shiver of excitement through his body. The CORE Freedom Ride, the ad explained, would test the progress of bus desegregation mandated by the *Morgan* and *Boynton* decisions. Putting small biracial groups on regularly scheduled interstate buses traveling through the South, CORE would deliberately violate state and local laws requiring racial segregation on buses and in terminals. "I couldn't believe it," Lewis recalled. "This was just what Bernard and I had written Fred Shuttlesworth about."[15]

During his years in Nashville, Lewis had developed a strong belief in something that he labeled "the Spirit of History," a phrase adapted from the writings of the German philosopher G. W. F. Hegel, whom he had studied in a first-year class taught by Professor John Lewis Powell. "Others might call it fate. Or destiny. Or a guiding hand," he explained. "Whatever it is called, I came to believe that this force is on the side of good, of what is right and just. It is the essence of the moral force of the universe. And at certain points in life, in the flow of human existence and circumstances, this force, this spirit, finds you or selects you, it chases you down, and you have no choice; you must allow yourself to be used, to be guided by this force and to carry out what must be done. To me, that concept of surrender, of giving yourself over to something inexorable, something so much larger than yourself, is the basis of what we call faith." The opportunity to become a Freedom Rider was one of these pivotal "points in life," he concluded. "Somehow, the Spirit of History was putting its hands on my life again."[16]

Rollins and Lewis wasted no time in applying to join the Freedom Ride, and LaFayette soon followed suit, or at least he tried to. CORE asked each applicant to include a recommendation from a teacher, pastor, or coworker and to write an essay outlining his or her commitment to nonviolence and the struggle for civil rights. Volunteers under the age of twenty-one also had to submit proof of parental permission. This last requirement foiled twenty-year-old LaFayette's bid to join the first group of Freedom Riders. Already exercised over her son's role in the Nashville sit-ins and stand-ins, his mother refused to sign the permission form, reminding him that she had sent him "to Nashville to study, not to aggravate white folks." His father was even more emphatic, thundering over the phone, "Boy, you're asking me to sign your death warrant."

If Lewis's parents had been asked to sign a permission form, they undoubtedly would have reacted the same way, questioning their son's sanity. But Lewis, having turned twenty-one in February, could apply without asking his parents for permission, or even informing them of the dangerous adventure he was about to undertake. His strong record as an NSM leader and his status as a jail-tested veteran who had been arrested five times during the past year virtually guaranteed that he would be chosen as one of Nashville's participants in the Freedom Ride. But he also benefited from a poignant essay that ended with a moving passage expressing his commitment to the nonviolent movement. "At this time," he wrote revealingly, "human dignity is the most important thing in my life. This is [the] most important decision in my life, to decide to give up all if necessary for the Freedom Ride, that Justice and Freedom might come to the Deep South."[17]

Both Lewis and Rollins received acceptance letters from CORE in mid-April, roughly three weeks before the Freedom Ride was scheduled to begin on May 4. The two-week-long Ride from Washington to New Orleans was loosely based on an April 1947 nonviolent direct action campaign called the Journey of Reconciliation. Designed as a test of compliance to the 1946 *Morgan* decision and as a means of extending CORE's influence into the South, the Journey of Reconciliation involved sixteen volunteers, eight white and eight Black, who traveled together on buses and trains from Washington through the Upper South states of Virginia, North Carolina, and Tennessee and the border state of Kentucky. Their disregard for local and state segregation statutes led to several arrests and some violence on the part of white segregationists, but their actions received little press coverage and resulted in few signs of progress.

In the decade that followed, interest in additional Journeys of Reconciliation faded as CORE, like many radical organizations, went into deep decline during the heyday of the Cold War. A limited resurgence and renewed interest in nonviolence came in the wake of the Montgomery Bus Boycott, but the opportunity to rebuild the organization as a major player in the civil rights struggle did not come until the resumption of nonviolent direct action during and after the sit-ins of 1960.[18]

*   *   *

The path to the Freedom Ride finally opened on February 1, 1961, the first anniversary of the original Greensboro sit-in, when James Farmer became CORE's executive director. One of CORE's founders in 1942, Farmer left the organization in the late 1940s to embrace the labor movement and later found work with the NAACP. The Journey of Reconciliation had taken place during his absence from CORE, and he had always regretted this missed opportunity.

This regret reached full force as he sat at his desk in New York that first morning waiting for reports from the Southern front. Sifting through a stack of accumulated correspondence, he noticed a number of inquiries about the lack of enforcement following the recent *Boynton* decision. Why, the letter writers asked, were Black Americans still being harassed or arrested when they tried to exercise their constitutional right to drink a cup of coffee at a bus terminal restaurant? At a late-morning meeting, Farmer relayed this troubling question to his staff, and to his surprise two of his field secretaries, Gordon Carey and Tom Gaither, were well aware of this unfortunate situation and had already come up with a tentative plan to address the problem of nonenforcement.

As Carey explained, during an unexpectedly long bus trip from South Carolina to New York in mid-January, he and Gaither had discussed the feasibility of a second Journey of Reconciliation. Thanks to a blizzard that forced them to spend a night on the floor of a Howard Johnson's restaurant along the New Jersey Turnpike, they had even gone so far as to map out a proposed route from Washington to New Orleans. And they had also come up with a catchy name for the project: "Freedom Ride."

Patterned after Gandhi's famous 1930 march to the sea—throughout the bus trip Carey had been reading Louis Fischer's biography of Gandhi— the second Journey of Reconciliation, like the first, would last two weeks. But, taking advantage of the Southern movement's gathering momentum, it would also extend the effort to test compliance into the heart of the Deep South. Despite the obvious logistical problems in mounting such an effort,

Farmer and everyone else in the room immediately sensed that Carey and Gaither were on the right track. Ten days later, CORE's National Action Committee approved Farmer's request to launch the Freedom Ride, endorsing the new director's bold plan to put "the movement on wheels . . . to cut across state lines and establish the position that we were entitled to act any place in the country, no matter where we hung our hat and called home."

The plan, as Farmer told the committee, was to "recruit from twelve to fourteen persons, call them to Washington, D.C., for a week of intensive training and preparation, and then embark on the Ride. Half would go by Greyhound and half by Trailways." The Riders would leave Washington on May 4, travel through Virginia, North and South Carolina, Georgia, Alabama, Mississippi, and Louisiana, and arrive—if all went well—in New Orleans on May 17, the seventh anniversary of the *Brown* decision.[19]

No one could be certain how much resistance the Riders would encounter along the route, especially in the Deep South, but an extensive scouting trip by Gaither in April revealed enough racial tension to deter all but the most courageous of Riders. This was the alarming message that Gaither received during a meeting with fifteen SNCC leaders in Charlotte, North Carolina, on April 21. While the SNCC leaders offered some support for CORE's planned Freedom Ride, they stopped short of a formal endorsement and warned that the Riders would almost certainly be met with violence at several points during their hazardous journey. Gaither, who relayed this and other warnings to Farmer in his report, identified the white supremacist strongholds where the Riders would be most likely to encounter violence, including the Alabama cities of Birmingham and Anniston, which he termed "a very explosive trouble spot without a doubt." Indeed, he concluded that in the Deep South, where police protection was unlikely, the Freedom Riders would be lucky to escape with their lives.[20]

With all of this in mind, Farmer selected the participants in the Freedom Ride with great care. The first two chosen were Jim Peck, a seasoned white veteran of the 1947 Journey of Reconciliation, and himself. Peck was an obvious choice, but Farmer's decision to put himself in harm's way raised more than a few eyebrows. Known more as an office and idea man than as a hands-on activist, CORE's forty-one-year-old leader had never exhibited much interest in risking arrest or imprisonment. Those who knew him well, however, understood his motivation. The Freedom Ride was Farmer's personal ticket to glory, his best chance to join King, A. Philip Randolph, and Marshall in the front ranks of civil rights leaders and, by doing so, raise CORE's profile as an important national organization. Having missed the 1947 ride, he wasn't about to miss this one.

In selecting the remaining Riders, Farmer and his staff tried to come up with a reasonably balanced mixture of Black and white, young and old, male and female, religious and secular, Northern and Southern, volunteers and CORE staff members. But the process became more complicated when three of those selected—Rollins and two New Orleans CORE activists who were languishing in a Louisiana jail—were forced to drop out before the Ride began. Nevertheless, the eleven Riders who joined Farmer and Peck for the training sessions in Washington on May 1 represented a wide range of backgrounds and movement experiences.

Two of the eleven—Genevieve Hughes, a twenty-eight-year-old white Cornell graduate from Chevy Chase, Maryland, and Joe Perkins, a twenty-seven-year-old Black army veteran from Kentucky—were CORE field secretaries. Four were white Northerners with limited experience in the South: Walter and Frances Bergman, a semiretired professor and a former elementary school administrator, both ACLU activists from Detroit; Ed Blankenheim, a twenty-seven-year-old carpenter's apprentice and part-time chemistry graduate student at the University of Arizona; and Albert Bigelow, a retired U.S. Navy captain, World War II veteran, and Harvard-trained architect who had become a prominent Quaker pacifist and antinuclear activist. Two others were Northern-born Black activists: Jimmy McDonald, a twenty-nine-year-old folk singer from New York City known for his vast repertoire of labor and freedom songs; and John Moody, a thirty-year-old Howard University student from Philadelphia and an active member of the SNCC-affiliated, Washington-based Nonviolent Action Group (NAG). Moody, however, withdrew from the Ride on the third day of training when all the talk about racism and savagery in the Deep South became too intense and threatening for him.

Moody's last-minute replacement was his nineteen-year-old Howard roommate, Hank Thomas, a fellow NAG activist from St. Augustine, Florida. A strapping six-foot-five football player, Thomas was the only individual to join the Ride without undergoing the full three days of nonviolent training. But his prior experiences in the Jim Crow South served him well, adding to the regional grounding of the other three Black Southerners who rounded out the Freedom Rider contingent: Lewis, who, in Rollins's absence, became the only Freedom Rider affiliated with the Nashville movement; the Reverend Benjamin Elton Cox, known as "Beltin' Elton," a twenty-nine-year-old Congregational minister from High Point, North Carolina, who had organized NAACP-sponsored sit-ins involving high school students; and eighteen-year-old Charles Person, a freshman at Morehouse College who had participated in several sit-ins as a member of the ACAHR and who had recently spent sixteen days in jail for his efforts. Along with Farmer's background as a native Texan, Lewis's and the other Black Southerners' familiarity with the racial scene below the Mason-Dixon Line would prove invaluable once the Ride headed south into a strange and dangerous land foreign to the other Freedom Riders.[21]

CHAPTER 4

———

Riding to Freedom

JOHN LEWIS knew next to nothing about his fellow Freedom Riders when he left Nashville on April 29, 1961, and he almost lost his chance to meet them when he missed the morning bus to Washington. Fortunately, Jim Bevel, accompanied by Bernard LaFayette, saved the day by driving him to Murfreesboro, where he caught another interstate bus. Lewis arrived in Washington on the morning of April 30, just in time to join the other Freedom Riders for three days of intensive preparation and training in nonviolence. As a protégé of James Lawson, he had already undergone nearly two years of such training and was probably better prepared than any of the other Riders, with the possible exception of Jim Peck. But he was eager to experience what the CORE trainers had to offer.

All thirteen Riders stayed at Fellowship House, a well-known Quaker meetinghouse and dormitory on L Street that had hosted generations of pacifists and social activists. "Inside was room after room filled with books and posters and pieces of art," Lewis recalled, "all centered around the themes of peace and community." To many of the Riders, such a scene was familiar, but the young Alabamian "had never been in a building like this," nor "among people like this."

In this enclave of interracial brotherhood, the Beloved Community that Lawson had conjured up suddenly seemed less abstract and more achievable, at least until Jim Farmer's rather heavy-handed welcoming speech complicated this vision. In greeting his fellow Riders, Farmer made it clear he was in charge and the Freedom Ride was first and foremost a CORE

project. Anyone unwilling to abide by CORE's strict adherence to nonviolence should withdraw from the project, he informed them in his best sten-
torian voice. As one of the three SNCC volunteers in the room, the others
being Charles Person and John Moody, Lewis was taken aback by Farmer's
emphasis on the primacy of CORE. But he appreciated the CORE leader's
passionate commitment to nonviolence, which became apparent during several minutes of sobering orientation.

Farmer eventually turned the podium over to a series of speakers, including one who briefed the Riders on the Constitution and federal and
state laws pertaining to discrimination in interstate transportation. A second speaker, a veteran activist with many years of experience in the Deep
South, vividly described the risks and challenges that the Riders would soon
experience—"what really was going to happen to us, including clobberings
and possibly death," as Farmer later put it. Thus began three grueling days
of training that, according to Lewis, "went by like a blur."

Despite being one of the youngest volunteers, Lewis—more than most
of the other Riders—took it all in stride. "We began by covering much of the
ground I'd already spent years learning from Jim Lawson," he remembered.
"We read and discussed Gandhi, Thoreau and the like. Then we moved on to
the specifics of the trip. We studied the structure of the Jim Crow system,
learned about the local and state laws we would encounter in the places
we were headed, listened to lawyers brought in by Farmer to lecture on
our rights under the *Boynton* decision and our legal recourses should those
rights be denied."[1]

All of this was a prelude to what CORE leaders considered to be the
most important part of the Riders' training: "intense role-playing sessions"
designed to give them a sense of what they were about to face. Coordinated
by Gordon Carey, the sessions were carefully constructed "sociodramas,"
as Farmer called them, "with some of the group playing the part of Freedom
Riders sitting at simulated lunch counters or sitting on the front-seats of a
make-believe bus. Others acted out the roles of functionaries, adversaries,
or observers. Several played the role of white hoodlums coming to beat up
the Freedom Riders on the buses or at lunch counters at the terminals."
After each session, the role-players' actions and reactions were evaluated by
the group, and over the course of the training each Rider got the chance to

experience the full range of emotions and crises that were likely to emerge during the coming journey. "It was quite an experience," Benjamin Elton Cox remembered. "We were knocked on the floor, we poured Coca-Cola and coffee on each other, and there was shoving and calling each other all kinds of racial epithets, and even spitting on each other, which would inflame you to see if you could stand what was going to come."

By the afternoon of May 3, the day before their scheduled departure, all of the Riders were emotionally drained. During the final hours of preparation, as pride and anticipation mingled with fear and apprehension, Farmer realized he had to do something to break the tension. Following a few freedom songs from Jimmy McDonald, he took the Riders downtown for an elaborate Chinese dinner at the Yen Ching Palace, an upscale Connecticut Avenue restaurant managed by NAG activist Paul Dietrich. It was an exotic experience for many of the younger Riders, including Lewis, who had never eaten Chinese food before. The whole scene somehow seemed appropriate for men and women about to explore the unknown. "As we passed around the bright silver containers of food," Lewis recalled, "someone joked we should eat well and enjoy because this might be our Last Supper." "Several in the group," he noted, "had actually written out wills in case they didn't come back from the trip." "As for me," he added, "just about all I owned was packed in my suitcase. There was no need for me to make out a will. I had nothing to leave anyone."[2]

The gallows humor of the Last Supper quip seemed to break the ice, and the gathering settled into a mood of genuine fellowship. By the time the steamed rice and stir-fried vegetables gave way to fortune cookies, it was clear the experiences of the last three days had created a family-like bond among the Riders. As the cookies and pots of tea were making their way around the table, Dietrich and several other NAG activists, including a Howard student named Stokely Carmichael, joined the group, just in time to hear a soul-searching speech by Farmer. Obviously pleased with what had happened since the Riders had arrived in Washington, he wanted them to know he had faith in their ability to meet any challenge. But he went on to insist he was the only one "obligated to go on this trip," that "there was still time for any person to decide not to go." With this unsettling benediction, Lewis and the other Riders filed out of the restaurant in near silence. Although the long-awaited Freedom Ride was scheduled to leave, no one knew how many Riders would actually appear at the bus station in the morning.

Farmer feared several Riders would drop out before the departure, but once he arrived at the breakfast table and saw the determination in the Riders' eyes, he realized the full contingent was "prepared for anything, even death." No one had withdrawn, and individually and collectively they appeared ready to do what had to be done, not in a spirit of selfless or reckless heroism but as a vanguard of ordinary citizens seeking simple justice.[3]

*   *   *

The morning scene at the downtown Trailways station—and at the Greyhound station across the street—gave little indication that something momentous was about to unfold. There were no identifying banners, no protest signs—nothing to signify the start of a revolution other than a few well-wishers representing CORE, NAG, and the SCLC. Despite a spate of CORE press releases, the beginning of the Freedom Ride drew only token coverage. No television cameras or radio microphones were on hand to record the event, and the only members of the national press corps covering the departure were an Associated Press correspondent and two local reporters from the *Washington Post* and the *Washington Evening Star*. The only other journalists present were three brave individuals who had agreed to accompany the Riders to New Orleans: Charlotte Devree, a white freelance writer and CORE activist from New York; Simeon Booker, a Black feature writer representing Johnson Publications' *Jet* and *Ebony* magazines; and Ted Gaffney, a Washington-based photographer and Johnson stringer. A fourth journalist, the *Baltimore Afro-American* editor Moses Newson, would later join the Ride in Greensboro, North Carolina.

Two weeks earlier the CORE office had sent letters describing the impending Freedom Ride to President Kennedy, FBI director J. Edgar Hoover, Attorney General Robert Kennedy, the chairman of the ICC, and the presidents of Trailways and Greyhound. But no one had responded, and as the Riders prepared to board the buses, there was no sign of official surveillance or concern. Once all the Riders had arrived, Farmer held a brief press conference to explain both the philosophy of nonviolence and CORE's "jail, no bail" policy. "If there is an arrest, we will accept that arrest," he told the handful of reporters, "and if there is violence we will accept that violence without responding in kind."

Farmer then turned to the Riders themselves, dividing them into two groups. Six, including Lewis, were assigned to Greyhound, and seven to Trailways. After checking their bags, the Riders received last-minute instructions. Each group would make sure one Black Freedom Rider sat in a seat normally reserved for white passengers, at least one interracial pair of Riders sat in adjoining seats, and the remaining Riders scattered throughout the bus. One Rider on each bus would serve as a designated observer and remain aloof from the others; by obeying the conventions of segregated travel, he or she would ensure at least one Rider would avoid arrest and be in a position to contact CORE officials or arrange bail money for those arrested. Most of the Riders, however, were free to mingle with the other passengers and to discuss the purpose of the Freedom Ride with anyone who would listen. Exercising the constitutional right to sit anywhere on the bus, or to seek service anywhere in the bus terminals, had educational as well as legal implications, Farmer explained, and the Riders were encouraged to think of themselves as teachers and role models.

Earlier in the week, Farmer had warned them they could be arrested at any time, so they had to be prepared for the unexpected. He had urged each Rider to bring a carry-on bag containing a toothbrush, toothpaste, and an inspiring book or two to help fill the hours behind bars. Many years later, Lewis remembered packing three books in the bag he placed under his seat: one by the Roman Catholic philosopher Thomas Merton, a second on Gandhi, and the Bible. All of these precautions and warnings took on new meaning as the buses actually headed south on Route 1.[4]

Every detail of that first day on the road was etched in Lewis's memory. "My seatmate was Albert Bigelow. He sat on the aisle," he remembered years later. "I sat on the window, watching the scenery as we pulled out of the terminal, wound through the city, then rolled across the Potomac and south into the open fields and farmland of Virginia. Ahead stretched thirteen days and 1,500 miles of Deep South highway. . . . Our first stop was Fredericksburg, an hour or so south of D.C., where we stepped off to see that the "WHITE ONLY" and "COLORED ONLY" signs had been removed from the terminal bathrooms and restaurant. 'Looks like they knew we were coming and baked us a cake,' someone said. There was no disruption as we used rest rooms traditionally designated for another race and ordered drinks at a counter that never would have served us before." Someone in a position of authority had decided there would be no trouble in Fredericksburg. Peck used the "colored" restroom, and Person, the designated Black tester for the day, used the white restroom and later ordered a drink at the whites-only lunch counter, all without incident. To the Riders' surprise, the service was cordial, and not a harsh word was spoken by anyone. This apparent lack of rancor in the state that had spawned the "massive resistance" movement only a few years earlier was almost eerie, and as the Riders reboarded the bus, they couldn't help wonder what other surprises lay ahead.

From Fredericksburg, the Riders traveled south and west to conduct tests in five other Virginia cities: Richmond, where they encountered no resistance and desegregated both bus stations before spending the night at the historically Black Virginia Union College; Petersburg, a center of movement activity led by the Reverend Wyatt Tee Walker, who had recently moved to Atlanta to become the executive secretary of the SCLC; Farmville, an ultraconservative town in Prince Edward County, where two years earlier local officials had shut down the public school system rather than submit to desegregation but now had hidden the bus terminal's Jim Crow signs with a fresh coat of paint; Lynchburg, a movement center that had experienced a jail-in earlier in the year—here the Riders once again saw no Jim Crow signs, but at the Trailways lunch counter they encountered a towering partition "making persons on one side virtually invisible to those on the other"; and finally, Danville, where the Riders were met with hostility and open resistance for the first time. At Danville's combined Greyhound-Trailways station, a Black waiter refused to serve Ed Blankenheim at the "colored counter," ultimately outlasting the Arizona activist, who reboarded the bus without being served. An hour later, when the Trailways Riders arrived, Peck renewed the challenge, and after a curt refusal and a brief standoff he convinced the station manager to relent.[5]

* * *

Every community, it seemed, had its own style of discrimination and strategy to send the Freedom Riders on their way without provoking a crisis. By mid-Sunday afternoon, May 7, the fourth day on the road, both buses had crossed the North Carolina line, leaving proud but perplexed Virginia to its own devices. The first overnight stop in the Carolinas was Greensboro, the fabled birthplace of the 1960 sit-in movement and a community where most white leaders had adopted a moderate, flexible approach to race relations. Although the local scene had become increasingly tense and racially polarized during the past year, the Riders entering the Greensboro Trailways station discovered that the "colored" lunch counter had been closed down earlier in the week and that all races were welcome at the white counter.

That evening the Riders were invited to a mass meeting at the Shiloh Baptist Church—the same Black church that had welcomed the Journey of Reconciliation riders in 1947. Shiloh's pastor, the Reverend Otis Hairston, was a fearless activist who had turned his church into an unofficial command center during the early stages of the sit-in movement. Now—along with George Simkins, the NAACP leader who had urged CORE to become involved in the Greensboro sit-ins, and Joseph McNeil, one of the city's four original sit-in participants—he gave Farmer a joyous welcome, offering him a platform to explain the strategy behind the Freedom Ride. When Farmer expressed both his fear that the desegregation fight had lost some of its "steam" and his determination to make segregation "so costly the South can't afford it," the sanctuary reverberated with amens. "Life is not so dear and sweet," Farmer added, "that we must passively accept Jim Crow and segregation. . . . If our parents had gone to jail we wouldn't have to go through the ordeal now. Our nation cannot afford segregation. Overseas it gives Uncle Sam a black eye. Future generations will thank us for what we have done."

On and on he went, crying out for a resurgence of the spirit that had nurtured the sit-ins. By the end of the evening, both Farmer and the audience were emotionally spent, but as the Freedom Riders and their hosts filed out of the sanctuary, the dual message of empowerment and responsibility was clear. Before they could hope to redeem the white South, Farmer and the Freedom Riders had to embolden the Black South, to stir things up to a point where a critical mass of activists demanded fundamental change. Coming at the end of four unexpectedly smooth and successful days on the road, Farmer's bold words thrilled Lewis. It was a stirring style of oratory that he aspired to—a style he would use to great effect later in his life. But in 1961, as one of the youngest of the Riders, he had not yet found his public voice. "We selected different spokespeople at each stop," he later explained, "but I was not eager to be one of them. Besides my natural shyness . . . I just didn't feel that it was my place to speak up. I was more than ready to speak through action, but words, well, I would just as soon leave them to others."[6]

From Greensboro, the Riders headed south through the small North Carolina communities of Salisbury, Rowan Mill, China Grove, and Kannapolis and on to Charlotte. The largest city in the Carolina Piedmont, Charlotte was a banking and textile center with a flair for New South commercialism. As in Greensboro, city leaders cultivated an image of moderation and urbane paternalism, but they did so with the expectation that all local citizens knew their place. The immutability of racial segregation, even in the most mundane aspects of life, was a given, and anyone who crossed the color line in Charlotte was asking for trouble. Person discovered just how true this was when he tried to get a shoeshine at the city's Union Station. As Peck later explained, the young Atlanta student "didn't even think of it as a test. He simply looked at his shoes and thought he needed a shine." After being rebuffed, he decided to remain in the whites-only shoeshine chair until someone either polished his shoes or arrested him. Within minutes, a policeman arrived and threatened to handcuff him and haul him off to jail if he didn't move. At this point, Person decided to avoid arrest and scurried back to tell the other Riders what had happened.

After an impromptu strategy session, the Riders designated Joe Perkins as the group's official shoeshine segregation tester. The whole scene carried a touch of the absurd—the Riders later referred to the incident as the South's first "shoe-in"—but Perkins agreed to sit in the shoeshine chair until somebody came and arrested him. A few minutes later, the CORE field secretary became the first Freedom Rider to be arrested. The formal charge was trespassing, and bail was set at fifty dollars. After a night in jail, Perkins went before a local judge who, to his amazement, rendered an acquittal based on the *Boynton* decision. Even so, as Perkins left the courthouse to rejoin the Ride, which had gone on to South Carolina, the same police officer who had arrested him at Union Station accosted him, advising him "to get the hell out of town," declaring he wasn't about "to let no New York nigger come down here and make trouble for us and our good nigras." Though tempted to argue the point, Perkins let the comment pass before catching a late-morning bus to Rock Hill, where the Riders were about to leave for Sumter after an overnight stay.[7]

Upon his arrival in Rock Hill, Perkins discovered that a great deal had happened during his absence. The North Carolina Piedmont was as far south as CORE's 1947 Journey of Reconciliation had dared to go, so when the Freedom Riders headed down Highway 29 from Charlotte to Rock Hill on Tuesday morning, May 9, they were entering uncharted territory. Rock Hill, a rough, cotton mill town that had been seething with racial tension since the celebrated jail-in three months earlier, turned out to be the first serious trouble spot for the Freedom Riders—and the scene of Lewis's first beating. Tom Gaither, who had spent considerable time there both in and out of jail, warned the Riders that the town was crawling with Klansmen. The relative ease of the journey through Virginia and North Carolina left many of the Riders unprepared for the rude welcome they received in Rock Hill, but Lewis, who had traveled to the troubled town earlier in the year to visit Diane Nash and other jailed SNCC colleagues, was not surprised.

"I could tell we were in real trouble as soon as I stepped off the bus," he recalled. "As Al Bigelow and I approached the 'white' waiting room in the Rock Hill Greyhound terminal, I noticed a large number of young white guys hanging around the pinball machines in the lobby. Two of these guys were leaning by the door jamb to the waiting room. They wore leather jackets, had those ducktail haircuts and were each smoking a cigarette. 'Other side nigger,' one of the two said, stepping in my way as I began to walk through the door. He pointed to a door down the way with a sign that said 'COLORED.' . . . 'I have a right to go in there,' I said, speaking carefully and clearly, 'on the grounds of the Supreme Court decision in the *Boynton* case.' I don't think either of these guys had ever heard of the *Boynton* case. Not that it would have mattered. 'Shit on that,' one of them said. The next thing I knew, a fist smashed the right side of my head. Then another hit me square in the face. As I fell to the floor I could feel feet kicking me hard in the sides. I could taste blood in my mouth. At that point Al Bigelow stepped in, placing his body between mine and these men, standing square with his arms at his sides. . . . They hesitated for an instant. Then they attacked Bigelow, who did not raise a finger as these young men began punching him. It took several blows to drop him to one knee. At that point several of the white guys by the pinball machines moved over to join in. Genevieve Hughes stepped in their way and was knocked to the floor."

Whether out of chivalry or just plain common sense, a police officer who had witnessed the entire assault finally intervened and grabbed one of the assailants. "All right, boys," he stated with some authority. "Y'all've done about enough now. Get on home." After a few parting epithets, the boys retreated to the street, leaving the Riders and the policeman to wait for several other officers who had been called to the scene. To Lewis's surprise, one of the officers appeared to be sympathetic to the injured Riders and asked them if they wanted to file charges against their attackers. But they declined the offer, upholding the Gandhian tradition of refusing to punish individuals motivated by systemic injustice. Though still shaken, Lewis, Bigelow, and Hughes then staggered into the terminal restaurant to join the rest of the Riders. Lewis, who had suffered bruised ribs and cuts around his eyes and mouth and on the back side of his head, was in need of immediate medical attention, but he stubbornly insisted on remaining at the restaurant until he finished his hard-earned cup of coffee.

Several hours later, at a dormitory at Friendship Junior College, someone fetched a first-aid kit and placed bandages over the wounds on Lewis's face, but he continued to downplay his injuries. No bones had been broken, he insisted, displaying the quiet courage for which he would later become famous. Most important, he pointed out, no pledges had been violated. The Freedom Riders had passed their first major test, refusing to strike back against an unprovoked assault. At a mass meeting held at the college that night, the Reverend C. A. Ivory, Rock Hill's most outspoken civil rights activist, praised the courage and restraint of the bloodied but unbowed Freedom Riders, all but ensuring that the episode would become part of the civil rights lore that celebrated Lewis's stoic dignity in the face of violence.[8]

* * *

Lewis's search for the Beloved Community was well underway in May 1961, but on the night of the Rock Hill assault it took on an added international dimension when he received a telegram from the American Friends Service

Committee. The Quakers, he later explained, had "tracked me down by calling Nashville. My application for foreign service had been accepted. I was a finalist. Included with the telegram was a money order for a plane ticket to Philadelphia, where I was scheduled for an interview the next day at the group's national headquarters." This was great news, but it presented him with a dilemma: to make the interview, he would have to abandon the Freedom Ride. "This was a tough decision," he acknowledged, "and I didn't have much time to make it. Since first learning of the Friends program, I'd often imagined actually living in Africa, reconnecting to my heritage, to the native land. Who could have dreamed someone like me, a sharecropper's son from a poor farm in Alabama, could have an opportunity like that? Now the opportunity had arrived, but the timing was terrible."

After weighing the two options—staying on the Ride or traveling to Philadelphia—he came up with a compromise that would allow him to do both. He decided to go to Philadelphia, but with the understanding that his stay there would be limited to three or four days. "If all went as scheduled," he reasoned, "that would allow me to rejoin the ride the following Sunday in Birmingham—May 14, Mother's Day. The heart of the journey would still be ahead of us." He hated to miss the next part of the Ride, which would wind its way through South Carolina, Georgia, and northeastern Alabama, but as he said goodbye to his fellow Riders on the morning of May 10 before leaving to catch a plane at the Charlotte airport, he promised he would be with them in spirit, rejoining the Ride as soon as possible. By that evening, Lewis had completed his initial interview, as the Ride had proceeded through Chester and Winnsboro, where Hank Thomas and Peck were arrested during a lunch- counter test, and on to Sumter for a two-day rest stop.

The interview and a required physical both went well, despite the examining doctor's concern about the cuts and bruises on Lewis's body. "After two days and nights in Philadelphia," Lewis reported, "I was told I'd been accepted—but not for Africa. My assignment was India. Should I agree to go, I'd be leaving late that summer. I was a little disappointed, but India, too, would offer an enriching experience. This was, after all, the home of Gandhi. Jim Lawson had had his own life-changing experience there. I accepted the assignment, then rushed to the airport for an Eastern Airlines flight down to Nashville, where I planned to then go by car to Birmingham to rejoin the group. The Freedom Ride was once again all that I was thinking about."[9]

Although Lewis did not know it at the time, he was not the only person fixated on the Ride. While he was in Philadelphia and Nashville, the leaders of the Alabama Knights of the Ku Klux Klan were finalizing plans of their own. The Klansmen had known about the Freedom Ride since mid-April, thanks to a series of FBI memos forwarded to the Birmingham Police Department. Police Sergeant Tom Cook—an avid Klan supporter and anti-Communist zealot who worked closely with Eugene "Bull" Connor, Birmingham's ultra-segregationist commissioner of public safety—provided the organization with detailed information on the Ride. Thus, even though press reports on the Freedom Ride were sketchy and the Klansmen knew next to nothing about CORE, they knew enough to sound the alarm. In a flurry of secret meetings in April and early May, the Klan leaders—with Cook's and Connor's help—prepared a rude welcome for the invading "niggers" and "nigger lovers."[10]

During Lewis's absence, the Freedom Ride, after a brief period of calm, took a dangerous turn as it proceeded through the Deep South. The stop in Sumter, where the Riders were hosted by the small but active CORE chapter at all-Black Morris College, went well. With Lewis in Philadelphia and Cox on his way to High Point, North Carolina, to honor a commitment to preach a Mother's Day sermon, the Ride needed reinforcements and found them at Morris College, where three students volunteered to join the Ride. When one additional volunteer—Ike Reynolds, CORE's Detroit-based field secretary—joined the group, the number of Riders rose to fifteen, eight of whom were Black. With the new recruits in hand, Farmer and the other CORE staff members spent most of the second day in Sumter assessing the experiences of the previous week and refining the plan for the remainder of the Ride.

In gauging the future, they had to deal with a number of unknowns, including the attitudes of Black leaders and citizens in Deep South communities that would inevitably be affected by the Ride. Would the Freedom Riders be welcomed as liberators? Or would they just as likely be shunned as foolhardy provocateurs by Black Southerners who knew how dangerous it was to provoke the forces of white supremacy? How many adults were ready to embrace the direct action movement their children had initiated? CORE leaders were hopeful, but after a week on the road they still regarded the Black South as something of a puzzle.

Equally perplexing, and far more threatening, was the unpredictability of white officials in the Deep South—and in Washington. What would the police do if the Freedom Riders were physically attacked by segregationist thugs? Would Southern officials enforce the *Morgan* and *Boynton* decisions, now that they knew that at least some members of the public were aware of the Freedom Ride? Perhaps most important, how far would the Justice Department go to protect the Freedom Riders' constitutional rights, knowing that direct intervention would be politically costly for the Kennedy administration? The probable answers to all of these questions remained murky as the Riders set out on the second week of their southward journey.

After a trip through the historic midsection of South Carolina that skirted Edgefield County, the home of the early twentieth-century demagogue "Pitchfork Ben" Tillman and the 1948 Dixiecrat standard-bearer Strom Thurmond, the Riders crossed into Georgia for an overnight stop in Augusta. There, and in the college town of Athens the next day, they "were served courteously" and without incident, leaving Peck to marvel that "a person viewing the Athens desegregated lunch counter and waiting room during our fifteen-minute rest stop might have imagined himself at a rest stop up North rather than deep in Georgia." After similar episodes at the Atlanta bus stations later in the day, Peck concluded, "Our experiences traveling in Georgia were clear proof of how desegregation can come peacefully in a Deep South state, providing there is no deliberate incitement to hatred and violence by local or state political leaders."[11]

The welcoming scenes at the Atlanta bus stations, where a crowd of sit-in veterans rushed forward to greet the Riders as conquering heroes, provided a moving affirmation of the movement's rising spirit. That night, this spirit was on full display as the Riders had dinner with Martin Luther King Jr. and the SCLC's senior staff. During the dinner, King, who had just returned from a trip to Montgomery, was at his gracious best, repeatedly praising the Freedom Riders for their courage and offering to help in any way he could. As he listened to the Riders relate personal stories of commitment, he interjected words of encouragement and assurances that their behavior, especially the restraint exercised by Lewis and others in Rock Hill, represented "nonviolent direct action at its very best." He told them he was proud to serve on CORE's national advisory board, and before saying goodnight he made a point of shaking hands with each Rider.

Moved by King's show of support and affection, some of the Riders began to hope that he might join them on the bus the following morning. But they soon learned he had no intention of becoming a Freedom Rider. At one point during the dinner, King privately confided in the journalist Simeon Booker, warning him that the SCLC's sources in Alabama had uncovered evidence of a Klan plot to disrupt the Ride with violence. "You will never make it through Alabama," an obviously worried King predicted. Booker did his best to laugh off the warning, facetiously assuring the SCLC leader that he could always hide behind Farmer, who presented attackers with a large and slow-moving target. But later, when Booker told Farmer what King had said, he learned the CORE leader had already been apprised of the situation in Alabama.

Undaunted, Farmer was determined to lead the Riders into Alabama and beyond. But later that night he received a phone call from his mother in Washington: his father had died, and she begged him to come home immediately to preside over the funeral. Overcome with what he later called a "confusion of emotions," Farmer reluctantly decided to fly to Washington the next morning. "There was, of course, the incomparable sorrow and pain," he recalled. "But frankly, there was also a sense of reprieve, for which I hated myself. Like everyone else, I was afraid of what lay in store for us in Alabama, and now that I was to be spared participation in it, I was relieved, which embarrassed me to tears." On Sunday morning, less than three hours before the first bus to Birmingham was scheduled to depart, a sheepish Farmer turned over the leadership of the Freedom Ride to Peck and Perkins. Sitting around the breakfast table, the Riders didn't know quite how to respond to Farmer's announcement. They could hardly begrudge their grieving leader the chance to attend his father's funeral, and they were confident he would keep his word and rejoin the Ride later in the week. But some of the more nervous Riders weren't sure what shape they would be in when he returned.

Even the grizzled veteran Peck wondered if he would ever see his old friend again. He and Farmer had been through a lot together—surviving the depths of the Cold War and CORE's lean years, not to mention the first ten days of the Freedom Ride. Now he had to go on alone, perhaps to glory, but more likely to a rendezvous with violence, or even death. When Peck phoned Fred Shuttlesworth in Birmingham to give him the exact arrival times of the two freedom buses, the normally unflappable minister offered an alarming picture of what the Riders could expect once they reached Birmingham. The city was alive with rumors that a white mob planned to confront the Riders. Shuttlesworth was not privy to FBI surveillance of the Klan in Birmingham and Anniston and did not know any of the details, but he urged Peck to be careful.[12]

* * *

The two groups of Freedom Riders left Atlanta an hour apart on May 14, the Greyhound group at 11:00 a.m. and the Trailways at noon. The trip to Birmingham, with a brief rest stop in Anniston, would take four hours. More than half empty, the Greyhound had fourteen passengers on board: seven Freedom Riders, two journalists, and five regular passengers, including two undercover plainclothes agents of the Alabama Highway Patrol carrying a concealed microphone through which they could eavesdrop on the Riders, gathering information that could be passed on to the state's ultra-segregationist governor John Patterson.

The Trailways bus also carried "undercover" passengers, several men dispatched by the Birmingham klavern of the Ku Klux Klan. The Klansmen did not identify themselves, but the bus was barely out of the Atlanta terminal when they began to make threatening remarks. "You niggers will be taken care of once you get in Alabama," one Klansman sneered. Once the bus crossed the state line, the comments intensified, and during the rest stop in Anniston the epithets and threats turned into violence. After informing the Trailways Riders that the Greyhound group had been attacked an hour earlier, the driver—flanked by eight "hoodlums," as Peck later called them—snarled, "A mob is waiting for our bus and will do the same to us unless we get these niggers off the front seats." When one of the Riders reminded the driver they were interstate passengers who had the right to sit wherever they pleased, the Klansmen went on the attack, pummeling Peck and several other Riders and leaving one, sixty-one-year-old Walter Bergman, unconscious. This was only the beginning of two hours of intimidation and a prelude to the violence that awaited them in Birmingham.

The situation was even worse on the Greyhound, which was surrounded by an angry mob at the Anniston terminal and later waylaid on a highway six miles west of town by a caravan of pursuing Klansmen. Disabled by slashed tires, the bus was firebombed with a Molotov cocktail while the passengers were trapped inside. Intervention by the highway patrolmen on board, combined with an exploding gas tank that forced the marauding Klansmen to withdraw, saved the passengers' lives, but several Riders were either beaten or overcome with smoke inhalation, and two ended up in the hospital. After the Klansmen threatened to blow up the hospital if the injured Riders were not removed from the building, a convoy of cars dispatched by Shuttlesworth and driven by his church deacons rescued the Riders and drove them to Birmingham. In the meantime, the Trailways Riders were attacked by a mob of Klansmen and other white supremacists after Bull Connor promised to withhold police protection for fifteen minutes while they beat the arriving Riders into submission. The brutal assault, witnessed by several newspaper and television reporters, injured several Riders and put Peck in the hospital with head wounds that required surgery and more than fifty stitches. Speaking to reporters from his hospital bed, a groggy but defiant Peck declared, "The going is getting rougher, but I'll be on that bus tomorrow headed for Montgomery."[13]

By nightfall, the rest of the Riders from both groups had found refuge at Shuttlesworth's Bethel Baptist Church parsonage, where they contemplated what to do next. At a mass meeting held at Bethel Baptist that evening, the Riders, several of whom were physically or emotionally battered, spoke in emotional tones about what they had experienced during ten days on the road. Although fear of the police and the suspicion that the violence was not yet over kept the audience small, the fifty or so who were there witnessed an inspiring outpouring of movement culture. For more than an hour, the sanctuary reverberated with amens and shouts of encouragement, until Shuttlesworth rose to cap off the evening with a brief sermon. "This is the greatest thing that has ever happened to Alabama, and it has been good for the nation," he insisted, momentarily puzzling many of his listeners. "It was a wonderful thing to see these young students—Negro and white—come, even after the mobs and the bus burning. When white and Black men are willing to be beaten up together, it's a sure sign they will soon walk together as brothers. . . . No matter how many times they beat us up, segregation has still got to go. Others may be beaten up, but freedom is worth anything."

The immediate reaction to the drama being played out in Alabama was one of shock and disbelief. Newspapers across the nation and the world carried headlines, and in some cases photographs, of what had happened in Anniston and Birmingham. In Washington, President Kennedy, who was busy preparing for a trip to Europe and his first summit meeting with the Soviet premier Nikita Khrushchev, did not appreciate the embarrassing crisis in Alabama that CORE, in his mind, had deliberately precipitated. From the administration's perspective, the timing of the confrontation could not have been worse. After reading the Monday-morning headlines, Kennedy exploded in a conversation with Harris Wofford. "Can't you get your goddamned friends off those buses?" he asked. "Stop them."[14]

The reaction among Nashville's student activists was, of course, dramatically different from the president's. They were appalled by what had happened—especially Lewis, the only NSM member who had participated in the Freedom Ride. Having returned to Nashville from Philadelphia on Saturday night, he found himself in the midst of a milestone event. After fourteen weeks of stand-ins, the last of the holdouts among Nashville's theater owners had finally capitulated and agreed to desegregate. The next day—as the Freedom Riders were making their way from Atlanta to Birmingham—the NSM held an outdoor party to celebrate its victory. For a time, it was a jubilant celebration, Lewis recalled, "as several dozen of us sat outside in Nashville's gorgeous spring sunshine, eating and laughing and listening to Bevel make a passionate speech about our stand-in campaign."

But just as Bevel was finishing up, "a report came over the radio that stunned us all to silence." The Greyhound carrying seven Freedom Riders and two sympathetic journalists to Birmingham had been bombed a few miles outside Anniston. "I felt shock. I felt guilt," Lewis wrote years later. "That was my bus, my group. It was devastating to hear this news, and it was torture to hear it only in the sketchiest terms. There were no details—no reports about injuries or deaths. I could only imagine, and imagination coupled with fear is a tortuous thing. Later I would learn what had happened.

The next morning every newspaper in the nation, and many more around the entire world, would carry a front-page photograph of the Greyhound bus in Anniston, Alabama, flames licking out its exploded windows, a column of thick black smoke billowing toward the sky."

By late Sunday afternoon, even before he had seen the frightening picture of the burning bus, Lewis had also learned that another group of white people had mobbed the Trailways bus in Birmingham and nearly killed Peck. Lewis got word from CORE that he should not rejoin the Freedom Ride that night as planned; he should wait until the organization was sure the Ride would continue. This made sense, but he and the other NSM leaders were impatient and wanted to do something right away to salvage the Ride. "All that evening and into the early hours of Monday morning," Lewis remembered, "we discussed and debated what to do. Should we reinforce the Ride? If so, how many of us would go? When? And where would the money come from to pay our way?"[15]

Later that morning, all of their deliberation and tentative plans appeared to be moot after word came that Farmer had canceled the rest of the Ride. This report, which proved false, sent Lewis into a tailspin: "I couldn't believe it. I understood the thinking behind the decision, but it defied one of the most basic tenets of nonviolent action—that is, that there can be no surrender in the face of brute force or any form of violent opposition. Retreat is one thing, surrender is another." In actuality, the Freedom Riders in Birmingham, in consultation with Farmer, were still mulling over their options. When they gathered at the Bethel parsonage on Monday morning, the situation appeared less desperate than it had only a few hours earlier. Having survived the initial shock of the attacks, the Riders had regained at least some of the spirit that had brought them to the Deep South in the first place.

Suffering from severe smoke inhalation, Mae Frances Moultrie, one of the Morris College students who had joined the Ride in Sumter, decided to return directly to South Carolina. But the other Riders—including Peck, the most seriously injured of the weekend casualties—were more or less ready to travel on to Montgomery. By a vote of eight to four, the group decided to continue the Freedom Ride, hopefully all the way to New Orleans. Peck's resolute determination seemed to steel their courage, especially after he refused to fly home immediately. Arguing that "for the most severely beaten rider to quit could be interpreted as meaning that violence had triumphed over nonviolence," Peck forged a near consensus that led to a meeting to plan the next leg, from Birmingham to Montgomery. By the end of the meeting, they had decided to leave in a single contingent on a Greyhound bus departing at three that afternoon.

Unfortunately for the Riders, this plan depended on two factors: finding a Greyhound bus driver willing to take the risk of riding with them; and obtaining a guarantee of state police protection from Governor Patterson. Both of these requirements proved to be unobtainable, even after Attorney General Robert Kennedy consulted with Shuttlesworth and personally negotiated with the governor, the manager of the Birmingham Greyhound station, and the Teamsters Union. At one point during a conversation with the station manager, an exasperated Kennedy shouted, "The Government is going to be very much upset if this group does not get to continue their trip." But even this warning from the president's brother fell on deaf ears, and for several hours on Monday afternoon there was a tense standoff at the Greyhound bus station between the Riders and roving Klansmen backed up by Bull Connor and his rogue police force. The Riders only lost heart and backed down after they heard a radio report that Patterson refused to offer them protection.

"The citizens of this state are so enraged," the governor claimed, "that I cannot guarantee protection for this bunch of rabble-rousers." The only solution, Patterson declared, was for the Riders to leave the state immediately; he might provide them with an escort to the state line, but certainly not to Montgomery, where they were sure "to continue their rabble-rousing." Hearing this, the Riders decided further effort to ride a bus to Montgomery would be futile. Instead, they would fly to Montgomery and catch a bus to Mississippi from there. Some of the Riders, having seen more than enough of Alabama, preferred to fly all the way to New Orleans—in effect ending the Ride two days early. Others suspected that the choice was beyond their control and that in all likelihood they would end up on the first available flight out of the city.

When the Riders arrived at the airport late that afternoon, they had to brave a gathering mob of Klansmen—only partially restrained by the police—

before boarding a plane to Montgomery. Minutes later a bomb threat sent them scurrying back into the terminal, where they waited nearly six hours before boarding a flight to New Orleans. Even this belated departure required the timely intervention of John Seigenthaler, a Tennessee-born Justice Department official dispatched to Birmingham by Robert Kennedy. As Seigenthaler introduced himself to the beleaguered Riders that evening, he could see right away that a long day of indignities and threats had exacted a heavy toll. Their downcast eyes told him they were fed up with Alabama and its hate-mongering politicians and Klansmen; they just wanted out. At least five of the Riders—Peck, Person, Reynolds, Hughes, and Walter Bergman— were still weak from the attacks and had no business being out of bed, but there they were, huddled in a corner trying to cope in the face of physical and emotional pain.

By midnight the Riders, accompanied by Seigenthaler, were safely out of Alabama, but an additional ordeal awaited them. As they walked from the plane to the New Orleans terminal, they passed through a cordon of police officers shouting racial epithets. Only after Seigenthaler identified himself as a federal official did the police cease their harassment, allowing the Riders to make their way to a welcoming committee of local CORE volunteers. Several of the Riders, with tears of joy streaming down their faces, looking much like returning prisoners of war, collapsed into the outstretched arms of their comrades. Against all odds, they had made it to New Orleans after all. The great CORE Freedom Ride of 1961 was over, or so it seemed.[16]

* * *

Lewis and his NSM colleagues had conflicting emotions when they learned what had happened: though relieved that the Riders were safe, they were severely disappointed that the CORE Freedom Ride had ended on a sour note, failing in its mission to demonstrate that the Deep South was ready for nonviolent direct action. Yet even before the airborne escape to New Orleans, the Nashville students had decided that they could not allow the Freedom Ride to end in retreat and defeat. On Monday afternoon, May 15, more than a full day before the flight to New Orleans, Nash had called Farmer to see if he "had any objections" to the NSM "going in and taking up the Ride where CORE left off." Nash, Lewis, and others later insisted that the call was simply a means of letting "him know our intent and to ask for his support— not his permission." Whatever her intention, Nash clearly caught Farmer off guard. "You realize it may be suicide," he stammered into the phone. This warning only confirmed her suspicion that Farmer was out of touch with the spirit of the student-led movement. "We fully realize that," she replied, brushing off his objection, "but we can't let them stop us with violence. If we do, the movement is dead." Impressed by her poise and determination, a still-wary Farmer reluctantly pledged his support.

By Monday night the die was cast, but working out the logistics of re-suming the Ride consumed a day and night full of meetings. With Nash and Lewis leading the way, the NSM obtained an enthusiastic endorsement from Lawson—who was away visiting his family in Ohio but promised to join the new Ride as soon as he returned—and, after some resistance, a measure of support from the rest of the NCLC. "As always," Lewis recalled, "there was caution and resistance from several of the older NCLC members taking part in our meetings. We needed their support, at least in terms of money, and they were using that as a lever for their position. As far as I was concerned, it was time to *go*. The money and everything else we were debating were trivial, tedious. Time was wasting. This was a crisis, and we needed to act."

By midnight, the discussions were over, and the NCLC had authorized payment of the $900 needed to buy bus tickets for the twenty-one Riders selected by the NSM's current chairman, Jim Bevel. The Riders, it was de-cided, would be dispatched in two groups—ten students by bus, and the other eleven, who would leave a day or two later, split between several trav-eling by train and the remainder by car.[17]

With the ticket money in hand, an elated Nash made two phone calls, one to the SNCC headquarters in Atlanta and a second to Shuttlesworth in Birmingham, letting them know that a new batch of Freedom Riders would soon be on its way, perhaps as early as Wednesday morning. "The students have decided that we can't let violence overcome," she informed Shut-tlesworth. "We are going to come into Birmingham to continue the Freedom Ride." Suspecting the Nashville students had no idea what they were getting themselves into, the Birmingham minister offered a stern warning. "Young lady, do you know that the Freedom Riders were almost killed here?" he asked. Nash assured him that she did, adding, "That's exactly why the ride must not be stopped. If they stop us with violence, the movement is dead. We're coming. We just want to know if you can meet us."

Several hours later, Nash had a similar telephone conversation with Seigenthaler. Awakened at 4:00 a.m. by a frantic call from Burke Marshall, Robert Kennedy's special deputy for civil rights, who had heard a rumor that a new Freedom Ride was about to begin, Seigenthaler was charged with the task of stopping the Ride. "You come from that goddamn town," Marshall told him. ". . . If you can do anything to turn them around, I'd appreciate it." A groggy Seigenthaler soon placed a call to George Barrett—an old Nashville friend and labor lawyer with close ties to the local movement and Highlander Folk School—asking him to call Nash and plead with her to call off the Ride. Barrett had no luck with his plea but later gave Seigenthaler her phone number. During the awkward call that followed, Nash refused to alter the NSM's plan, insisting that delaying the hour of freedom was out of the question. Exasperated, Seigenthaler predicted, "You're going to get your people killed." Once again she was unmoved. If the first wave of Nashville Freedom Riders were to die, she calmly informed him, "then others will follow them."[18]

On Tuesday morning, a few minutes after the first group of ten Riders boarded a bus for Birmingham, Shuttlesworth—following Gandhian protocol—informed the press that they were coming. The first group included eight Black students, with Lewis as the designated leader, and two Northern white exchange students, Jim Zwerg from Wisconsin and Salynn McCollum from New York. Before leaving Nashville, Lewis counseled the other Riders to behave like normal passengers and to avoid any overt challenges to segregation during the ride to Birmingham. But Zwerg and Paul Brooks, Lewis's classmate at ABT, refused to cooperate, sitting together as a conspicuous interracial duo near the front of the bus. This did not seem to bother the bus driver or any of the regular passengers, but when the bus reached the Birmingham city limits, a boarding party of police officers arrested Zwerg and Brooks for violating Alabama law.

The bus arrived at the terminal at 12:15, too late for the Riders to be transferred to the noon bus to Montgomery. But a late arrival was the least of the Riders' problems. At the terminal, the police temporarily sealed the bus, taping newspaper over the windows to conceal what was going on inside. After examining each passenger's ticket before letting anyone off, the police maintained an armed guard over the seven remaining "suspects." When Lewis, as the spokesman for the group, stood up and objected, a policeman poked a billy club into his stomach, shoving him back into his seat. By this time, Zwerg and Brooks had been carted off to the city jail, and McCollum, avoiding identification as a Freedom Rider, had disembarked with the other passengers. Rushing undetected through the crowd, she called Nash from a pay phone. Trying not to panic, Nash immediately phoned Burke Marshall in Washington. Why, she asked, were the Freedom Riders being forcibly detained by the Birmingham police? Caught off guard, Marshall promised to investigate, but he couldn't resist reminding Nash that she and the Nashville students had been warned that Birmingham was a dangerous place.

As news of the Riders' arrival spread, a large crowd of white protesters began to gather at the terminal, providing the police with a rationale for protective custody. The only way to ensure the Riders' safety, the officer in charge insisted, was to keep them on board. Outside the bus, the press was being told the Riders were being detained so they could be safely transferred to a Montgomery-bound bus later in the afternoon. At five minutes after four, Police Chief Jamie Moore shepherded the Riders through two rows of police officers and into the terminal building. With the crowd straining to get a piece of them, the seven students made their way into the white waiting room, where they were welcomed by McCollum and Shuttlesworth, both of whom ignored the police chief's warning that interracial mingling would incite the crowd. Shuttlesworth then led the Riders to the terminal's whites-only restaurant, but the door was locked. Cordoned off by the police, the Riders retreated to the terminal's white restrooms, which, to their relief, were open. Preoccupied with the surging crowd, the police made no move to prevent this historic desecration of segregated toilets. Later, back in the white waiting room, Shuttlesworth and the Riders celebrated their small victory with round after round of freedom songs.

Earlier in the afternoon, Governor Patterson's radio broadcast had excoriated the Nashville-based Riders as troublemakers and criminals, ending with the declaration that no one could "guarantee the safety of fools." Later, just before the 5:00 p.m. bus to Montgomery began loading passengers, Bull Connor strode into the waiting room. Lewis later claimed that he immediately recognized this menacing figure, "even though I'd never seen him before in my life. He was short, heavy with big ears and a fleshy face. He wore a suit, his white hair was slicked straight back above his forehead, and his eyes were framed by a pair of black, horn-rimmed glasses." At first Connor seemed content to mingle with the police guards, but as soon as Lewis and the other Riders began to move toward the loading platform, he stepped in and ordered his officers to place the unwanted visitors in "protective custody." Pointing to the unruly crowd, he assured the students he was arresting them for their "own protection." When Shuttlesworth stepped forward to object, Connor directed Chief Moore to arrest him as well. All of the "agitators" were then led to a line of waiting paddy wagons that whisked them off to Birmingham's notorious Southside jail.

At the jail, guards separated the detainees by gender and race. With the exception of Shuttlesworth, all of the men ended up in a dark and crowded cell that Lewis likened to a dungeon: "It had no mattresses or beds, nothing to sit on at all, just a concrete floor." At 10:00 p.m., Shuttlesworth was released on bond, but the other prisoners remained in jail, even though no formal charges had been brought against them. Isolated from the outside world with no access to the press—or to Nash, who was desperately trying to find out what had happened to them—Lewis and his cellmates adopted a strategy of Gandhian noncooperation. Although they had not eaten since morning, the students defiantly refused to eat or drink anything. And since sleeping under these conditions was virtually impossible, they decided to pass the time singing freedom songs, a morale booster that had served them well during the Nashville demonstrations. After all, they informed the guards, it was May 17—the seventh anniversary of *Brown*, a day worth celebrating in or out of jail. "We went on singing," Lewis later confessed, "both to keep our spirits up and—to be honest—because we knew that neither Bull Connor nor his guards could stand it."[19]

This passive-aggressive serenading went on pretty much all night and throughout much of the next day and evening, until Connor had had enough. At 11:30 p.m. he appeared at the city jail, grim-faced and barking orders at people on both sides of the bars. Accompanied by five police officers and two local reporters, he announced he was tired of listening to freedom songs. It was time for the students to go back to Nashville where they belonged. As the police began rounding them up, the students, following their training in Lawson's workshops, responded with passive resistance. "We refused to cooperate," Lewis recalled with pride many years later. "We let our bodies go limp, forcing the officers to drag us from the jail and out into the night."

Eventually the police managed to load the students into two cars, and with Connor sitting in the front seat of the lead car and Lewis sitting behind him, they headed north on Highway 31, the same road the students had traveled by bus on Wednesday morning. After leaving the city lights behind, Connor tried to engage several of the students in friendly small talk but made no effort to reveal his exact plans for them. At first they feared they were headed for some sort of staged ambush, but as Connor continued his jovial chatter they began to relax. Most of the conversation was between Connor and the feisty Birmingham native Catherine Burks, who refused to be intimidated by a man she later claimed "was a powerful dictator but didn't have any power over me." After Connor hinted that he planned to take the students all the way to Nashville, Burks suggested that, in the spirit of Christian fellowship, he should join them for breakfast before returning to Alabama. At one point she even offered to cook for him.

To Lewis, sitting directly behind the driver's seat, this unexpected banter was somewhat reassuring, but the strained joviality came to an abrupt halt when the convoy reached the small border town of Ardmore, Alabama. "This is where you'll be getting out," Connor informed them, adding, "There is the Tennessee line. Cross it and save the state and yourself a lot of trouble." As several officers stacked their bags by the side of the road, Connor quipped, "You'all can catch a train from here, or maybe a bus." As the cars disappeared into the night, Burks defiantly shouted to Connor that they would be back in Birmingham by "high noon." But neither she nor any of the other stranded students had any idea how they would do that. It was 4:00 a.m., and for a while they "just stood there in the dark" wondering whether they were about to be ambushed or even lynched, but before long they headed down the tracks in search of help.[20]

Failing to find a railroad depot, they eventually stumbled on a cluster of houses Lewis later described as "broken-down shacks." "A mile or so up and across the tracks," he recalled, "we knocked on the door of a small weather-beaten little house, and an elderly Black man opened the door. He looked very puzzled, very frightened. Here were seven young men and women standing on his front step with suitcases in their hands. . . . 'We're the Freedom Riders' I told him. 'We are in trouble and we need your help. Would you help us?' He shook his head. 'I can't let you in.' But then, the door opened wider and a small woman stepped up beside him. . . . They reminded me of so many older members of my family in Pike County. You could tell they had both worked very hard all their lives. 'Honey,' she said to her husband. 'Let them in.'"

Once inside, Lewis called Nash to tell her what had happened. Stunned, she said she could send a car to bring them to Nashville, or she could find some way to send them directly back to Birmingham. The choice was up to them, she declared, but the situation was complicated by the fact that eleven new Freedom Riders would soon be on their way to Alabama. All seven students, Lewis assured her, were eager to return directly to Birmingham as soon as possible. Nash was not surprised and immediately dispatched a rescue car driven by Leo Lillard, a recent Tennessee State graduate who would prove to be an invaluable trainer for the scores of Freedom Ride recruits who passed through Nashville later in the year. A notoriously fast driver, Lillard arrived in Ardmore by late morning. Piling into his four-door sedan, the seven students thanked the elderly couple for their help before roaring down the same highway that had seemed to seal their fate only a few hours earlier.

The car was crowded, and whenever they passed another vehicle they took the precaution of "squeezing down in the seats, out of sight," just in case the Alabama state police or Klan vigilantes were looking for them. Nevertheless, the mood in the car was upbeat, even jubilant, especially after they heard a radio report that Connor had boasted that he had resolved the crisis by personally returning the would-be Freedom Riders to their college campuses in Tennessee. Burks and several others mused about how shocked Connor was going to be when he saw them back in Birmingham, and a few minutes before 3:00 that afternoon—a mere fifteen hours after being rousted from their jail cells—Lillard pulled into the driveway of Shuttlesworth's Bethel Baptist parsonage. As Shuttlesworth rushed out to greet them, other familiar faces began to appear in the background. All eleven of the reinforcements that Nash had mentioned on the phone were at the parsonage. After a rollicking reunion on the lawn, Lewis called Nash to tell her that nineteen Riders were ready to board the first available bus to Montgomery.[21]

After organizing a carpool to transport the Riders to the downtown Greyhound station, Shuttlesworth sent word to law enforcement officials and the press that a new Freedom Ride was about to begin. By late afternoon, news of the Ride had spread across town and even to Montgomery and Washington. The reaction at all levels was a combination of surprise and head-shaking frustration. Despite their differences, local, state, and federal officials shared a common resolve to bring the Freedom Rider crisis to a close. In downtown Birmingham, Connor and the police were growing tired of a cat-and-mouse game with troublemakers who didn't seem to respond to the traditional forms of control and intimidation. Under increasing political pressure to maintain law and order, they knew they could not afford another public relations disaster like the Mother's Day riot. Yet they were not about to let the Freedom Riders run roughshod over the hallowed strictures of racial segregation.

Governor Patterson was playing an equally difficult game, trying to extract political capital out of the crisis without having it blow up in his face. Dodging federal entreaties that he guarantee the Freedom Riders' safety, he was determined to defend the shibboleths of states' rights and to teach the Riders, the Kennedys, and other potential meddlers from the North a lesson. But to do so was proving more challenging than he or anyone in his circle had anticipated. The situation was no less frustrating for the Justice Department officials who spent most of Thursday organizing a federal peacekeeping force that could forestall wholesale violence in Alabama. Faced with a politically unpalatable scenario, Robert Kennedy and his staff continued to search for some means of ending the crisis before the peacekeeping force was deployed. Hoping for a miracle, they privately welcomed Connor's attempt to take the situation in hand. Despite the initial fear that Connor had snapped—"Jesus Christ, Bull has kidnapped them. He's going to kill them," a panic-stricken Seigenthaler had reported early Friday morning—administration leaders were actually relieved to learn that Connor had driven the jailed Riders back to Tennessee. But now, with their return to Birmingham and with new Riders popping up all over the place, the crisis was more dangerous than ever.[22]

CHAPTER 5

———

Mississippi Bound

W
ITH THE FREEDOM RIDERS mobilizing, Bull Connor raging, John Patterson hiding, and crowds of angry white protesters gathering, the prospects for a timely resolution of the crisis seemed to be slipping away. By the time Fred Shuttlesworth and the Freedom Riders arrived at the Greyhound terminal late Friday afternoon, May 19, 1961, a number of newspaper and television reporters, as well as several hundred onlookers, were already at the scene. For the fourth time in six days, a large crowd had gathered to protest the Freedom Riders' presence in Alabama. Later in the day, the size of the crowd would grow to three thousand and beyond, and the rising anger of the most militant protesters would eventually force the police to use their new K-9 corps to maintain order. At first, as the Riders piled out of the cars and headed toward the loading dock, the protesters seemed more stunned than anything else. "They pushed in at us as we entered the terminal," John Lewis remembered, "but no one touched us."

After Greyhound officials failed to find a driver brave enough to drive the afternoon bus to Montgomery, the Riders retreated to the white waiting room, where they sang freedom songs and prayed as the police strained to keep the swell of protesters from getting completely out of hand. Most of the protesters remained outside the terminal, but the police made a point of allowing some, including several men dressed in Klan robes, to wander around the waiting room with impunity. Standing smugly only a few feet from the Riders was Imperial Wizard Robert Shelton, decked out in a black robe with an embroidered snake on the back. For nearly three hours, the police stood by and watched as Shelton's Klansmen indulged in petty acts of provocation, such as "accidentally" stepping on the Riders' feet, spilling drinks on their clothes, and blocking access to the restrooms. But as darkness approached, Chief Jamie Moore decided to clear the room of everyone but the Riders. By nightfall, the scene in and around the terminal had taken on an eerie tone. "We could see them through the glass doors and streetside windows," Lewis remembered, "gesturing at us and shouting. Every now and then a rock or a brick would crash through one of the windows near the ceiling. The police brought in dogs and we could see them outside, pulling at their leashes to keep the crowd back."[1]

Unbeknownst to the Riders under siege, a few hours earlier the Kennedy administration had brought Governor Patterson to the bargaining table by threatening to send a large federal peacekeeping force to Birmingham. By early evening, John Seigenthaler was at the governor's office in the state capitol in Montgomery negotiating a plan to protect the Freedom Riders with state and local law enforcement officers. After several false starts and harangues by the governor, Seigenthaler began to make headway with the argument that it was in Alabama's interest to hand the Freedom Rider problem over to Mississippi as soon as possible. When Patterson insisted that no one could guarantee the Riders' safe passage from Birmingham to the Mississippi border, Floyd Mann, Alabama's director of safety, surprised the governor with the assertion that the state highway patrol was up to the task. Over the next few minutes, with Seigenthaler's encouragement, Mann guided Patterson toward acceptance of the responsibility for the Riders' safety. The agreed-on plan called for a combined effort of local and state officials. The Birmingham and Montgomery police would protect the Riders within city limits, and the state police would provide protection on the open highways, with Mann himself on the bus as added insurance.

When Robert Kennedy called Patterson to inquire if the pledge of protection was genuine, the governor yelled out, "I've given my word as Governor of Alabama." Unfortunately, later in the evening Patterson had second thoughts about letting the Freedom Riders slip from his grasp. While Mann was busy conferring with local and state police commanders in a legitimate effort to live up to the agreement, Patterson was effectively undercutting the plan with some last-minute political maneuvering. Before he left his office that evening, he ordered his attorney general to track down circuit judge Walter B. Jones to prevail on him to issue an injunction against the Riders. An arch-segregationist, Jones readily complied.

By Saturday morning, Alabama officials essentially had two contradictory plans in place, one that tacitly recognized the Riders' right to travel and another that branded them as outlaws subject to arrest. If the agreement with the feds fell apart or became too costly politically, they could simply revert to hard-line resistance. Robert Kennedy, unsure that he could trust Patterson, placed an early-morning call to Shuttlesworth, suggesting the students' best option was to follow the CORE Riders' example and fly to New Orleans. Alabama was dangerous enough, the attorney general insisted, but traveling through Mississippi would be even worse, facetiously reminding Shuttlesworth that even "the Lord hasn't . . . been to Mississippi in a long time." The Alabama minister shot back, "But we think the Lord *should* go to Mississippi, and we want to get him there." These words dredged up one of Kennedy's worst fears: that Shuttlesworth himself had decided to join the Freedom Ride. And he was right.

As the Riders prepared to board a morning bus to Montgomery after a long and sleepless night in the terminal, Shuttlesworth was with them. When the police closed ranks around the bus, Shuttlesworth could not resist commenting on the irony of the situation. "Man, what's this state coming to!" he shouted to the police. "An armed escort to take a bunch of niggers to a bus station so they can break these silly laws." After a few parting taunts directed at the line of officers—including the jibe, "We're gonna make a steer out of Bull"—he attempted to board the bus along with the other Riders. But Chief Moore stepped in front of the door and ordered him to go home. After Shuttlesworth produced a ticket, Moore repeated the order, and when the minister once again failed to back away from the bus, the chief arrested him for refusing to obey a police officer.

As Shuttlesworth was being led away, a phalanx of police cruisers and motorcycles pulled in front of the loading platform, signaling that the escort was ready to leave. Afraid of being left behind, several reporters made a mad dash for their cars, just in time to join the convoy that was soon barreling down the streets of Birmingham. After five days of turmoil and delay, the

Freedom Ride was back on track moving southward toward Montgomery, a historic capital city with a divided heritage. Having served as both "the cradle of the Confederacy" and the unwilling nurturer of nonviolent struggle, Montgomery presented the Freedom Riders with a unique set of challenges no less daunting than those encountered in Birmingham.[2]

* * *

The Freedom Riders' departure from Birmingham on the morning of May 20 resembled a staged Hollywood chase scene. Since none of the Riders had been briefed on the plan to protect them, there was high anxiety on the bus, at least in the early going. When the Greyhound reached the southern edge of the city, there was a moment of panic as the police escort pulled to the side of the road, but within seconds several highway patrol cars appeared in front of the bus. Overhead a low-flying highway patrol plane tracked the bus's progress down Highway 31, with the rest of the convoy—the cars carrying FBI observers, Floyd Mann's plainclothes detectives, and several reporters—following close behind.

Additional highway patrol cars were stationed all along the route at intervals of fifteen miles, and at each checkpoint a new patrolman took the lead. All of this was reassuring, and by the time the bus passed over the Shelby County line, many of the Riders had begun to relax. State officials had promised the Justice Department that the bus run to Montgomery would include all the normal stops, but in fact there were no stops. No one on the bus, however, voiced any objection to the express-like pace of the trip. For the first time in days, the Nashville students felt relatively safe. "No one on the bus said much," recalled Lewis, but "the mood was very relaxed. . . . It was a pleasant ride; a nice Saturday morning drive." Exhausted from several sleepless nights, some of the students "actually dozed off" during the last half of the journey.[3]

"In less than two hours," Lewis remembered, "we reached the Montgomery city limits, and suddenly, as if on cue, the patrol cars turned away, the airplane banked off toward the horizon, and we were on the road alone. There were no Montgomery police cars to meet us. There was nothing on the road but our bus. As we slowed to the city speed limit and began turning toward the downtown station, it felt eerie, very strange. The Montgomery

Greyhound terminal looked almost deserted as we pulled up to the loading dock. The only people I could see were a couple of taxi drivers sitting in their cabs, a small group of reporters waiting on the platform, and a dozen or so white men standing together over near the terminal door. 'This doesn't look right,' I said to William Harbour as we stepped off the bus. I didn't like the looks of those men by the door. The journalists moved in. An NBC reporter and his cameraman stepped up to speak to me. . . . Norm Ritter, a writer from *Life* magazine, started to ask me a question, but I didn't hear it. I was looking past Ritter, to those white men, who were suddenly coming toward us fast."

Facing Lewis, Ritter was about to become the first target of an angry mob: "Ritter saw the look on my face, I guess, and turned around. I remember how he lifted his arms, holding them out wide, as if to protect us, as if he could hold these men back by himself. There was a low wall behind us, with about an eight-foot drop to a concrete ramp below. I backed the others toward the wall. 'Do not run,' I told them. 'Let's stand here together.' And then, out of nowhere, from every direction, came people. White people. Men, women and children. Dozens of them. Hundreds of them. . . . They emerged from everywhere, from all directions, as if they'd been let out of a gate. . . . They carried every makeshift weapon imaginable. Baseball bats, wooden boards, bricks, chains, tire irons, pipes, even garden tools—hoes and rakes. One group had women in front, their faces twisted in anger, screaming, '*Git them niggers*, GIT *them niggers!*' It was the press, though, who got it first. The NBC cameraman, a guy named Mac Levy, was kicked in the stomach by a fat man with a cigar in his teeth. Levy's camera . . . fell to the ground and someone picked it up and began beating him with it. . . . One reporter . . . had blood just gushing from his head. Now the mob was moving toward us."[4]

By this time, most of the Riders had left the bus, and several pairs of seatmates had joined hands to form a human chain on the loading platform. But the surging mob quickly overwhelmed them. Pressed against a retaining wall, most of the Riders either jumped or were pushed over the railing into the parking lot below. Some landed on the hoods or roofs of cars before scrambling to their feet and staggering toward the street in front of the terminal. With most of the attackers still on the loading platform, those fortunate enough to make it to the lower level gained at least some chance of escape, frantically running from the area and trying to find someone willing to drive them to Ralph Abernathy's First Baptist Church or some other safe haven. After briefly huddling on the curb, the seven female Riders spied a parked taxi with a Black driver behind the wheel and jumped in the cab. When the driver refused to take the two white women in the group—Susan Wilbur and Susan Hermann—several members of the mob dragged them onto the sidewalk and began beating them. Somehow Wilbur and Hermann managed to escape serious injury, but others, including Lewis, were less fortunate.

The first to be assaulted was Lewis's seatmate Jim Zwerg, who bowed his head in prayer as the attackers moved in. Attracting attention as the only white male Rider, he was knocked to the pavement amid screams of, "Filthy Communists, nigger lovers, you're not going to integrate Montgomery!" According to Fred Leonard, who was standing only a few feet away, "It was like those people in the mob were possessed. They couldn't believe that there was a white man who would help us. . . . It's like they didn't see the rest of us for about thirty seconds. They didn't see us at all." As the other Riders looked on in horror, several white attackers later identified as Klansmen kicked Zwerg in the back before smashing him in the head with his own suitcase. Dazed and bleeding, Zwerg struggled to get up, but one of the Klansmen promptly pinned his arms back while others punched him repeatedly in the face. "Some men held him while white women clawed his face with their nails," Lucretia Collins, who witnessed the assault from the back seat of a departing taxicab, recalled. "And they held up their little children—children who couldn't have been more than a couple years old—to claw his face. I had to turn my head because I just couldn't watch it." Eventually, Zwerg's eyes rolled back and his body sagged into unconsciousness. After tossing him over a railing, his attackers went looking for other targets.

Turning to the Black Freedom Riders huddled near the railing, several of the Klansmen rushed forward. The first victim in their path was William Barbee, the only Rider who had not traveled to Montgomery on the Greyhound. Sent ahead "to arrange for cars and other necessities," he was at the terminal to welcome his friends when the riot broke out. Standing next to Lewis and Bernard LaFayette, Barbee had only a moment to shield his face before the advancing Klansmen unleashed a flurry of punches and kicks that dropped him to the pavement. While one Klansman held him down, a second jammed a jagged piece of pipe in his ear, and a third bashed him in the skull with a baseball bat, inflicting permanent damage that shortened his life. Moments later, Lewis went down, struck by a large Coca-Cola crate. "I could feel my knees collapse and then nothing," he remembered. "Everything turned white for an instant, then black."[5]

The violence continued to spread as Lewis's limp body lay on the loading platform, and it only began to subside after the belated arrival of law enforcement officials. "By the time I regained consciousness," he remembered, "the scene was relatively under control. Floyd Mann, Alabama's public safety director, had pushed his way into the mob, tried pulling some men off William Barbee's body, then raised a pistol and fired into the air, warning the crowd away. Montgomery police commissioner L. B. Sullivan and his men finally arrived—Sullivan had reportedly sat in his car around the corner during the worst of the attack, calmly waiting while the mob had its way. Also now on the scene was the attorney general of Alabama, a man named MacDonald Gallion. As I got to my feet, he stood over me and read aloud an injunction forbidding 'entry into and travel within the state of Alabama and engaging in the so-called 'Freedom Ride' and other acts or conduct calculated to promote breaches of peace.' . . . I hardly listened to those words. My head was spinning, both with thoughts about the carnage that had occurred and with pain. I was bleeding pretty badly from the back of my head. I couldn't believe how much blood there was."

Once Lewis's head began to clear, he realized he was not the only seriously injured Freedom Rider at the bus station: "I looked around. Pieces of our belongings were scattered on the asphalt—a shoe here, a composition book there. I could see only two other riders—Barbee and Zwerg. The others, I later learned, had made their way into the surrounding black community, many to a nearby Presbyterian church. Zwerg looked horrible. Barbee looked almost as bad. They clearly needed to go to a hospital right away. But when I tried getting Zwerg to his feet and asked a police officer for help in finding an ambulance, he shrugged, 'He's free to go,' the policeman said, but it was up to us, he said, to find our own transportation. Barbee and I were able to find a black cabdriver who would give us a ride, but the man refused to carry Zwerg, again because of the segregation statutes. Zwerg was eventually driven to a local hospital, St. Jude's, by another driver, a black man, who chose to ignore those laws. Barbee and I were taken to the office of a local doctor, who treated us both. . . . By the time the doctor was done, a volunteer driver had arrived to take me to the home of a local minister named Solomon Seay."

Lewis would never forget his sense of relief and the welcoming, joyous scene at Seay's house. "I was greeted with cheers and hugs," he remembered, "the same reception each of the riders received as we all arrived that afternoon. The phone was ringing constantly, with news of response from the world beyond Montgomery. Jim Lawson was on his way down from Ohio. Diane [Nash] was coming in from Nashville. Dr. King was reportedly on his way." Rather than crushing the spirit of the Freedom Riders, the fiasco at the bus station had created an opportunity to strengthen the movement's solidarity and resolve. It also reinforced the sense of crisis required to sustain the Kennedy administration's involvement in protecting the Riders. "The Kennedys were livid," Lewis recalled. "Patterson had promised to protect us, then turned around and not only allowed us to be ambushed, but then sent his attorney general to the scene to serve us with injunctions. Warrants were now out for our arrest, even as the mob back at the bus station, which had grown to over a thousand, was still rioting—setting parked cars on fire, roaming the surrounding neighbor-hood and beating any black person they could find. . . . As the violence and the afternoon wore on, Police Commissioner Sullivan leaned on a car, chatting with reporters who asked him to sum up the situation. 'I really don't know what happened,' he told them. 'When I got there, all I saw were three men lying in the street. There was two niggers and a white man.'"[6]

* * *

When it became clear that the Montgomery police had done little or nothing to protect the Freedom Riders, an angry Robert Kennedy called John Patterson for an explanation. The governor, who had not spoken to the attorney general for two days, dodged the call. For Kennedy, this was the final straw. Politics aside, no governor could be allowed to thumb his nose at the federal government while countenancing the wanton disruption of civil order. The force of federal marshals that he and his brother had hoped would never be used, he now realized, was the only available deterrent to continued disorder and disrespect. With his brother's summit meeting with Khrushchev in Vienna less than two weeks away, he could not allow the image and authority of the United States to be undercut by a mob of racist vigilantes or, for that matter, by a band of headstrong students determined to provoke them. Like it or not, he had to do something dramatic to bring the Freedom Rider crisis to a close. In a telegram to Patterson, he asserted that the administration now "had no alternative but to order" a large federal force to protect "persons and property" in Montgomery. The marshals would soon be on their way.

Civil rights leaders welcomed federal intervention, but for the Freedom Riders themselves, the biggest story of the day was the unreported transformation of a limited project into a full-fledged movement. The seeds of this transformation had been planted the previous Tuesday, May 16, when the Nashville students had stepped in for the CORE Riders, but it was not until Saturday afternoon that a true movement culture began to take hold among the Riders. As the survivors of the riot gathered at the Reverend Seay's house, the scene began to resemble a religious revival. Surviving a trial by fire had somehow dispelled the mystique of massive resistance, and despite fears of future violence, as well as concern for those who had already been injured, the importance of sustaining the Freedom Ride was clearer than ever. The presence of Lewis and other injured Riders only served to reinforce the growing realization that the stakes had been raised and that there could be no turning back in the face of danger.

Speaking from his hospital bed at St. Jude's, a heavily bandaged Zwerg assured reporters that "these beatings cannot deter us from our purpose. We are not martyrs or publicity seekers. We want only equality and justice, and we will get it. We will continue our journey one way or another. We are prepared to die." Lying one floor below, in St. Jude's Black ward, William Barbee echoed Zwerg's pledge: "As soon as we've recovered from this, we'll start again. . . . We'll take all the South has to throw and still come back for more." As Diane Nash argued in a series of messages sent to the offices of SNCC, the SCLC, CORE, and the NAACP, surely it was time for movement leaders to put aside whatever reservations they had about the wisdom of the Freedom Ride and rally behind the students in Montgomery.

The response to Nash's plea was overwhelmingly positive, and within a few hours a plan for a mass rally of Freedom Rider supporters was in place. The Sunday-evening rally would be hosted by the Reverend Ralph Abernathy and the congregation of the First Baptist Church. Movement leaders and newspaper and television reporters from across the nation were invited to witness and testify to the breadth and depth of support for the Riders. Martin Luther King Jr. ignored Robert Kennedy's plea for him to stay away from Montgomery, and Jim Farmer and Shuttlesworth also agreed to speak at the rally, much to the dismay of local, state, and federal authorities.

When King's plane arrived around noon, an armed guard of fifty federal marshals escorted him to a private meeting with Lewis, Nash, and LaFayette at an outlying Black church, before proceeding on to Abernathy's downtown parsonage. Later in the afternoon twelve of the marshals returned to the airport to provide an escort for Shuttlesworth, who soon joined King, Abernathy, and the Freedom Riders who had gathered in the basement library at First Baptist. "This was the same room in which I had met with Dr. King and the Reverend Abernathy in the summer of '58 when we had discussed my enrollment at Troy State," Lewis recalled. "Now, here I was again. Preparing for another meeting with those two men, under entirely different circumstances, and not so privately."

Although the mass meeting was scheduled to begin at 8:00 p.m., the faithful began to arrive at First Baptist as early as 5:00. At that point only a few white protesters were in sight of the church, and the early-comers had no trouble making their way to the sanctuary. Outside, a dozen marshals wearing yellow armbands stood quietly by, warily observing the surrounding streets. But there were no city police officers, highway patrol officers, or National Guardsmen on the scene to restrain any potential disorder or violence. Along with the token federal presence, which would prove to provoke rather than deter civil disorder, the absence of local or state law enforcement officers virtually guaranteed an assault on the church. Despite all the rhetoric of the past twenty-four hours, federal authorities in Washington and at nearby Maxwell Field, where the marshals were bivouacked, seemed reticent to do anything beyond the minimum effort to forestall disaster. Even as dusk approached and the crowd outside the church swelled to two thousand and beyond, the Kennedys stuck to the plan of waiting for Patterson's call to the National Guard for assistance.

By 8:00 p.m., fifteen hundred people were inside the sanctuary, and the rising sound of hymns and amens signaled the beginning of the program. The vast majority of the crowd inside the church was Black—the only white people being news reporters and television camera crews, as well as a handful of racial liberals such as the English writer Jessica Mitford. Many of the local Black citizens who had come to support the Freedom Riders were veterans of the mass meetings that had sustained the bus boycott five years earlier, but nothing quite like this had been seen in Montgomery for a long time. With King still downstairs polishing the speech that he had written on the plane, the Reverend Seay opened the program with a description of how the Freedom Riders, who had gathered at his home to restore their energy for the coming struggle, had inspired him with their courage. The Freedom Riders were in the sanctuary, he told the crowd, but he did not dare introduce them because an unjust law had made them fugitives. The only "Freedom Rider" that he could safely identify was Diane Nash, who had been given a seat of honor near the front of the sanctuary. Eventually, without naming names, he asked a couple of the Riders to make brief statements, but the fear of arrest kept them in the background for most of the evening. As an extra precaution, all of the Riders were dressed in choir robes to make them more difficult to identify.

While Seay presided over the emotional opening of the mass meeting, a drama of a different sort was developing downstairs, where a conclave of ministers—including King and Abernathy—was growing increasingly concerned about the size and mood of the crowd outside. The last few parishioners who had straggled into the church had encountered racial epithets and a shower of rocks, and some protesters were beginning to smash the windows of cars parked nearby. Even more alarming to King was the rumor that a group of armed Black taxicab drivers was planning to confront the white protesters. No one had been hurt, and so far the cabdrivers had kept their distance from the mob, but the situation was serious enough to prompt King to venture outside to see for himself. Ignoring the strong objections of his aides, he and a few volunteers spent several minutes circling the church and eyeing the crowd across the street. Eventually someone recognized the famous Atlanta preacher and began screaming, "Nigger King!" Before long, rocks and other missiles were being thrown in King's direction—including a metal cannister that one of his aides feared was a bomb. As the aide tossed aside what turned out to be an empty tear gas canister, King and the others scurried back inside the church.

A few minutes later, Farmer and Shuttlesworth arrived, having somehow managed to make their way safely through the mob outside. Farmer immediately walked over to Lewis, the only other original CORE Freedom Rider in the sanctuary, and embraced him, and then introduced himself to Nash, whom he had never met. Following a rush of amens, Farmer stepped to the pulpit for a few salutary words before retiring to the basement to join King, Abernathy, and a few others who were busily assessing the situation. Over the next hour the situation outside the church grew increasingly ominous. As rocks, bricks, and Molotov cocktails rained down on the church grounds, the hopelessly outnumbered marshals bought a few minutes of time by firing several rounds of tear gas into the crowd. With each round the crowd fell back for a moment, only to advance again as soon as the air cleared.

Inside the church, the Reverend Seay led the congregation through several rousing choruses of "Love Lifted Me" in a spirited attempt to stem a full-scale panic. "I want to hear everybody sing," Seay roared from the pulpit, "and mean every word of it." Sing they did, but the stanzas of faith and hope did not stop them from preparing to defend themselves and their families. Anticipating trouble, many of the men—and some of the women—had come to the church armed with knives and pistols, and there was little doubt that they would use them against the white mob if necessary. "We riders were nonviolent, steeped and trained in the teachings of Gandhi," Lewis later explained, "but most of the people of Montgomery were not."[7]

* * *

All of this, plus the news that some members of the mob had broken through the line of marshals and were banging on the church door, prompted King to ask his aide Wyatt Tee Walker to call Robert Kennedy. After Walker, and then King, told Kennedy that their situation was growing desperate, the attorney general assured them that a large contingent of marshals was on its way. When King tried to press him for details, Kennedy tried to change the subject. Wasn't it time to call off or at least postpone the Freedom Ride? he asked. Not sure how to respond to this request, King explained that he could not speak for the Freedom Riders; he would, however, broach the subject with Farmer and Nash. In the meantime, the people in the church needed protection. If the marshals "don't get here immediately," King exclaimed, "we're going to have a bloody confrontation." Fortunately, the marshals' arrival soon brought what was becoming an awkward conversation to a close. They would not talk again until after midnight, more than three long hours later.

By 9:00 p.m., even with the reinforcements trying to hold back the mob, the besieged congregation had to contend with clouds of tear gas that had drifted into the sanctuary. The marshals, most without gas masks, also found themselves gasping for air. Forced to withdraw from the area in front of the church, they could not prevent an aroused vanguard of protesters from reaching the church door and shattering a large stained-glass window with a brick. At Seay's insistence, the children were evacuated to the basement, just in time to escape a volley of rocks that broke several windows. Before long, however, no one in the church, not even those in the basement, could avoid the sickening fumes of the tear gas that had seeped through the building's exterior. Despite the marshals' good intentions, the rescue was turning into a fiasco.

Even so, there was no wholesale panic in the church. Over the next hour, as the outnumbered marshals struggled to keep the mob at bay, the besieged parishioners at First Baptist continued to tap an inner strength that defied the logic of their precarious position. Even in the face of tear gas and surging rioters, hymns and freedom songs filled the sanctuary. Years later Lewis marveled at the courage and strength of the movement leaders who spoke so movingly to the faithful that night. "Wyatt Walker spoke first. Then Abernathy. Then Farmer. And then up stepped Dr. King," he recalled. "He praised the congregation's courage. He criticized John Patterson. He encouraged the people to remain confident. He told them that they would triumph, that there could be no other way. 'Alabama will have to face the fact,' he said, 'that we are determined to be free.' There were shouts of 'Amen!' and 'Praise God!' 'Fear not,' he said, 'we've come too far to turn back.' There was singing and celebration."

King went on to urge the audience to launch "a full-scale assault on the system of segregation in Alabama," adding, "The law may not be able to make a man love me, but it can keep him from lynching me. . . . Unless the federal government acts forthrightly in the South to assure every citizen his constitutional rights, we will be plunged into a dark abyss of chaos." Departing from his prepared text, he placed much of the blame on Patterson, who bore the "ultimate responsibility for the hideous action in Alabama." "His consistent preaching of defiance of the law," King claimed, "his vitriolic public pronouncements, and his irresponsible actions created the atmosphere in which violence could thrive. Alabama has sunk to a level of barbarity comparable to the tragic days of Hitler's Germany."[8]

In the meantime, Robert Kennedy and Governor Patterson were engaged in a bitter phone conversation about who was to blame for the crisis in Montgomery and how it could be curtailed before there was more bloodshed and violence. At 10:00 p.m., when Patterson learned through a concealed wiretap that Kennedy was preparing to send in a division of regular army troops to quell the riot, the governor blinked and placed the city of Montgomery under what he called "qualified martial rule." Almost immediately, a swarm of city police officers rushed in, followed by more than a hundred National Guardsmen who formed a protective shield in front of the church. Together the police and the Guardsmen cleared the immediate area, and a few minutes later the commander of the Guard, Adjutant General Henry Graham, announced that the sovereign state of Alabama had everything under control and needed no further help from federal authorities.

In actuality, dispersing the mob proved more difficult than Graham or anyone else anticipated. While most of the mayhem was over by 10:15, sporadic violence continued for several hours. Indeed, for the besieged gathering inside the sanctuary, the joyous news of the National Guard's arrival was soon tempered by the realization that their rescuers were white Alabama segregationists, not federal troops. Marching into the church with several of his aides, Graham presided over a formal reading of Patterson's declaration of martial law, which predictably began with the hostile phrase "Whereas, as a result of agitators coming into Alabama to violate our laws and customs . . ." As a murmur of indignation spread through the sanctuary, Graham stepped forward to inform the crowd that the siege was not over, that in all likelihood they would have to remain in the church and under the protection of the National Guard until early morning. Liberation had turned into protective custody. To the Freedom Riders, who had already experienced the protective custody provided by Bull Connor, the scene was all too familiar. "Those soldiers didn't look like protectors now," Lewis later commented. "Their rifles were pointed our way. They looked like the enemy."[9]

This uncomfortable standoff lasted until 4:30 in the morning. Finally, after being pressured by Justice Department officials, a convoy of National Guard trucks and jeeps pulled up in front of the church and began loading an exhausted cargo of men, women, and children. Among them were Lewis and the Freedom Riders, who in the early-morning confusion were taken to a scattering of homes in the Black community. But by Monday afternoon, virtually the entire Freedom Rider contingent had regrouped at the home of Dr. Richard Harris Jr., a prominent Black pharmacist and former neighbor of King's. Joined by an array of movement leaders—including King, Abernathy, Walker, Nash, CORE attorney Len Holt, and Ed King of SNCC—the Riders turned Harris's large brick home into a combination refuge and command center.

During the next two days, Harris's sprawling den became the backdrop for a marathon discussion of the future of the Freedom Ride. The conversation ultimately touched on all aspects of the Freedom Riders' situation, from narrow logistical details to broad philosophical considerations of nonviolent struggle. But the first order of business was finding a solution to the Riders' legal problems. In an ironic twist, Patterson's declaration of martial law had suspended normal civil processes, temporarily negating Judge Jones's injunction within the city limits of Montgomery. The Riders were still subject to arrest everywhere else in Alabama, however. In an effort to remedy this situation, movement attorneys Fred Gray and Arthur Shores went before federal district judge Frank Johnson on Monday afternoon, May 22, seeking to vacate the injunction.

Held at the federal courthouse adjacent to the Greyhound terminal, the hearing required Lewis, who was chosen to serve as the Riders' designated plaintiff and primary witness, to pass by the scene of the Saturday-morning riot. Still bruised and heavily bandaged, Lewis was called on to explain the motivations behind the original CORE Ride and the Nashville Ride. "A day earlier, in the wake of the attacks that week, which had clearly involved the Klan," Lewis recalled, "Judge Johnson had signed a federal restraining order against Klan groups in Montgomery. Now, as he sat on the bench to consider both lifting the injunction against our ride and issuing an injunction guaranteeing our protection as we continued our journey, there were federal marshals in the courtroom assigned to protect the judge's life."

Years later, Lewis described the extraordinary scene in Johnson's courtroom: "I had been in court before, but this was the first time I had actually testified. Judge Johnson asked me to explain what I had experienced during the Freedom Ride so far and why we wanted to carry the ride on into Mississippi. I was nervous. This was an imposing scene.... This was different than a press conference, or a crowd massed for a rally, or a church filled on Sunday morning. This was a courtroom, the seat of the law, and it was the law itself, come down from the Supreme Court in Washington, that was at issue this day. That was how I answered the judge's question, by stating that we had begun this ride to see that the law was carried out, and we wanted to continue it for the same reason. That, apparently, was good enough for Judge Johnson, who lifted the injunctions against us and allowed us to leave the courtroom without the shadow of arrest over our heads."[10]

* * *

The Ride could now continue, but that night, at a meeting held at the Montgomery YMCA, there were a number of important matters to attend to, including working out clear lines of organizational authority and responsibility. Complicated by generational and ideological divisions, the ongoing discussion among students and older movement leaders took several unexpected turns on Monday evening. Ignoring the democratic sensibilities of the students, Farmer took immediate charge of the meeting. "He talked loud and big," Lewis remembered, "but his words sounded hollow to me. His retreat after the attacks in Anniston and Birmingham had something to do with it, I'm sure, but he just struck me as very insincere. It was clear to everyone that he wanted to take the ride back now, when we all knew that without our having picked it up, there would have been no more Freedom Ride. It didn't matter to me at all who got the credit; that wasn't the point. But from where Farmer stood, that seemed to be all that mattered. He saw this ride in terms of himself. He kept calling it 'CORE's ride,' which amazed everyone."

Some students openly challenged the CORE leader's proprietary claims, while others quietly wrote him off as an organization man hopelessly out of touch with the democratic spirit of the modern movement. But most of the attention ultimately focused on Martin Luther King Jr., whose recent support of the CORE and Nashville Freedom Rides had triggered speculation that at some point he might become a Freedom Rider himself. Earlier in the week, Nash had broached the subject during a phone conversation with him, suggesting his presence on one of the freedom buses was essential to the movement, but before the Monday-night meeting there was no organized effort to persuade him to join the Freedom Ride. Though discouraged by King's noncommittal response to her initial entreaty, Nash decided to try again in Montgomery.

"Diane, true to form—fearless and straightforward—confronted him with the question of whether he would join us," Lewis observed, with mixed emotions. "No, Dr. King said, he could not go. He was on probation, he explained, from his arrest in Atlanta. 'I'm on probation, too,' one of our group shouted. 'Me, too,' yelled another. 'We're all on probation,' said someone else. Dr. King did not budge. 'I think,' he answered with some irritation in his voice, 'I should choose the time and place of my Golgotha.' That did it. Several of our group stood up, shook their heads and moved toward the door. The rest followed. On the way out I heard for the first time a phrase that would be repeated often in the coming years used to mock Dr. King for his loftiness in the movement and for quoting the Scripture, invoking God and Jesus in terms of his own situation. 'De Lawd!' That's what someone muttered as we left the YMCA room that night. There was anger in the phrase, criticism of Dr. King for somehow comparing himself to Christ. There couldn't have been a more concise way to capture the split that was widening between the generations in the movement than that simpler phrase: De Lawd."

Lewis did not agree with this denigration of King, then or later, but he did have some understanding of why his SNCC friends were so disappointed. Later that evening, he and Abernathy did their best to smooth things over with the most disillusioned students, but for some King's mystique was permanently dispelled. In the years to come, the break between the student movement and King would become increasingly problematic for Lewis, who tried to balance his loyalty to SNCC with his admiration for the SCLC leader.[11]

On Tuesday morning, the movement conclave at Harris's house continued to wrestle with the issues of organizational harmony and personal commitment, but the scene inside the house was calm compared with what was going on elsewhere. In the streets of Montgomery, there was sporadic violence, multiple bombs threats, and "roving gangs of white youths," enough mayhem to force General Graham to dispatch 150 additional National Guardsmen to trouble spots around the city. Most of the action, however, was in the corridors of power in Montgomery, Jackson, and Washington. With martial law still in effect and with the resumption of the Freedom Ride scheduled for Wednesday morning, Tuesday was a time for public posturing and behind-the-scenes negotiation among government officials. Earlier in the week, former Mississippi governor James Coleman had warned Burke Marshall that he feared the Freedom Riders would "all be killed" if they tried to cross the state without a military escort. Even Medgar Evers, the Mississippi NAACP's state field secretary, confessed to reporters that he hoped the Freedom Riders would postpone the trip to Jackson—that under the present circumstances it was simply "too dangerous" to force a confrontation with Mississippi segregationists.

Heeding these warnings, the Justice Department—in close collaboration with Patterson, Mississippi's governor, Ross Barnett, and the state's powerful U.S. senator, James O. Eastland—organized a military operation "worthy of a NATO war game," as one historian later put it. Unfortunately, this collaboration also produced a tacit understanding that once the Freedom Riders arrived in Jackson, there would be no federal interference with local law enforcement. The Freedom Riders would be safe during their journey from Montgomery to Jackson, but once they were in the Mississippi capital, the police would be free to make mass arrests. Though hardly pleased with the prospect of jailed Freedom Riders, Robert Kennedy assured Eastland that the federal government's "primary interest was that they weren't beaten up."

Kennedy and his Justice Department colleagues regarded the deal as an unpleasant but necessary resolution to a crisis that had already taken up too much of the administration's time and energy. In their eyes, the decision to accede to Eastland's demands was simply a postponement of the day of reckoning and not a surrender. Sometime in the future the federal government would find a way to guarantee the right to travel from state to state without accommodating outdated segregationist laws. But under the current conditions of Cold War politics, administration leaders did not feel they could afford a prolonged crisis that would embarrass the nation in front of the world.[12]

The decision to seek freedom later, rather than freedom now, was not, however, relayed to the Freedom Riders themselves, who continued to hope that the federal government would protect their constitutional rights by immediately enforcing the *Morgan* and *Boynton* decisions. This expectation became clear during a Tuesday-morning press conference featuring King, Farmer, Abernathy, and Lewis. Determined to sustain the momentum of the Freedom Ride and eager to demonstrate the solidarity that had formed over the past week, the four civil rights leaders abandoned the security of Harris's house to brief the press on their plans. Surrounded by federal marshals and a crush of reporters, they explained why they and their organizations were committed to resuming the Freedom Ride.

King then read a joint declaration vowing that the Freedom Riders would soon board buses bound for Mississippi, with or without guarantees of police protection. Before their departure, he announced, the Riders would participate in a nonviolent workshop led by Nashville movement leader James Lawson. "Freedom Riders must develop the quiet courage of dying for a cause," he declared, his voice cracking with emotion. "We would not like to see anyone die. . . . We all love life, and there are no martyrs here—but we are well aware that we may have casualties. . . . I'm sure these students are willing to face death if necessary."

Sitting to King's immediate left, Lewis felt King's rousing words struck just the right tone, signaling a new departure for the Freedom Rides. "It was no longer just us, the core group from Nashville," he observed. "Now, students were flooding into Montgomery from all across the South, from as far west as New Orleans and as far north as D.C. The nature of the ride had shifted now, with control moving from CORE to the students. It had become a more spontaneous event, less like a precise, military-like assault and more like an organism with a life of its own, a thing that seemed to be growing on its own accord, with students arriving by the score even as we met with the press, all of them piling into Dr. Harris's house, eager to get on the bus, ready to fill Mississippi's jails, if need be. But we would go first, the two dozen or so of us who were set to board a pair of buses the next morning."[13]

* * *

The federal presence in Alabama and Mississippi was both everywhere and nowhere on Wednesday morning, May 24. Having asserted the power and authority of the national government, the Kennedy administration had withdrawn, at least temporarily, to the sidelines. The short-term, if not the ultimate, fate of the Freedom Ride had been placed in the hands of state officials who, paradoxically, had promised to protect both the safety of the Riders and the sanctity of segregation. When the Trailways group of Riders left Harris's house at 6:15 a.m., they were transported by a half dozen jeeps driven by Alabama National Guardsmen. This unimpressive show of force raised a few eyebrows among the Riders, but as the convoy approached the downtown Trailways terminal, the now familiar outline of steel-helmeted soldiers came into view. In and around the terminal, more than five hundred heavily armed Guardsmen and a number of FBI agents and plainclothes detectives stood watch over several clusters of white bystanders.

As the Riders filed out of the jeeps, the scene was tense but quiet until the crowd spotted King, who had agreed to escort the Trailways group into the terminal. King, still uncomfortable with his refusal to join the Ride, was determined to provide the disappointed students with as much visible support as possible. During an early-morning prayer meeting at Harris's house, he and Abernathy had blessed the Riders, and in a show of solidarity his brother, A. D. King, had flown in from Atlanta to help desegregate the Trailways terminal's snack bar. With some members of the crowd scream-ing words of indignation, King led the combined SCLC–Freedom Rider entourage through the white waiting room and up to the counter, where he and others ordered coffee and rolls. As several reporters and camera crews pressed forward to record the moment, "the white waitresses re-moved their aprons and stepped back" while Black waitresses from the "Negro lunch counter stepped up and took the orders," thus breaking a half-century-old color bar. Local and state officials, it seemed, had put out the word that nothing was to get in the way of the Freedom Riders' exit from Montgomery.

Upon arriving at the loading bay, the group of twelve Riders—which included Lawson, Jim Bevel, LaFayette, and C. T. Vivian—discovered there were no regular passengers waiting for the morning bus to Jackson. Alabama Guardsmen were only allowing Freedom Riders and credentialed reporters to board the bus. After General Graham stepped onto the bus to advise them that they were about to embark on "a hazardous journey," six Guardsmen joined the Riders and reporters, as an array of jeeps, patrol cars, and police motorcycles prepared to escort the bus to the city limits, where a massive convoy of vehicles was waiting. Once the bus reached the city line, the magnitude of the effort to get the Freedom Riders out of Alabama without any additional violence became apparent. In addition to several dozen highway patrol cars, there were two helicopters and three U.S. Border Patrol planes flying overhead, plus a large contingent of press cars jammed with reporters and photographers. As the Riders would soon discover, nearly a thousand Guardsmen and several FBI surveillance units were stationed along the 140-mile route to the Mississippi border.

During the journey to Jackson, Lawson and several other Riders made it clear that they did not appreciate the heavy-handed style of protection being imposed on a Freedom Ride designed to test the constitutional right to travel freely from place to place. "This isn't a Freedom Ride, it's a military operation," Bevel yelled out, a sentiment echoed by LaFayette, who confessed, "I feel like I'm going to war." When they reached the Mississippi line, they discovered just how true this was. Matching their Alabama cousins, Mississippi authorities had assembled a small army of National Guardsmen and highway patrol officers. If this was not bracing enough, word soon came that Mississippi authorities had uncovered a plot to dynamite the bus as soon as it entered the state. This and other unconfirmed threats caused an hour's delay, but by 2:00 p.m. the bus had finally arrived at the Jackson Trailways terminal.[14]

At the Jackson terminal, the Riders, Black and white, filed into the white waiting room, and several promptly used the white restroom. When they ignored police captain J. L. Ray's brusque order "to move on," all twelve were placed under arrest, charged with inciting to riot, breach of peace, and failure to obey a police officer. Significantly, there was no mention of violating state or local segregation laws, a strategy designed to avoid a court challenge to those laws. As several reporters, a contingent of National Guardsmen, and a cheering crowd of white protesters looked on, the police jammed the Riders into paddy wagons and hauled them off to the city jail. A few minutes later, they all refused an NAACP offer to post a $1,000 bond for each defendant.

While all this was going on, Lewis and the Greyhound group were still en route. They had caused quite a stir before leaving Montgomery, when state officials complained that they knew nothing about a second freedom bus to Jackson. With Lucretia Collins as the designated leader, the bus left the Greyhound terminal adjacent to the federal courthouse at 11:25 a.m. amid the jeers of a large crowd of protesters who had to be restrained by National Guardsmen. Out on the highway, a hastily organized escort of highway patrol cruisers and helicopters shadowed the bus, and National Guardsmen on full alert still lined the route. Years later Farmer recalled the sight of the Mississippi Guardsmen's "rifles pointed toward the forests." To him the scene conjured up images of "runaway slaves a century ago, sloshing through water and hiding behind trees as they fled pursuing hounds."

Lewis had a similar reaction to the Mississippi part of the journey. "I'd never been to Mississippi before," he later explained. "All my life I had heard unbelievably horrible things about the place, stories of murders and lynchings, bodies dumped in rivers, brutality and hatred worse than anything I'd ever heard of growing up in Alabama or attending college in Tennessee. Now I was here, and it was unsettling seeing crowds of onlookers standing by the roadside, held back by those armed troops, some of whom wore big bushy beards that made them look like Confederate soldiers." As the bus approached Jackson, Lewis remembered, "our anxiety began to rise . . . and so, as we always did when the tension increased, someone started a song, and we all joined in: *I'm taking a ride on the Greyhound bus line, I'm riding the front seat to Jackson this time. Hallelujah, I'm a-traveling, Hallelujah, ain't it fine. Hallelujah, I'm a-traveling down freedom's main line.*"

The freedom songs calmed their nerves—until they actually arrived in Jackson. The second round of arrests followed the same pattern as the first, with the Jackson police swooping in and apprehending all fifteen Riders within three minutes of their arrival. Farmer led the exodus off the bus, with Lewis and the other Riders walking close behind him. Lewis had just enough time to make it to a urinal in the white men's room before being arrested. When the arresting officer told him to move, Lewis said, "Just a minute. Can't you see what I'm doing?" That only angered the officer, who barked, "I said *move! Now!*" Escorted to a paddy wagon, he was whisked off to the Jackson city jail, where he was incarcerated with the other twenty-six Riders arrested that day. On the way to jail, the Riders serenaded the paddy wagon guards with chorus after chorus of the movement anthem "We Shall Overcome," emphasizing the line "We are not afraid!"[15]

* * *

Two days later, the arrested Riders appeared before Judge James L. Spencer, who, as Lewis recalled, turned his back on the Riders' two Black attorneys and then "wheeled around, smacked his gavel on the bench and gave us each a $200 fine and sixty days in jail." Even though Spencer—hoping that the convicted troublemakers would simply pay the fine and flee the state—immediately suspended the jail term, the Riders refused to pay the fine or to accept bail. Disgusted, Spencer sent them all back to the city jail, where they remained for three days before being moved across the street to the Hinds County jail.

By the time the next onslaught of Riders—nine on a bus from Memphis and eight more from Montgomery—had arrived in Jackson on May 28, Lewis and the others arrested four days earlier had already been transferred to the Hinds County Penal Farm in Raymond, fifteen miles west of the capital. Isolated from public scrutiny or press coverage, the original arrestees were now at the mercy of the Raymond guards. There, Lewis recalled, the Riders "were crammed into cells even smaller than the jail's. There were not enough beds for all of us, and so we slept on the floor, on tables, on benches, anywhere we could stretch out our bodies."

During their two weeks at Raymond, Lewis, Farmer, Lawson, and the other Riders incarcerated there received only fragmentary bits of news about what was happening in the wider world. But as Lewis later confirmed, they did learn that "the Freedom Ride had burst wide open . . . mushrooming and multiplying into Freedom *Rides,* dozens of them." This influx would eventually involve "buses filled with literally hundreds of Freedom-Riding Northerners arriving in Jackson each day from every direction. Quakers, college professors, rabbis, pacifists, unionists, communists, conscientious objectors, clergymen—they were flooding in from Minnesota, Wisconsin, California, as well as from points east and south, merging with the students of SNCC and CORE and overflowing the jails of Jackson." All told, 436 Freedom Riders participated in more than sixty different Rides during the spring and summer of 1961, and more than 300 of them ended up in prison in Mississippi.[16]

This unprecedented flood of movement activity altered the nature and meaning of citizen politics in the United States: first by goading white supremacist politicians into harsher and ultimately self-defeating forms of intimidation and violence; second by forcing the Kennedy administration to take a firm stand on behalf of racial justice and the enforcement of constitutional law on matters of racial equality; and third by successfully challenging the widespread public presumption that disrupting civic order in the name of civil rights was fundamentally un-American and morally wrong. In the wake of the Freedom Rides, which demonstrated the discipline, restraint, and courageous spirit of nonviolent activism, it became extremely difficult to assert the moral equivalence of Gandhian disruption and the vigilantism of the Ku Klux Klan.

As Lawson warned his disciples, the legitimization of nonviolent direct action required a considerable amount of sacrifice and unmerited suffering. Lewis had already experienced a measure of such sacrifice and suffering, but any doubt he might have harbored about the truth of Lawson's claim was dispelled during his incarceration in Mississippi. Two weeks after his arrival at Raymond, the real test of his commitment to the cause began when he and several dozen other Riders were transferred to the infamous Parchman Prison Farm in Sunflower County. As Lewis recalled his wild and frightening ride to Parchman, "On the fifteenth of June, well past midnight, we were marched out into the darkness, forty-five of us, and put into windowless truck trailers—herded like horses, like cows, into these airless, seatless containers. . . . We had no idea where we were going. And then, after about two hours, we were a hundred miles northwest of Jackson, in the middle of nowhere. The doors were opened, and we stepped out into the light of dawn to see a barbed-wire fence stretching away in either direction. And armed guards with shotguns. And beyond the guards, inside the fence, a complex of boxy wooden and concrete buildings. And beyond them, nothing but dark, flat Mississippi delta."[17]

Lewis had heard of Parchman, which had been a menacing symbol of Mississippi's penal system since its founding in 1901, and he knew about its reputation. But nothing in his past had prepared him for the forbidding nature of the scene that morning. As the Freedom Riders' eyes adjusted to the morning light, the imposing figure of Superintendent Fred Jones appeared at the gate. "We have some bad niggers here," Jones drawled. "We have niggers on death row that'll beat you up and cut you as soon as look at you." Moments later the guards began pushing the Riders toward a nearby processing building, but the forced march was soon interrupted by a scuffle in the rear of the line. Terry Sullivan and Felix Singer, two white Freedom Riders who had remained in the back of one of the trucks and then gone limp in defiance of the guards, were being dragged to the processing center by their feet. The guards were unimpressed. "What you actin' like that for?" one guard asked. "Ain't no newspaper men out here." Lewis, standing just a few feet away, heard another guard chime in, "Go ahead and sing your goddamn freedom songs now. We got niggers here that will eat you up. So you go on and sing your songs inside now."[18]

Taken to the basement of the processing center, the Riders soon found themselves under the control of a man who introduced himself as Deputy Tyson. Later described by Stokely Carmichael as "a massive, red-faced, cigar-smoking cracker in cowboy boots," Tyson would become an all too familiar figure to the Riders during their stay in Parchman. Without any explanation other than a smirk, Tyson ordered them to remove all of their clothes. "For two and a half hours we stood wearing nothing," Lewis remembered. "When we were finally led, two by two, into a shower room guarded by a sergeant with a rifle, I thought of the concentration camps in Germany. This was 1961 in America, yet here we were, treated like animals for using the wrong bathroom."

This scene would be repeated throughout the summer as hundreds of Freedom Riders were taken to Parchman. All would be strictly isolated from the regular prisoners for fear they might infect them with radical ideas, and none would be allowed to work in the fields, an unintended mercy that saved them from the physical toll of hard, back-breaking labor. Instead, a combination of boredom and isolation, interrupted by periodic harassment, was their punishment. "The monotony was tremendous," Lewis remembered. "We had no reading material other than the Bible, a palm-sized copy of the New Testament, which was given to each of us by the local Salvation Army. . . . There were walls between the cells, so we could not see one another. Only when we were taken out to shower, which was twice a week, did we see anyone but our cellmate. Once a week we could write a letter, which I always made as long as I could." Long or short, Lewis's letters helped to alleviate his sense of isolation, though some letters were more difficult to write than others. One memorable letter was sent to the ABT administration explaining where he was and why he had missed his graduation ceremony in early June, and another went to his disappointed parents, offering an abject apology for spoiling their plan to come to Nashville to attend the ceremony.[19]

The tight regimen at Parchman was mandated by the state's publicity-conscious governor, Ross Barnett, who found himself under increasing pressure from a federal government desperate to avoid a repeat of the violence that had greeted the Freedom Riders in Alabama. With their eyes on the Cold War and on the expressions of disapproval from around the world, the Kennedy brothers pulled out all the stops to make the Freedom Rider crisis go away.[20]

On May 29, even before the massive expansion of the Freedom Rides and the alarming transfer of Riders to Parchman, the Justice Department petitioned the ICC to implement a formal, binding order desegregating interstate transit facilities. The hope was that local and state officials, and bus and rail companies, would take down the "Colored Only" and "Whites Only" signs that had been hanging in terminals for generations, and see to it that interstate passengers of all races could sit anywhere they pleased. "Just as our constitution is color blind, and neither knows nor tolerates classes among citizens," the petition advised, "so too is the Interstate Commerce Act. The time has come for this commission, in administering that act, to declare unequivocally by regulation that a Negro passenger is free to travel the length and breadth of this country in the same manner as any other passenger."

The Kennedys realized that the ICC was a notoriously slow-moving agency, and that at best it would be several months before the commissioners responded to the petition. But they hoped the civil rights community, which had been calling for such an ICC order for more than a decade, would accept the petition as an act of good faith and immediately call off the Freedom Rides planned for the near future. Robert Kennedy's earlier call for a "cooling off" period had been rejected by CORE's leaders; Farmer's response was, "Please tell the attorney general that we've been cooling off for 350 years. If we cool off any more, we will be in a deep freeze. The Freedom Ride will go on." Kennedy now calculated that the submission of the petition might bring Farmer and the Riders around. But he was wrong. The incarcerated Riders' new freedom song, which they sang incessantly to the consternation of their guards, was "Buses Are a Comin'," and the freedom buses continued to roll into Mississippi until mid-August.

Hampered by the fear of alienating powerful Southern Democrats like Barnett, Eastland, and Patterson, the Kennedys felt they had to tread lightly in the Deep South. They were also hamstrung by the reality that the legal battle surrounding the Freedom Rides was being played by the rules of local and state law, not federal or constitutional law. The legal situation also hindered the Freedom Riders' Gandhian strategy of crippling Mississippi's criminal justice system by overflowing its jails. Under Mississippi law, incarcerated prisoners lost the right to appeal their conviction if they remained in jail for more than thirty-nine days. With this in mind, CORE worked out an elaborate plan of staggered bail-out dates.

For Lewis, the release date was July 7, a little over three weeks after he had entered Parchman. After a round of bittersweet goodbyes, he left his cellmate—Bill Harbour, a nineteen-year-old Tennessee A&I student from Piedmont, Alabama—and the other Riders remaining behind bars and boarded a bus. On the trip to Jackson, where he would take a train on to Nashville, he had time to reflect on what he and others had experienced during the past two months. "I thought about the fact that we had just about literally been through hell," he recalled, "first in Anniston, then in Birmingham, then in Montgomery, and now here at Parchman." Yet the journey had been well worth all the pain and sacrifice. "Freedom Riders were flooding the South now," he told himself, "scores of buses filled with black and white passengers bound to break down the walls of segregation in these states."

The fledgling movement that Lewis had joined three years earlier had gained considerable momentum during the Freedom Ride campaign. Indeed, the work on behalf of racial justice had achieved a scope and importance unimaginable in the 1950s, and Lewis was proud of the part he had played in helping to bring this about. But he also knew "that work was just beginning . . . that we were in for a long bloody fight here in the American South." On the train ride to Nashville, he finally made the decision to turn down the tempting opportunity to spend two years in India. His calling, he now realized more than ever, was to devote his life to the civil rights struggle, "to stay in the middle of it."[21]

* * *

Once he was back in Nashville, Lewis was reminded that the Freedom Rides, as important as they were, did not address much of the unfinished business of desegregation left over from the sit-ins and stand-ins of the previous year. One prime example was the refusal of the city's major grocery stores to hire Black employees. Other patterns of segregation and blatant discrimination persisted at local hotels, libraries, and parks. During the summer of 1961, these businesses and institutions, along with every other "business or public service in the city that practiced racial segregation," became a target for the NSM. Immediately after his return, Lewis threw himself into the NSM's ambitious new project, Operation Open City.

With Nash and Bevel no longer in the city, Lewis was the obvious choice to lead the Open City campaign, in part because he had broad experience both inside and outside Nashville. "For the first time," he noted, "we were joined on the picket lines by large numbers of non-Nashvillians—students, mostly Northerners, coming or going from the Freedom Rides. They were eager to be involved in what we were doing in Nashville, and they jumped right in, which would have been a good thing except for the fact that many of them were untrained in our practices and procedures. . . . What we had achieved in Nashville up to then . . . was due to the discipline and care with which we approached our demonstrations. That summer, though, I could see that discipline eroding, crumbling a little at the edges where the outsiders were stepping in."

Carmichael, the outspoken NAG activist who would serve as Lewis's counterpoint in SNCC for the rest of the decade, was "one of the worst offenders," according to Lewis, indulging in reckless "name-calling and taunting and cursing" when confronting white segregationists on the picket line. "He loved nothing more than to scare the hell out of people," Lewis observed. "And he was good at it. He had a sharp tongue, and he knew how to use it, to poke and prod and provoke." Both during and after his stay in Parchman, Carmichael challenged SNCC's once sacrosanct commitment to nonviolence, much to Lewis's dismay. Another troubling visitor to Nashville with little faith in nonviolence was Jim Forman, a talented but cynical Black journalist and former schoolteacher from Chicago, who would become SNCC's executive secretary later in the year.

Forman eventually moved on to an extended visit with the controversial proponent of armed defense, Robert Williams, in Monroe, North Carolina, but Carmichael remained for most of the summer. Both Forman and Carmichael were vocal participants in a SNCC meeting that grew out of a student leadership seminar titled "Understanding the Nature of Social Change," a star-studded gathering of Black intellectuals featuring the sociologist E. Franklin Frazier, the psychologist Kenneth Clark, and the historian Rayford Logan. Sponsored by the New World Foundation, the three-week-long seminar was held in Nashville beginning on July 30. At a spin-off meeting, the major topic of discussion was a proposed reallocation of SNCC's time and resources to voter registration, as opposed to its current emphasis on nonviolent direct action. But most of the sessions at the larger conference, originally conceived by Tim Jenkins, a Black Howard University graduate student serving as president of the National Student Association, dealt with the student-led movement's naïveté "about how," in Jenkins's words, "the political system actually worked . . . or failed to work." Thus, despite the pretense of academic detachment, the prescribed necessity of deferring to the federal government's wishes hovered behind many of the presentations and discussions.

Two weeks earlier at a contentious SNCC meeting in Baltimore, a proposal to establish a series of voting rights projects had run into strong opposition from direct action advocates who resented the Kennedy administration's less-than-subtle effort to steer the SNCC students toward voting rights by dangling the promise of funding from the Taconic Foundation, tax exemptions, and enhanced legal and physical protection if they did so. The administration's motivation—which became clear in a June 16 meeting with Lawson, Nash, and other student movement leaders in Robert Kennedy's office, with the famed singer and Kennedy insider Harry Belafonte there to represent the Taconic Foundation—was both political and practical, grounded in the questionable assumption that voting rights work in the Deep South would provoke less violence than direct action campaigns like the Freedom Rides.[22]

This heated debate resumed in Nashville, where Lewis and several other NSM leaders were ready to take on the voting rights advocates. "I didn't take the trip to meet with Belafonte," Lewis recalled, "but I heard all about it. And I didn't like it. Neither did Diane, or Marion [Barry], or Bevel or Bernard, all of whom spoke firmly in defense of sticking to our roots. As far as we were concerned, the very future of SNCC was on the line here. Direct action was what had gotten us this far; SNCC had been created and built on the foundation of confrontation—disciplined, focused, aggressive, nonviolent confrontation."

Lewis listened patiently while the other side, led by Jenkins (who turned out to be a close friend of the deputy attorney general Burke Marshall) and Charles Jones, a student activist from Charlotte, North Carolina, made its case. But nothing that Jenkins or anyone else said changed his mind or alleviated his suspicion that the administration was, in effect, trying "to buy us out, to make us beholden to the very government we were confronting." One NSM member put it more bluntly, arguing that the voter registration offer was "nothing more than a device to 'get the niggers off the streets.'" "To me the matter was simple," Lewis later wrote. "We had gotten this far by dramatizing the issue of segregation, by putting it on stage and *keeping* it on stage. I believed firmly that we needed to push and push and not stop pushing. . . . I believed in *action*. Dr. King said early on that there is no noise as powerful as the sound of the marching feet of a determined people, and I believed that. I *experienced* it."[23]

Nothing was settled by the close of the Nashville meeting, but Lewis and the other SNCC leaders found more room for agreement when they reconvened on Friday, August 11, at the Highlander Folk School. Several of the SNCC leaders, including Lewis, had been to Highlander before, and they knew it was a place for open discussion and honest disagreement. As the discussion deepened over the weekend, some worried that SNCC was in danger of dividing into two separate organizations or of disappearing altogether. Jenkins and Jones were adamant that voting rights should be SNCC's first priority, while Nash, Lewis, and the Freedom Rider faction were no less certain that direct action represented the heart and soul of the organization and the movement.

Fortunately, Ella Baker was on hand to serve as a mediating influence, just as she had done at SNCC's founding conference in Raleigh fourteen months earlier. On Sunday, after three days of wrangling, Baker, the one veteran organizer trusted by both factions, fashioned a workable compromise that divided SNCC into two equal "wings." Nash, everyone agreed, would lead the direct action wing, and Jones would lead the voting rights wing. Though no one was completely satisfied by this division, most, including Bernard LaFayette, tried to make the best of the situation. Assuming his usual calming role, LaFayette reminded his departing colleagues that "a bird needs two wings to fly."

Years later, after he became the nation's most celebrated voting rights advocate, Lewis looked back on the compromise forged at Highlander with a sense of irony. Though ratified reluctantly against his better judgment, it was one of the most fortuitous milestones of his life, a turning point that opened a path for SNCC to establish local voting rights campaigns in dozens of the Deep South's most backward counties and to participate in the regionwide Voter Education Project (VEP) that would expand and transform the Southern Black electorate over the next three decades, and that Lewis himself would direct for seven years. Several fledgling SNCC voting rights efforts had already begun, most notably by Bob Moses in McComb, Mississippi, and Charles Sherrod in the southwest Georgia town of Albany. But for most SNCC activists, including Lewis, the creation of the voting rights wing at Highlander marked a radical new departure.[24]

In the short run, however, the most important departure was the Freedom Riders' return to Jackson for a mass arraignment on August 14, the day after the Highlander meeting. For Lewis, as for 191 other formerly incarcerated Riders, returning to Jackson—even for a few days—was a potentially traumatic experience. But they all felt compelled to show up, as CORE stood to forfeit several hundred dollars of bail money for each Rider who failed to appear for arraignment. To CORE's relief, only six Riders missed the dreaded arraignment, unexpectedly providing movement leaders with an opportunity to hold a mass "freedom rally" at a Black Masonic temple. Hosted by the Jackson Non-Violent Movement, the rally featured Farmer and several others who addressed a crowd of more than a thousand, including all of the Riders about to be arraigned. Assuring them that the critics who claimed that the Freedom Rides had "run out of steam" were wrong, Farmer told the crowd that they were part of a growing national movement. The return to Jackson had pumped new life into the Freedom Rides, he insisted, "which now must continue no matter how much it costs."

Lewis and the other Riders left the rally exhilarated, but these feelings of emotional uplift would soon be tested by the challenges of a hostile courtroom. At the arraignment, presided over by Judge Russell Moore, the Riders' lead attorney, William Kunstler, filed several defense motions, including a declaration that the local statutes involved in the Freedom Riders' arrests "were unconstitutional on their face and a violation of the U.S. Constitution." But Moore swiftly rejected all of Kunstler's motions and brought the defendants forward in pairs to register their pleas and assign trial dates. Beginning on August 22, the trials would consume twenty-two weeks of the court's docket, stretching into mid-January 1962.

Lewis, who would have to wait several weeks for his day in court, left the state along with many others by nightfall. For him, as for all of the Riders, the chances of acquittal were slim, and there seemed to be no way for CORE to escape the crushing financial burden presented by the protracted trial schedule. Imposed by a system determined to halt the Freedom Rides, the scheduled appellate trials promised to consume virtually all of CORE's resources, making it all but impossible to extend the Rides to other areas of the South. And with more than a hundred Riders still languishing in Mississippi jails, there would almost certainly be many more trials to follow. Barring intervention by the federal courts, which seemed highly unlikely, the legal tangle related to the Jackson arrests would take months, and even years, to unravel.[25]

The Freedom Riders' best hope was a timely positive ruling by the ICC, which began public hearings on the Justice Department's petition the day after the arraignment. Most of the groundwork for the hearings already had been laid in lengthy behind-the-scenes negotiations between the commissioners and the Justice Department, sustaining Robert Kennedy's hope that the potentially powerful regulatory agency would eventually provide a politically and legally palatable solution to the Freedom Rider crisis. But the attorney general was running out of patience with the Republican-dominated commission. He wanted nothing less than a broadly enforceable order that would supersede the indefinite mandates of the Motor Carrier Act of 1935 and the obvious limitations of the *Morgan* and *Boynton* decisions. Historically, the conflicting provisions of state and federal laws on matters of Jim Crow transit had tilted toward segregation, in part because only the state statutes included specific commands. Thus meaningful desegregation would require a detailed and directive order along the lines proposed by the Kennedy administration.

To bring this about, the administration mounted a broad-gauged appeal emphasizing the national security aspects of the struggle for civil rights. The immediate need for a sweeping ICC desegregation order, Deputy Attorney General Marshall insisted, transcended considerations of racial equity or legal precedent. Secretary of Defense Robert McNamara also weighed in, arguing that the enforcement of segregation on buses and trains posed a serious threat to the morale of Black military personnel assigned to Southern bases. Secretary of State Dean Rusk, a native Georgian familiar with Southern laws and customs, went even further, reminding the commission that the persistence of segregated transit facilities was a major embarrassment for a nation promoting democracy and freedom in a largely nonwhite world.

Several civil rights organizations also tried to push the commission toward a righteous and timely decision. To make sure that the commissioners realized what was at stake, CORE set up a line of sign-carrying Free-dom Riders outside the ICC building on the first morning of the hearings. Speaking for the SCLC, King challenged the ICC to issue a sweeping ruling that included a "blanket order" against segregation in bus, rail, and air ter-minals. "The Freedom Rides had already served a great purpose," he told reporters, highlighting "the indignities and injustices that the Negro people still confront as they attempt to do the simple thing of traveling as inter-state passengers." But he insisted a clear and broad ICC mandate held the power to go even further. If strict compliance were enforced for interstate travelers, all segregated travel would "almost inevitably end," even among intrastate travelers. "This will be the point where Freedom Rides will end," he predicted.[26]

* * *

Lewis kept close tabs on the governmental drama playing out in Washington. But he also continued to confront his own drama back in Nashville, where he spent most of late August and early September either on a picket line or in jail. Somehow he also found time to continue his education, enrolling at Fisk for the fall semester. LaFayette became his roommate, as they both took advantage of an agreement between ABT (which was not accredited) and Fisk that offered ABT graduates the opportunity to earn an accredited bachelor's degree by taking two years of courses at Fisk. No longer inter-ested in a career as a preacher, Lewis felt he needed a liberal arts degree as a basis for doing something else. Pursuing a philosophy degree at Fisk would also keep him in Nashville, which was exactly where he wanted to be as the Open City campaign continued its assault on Jim Crow.

There was still so much left for the NSM to do. On September 8, Lewis—the recently elected chairman of the NSM's central committee—and several dozen other students formed picket lines both outside and inside the state capitol protesting the expulsion of fourteen Freedom Riders from Tennessee State. He was one of eleven who formed a double line in front of Governor Buford Ellington's office, a bold action that received considerable attention in the press. Inspired by the Freedom Rides, the student-led movement was becoming increasingly militant, as Martin Luther King Jr. noted in a *New York Times Magazine* essay published two days after the capitol protest in Nashville. King credited the Black student vanguard with delivering the message that "the time for freedom has come." "The young Negro is not in revolt, as some have suggested, against a single pattern of timid, fumbling, conservative leadership," the SCLC leader insisted. "Nor is his conduct to be explained in terms of youth's excesses. He is carrying forward a revolutionary destiny of a whole people consciously and deliberately. Hence the extraordinary willingness to fill the jails as if they were honors classes and the boldness to absorb brutality, even to the point of death, and remain nonviolent."

Lewis found this last statement especially perceptive and in keeping with his own sense that the Freedom Riders had turned Parchman into a veritable university of nonviolence. He was also thrilled by King's expansive interpretation of the student movement's lofty aims. "The students are not struggling for themselves alone," King explained. "They are seeking to save the soul of America. They are taking our whole nation back to those great wells of democracy which were dug deep by the Founding Fathers in the formulation of the Constitution and the Declaration of Independence. In sitting down at the lunch counters, they are in reality standing up for the best in the American dream."

Designed to prick the conscience of white America, King's words appeared at a critical moment in the Freedom Rider saga. Despite the essay's declarative title—"The Time for Freedom Has Come"—in reality the timing of freedom's arrival in the Jim Crow South was still very much in doubt. To bring the Freedom Rides to a successful conclusion, movement leaders would need every influential ally they could muster, especially in the legal arena. On September 11, the day after King's essay appeared, the arraignment of seventy-eight additional Freedom Rider defendants in Jackson intensified the legal and financial pressure bearing down on CORE. It was now clear that the legal struggle over the Freedom Riders' fate would continue for at least nine more months, prompting a confident Governor Barnett to declare that the "outside agitators" who had invaded the state were finally learning the full meaning of Mississippi justice.

The next day, Barnett's words took on added weight when Bevel, who had encouraged four Jackson high school students to demonstrate in support of the Freedom Rides, went on trial for contributing to the delinquency of a minor. Following a swift conviction, Judge Moore issued the maximum sentence of $2,000 in fines and six months in jail. Refusing to file an appeal and post bail, Lewis's close friend and comrade was behind bars by early afternoon. And he was not alone. Earlier in the day, the Jackson police had arrested fifteen new Freedom Riders at the Trailways terminal. All of those arrested— twelve white and three Black Riders—were Episcopal priests affiliated with the Episcopal Society for Cultural and Racial Unity, an Atlanta-based group of racially liberal clergymen and lay leaders. The spread of the student movement's passion to older activists attracted a great deal of attention in the national press, especially after it was reported that one of the Episcopal Riders was Robert L. Pierson, the thirty-five-year-old son-in-law of Nelson Rockefeller, the liberal Republican governor of New York.[27]

For King, Farmer, and other movement leaders, the new arrests were both encouraging and concerning, considering that the movement's limited resources were approaching the breaking point. In mid-September, the success of the Freedom Rides was still very much in doubt. Then, on September 22, everything changed when the ICC announced that it had decided to implement the long-awaited transit desegregation order. Endorsing virtually every point in the attorney general's petition, the commission declared that, beginning on November 1, all interstate buses would be required to display a certificate that read, "Seating aboard this vehicle is without regard to race, color, creed, or national origin, by order of the Interstate Commerce Commission." Additionally, all terminals serving interstate buses would be required to post and abide by the new ICC regulations. The ruling applied only to interstate bus transportation and did not extend to air or train travel, but within these limitations the commissioners had gone about as far as anyone in the administration or the movement could have reasonably expected.

In the wake of the ICC ruling, there was jubilation, both at the Justice Department and the White House and at the offices of CORE, the SCLC, SNCC, and even the NAACP, which at Thurgood Marshall's request had recently allocated $300,000 in emergency funds to cover the Freedom Riders' court costs. Movement leaders had been planning a march on Washington patterned after A. Philip Randolph's threatened 1941 march, in a desperate attempt to stage a "spectacular" demonstration of nonviolent commitment and solidarity. But now the march was canceled, and CORE began to plan a new wave of Freedom Rides designed to test enforcement of the ruling. At the CORE office in New York and at recruitment centers across the nation, the next six weeks would be a time of feverish activity and hopeful speculation about the future. Seven years after *Brown* and fourteen years after *Morgan v. Virginia*, a major federal agency other than the Justice Department or the Supreme Court had finally weighed in on the side of racial justice. Whether the rhetoric of equal treatment could be translated into something tangible remained to be seen. But this time, unlike the "with all deliberate speed" waffling of the 1955 *Brown* implementation decision, there was a firm date for compliance.[28]

Just before the SCLC annual conference opened in Nashville, King hailed the ICC ruling as proof that the Freedom Riders' struggle "had not been in vain." The desegregation of buses and terminals was imminent, he insisted, and the nonviolent movement would soon move on to other challenges, including doubling the number of Black voters in the South by the end of the year. To this end, King, with the SCLC board's approval, created the position of "Special Projects Director" and immediately hired Lawson to fill it. Over the coming months, Lawson told reporters, the organization planned to recruit a nonviolent army of ten thousand committed activists, each willing to put his or her body on the line, or in jail if need be. In the tradition of Gandhi's followers, the SCLC's nonviolent soldiers would attack social injustice wherever they found it, even in the darkest recesses of the Deep South.

Attending the convention, Lewis was transfixed by Lawson's vision of a righteous legion of nonviolent foot soldiers. It was what he had been waiting for since his first exposure to the philosophy of nonviolence in the Nashville workshops. Two weeks earlier, he, along with others who had participated in the first wave of Freedom Rides, had attended a mass rally and fund raiser in Pittsburgh heralded as a "Salute to the Freedom Riders." Now, on the first night of the SCLC conference, during the intermission of a benefit concert featuring Harry Belafonte, Miriam Makeba, and the Chad Mitchell Trio, he was being saluted again, joining nine other Nashville Riders as a recipient of a $500 Freedom Award.

For Lewis, standing in the spotlight, shaking King's hand, and listening to the thunderous applause reverberating through the cavernous Grand

Ole Opry auditorium transcended the honor being bestowed. The award also brought him a much-needed scholarship that would help pay his Fisk tuition, and best of all it came with a personal note from King telling him "how valuable" he had been "to the movement" and how much he "could contribute in the future." Perhaps, King added, once the boy from Troy had finished his studies at Fisk, he might return home to Alabama to direct the SCLC's operations in the state. Lewis was flattered, but at that moment he couldn't imagine abandoning his movement brothers and sisters in SNCC for a position at the SCLC. As much as he admired King, he could not see himself as part of a formal organization led by Baptist preachers, some of whom were more than twice his age and many of whom were wary of radical politics. He still thought of himself, first and foremost, as a student activist, an insurgent whose heart and soul remained with a band of young rebels determined to change the world.[29]

CHAPTER 6

———

SNCC on the March

J OHN LEWIS took his studies seriously, even though, as he wrote years later, "many of the professors at Fisk, as well as many of my fellow students, thought I was some sort of weird character, that I was not really in school, but was just using Fisk as a base of operations, that I was some sort of transient activist, just passing through." He later vehemently disputed this charge. "It all mattered to me," he insisted, "school *and* the movement." He was, however, something of an oddity, both at Fisk, where he was outnumbered by self-indulgent frat boys and sorority girls engaging in what he regarded as "trivial silliness," and within the NSM, where he was a self-described "holdover" from the first wave of James Lawson–trained activists.

Many of his closest friends in the local movement had moved on: Diane Nash and Jim Bevel, now an inseparable couple on the verge of marriage, were in Jackson; Paul Brooks had gone elsewhere, first to North Carolina to study Robert Williams's armed defense program and later to other civil rights hot spots; and Jim Zwerg was back in Wisconsin. Others were scattered across the South. Consequently, in the fall and winter of 1961, the NSM, in Lewis's estimation, "wasn't as mass as it had been a year earlier." He and a hard core of remaining activists (they jokingly called themselves "the Horrible Seven")—including the former Freedom Riders Fred Leonard and Bill Harbour—"had to work hard" to keep the NSM going, spending a good bit of their time recruiting new members. Nonetheless, the continuing Open City campaign managed to carry on with a measure of success, encountering some resistance but nothing like the violence erupting in places like Mississippi and southwest Georgia.[1]

The denouement of the Freedom Rides during the late fall and winter of 1961, and continuing through the spring and summer of 1962, brought both hope and despair to the movement. This confusing period began with the hundreds of testers whom CORE dispatched in sixteen states on November 1, 1961, the day the ICC order went into effect. Publicly, CORE leaders predicted near-universal compliance, but privately they conceded there was no way of knowing how the white South would respond to the order, or how vigilant the Justice Department would be in enforcing it.

Fortunately for CORE and devoted proponents of nonviolence like Lewis, as the reports trickled in during the first week of testing, it became clear that even the unseasoned testers were living up to the high standards of poise and discipline that had characterized the Freedom Rider movement since early May. Perhaps even more important, the reports indicated that most of the testers were encountering less resistance than expected. The best news came out of Virginia, Kentucky, Texas, and West Virginia, where the tests found total compliance. In Tennessee there was compliance in four of the five bus stations tested, and to Lewis's relief, at the Nashville stations there was full compliance and no resistance.

The reports from the Deep South, though decidedly mixed, were more troubling. Compliance was incomplete in many communities, and nonexistent in others. The worst offenders were small communities in Mississippi, Alabama, Louisiana, and Georgia, but there was trouble even in Atlanta, where Bevel, Jim Forman, Bernard LaFayette, and Charles Jones were arrested after trying to desegregate the restaurant at the Trailways station. Predictably, at the Birmingham bus stations, the required ICC postings were nowhere in sight. Before the testing, a defiant Bull Connor promised to arrest anyone who violated the city's segregation ordinances, and Governor John Patterson backed him up, warning that if the Freedom Riders "continue to invade our state and continue to try to run over us, we want to serve notice that we are going to defend ourselves and we are not going to take it lying down."

A similar attitude prevailed in McComb, Mississippi, where violent resistance to Freedom Riders and Bob Moses's voting rights campaign led to a U.S. District Court injunction prohibiting any future Rides in the city, and in Albany and southwest Georgia, where a successful organizing campaign led by two SNCC field secretaries, Charles Sherrod and Cordell Reagon, met resistance from Mayor Asa Kelley and Police Chief Laurie Pritchett. Unlike Connor, Pritchett was adept at handling the press and camouflaging whatever force was needed to keep segregation intact. Here Freedom Rides on November 1 and December 10 helped to propel a local struggle, formally organized as the Albany Movement on November 17. The Albany Movement soon enlisted thousands of Black citizens in a community-wide effort to hasten the demise of Jim Crow in one of the nation's most segregated cities. Before the year was over, there were scores of freedom-song-filled mass meetings and hundreds of arrests, including that of Dr. Martin Luther King Jr. during a December 15 prayer pilgrimage to city hall. But neither the Kennedy administration nor the national press seemed to be concerned about the efforts to suppress this unprecedented mass arousal. Perhaps even more alarming, the Albany Movement drew SNCC, the SCLC, and to a lesser extent the NAACP into a factional quagmire that taught movement leaders—especially King, who was accused of stealing the limelight from SNCC and its local recruits—a painful lesson about the difficulties of collaborative mass protest in the Deep South.

The ongoing struggle in Albany highlighted the potential for mass involvement in the nonviolent movement, but it also revealed the strains and stresses burdening the often-fractious civil rights coalition: King's almost inevitable monopolization of media coverage; differing approaches to leadership and discipline; disagreements on the proper role of white allies in the movement; and even questions about the sanctity of nonviolence. All of these issues were on the table in April 1962, when Lewis traveled to Atlanta for SNCC's second annual conference. "It was incredible to see how drastically the complexion of the organization had changed in such a short time," he observed. "So many faces were gone—Bernard, Bevel, and Diane . . . and many others who had been there in the beginning. In their place had risen new voices—Stokely [Carmichael], Forman, Sherrod, Ruby Smith—as well as a wave of white activists from various leftist groups. . . . Our cause remained the same, but our methods were all in question. You heard the term 'revolution' more than the word 'integration.' The spirit of redemptive love was being pushed aside by a spirit of rage. And the whole idea of nonviolence was up for debate." To Lewis's dismay, many of the 250 delegates at the conference expressed support for Forman's claim that there was nothing wrong with striking back when hit. This flew in the face of Gandhian philosophy and Lawson's teachings, but Lawson wasn't there to object. Despite his critical role in the founding of the organization, he was not invited to the Atlanta meeting.

Lewis's close association with Lawson was well known, and it was no secret that he was displeased by the tone and direction of the conference. Even so, his reputation as a courageous veteran of the Freedom Rides and the Nashville direct action campaigns was sufficient to get him elected to SNCC's executive coordinating committee. By accepting this leadership position, he demonstrated his continuing commitment to the organization, but he refused to be cowed by the critics of nonviolence, or by those who resented his openness to working with Martin Luther King Jr. and the SCLC. In May, at King's request, he attended an SCLC meeting in Chattanooga, where he was elected to the SCLC's board of directors. While King did not share Lewis's enthusiasm for the SNCC model of low-key leadership, he admired his young friend's courage and unshakable commitment to nonviolence. Unfortunately, their friendship would become increasingly problematic later in the year as the two competing organizations vied for control of the Albany campaign and other direct action initiatives.[2]

For a time, Lewis managed to avoid the mounting pressure of this rivalry by escaping to a summer SNCC project in the remote town of Cairo, Illinois, located at the confluence of the Mississippi and Ohio Rivers. "Though Illinois is considered a Northern state," Lewis later wrote, "Cairo, bordered by Kentucky and Missouri, was Southern in every way—very small, very rural, very segregated." In terms of both race and class, Cairo had a reputation as a tough town, and its political leaders had no patience for activists like Lewis, who tried to upend a long tradition of racial segregation and elite political control with a Nashville-style direct action campaign aimed at hotels, restaurants, theaters, bus stations, and public swimming pools. The local white response, though less violent than what was happening in the Mississippi Delta 250 miles to the south, was strong enough to put Lewis in jail on several occasions, and there was more than enough resistance to warrant Jim Forman's decision to send Danny Lyon, a talented SNCC photographer, to document what was going on. While Lewis was leading a prayer vigil outside Cairo's segregated public pool, Lyon snapped a memorable photo that ended up on one of SNCC's most celebrated posters. The poster's caption, "COME LET US BUILD A NEW WORLD TOGETHER," became a staple of SNCC media, enhancing both Lyon's and Lewis's stature within the movement.

For Lewis, there were lessons learned that summer, notably that the ex-Confederate South had no monopoly on white supremacist intransigence. But in Cairo he always felt a bit disoriented and physically detached from the main currents of the civil rights struggle. Most of the excitement related to the movement was taking place far to the south, either in Mississippi, where violence had escalated in the wake of the Freedom Rides and the early voting rights initiatives of the VEP, or in southwest Georgia, where the Albany Movement, hampered by internal dissension and a lack of support from the Kennedy administration, was lurching to a disappointing standoff. The Albany situation was especially discouraging. After scores of demonstrations and mass meetings, and after thousands of arrests—of both students and adults—the effort to desegregate the city and its surrounding counties was as far away from victory as it had been when the Albany Movement had appeared on the scene. In early July, when Lewis learned that King had been arrested and then released on bond against his will—and worst of all, had then left the city without securing any meaningful concessions from the local white establishment—he wished he had been there to help.

The unkindest cut of all, for Lewis, was the discovery that the Kennedys had seemingly forgotten the lessons they had learned from the Freedom Riders less than a year earlier. "Through all this, in Mississippi and Georgia, where our voter registration efforts were concentrated and where the backlash of violence was most brutal," he recalled, "the federal government was conspicuous by its absence. There were few words of support from Washington, and no physical support in the way of federal marshals. Pleas were pouring in to the White House for the government to step in and help. But those pleas were ignored. . . . 'Where are the Kennedys?' That was the question we were all asking."[3]

In early September 1962, Lewis—still wondering when the Kennedys would wake up and do the right thing—began his second year at Fisk. Three weeks later, the administration did show signs of a moral awakening when it backed up James Meredith's attempt to become the first Black student to enroll at the University of Mississippi. The ensuing "Battle of Oxford" pitted nearly three thousand rampaging white supremacists against federal marshals and military police—and ultimately against more than thirty thousand U.S. Army and Mississippi National Guard soldiers. The most forthright federal intervention in a civil rights–related conflict since the Eisenhower administration's deployment of troops during the 1957 Little Rock school desegregation crisis, it provided movement activists with a measure of hope for future federal protection.

Fortunately for Lewis and the NSM, the continuing Open City campaign was making headway without such protection. The primary targets that fall were Nashville's segregated hotels, where the students staged a series of lobby "sleep-ins." On one occasion, Lewis and the "sleeping" students had to dodge liquor bottles flung by white hotel guests, and there were a number of arrests. But Nashville's reputation as a moderate city was still intact, especially after *Jet* magazine ran a cover story in December 1963 changing the community's moniker from "Music City" to "Best City in the South for Negroes." This high praise was of questionable validity, but it made some sense when cities such as Albany were undergoing so much turmoil. "The story made much of the success we had accomplished," Lewis explained, "especially in light of the frustration and failure the movement had experienced in Albany." "For at least five years," the *Jet* article reported, with some exaggeration, "Whites and Negroes stood eyeball-to-eyeball in bitter confrontations over segregation in Nashville. There were times when brush-fire violence threatened to reduce the city to smoldering ashes. An eyelash before it was too late, the white power structure blinked. When their eyes had adjusted to the new light of revolution, they became more color blind. They watched their city desegregate in direct ratio to the pressures exerted by the Negro community."

Lewis welcomed *Jet*'s acknowledgment of the NSM's efforts but not the insinuation that Nashville had reached an acceptable plateau of racial equity and harmony. On the opposite side of the ledger, the more militant members of SNCC around the South no longer looked to the Nashville movement as a vanguard. This lack of respect surfaced at a SNCC conference held in Nashville in November, when several delegates all but scoffed at the level of conflict in the city. "Compared to a vicious battle" like the one that had occurred in Oxford a month earlier, "our success at desegregating movie theaters and grocery stores in Nashville could seem almost quaint," Lewis acknowledged.[4]

* * *

In SNCC, and in the SCLC, the focus that fall was not on the limited victories that had been won in cities like Nashville but rather on the stinging defeat in Albany and southwest Georgia. There was a general sense of crisis and looming failure—of lost momentum and tactical and strategic mistakes—that led to a thoroughgoing reconsideration of the core principles of the nonviolent direct action movement. In SNCC, everything from the need for strong leadership and discipline to the role of white activists—especially radical left-wing activists—was now a subject for debate. Lewis had little patience for any of this, most of which he regarded as a retreat from righteous action.

In the SCLC, the strategic reconsideration was narrower and much more to his liking. There the debate was limited to the question of how to repair the damage inflicted by the perceived defeat in Albany. In early January 1963, King convened a two-day strategic meeting in the small Georgia town of Dorchester, a few miles southwest of Savannah. Bringing together a dozen or so of the organization's leaders (Lewis, preoccupied with the struggle in Nashville, was not among them), he asked them to analyze the lessons learned in Albany. After considerable discussion, the gathering came up with several recommendations: the SCLC should concentrate its efforts on "certain aspects of segregation and aspects and areas where we could win a victory"; the focus should be on exerting pressure on the white business community, not just on politicians; and, as King put it, to remember "the key to everything is federal commitment." There was also widespread agreement that it was time to take bold risks, to attack segregation and discrimination in the toughest cities in the Jim Crow South, and before the meeting broke up King decided that all of these considerations pointed to a go-for-broke direct action campaign in Bull Connor's Birmingham. As his aide Andrew Young later observed, King also "went to Birmingham because Fred Shuttlesworth pleaded with him to do it."

While Lewis did not participate in the decision to take on Birmingham's segregationists, he understood and endorsed the rationale for doing so. "Shuttlesworth and King and Ralph Abernathy all knew that Bull Connor did not have the restraint or savvy of a Laurie Pritchett," Lewis noted. "And, unlike in Albany, where . . . our SNCC people had essentially come into a completely unorganized community, there was already a solidly entrenched activist infrastructure in black Birmingham, spearheaded over the years by Shuttlesworth." All of the elements needed for a major confrontation that would attract national attention were present in Birmingham, and more fuel was added to the fire on January 14, just after the close of the Dorchester meeting, when the incoming governor of Alabama, the arch-segregationist George C. Wallace, ended his inaugural address with the pledge, "Segregation now! Segregation tomorrow! Segregation forever."[5]

The Birmingham campaign—named Project Confrontation, or Project C for short—began on April 3 and continued through mid-May. No movement campaign had ever been attempted on such a massive scale. Through more than thirty consecutive days of protest, each capped with a rousing mass meeting, the project grew in intensity and meaning. Back in Nashville, Lewis scoured the *Nashville Tennessean* every day to find out what was happening two hundred miles to the south. As the primary leader of the continuing protests in Nashville, he didn't feel he could abandon his post and go to Birmingham. But both his heart and mind were with the activists of Project C. "The SCLC brought in leaders from all corners of the movement, including Diane and Bevel, who set about organizing student contingents," he remembered with pride. "All the tools that we had used in Nashville—sit-ins, boycotts, mass marches, rallies, mass meetings—were put in place in Birmingham."

Bevel and Nash, now husband and wife, were destined to play a critical role in the project's success. After King was arrested on Good Friday, April 12, and after he penned his famous "Letter from a Birmingham Jail," the project began to lose steam and was in jeopardy of collapsing, largely because there were no longer enough adults willing to fill the ranks of the daily marches. Widespread police intimidation and the fear of losing employment had taken its toll, and project leaders were left with no wholly acceptable means of remedying the situation. The only choice available, Bevel concluded, was to organize and train "a huge army of Birmingham's children." Without any formal endorsement from King or any other SCLC leader, Lewis noted, Bevel "went into the local Black schools and churches, using the NBC White Paper documentary 'The Nashville Sit-In Story'—the one for which we had been interviewed in 1960—to teach hundreds of teenagers the techniques of nonviolence. What Bevel was doing in Birmingham was little different from what we had done from the beginning in Nashville and, indeed, what we would later do in Selma. We considered it natural and necessary to involve children—adolescents—in the movement. We weren't far from being teenagers ourselves, and we shared many of the same basic feelings of adolescence: unbounded idealism, faith and optimism untrampled by the reality of the adult world. Young people identify more strongly than anyone else with the whole concept of freedom. They are free in the fullest sense of the word—free of major responsibilities that might hold them back. They have no mortgage, no marriage, no family, no children of their own, no job. They are, as we assumed ourselves to be, willing to risk everything for something noble and deserving, for the cause."

Young people, Lewis forgot to mention, were also up for a lark—for skipping school, for finding freedom and excitement in breaking the rules of their normal routine. But whatever their primary motivation, the Birmingham kids who joined what became known as the Children's Crusade rescued a civil rights campaign on the brink of failure. They did so, as it turned out, with considerable help from Bull Connor, who overreacted to their challenge by using high-pressure firehoses and attack dogs to control them—in full view of a national television audience. "I watched the images on television that night," Lewis recalled, "and, like the rest of America, I was absolutely stunned by what I saw. Snarling German shepherds loosed on teenage boys and girls, the animals' teeth tearing at slacks and skirts. Jet streams of water strong enough to peel the bark off a tree, aimed at twelve-year-old kids, sending their bodies hurtling down the street like rag dolls in a windstorm. . . . Those images, like the bombed bus in Anniston, or the photos of Jim Zwerg and me after the bus station attack in Montgomery, became timeless. They went out to the world, and no one who saw them would ever forget them."

It took less than a week for Connor's self-defeating tactics to bring Birmingham's business leaders to the negotiating table, and on May 8 their representatives signed an agreement accepting most of Project C's demands. The city's political establishment soon followed suit, and King and his staff left town with a major victory in hand. There would be recriminations about the reliance on the Children's Crusade, and it would take more than a year before the local Jim Crow structure was completely dismantled. But the entire nonviolent movement was energized by the triumph in Birmingham. Movement leaders began to plan additional civil and voting rights campaigns, and in cities like Nashville it became easier to recruit foot soldiers for the struggle. "We were still in the process of desegregating Nashville, still marching on our own," Lewis remembered, "and now there was Birmingham as a backdrop, as a context, as a frame of reference. . . . And our ranks began to grow immediately because of it. The attitude was, Hey, if they are standing up to fire hoses and dogs down there, the least we can do is march outside a restaurant up here."

There was also a noticeable change in the civil rights posture of the Kennedy administration in the wake of Birmingham. In January, the president told King he had no plans to introduce a major civil rights bill during the year. But he reversed himself by the end of May, preparing a sweeping bill that, if passed, would outlaw racial discrimination in all public accommodations. Since nothing like this had ever reached the floor of Congress, much less passed into law, Lewis and other movement leaders were skeptical that Kennedy would follow through with his new plan. But on the night of June 11, he delivered the most extraordinary speech of his presidency in a televised address that outlined the civil rights bill he would soon put before Congress. "Now the time has come for this nation to fulfill its promise," he declared. "The events in Birmingham and elsewhere have so increased the cries for equality that no city or state legislative body can prudently ignore them. . . . We face, therefore, a moral crisis as a country and a people. It cannot be met by repressive police action. It cannot be left to increased demonstrations in the streets. It cannot be quieted by token moves or talks. It is time to act in the Congress, in your state and local legislative bodies, in all of our daily lives. . . . A great change is at hand, and our task, is to make that revolution, that change, peaceful and constructive for all."[6]

Hearing these words—especially the reference to "revolution"—thrilled most movement leaders. But the same words simultaneously confirmed the worst fears of white supremacist zealots. A few hours before Kennedy's speech, Governor Wallace honored his pledge "to stand in the schoolhouse door" if that is what it took to stop the desegregation of the University of Alabama in Tuscaloosa. In a carefully orchestrated drama worked out behind the scenes, he stepped aside when confronted by Deputy Attorney General Nicholas Katzenbach and a corps of the federalized Alabama National Guard, allowing two Black students to register and reducing his pledge to symbolic resistance.

Later that night, just after midnight, in Jackson, Mississippi, an even darker drama unfolded when a forty-two-year-old Klansman named Byron de la Beckwith assassinated Medgar Evers, the state field secretary of the NAACP, with a high-powered rifle. Coming just hours after Kennedy's speech, the news that Evers, one of the South's most courageous civil rights activists, had been gunned down in the driveway of his home emotionally whipsawed much of the American public with a shattering sequence of hope and despair.[7]

*   *   *

The dizzying array of events on June 11 and 12 left Lewis, like so many others, in a state of high anxiety. What other shocking and unsettling developments were in the offing, he wondered? Would the racial and political landscape enter into a new equilibrium, or would it continue to present the movement with unexpected challenges and opportunities? Two days later, he found out when Chuck McDew submitted his resignation as chairman of SNCC. After taking over from Marion Barry in November 1960, McDew had proved to be a hardworking movement stalwart, but in recent months he had grown increasingly weary as he tried to meet his fundraising and other responsibilities as chairman.

As a member of SNCC's coordinating committee, Lewis attended an emergency meeting in Atlanta to choose McDew's successor. But before driving down from Nashville with four other SNCC leaders, he received a call from executive director Jim Forman alerting him to the probability that he would be elected the new chairman. Never having considered himself a potential leader at that level, Lewis was stunned. Although he later discovered that several other SNCC activists, including Charles Sherrod, had expressed interest in the position, his election appeared to be a foregone conclusion among those attending the meeting in Atlanta. After Forman nominated him, the resolution to accept him as the best choice to serve out the remaining ten months of McDew's term was approved with virtually no discussion. In trying to explain his selection, Lewis later speculated that his arrest record had been his primary asset. The major source of his popularity, he acknowledged, "wasn't my commitment to nonviolence so much as my actual experience, the fire that I had been through. At that point I had been arrested twenty-four times—seventeen in Nashville. That fact alone carried a lot of weight with my colleagues."[8]

Lewis's assumption of the chairmanship brought an immediate relocation to Atlanta, his first move since arriving in Nashville in 1958. After packing up the few belongings he had accumulated, he prepared to live on his own for the first time. His meager salary of ten dollars a week, plus a monthly housing allowance of fifty-four dollars, allowed him to rent a small, second-floor apartment in a brick building on Gordon Road, in a predominantly Black section of southwest Atlanta, a fifteen-minute bus ride away from SNCC's downtown office. Of course, as chairman he would spend much of his time traveling around the South; in fact, during his first week on the job, with his belongings barely unpacked, he flew to Washington for a meeting at the White House.

Ten days earlier, on the same day that President Kennedy had unveiled his civil rights bill, Dr. King had announced that the nation's civil rights leaders planned to hold a mass march in Washington sometime in the late summer. Patterned after A. Philip Randolph's famous 1941 March on Washington, which was canceled when President Franklin Roosevelt complied with Randolph's demand for the establishment of a Fair Employment Practice Committee, the proposed 1963 march had been in the works since January, when Randolph and Bayard Rustin first floated the idea. Like the 1941 march, the 1963 version was touted as an economically oriented march "for jobs and freedom," a decidedly different agenda from the public accommodations emphasis in Kennedy's pending civil rights bill.

Kennedy set up the June 22 meeting at the White House as a means of convincing Randolph, King, Jim Farmer, Roy Wilkins of the NAACP, Whitney Young of the National Urban League, and Lewis representing SNCC to cancel the march and concentrate on getting the administration's civil rights bill passed. The president invited more than thirty civil rights leaders to the meeting, but his attention was directed primarily at Randolph and the other members of what later became known as the "Big Six." As the youngest and least well known of this select group, Lewis deferred to his colleagues and did not say much during the two-hour meeting. But he listened intently as Kennedy made the administration's case against going ahead with the march. "The president got right to the point," he recalled. "He was concerned about all the violence and unrest he was seeing in the South. He was mightily concerned about the success of the civil rights bill, and he didn't see how this march was going to help anything. 'We want success in Congress,' he told us, 'not just a big show in the capital.' He said this bill had a much better chance of passing if black people stayed off the streets."

Lewis was shocked by Kennedy's apparent naïveté about the grassroots nature of the Southern struggle, but he was heartened by Randolph's unequivocal response. "The Negroes are already *in* the streets," Randolph pointed out, adding that it was "very likely impossible to get them off. If they are bound to be in the streets in any case, is it not better that they be led by organizations dedicated to civil rights and disciplined by struggle rather than leave them to other leaders who care neither about civil rights nor about non-violence?" The march would take place, he declared, whether or not the administration sanctioned it.

Later in the meeting King, Wilkins, and several others expressed essentially the same sentiment, and Lewis came away from the discussion with renewed respect for the leaders of organizations whose conservatism had often disappointed him in the past. At the same time, however, the meeting heightened his awareness of the stark differences between SNCC's approach to direct action and the more conservative approaches of the other organizations. Before the meeting, most of Lewis's SNCC colleagues had considered both the march and the White House gathering to be a waste of time and had only reluctantly agreed to endorse his trip to Washington. As he noted years later, he was virtually the only SNCC leader with any interest in supporting the march or discussing the matter with the administration. "I thought the march was a good idea," he remembered. "I felt that *any* form of action, any form of drama of this kind, was helpful and effective. I think that whenever you can get a large group of people together, whether it's to march, or to have a prayer vigil, or to sit in, you should. Whenever people have an opportunity to dramatize their feelings, to point out an issue, to educate others and alert them and open their eyes, I think they should *do* those things."

Yet both before and after the White House meeting, he shared his SNCC colleagues' doubts about the value of a mass march that did not reflect the insistent militancy of the activists bearing the brunt of the freedom struggle. "At SNCC," he explained, "we had little patience with meetings and talk and inflated, empty gestures. That had been the standard procedure for the previous one hundred years. We were about something different—aggressive action. More than any of the other groups invited to meet with Kennedy, we were the one with our people out on the front lines, being beaten and jailed and killed all across the South with little response or protection from the federal government. . . . The feeling among most of the rank and file of SNCC was that if we did take part in this march, we should do it *our* way, which would be to turn this demonstration into a protest rather than a plea. Stage sit-ins all across Washington. Tie up traffic. Have lie-ins on local airport runways. Invade the offices of southern congressmen and senators. Camp on the White House lawn. Cause mass arrests. *Paralyze* the city."[9]

This was just the kind of scenario that terrified the Kennedy administration, and even Lewis had serious reservations about the wisdom of unleashing a full-scale nonviolent invasion of the nation's capital at a time when the political establishment was moving toward acceptance of civil rights legislation. But after his return to Atlanta, he and Forman and other SNCC leaders deliberated on the best approach to the march and produced a middle-ground form of militancy that would exert pressure in Washington without provoking widespread panic. This deliberation led to the first real enthusiasm for SNCC participation in the march. Forman, who was now fully on board, agreed to accompany Lewis to a July 2 movement-wide planning meeting in New York.

The New York meeting turned out to be an important milestone in Lewis's development as a civil rights leader. It was his first trip to the nation's largest city, and his first opportunity to visit Harlem. "The one thing I will never forget about that trip," he recalled, "was the great sense of anger and hopelessness I felt in Harlem. It was very different from the South, where we were moving and marching and acting with a sense of community and purpose. In Harlem I saw boarded-up buildings, metal grates on store windows, a different kind of poverty from the poverty we had in the South—a starker, dismal, urban kind of poverty. I felt a great sense of despair. I passed a crowd of people on a corner, listening to a speaker chant and rave about what they were going to do with 'Whitey,' and it seemed very sad, very hopeless."

There were more revelations at the gathering held several miles away at the Roosevelt Hotel. Many of the same leaders who had attended the White House meeting two weeks earlier were on hand, but the personal dynamics were strikingly different this time as the dictates of organizational hierarchy and competition held sway. An ideological cleavage between a conservative faction led by Wilkins and Young and a much more liberal faction led by King, Farmer, Randolph, and Rustin, with Lewis playing a supporting role, dominated the meeting. Wilkins, whom Lewis found to be aggressively condescending, was determined to eliminate Rustin's role in organizing or presiding over the march, ostensibly because of his reputation as both a radical ex-Communist and a homosexual. In the end, after several awkward and divisive exchanges, King, Farmer, and Randolph forced Wilkins to relent, and the group agreed to name Randolph as the director of the march with Rustin as his deputy. There was also considerable debate over how dramatic and protest-like the march should be, with Wilkins and Young pitted against Farmer and Lewis, who did not want to return to their organizations with a plan for a timid event. This particular point was left unresolved, but at least everyone agreed on August 28 as the date of the march.

As soon as the meeting broke up, the press descended on Lewis and the other participants. Lewis, who said very little during the meeting, was nonetheless forthright in his comments to the reporters, both then and in the days that followed. He insisted that SNCC had no intention of calling off its mass demonstrations before seeing "definite signs of progress." "It would be very dangerous if we did," he explained, "because it would lead to violence. Demonstrations will continue regardless, but if the Negro leaders attempted to halt them before equal rights are assured, the demonstrations would merely continue without leaders." "We do not want violence and we do not advocate it," he added. "But we will not slow down because of the possibility. Violence represents the frustration of the Negro community and the slow pace of progress in achieving real democracy; the only way to avoid this is to show tangible proof to the American Negro that his life is getting better."

Lewis's straightforward responses to reporters' questions about his organization's position on continued protests and the impending event in Washington pleased Forman and most other SNCC leaders. But once Lewis was back in Atlanta, Forman couldn't resist criticizing the notoriously modest chairman's reluctance to join the other members of the Big Six in the limelight. "You've got to get out *front*," Forman counseled, after showing Lewis a newspaper photo in which he was at the far "end of the group, almost out of the frame." "Don't let King get all the credit. Don't stand back like that. Get out front." Worrying about who gets credit was not part of Lewis's approach to leadership, but he felt he was already out front in the ways that really mattered, in ceaselessly representing SNCC wherever the foot soldiers of the movement needed encouragement and direction.[10]

Throughout the summer of 1963—which saw eight hundred protests and twenty thousand arrests during the ten weeks following Kennedy's June 11 civil rights speech, more than during any previous period of movement activity—Lewis was constantly on the move visiting and nurturing pockets of resistance to Jim Crow. From Pine Bluff, Arkansas, and Greenwood, Mississippi, in the west, to Danville, Virginia, and Cambridge, Maryland, in the east, he appeared in person, delivering speeches and conducting nonviolent workshops aimed at shoring up local movements. "There were so many hotspots that summer," he remembered, ". . . sometimes I had to check to make sure where I was." Unlike McDew, who spent much of his chairmanship raising funds, Lewis was a hands-on leader personally connected to the bone and marrow of the struggle. "I was a walking example of the things that SNCC stood for, the things that SNCC was trying to do," he later explained. "When people saw me, they saw arrests and beatings and nonviolence."

In late July, Lewis spent several days in Selma, Alabama, where Bernard LaFayette was spearheading a SNCC voting rights project. LaFayette, who had been in the Black Belt town since January, faced considerable resistance from local white citizens led by Selma's combative sheriff Jim Clark. Starting from ground zero in a county where it was virtually impossible for Black people to register to vote, LaFayette organized voter education workshops that attracted scores of potential Black voters and even held mass rallies, one of which attracted more than seven hundred brave souls who came to hear Bevel speak. At that point only a handful of Black registrants had been added to the local electorate, but Lewis—who also spoke at a mass rally during his visit—left Selma with renewed hope that progress toward democracy was possible even in the darkest recesses of the Deep South.

From Selma he traveled to Cambridge, a small town in Maryland's isolated Eastern Shore region, where Gloria Richardson, the director of the Cambridge Nonviolent Action Group, was in the midst of an ambitious series of demonstrations aimed at challenging racial discrimination in housing, employment, education, and public accommodations. Here, as in Selma, white resistance led by the police had turned violent, leading to mass arrests, rioting in Black neighborhoods, and the dispatch of four hundred National Guardsmen to the city in an effort to restore order. Concerned that the volatile situation in Cambridge was about to explode, Robert Kennedy invited both Richardson and Lewis, along with an aide representing the governor of Maryland, to an emergency meeting at the Justice Department building on July 22. The meeting led to the signing of the Cambridge Accord the next day, which promised gradual desegregation and several antidiscrimination measures in exchange for an end to the demonstrations. For Lewis, however, the most memorable aspect of the meeting was a brief private conversation with Kennedy that produced a startling confession. "John," the attorney general revealed, "the people, the young people of SNCC, have educated me. You have changed me. Now I understand." "That was something to hear," Lewis recalled, "coming from the man who had been reviled by so many of us—including me—for his foot-dragging in response to our needs in the South. That showed me something about Bobby Kennedy that I came to respect enormously—the fact that, though he could be stern, firm, even ruthless, in some people's opinion, he was willing to listen, and learn, and change."

Kennedy's surprising statement led Lewis to wonder if his criticisms of the administration's recalcitrance on civil rights matters had been too harsh, but disturbing events in central and southwest Georgia soon dispelled such thoughts. In early August, the administration seemed unwilling and unable to do anything to mitigate a dangerous situation in Americus, where four SNCC voting rights activists—including Don Harris, who would later become one of Lewis's closest friends—were arrested and charged with "seditious conspiracy," a capital crime that carried the death penalty under Georgia's 1871 Anti-treason Act. Although a judicial ruling eventually reduced the charge to a noncapital felony, the four activists suffered severe beatings and served eighty-four days in a local jail. The state's decision to invoke the antitreason statute as a barrier to Black voter registration—and the federal government's apparent indifference to this outrageous escalation of white supremacist resistance—reminded Lewis that, as one historian later put it, SNCC's voting rights organizers were "engaged in a life-or-death struggle." Equally disturbing was the Justice Department's prosecution of nine nonviolent Albany picketers charged with conspiracy to obstruct justice. In mid-August, just two weeks before the scheduled March on Washington, a federal grand jury in Macon issued an indictment in the Albany Nine case, providing a convenient means of reassuring anxious white Southerners that the administration was "even-handed" in its approach to civil rights agitation.

In the wake of the Albany Nine prosecution and indictment, Lewis and other SNCC leaders considered holding demonstrations outside the Justice Department building as part of the March on Washington. But Randolph and Rustin persuaded them to forgo this confrontational strategy, reminding them that Lewis, as SNCC's chairman, would have the opportunity to speak his piece on the Justice Department's failings and related matters at the Lincoln Memorial on August 28.[11]

* * *

Lewis knew that his speech at the march would be the most important public statement of his life, and he was also aware than many SNCC activists remained opposed to the organization's involvement in what they feared would be a pro-administration showcase orchestrated by moderate civil rights organizations hoping to curry favor with the government. To some degree, Lewis shared these fears. "All this arranging and orchestrating was alarming to many of us at SNCC," he explained years later. "The sense of militancy, which was so central to most of our efforts, which was so much a part of our definition of ourselves, was being deflated. Civility had become the emphasis of this event. It was becoming a march *in* Washington, not *on* Washington. The whole thing seemed to have been co-opted by the government—co-opted very deftly.... The Kennedy administration seemed to be trying to silence us in a way, to cool us off, to take steam out of the movement, to get rid of the *drama*."

Even so, Lewis was convinced that it would be foolish for SNCC to withdraw from the march and miss an opportunity to deliver an important message to the nation and the world. An opportunity like this might never come again, so Lewis poured all of his passion and energy into crafting a speech that would match the seriousness of the occasion. He knew about what the great Black contralto Marian Anderson had accomplished with her groundbreaking concert at the Lincoln Memorial on Easter Sunday 1939, and he wanted to follow her lead in using this sacred backdrop to frame a plea for freedom and democracy. He began in mid-August by dictating textual phrases and talking points to Nancy Stearns, a white staff member in SNCC's Atlanta office, and later talked through his ideas with Forman, Julian Bond, and several others. He wanted to be true to his own personal beliefs, but he knew the speech also had to capture the militancy and urgency felt so strongly among the SNCC rank and file. "I wanted a strong speech, one that went beyond supporting a particular legislation," he insisted. "I wanted a civil rights bill—certainly—a strong bill. We all wanted that. But we weren't going to beg for it.... We wanted to send as strong a message as possible to the Kennedy administration that we felt the President was being too cautious, doing far too little when it came to meeting the needs of Black Americans. Ever since his campaign in 1960 he had been talking about how he was going to do this and that in terms of civil rights legislation, and in actuality he had done virtually nothing. Meanwhile we were out in the streets across the South, taking a whipping."

Though well known for his gentle and forgiving nature, Lewis approached the Washington speech with an air of uncompromising toughness. "My words needed to be forceful—I knew that," he explained. "I didn't want to be part of a parade. I wanted to see discipline and organization on this day, but I wanted it to have an air of militancy as well, even some disruption if necessary—*disciplined* disruption. . . . I wanted this march to have some sting, and if the only place for that sting would be in my speech, then I needed to make sure my words were especially strong."

By Friday, August 23, when Lewis left Atlanta for a march organizers' meeting in Harlem, he had a complete draft in hand. But he wasn't satisfied with what he had written. Fortunately, there were a number of other SNCC activists who had come to New York to help Rustin and his lieutenants work out the final organizational details, and to attend a fund raiser at the Apollo Theater featuring Thelonious Monk and a glittering array of other musicians. Lewis was excited about seeing the concert, but he spent much of his time that weekend going over the speech with an ad hoc committee of SNCC advisers, notably Courtland Cox, Joyce Ladner, and Eleanor Holmes, plus Tom Kahn, a white assistant to Rustin. The advice was spirited and helpful, including a suggestion by Cox that the speech should point out the failure of both political parties to address civil rights issues in a meaningful way, and Kahn's idea that Lewis should compare the movement's plans to General William Tecumseh Sherman's 1864 March to the Sea. Lewis incorporated both suggestions into the speech, pointing out that civil rights leaders needed to ally with a principled political party and characterizing the movement as "an army—a nonviolent army—bent on nothing less than destruction—the destruction of segregation."

Lewis had already sprinkled the speech with references to "revolution," and now he had a vivid image of resolute, "scorched earth" action to give life to his words. He also accepted advice to include specific references to the current crises in Albany, Americus, and Danville, Virginia, and to express outrage over certain glaring weaknesses in the administration's civil rights bill, especially its provision that voter registration would only be available to citizens who had completed at least six years of formal education. By Sunday night, Lewis was pleased with the revisions, and when he took the train to Washington the next morning, he felt he was ready to present SNCC's position at the march on Wednesday. The final draft, parts of which he would never deliver, began with a bold assertion about the march's purpose and the desperate economic circumstances of many Black Americans: "We march today for jobs and freedom, but we have nothing to be proud of, for hundreds and thousands of our brothers are not here. They have no money for their transportation, for they are receiving starvation wages, or no wages at all."

He then went on to attack the inadequacies of the current civil rights bill: "In good conscience, we cannot support wholeheartedly the administration's civil rights bill, for it is too little and too late. There's not one thing in the bill that will protect our people from police brutality. This bill will not protect young children and old women from police dogs and fire hoses, for engaging in peaceful demonstrations. . . . The voting section of this bill will not help thousands of Black citizens who want to vote. It will not help the citizens of Mississippi, of Alabama and Georgia, who are qualified to vote but lack a sixth-grade education. 'ONE MAN, ONE VOTE,' is the African cry. It is ours, too. It must be ours."

From there, he turned to the historic nature of the march and the dire political situation that had made it necessary: "For the first time in one hundred years this nation is being awakened to the fact that segregation is evil and that it must be destroyed in all forms. Your presence today proves that you have been aroused to the point of action. We are now involved in a serious revolution. This nation is still a place of cheap political leaders who build their careers on immoral compromises and ally themselves with open forms of political, economic and social exploitation. What political leader here can stand up and say, 'My party is the party of principles?' The party of Kennedy is also the party of Eastland. The party of Javits is also the party of Goldwater. Where is *our* party? . . . In Albany, Georgia, nine of our leaders have been indicted not by Dixiecrats but by the federal government for peaceful protest. . . . I want to know, which side is the federal government on?"

Lewis knew this bold and inflammatory rhetoric would infuriate the Kennedys and embarrass a significant portion of the civil rights coalition sponsoring the march. But he didn't stop there, moving on to a call for radical change and direct action. "The revolution is at hand," he declared, "and we must free ourselves of the chains of political and economic slavery. The nonviolent revolution is saying, 'We will not wait for the courts to act, for we have been waiting for hundreds of years. We will not wait for the President, the Justice Department, nor Congress, but we will take matters into our own hands and create a source of power outside of any national structure, that could and would assure us a victory.' To those who have said, 'Be patient and wait,' we must say that patience is a dirty and nasty word. We cannot be patient, we do not want to be free gradually. We want our freedom, and we want it *now*."

The next section of the speech clarified the nonviolent movement's agenda and chosen strategy, introducing the concept of a Beloved Community. "In the struggle," he insisted, "we must seek more than civil rights, we must work for the community of love, peace and true brotherhood. Our minds, souls and hearts cannot rest until freedom and justice exist for *all* people." He knew full well that many of his SNCC colleagues had long since moved away from a spiritual and philosophical attachment to nonviolence as a way of life; that for them the primary goal of the movement was no longer love or interracial brotherhood but rather a thoroughgoing redistribution of power. But he decided to speak from the heart as a matter of personal privilege, hoping that his vision of a freedom struggle beyond the acquisition of governmentally sanctioned civil rights would inspire others to join the fight for a Beloved Community.

His objective was a sweeping transformation of existing institutions and ways of life, one that could only be achieved through considerable commitment and sacrifice—and a massive mobilization of love and goodwill. This point was made clear in the closing paragraphs of the speech. "The revolution is a serious one," he reminded his prospective converts. "Mr. Kennedy is trying to take the revolution out of the streets and put it into the courts. Listen, Mr. Kennedy. Listen, Mr. Congressman. Listen, fellow citizens. The Black masses are on the march for jobs and freedom, and we must say to the politicians that there won't be a 'cooling-off' period. All of us must get in the revolution. Get in and stay in the streets of every city, every village and every hamlet of this nation until true freedom comes, until the revolution is complete. . . . The time will come when we will not confine our marching to Washington. We will march through the South, through the heart of Dixie, the way Sherman did. We shall pursue our own 'scorched earth' policy and burn Jim Crow to the ground—nonviolently. We shall fragment the South into a thousand pieces and put them back together in the image of democracy."[12]

* * *

When Lewis checked into Washington's Statler Hilton Hotel on Monday afternoon, he found himself in the midst of frantic preparations for the march. There was widespread anxiety about the possibility of violence on Wednesday, especially among the Washington police; an order to ban liquor sales throughout the district on the day of the march had been issued; fifteen thousand soldiers were on alert in case they were needed for riot control; and part of the Washington Senators' homestand had been canceled. Only Rustin was an island of calm—or at least he was until he saw an advance copy of Lewis's speech. Late Tuesday afternoon, after discovering copies of Whitney Young's speech on a table in the Statler Hilton lobby, Courtland Cox decided it would be great to do the same for Lewis's speech. Bond agreed, and—without consulting Lewis—ran off a number of copies, which he placed alongside the stack of Young's copies. Within minutes, a copy was in the hands of Washington's Roman Catholic archbishop, Patrick O'Boyle, who had been asked to deliver the march's opening invocation. After a quick reading, the distraught prelate contacted Burke Marshall at the Justice Department and then called Rustin, expressing his outrage at Lewis's use of incendiary words. If Lewis was allowed to deliver the speech, O'Boyle warned Rustin, he would withdraw from the event. That evening, when Lewis returned to his room, he found a note from Rustin asking him to come downstairs immediately for a discussion of something very important. But even before Lewis got out the door, Rustin called to make sure he understood how urgent the matter was. "We have a problem," Rustin blurted out, before explaining: "It's your speech. Some people are very concerned about some of the things you're going to say in your speech. You need to get down here. We need to talk."

Once Rustin explained the problem, Lewis was actually relieved that the march leader had no quarrel with the vast majority of the speech. The references to "revolution," "cheap political leaders," and "Sherman's march" were all fine as far as Rustin was concerned. The sticking point for him, and for O'Boyle, was Lewis's disparagement of "patience." "Apparently, my calling patience a 'dirty and nasty word' had sent O'Boyle through the ceiling," Lewis recalled. Seeing that Lewis looked puzzled, Rustin cut to the chase: "This is offensive to the Catholic Church . . . Catholics *believe* in the word 'patience.'" Though Lewis still didn't quite understand why anyone would care about such a trivial point, he agreed to remove the reference from his text. Rustin was pleased but warned there would almost certainly be additional objections to overcome later in the morning after others had a chance to examine the speech.

During a breakfast meeting at the hotel, and later during a meeting with congressional leaders at the Capitol, there was no mention of Lewis's speech. As noon approached and as hundreds of thousands of marchers gathered on the mall and around the reflecting pool in front of the Lincoln Memorial, march leaders were preoccupied with making their way to the speakers' stand without being swallowed up by the surging crowd. For a time Lewis thought he was home free, that he would be able to deliver his entire speech as planned, unedited and uncensored. But early in the afternoon, as the crowd was being entertained with a musical prelude featuring Joan Baez, Bob Dylan, Odetta, and Mahalia Jackson, he was summoned to a private meeting inside the memorial behind Lincoln's statue.

Rustin, King, Wilkins, Young, and several other march leaders were there. The speech, he was told, was unacceptable. As he later explained, "Word had come that alarms were sounding in all quarters. Walter Reuther was irate that I had dared to criticize the President's civil rights bill. Bobby Kennedy had talked to O'Boyle that morning and had spoken with Burke Marshall about the speech. He, too, was upset. Roy Wilkins was having a fit, saying he just didn't understand us SNCC people, that we always wanted to be *different*. He got up in my face a bit, saying we were 'double-crossing' the people who had gathered to support this bill. But I didn't back down. I told him I had prepared this speech, and we had a right to say what we wanted to say. 'Mr. Wilkins,' I told him, 'you don't understand. I'm not just speaking for myself. I'm speaking for my colleagues in SNCC, and for the people in the Delta and in the Black Belt. You haven't been there, Mr. Wilkins. You don't *understand*.' He started shaking his finger at me, and I shook mine right back at him. For a moment, it was getting to be a real scene."

At that point, Rustin jumped in between them and decided to clear the room except for an ad hoc committee of four—Randolph, Rustin, King, and the Reverend Eugene Carson Blake of the National Council of Churches. Archbishop O'Boyle, assured that "patience" had been stricken from Lewis's text, was about to deliver the invocation, so there was no time for a free-for-all discussion. Each of the four remaining men took issue with parts of Lewis's speech; King, for example, didn't like the reference to Sherman's march, admonishing his young disciple: "John, I know who you are. I think I know you well. I don't think this sounds like you." Blake was totally opposed to using the words "revolution" and "masses," which he derided as "Communist talk," but Randolph disagreed, chiming in that he had used those same words in public many times over the years. He then had to excuse himself, as he was needed on the speakers' platform to open the proceedings, but the discussion went on.

Minutes later Randolph returned, only to discover than Forman and Cox were now in the room, ready to defend Lewis's right to say anything he wanted. At one point, they turned to Rustin, threatening that if one word of their chairman's speech was altered, it "would be over their dead bodies." With this, Randolph had heard enough. "I have waited twenty-two years for this," he declared, his normally deep voice softened with sadness. "I've waited all of my *life* for this opportunity. Please don't ruin it." Turning to Lewis, he pleaded for compromise and understanding: "John, we've come this far together. Let us *stay* together." Years later, Lewis recalled the moment of decision as no decision at all: Randolph "looked as if he might cry. . . . This was as close to a plea as a man as dignified as he could come. How could I say no? It would be like saying no to Mother Teresa." Breaking the tension, he promised Randolph that he "would fix it."

For the next hour or so, Lewis stood over Forman, who was seated at a typewriter; there was no one else in the room as the two of them slowly but surely made their way through "every sentence, every phrase." At times they could hear a muffled version of the speeches being delivered at the top of the memorial's steps, but their focus was on eliminating controversial passages without sacrificing the intended message. In the end, the references to Sherman, "cheap politicians," and the civil rights bill being "too little and too late" were gone, as was the provocative query, "Which side is the government on?" Yet plenty of militancy remained. "I was angry," Lewis remembered. "But when we were done, I was satisfied. So was Forman. The speech still had fire. It still had bite, certainly more teeth than any other speech made that day. It still had an edge, with no talk of 'Negroes'—I spoke instead of 'black citizens' and 'the black masses,' the only speaker that day to use those terms."[13]

When Lewis stepped up to the podium to deliver his speech, the scene before him almost took his breath away. As many as a quarter million people, roughly 80 percent of whom were Black, had jammed together all along the reflecting pool and beyond, almost to the Washington Monument three-quarters of a mile away. Lewis had never seen, much less spoken to, a crowd of this size. But neither had anyone else who was there that day. Almost four times as large as the crowd that had gathered to hear Marian Anderson sing from the steps of the Lincoln Memorial in 1939, the sheer size of the gathering made Lewis feel that all the wrangling over his speech was trivial compared with the human drama of democratic promise set before his eyes. He spied a number of celebrities on or near the stage—Josephine Baker, Jackie Robinson, Marlon Brando, Paul Newman, and others—and as the roar of the crowd greeted him, he looked to his right and saw a small group "of SNCC people hollering and yelling, cheering me on." Mostly, though, he saw the multitude of expectant people waiting for his words. "We are here," he thought to himself. "We the people are *here*."

"As I began," Lewis recalled, "I actually wondered if I'd be able to speak at all. My voice quavered at first, but I quickly caught the feeling, the call and response, just like church. The crowd was with me, hanging on every word, and I could feel that. I soon had the rhythm, as the words went out and the sounds of support came back." As he made his way through the speech, he felt a strange combination of exhilaration and resentment: "The speech itself felt like an act of protest to me. After going through what I had been through during the previous sixteen or so hours, after feeling the pressures that had been placed on me and finally stepping out and delivering these words, it felt just like a demonstration, just like a march. It felt like defiance. I had been rubbed the wrong way, and I think it was evident in my tone that after-noon, even in my facial expression. I felt defiance in every direction: against the entrenched segregation of the South; against the neglect of the federal government; and also against the conservative concerns of the establishment factions, black and white alike, that were trying to steer the movement with their own interests in mind rather than the needs of the people. By the time I reached my closing words, I felt lifted both by a feeling of righteous indignation and the heartfelt response of those hundreds of thousands of men, women, and children before me, who burst into cheers with each phrase." Some of the loudest cheers, he later learned, came from "the poor farmers and sharecroppers whom SNCC organizers brought from Mississippi, Alabama, and southwest Georgia." For them, the South Carolina SNCC leader Cleve Sellers observed, "the march was a tremendous inspiration" helping "them believe that they were not alone" in their struggle.[14]

After accepting congratulatory handshakes from Rustin and many others on the platform, Lewis took his seat and listened to the program's two remaining speeches, one by Rabbi Joachim Prinz and another by Dr. King. In the flush of so much excitement, with his pulse racing, he had difficulty concentrating on the actual words closing out the program, but he heard enough of King's "I have a dream" refrain to know that he had been part of something special, that at least some of what was said that day would live on in the hearts and minds of many Americans.

Within an hour, as the huge crowd dispersed and headed home, Lewis, King, and the rest of the speakers were taken to the White House for a postmarch meeting with President Kennedy, who had watched the whole affair on television. Though understandably nervous about the president's reaction to his speech, Lewis braved the receiving line and shook his hand. The president's only comment was a noncommittal "I heard your speech," but Lewis left the encounter with a strong sense of presidential disapproval. In his general remarks, Kennedy mentioned the civil rights bill but avoided any specific promises. "I think his overriding feeling about the day," Lewis observed, "was relief that it was finally over, without crisis, incident or explosion, without any damage done."

In the press coverage that followed, there was little mention of the substance of the speeches by Lewis or anyone else. Even King's soaring rhetoric elicited surprisingly little public commentary. A few observers noted Lewis's willingness to address important and pressing issues, but most all but ignored the specifics of what he had to say. Almost all of the emphasis was on the peaceful, respectable nature of the march—on the good behavior exhibited by the civil rights movement and its followers. The civil rights bill also got lost in this cloud of praise, and for several weeks, as it became mired in congressional subcommittee wrangling, the bill almost dropped "almost out of sight," to use Lewis's words.

Only in the Black community did the march's program stir heated debate and controversy. Both King and Lewis were taken to task by Malcolm X, who labeled the event the "Farce on Washington." Referring obliquely to Lewis's censored speech, the Nation of Islam leader issued a scathing rebuke to the march's top-down organizers: "They told those Negroes what time to hit town, how to come, where to stop, what signs to carry, what song to sing, what speech they could make, and then they told them to get out of town by sundown." Even within SNCC, there was considerable criticism of Lewis's decision to accommodate the organizers' demands to scale back his radical language. Similarly, King had to endure severe criticism leveled at the allegedly conciliatory tone of his remarks. Why, several Black observers asked, did he fail to condemn a federal government that refused to intervene when Southern civil rights activists were subjected to unwarranted arrests and vigilante violence?[15]

Though disappointed with the overall reaction to the march, Lewis rejected much of the criticism aimed at either him or King. Granted, he had not been able to say all that he wanted to say, but even the amended speech in his estimation represented a new toughness in the movement's public posture toward the Kennedy administration and its moderate and conservative supporters. And he adamantly refused to criticize King's "message of hope and harmony." As he later wrote, "I have always believed there is room for both outrage and anger *and* optimism and love." It pained him that many of his SNCC colleagues did not share his belief in balancing such conflicting emotions, and over time this disagreement would weaken his faith in the organization.

At the time, Lewis was disappointed that the march was, in his words, "a failure in terms of specifics, in terms of prompting meaningful action on the part of the government or moving the segregationists in the South from their entrenched positions." Yet his long experience in the movement— from the sit-ins and Freedom Rides to the recent crisis in Birmingham—had taught him to respect the ultimate power and value of mass arousal. In his view, the March on Washington, for all its limitations, had produced "a truly stunning spectacle in terms of showing America and the world the size and the strength and the spirit of our movement." A milestone in the civil rights struggle's path to national prominence and visibility, the march laid a foundation on which later initiatives could be mobilized. Never again could the movement be relegated to the shadows of American life.[16]

CHAPTER 7

———

"Bombingham" and Freedom Summer

URING THE LATE SUMMER of 1963, John Lewis had no illusions about the difficulty of the path forward. In the absence of a comprehensive and strictly enforced civil rights act—a law backed up by a regionwide campaign of direct action—the rate of progress, he feared, would remain painfully slow. He knew what to expect, or at least he thought he did: grinding, gradual change built on the sacrifices of brave and determined activists. What he did not expect was "the season of darkness" that descended on the movement less than a month after the March on Washington. In mid-September, he took time out to spend a few days with his family in Pike County. That was where he heard a radio news broadcast about a Sunday-morning bombing at the Sixteenth Street Baptist Church in Birmingham. Minutes later he learned some of the details from Jim Forman, who called from Atlanta to urge him to head for Birmingham as soon as possible. Julian Bond was already on his way, and Forman hoped the two of them could help to forestall any additional violence. The blast had destroyed part of the church, injured twenty-one children, and killed four little girls.

When Lewis arrived at Kelly Ingram Park, the local movement staging ground adjacent to the church, he encountered a heartrending scene of grief and disbelief. "It was unreal to stand there and try to absorb what had happened," he remembered. "I looked at the people standing on the sidewalk across the street, these Black men and women of Birmingham, who had been through so much, and I knew that they had to be asking themselves,

How much *more?* What *else?* What's *next?*" Three days later, he attended the funeral for the four little girls, a deeply solemn service that attracted eight thousand mourners to the church and park grounds. "So many tears. So much grief." he observed. "It was almost too much." Prior to the funeral, Rustin and several other SCLC advisers had considered but ultimately rejected a plan to call for a brief national work stoppage during the services, and similarly Lewis, along with Bevel and Nash, had argued that the situation demanded direct action—perhaps "blocking the streets around the funeral to tie up the city." But Fred Shuttlesworth convinced them that this was a bad idea. It would be better, he insisted, to keep the focus on the girls and their grieving families and avoid any actions that might detract from the dignity of the mourning.

Martin Luther King Jr.'s eulogy, delivered in the most difficult of circumstances, managed to lift Lewis and many others out of their despair. Speaking to the militant white segregationists of the benighted South, he declared, "You can bomb our homes, bomb our churches, kill our little children, and we are *still* going to love you." And for the mourners waiting for consolation and direction, he counseled, "At times life is hard, as hard as crucible steel. In spite of the darkness of this hour, we must not lose faith in our white brothers." The site of numerous racially motivated bombings over the years, Birmingham—or "Bombingham," as it was sometimes known—harbored some of the South's most violent Ku Klux Klansmen, and few in the crowd doubted that they were the culprits behind the Sixteenth Street bombing. And they were right, though it would take more than four decades to bring all four of the Klan bombers to justice.

Lewis considered King's plea for forgiveness and reconciliation to be a supreme act of moral courage. Nash agreed with him that King had struck just the right tone, but the two Nashville Movement veterans also wanted to turn the emotion of the moment into purposeful action. During an interview with a *Washington Post* reporter the day after the bombing, they mentioned the possibility of organizing "a mass march on Montgomery, a nonviolent siege of the state capital." After appearing in the *Post* and spreading to other newspapers, the idea gained momentum and a catchy name coined by Nash, "Move on Alabama." On the evening following the funeral, Nash and Lewis discussed the idea with King and several other SNCC and SCLC activists. By this time Nash had worked out a concrete plan to bring Montgomery to a standstill—perhaps even to drive Governor George C. Wallace out of the statehouse. The plan was to "shut down everything." King and everyone else listened attentively as Nash laid out her proposal, but by the end of the meeting it was clear that the SCLC's leaders were unwilling to support such a daring and risky venture. If we are "going to launch a 'move' anywhere," Lewis reported to SNCC headquarters, it is "going to have to be essentially on our own."[1]

In the wake of the March on Washington, the ideological separation between SNCC and the rest of the civil rights movement was wider than ever. Lewis and SNCC were now clearly well outside the mainstream, which meant they found themselves virtually ineligible for support or financial backing from the liberal foundations that had stepped up to fund the rest of the movement. In the fall of 1963, the Taconic Foundation, headed by Stephen Currier, a wealthy Mellon family in-law, sponsored several "civil rights breakfasts" where the distribution of funds to civil rights organizations was discussed. The total pot of available money was $800,000, enough to convince Lewis and Forman to attend the first breakfast. But it soon became clear that Roy Wilkins and the NAACP held much of the power to determine how the money would be distributed, which meant that SNCC stood to receive only a small fraction of the funding. In the end, every major organization other than SNCC received at least $100,000, while SNCC's share turned out to be a paltry $15,000. SNCC leaders, accustomed to operating on a shoestring budget, had always been wary of swapping independence for financial backing. But as the new year approached, SNCC's lack of financial resources continued to limit the organization's options and operations in the field.

SNCC also had to deal with the shock of John F. Kennedy's death. While the nation mourned its fallen leader following his assassination in Dallas in late November, the launching of a major campaign that would disrupt the civic order did not seem wise or appropriate, even to the most radical members of SNCC. Lewis, who had more faith in Kennedy than most of his colleagues, was "devastated." He was in Nashville driving to the airport to catch a flight to Detroit when he heard the news. "I felt lost, faint really," he recalled. "I just wanted to go back to my apartment and forget about every-thing for a while. I've often felt like this at times of great crisis in my life. I want to go to a familiar place. I want to be home." As he later revealed, "I had my differences with the man, but I liked John Kennedy. I admired him. He truly had ideals, which not all politicians do. He was a symbol of hope, of change. He represented a period of great expectations for this entire country, including us—*most* of us—in the movement."

Nevertheless, considering the dangerous level of vigilantism plaguing the Deep South at the time, Lewis and other SNCC leaders did not feel they had the luxury of waiting very long before resuming a full slate of protests. The option of implementing Nash's proposed "Move on Alabama" remained open for consideration, but the nonviolent assault on Montgomery would not take place as planned. Lewis saw to it that "there would be a move. . . . But it would not be that fall, and it would not be in Alabama." Instead, it would come in Mississippi the following year.[2]

* * *

SNCC had actually been preparing for a major initiative in Mississippi since the summer of 1963. The evolving plan, conceived by SNCC's voter educa-tion specialist Bob Moses and the innovative white organizer and former Stanford dean Al Lowenstein, involved promoting voting rights by holding a "mock election" at the same time as the virtually all-white, official state election scheduled for September. Modeled after the protest votes held in South Africa earlier in the decade, the SNCC project came to be known as the Freedom Vote. The ambitious project, which recruited actual candi-dates and used actual ballot boxes, was administered by SNCC volunteers and allied members of the Council of Federated Organizations (COFO), an umbrella organization founded in Jackson in 1962. Aaron Henry, the state chairman of the Mississippi NAACP, became the Freedom Party's candidate for governor, and Ed King, a white minister affiliated with historically Black Tougaloo College in Jackson, agreed to be his running mate, forming the first interracial ticket in the state's history. The most innovative part of the proj-ect, one that would have long-term consequences for the movement, was the inclusion of eighty white college students from outside the South. By the following summer—designated "Freedom Summer" by movement leaders—

the number of student volunteers would swell to nearly a thousand, radically altering the racial dynamic of the Mississippi freedom struggle.

Most of the excitement in the fall of 1963 was in Mississippi, but there was also rising movement activity in St. Augustine, Florida, where a local sit-in movement had erupted in July, and in Alabama, primarily in Selma and the surrounding Dallas County. The Selma voting rights project had been spearheaded earlier in the year by Bernard LaFayette, but after he returned to Nashville in September to resume his college studies, Worth Long, Prathia Hall, and John Love took the helm. Working with a small but dedicated group of Black college and high school students, the SNCC organizers promoted a series of demonstrations, including several sit-ins at downtown stores on September 16, the day following the Birmingham church bombing.

The reaction from Sheriff Jim Clark and his deputies, augmented by more than a hundred state patrol officers led by Colonel Al Lingo, was immediate and brutal, leaving several protesters badly beaten and sixty-three others in jail. A group of Black teenagers then picketed the Dallas County Courthouse, and they, too, were arrested. Nightly mass meetings held at several Black churches followed, as local adult leaders stiffened their resolve to stand up to the local power structure. One of their requests, delivered to the commanding officer of nearby Craig Air Force Base, was to declare Selma off-limits to military personnel, a request reinforced by a strongly worded telegram from Lewis to Secretary of Defense Robert McNamara. When McNamara's office gave the complaint a perfunctory dismissal, Lewis and Forman decided that it was time to travel to Selma to have a closer look.

The scene in Selma, as later described by Lewis, was fraught with rising tension and the threat of violence: "The night we arrived, September 23, I attended a mass meeting at the town's Tabernacle Baptist Church and spoke to an audience of more than a thousand people. Outside, fifty of Colonel Lingo's troopers, armed with machine guns, surrounded the building. I envisioned another night-long shut-in siege, like the one in Montgomery during the Freedom Ride. For a time, it looked like I might be right. But eventually, late that evening, we were allowed to leave, with no arrests." The following morning, however, thirty protesters were arrested and placed in the city jail.

Lewis and a large number of local followers soon responded with a mass demonstration and march. "I carried a sign that read ONE MAN, ONE VOTE," Lewis recalled, "the first appearance of what was now SNCC's official slogan. The phrase had really struck a chord after my March on Washington speech, and now it was printed on the top of all our letterheads, as well as on most of our picket signs." Unimpressed by SNCC's slogan, Lingo's troopers promptly arrested Lewis and most of the other marchers for unlawful assembly. Armed with electric cattle prods, the troopers "reached out with those weapons to herd us along." "I was quick enough to dodge," Lewis noted, "but others weren't so lucky. I could hear sharp cries of pain as we were loaded on the bus."

Taken to the Selma prison farm, Lewis remained there amid gulag-like squalor and deprivation for a week before being released. Local authorities, who steadfastly refused to acknowledge the legitimacy of the voting rights campaign, seemed willing to resort to just about any level of force and intimidation to quell the local movement. But Lewis and his supporters were determined to carry on with the fight. When the local registrar's office was open for registrants on the first and third Mondays of the month—the days known as "Freedom Mondays" in the Black community—the lines of men and women waiting to register often "stretched around the block."

This spectacle became an object of interest to news and television reporters, FBI agents, Justice Department observers, and local deputies and white vigilantes who routinely showed up to harass and sometimes assault the Black citizens standing patiently in line. Other witnesses, such as James Baldwin, came from as far away as New York to lend aid and comfort to the prospective registrants. But public attention didn't seem to inhibit Clark and Lingo's heavy-handed approach to maintaining civic order and the status quo. Pushing peaceful registrants down the courthouse steps, using their billy clubs to beat them into submission, shocking them with cattle prods, threatening to cripple and even murder them—these became almost daily occurrences in downtown Selma.

Lewis was heartsick by the time he left Selma in early October, but also deeply moved by the bravery of so many ordinary people displaying extraordinary courage. He returned to Selma several times that fall to monitor the situation, but increasingly his focus, and that of SNCC generally, was on Mississippi.[3]

Lewis and SNCC wanted to capitalize on the success of the 1963 Freedom Vote, which drew more than ninety thousand Black Mississippians to the unofficial "polls." At this point, no one could be confident about the fate of the Kennedy civil rights bill that had become the ward of the new president, Lyndon B. Johnson. The wily Texan promised to do everything in his power to see the bill enacted into law—to "honor President Kennedy's memory" by passing the bill without delay—and he clearly had the requisite political skills to bring the government's professed commitment to civil rights to fruition. But Lewis and SNCC had good reasons to be concerned. During the week following the assassination, Johnson invited several civil rights leaders— including King, Jim Farmer, Wilkins, and Whitney Young—to a meeting at the White House. But no invitation was tendered to Lewis and SNCC, which was scheduled to hold its annual conference in Washington later that week. Even before this snub, Lewis and many other SNCC activists worried that even if the civil rights bill survived politically, it would be gutted and unrecognizable by the time it became law, sharing the fate of the toothless 1957 and 1960 civil rights acts. As Senate majority leader, Johnson had been a major factor in the compromises that limited the effectiveness and scope of previous civil rights legislation, and there was little reason to believe that he would act any differently this time around.

Such suspicions helped to fuel the determination among movement leaders to step up the pressure on Johnson and his administration, and to many of them the risky but potentially decisive Freedom Summer experiment appeared to be the best means of doing so. Lewis, in particular, invested his hopes and dreams in the coming move on Mississippi. Well aware that many members of SNCC had lost faith in nonviolence, interracial cooperation, and anything resembling the dream of an inclusive Beloved Community, he regarded the multiracial, multigenerational, and interregional nature of the Freedom Summer campaign as a way to renew the moral fiber of the movement. Politically and spiritually, it seemed to signal the rise of a new dawn of democratic promise. Mississippi, long considered to be the worst state in the nation when it came to protecting civil and human rights, might now become a shining example of hard-won but fundamental social change, or so Lewis hoped.

This hope for the future was tempered by the growing atmosphere of fear that followed John Kennedy's assassination. SNCC staff members working in the Deep South suddenly felt more vulnerable. If a president could be killed, surely the same thing might happen to radical activists out in the field with little or no protection. "There was concern that the killing of Kennedy might prompt a crackdown on 'radical' organizations such as ourselves," Lewis observed, "that, as Forman put it . . . 'anyone left of center will be subject to a purge.'" This concern, and the broader fear that the federal government was unwilling to protect civil rights activists in dangerous places like Mississippi, factored into the rationale for including a large number of white students in the Freedom Summer campaign.[4]

* * *

Bob Moses, among others, argued that one way to draw a sympathetic response from the American public was to place white as well as Black activists in harm's way. While no one wanted anyone to die in Mississippi, the realization that not only Black citizens were at risk was thought to be a way of cultivating white Americans' awareness of the reality of violence as a bulwark of the vaunted "Southern way of life." The thought that a victim of vigilante or police violence in Mississippi might be the kid who grew up next door was possibly the shock that white America needed. Lewis, who conceded that the strategy of nonviolence depended on the perception that violent resistance to change was not only possible but probable, agreed with Moses that the risk of dispatching white students to Mississippi or anywhere else in the South was worth taking. "We knew we needed help," he later explained, "and that help, we decided, should come from *white* America—not in the form of money, not in the form of moral support, but in the flesh-and-blood form of their own sons and daughters."

If the Beloved Community was ever going to emerge from the welter of conflict and struggle in America, he reasoned, Black and white citizens would first have to share the burdens of sacrifice and loss. While many of his SNCC colleagues were uncomfortable with this calculation, Lewis, like Moses, was convinced "that the movement should not be about black against white"; instead "it should be black *and* white, united against something that was simply wrong." "I always felt," he insisted, "that it was important that white people be involved with us, that they bear witness not just from a distance but by standing beside us, suffering with us and, ultimately, succeeding with us."[5]

Preparations for Freedom Summer occupied much of Lewis's time during the winter and spring of 1964. Voter registration projects run by SNCC and CORE were already in place in several Mississippi counties at the beginning of the year, but there was a lot of work to do before the movement would be ready to oversee a full-scale campaign involving hundreds of out-of-state volunteers. In late January, Lewis and Forman traveled to Hattiesburg, where they joined a number of civil rights leaders and several dozen clergymen for the first movement-sponsored Freedom Day, a mass march and rally designed to draw media attention to the voting rights effort. On the eve of the march, Lewis delivered a rousing speech to a crowd of several hundred supporters, and the next day he participated in a picket line outside the county courthouse. This open defiance shocked and enraged local authorities, but by the end of the day only one person, Moses, had been arrested, a show of restraint prompted by the presence of several network television camera crews. Freedom Days in several other Mississippi communities followed, despite a noticeable resurgence of white supremacist violence.

In April, the state legislature eliminated the Freedom Day tactic by outlawing picketing outside state government buildings. But the Mississippi movement found other ways of keeping voter registration in the public eye, notably by encouraging national entertainment and sports celebrities to boycott the state unless audiences were fully integrated, and by attracting an interracial audience to a high-profile Joan Baez concert at Tougaloo College. The political response to these and other violations of Mississippi law and racial etiquette bordered on hysteria, as the state braced itself for the coming invasion of militant activists.

Meanwhile, Lowenstein, Lewis, Moses, and other Freedom Summer coordinators were busy recruiting hundreds of volunteers willing to spend the summer in Mississippi either working on voter registration or teaching in "Freedom Schools." Despite the growing realization that the federal government had no intention of providing protection for the summer volunteers, the plan of action continued to expand. Most important, at the April COFO convention, delegates from across the state voted to reach beyond the unofficial Freedom Vote held the previous fall to form the Mississippi Freedom Democratic Party (MFDP). Lewis hailed this development as a major stride toward political legitimacy and maturity among Black Mississippians, even though the intention to participate in the state Democratic Party's upcoming conventions and primaries would surely be stymied by race-conscious party officials. The ultimate goal, which he understood and supported, was to spend the summer "educating and organizing Black voters across the state, to bring them into the MFDP and to have them choose their own delegates" to the Democratic National Convention to be held in Atlantic City, New Jersey, in August.[6]

As it turned out, Mississippi would experience a great deal of turmoil before anyone, Black or white, showed up in Atlantic City. Part of this turmoil originated far to the north, at Western College, in Oxford, Ohio, where several hundred Freedom Summer volunteers gathered in early June. As soon as the weeklong training sessions began, serious conflict arose between the predominantly Black and Southern-based staff and the overwhelmingly white students, many of whom came from privileged backgrounds and elite universities, and most of whom had little or no experience either in the South or in Black communities. One of the major goals of the Western sessions was to prepare the student volunteers, 90 percent of whom were white, to interact with Black Mississippians in an egalitarian, condescension-free manner. This proved to be a difficult task, partially because there was considerable resentment among the trainers, especially the SNCC veterans, who were upset not only by some of the class-based smugness they encountered but also by the disproportionate press coverage extended to the white student volunteers. Years later Lewis captured the core of this resentment, which would only grow stronger once the white students actually arrived in Mississippi: "Hey, we've been down here all these months, all these years, working our butts off day in and day out, and these white kids come down and stay a week or two and they get all the headlines, they get all the credit."

At the time, Lewis worried that such feelings would exacerbate the already tense relations between many Black and white activists working for

SNCC. Roughly 20 percent of SNCC's staff was white, and Lewis considered several of his white colleagues to be among the most trusted and valuable members of the organization. But a significant portion of SNCC, having fallen victim to the rising "anger and rage about Whites in general," was ready to tie the organization to racial identity, even to the point of expelling most or all of its white members. One striking example of this mentality was Stokely Carmichael's decision to exclude whites from any involvement in the Freedom Summer district under his supervision. Lewis vehemently opposed the decision, and Carmichael soon backed down from his all-Black pledge. But the controversy saddened Lewis and other proponents of inter-racial cooperation and harmony.

At the November 1963 SNCC conference in Washington, Bayard Rustin, anticipating this separatist impulse, had tried to establish a middle ground by encouraging white staff members to concentrate on or even limit their work to predominantly white communities. With this in mind, Sam Shirah, a white SNCC staff member born, like Lewis, in Troy, Alabama, founded the Southern Student Organizing Committee (SSOC) in the spring of 1964. Conceived as a SNCC spin-off and designed to mobilize support among white Southern college students, SSOC served as a way station for whites who felt increasingly uncomfortable with SNCC's separatist trajectory. Predictably, Lewis was never a fan of what he called SNCC's "all-white shadow," a relatively ineffective organization that struggled until its dissolution in 1969. But in 1964 there wasn't much he could do to stem the rising tide of identity politics in an organization destined to abandon interracialism, one of its key founding principles.[7]

*   *   *

What Lewis could do was to work as hard as possible to ensure the success of Freedom Summer. In the weeks leading up to the training sessions in Oxford, he traveled to a number of college campuses, where he recruited and screened volunteers. He was looking for students interested in going to Mississippi for the right reasons, those motivated by genuine concern for the cause of civil rights and the future of American democracy. And he wanted to make sure they had a good sense of the dangers of civil rights work and of what they would face on the bloody ground of Mississippi. He also asked them point blank if they were averse to taking orders from Black supervisors, many of whom would be far less educated than they were. All of the community voting project directors, he warned them, were Black, and many had never traveled outside the state. Students who agreed to go to Mississippi would be entering a battleground beyond the American mainstream, an exotic destination unlike any place they had ever seen. While he didn't want to scare them off, he wanted them to enter the struggle with their eyes open.

In late April, Lewis took a day off from recruiting to address the annual convention of the American Society of Newspaper Editors. He wanted the media to know what was coming and why the movement was determined to grab the attention of the federal government and the American public. So he told them about the recent violence against Black Mississippians, about the administration's indefensible appointment of Harold Cox and other segregationist federal judges, about the freedom schools and voter registration projects, about the new MFDP, and about the legion of students that would soon descend on the state. He warned them that the time had come for federal officials to decide whether they had the courage to ensure true democracy and voting rights for all citizens. They "must make that choice this summer," he insisted, "or make us all witnesses to the lynching of democracy."[8]

SNCC was all in when it came to waging the struggle in Mississippi, and to prove the point, in May the organization moved its headquarters from Atlanta to two "command centers" closer to the action, one in Jackson and another in the Delta town of Greenwood. This was a daring move, fraught with danger, but it was something that Moses had been advocating for some time, and that Lewis had come to see as a necessary step in engaging the evil of Jim Crow. For a time in June, the real headquarters shifted temporarily to Western College, where more than one hundred SNCC staff members joined forty CORE activists and a handful of other trainers, plus a large contingent of ministers, lawyers, doctors, and nurses. Missing, however, was any significant representation from the NAACP or the SCLC. Lewis and Farmer were essentially in charge, without the constraints of dealing with Wilkins. King lent support from afar, but he knew SNCC and CORE were better suited than the SCLC to oversee the nonviolent but gritty warfare that was about to begin. Having cooperated closely during the Freedom Rides of 1961, the two direct action organizations, led by fellow Freedom Riders Lewis and Farmer, worked well together.

Overseeing an intense training regimen, they mobilized an array of lecturers and mentors ranging from Moses to Rustin. Even John Doar was on the scene representing the Justice Department, sent primarily to warn the volunteers that they would be on their own in Mississippi, that they should not expect any protection from the federal government. Moses also offered a sobering bit of realism. "Don't come to Mississippi this summer to save the Mississippi Negro," he told them. "Only come if you understand, really understand that his freedom and yours are one." He had no idea how many Black voters would be registered, or how many pupils the freedom schools would attract, but in Mississippi just making it through the summer as Black and white activists bound in solidarity would be a victory worth celebrating. Freedom Summer was only the first stage of a long struggle for liberation and justice in a state that historically had seen precious little of either.

While this message led to a handful of dropouts, the vast majority of the volunteers left Oxford with feelings of exhilaration and common purpose. With freedom songs ringing in their ears, but with a measure of fear and trepidation in their thoughts, the first group of Freedom Summer volunteers boarded buses on June 21. Lewis, who knew much more than the students did about the dangers awaiting them in Mississippi, had great difficulty enjoying either the departure or the journey south. Struck with "a palpable sense of fear," he later acknowledged that he "felt a huge personal responsibility for these young men and women," many of whom he had recruited.[9]

This sense of dread intensified three days later when three Freedom Summer volunteers disappeared near the Klan-infested town of Philadelphia in Neshoba County. Mickey Schwerner, a twenty-four-year-old white CORE field secretary from Brooklyn whom Lewis had known for some time; James Chaney, a twenty-one-year-old Black CORE worker from nearby Meridian; and Andrew Goodman, a twenty-year-old white Queens College student whom Lewis had met the previous week in Oxford, were investigating the burning of a Black church in Longdale when they were arrested for speeding by Neshoba County deputy sheriff Cecil Price, a member of the White

Knights of the Ku Klux Klan. They were taken to jail in Philadelphia and then released, but were later apprehended by Price and two carloads of Klansmen, who proceeded to torture and murder the three young civil rights activists before burying them beneath an earthen dam a few miles outside Philadelphia. Their bodies would not be discovered until August 4, more than six weeks later, and in the interim Neshoba County became the scene of a massive search led by the FBI. Their blue Ford station wagon, burned and dumped into a swampy creek, was discovered two days after their disappearance. But there was no sign of the missing men.

Lewis got word that the three activists were missing while he was attending an uncle's funeral in Troy. "I couldn't believe it. Not already," he recalled. "We hadn't even gotten started yet. Half our eight hundred volunteers were still up in Oxford, getting set to board buses south for their assignments, and already we had three missing." Rushing to Meridian, he joined a search party that included Farmer, a CORE leader from Chicago named George Raymond, the Black comedian and activist Dick Gregory, and several dozen others. By the time they reached Philadelphia, the town was crawling with reporters, heavily armed state police officers, and menacing-looking men deputized by Price's boss and fellow Klansman, Sheriff Lawrence Rainey. Taken to Rainey's office for a briefing, Lewis, Farmer, and Raymond got a taste of the outright defiance that was all too common among Mississippi law enforcement officers.

"The atmosphere was tense," Lewis remembered. "Rainey and Price did nothing to hide their contempt for us. They sneered. They smirked." When Lewis asked to see the burned car and the remains of the church in Longdale, he was told by the attorney representing the sheriff's office that such visits were impossible, ostensibly because of fear that the civil rights leaders might tamper with the evidence. To Lewis, this claim implied that a crime had been committed, but the attorney quickly quashed the implication. "You know," the attorney drawled, "those boys may have decided to go up north or someplace and have a short vacation. They'll probably be coming back shortly."

The smirk on the attorney's face and the cavalier attitude of Rainey and Price set off an alarm in Lewis's head. It was likely, he now believed, that these men were responsible for Goodman, Schwerner, and Chaney's disappearance, or at the very least they knew who was responsible. That evening a widening search of the wooded areas outside Philadelphia turned up nothing, prompting the Freedom Summer organizers to ask President Johnson and Attorney General Robert Kennedy to conduct a full-scale investigation of the case. Johnson, who was in the final stages of mobilizing congressional support for his civil rights bill, responded immediately, ordering his defense secretary Robert McNamara to dispatch two hundred sailors to Neshoba County to expand the search. At the same time, the attorney general ordered J. Edgar Hoover to send more than 130 additional FBI agents to the state.

Judging by past experiences with Hoover, Lewis and most other movement leaders had no faith in the FBI's investigative capacity when it came to civil rights matters. But they were pleased that the federal government had at least acknowledged the gravity of the racial violence in Mississippi. The Freedom Summer organizers were also gratified that the case of the missing volunteers was attracting widespread public attention, though in a press conference that week Lewis noted the bittersweet nature of this development. "It is a shame," he told the reporters, "that national concern is aroused only after two white boys are missing." For better or worse, the developing reaction to the situation in Mississippi seemed to confirm the wisdom of Moses's plan to put whites alongside Blacks in the line of fire.[10]

*   *   *

Ten days later, on July 2, the House of Representatives gave final approval to the Senate version of the civil rights bill and immediately submitted it to President Johnson for his signature. Lewis, along with a number of other movement leaders, was invited to Washington for the signing ceremony, but he didn't feel right about leaving the volunteers at that time, even for a few days: "I decided to stay in Mississippi instead. This was where I wanted to be, not on some stage someplace." When word came that the bill was about to become law, he was in Greenwood overseeing an interracial group of volunteers working at a playground. The news, he later remembered, had surprisingly little effect on him and the volunteers: "We felt glad, but not joyous. There was no sense of celebration. We were still in the middle of a war down there, a campaign that was just beginning. The news from Washington felt as if it were coming from another country, a very distant place."

While he welcomed the passage of the Civil Rights Act and understood its historical significance, Lewis "worried that with the signing of this act, a lot of people might think our work was done," that "now that we had this law," there would be "no need to push anymore, no need to protest. . . . Now we could just leave it to the Justice Department to enforce it." Lewis rejected this assumption, knowing the act was essentially limited to public accommodations and did not address racial discrimination in employment, housing, or education. Skeptical that Justice Department enforcement would be vigilant, he expected stiff resistance. After six months of lobbying and arm-twisting, Johnson had only managed to convince eight Southern representatives and one Southern senator (Ralph Yarborough of Texas) to support the bill; the other 115 congressional politicians representing the region voted no.

In Mississippi, Lewis suspected, the Civil Rights Act would have little or no effect on the character of race relations and white supremacist politics for the foreseeable future. And he was right: "We were steeled for a season of violence in Mississippi that summer, and we got it. Between June 15 and September 15 our people reported more than 450 'incidents,' ranging from phone threats to drive-by shootings. There were more than a thousand arrests . . . eighty beatings . . . thirty-five shootings . . . thirty-five church burnings . . . thirty bombings. The Klan was quite simply running amuck. It was open season on civil rights workers, with very little response from local or federal authorities." The only reason the actual body count remained relatively low was the influence of the national newspaper and television reporters who fanned out across the state chronicling and exposing many of the white supremacists' threats and acts of violence. "As bad as the violence was that summer," Lewis concluded, "God knows what it would have been like without the presence of the press. And we used that weapon in every way we could."[11]

The relentless and often violent resistance from white Mississippians, though rooted in race, also stemmed from an antipathy toward an emerging student counterculture associated with the unconventional behavior and political radicalism of "outside agitators." The volunteers who staffed the Freedom Schools and voter registration campaigns were seen as an invading army of bohemian cultural misfits determined to flout traditional social conventions with their long hair, sexual promiscuity, freedom songs, and "beatnik" mores. Even some Black Mississippians raised their eyebrows at the prevailing lifestyle among the volunteers. A larger concern for Lewis, however, was the danger of approaching the local population, especially in rural Black communities, with an air of condescension. Thus he encouraged the volunteers and staff members affiliated with SNCC to blend in as much as possible. "Overalls became the standard outfit for our Black volunteers." he noted. "Blue denim bib overalls with a white T-shirt underneath became the symbol of SNCC. And it was practical. It fit our lifestyle of sleeping on sofas and floors and walking miles and miles of dusty roads. It also identified us with the people we were working with—farmers and poor people. The more political members among us liked the fact that overalls symbolized the proletariat point of view, the worker, the masses. Some SNCC people felt uncomfortable in overalls but most of us had grown up poor ourselves, so wearing dungarees was nothing new. I had left my overalls behind when I moved from rural Alabama to go off to college, but that summer in Mississippi I put them back on."

Other than a few brief visits to Atlanta, New York, and Washington, Lewis spent the entire summer in Mississippi, mostly working out of the SNCC office in Greenwood, in Leflore County, on the eastern edge of the Delta. He lived with the Greenes, Black schoolteachers who opened their house to the movement, and sometimes shared a room with Carmichael and other members of the SNCC staff. The Greenes' home was a classic "freedom house," with various movement people coming and going all the time, a safe haven from the tension and violence of the surrounding countryside. When Lewis and others ventured out to work with local Black residents on voter registration and citizenship training, they encountered "hot, tiring, tedious work," as he described it, "walking door-to-door, canvassing and convincing people to come to class at one of our Freedom Schools, to come to the courthouse to register to vote. Standing in unmoving lines outside those antebellum courthouses for hours on end, facing heat and hunger and profane harassment and worse."[12]

Fortunately, the resolute courage that he observed among the local population that summer was more than enough to sustain his spirit and keep him going. One of SNCC's highest priorities was to support the MFDP in its effort to gain a foothold in the state Democratic Party, and Lawrence Guyot, a SNCC field secretary from Pass Christian, Mississippi, became the MFDP's chairman. The vice chairperson was Fannie Lou Hamer, a remarkable forty-six-year-old woman from Sunflower County who became one of SNCC's most effective organizers during Freedom Summer. An impoverished share-cropper who left school at the age of twelve, Hamer used her powerful and eloquent voice, in both speech and song, to inspire her fellow Black Mississippians to stand up to the white power structure. In the process, she grew close to Lewis, who admired her grit and determination. Never a shrinking violet, Hamer did not hesitate to scold Lewis and the Freedom Summer visitors with admonitions: "Now, John Lewis. . . . Now, Jim Forman," she warned, with a teasing lilt to her voice, "let me tell you all, if you're going to come to Mississippi, you can't just come here and stay for one day or one night. You've got to stay here for the *long* haul. . . . I know Mississippi, and you'd better be ready to move *in*."

The MFDP's immediate goal was to encourage Black participation in Democratic Party precinct meetings in preparation for full participation at the Democratic National Convention to be held in Atlantic City in late August. When white citizens stonewalled this initiative, the focus shifted to the selection of delegates at local MFDP meetings, and to a final selection of convention delegates at a statewide MFDP conference in Jackson on August 6. Lewis did what he could to support this effort, speaking at MFDP rallies across the state, sometimes accompanied by Dr. King, but almost always in collaboration with Guyot and Hamer. The rising spirit of political mobilization was infectious and exhilarating, sending waves of excitement through the SNCC staff. But other organizations, notably the NAACP and the National Urban League, had a different reaction. Sharp critics of the Freedom Summer campaign from the start, Wilkins and Young refused to support the MFDP and even called for a national moratorium on civil rights demonstrations. Continued agitation in Mississippi, they argued, would jeopardize President Johnson's reelection and the future of the movement. At Wilkins's urging, an emergency meeting of civil rights leaders was held in New York to discuss the matter. Once the meeting began, Lewis was shocked to discover that only he and Farmer opposed the moratorium; even King, Rustin, and A. Philip Randolph came out in favor of Wilkins's proposal.

This willingness to stall the movement's momentum violated one of Lewis's fundamental beliefs. "The right to demonstrate was, to me, something that must never, never be compromised," he later explained. "The right to challenge authority, to raise questions, point up issues, draw attention to needs, demand change, is at the basis of a truly responsive, representative democracy. People simply must never give up their right to protest. . . . Almost all of my SNCC colleagues felt the same way. We were created, in a way, to be a thorn in the flesh of the American body politic and of the established, traditional civil rights movement. Forming a consensus with other groups had never been a priority for us."[13]

The federal government was well aware of SNCC's reputation for independent-minded radicalism, and during the summer of 1964 a number of federal officials from the president on down tried to pressure the organization to soften its stance. The Selective Service System suddenly undertook a vigorous investigation of Lewis's draft status. Having been rejected for conscientious objector status in 1961, Lewis had appealed his 1-A classification and was awaiting a decision. During Freedom Summer, Selective Service officials began an unusually thorough process of interviewing scores of his acquaintances in Alabama, Georgia, and Tennessee, all in an apparent effort to find something damning in his background. After the investigation was complete, he met with a Justice Department hearing officer in September, and a year later he received notification, much to his surprise, that he had won his appeal, making him the first Black man in Alabama history to be granted conscientious objector status.

A more general assault on SNCC emanated from Hoover and the FBI. Early on, Hoover and the bureau identified SNCC as one of the most dangerous predominantly Black organizations in the nation, placing it in the same category as the Nation of Islam. In late June 1964, just as the Freedom Summer campaign was getting started, Hoover explained his concerns in a lengthy interview with a *New York Times* reporter. Published under the sensational headline "Hoover Says Reds Exploit Negroes," the interview demonized SNCC's role in Freedom Summer as a front for Communist subversion, citing as evidence the organization's alliance with the left-wing, pro-labor National Lawyers Guild. When asked to comment on Hoover's charges, Lewis suggested the director should spend less time tar brushing civil rights activists with a mythical association with the "Red Menace" and more time apprehending "the bombers, midnight assassins and brutal racists who daily make a mockery of the United States Constitution."[14]

The search for Goodman, Schwerner, and Chaney drew a great deal of attention in the month following Lewis's retort, but the trail remained cold until the discovery of three mutilated corpses on August 4. All three had been shot before being buried beneath a cattle pond dam a few miles southwest of Philadelphia. The funerals that followed were gut-wrenching, agonizing affairs for the victims' families and friends, and for Lewis and the Freedom Summer staff and volunteers. At Chaney's funeral in Meridian, a mixture of sorrow and anger enveloped a crowd of more than seven hundred mourners, and Dave Dennis, a former Freedom Rider and the leader of Mississippi CORE, spoke for many of them in his eulogy. "I've got vengeance in my heart tonight," he declared, his voice rising in high-pitched anguish, "and I ask you to feel angry with me. I'm sick and tired, and I ask you to be sick and tired with me. The white men who murdered James Chaney are never going to be punished. . . . If you go back home and sit down and take what these white men in Mississippi are doing to us . . . if you take it and don't do something about it . . . then God damn your souls!"

Though understandable, this kind of rhetoric was unacceptable to Lewis, who worried that violent retaliation against white people would soon follow and just make matters worse. Turning away from nonviolence, which was how some listeners interpreted Dennis's words, would only compound the tragedy of racially motivated murders. There was already a dangerous trend toward disillusionment and resignation throughout the movement, Lewis acknowledged. "Out of frustration, bitterness, outright hostility to the system, to the government, to white people in general, every day," he later wrote, "the more radical arm of the movement was swelling a little more." And in this case, by radical he meant that previously balanced and well-focused nonviolent activists had grown too outraged and angry to keep their eyes on the prize. Two days later, at Goodman's funeral in Manhattan, Lewis was relieved to hear Rabbi Arthur Lelyveld, a Goodman family friend who had represented the National Council of Churches in Mississippi during Freedom Summer, make a plea for peace, reconciliation, and nonviolence. "Not one of those young people who are walking the streets of Hattiesburg or Camden or Laurel or Gulfport or Greenville," the rabbi insisted, "not one of them, and certainly neither Andy nor James nor Michael would have us in resentment or vindictiveness add to the store of hatred in the world. They pledged themselves in the way of nonviolence. They learned how to receive blows, not how to inflict them. They were trained to bear hurts, not to retaliate. Theirs is the way of love and constructive service."

That night Lewis spoke at Schwerner's funeral at a church on East Thirty-Fifth Street in Manhattan, as did Farmer and Dennis. Speaking from the heart, he delivered a passionate but comforting eulogy echoing Rabbi Lelyveld's words. He also listened carefully to Dennis, who repeated what he had said in Meridian—tortured expressions of pain and anger and outrage. In the end, Lewis wasn't sure which message "reached more hearts" that night. Indeed, as he later confessed, even he "wondered how long we could keep the faith." "How long," he asked himself, "could we believe in government that allowed things like this to happen? I had asked in my speech at the March on Washington which side the federal government was on. And now, a year later, the answer was no clearer."[15]

CHAPTER 8

Atlantic City and Africa

T HE NEXT CHAPTER in the movement's struggle to gain access to the levers of governmental power took place on August 6, 1964, at the MFDP's state convention in Jackson. Convened on the eve of James Chaney's funeral in Meridian, the Jackson gathering tried to rise above the grief that had enshrouded Freedom Summer following the gruesome discovery in Neshoba County. Some of the twenty-five hundred attendees fought through tears and anger as they selected sixty-eight delegates to attend the upcoming Democratic National Convention. Sixty-four of those chosen were Black, and four were white, including the Reverend Ed King. The backgrounds of the Black delegates ran the full gamut of class and life experiences, ranging from sharecroppers like Fannie Lou Hamer to middle-class professionals and business leaders.

The MFDP convention "was an electrifying event" for John Lewis, who addressed the throng wearing his classic SNCC blue overalls and a white T-shirt. Fannie Lou Hamer and Lawrence Guyot also spoke, as did Joseph L. Rauh Jr., a liberal labor lawyer who, acting as general counsel for the Leadership Conference on Civil Rights, had come to Mississippi earlier in the summer to advise the MFDP. Throughout the day and early evening, "there was chanting and cheering and waving placards as each speaker rose to address them." By the end of the meeting, "the optimism was unbounded," Lewis observed, in part because "the sixty-eight men and women chosen that night to travel to Atlantic City represented much more than one state or one political party. They represented all of us, every American—black or white—who believed in the concept of inter-racial democracy."

Lewis was well aware, of course, that a daunting challenge lay ahead. Somehow the MFDP would have to find a way to convince President Lyndon Johnson and the leaders of the Democratic Party that it was time to make Mississippi's official delegation truly representative of the state's biracial population. Since it was clear that the all-white delegation selected by the Mississippi Democratic Party had no intention of sharing its seats with the MFDP, conflict over the final composition of the delegation was inevitable.

In preparation for the expected struggle in Atlantic City, Rauh, assisted by a number of ACLU and National Lawyers Guild attorneys, spent much of the summer preparing legal briefs substantiating the MFDP's claim to most or all of the state's delegates. With the help of Ella Baker, the sixty-year-old godmother of SNCC, Rauh also mobilized support for the MFDP from other state delegations, securing written pledges of support from several states before the convention.

By the time the buses carrying the MFDP delegation arrived in Atlantic City on Friday, August 21, there was a "sense of elation and excitement" among the delegates. Lewis, who arrived the same day after flying to Philadelphia and taking a long cab ride to the Jersey shore, was amazed by what he witnessed outside the civic center where the convention was scheduled to open on Monday. The MFDP contingent was practically dancing on the sidewalk, anticipating a victory they had been seeking for far too long. "How could we not prevail?" Lewis thought to himself. "The law was on our side. Justice was on our side. The sentiments of the entire nation were with us. I couldn't see how those convention seats could be kept from us."

Neither Lewis nor the MFDP delegates were taking any chances, however. Both before and after the opening gavel, they conducted a carefully orchestrated campaign to publicize their case. "While the Freedom Party delegates were inside the hall attending hearings, meetings and caucuses," Lewis explained, "we maintained a vigil outside, staging rallies, giving interviews to the press, pointing out the burnt carcass of the Ford, which had been towed all the way from Greenwood, and carrying placards bearing the photographs of Schwerner, Goodman, and Chaney, whose killers were still at large."[1]

The first test came on Saturday, August 22, when the request to replace the all-white Mississippi delegation went before the 108-member Credentials Committee. The MFDP's strategy, known as "eleven and eight," was to have the decision placed before the entire convention after reaching the required threshold of convincing eleven committee members to do so. Once that was accomplished, a roll-call vote from all of the delegates would be mandatory if as few as eight states requested it. MFDP leaders were confident of victory if they could secure a roll-call vote, but they knew it was going to be difficult to reach the magic number of eleven supporters on the committee. They suspected that the decision would hinge on the committee's reaction to testimony presented in a televised hearing that afternoon.

The scene in the crowded hearing room was fraught with tension and drama, which Lewis observed on closed-circuit television in a nearby room. The hearing room was jammed with committee members and delegates, including the MFDP delegation. "The members of Mississippi's regular Democratic Party were there as well," Lewis recalled, "white plantation owners and businessmen looking across the aisle at women whom they knew only as maids and cooks, and men they knew only as field hands." Rauh, as a Credentials Committee member representing the District of Columbia, presented the MFDP's case before turning the microphone over to a series of witnesses brought in to document the "story of tragedy and terror in Mississippi."

The testimony began with Aaron Henry and Ed King and culminated with the simple but powerful words of the delegation's vice-chair, Fannie Lou Hamer. The stories Hamer told were searing, amplified by the ring of truth. Lewis, like many Americans, would never forget what he witnessed that day as she held forth on the true meaning of democracy, and on the pain and disrespect that she had experienced as a poor Black woman trying to exercise her rights as a citizen in Jim Crow Mississippi: "Under the heat of the glaring television lights, with sweat rolling down her face, she began slowly, describing the murder of Medgar Evers and the riots at Ole Miss. Rita Schwerner sat beside Fannie Lou as she spoke, a reminder of the three deaths earlier that summer. Finally Fannie Lou detailed her own experiences—the savage beatings she had endured in pursuit of the vote, the cruel humiliations, the violent violations of her basic rights as a human being and as an American citizen. With tears welling in her eyes—with tears filling the eyes of almost everyone watching—she asked, in the unrehearsed, down-to-earth, plain language of an everyday American, the question we all wanted answered: '. . . if the Freedom Democratic Party is not seated now, I question America. Is this America, the land of the free and the home of the brave, where we have to sleep at night with our telephones off the hooks because our lives be threatened daily because we want to live as decent human beings, in America?'"

Hamer's testimony was riveting—too riveting, as it turned out, for Johnson. Watching the television broadcast in the White House, he panicked at the thought of one Black woman from Mississippi disrupting his plans for reelection. Several advisers had warned him that seating and legitimizing the MFDP delegation would cost him hundreds of thousands of white Southern votes, not only in Mississippi but across the region, and he was afraid they were right. Halfway through Hamer's speech, he ordered the television networks carrying the hearing to switch their coverage to a special address from the White House. When he told the network executives that he had an important announcement to make that couldn't wait, they complied, even though his ulterior motive was obvious.

Fortunately for the MFDP, Hamer's words had already captured the attention of part of the nation, and millions more would become captivated by her truth-telling message that evening when all three major networks replayed highlights from her speech. Despite Johnson's trickery, the public response to Hamer's plea was overwhelming. The delegates to the convention received "an avalanche of telegrams from across the nation," as Lewis put it, guaranteeing that Johnson would have to work out some form of compromise to seat at least some of the MFDP delegates. Lewis and others worried that Johnson would utilize all of his political skills to arrange a compromise that would fall far short of the MFDP's expectations, and their fears soon proved justified.[2]

*   *   *

After the president appointed a special subcommittee chaired by Minnesota attorney general and future presidential candidate Walter Mondale, the MFDP delegates were presented with a proposal offering two "at-large" seats to Aaron Henry and Ed King. The proposal included a stipulation that all of the state's delegates would have to sign a loyalty oath pledging their support to the party's presidential ticket, a clear warning to the white Mississippi delegates who had already announced their commitment to the Republican nominee, Senator Barry Goldwater, who had won their support by opposing the Civil Rights Act. As an additional concession to the MFDP, the proposal also prohibited racial discrimination in the delegate selection process for future Democratic national conventions. Finally, as an added inducement to accept the offer, Johnson unofficially informed the MFDP that his selection of their favored vice-presidential candidate, the longtime civil rights advocate Senator Hubert Humphrey of Minnesota, hinged on their acceptance of the two at-large seats. Otherwise, he would choose a running mate far less acceptable to the civil rights community.

Walter Reuther, the liberal head of the United Auto Workers union, along with Humphrey himself, led the effort to drum up support for the compromise proposal, buttonholing delegates all across the convention center. There was nothing subtle about the effort, and the stakes were high. From the moment the proposal surfaced, the civil rights leaders attending the convention were split over whether to accept Johnson's offer. Gathering at the Union Temple Baptist Church a few blocks from the convention center, representatives of the SCLC, CORE, SNCC, and the NAACP held what Lewis later termed "an emergency summit meeting." Roughly half of those at the meeting argued for acceptance of the compromise, but the other half felt just as strongly that the president's offer was insulting and tantamount to blackmail. Andrew Young of the SCLC led the pro-compromise pragmatists, while Jim Forman, Lewis, and Cleveland Sellers of SNCC took the lead for the other side.

Trying to avoid a full-blown schism, Lewis weighed his words carefully and did his best to cool Forman and Sellers down. But he shared his SNCC colleagues' deep disappointment that any movement leader would seriously consider accepting the compromise. "The idea that Johnson was dictating everything here, from the number of delegates to who those delegates would be, was outrageous to me," he later wrote. "But beyond that was the simple fact that too many people had worked too hard for too long to be told that they would now be treated as honorary guests and nothing more. That was too much, and that's what I told Andy. 'We've shed too much blood,' I said.

'We've come much too far to back down now.' Anyone who had been in Mississippi that summer, I said, would feel the same way."

At the same time, Lewis made it clear that the decision should be left up to the MFDP delegates themselves, that neither SNCC nor any other group should tell them what to do. So he and SNCC stepped back to let the Mississippians find their way to a satisfactory resolution. What he did not fully understand or expect, however, was how much pressure the Johnson forces were willing to exert to get their way. Wiretapping the rooms where the MFDP delegates and movement leaders were meeting, the president's men took every advantage to counter their opponents' tactics. They also pressed Roy Wilkins, Bayard Rustin, and even Martin Luther King Jr. into service as lobbyists for the compromise. It was a matter of "practical politics," the moderate civil rights leaders told the delegates, a means of ensuring the election of a president who would advance the cause of civil rights. After considerable hesitancy, the MFDP's most trusted attorney, Joseph Rauh, joined the lobbying effort, largely because he believed it was crucial to secure Humphrey's selection as Johnson's running mate. Rauh, who was later cast as a turncoat by many MFDP delegates and supporters, would come to regret this decision. But at the time he thought he was acting in the best interests of the broader movement.

When the MFDP delegation met to vote on whether to accept the two-seat offer, only a handful of delegates, led by Aaron Henry and Ed King, argued in favor of acceptance. And when the vote was actually taken, even they voted to turn Johnson down, making the rejection unanimous. Lewis and his SNCC colleagues were elated, particularly after the MFDP delegates staged a sit-in on the convention floor on Tuesday evening, the second night of the convention. Since the all-white Mississippi Democratic Party delegates had withdrawn from the convention after being required to sign a loyalty oath to the Democratic ticket, the seats reserved for the Mississippi delegation were empty until the MFDP insurgents sat in them. Security guards promptly escorted them out of the hall, but the next night, after the chairs were removed, they returned to stand defiantly in the same space. This time they were left alone and allowed to witness firsthand the nominations of Johnson and Humphrey. Lewis remembered them standing there "forlorn and abandoned," silent but determined witnesses to a political drama gone wrong.[3]

The next morning, as Lewis and the Democrats left Atlantic City to return home, he felt that he, too, had become a historical witness—one who had just experienced a major turning point in the struggle for civil rights. "I'm absolutely convinced of that," he wrote nearly a quarter century later. "Until then, despite every setback and disappointment and obstacle we had faced over the years, the belief still prevailed that the system would work, the system would listen, the system would respond. Now, for the first time, we had made our way to the very center of the system. We had played by the rules, done everything we were supposed to do, had played the game as exactly as required, had arrived at the doorstep and found the door slammed in our face."

The MFDP had lost, having been crushed by power politics, but the biggest losers, Lewis concluded, were Lyndon Johnson and the American people. In the election later that fall, Johnson lost the support of the white Democrats of the Deep South, but losing the electoral votes of the five Southern states won by Barry Goldwater was of little consequence. To Lewis, the loss that mattered—that changed the course of American history—was the loss of faith among the American people. "That loss of faith would spread through Lyndon Johnson's term in office, from civil rights and into the issue of Vietnam," he observed in 1998. "That loss of faith in the President would eventually grow into a loss of faith in the federal government as a whole, and it would extend out of the 1960s, into the '70s and '80s, and on up to today."

Lewis's reductionist interpretation of post-1964 American politics might be flawed and incomplete. But he was on solid ground when he detected a fundamental shift in the movement's orientation toward political and social reform. The betrayal of the MFDP in Atlantic City, in his view, "was a major letdown for hundreds and thousands of civil rights workers, both black and white, young and old people alike who had given everything they had to prove that you could work through the system. They felt cheated. They felt robbed. It sent a lot of them outside the system. It turned many of them into radicals and revolutionaries. It fueled the very forces of protest and discontent that would eventually drive Lyndon Johnson out of office. It was a classic tragedy—a man unwittingly bringing about his own downfall by what he thought was the right decision."

The tragic legacy of Atlantic City influenced relationships and behavior throughout the movement, especially in SNCC, where solidarity born of common struggle began to decline in the face of suspicion and recrimination. "The movement started turning on itself," Lewis recalled with sadness. "Fingers of betrayal were pointed left and right. The 'white liberals' were not to be trusted—that was one lesson many said they had learned. Men like Joe Rauh were dismissed as manipulators, clever double-crossers. 'Double crossers'—you heard that word a lot, along with 'Uncle Tom.' Anyone who trusted the white man at this point, who believed we could work together, was a fool, a Tom." Even some of Lewis's most trusted allies succumbed to this separatist mistrust. Bob Moses, the architect of Freedom Summer and a longtime advocate of interracial cooperation, "left Atlantic City vowing never to speak to a white man again. Within a year he would change his name and move to Africa."[4]

* * *

By the beginning of September, Lewis was feeling increasingly isolated and discouraged. The MFDP was still intact, but Freedom Summer was over, an experiment that had run its course, leaving little sense of accomplishment. Seventeen thousand Black men and women had filled out voter registration forms, and the freedom schools had provided at least a glimpse of what a more democratic Mississippi might look like. But the stark realities of Black life and political power across the state remained unchanged. "For all the positive seeds that were planted that summer," Lewis observed, "the end result for most of the people who experienced it was pain, sorrow, frustration, and fear. No one who went into Mississippi that summer came out the same. So many young men and women, children really, teenagers eighteen and nineteen years old, went down there so idealistic, so full of hope, and came out hardened in a way, hardened by the hurt and hatred they saw or suffered, or both. So many people I knew, so many people I *recruited*, came out of that summer wounded, both literally and emotionally."

And yet, when seen through a broader lens, Freedom Summer also created, in Lewis's view, an "atmosphere of openness and breaking down barriers" that went beyond interracial cooperation, "that extended into everything from sexuality to gender roles, from communal living to identification with working classes." Paradoxically, the same experience that produced so much heartache also produced a model of movement culture that transformed citizen politics later in the decade. "I have no doubt," Lewis asserted, "that the Mississippi Summer Project, in the end, led to the liberating of America, the opening up of our society. The peace movement, the women's movement, the gay movement—they all have roots that can be traced back to Mississippi in the summer of '64."[5]

Lewis's recognition of Freedom Summer's ultimate legacy would come later, of course. In the immediate aftermath of the Atlantic City fiasco, as chairman he had to deal with the fragmentation of SNCC. He did his best to stay above the fray, reminding himself and others that nothing would be gained by giving in to self-indulgent despondency. As he later explained, "When I first got involved in the movement as a teenager, I recognized that this struggle was going to be long, hard and tedious, and that I would have to pace myself and be patient where necessary, while continuing to push and push and push, no matter what." Even so, he was both physically and mentally exhausted by the end of the summer, as close to burnout as he had ever been.

Lewis needed a break from the intensity of the movement, and fortunately, Harry Belafonte, a longtime SNCC supporter, had devised a plan for just such a hiatus. Earlier in the summer, he had approached Lewis and Forman on behalf of Sékou Touré, the president of the West African nation of Guinea. Touré had asked Belafonte to organize a visiting delegation of civil rights activists, young men and women who could come to Guinea to meet some of their African counterparts. When Belafonte extended the invitation to the SNCC leaders, they leaped at the chance to form a delegation. After raising most of the money needed to fund the trip, Lewis and Forman selected twelve individuals to make the journey; besides the two of them, the group included Don Harris, Bob and Dona Moses, Julian Bond, Fannie Lou Hamer, Bill Hansen, Ruby Doris Robinson, and Prathia Hall. Of the ten, only Harris had visited Africa before, in 1961 as an Operation Crossroads Africa volunteer in Northern Rhodesia. Most, like Lewis, had never traveled outside the United States.

For all of the SNCC representatives, but particularly for Lewis, the trip to Africa was much more than a vacation. It was also an unprecedented opportunity to connect with African activists on their home ground. "I had met with African students in America many times, on college campuses around the country," Lewis later noted. "I'd read the newspapers and watched television reports and had a basic sense of current events across Africa, the wave of liberation movements there. I felt a sense of communion, a sense of fellowship with these rising nations of Africa, and especially with the young men and women who were so much at the heart of it all."

Accompanied by Belafonte and his wife, Julie, the SNCC delegation flew from New York to Dakar, Senegal, on September 11. Greeted at the Dakar airport with a reception and signs that read "WELCOME SNCC TO SENEGAL," they soon flew on to Conakry, the capital of Guinea. Touring Guinea and meeting Touré, a Muslim intellectual who would remain president until his death in 1984, Lewis and his colleagues encountered revelation after revelation in the six-year-old independent nation that was sliding into autocracy. Yet even before they met Touré, there was a string of surprises, beginning with the crew of the Air Guinea flight into Conakry. The flight, Lewis observed, "was piloted by two black men and staffed by black flight attendants. With all the flying I'd done in the United States, this was the first time I'd ever seen black pilots. And that was just the beginning. In every city I visited, I was struck by the sight of black police officers, black men behind the desks in banks, black people not just on bicycles but also behind the wheels of Mercedes. Black people in *charge*."[6]

After a week in Guinea, most of the SNCC group returned to the United States, but Lewis and Harris remained in Africa for two more months, traveling through Liberia and Ghana (where they spent time with the expatriate African American actor and radical activist Julian Mayfield, whose wife worked for Ghana's president Kwame Nkrumah) in West Africa and on to Ethiopia, Kenya, Zambia, and Egypt. Their unexpected three-day stop in Kenya—the result of a mechanical failure on the southward flight to Zambia—led to the biggest surprise of the entire journey. Sitting in a courtyard café at the New Stanley Hotel in Nairobi, they were stunned to encounter Malcolm X, who was visiting Kenya after attending a nonaligned nations conference in Cairo, where he touted the Organization of Afro-American Unity (OAAU) as a means of bringing the plight of Black America to the attention of the United Nations. The three men spent the afternoon and part of the following day together, talking about everything from the state of the movement and the world to the Nation of Islam, the Black nationalist organization that Malcolm X had helped lead before his resignation earlier in the year. Much of the conversation focused on Malcolm X's new emphasis on class as opposed to race, and on his eleven-nation African tour devoted to informing Africans about the current civil rights struggle in the United States.

To Lewis and Harris's surprise, he praised their efforts during Freedom Summer and the Democratic National Convention. This was not the Malcolm X who had often ridiculed the movement in the past. He seemed optimistic and cooperative, and supportive of a new solidarity that would advance the cause of civil rights. He encouraged them to think globally and to engage with the anti-imperialistic struggles in Africa and other parts of the so-called Third World. Although the two SNCC leaders had met him before, they had never had the opportunity to talk with him in such depth and candor, and they came away from the meeting with a new appreciation for his potential as a valuable partner in the struggle for civil and human rights. Their only major concern was his obvious nervousness about his personal safety. Both his behavior and some of his comments communicated that he felt he was in danger of being killed by agents of Elijah Muhammad, the imperious founder of the Nation of Islam. Four months later, on February 21, 1965, he was shot to death at the Audubon Ballroom in Manhattan as he was preparing to deliver an address to the OAAU. The following week, Malcolm X's funeral at the Faith Temple Church in Harlem attracted more than a thousand mourners, but only three civil rights leaders chose to attend—Jim Farmer, and Lewis and Forman representing SNCC.

Following the impromptu meeting with Malcolm X, Lewis and Harris proceeded on to Lusaka, the Zambian capital, to attend a weeklong celebration of national independence. Having spent most of 1961 in what was then Northern Rhodesia, Harris was thrilled to witness the formal transition from British colony to independent nation. The pomp and circumstance of the ceremony was elaborate and joyous as 175,000 people crowded into the newly constructed Independence Stadium to celebrate amid marching bands, fireworks, flaming torches, and Zambia's first president, Kenneth Kaunda. "I'd never seen anything like it in my life," Lewis later commented, "this nation of black and brown people tasting their moment of history, celebrating their first step into liberation. I remember thinking that this needed to be felt in Alabama and Mississippi. This needed to *happen* in those places."

With their racial and international education almost complete, Lewis and Harris traveled home through Ethiopia, Egypt, Italy, and France. Arriving in the Ethiopian capital of Addis Ababa on November 2, the eve of the American election, they listened to the returns broadcast over Voice of America radio. Pleased that Johnson won a resounding victory over the conservative Republican Goldwater, they nonetheless felt a twinge of regret that they had not been able to cast their own votes on behalf of freedom and liberal democracy, an ironic twist for two voting rights activists eligible to vote in a presidential election for the first time. From Addis Ababa they flew to Cairo, where they visited the pyramids at Giza and stayed with W. E. B. Du Bois's stepson David Graham Du Bois, a journalist who introduced them to a number of independence movement activists from across the African continent. After several days in Cairo, they moved on to Rome and Paris, a heady experience for two young Americans whose previous experience with northern Africa and Europe was limited to images in *National Geographic* magazine. In Paris, he and Harris spent a dazzling evening of nightclub hopping with Hazel Scott, the Trinidadian-born jazz singer, pianist, civil rights activist, and former wife of Harlem congressman Adam Clayton Powell Jr. Finally, after seventy-two days abroad, they flew to New York, landing at LaGuardia Airport on November 22, the first anniversary of John Kennedy's assassination.[7]

*　*　*

After their return, Lewis and Harris wrote a long report detailing what they had done and learned in Africa, and in several interviews with the press they tried to convey how enlightening and eye-opening the trip had been. At the same time, they inquired about what had happened in SNCC while they were gone. Things had not been going well before they left, but they soon discovered that the situation had grown much worse during their ten-week absence, deteriorating to the point of crisis. "By the time I returned that November," Lewis recalled, "SNCC was shaking at its very roots, fragmenting and threatening to fall apart under its own weight."

Part of the problem was the growth in membership since the beginning of Freedom Summer. A number of summer volunteers had decided to remain in Mississippi as field workers, expanding the once meager staff to more than two hundred. SNCC was no longer a small group that fostered intimate connections. Before 1964, they had "considered themselves a band of brothers and sisters, a circle of trust," and the organization generally had rendered decisions through hard-earned consensus. Their meetings, Lewis remembered fondly, had resembled "'soul sessions'—freewheeling, wide-ranging, 'anything goes' discussions through which we would finally arrive at a conclusion or decision accepted by everyone." "That type of process is workable," he pointed out, "when the participants all know and trust one another. But it becomes a problem when the participants were strangers. And that's what had happened by the fall of 1964—there were a lot of people in SNCC who simply didn't know one another."[8]

The factionalism that now disrupted the organization was partly a matter of race, Black versus white, but even more pervasive was an ideological and experiential split between what Lewis called "salt-of-the-earth Southern black men and women" and "Northern, college-educated intellectuals." The latter group tended to be more political and militant than their Black Southern colleagues, placing a much greater emphasis on Black nationalism and racial identity. The Black Southerners, he explained, "saw less need to take on the trappings of Africa, or to assert their Blackness through things such as clothing and appearance. They didn't feel the same need to discover and assert their Black identity, I guess, because they had never lost it in the first place."

The relationship between racial identity and politics had become an issue of considerable interest to Lewis since his experiences in Mississippi during Freedom Summer, and especially after his recent encounter with Africa. As he revealed to the Justice Department official Harris Wofford in March 1965, Lewis now realized that "campaigns to win the right to vote in the Black Belt had as large an impact—and required no less courage than—the earlier sit-ins and Freedom Rides." He also told Wofford that "the African trip had given him a new perspective, in which he felt more American and attached more importance to the attainment of political power." A month earlier, during a SNCC staff meeting at which he was reelected as chairman and presided over a strengthening of SNCC's executive committee, he responded to the rising politics of race within the organization by clarifying his belief in interracial cooperation. While he insisted on a continued role for white activists in SNCC, he conceded that "the organization must be black-led and black-dominated." As he later explained to the Atlanta journalist Pat Watters, it was important for the African American freedom struggle to be controlled "by people who are the victims—because they have insights that the non-whites can't have." Driven in part by the perceived necessity of taking a middle-of-the-road position that would forestall the efforts of those who wanted SNCC to be a Black-only organization, this statement was as close as he would ever come to an acceptance of racial hierarchy.

Lewis also had to deal with a growing divide over matters of structure and leadership. One group, a solid majority of the SNCC staff, chafed at any suggestion that the organization needed more structure or direction from the top. Known as the "Freedom High" faction, they practiced a highly individualistic, self-directed form of activism. As Lewis characterized the core of their approach to movement culture, "No one is responsible to anyone or answerable to anything other than his or her own instinct, his own spirit—a spirit fueled by the righteous, sweeping sense of almighty *freedom*. Freedom High. It meant exactly what it said. You were *high* on freedom." At the other end of the spectrum, another group wanted to bring a measure of order and discipline to the organization. Finally, in the middle, there were those, including Lewis, who sought a creative balance between structure and individual freedom.

There were also disagreements over how to handle the Communist influence and infiltration issue, the problem of declining funding, and how to deal with charges of radicalism being leveled at SNCC by conservative, moderate, and even liberal observers, including some civil rights leaders. All of these issues and several others were hashed out at several meetings held while Lewis was in Africa. Courtland Cox, who was in charge of the SNCC office while Lewis and Forman were abroad, convened the first of these gatherings in October. Held at the Gammon Theological Seminary in Atlanta, this "emergency" meeting was open to all SNCC members, not just the staff, a decision guaranteeing the meeting would turn into a free-for-all. Forman returned from Africa just in time to participate, but he had no luck in bringing order out of the chaos. For five days, the discussion, mostly about leadership, went back and forth treading the same ground, with accusations, recriminations, finger-pointing, and shouting matches filling the air. The stated agenda included consideration of a Freedom Summer–style "Black Belt Summer Project" to be held in several Deep South states during the summer of 1965, but the unruly group never got around to it.

The Freedom High faction, led by Stokely Carmichael and Cox, dominated much of the deliberation, which eventually centered on their proposal to dismantle most of the organization's structure and hierarchy. Their suggestions included abolishing the central and executive committees and the chairmanship; and closing the Atlanta office and substituting "a loosely knit, geographically scattered, rotating circle of 'leaders.'" Several Southern Black staff members countered with calls for more structure and centralized authority. But the meeting adjourned with no clear resolution of any of the controversies that had sparked so much divisiveness. The one individual who might have cut through the tension with some therapeutic words of wisdom was Moses, the most revered figure in SNCC. But he chose to sit through it all silent as a stone, a testament to his lingering feelings of guilt about his guiding role in what he saw as the Freedom Summer fiasco.[9]

A month later, just before Lewis's return, many of the same issues plagued a weeklong staff retreat held in Waveland, Mississippi, a gulf coast town near the Louisiana border. This time the debates were more structured, with a number of the 160 attendees presenting position papers on an array of topics ranging from the racial composition of the staff to the role and treatment of women in the movement. Casey Hayden and Mary King, two white feminists who had been fuming about the organization's condescension toward female staff members, presented a provocative paper attacking "assumptions of male superiority," claiming that such attitudes were "as widespread and deep-rooted and every much as crippling to the woman as assumptions of white supremacy are to the Negro." Some of the male staff members took exception to this complaint to the point of openly ridiculing it. Carmichael, for one, responded with the sexist quip that the only position for women in SNCC was "prone." The suspicion that he was being facetious did little to assuage the feelings of Hayden, King, and the other women in the room.[10]

Lewis knew nothing about any of this until he was briefed following his return. But once he heard what had happened, both at the Atlanta meeting in October and later at Waveland, he feared that SNCC faced a dark future. Years later, when he looked back on this period of trials and tribulations, he tried to explain the root cause of the malaise. "There was no question that we had other important issues to settle, issues that cut to the very core of how we defined ourselves," he wrote. "But none of those issues mattered as much to me as how we felt about and related to one another.... The biggest problem we had, as I saw it, was the loss of that unity of spirit and purpose that we had shared in the beginning, the loss of faith in one another. We had become riddled with infighting and suspicion and rumors and behind-the-scenes politics—in other words, we were becoming much like the organizations we had opposed for so long."

Lewis made a valiant effort to repair the damage inflicted while he was away. But he had a difficult time heading off the swirl of rumors and recriminations that seemed to expand with every passing week. He also couldn't help but feel partially responsible for the organization's declining morale and civility. As soon as his plane touched down in Atlanta, he had to deal with complaints that his extended sojourn in Africa had left SNCC vulnerable to dissension and misinformation. Bond, Bill Hansen, Charles Sherrod, and a host of others, some of whom were among his closest friends, chastised him for staying away for too long. "I should have been more savvy," he remembered them saying, "more politically astute ... I shouldn't have been so naive ... so trusting." It was his nature to be trusting, and he couldn't operate any other way. But he knew there was considerable validity in the criticism of his absence. For some, his reputation for dependability—for being the most diligent of activists—would never recover.[11]

As the year drew to a close, Lewis tried to make up for lost time. But he was confounded by a series of frustrations, including a persistent rumor that Carmichael was plotting a "coup" that would remove him as chairman. There was also a rumor that he was leading the organization toward a covert alliance with the Communist Party. At one point, several observers outside SNCC even claimed that Lewis and Harris had not been in Africa at all, that they had actually made a secret trip to Red China. Lewis didn't want to dignify this ludicrous claim with a denial, but the situation in the white South was so tense that he knew there were some who actually believed it.

Lewis was more concerned with the mix of news from the Southern front. On December 4, he received word that twenty-one white Mississippians had been arrested for their involvement in the abduction and murder of Goodman, Schwerner, and Chaney. But a week later, U.S. district judge Harold Cox, a notorious white supremacist, dismissed all of the charges. That same week, Lewis was elated when Dr. King became the second African American (the diplomat Ralph Bunche was the first, in 1950) to be awarded the Nobel Peace Prize. Yet even this bit of good news was spoiled when Lewis discovered that very few of his SNCC colleagues felt the same way. Resentment of—and even outright contempt for—King was palpable among many SNCC activists. Though still chairman of the organization, Lewis had become a lonely figure cut off from most of his comrades.

In mid-December, in an attempt to boost SNCC's perilous financial situation, Lewis traveled to New York and Philadelphia on a four-day fundraising trip. But his efforts were hampered by widespread speculation among potential donors and supporters that SNCC was on the verge of splitting into two or more separate organizations. Alarmed, he decided to send an open letter to SNCC's entire membership countering the breakup rumor and other falsehoods.

The three-page letter began with a brief recap of his African trip and a statement that this recent experience had confirmed his belief "that the social, economic, and political destiny of the black people of America is inseparable from that of our brothers of Africa." He then moved on to debunk the rumors circulating through and around the organization—the impending coup, Communist infiltration, the alleged trip to Peking, and the speculation that he was planning to leave SNCC to resume his studies at Fisk. He insisted he "had no plans for leaving the Movement to enter school" in the coming year. "I will be involved in the struggle one way or another till every victory is won," he promised.[12]

SNCC was in peril, he conceded, but not because of any fundamental weaknesses in the organization's programs. The financial situation was dire and growing worse with all the uncertainty about SNCC's future. "In addition," he warned, "we are under attack from many quarters—the press and other civil rights groups. We must understand these rumors and the 'red-baiting' as effective and destructive political gimmicks, and we cannot take this lightly. The situation demands that we reassure our friends, supporters, and the American public that we are a unified, effective, strong and vital force on the American scene for social, economic, and political change." This last assertion about SNCC's unity and effectiveness represented a bit of wishful thinking on his part. But the deeper truth he wanted to stress was the value and unique character of SNCC's work in the field. "I am asking of all the staff to speak the truth of the work and programs of SNCC," he declared. "We have nothing to make apologies for. Our projects and programs are worthy of support." He then laid out his schedule for the next month, during which he would visit all of the organization's ongoing projects, from eastern Arkansas and Mississippi to central Alabama and southwest Georgia.

Lewis's strategy was to implore his colleagues to produce fewer words and more action. Turning to the work at hand—the work that had led movement activists to get involved in the first place—was, he believed, the best way to resolve a crisis born of dissension and doubt: "I still believed, as always," he later stated, "that nothing would unify us, nothing would shore up our crumbling foundation, like another battle. We needed, that December, to turn our energy and passions not on one another but on a deserving target."[13]

CHAPTER 9

Selma and Bloody Sunday

T HE TARGET that John Lewis settled on—the local movement he hoped would renew SNCC's flagging spirit—was the voting rights struggle in Selma. For nearly two years, the central Alabama project that Bernard LaFayette had initiated in January 1963 had met with stiff resistance from the white supremacist political and law enforcement leaders of Selma and the surrounding Black Belt counties of Dallas, Perry, Wilcox, and Lowndes. Even so, the project had fostered several local movements that justified Lewis's decision to extend SNCC's mobilization effort there into the new year. Despite the rising threat of violence, he was not about to abandon the brave foot soldiers who had courageously responded to SNCC's call to action, especially now that he was convinced SNCC had a great deal to gain in terms of solidarity and morale by doubling down in central Alabama.

One complicating factor, however, was the looming presence of Dr. Martin Luther King Jr. and the SCLC. Most of Lewis's SNCC colleagues resented the SCLC's tendency to take over existing protest campaigns after SNCC had completed the hard and often dangerous work of grassroots organizing. That is what happened in Albany, Georgia, in 1962, and there was widespread concern in SNCC that it would happen again in Selma. Lewis was always open to collaboration with King and the SCLC, but very few others in SNCC shared his view.

By early 1964, the SCLC had developed a tentative plan to replace SNCC as the primary organization working for voting rights in Selma and central

Alabama. The plan finally became public in December, when the leadership of the Dallas County Voters' League—known as the Committee of Fifteen—formally invited the SCLC to oversee their voting rights campaign. On December 28, at a meeting attended by leaders from several civil rights organizations, the SCLC staff announced that King would kick off its Selma campaign with a public address in the city on January 2. Speaking for the organization, Andrew Young predicted that it would take at least six months for the campaign to bring a measure of democracy to the "most oppressive" community in the South.

This bold move sent ripples of anger through SNCC's ranks, even though the organization's chairman steadfastly refused to join the chorus of criticism. To Lewis, any activity that benefited the movement as a whole took precedence over the sectarian interests of any one organization. Having witnessed the harshness of the white regime in Selma on several occasions during the past two years, he suspected it would take more than one organization to bring political democracy to the city. As in the past, he welcomed collaboration between SNCC and the SCLC, the organization his mentor had created in 1957. If the competition moving into Selma had been the NAACP or the National Urban League, he might have made a different judgment. But he considered working with King to be an honor and a privilege, whatever organizational complications arose. After all, he had been a member of the SCLC's board of directors since 1962, even though many among SNCC's leaders and rank and file believed this laid him open to charges of divided loyalty and conflict of interest. Such suspicions had been rife throughout his chairmanship, but during the Selma crisis, when the tension between SNCC and the SCLC reached new heights, they would prove to be increasingly difficult to quell.[1]

When King arrived in Selma on January 2, more than seven hundred Black citizens, including Lewis and a small contingent from SNCC, jammed into Brown Chapel AME Church to hear him issue a challenge to the city's white supremacist power structure. King didn't disappoint those who came to witness a righteous call for protest and defiance. As Lewis recalled King's words, there was "a laying down of the gauntlet." In two weeks' time, the SCLC leader promised, the movement would hold massive street demonstrations in and around Selma. "We will seek to arouse the federal government by marching by the thousands," he declared, counseling the crowd: "We must be willing to go to jail by the thousands."

Within a week, the Johnson administration, which had previously signaled that it would not introduce voting rights legislation until 1966, announced that it was accelerating the voting rights legislative schedule by a full year. If all went well, 1965 would be the year for the long-awaited voting rights act. Although this was welcome news in movement circles, few members of SNCC or the SCLC had much confidence that Lyndon Johnson, the man who had thwarted the MFDP's hopes in Atlantic City, would actually deliver on his promise. At this point, no one in either organization was inclined to let up on the pressure being exerted in Selma. SNCC continued to maintain its Alabama headquarters in a downtown Selma office, and the SCLC promptly opened a "command center" divided between Brown Chapel and a second church nearby.

The Reverend Hosea Williams, a veteran organizer from Georgia, and Jim Bevel, Lewis's former SNCC colleague, were put in charge of the SCLC operation, fortunate choices that for a time inhibited any overt conflict between the two organizations. With Lewis temporarily retiring to the background, Bevel (who Lewis insisted "would always be one of us") served as "the spearhead, wearing that skullcap and his SNCC-style overalls, preaching as much as speaking, gathering the masses, getting the people of Selma and the surrounding counties—hundreds of people, thousands—ready to be out in front of that courthouse every day beginning the middle of the month."

By the time King returned to Selma on January 14, the expectations of a major mobilization and an impending confrontation had risen to an unprecedented level, not only among SCLC and SNCC staff members but also among the mass of eager Black registrants, commonly known in Selma as the "foot soldiers" of the voting rights movement. The dominant spirit here, Lewis observed, was strikingly different from what it had been in Birmingham in 1963, "where there were lots of generals on the scene, lots of staff and leaders—the Fred Shuttlesworths and the Dr. Kings—carefully planning every move, all of it very organized from the top down. Selma was more of

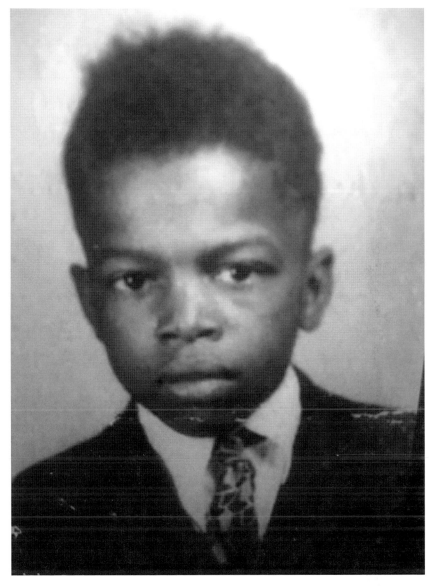

Eleven-year-old John Lewis, the "Boy Preacher" of Pike County, Alabama, wearing his Sunday best, 1951. (Courtesy of the Lewis Family)

Blood-spattered Freedom Riders John Lewis and Jim Zwerg wait to be taken to a hospital after being attacked by a white mob at the Montgomery, Alabama, Greyhound bus station, May 20, 1961. (Everett Collection Inc / Alamy Stock Photo)

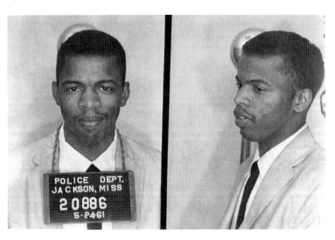

John Lewis's Freedom Rider mugshot taken after his arrest for "breach of peace" in Jackson, Mississippi, May 24, 1961. (Kypros / Getty Images)

Civil rights leaders, including the organizational heads known as the Big Six, meet at the NAACP headquarters in New York to plan the March on Washington for Jobs and Freedom, July 29, 1963. *Left to right:* Bayard Rustin, Jack Greenberg (NAACP Legal Defense Fund), Whitney Young, James Farmer, Roy Wilkins, Martin Luther King Jr., John Lewis, and A. Philip Randolph. (Everett Collection Inc / Alamy Stock Photo)

John Lewis, chairman of the Student Nonviolent Coordinating Committee, speaks at the Lincoln Memorial to a March on Washington crowd estimated at 250,000, August 28, 1963. (Bettmann / Getty Images)

John Lewis (*right*) and Hosea Williams lead a group of six hundred marchers across the Edmund Pettus Bridge in Selma, Alabama, March 7, 1965. (Alabama Department of Archives and History, Donated by Alabama Media Group / Photo by Tom Lankford, *Birmingham News*)

Bloody Sunday in Selma, Alabama, March 7, 1965. John Lewis (on the ground wearing a tan raincoat) and other marchers were attacked by state troopers after crossing the Edmund Pettus Bridge. Lewis suffered a fractured skull during the attack. (Everett Collection Historical / Alamy Stock Photo)

After five days on the road, the Selma-to-Montgomery marchers approach the steps of the Alabama State Capitol in Montgomery, March 25, 1965. Followed by an estimated thirty thousand marchers, Lewis and other leaders can be seen in the front row. *Left to right:* John Lewis (wearing light-colored vest), Ralph Abernathy, Ruth and Ralph Bunche, Martin Luther King Jr., Coretta King, Fred Shuttlesworth, and Hosea Williams (holding child). (Alpha Historica / Alamy Stock Photo)

Sitting in his office at the Southern Regional Council headquarters in Atlanta, Voter Education Project director John Lewis holds up a VEP poster with the message, "Hands that pick cotton . . . now can pick our public officials," October 10, 1971. (Bettmann / Getty Images)

John Lewis and other civil rights leaders walk across the Edmund Pettus Bridge in Selma, Alabama, to commemorate the twentieth anniversary of Bloody Sunday and the Selma-to-Montgomery march, March 3, 1985. *Left to right:* Bernard LaFayette, Lewis, Jesse Jackson, Joseph and Evelyn Lowery, Coretta King. (Bettmann / Getty Images)

Atlanta City councilman John Lewis talks to reporters after upsetting Julian Bond in the Democratic primary runoff election for Georgia's Fifth Congressional District seat, September 3, 1986. His wife, Lillian, is standing to his left. (Bettmann / Getty Images)

Representative John Lewis is handcuffed and arrested in front of the Sudanese embassy in Washington after participating in a demonstration protesting the Sudan government's policy of genocidal warfare in the province of Darfur, April 27, 2009. (ZUMA Press, Inc. / Alamy Stock Photo)

John Lewis receives the Presidential Medal of Freedom from President Barack Obama, February 15, 2011. (Abaca Press / Alamy Stock Photo)

John Lewis speaks at a rally in Washington commemorating the fiftieth anniversary of the Voting Rights Act, July 30, 2015. (REUTERS / Alamy Stock Photo)

Representative John Lewis, speaking in the House Chamber, holds up a copy of the U.S. Constitution to remind his colleagues of their sworn duty to abide by its principles, March 3, 2016. (US Senate / Alamy Stock Photo)

John Lewis visits the Black Lives Matter Plaza, just north of the White House in Washington, D.C., June 7, 2020, six weeks before his death. (NurPhoto SRL / Alamy Stock Photo)

A horse-drawn carriage takes John Lewis on his final crossing of the Edmund Pettus Bridge in Selma and on to the Alabama State Capitol in Montgomery, July 26, 2020. (Tribune Content Agency LLC / Alamy Stock Photo)

a bottom-up campaign, of the people acting with minimal direction from leaders."[2]

*   *   *

This was the kind of grassroots campaign that Lewis and many of his SNCC colleagues had been encouraging since the organization's founding five years earlier. When the first Selma march commenced on January 18, Lewis walked alongside Dr. King with his head held high, confident the movement that had experienced so much dissension and disappointment during the past six months was entering a new stage of solidarity. The foot soldiers, more than four hundred strong that day, gave him renewed hope that he and his fellow activists would indeed, in the words of the movement's anthem, "overcome," regardless of how intransigent or violent their opponents might be.

As expected, on the day of the first march, the white supremacist opposition surrounding the Dallas County Courthouse steps was daunting, made up not only of local reactionaries but also of right-wing, racist leaders from around the nation. Even George Lincoln Rockwell, the führer of the American Nazi Party, was on hand with several of his uniformed stormtroopers, all screaming racial epithets at the marchers, most of whom were lined up in an alley per Sheriff Jim Clark's order. After several hours of waiting to be admitted to the voter registration office, the marchers withdrew, mercifully without suffering any physical attacks or injuries. "No one was let into the courthouse," Lewis remembered, "No one was registered to vote. But the line had been drawn, and that was enough."

The violence came later that afternoon when Dr. King tried to breach the color bar at the previously whites-only Hotel Albert. As King signed the register as the hotel's "first-ever Black guest," Jimmy George Robinson, a member of the militantly white supremacist National States Rights Party, lunged at the civil rights leader and began wildly kicking and punching him. Standing nearby, Lewis responded instinctively, grabbing Robinson and immobilizing him with a bear hug. This rush to King's defense, Lewis later confessed, was one of the strangest experiences of his life. "I'm not a physical person," he explained. "I've never been in a fight in my life. I've been hit—many, many times—but I've never hit back. At that moment, though, something shot up in me, something protective, something instinctive. . . . I don't think I've ever come as close to hitting someone as I did at that moment. Maybe it was because Dr. King meant so much to me, I don't know, but that moment pushed me as close as I have ever been to the limits of my nonviolent commitments."

Lewis's commitment to nonviolence would be tested almost daily during the two weeks that followed. As the courthouse marches continued, an exasperated Sheriff Clark responded with increasing harshness, ordering mass arrests and doling out punishment whenever his anger got the best of him. On the second day of marching, as national news reporters looked on, Clark grabbed fifty-three-year-old Amelia Boynton "by the back of her collar and pushed her roughly half a block into a patrol car." One of the most revered members of Selma's Black community and the mother of Bruce Boynton, the plaintiff in the 1960 *Boynton v. Virginia* case that helped trigger the Freedom Rides, she ended up in jail, as did sixty-seven other protesters, including Lewis, the following day. Lewis's arrest came after he asked Clark if the protesters could enter the courthouse through the front door. Clark gave him one minute to move away from the front steps before arresting him and everyone in his group. Lewis spent the next five nights at a county work farm on the outskirts of the city as the daily downtown marches continued.[3]

Upon his release on January 25, Lewis returned to the courthouse, where he witnessed an unexpected altercation between Clark and a Black hotel maid named Annie Lee Cooper. A feisty, 235-pound woman, Cooper, after being shoved by Clark, sent the sheriff reeling with a punch to the head. Subdued by Clark's deputies, Cooper dared the sheriff to strike her with his billy club, which he proceeded to do in full view of the national press. As an apostle of nonviolence, Lewis could not condone Cooper's action, but neither could he bring himself to chastise a momentary loss of control by a loyal foot soldier he had come to know and admire in recent weeks.

Later in the week, Lewis traveled to the West Coast for several days of much-needed fundraising, though this effort was hampered by his admission that SNCC was only minimally involved in the Selma protests. It was the SCLC's "show," he conceded, a fact underscored by Dr. King's high-profile arrest during his absence. Just before the arrest, the SCLC leader reminded the marchers what they were fighting for. "If Negroes could vote," he declared, "there would be no Jim Clarks, there would be no oppressive poverty directed against Negroes, our children would not be crippled by segregated schools, and the whole community might live together in harmony."

Arrested along with King were 250 other marchers, and later in the day 500 Selma schoolchildren joined them behind bars. Over the next two days, Clark arrested several hundred more students, escalating a crisis that was clearly out of control. The most alarming development for the white supremacist status quo was the recent spread of the protests to Marion, the county seat of Perry County, twenty-seven miles northwest of Selma. Six hundred and fifty marchers filled the streets of Marion on February 2, and on the following day there were seven hundred arrests that more than filled the county's jails.[4]

And if this were not enough to put central Alabama's white citizens on edge, on February 4 Selma received an unexpected visit from Malcolm X, widely considered among whites, and even among many Blacks, the most incendiary Black radical in the nation. From their conversation in Kenya the previous fall, Lewis knew that Malcolm X had adopted a new, more accepting attitude toward interracial cooperation and harmony—an attitude that the former Nation of Islam leader demonstrated in a brief speech at Brown Chapel attended by hundreds of local Black residents and dozens of leading civil rights figures, including Coretta King and Fred Shuttlesworth.

Yet even Malcolm X's scaled-down rhetoric was far more fiery and direct than the citizens of Selma, Black or white, were accustomed to hearing. In struggling for voting and other civil rights, he insisted, Black citizens had moral and political justification to seek their goals "by any means necessary." At a press conference held later that day, he elaborated on his militancy, warning whites "that the people in this part of the world would do well to listen to Dr. Martin Luther King and give him what he is asking for and give it to him fast." Otherwise, sooner or later they would face revolutionary forces employing more coercive and violent forms of insurgency. At the time, he had no way of knowing that seventeen days later, long before the violent resistance in Selma reached its apex, violence from a different source—a brutal internecine struggle in the Nation of Islam—would end his life at the age of thirty-nine.

Even before Malcolm X's admonition, the events in Selma were a subject of growing concern in Washington. Representatives and senators in both parties had begun to exert pressure on the administration to clarify its plan for voting rights legislation, and on the same afternoon as Malcolm X's speech, President Johnson told reporters "that all Americans should be indignant when one American is denied the right to vote," and he confirmed his commitment to use "the tools of the Civil Rights Act of 1964 in an effort to secure the right to vote." The next morning, the *New York Times* published Dr. King's "Letter from a Selma, Alabama Jail" calling on the nation to provide the SCLC with the financial support needed to sustain its voting rights campaigns in Selma and other Southern communities. "THIS IS SELMA, ALABAMA," he declared, "THERE ARE MORE NEGROES IN JAIL WITH ME THAN THERE ARE ON THE VOTING ROLLS."[5]

Later that day, a fifteen-member fact-finding delegation of liberal House members led by Michigan congressmen Charles Diggs and John Conyers arrived in Selma. Even some local white residents—including Roswell Falkenberry, the publisher of the *Selma Times-Journal,* and Selma's young mayor, Joe Smitherman—had called for a congressional investigation of the Selma crisis, though Smitherman and others criticized the delegation's visit as a publicity stunt designed to placate outside agitators. Soon after their arrival, King unexpectedly decided to post bail and met with them, along with Lewis, promising to come to Washington to lobby for voting rights legislation the following week. Meanwhile, Clark arrested five hundred more marchers, prompting Lewis to call Johnson's aide Clifford Alexander to complain about the arrestees' intolerable treatment in jail.

At the same time, Friends of SNCC chapters in New York, Chicago, and Washington held sit-ins in federal buildings to protest the government's inaction in Selma. At the federal courthouse in New York, for example, several Friends clashed with U.S. marshals, with punches being thrown by both sides. "That bothered me a lot," Lewis recalled. "This was just one more sign of the growing sense of impatience and militancy spreading throughout the movement, especially within SNCC. It did not bode well."

Lewis understood the growing frustration, especially in Selma, where Sheriff Clark's brutality was increasingly evident. A week after the sit-ins and the congressional delegation's visit, Clark arrested more than 160 teenagers, whom he ordered on a "forced run of more than two miles out into the countryside." Along the way Clark's deputies prodded the kids with billy clubs and electric cattle prods. Disgusted, Lewis issued a damning press release condemning Clark's extremism: "Sheriff Clark proved today beyond a shadow of a doubt that he is basically no different from a gestapo officer during the Fascist slaughter of the Jews. This is but one more example of the inhuman, animal-like treatment of the Negro people of Selma, Alabama. The nation has always come to the aid of people in foreign lands who are gripped by a reign of tyranny. Can this nation do less for the people of Selma?"[6]

* * *

More evidence of Clark's violent style of intimidation surfaced on February 16, when Lewis led a group of twenty-five protesters to the courthouse. In the front line standing on the steps was the Reverend C. T. Vivian, a former Freedom Rider and Lewis's old friend from Nashville, who confronted Clark and his deputies with bold words. "You're racists the same way Hitler was a racist!" Vivian declared, before daring Clark to hit him. Avoiding several deputies who stepped in to block their boss from taking "the bait," Clark lunged forward, punching Vivian in the mouth so hard that he broke a finger in the process. Bloodied, Vivian tumbled down the steps before being arrested and carted away.

Vivian was released the next day, and that evening King delivered a fiery speech at Brown Chapel calling for increased militancy, including nighttime marches and an expansion of SCLC-sponsored demonstrations to towns in neighboring counties. One of King's lieutenants, James Orange, had already spearheaded a series of demonstrations in the Perry County town of Marion, prompting a sharp reaction from local white officials, who asked Governor George Wallace to dispatch Colonel Al Lingo and a group of state troopers to the town. By the morning of February 18, when the troopers arrived and arrested Orange, the stage was set for a major confrontation. After 450 Black protesters gathered at Marion's Zion Methodist Church that evening to hear Vivian and another SCLC staff member, Willie Bolden, speak, the crowd began a march to the city jail to serenade Orange with freedom songs. But before they had marched a block, a force of troopers and local police, plus Clark and several of his deputies, ordered them to return to the church.

Seconds later, however, after one of the marchers knelt to pray, the white law enforcement officers started beating the marchers indiscriminately. A group of white onlookers then turned on the reporters and camera crews standing nearby, cracking heads and smashing equipment. Richard Valeriani of NBC News received a deep gash on his head and ended up in the hospital, but the worst violence was to come.

Jimmie Lee Jackson, a twenty-six-year-old army veteran, tried to flee from the assault, running alongside his grandfather, who had been struck in the head. They thought they had found refuge at the nearby Mack's Café, where Jackson's mother worked, but the state troopers pursued them into the café, where they assaulted several patrons, including Jackson's mother. When Jackson tried to shield his mother from further harm, a state trooper named James Fowler shot him twice in the abdomen. Jackson staggered into the street and collapsed on the pavement, where he remained bleeding and gasping for breath for thirty minutes before local police took him to a county infirmary. Removed to a Selma hospital later in the evening, he was listed in critical condition and not expected to live. He would die eight days later, on February 26. By then, he had become a frightening symbol of what could happen to an unarmed Black man who ran afoul of white law enforcement in the Alabama Black Belt.[7]

When Jackson was shot, Lewis was nearly two hundred miles away in Atlanta in transit to a SNCC meeting in Americus. While on the road, he heard a radio broadcast by Governor Wallace announcing a ban on all night marches and pronouncing the Marion incident the work of "professional agitators with pro-communist affiliations." Two days later, while driving back to Atlanta, Lewis received an even bigger shock when he heard the news that Malcolm X had been assassinated at the Audubon Ballroom in Harlem while speaking to members of the Organization of Afro-American Unity. The world had gone mad, Lewis thought to himself, a fear seemingly confirmed when he heard that Malcolm X had probably been killed by "his own people," the Black Muslims whom he had served so faithfully until breaking with the group's autocratic leader, Elijah Muhammad. Later in the week, he flew to Cleveland for the funeral, an eerily emotionless memorial that he found grim and depressing.

Jimmie Lee Jackson's funeral was no less depressing but far more emotional. Held on the last day of February in a small church in Marion, with four hundred mourners inside the sanctuary and six hundred more standing in the rain outside, the memorialization of the first person to die as a result of the white resistance to the Selma campaign took Lewis and many others to the edge of despair. After eulogies by King and Bevel, the mourners walked down a dirt road to the cemetery where Jackson was laid to rest. During what turned out to be a fateful procession, Bevel came up with a daring plan to carry Jackson's body all the way to Montgomery. The idea, later summarized by Lewis, was to "walk the entire fifty-four miles from Selma and lay this young man's casket on the capitol steps. Confront the governor. Confront the state of Alabama. Give them something they couldn't turn their heads away from."

During a series of meetings held over the next four days, Bevel's idea "caught fire" among the SCLC's leaders, including King, but other than Lewis, SNCC wanted no part of it. Jim Forman led the charge against the proposed march, convinced that it would be far too risky and do little or nothing for the mass of disfranchised people in central Alabama. But the SCLC would not be deterred as Bevel announced on March 3 that a march led by Dr. King would leave Selma for Montgomery the following Sunday. In response, Forman sent a protest letter to King bearing Lewis's signature. "We strongly believe that the objectives of the march do not justify the dangers," the letter stated, ". . . consequently the Student Nonviolent Coordinating Committee will only live up to those minimal commitments . . . to provide radios and cars, doctors and nurses, and nothing beyond that."[8]

Lewis strongly disagreed with his organization's withdrawal and said so at a SNCC executive committee meeting in Atlanta later in the week. Unable to convince his colleagues that SNCC had a moral obligation to participate in the march, he nonetheless declared his intention to be involved. "I grew up in Alabama." he explained. "I feel a deep kinship with the people there on a lot of levels. You know I have been to Selma many, many times. I've been arrested there. I've been jailed there. If these people want to march, I'm going to march with them. You decide what you want to do, but I'm going to march." In the end, he accepted a compromise that provided for his participation but only as an individual, not as a representative of SNCC. But he didn't like it. "That hurt me," he recalled. "I never imagined that my own organization, SNCC, would ever step aside and tell me to walk alone.... For the first time since I had become part of the movement I was walking alone, in a sense I would be walking with the people, but *my* people—the people of SNCC—would not be with me."

Just after the meeting closed around midnight, Lewis joined two colleagues, Bob Mants and Wilson Brown, for the four-hour drive to Selma. It was now the day of the march, Sunday, March 7, and after a few hours of restless sleep at SNCC's Selma Freedom House, he packed his backpack and headed for Brown Chapel, the staging ground for the fifty-four-mile march to Montgomery. Nearly six hundred marchers were there, waiting for instructions from Bevel, Williams, Young, and other members of the SCLC's staff. King was not there, having chosen to honor a commitment to preach at his home church in Atlanta, but he hoped Young could convince the crowd to delay the march until after his return to Selma the next day.[9]

It was later revealed that King's absence was also a response to a series of death threats that had surfaced during the past week, but whatever his motivation, neither he nor Young, nor anyone else in the SCLC, had the power to delay the march. The people of Selma, it became clear on that fateful afternoon, were going to march, with or without the SCLC's blessing. After King was informed there was no way to stop the march from going forward as originally planned, he instructed Young to choose himself, Bevel, or Williams to join Lewis as coleader of the march. A coin toss soon put Williams on the front line with Lewis, and by midafternoon the assembled mass was ready to head eastward out of town across the Edmund Pettus Bridge and down Highway 80 to Montgomery. At that point, no one knew how far they would actually march on the first day, or what resistance they would encounter along the way. "We expected a confrontation," Lewis remembered. "We knew Sheriff Clark had issued yet another call the evening before for even more deputies. Mass arrests would probably be made. There might be injuries. Most likely, we would be stopped at the edge of the city limits, arrested and maybe roughed up a little bit. We did not expect anything worse than that."

Before leaving the church grounds, Lewis acknowledged the reporters present by reading a short statement about why the march was important.

The assemblage then bowed their heads and knelt on one knee as Young offered a prayer. And then they were off, walking two abreast past the all-Black Carver housing project and down Water Street to the bridge crossing the river. With Lewis and Williams leading the way, the marchers grew silent as they passed by a surly group of armed white men standing in front of the city newspaper office. Turning onto a narrow sidewalk, they crossed over the west side of the bridge until they reached the peak in the middle, stopping first to look down at the water below and then east toward the end of the bridge, where a small army awaited them. There, in Lewis's words, "stood a sea of blue-helmeted, blue-uniformed Alabama state troopers, line after line of them, dozens of battle-ready lawmen stretched from one side of U.S. Highway 80 to the other." And behind them was "Sheriff Clark's posse—some on horseback, all wearing khaki clothing, many carrying clubs the size of baseball bats."

Standing a hundred feet above the mud-colored river, Williams gulped and asked Lewis if he could swim. Lewis said no, and Williams confessed that neither could he. So with no safe route of escape and hundreds of marchers trailing behind them, they had no choice but to move forward to the end of the bridge, where Major John Cloud of the state police was standing holding a bullhorn. "This is an unlawful assembly," Cloud bellowed. "Your march is not conducive to the public safety. You are ordered to disperse and go back to your church or to your homes." When Williams asked to have a word with the major, the response was, "There is no word to be had." Cloud then gave them two minutes to turn around and disperse, but complying was all but impossible. Lewis suggested that they all kneel in place and pray, but before the idea could be acted on, less than a minute after Cloud's warning, the troopers were ordered to advance.

The mayhem that followed would be seared in Lewis's memory, and in the memories of the millions of Americans who watched the videotape of what became known as Bloody Sunday. "The troopers and possemen swept forward as one," Lewis remembered, "like a human wave, a blur of blue shirts and billy clubs and bullwhips. We had no chance to turn and retreat. There were six hundred people behind us, bridge railings to either side and the river below. I remember how vivid the sounds were as the troopers rushed toward us—the clunks of the troopers' heavy boots, the whoops of rebel yells from the white onlookers, the clip-clop of horses' hooves hitting the hard asphalt of the highway, the voice of a woman shouting, 'Get 'em! *Get* the niggers!'"

Lewis was one of the first to go down, clubbed on the left side of his head by a burly trooper. "I didn't feel any pain," he later insisted, "just the thud of the blow, and my legs giving way. I raised an arm—a reflex motion—as I curled up in the 'prayer for protection' position. And then the same trooper hit me again. And everything started to spin." As he strained to remain conscious, a cloud of highly toxic C-4 tear gas wafted over him and the other marchers. Choking and coughing, he slid into nausea and an eerie, out-of-body feeling: "I remember how strangely calm I felt as I thought, This is it. People are going to die here. *I'm* going to die here." Though no one actually died as a result of the assault, many were struck down or trampled as the marchers retreated in terror. Thirteen, including Lewis, would require hospitalization, and scores of others suffered serious injuries both physical and psychological.[10]

As Roy Reed of the *New York Times* described the scene on the bridge, "The first 10 or 20 Negroes were swept to the ground screaming, arms and legs flying. . . . Those still on their feet retreated. The troopers continued pushing, using both the force of their bodies and the prodding of their nightsticks. A cheer went up from the white spectators lining the south side of the highway. The mounted possemen spurred their horses and rode at a run into the retreating mass. The Negroes cried out as they crowded together for protection, and the whites on the sidelines whooped and cheered."

From inside the melee, Lewis regained enough consciousness to witness some of the worst of the carnage. "There was mayhem all around me," he recalled years later. "I could see a young kid—a teenaged boy—sitting on the ground with a gaping cut in his head, the blood just gushing out. Several women, including Mrs. Boynton, were lying on the pavement and the grass median. People were weeping. Some were vomiting from the tear gas. Men on horses were moving in all directions, purposely riding over the top of fallen people, bringing their animals' hooves down on the shoulders, stomachs and legs. The mob of white onlookers had joined in now, jumping cameramen and reporters." The brutal pursuit continued for several agonizing minutes. "I was up now and moving back across the bridge, with troopers and possemen and other retreating marchers all around me," Lewis remembered. "With nightsticks and whips—one posseman had a rubber hose wrapped with barbed wire—Sheriff Clark's deputies chased us all the way back into the Carver project and up to the front of Brown Chapel, where we tried getting as many people as we could inside the church to safety. I don't even recall how I made it that far, how I got from the bridge to the church, but I did."

Both on the church grounds and in nearby streets, the assault continued for half an hour until Selma's public safety director, Wilson Baker, intervened. By that time, Lewis noted with alarm, some of the marchers had begun to "fight back . . . with men and boys emerging from the Carver homes with bottles and bricks in their hands, heaving them at the troopers, then retreating for more." Soon a group of angry Black men and women "collected in front of the church, with SNCC and SCLC staff members moving through and trying to keep them calm. Some men in the crowd spoke of going home to get guns. Our people tried talking them down, getting them calm." Meanwhile, "kids and teenagers continued throwing rocks and bricks." As ambulances shuttled between the church and Good Samaritan Hospital, a Catholic facility staffed mostly by Black doctors and nurses, several friends urged Lewis to join the wounded at the hospital. But he refused and remained on site into the evening, when he and Williams convened a mass meeting in Brown Chapel.

Although a band of state troopers continued to surround the church, more than six hundred souls—including a number of heavily bandaged survivors of the afternoon assault—packed the sanctuary to listen to what the march's leaders had to say. After Williams offered a few words to calm the crowd, Lewis—with his head "throbbing" and his hair "matted with blood," and still wearing a trench coat "stained with dirt and blood"—made his way to the pulpit. "I don't know how President Johnson can send troops to Vietnam" and other parts of the world, he declared, yet "he can't send troops to Selma, Alabama." Hearing cries of "Yes! and Amen," he went on to predict, "Next time we march, we may have to keep going when we get to Montgomery. We may have to go on to *Washington*." This bold statement, which appeared in the *New York Times* the next morning, elicited a prompt response from the Justice Department, which pledged to send FBI agents to

Selma to investigate whether law enforcement officers and others had used "unnecessary force" to block the march to Montgomery.

Lewis was then taken to Good Samaritan, where X-rays revealed he had suffered a fractured skull and a severe concussion. Admitted for observation and treatment, he was resting in his hospital room when the ABC television network shocked its viewers that evening with a special fifteen-minute news bulletin showing extended film footage of the savage attack on the marchers. Wedged in between sections of the movie *Judgment at Nuremberg*, the footage as shown had a surrealistic quality that left many Americans wondering if what they were watching was real. It was, of course, all too real, including a film clip in which Sheriff Clark could be heard screaming, "Get those goddamned niggers. And get those goddamned *white* niggers."[11]

* * *

The assault's impression on the American public was profound and disturbing, triggering a migration of supporters to Selma from across the nation, some coming by plane or train and some by car. Soon there was a round-the-clock vigil outside Brown Chapel, as SCLC leaders warily planned their next move. On the Monday morning after the assault, the SCLC filed a motion with the federal district court in Montgomery seeking an injunction barring Alabama officials from interfering with the proposed Selma-to-Montgomery march. District Judge Frank Johnson, who had issued rulings favorable to the movement in the past, was expected to grant the injunction, though no one knew how long he would deliberate on the matter. The SCLC's leaders were ready to move on with the march and hoped for a quick ruling, but when a preliminary ruling came that afternoon, they were disappointed. Judge Johnson insisted he could not grant an injunction without a hearing, and the earliest possible day for a hearing would be Thursday, March 11.

This unexpected delay triggered an emergency meeting early Monday night, during which King and his senior staff met with Jim Farmer of CORE and Forman and two others representing SNCC. Lewis, still in the hospital and heavily sedated, could not participate in the meeting to consider, as he later described the choice, "whether they should risk losing the judge's support by staging a march before getting his approval, or risk losing credibility and momentum by waiting patiently until he issued his injunction." Farmer, Forman, and his SNCC colleagues were in favor of proceeding without delay. The SCLC was split, with Williams siding with SNCC and CORE, but with King and his other aides advocating patience and acceptance of the judge's preliminary order. Forman was the judge's most vehement critic, labeling the order "legal blackmail," but almost everyone in SNCC, including Lewis once he was informed about the back-and-forth at the meeting, favored an immediate resumption of the march. That Forman and other SNCC activists were now eager to participate in a march they had scorned earlier was a testament to their outrage over what had happened to Lewis and so many other marchers. Within hours of the assault on Bloody Sunday, dozens of SNCC staff members and field workers traveled to Selma, some on a chartered plane from Atlanta; they were ready to march.

At the end of the meeting, King rendered his decision to abide by the court order. There would be no march the next day, or so everyone at the meeting believed as they filed out to attend a mass meeting in the Brown Chapel sanctuary. Speaking from the pulpit to a highly emotional crowd jammed into the church, King impulsively changed his mind and announced he would lead the march the next afternoon. There was euphoria, undoubtedly mixed with anxiety, in the hall, and confusion among movement leaders on all sides. Retiring to the home of a local Black dentist, Dr. Sullivan Jackson, SCLC and SNCC leaders held a meeting that lasted into the early hours of Tuesday morning as they worked out the logistical details of the march and also tried to fashion a compromise that would satisfy federal officials. King spoke to Attorney General Nicholas Katzenbach by phone and a few hours later met with the Justice Department's leading civil rights specialist, John Doar, and ex–Florida governor LeRoy Collins, the director of the department's Community Relations Service. President Johnson had sent both Doar and Collins to Selma to serve as liaisons between the movement and local and state officials, and Collins in particular did what he could that morning to rein in Sheriff Clark and Al Lingo.

Still in the hospital, Lewis took no part in any of this and had no idea what King and his staff were actually planning to do once the march commenced. Unbeknownst to him, and to the rest of the SNCC activists at the scene, at some point during the nightlong deliberations and negotiations,

King had decided to end Tuesday's march at the east end of the Edmund Pettus Bridge.[12]

When King and more than two thousand followers marched across the bridge on Tuesday afternoon, they approached a phalanx of law enforcement every bit as impressive as the one the march had encountered on Sunday. Once again there were hundreds of troopers and possemen wearing full battle gear and blocking the roadway east to Montgomery. But this time there was no advance as the marchers reached the end of the bridge and knelt to pray. They then sang "We Shall Overcome," before gazing down the highway. What they saw shocked them: suddenly the mass of troopers and possemen, apparently by order of the governor, stepped aside, creating an open eastward path. But what happened next was even more shocking. Instead of moving forward, King turned around and walked back over the bridge, making his way through the stunned marchers as best he could. Although he would later explain that earlier in the day he had reached an agreement with federal officials that the Tuesday march would only be symbolic, that the marchers would stop at the end of the bridge and not go any farther until Judge Johnson issued an injunction, no one in the crowd, other than King's top aides, knew about the agreement at the time.

March 9, 1965, would forever be known as Turnaround Tuesday, one of the oddest episodes in movement history. Lewis, who would not be released from the hospital until Tuesday night, did not witness the turnaround. But he was soon inundated with complaints from marchers who "were shocked and confused." "They had no idea what was going on," he later noted. "They had come to put their bodies on the line, and now they were backing down, retreating, going home. They followed Dr. King—what else could they do. But they were disappointed. Many were openly angry." Forman and many other SNCC staff members were also angry, convinced that King and the SCLC had tricked them into participating in a farcical and cowardly act. Forman, in particular, lashed out and vowed that SNCC was done working with the SCLC. As Lewis later described Forman's response, "There would be no waiting for any judge's injunction. SNCC was finished with waiting, finished with Selma. It was time to do something on our own. . . . Within twenty-four hours he shifted our manpower and focus from Selma to the streets of Montgomery, where SNCC-led student forces from Tuskegee

Institute and Alabama State University began laying siege to the state capitol with a series of demonstrations more overt and aggressive than anything seen in Selma. Taunting, provoking, clashing with mounted policemen—the SNCC protests that week in Montgomery would prove to be nothing like our nonviolent campaign in Selma."

All of this created an open breach between Lewis and many of his SNCC colleagues. Almost alone among SNCC's leadership, he supported King's actions on Turnaround Tuesday. "I had no problem with what King did," he insisted. "I thought it was in keeping with the philosophy of the movement, that there comes a time when you must retreat, and that there is nothing wrong with retreating. There is nothing wrong with coming back to fight another day. Dr. King knew—we all knew—that Judge Johnson was going to give us what we were asking for if we simply followed procedure, followed the rules."[13]

Lewis's physical condition remained shaky—the doctors at Good Samaritan urged him to see neurological specialists in Boston as soon as possible—and the widening gulf between him and the rest of SNCC's staff saddened him. But he was heartened by the American public's response to the violence and repression of Bloody Sunday. During the two days since the assault, public demonstrations in support of the Selma marchers had been organized in more than eighty cities across the nation, and sentiment in favor of a strong voting rights act was reaching new heights. This was particularly evident in Congress, where more than sixty members of the House sent a telegram to the president demanding "immediate submission of a voting rights bill." Thus, "despite all the buzz among my SNCC colleagues" about "betrayal," Lewis felt "exhilarated" by what was happening. When asked about the "split" between SNCC and the SCLC at a mass meeting on Tuesday evening, he refused to comment on the matter other than by reminding reporters that the two organizations had always gone their separate ways. "SCLC is not the enemy," he added. "George Wallace and segregation are the enemy."

Earlier in the day, just before Lewis's release from the hospital, more than four hundred ministers who had come to Selma to show their support for the voting rights movement participated in a march from Brown Chapel to the downtown business district. Lewis was thrilled by this unprecedented demonstration of support, but his mood darkened the next morning when he learned that while walking down a street after having dinner at a downtown café, one of the visiting ministers, James J. Reeb, a white Unitarian from Boston, had been struck in the head with a baseball bat by an angry white supremacist. Left with a massive blood clot in his brain, Reeb was rushed to a Birmingham hospital, where he died two days later.

The day Reeb died was also the day the hearing in Judge Frank Johnson's Montgomery courtroom began. The hearing lasted five days, concluding on Tuesday after a one-day hiatus on Sunday. Lewis testified on Friday, the second day of the hearing, providing a vivid description of the Bloody Sunday assault and watching a three-minute film clip showing some of the violence. On Saturday, Lingo stunned the judge when he confirmed that Governor Wallace commanded him to stop the march by any means necessary and, in effect, to "teach other niggers" to stay away from any marches "on a public highway in Alabama." "I was ordered," Lingo said point blank, "to cause the scene that the troopers made."[14]

* * *

That afternoon, Wallace was meeting with President Johnson at the White House, where he tried to convince him to intervene to stop the march. Johnson refused, and during a press conference after the meeting, he offered the governor a stern lesson in civics and constitutional history. "The demonstrations in Selma . . . are a protest against a deep and very unjust flaw in American democracy itself," the president declared, adding, "Ninety-five years ago our Constitution was amended to require that no American be denied the right to vote because of race or color. Almost a century later, many Americans are kept from voting simply because they are Negroes. Therefore, this Monday I will send to the Congress a request for legislation to carry out the amendment to the Constitution."

This long-awaited declaration was just what Lewis needed to boost his spirits, and on Sunday he flew to New York, where he and Forman spoke at a massive voting rights rally in Harlem. Similar rallies were held in a number of cities that weekend, including Montgomery and Washington, where there were sit-ins and picket lines at the Justice Department building and in front of the White House.

On Monday, Lewis was back in the Montgomery courtroom, where everything seemed to be going the movement's way. It was now clear that

Judge Johnson planned to grant the injunction, and before adjournment he asked the plaintiffs to submit a detailed plan for the march. That afternoon, Lewis joined Young, Williams, the NAACP attorney Jack Greenberg, and several others at a Montgomery motel, where they hashed out the details of what they wanted to do—"the number of people we expected to march, the route we would follow and the number of days it would take." He then returned to Selma to attend a rally at the Dallas County Courthouse, where King memorialized the Reverend Reeb in front of a crowd of two thousand. Sheriff Clark and his deputies kept close watch over the marchers but did not try to break up the rally or stop King from speaking.

In the streets of Montgomery, however, Monday afternoon witnessed a violent confrontation between SNCC-led student demonstrators and a force of police officers and mounted deputies. When the white law officers tried to disperse the demonstrators, some of the students fought back with rocks and bricks and bottles, prompting a mounted charge of deputies "swinging clubs and whips." When Lewis learned what had happened, he was heartsick, deeply disturbed by the students' breach of nonviolent discipline and appalled by the violent, aggressive tactics employed by the Montgomery deputies. Concerned that the conflict in central Alabama was escalating out of control, he called for a march to the state capitol to protest the rough treatment suffered by the students.[15]

Led by Lewis, Forman, and King, the march would take place on Tuesday afternoon, but by then the roller coaster of emotions within the movement had soared upward thanks to a remarkable speech delivered by President Johnson. On Monday evening, Lewis, along with King and several other SCLC leaders, gathered around the television in Dr. Sullivan Jackson's living room to watch Johnson give a special address to Congress. Both Lewis and King had been invited to Washington to be part of the live audience, but they declined, feeling they were needed in Selma. Neither man expected much from the speech, which they feared would offer nothing but empty platitudes and self-serving political posturing. But they were pleasantly surprised.

Lewis later characterized the March 15 speech—written primarily by the president's liberal aide, Richard Goodwin—as the "finest" of Johnson's career and "probably the strongest speech any American president has ever made on the subject of civil rights." It began with an eloquent allusion to the historical importance of the struggle for voting rights in Selma. "At times history and fate meet at a single time in a single place to shape a turning point in man's unending search for freedom," Johnson declared. "So it was at Lexington and Concord. So it was a century ago at Appomattox. So it was last week in Selma, Alabama." The rest of the forty-five-minute speech was full of stirring words never before uttered by an American president.

At one point, Johnson insisted that, through their "actions and protests" and "courage to risk safety and even to risk . . . life," Black Americans "have awakened the conscience of this nation." "Equality depends," he added, "not on the force of arms or tear gas but upon the force of moral right." After several more moral pronouncements interrupted by applause, Johnson ended on a crescendo of emotion that left many of his listeners—including Dr. King back in Selma—with tears of joy. "What happened in Selma is part of a far larger movement which reaches into every section and state of America," Johnson informed Congress and the nation. "It is the effort of American Negroes to secure for themselves the full blessings of American life. Their cause must be our cause too. Because it is not just Negroes, but really it is all of us who must overcome the crippling legacy of bigotry and injustice. And we *shall* overcome."[16]

Lewis, like King, was overcome with emotion, especially after Johnson closed by quoting one of the movement's most hallowed freedom songs. "Lyndon Johnson was no politician that night," he recalled. "He was a man who spoke from his heart. His were the words of a statesman." Not everyone in the movement shared his sanguine view. Forman, for one, refused to praise the president, telling reporters that Johnson's "We shall overcome" reference had "spoiled a good song." At a mass meeting in Selma the next night, Forman continued his harsh criticism, claiming, "There's only one man in the country that can stop George Wallace and those posses. These problems will not be solved until that man in that shaggedy old place called the White House begins to shake and gets on the phone and says, 'Now listen, George, we're coming down there and throw you in jail if you don't stop that mess. . . .' I said it today, and I will say it again. If we can't sit at the table of democracy, we'll break the fucking legs off."

Lewis winced upon hearing Forman's intemperate words, not only because his colleague had used a four-letter word in a church setting but also because his statement violated the spirit of nonviolence. Forman's message, Lewis later pointed out, "was not the *message* of the movement, at least not of the movement that I was a part of." What worried Lewis the most was that he feared Forman's style of leadership "pointed the way down a road SNCC was headed that I knew I would not be able to travel." While he was not about to give up his efforts to keep SNCC on a nonviolent path, he knew there would be tough days ahead as long as Forman was the organization's executive director.

Of course, Lewis also knew that words were less important than actions, whether they came from a movement leader or a president or a judge. Indeed, he was reminded of this truth a few minutes after Forman finished his speech. With King at the podium, an SCLC staff member rushed into the hall to relay an important message to his boss: Judge Johnson had just issued an injunctive ruling prohibiting any governmental interference with the proposed march. The written order delivered the next morning roundly condemned the actions of Sheriff Clark as unwarranted "harassment, intimidation, coercion, threatening conduct, and sometimes, brutal mistreatment." The governor and the state police, though only mentioned in passing, were also chastised and enjoined by implication. "The attempted march along U.S. Highway 80," Judge Johnson insisted, "involved nothing more than a peaceful effort on the part of Negro citizens to exercise a classic constitutional right: that is, the right to assemble peaceably and to petition one's government for the redress of grievances."[17]

Judge Johnson's action empowered the SCLC to go forward with the march, which, according to the plan submitted to the district court, was scheduled to commence on Sunday, March 21, five days after the delivery of the order. Following through with the proposed march had become essential to the voting rights movement's image and credibility. But in the larger scheme of things, the most important actions in mid-March took place in Washington, where the Johnson administration was moving to turn the president's promises into something tangible. Many voting rights activists had reserved judgment following Johnson's March 15 speech, waiting to see if the president's actions matched his words. But even the most skeptical observers were gratified by the flurry of preliminary legislative activity that occurred during the third week of March.

The hard work of hammering out the details of a voting rights bill that was passable yet strong enough to win the support of liberal members of the House and Senate, not to mention movement leaders, had actually begun earlier in the month. Spearheaded by Attorney General Katzenbach and Deputy Attorney General Ramsey Clark, several draft proposals for the bill received careful scrutiny at a series of meetings where all manner of alterations and refinements were made. A penultimate draft reached House and Senate leaders the morning after the president's speech, and within a day a slightly revised bill was formally presented to both houses. Hearings convened by the Senate Judiciary Committee and a subcommittee of the House Judiciary Committee began almost immediately, and many observers began to predict "swift passage of the bill with few amendments." All of this momentum emerged well before the first marcher headed down Highway 80 on March 21.[18]

* * *

Back in Alabama, and at the SCLC and SNCC offices in Atlanta and NAACP headquarters in New York, there was momentum of a different sort as movement organizers coordinated a complex web of planning and preparation for the five-day march. Lewis, despite the lingering effects of his head injuries, was in the thick of it, attending to one logistical challenge or another. The week before the march, he recalled, saw "a swirl of activity, much like preparing an army for assault. Marchers, not just from Selma but from across the nation, were mobilized and organized, route sections and schedules were mapped out, printed up and distributed, tents big enough to sleep people by the hundreds were secured. Food. Security. Communications. There were thousands of details to take care of, and thousands of dollars, most of it raised by the SCLC, to be spent."

Feeding, housing, and protecting the marchers were serious concerns that required close attention and elaborate organization. There would be several crews charged with cooking and transporting food to the nightly campsites, a staff of doctors and nurses provided by the Medical Committee for Human Rights, and an extensive security force provided by the federal government, which stationed more than eighteen hundred Alabama National Guardsmen along the fifty-four-mile route, with two thousand army personnel dispatched to back them up. There were also hundreds of FBI agents and U.S. marshals on site, as well as helicopters and low-flying planes patrolling the skies above Highway 80. The security plan even involved demolition teams that inspected bridges and roadways for explosives.

All of this was in place by Saturday evening, March 20, the night before the march. Lewis and two hundred others spent the night sleeping at Brown Chapel, and he and several others gave brief speeches before turning in. Unsure of exactly how many marchers would show up, the organizers were gratified to see more than three thousand people in front of the church the next morning. Following a rousing speech by King, the marchers gathered closely behind a front line of movement leaders that included Ralph and Juanita Abernathy, Lewis, Forman, Williams, Young, A. Philip Randolph, Ralph Bunche, the comedian Dick Gregory, Rabbi Abraham Heschel, and King and his wife, Coretta. Unlike the marches on Bloody Sunday and Turnaround Tuesday, this march had a festive air, with each individual in the front line wearing a Hawaiian lei around his or her neck. As they marched toward the Edmund Pettus Bridge, a truck bearing television lights and cameras rolled in front of them capturing every step taken by the Kings and those around them. The cameras also captured a broad cross-section of America, Black and white, young and old, marching for freedom and simple justice. Bevel's original plan to carry Jimmie Lee Jackson's body to Montgomery had been scrapped, but Jackson's grandfather was there among the marchers, as were Doar and Clark representing the Justice Department.

When the marchers reached the east end of the bridge, they saw essentially the same array of state and local law enforcement that had blocked the roadway two weeks earlier. But this time there was no attempt to obstruct the mile-long procession. Accompanied by several trucks and jeeps filled with National Guardsmen and army soldiers, the marchers passed through safely, reaching the Selma city limits and beyond without incident. Once they entered the rural countryside, the marchers encountered periodic verbal harassment from passing motorists, and at one point a showering of "hate leaflets" dropped from a private plane. But by nightfall they had completed seven miles and stopped to camp for the night at an eighty-acre farm owned by David Hall, a Black employee of the Carver housing project back in Selma.

Lewis managed to walk the seven miles, but—per an arrangement with his doctors, who feared that five nights of sleeping on hard ground along the route would be too much of a strain on his precarious health—he returned to Selma for the night. Transported back to the march each morning, he would repeat the pattern of sleeping in Selma throughout the five days of marching. On the morning following the first night on the road, more than two thousand other marchers returned to Selma, abiding by an agreement with Judge Johnson that no more than three hundred marchers would march on the narrow two-lane roads of Lowndes County on the second day.[19]

On the third day, the number of marchers was once again over three thousand, and despite dreary and cold rainy weather, the mood remained upbeat and almost euphoric. Lewis was thrilled beyond measure. "To me," he later wrote, "there was never a march like this one before. . . . The incredible sense of community—of *communing*—was overwhelming. We felt bonded with one another, with the people we passed, with the entire nation. The people who came out of their homes to watch as we passed by—rural people, almost all of them black, almost all of them dirt poor—waved and cheered, ran into their kitchens and brought us out food, brought us something to drink. More than a few of them put down what they were doing and joined us."

On the fourth day, the marchers covered sixteen miles, stopping for the night at the City of St. Jude, a Catholic conference center located just outside the Montgomery city limits. By this time, the number of marchers had risen to unprecedented levels, as had the number of television and newspaper reporters trying to capture the unfolding drama. Watching the mass of marchers arrive at St. Jude, Roy Reed of the *New York Times* felt he was witnessing "a grandeur that was almost biblical."

That night, the march organizers staged a massive outdoor rally and concert, a star-studded affair featuring more than a dozen entertainers who performed on "a makeshift stage fashioned from stacks of coffins loaned by a local black funeral home." The performers included Sammy Davis Jr., Nina Simone, Johnny Mathis, Joan Baez, Leonard Bernstein, Tony Bennett, Ossie Davis, and Harry Belafonte, the man responsible for bringing all of these celebrities together. Lewis—sitting there under the stars for four hours, listening to the music, the speeches, and the joyous laughter of the crowd—characterized the evening as a glorious "spectacle, a salute to Selma." When one reporter tried to denigrate the event by suggesting the entertainers' presence had turned "a serious march into a circus," the actress Elaine May shot back: "The only real circus is the state of Alabama and George Wallace."[20]

The next morning, March 25, marked the end of the march, as Lewis and nearly forty thousand others walked the six miles from St. Jude to the Alabama State Capitol. The historic walk took them past the federal courthouse; around Court Square, where slaves had been bought and sold a century earlier; and up the length of Dexter Avenue, past the Baptist church that King had pastored during the Montgomery Bus Boycott and on to the nearby Greek Revival–style capitol, where Jefferson Davis was sworn in as president of the Confederate States of America in 1861. As they approached the capitol, Lewis "could see the Alabama state flag flying high above the rotunda dome, along with the flag of the Confederacy. But the American flag was nowhere in sight. Neither was George Wallace, though we learned later that he watched the entire afternoon, peeking out through the drawn blinds of the governor's office."

What Wallace witnessed that afternoon must have shaken his confidence. After nearly a century and a half of racial discrimination and Black disfranchisement, "We the People" had finally arrived in Montgomery to serve notice that a new day of democracy was dawning. With the crowd blanketing several blocks west of the capitol, a procession of orators ranging from Farmer, Bayard Rustin, and Rosa Parks to Bevel, Lewis, and King held forth on the meaning of the march. King, who spoke last, delivered what Lewis and many others regarded as one of the greatest speeches of his career. His eloquence reached a climax in a final burst of words, some borrowed from "The Battle Hymn of the Republic." "How long will justice be crucified and buried?" he asked. "I come to say to you this afternoon, however difficult the moment, however frustrating the hour, it will not be long. Because truth crushed to earth will rise again. How long? Not long! Because no lie can live forever. How long? Not long! . . . Because the arc of the universe is *long*, but it bends toward justice. How long? Not long! Because mine eyes have seen the glory of the coming of the Lord. He is trampling out the vintage where the grapes of *wrath* are stored. He has loosed the fateful lightning of his *terrible* swift sword. His truth is marching on. Glory! Hallelujah! Glory! Hallelujah!"[21]

King's speech left Lewis in tears of joy. Perhaps we shall indeed overcome—perhaps the Beloved Community is not beyond our reach after all, he thought to himself. Yet he knew, even in that hopeful moment, that tough times lay ahead, that the forces of reaction remained powerful and that the passage of a strong voting rights act was not yet ensured. In fact, the optimism inspired by King's words proved to be fleeting, foundering later that evening when a carload of Klansmen shot and killed thirty-nine-year-old Viola Gregg Liuzzo, a movement volunteer and mother of five from Detroit who was transporting marchers back and forth from Selma to Montgomery. On her return from Selma, just a few miles west of Montgomery, a shotgun blast ended Liuzzo's life, all but destroying the euphoria that Lewis and others had felt at the end of the march.

Also disillusioning was the discovery later in the year that one of the four Klansmen responsible for her death was Gary Thomas Rowe Jr., an undercover FBI informant and provocateur who four years earlier had taken part in the savage beating of Jim Peck and other Freedom Riders at a Birmingham bus terminal. Adding insult to injury, the FBI not only tried to shield Rowe from prosecution but also conducted a systematic campaign to smear Liuzzo as a Communist, a heroin addict, and a civil rights "whore" obsessed with interracial sex.

This betrayal sorely tested Lewis's faith in government as a potential guarantor of civil rights. The same federal government that had recently aligned itself behind the voting rights struggle had also sabotaged Fannie Lou Hamer and the MFDP in Atlantic City in 1964, and now, less than a year later, had been party to the murder and character assassination of a blameless movement volunteer. No wonder Lewis was in a state of considerable confusion by the time he left Alabama in late March 1965. Would they see the dawning of a true democracy or continued dissembling by federal authorities? As the congressional struggle over voting rights approached the time of decision, neither Lewis nor anyone else in the movement could be sure about the future of freedom in the Deep South.[22]

CHAPTER 10

———

Leaving SNCC

I N THE WAKE of the Selma-to-Montgomery march in 1965, SNCC's leaders turned their attention to Mississippi, where the MFDP was continuing to challenge the authority of white supremacist Democrats. John
Lewis and the SNCC executive committee were determined to liberate the
state at whatever risk or cost. To demonstrate their commitment, they decided to hold SNCC's spring 1965 staff meeting in Holly Springs, a county
seat located just south of the Mississippi-Tennessee border.

At the top of the agenda was a discussion of how SNCC should respond
to the Johnson administration's War on Poverty and related Great Society
programs. But from the outset, an ongoing personnel controversy dominated the meeting. "The weekend had hardly begun," Lewis observed, "when
internal issues again erupted. This time the concern was the role in SNCC
of what had become known as floaters—staffers or volunteers who had no
specific assignment or designated site but who were free to go from place to
place as they felt fit, filling whatever need might be calling."

The root of the problem was the prevalence of the movement philosophy
known within SNCC as "Freedom High." Lewis, along with Jim Forman and
many of the long-standing SNCC veterans, expressed deep concern about
the growing influence of the Freedom High faction; thus, at Holly Springs
they authorized a management program that would rein in the more self-
indulgent members of the organization. At one point Lewis, in uncharac-
teristically harsh language, advised the Freedom High activists "to shape up
or ship out." But in the end, the proposed program failed miserably, in large

part because most of the staff came to regard it as a high-handed purge. This backlash only made things worse, severely weakening Lewis's stature as a trusted leader.[1]

As the year wore on, Lewis tried to move past the Holly Springs fiasco, focusing on more important matters such as shoring up local movements as far afield as Gary, Indiana, and Jackson, Mississippi. He also kept busy monitoring the progress of the Johnson administration's voting rights bill, an early version of which passed the Senate on May 26. The legislative wrangling over the bill would consume much of the summer, with President Lyndon Johnson twisting arms and jawboning all the way. Finally, on August 3 and 4, the House and then the Senate passed a strong revision of the bill by a wide margin. Elated, Johnson scheduled the signing ceremony for the afternoon of August 6, inviting Lewis and Jim Farmer to a private meeting at the White House that morning.

The meeting was brief, barely twenty minutes long, but it was long enough for the president to dispense a bit of practical advice. Leaning forward in his chair, he gave Lewis some down-home marching orders: "Now John, you've got to go back and get all those folks registered. You've got to go back and get those boys by the *balls*. Just like a bull gets on top of a cow. You've got to get 'em by the balls and you've got to *squeeze*, squeeze 'em till they *hurt*."

At the Capitol a few hours later, in the same room where Abraham Lincoln had signed the Emancipation Proclamation in 1863, Lewis experienced one of the most "powerfully moving" moments of his life. In a letter to Johnson that evening, he insisted that the Voting Rights Act was "a milestone and every bit as momentous and significant . . . as the Emancipation Proclamation." "That day," he later wrote, "was a culmination, a climax, the end of a very long road. In a sense it represented a high point in modern America, probably the nation's finest hour in terms of civil rights." The Voting Right Act held out so much promise, with its powerful provisions designed to counter traditional forms of disfranchisement such as literacy clauses and poll taxes, to substitute federal examiners for local registrars when discriminatory intentions were suspected, and to require federal preclearance of all changes to voting regulations in jurisdictions with histories of systemic suffrage discrimination based on race. As Lewis put it, "this law had teeth," and Johnson was justifiably proud of his legislative accomplishment protecting the right to vote, which he described in his public remarks as "the most powerful instrument ever devised by man for breaking down injustice and destroying the terrible walls which imprison men because they are different from other men."

Lewis left the signing ceremony clutching a commemorative pen, along with a measure of hope for full enforcement and a brighter future. But it didn't take long for him to return to the harsh realities of the voting rights struggle on the ground. Two days after his Washington high, he was in jail in Americus, Georgia, where he had led a rally in support of two Black women arrested for joining a voter registration line reserved for white citizens. "As always," he shrugged, "when it came to the Deep South, passing laws was one thing, enforcing them was another."[2]

Later that week, a major race riot in Watts, a predominantly Black and impoverished section of South Central Los Angeles, reminded Lewis and others that the South had no monopoly on racial discrimination and Black despair. After years of tension between Watts residents and the city's overwhelmingly white police force, a routine traffic stop involving a white police officer and a Black motorist suspected of drunk driving triggered an altercation that soon spread throughout the surrounding neighborhoods. Six days of rioting, arson, and looting followed, prompting four thousand arrests, destroying more than a thousand buildings, and leaving thirty-four dead. By the time the National Guard restored order on August 18, televised scenes of Black protesters burning down their own neighborhood had seared the national psyche, instilling widespread fear, especially among white citizens.

Many observers, including President Johnson, were shocked by the intensity and scope of the Watts uprising, but Lewis was not. In fact, he had all but predicted such carnage in a *New York Herald Tribune* article published in late May. Run under the headline "SNCC's Lewis: We March for Us . . . and for You," the article warned that voting rights alone, though clearly important, could not solve many of the most troubling problems afflicting Black Americans: "Where lack of jobs, intolerable housing, police brutality, and other frustrating conditions exist . . . violence and massive street demonstrations may develop. . . . If the government cannot answer our questions and help us to solve some of these problems, I can only see many long, hot summers ahead."

Lewis knew all too well that the problem of "fear and deprivation" among Black Americans "north and south" represented an enormous challenge to the proponents of nonviolent struggle. Despite the great legislative victories of 1964 and 1965 and the rousing solidarity of the Selma-to-Montgomery march, the frustration level in many Black communities and organizations was rising during the summer and fall of 1965. Lewis saw this troubling new reality at every turn, both inside SNCC and elsewhere. "Now that we had secured our bedrock, fundamental rights—the rights of access and accommodation and the right to vote—the movement was moving into a new phase, a far stickier and more complex stage of gaining equal footing in this society," he recalled years later. "The problem we faced now was not something so visible or easily identifiable as a Bull Connor blocking our way. Now we had to deal with the subtler and much more complex issues of attaining economic and political power, of dealing with attitudes and actions held deep inside people and institutions." "Combating segregation is one thing," he insisted. "Dealing with racism is another."[3]

* * *

The external challenges posed by a persistent white supremacist culture tested SNCC's human and financial resources to the limit. But the organization also faced almost insurmountable internal problems in the aftermath of Selma and the 1965 voting rights campaign. Lewis spent much of the summer away from the SNCC office in Atlanta, traveling widely in a desperate effort to boost the organization's funding and morale. At almost every stop, however, he discovered that SNCC's structure and solidarity were slipping away. The divisions and disagreements that had plagued the gathering at Holly Springs in April had only grown worse, and Lewis feared SNCC was on the verge of coming apart. An organization that had always prided itself on being skeptical of strong leadership was now in danger of dissolving into chaos. As Lewis described the dilemma, "The same freedom we had thrived on in our early years was now pulling us to pieces."

Lewis's concerns were heightened by a rapidly developing situation in Lowndes County, Alabama, an overwhelmingly Black county that straddled the route from Selma to Montgomery. Rural and poor, and ruled by a reactionary white power structure that did not allow a single Black resident to register to vote before 1960, Lowndes was the focus of a spirited SNCC-led voting rights campaign initiated during the Selma-to-Montgomery march. Led by Stokely Carmichael, the campaign soon took a radical turn, veering away from SNCC's historical attachment to nonviolence, interracial cooperation, and coalition building within the Democratic Party.

By midsummer, Lowndes's SNCC staffers were openly carrying weapons in response to police violence, which included the August 20 murder of Jonathan Daniels, a white Episcopal seminarian and civil rights activist from New Hampshire. Lowndes, Carmichael would later write, "was a truly totalitarian society," an "insulated police state" that forced the SNCC activists and their local Black partners to prepare for armed conflict. By the end of the year, both sides had backed off from actual violence and turned to political struggle between a nearly all-white local Democratic Party and an all-Black independent party initially called the Lowndes County Freedom Organization (LCFO). After adopting the black panther as its symbol in December, the SNCC-led group became known as the Black Panther Party, a name that would later spread to militant Black political organizations in California and elsewhere.

None of this sat well with Lewis, who during the fall of 1965 continued to urge Lowndes County's Black voters to eschew the LCFO and participate in the Democratic primary. This enraged Carmichael, who later confessed, "After that I wanted his blood." His opposition to Lewis involved more than a personal grudge, however. He had long since given up on the Democratic Party as a reliable movement ally, having opposed the MFDP's effort in Atlantic City to convince white liberals that Blacks deserved representation in the party. Backed by a growing, increasingly radical "New Left" faction of predominantly Northern-born SNCC activists, he decided to rescue the organization from Lewis and what one observer described as "the gospel-singing SNCC kids from the South."

Lewis tried to counter this disdain for nonviolence and interracial cooperation, but there wasn't much he could do to reassert the authority of SNCC's founding principles. "As a group built on the philosophy of consensus," he later explained, "we had never resorted to rules and regulations."

SNCC's Freedom High faction, which celebrated individual initiative at the expense of structure and centralized authority, had been in ascendance since 1964, and there was no way to reverse this trend short of splitting the organization in two. In any event, Lewis's preference had always been to lead by example, and he had never been adept at heavy-handed leadership. It was simply not his style or strength. Besides, by his calculation, he had too many other pressing concerns during the second half of 1965 to devote much time and energy to what in all likelihood would be a futile effort to rein in Stokely and the unruly Freedom High activists.[4]

At that time, one of Lewis's highest priorities was to connect the civil rights movement to the growing movement against American involvement in the Vietnam War. Like his mentors, James Lawson and Martin Luther King Jr., he viewed pacifism as a natural complement to the philosophy of nonviolence. While he was not sure that he was unconditionally opposed to all wars, he decided early on that the American war effort in Vietnam was both immoral and detrimental to the well-being of Black Americans. His opposition to the war was well known among his friends in SNCC, and most of them agreed with him, applauding his concerted effort to achieve conscientious objector status, which was finally granted in December 1965. Earlier, during the fall, he had begun to include brief references to his antiwar views in his speeches to SNCC audiences. When he felt reasonably sure that no reporters were present, he questioned how President Johnson could justify "sending tens of thousands of troops to fight this war in Vietnam to 'protect the rights' of the people of South Vietnam" when "the rights of Black people across the nation continued to be violated without protection."

At this point, none of the major civil rights organization had taken a public stand against the war, but SNCC began to consider doing so at its November staff meeting in Atlanta. During the meeting, Lewis made a strong argument for taking a public antiwar position based on the philosophy of nonviolence. Most of the staff agreed with Lewis, but many were less philosophical and more concerned that Black soldiers "were being sent to fight a war for a white society that oppressed and exploited them," a point of view reinforced by a "NO VIETNAMESE EVER CALLED ME NIGGER" poster mounted on the wall of SNCC's Atlanta office.

Following the November meeting, Lewis, Forman, and Courtland Cox jointly drafted a formal antiwar statement that was circulated among the SNCC staff. Some members, including Marion Barry, came out against releasing the statement, fearing it would hinder the financially strapped organization's fundraising efforts. But by early January there was wide support for going public. Without giving any hint of what Lewis planned to discuss, SNCC called a press conference to deliver the organization's antiwar message. Forthright in its condemnation of the government's policies, Lewis's bold statement produced a noticeable buzz among shocked reporters, especially when he spoke out against the draft. "We are in sympathy with, and support the men in this country who are unwilling to respond to a military draft which would compel them to contribute their lives to United States aggression in Vietnam in the name of 'freedom' we find so false in this country," he declared, adding, "We take note of the fact that 16 percent of the draftees from this country are Negroes called on to stifle the liberation of Vietnam, to preserve a 'democracy' which does not exist for them at home."

The fallout from the press conference was immediate and overwhelmingly negative. In a nation unaccustomed to linking civil rights advocacy with opposition to the war and the draft, the public reaction was a combination of "outrage and alarm," Lewis recalled. Both the FBI and the House Un-American Activities Committee were put on alert as a safeguard against SNCC radicalism, and Lewis's draft classification as a conscientious objector suddenly became I-A, meaning "available for service." Worst of all, Roy Wilkins of the NAACP and Whitney Young of the National Urban League dutifully lined up behind the Johnson administration, condemning SNCC's antiwar statement as "outrageous." Many other civil rights leaders, including King, remained silent, leaving SNCC to fend for itself.[5]

* * *

Another significant diversion that affected Lewis's life during the fall of 1965 was an unexpected turn toward electoral politics. During SNCC's early years, there was little thought of advancing civil rights through officeholding. But in February 1965, Bayard Rustin published an influential essay in *Commentary* magazine with the provocative title "From Protest to Politics:

The Future of the Civil Rights Movement." Rustin's agenda went well beyond the mere extension of voting rights to include coalition building, active participation in public policy debates, and officeholding at all levels of government. Coming from one of the principal architects of the nonviolent direct action phase of the movement, this sage advice drew wide attention and some enthusiasm among civil rights activists.

One of the first to act on Rustin's suggestions was Julian Bond, SNCC's longtime communications director and Lewis's close friend and adviser. Taking advantage of the 1963 Supreme Court ruling *Gray v. Sanders,* which mandated "one man, one vote" redistricting throughout Georgia, Bond decided to run for a legislative seat representing District 136, a new district in inner-city Atlanta. The fact that the district's population was 98 percent Black augured well for Bond's chances, though his Republican opponent, an Atlanta University administrator appropriately named Malcolm Dean, was also Black.

Lewis had no experience with political campaigning, but an unusually light travel schedule in October allowed him to devote much of his free time to Bond's campaign. "I went house to house, knocking on doors, just talking to people. No speeches," he remembered. "I visited barbershops and beauty shops, encouraging people to vote for Julian." On election day, Lewis was elated when his friend won a landslide victory, garnering 82 percent of the vote.

At that point, SNCC's first venture in electoral politics appeared to be a success, and Bond was scheduled to be sworn in as a member of the Georgia House of Representatives in mid-January. But the furor following the release of SNCC's antiwar statement on January 6 placed a major obstacle in his path. In his role as SNCC's communications director, he was responsible for explicating the meaning of the statement for the press and the public. And he did this with skill and a calm demeanor, until one reporter caught him off guard with a personal question, "asking him what *he* thought of the statement. Did he support it?" Without thinking much of it, he responded, "Sure, I support it." A firestorm of criticism ensued, with a number of his legislative colleagues issuing charges of treason. When he showed up at the swearing-in ceremony four days later, the House, by a vote of 184 to 12, denied him his seat on the grounds that he had "violated his oath to uphold the Constitution of Georgia and the United States."

SNCC rushed to Bond's defense, protesting that the refusal to seat him was blatantly illegal. No one was more upset than the normally unflappable Lewis, who suspected race had been a major factor in the legislature's decision to exclude his friend and colleague. Even in his memoir, written more than thirty years later, Lewis's outrage was palpable. "It was astounding," he explained. "It wasn't even legal. Once again, we were getting screwed. Once again, the system was making a mockery of justice. Was it any wonder that people in the movement were bailing out right and left, abandoning all hope of appealing to and working through a system that could do something like this? It was a replay of what had happened to the MFDP in Atlantic City. It was an echo of all the 'not guilty' verdicts sneeringly returned in Deep South courtrooms where white men stood trial for the blatant murders of blacks."

In the short term, the best SNCC could do was to support Bond in a second, special election, which he won handily. But once again the legislature denied him his seat. He then turned to the courts for justice, eventually attracting a national following, especially among antiwar and civil rights activists, including King, who organized a massive march on his behalf. After a federal district court ruled against him, affirming the legislature's claim that his antiwar statements breached his oath of office, Bond appealed to the U.S. Supreme Court.

In early December 1966, a unanimous Court ruled in his favor, and a month later he finally took his seat in the Georgia legislature, becoming the first member of SNCC to hold public office. By then he was a national figure and a rising star on the college lecture circuit. Despite repeated attempts to gerrymander him out of office, he would go on to serve three two-year terms in the Georgia House (1967–1974) and six terms in the state senate (1975–1987).[6]

Despite the troubles that delayed Bond's legislative career, Lewis took a great deal of satisfaction from his friend's entry into politics. He hated to lose a communications director whose skills had been essential to SNCC's six years of growth and success. But by early 1966 he feared he too would soon find himself outside the SNCC orbit. Perhaps Rustin was right about the importance of making the transition from protest to politics. For the past two years, he and Bond had grown increasingly uncomfortable with the organization's trajectory. The old enthusiasm for nonviolent struggle and racial integration was fading fast, and there didn't seem to be much they could do about it.

The decline, as Lewis saw it, involved more than an erosion of the philosophical imagination that had produced and sustained the dream of the Beloved Community. There was also, he recalled, a "growing climate of suspicion and mistrust within our ranks. The 'band of brothers' was becoming a distant memory." And the situation was getting worse with every passing week. "It had been Selma that held us together as long as we did," he later concluded. "After that, we just came apart."

Lewis felt that, as SNCC's chairman, he had a responsibility to keep the organization vital and intact. He still believed in its mission as a grassroots vanguard of nonviolent revolution—and as an important counterweight to the movement's older, more cautious organizations. But during the spring of 1966, Lewis's status within SNCC became untenable. In March, when he attended a Washington planning meeting for the upcoming White House Conference on Civil Rights, he drew sharp criticism from a number of staff members. They thought his absence from the conference would send a blunt message to President Johnson: that there would be no kowtowing to an administration that had let them down on so many occasions. Lewis strongly disagreed, arguing that "in any situation where people are prepared to talk about problems . . . it is imperative to listen, to at least hear what they have to say. That is an essential part of the philosophy of nonviolence, that you are as open to receive as to deliver, that you are willing and able to keep all possible doors open."

In the same spirit, Lewis resisted the repeated calls for him to resign his position on the SCLC's board of directors. Carmichael and Cox led the charge, mocking Lewis's continuing devotion to King, who had become unpopular among many SNCC activists. Lewis's willingness to cooperate with the SCLC, as he had done in Selma, was seen as a sign of weakness by the organization's more militant members. Many of these self-styled radicals were also critical of his deep attachments to nonviolence and interracial collaboration, as well as of his obvious lack of enthusiasm for Black nationalism. In their eyes, his shortcomings involved sins of both omission and commission. He was opposed to establishing SNCC projects in Northern cities or engaging in armed self-defense. Yet he had a single-minded passion about the moral power of love, forgiveness, and reconciliation. "He was the perfect embodiment of SNCC's original devotion to religious nonviolence and interracial coalition," the historian Robert Weisbrot argued in 1990. "By May 1966 such values were an embarrassment to many SNCC members, a reminder—along with Lewis himself—of an earlier, more naïve time." The journalist Milton Viorst once made a similar observation, concluding, "If the chairman was to be SNCC's symbol to the outside world, Louis was no longer qualified, because SNCC's policies had moved so dramatically away from his beliefs."

Lewis could see what was happening, but he was not willing to save his chairmanship if survival required abandoning his core beliefs. His loyalty to the nonviolent freedom struggle was deeper than his loyalty to SNCC or any other organization. Years later he summed up his dilemma: "I still had faith in the principles that we had applied to the formation of SNCC. But SNCC itself had now abandoned them." He believed in struggle and refused to go down without a fight. But he felt he would be lucky if his chairmanship lasted another year. "Most of the 'old' SNCC members, those who had been with us through the sit-ins and the Freedom Rides, still respected me," he noted. "But many of the newer, younger members, those who had only heard about the early years, but who weren't actually there, really didn't know who I was, what we were—or, at least, what we had been. Some of those newer members saw me at Selma, crossing that bridge, having my head beaten in, and they just shook their heads, dismissing me as a 'Christ-loving damn fool' and an 'anachronism.'"[7]

In late March, Lewis renewed his image as a fearless proponent of direct action by leading a sit-in on behalf of Black suffrage and liberation in South Africa. Arrested along with four other SNCC activists at the South African consulate in New York, he foreshadowed the future American movement against apartheid that would become prominent two decades later. This episode momentarily raised his hopes for a return to SNCC's glory days, and several weeks later, in late April and early May, he enjoyed a brief respite from SNCC's troubles after accepting an invitation to speak to a student peace group in Norway. But by the time he returned, just before the opening of SNCC's spring staff conference on May 8, the organization's unfolding drama had taken an unexpected turn.[8]

* * *

After five years as executive secretary, Forman had decided to resign, and Carmichael had launched a campaign to replace Lewis as chairman. Lewis was shocked by both developments, though he was relieved he would no longer have to deal with Forman's unsettling influence. They had never been in agreement on important issues such as strict adherence to nonviolence or the importance of interracial collaboration. True to form, a year after stepping down, Forman would help H. Rap Brown negotiate an ill-fated merger between what was left of SNCC and the revolutionary Black Panther Party led by Huey Newton and Bobby Seale.

Near the end of the weeklong staff conference, which was held at a church retreat center in Kingston Springs, Tennessee, there was an election to fill several key staff positions, including executive secretary and chairman. After Carmichael refused to accept a nomination to replace Forman, his intention to oust Lewis as chairman was clear. Before the vote, there was what Lewis later described as "a very emotionally charged open discussion with people standing up and speaking out about changes we needed to make." The most heated issue was whether to expel white members from the organization, a controversial proposal advanced earlier in the year by Bill Ware, a Black Mississippian and admirer of Malcolm X. After Lewis argued forcefully that it would be wrong and foolish for SNCC to embrace Black separatism, the backlash began. "I was criticized for spending so much time visiting college campuses around the country—'white' college campuses," he recalled. "I was also criticized for going to Washington for that planning session in March. I was attacked for my SCLC affiliation and my allegiance to Dr. King. Even my religious orientation was attacked."

Lewis considered many of the comments to be "very low and nasty, very bitter and mean," as several of his harshest critics shouted that SNCC needed a chairman who would stand up to Lyndon Johnson and King and tell them to "kiss our ass." Most of the gathering just sat and listened, so it was difficult to tell how much support Lewis had. When the vote was taken, he was pleasantly surprised that he was reelected by a wide margin, sixty to twenty-two, with a large number of abstentions. Or so it seemed.

After the vote, many of the members thought the meeting was over and returned to their cabins for the night. But it was not over. Without any warning, Worth Long, a veteran of the Selma voting rights project but no longer a staff member, questioned the validity of the election, raising a procedural objection that led to further discussion and a second vote. Lewis suspected that Long was fronting for Forman and Carmichael, but for a while he kept silent as many of those remaining at the meeting made the case against his reelection. Eventually, however, he lost his composure and "overplayed his hand," as Milton Viorst later put it, threatening to resign from SNCC if he were not reelected chairman. In Viorst's words, "In an organization riddled with suspicion of overbearing leaders, this statement was catastrophic."

Since most of Lewis's strongest supporters had already left, the result was almost a foregone conclusion. The prosecution, Lewis later wrote, "went on for several hours, people raising their voices and shouting, all these feelings bursting out, just a torrent of pent-up frustration and anger." At 5:30 a.m. the verbal assault ended, and Carmichael was elected chairman by acclamation. Lewis had been "de-elected," as he put it, the victim of an organizational coup that would have profound implications for SNCC's future. There was more than personal intrigue behind Lewis's ouster; it also reflected a dramatic shift in the organization's philosophical orientation, a shift that had begun as early as 1964. "What happened that night was the beginning of the end of SNCC," he told Pat Watters in 1970. "Breaches were created, wounds were opened that never were healed. I didn't consider it a repudiation of me. It was just a very sad thing, a very tragic thing for SNCC."

Lewis did his best to be a good loser, but it was difficult to overcome feelings of disappointment and rejection. "As much as I tried not to feel it," he revealed in his memoir, "this was a serious blow, a personal thing, and it affected me very much. My life, my identity, most of my very existence, was tied up in SNCC. Now, so suddenly, I felt put out to pasture. I was able to reason it out, to rationalize and understand it, especially with other people around, but when I was alone, it hurt. It hurt more than anything I'd ever been through."[9]

In the immediate aftermath of the Kingston Springs conference, Lewis was tempted to resign and distance himself from the organization. But he decided to stick it out at least for a while, hoping he could serve SNCC in some other capacity. When he returned to the Atlanta office, he learned he had been named director of the Committee for International Affairs, which he had created earlier in the year as a liaison to freedom struggles in the Third World. Although he doubted Carmichael and the new executive secretary, Ruby Doris Smith, had much interest in the committee's work, he accepted his demotion with as much grace as he could muster. On May 24, he joined Forman at an Atlanta press conference to present a united front and to put a favorable gloss on the change in leadership. In the spirit of solidarity, he even appeared with Carmichael at a Washington fund raiser. "It felt sort of odd sitting there watching him take charge," he confessed. "I had to swallow some pride . . . but I told myself it was toward a greater good, toward some sense of peace."[10]

Two weeks later, SNCC became embroiled in a major drama taking place in Mississippi. On June 5, James Meredith, a quixotic and fiercely independent activist who had desegregated the University of Mississippi in 1962, had set out with four friends on a 220-mile March against Fear from Memphis to Jackson. On the second day of the march, the group crossed the Mississippi line and headed south into the Delta on Highway 51, but twelve miles down the road, Meredith was gunned down by a forty-four-year-old white supremacist and World War II veteran named Aubrey James Norvell. Three shotgun blasts put Meredith in the hospital, provoking enough outrage to energize a large contingent of civil rights leaders determined to continue the march all the way to the state capitol in Jackson.

Carmichael and King were among the leaders responding to the call, and as the three-week-long march progressed, they had ample opportunity to air their differences at the nightly mass rallies at campsites along the route. King and his lieutenants preached the gospel of nonviolence, often using a ritualistic call and response. "What do we want?" King asked, and the crowd roared back, "Freedom!" When the march reached Greenwood on June 17, Carmichael countered with a rhythmic and dramatic call-and-response ritual of his own: "What do you want?" he asked over and over again, and each time the crowd shouted, "Black Power!"

Lewis was not there to witness this seminal moment in movement history; he was working in the SNCC office in Atlanta and didn't join the march until it reached Canton on June 24. But he had a preview of Carmichael's Black Power strategy on June 11, when he overheard a phone conversation between the chairman and Cleveland Sellers. Lewis couldn't hear it all, but he heard enough to know that Carmichael planned to lay a trap that would embarrass King and the SCLC. "That was the last straw," he recalled, with some sadness. "There was nothing left to hold on to here. Until then I had held on to a thin thread of hope that SNCC could still turn itself around. But this was too much. I could never be a party to anything that involved deviousness and deceit. That afternoon, I submitted my resignation, effective July 22."

In the weeks that followed, the Black Power slogan reverberated through the press, striking fear and confusion among many white people and eliciting fierce criticism from a range of civil rights leaders from King and Rustin to Wilkins and Thurgood Marshall. When an Associated Press reporter asked Lewis what he thought, he could not resist weighing in on his successor's recklessness. The ambiguous phrase "Black Power" frightened people to no purpose, he offered, adding, "As an organization we don't believe in sloganeering. We believe in programs." In his criticism of Carmichael, Lewis was obviously trying to avoid inflammatory language, but he had no control over the story's provocative headline: "John Lewis Breaks with SNCC over Phrase Black Power."

The break with SNCC was now almost complete. But when he heard that Mississippi state troopers had assaulted the marchers with clubs and tear gas as soon as they tried to set up camp in Canton, he felt he had to go there to do what he could to help. When he arrived, the scene reminded him of the carnage on Bloody Sunday fifteen months earlier. As he made his way through the crowd, he was surprised when none of his SNCC colleagues said anything about his negative statement on Black Power, and he was even more surprised when Carmichael encouraged him to address the crowd at a mass meeting that night. Most of the marchers knew nothing about his resignation letter or his impending departure from SNCC, but he knew that this would almost certainly be his last speech for the organization.

As Lewis rose to speak, he was almost overwhelmed by emotion tinged with a certain sadness, a mournful regret that the Beloved Community seemed farther away than ever. He later confessed to the *New York Times Magazine* feature writer Paul Good, who was standing on the edge of the crowd listening and taking notes, that he "felt like an unwanted guest that night." Good's poignant essay, which appeared the following summer, captured the pathos of the moment: "Even as he spoke, listeners sloshed away. The speaker's credentials were in order, but his time was out of joint. He spoke the old words of militant love, but the spiritual heart of the movement that for years had sent crusaders up and down American roads, trusting in love, was broken and Lewis had become that most expendable commodity, a former leader. It was not so much that he was losing his audience; the audience was already lost."[11]

On July 22, less than a month after the Canton speech, Lewis cleared out his desk at the Atlanta office and said goodbye to SNCC. "So there I was," he explained, "twenty-six years old and starting my life over, broke, with no job, no skills, no wife, no children, no place even to call home." He knew he wanted to stay close to the movement, to continue the struggle, but beyond that his plan for the future was uncertain.

He also knew that returning to his family in Pike County was not a realistic option. While he cherished his family, his ideals and passions—the things that mattered most to him—were not "a part of their world." "My family," he later explained, "had never really been connected to or understood my involvement in the movement. To them, it was as if I was living in a foreign country. Their lives were very simple, very insular, very close to the earth. They didn't look too far beyond their immediate surroundings." Besides, going back home for anything more than a brief visit would put his family in danger. Among the white residents of Pike County, he was a notorious figure, a marked man, an agitator.

Lewis wasn't sure he wanted to stay in Atlanta either. Perhaps, he thought, he could return to Fisk to complete his bachelor's degree. But that would require a bit of money, much more than an unemployed civil rights worker could muster. His meager salary at SNCC had barely kept him alive, so he had no savings. He desperately needed a job, preferably one that would allow him to work for social change while earning a decent income. But how and where he would find such a job was a puzzle until he received an unexpected phone call from Carl Holman, the editor of a weekly newspaper, the *Atlanta Inquirer*, and formerly a professor at Clark College.

Holman was also a member of the board of directors of the Field Foundation of New York, a philanthropic organization that had funded child welfare programs and civil rights initiatives such as the Voter Education Project begun in 1962. The executive director of the Field Foundation, Leslie Dunbar, was the former head of the Southern Regional Council (SRC), a prominent white liberal organization that had promoted civil rights and racial integration since the 1940s. As soon as he learned that Lewis had left SNCC, Dunbar seized the opportunity to recruit him for a position with the Field Foundation. When Holman asked Lewis if he would consider leaving the South and moving to New York, the deposed SNCC leader knew he had found a pathway to a new and potentially fulfilling chapter of his life.[12]

CHAPTER 11

———

Transition and Tragedy

O N AUGUST 1, 1966, John Lewis began his golden exile in New York as the new associate director of the Field Foundation. His new home, a fourth-floor walk-up apartment on West Twenty-First Street, in the gritty Chelsea section of Manhattan, was a long way from the Deep South, geographically and culturally. Predictably, it took some time for him to get used to the pace and feel of Northern city life. His neighborhood was mixed, with a "good number of blacks and a few Puerto Ricans." But this was his first experience with living in a predominantly white setting. At times, he seemed lost, but as he later observed, "it actually felt good, in an odd, liberating kind of way. This was a time of transition for me, a time when I needed to be lost for a while. And there is no better way for a boy from the rural South to be lost than to pick him up and put him in a place like Manhattan."

He often felt lonely and homesick, and even likened himself to the novelist Ralph Ellison's "invisible man." "I didn't know any of my neighbors," he noted, "and they didn't know me." He did spend some time with Julie Prettyman, an old friend who ran SNCC's New York office. But mostly he found refuge in his work, for which he was paid $200 a month, five times his SNCC salary. He got along well with the foundation's staff of five, and he soon grew fond of Leslie Dunbar, whom he respected and admired. His primary task was to evaluate grant proposals and programs administered by community organizations dealing with social welfare and civil rights issues. He spent most of his time in the foundation's Park Avenue office, but he also traveled widely to talk with prospective grantees, sometimes in upstate New York but mostly in the South.[1]

At one point, Andrew Young and Martin Luther King Jr. visited the foundation office to solicit funds for an SCLC citizen education project, and on another occasion, Jim Bevel visited and spent a night in his apartment. They had fun talking about the "old days" and Bevel's current plan to push the SCLC toward open condemnation of the Vietnam War, an idea that Lewis applauded. But when he tried to convince Lewis to accept a staff position at the SCLC, the response was unequivocal. In Lewis's recounting of the conversation, he told Bevel, "There was no way I would ever consider that. . . . I could never go back and play a smaller role with another civil rights group than I had played with SNCC. I had been the national chair of a major organization. I'll admit it, it was a matter of pride, to a large degree."

Lewis kept tabs on SNCC through frequent letters and phone calls to and from old movement friends, especially Julian Bond, who kept up a steady stream of correspondence. Most of what Lewis heard or read saddened him. In the months since his departure, SNCC had moved further and further away from its traditional commitments to nonviolence and interracial cooperation. Black separatists like Julius Lester and H. Rap Brown had essentially taken over the organization by May 1967, when Brown replaced Stokely Carmichael as chairman and the last remaining white staff members were expelled. By then, SNCC had, in effect, abandoned the civil rights movement to become part of the radical New Left, driving virtually all of Lewis's old friends and colleagues out of the organization.

One of his closest movement friends, Don Harris, had left SNCC in 1965 to attend Harvard Law School. His wife, Kate, was the daughter of the famed Black social psychologist Kenneth Clark, the "doll man" whose work was instrumental to the NAACP's brief in the 1954 *Brown v. Board of Education* case. Clark still resided in suburban New York, in a beautiful home on the Hudson River, and Lewis sometimes joined Don and Kate there on weekend outings. On one occasion, he even met them at Oak Bluffs, a seaside resort on Martha's Vineyard, for an adventurous New England weekend.[2]

Lewis's memorable vacations with Kate and Don Harris helped to relieve his loneliness, but the most unforgettable experience during his fourteen-month sojourn in New York came in April 1967, when he witnessed one of

King's greatest speeches. The setting was the colossal Riverside Church in the Morningside Heights section of Upper Manhattan, and the theme was the moral bankruptcy of the Vietnam War. Sponsored by the Clergy and Laymen Concerned about Vietnam, the speech explored the unfortunate "connection between the war in Vietnam and the struggle I and others have been waging in America." "A few years ago," King reminded the crowd of two thousand, "there was a shining moment in that struggle. It seemed as if there was real promise of hope for the poor, both black and white, through the poverty program. . . . Then came the buildup in Vietnam, and I watched this program broken and eviscerated as if it were some idle political plaything of a society gone mad on war."

This was the speech that Lewis had been waiting to hear ever since he had publicly declared SNCC's opposition to the war in 1965. At the beginning of his speech, King acknowledged SNCC's courageous stand, confessing he had finally found the resolve to "break the betrayals of my own silences and to speak from the burnings of my own heart." This admission, couched in the spirit of love and redemption, reminded Lewis why he was so devoted to King. "I had heard Dr. King speak many, many times, and I had no doubt that this speech was his finest," he noted in his memoir. "It was deep, comprehensive, thoughtful and courageous. It was about what we were doing in Vietnam, but beyond that it was about what we were doing on this *earth*. He was saying that those bombs that were being dropped in Vietnam would detonate here, that they were being dropped on the hopes and dreams of the American people."

Lewis came away from the Riverside speech with renewed faith in the moral power of nonviolence—and with the recognition that his urge to reengage with the ongoing struggle in the South was growing stronger. "I wasn't in the midst of the movement anymore, not at the moment," he told himself, "but I knew I would get back to it. . . . People were beginning to talk about the South as being the stage for the next big wave of change in America. I believed that the next decade would see the whole nation looking to the South for direction and leadership. I wanted to be a part of that." Besides, he decided, "New York was just too big for me. I didn't feel as if I could get my hands around it. In the South, communities seemed comprehensible, manageable, workable. . . . I knew that the South was where I belonged. I needed to go back."[3]

* * *

Lewis also needed a good job to sustain him when he got there, and in October 1967 he found just that. When Paul Anthony, the executive director of the Southern Regional Council (SRC), heard a rumor that Lewis was thinking about returning to the South, he booked a flight to New York to offer the SNCC veteran a position as director of the SRC's Community Organization Project. Lewis wasted no time in accepting the offer. After submitting his resignation to Leslie Dunbar and thanking him for his many kindnesses, he headed south to Atlanta.

Georgia, Lewis soon discovered, was not the same place he had left in the summer of 1966. State politics had veered sharply to the right, and the notorious hard-line segregationist Lester Maddox had replaced the moderate Carl Sanders as governor. To make matters worse, here, as elsewhere, the civil rights movement was in complete disarray, with Black nationalists and proponents of armed self-defense squaring off against less militant organizations such as the NAACP, the SCLC, and the National Urban league. Dedicated to interracial cooperation and liberal reform, the SRC's staff of forty professional "do-gooders," as Maddox called them, faced the daunting task of navigating the troubled waters of Black frustration and white resistance.

Lewis's Community Organization Project spearheaded the development of cooperatives, credit unions, and community development programs all across the South. It was the kind of grassroots organizing that Lewis had been advocating for years, a mixture of resource development, democratic empowerment, and self-help. With his partner, Al Ulmer, a white North Carolinian and Peace Corps veteran, he visited both urban and rural communities, but mostly the latter. "We traveled all over the South, Al and I, into little towns and farming areas," he remembered, "many of the same places I'd spent time in during the first half of the decade. Selma, Greenwood, Americus—they were the same, but they were different now, too. Sleepier, sedate, calmer, quieter. No marching, no battalions of troopers, no press. The press had moved north now, following the movement and the action into the cities. The 'revolution,' riots, Black Panthers, campus unrest, Vietnam—these were the big stories now. The civil rights movement was old news."

Though seldom glamorous, organizing cooperatives was richly fulfilling for Lewis. "It was hands-on work," he recalled, "and I loved it." Most of the communities he visited, he concluded, faced problems "that wouldn't be helped by marching and singing. The people living there could finally vote, but other needs—food and shelter and jobs—were wanting. My job was about helping these people join together, helping them help one another to fill those needs." He was reaching out to people who often reminded him of his own family in Pike County. In effect, he had found a way to go home, to renew his ties to working-class and rural Black culture.

Lewis's experiences in the field also reinforced his commitment to the social gospel, extending the lessons he had learned in James Lawson's workshops, the sit-ins and marches, and the Freedom Rides. He thought a lot about this during the fall of 1967, as he wrote a long essay about the civil rights movement as "a religious phenomenon." With this essay, he finally completed the Fisk philosophy degree that had been on hold since 1963. The topic was essential to his understanding of how the nonviolent movement had taken hold earlier in the decade. As he once explained in a conversation with Pat Watters: "Redemptive love was the heart of the movement, the appeal to the best instincts of human beings. Redemptive love came naturally to Negro Southerners. The role and place of the Negro church was the idea of salvation. Many Negroes, young and old, were involved in the movement out of a strong, moral, religious feeling, conviction. Sharecroppers, poor people, would come to the mass meetings, because they were in the *church*. People saw the mass meetings as an extension of the Sunday services."[4]

Lewis also found time to renew his close friendships with Bond, who was serving his first term as a Georgia state senator, and Bernard LaFayette, who was working out of the SCLC's Atlanta office after a year in Chicago organizing an open housing movement. Knowing their friend was prone to working himself into exhaustion, both men tried to invigorate Lewis's social life with party invitations and introductions to young single women.

In December 1967, LaFayette introduced Lewis to Lillian Miles, a librarian who worked with Julian's mother at the Atlanta University Library.

Educated at California State College in Los Angeles and the University of Southern California, Lillian was bright and cosmopolitan, having spent two years in the Peace Corps in Nigeria and done a stint with Operations Crossroads Africa. When Lewis invited her to his birthday party in February, she showed up in a chic green-and-beige minidress emblazoned with peace signs. Later that evening, when he discovered she admired King as much as he did, Lewis was hooked. They soon became a couple, often double-dating with Julian and Alice Bond, and ten months later they married in a ceremony officiated by Martin Luther King Sr. at Ebenezer Baptist Church. Don Harris was the best man, Julian was an usher, and dozens of other SNCC and SCLC friends were among the three hundred guests at the church.[5]

The late-December wedding provided a sweet ending to a sour year in Lewis's life. From the previous spring on, a series of unexpected, and in some cases tragic, events had shaken his normally optimistic view of the future. His ideals of peace and love were under steady assault by a number of forces—escalating violence in Vietnam and in the streets of American cities, political and social polarization, governmental repression of dissent, and deepening disillusionment among Black and impoverished Americans who had expected more from the civil rights and Great Society legislation of the previous four years.

Lewis was particularly saddened by the fragmentation and decline of a civil rights movement that had once held so much promise. "I was dismayed by what I was seeing," he explained. "On almost every front, the attitude of nonviolence and the belief in a biracial democracy, in the Beloved Community, were being abandoned. Dr. King was doing his best to stay the course, but even his efforts were beginning to falter. Along with everyone else, he had shifted his sights to the North, mounting a campaign in Chicago that was a disastrous failure and mobilizing a Poor People's Campaign that couldn't seem to quite get off the ground. . . . There was no place for me in that movement, not as it had become."

* * *

For a time, Lewis felt he had found a refuge in national Democratic politics. He had never put much stock in electoral politics, other than campaigning for Bond in 1966. But in March 1968 he became deeply involved in Bobby

Kennedy's campaign for the Democratic presidential nomination. Senator Eugene McCarthy of Minnesota had announced his candidacy in November 1967 as an antiwar alternative to President Lyndon Johnson, and there was widespread speculation that eventually Kennedy, who had been elected to the Senate from New York in 1966, would throw his hat into the ring as well. On March 16, four days after McCarthy exposed Johnson's vulnerability by winning 42 percent of the vote in the New Hampshire primary, Kennedy entered the race.

Lewis was in Jackson, Mississippi, when he saw Kennedy's televised announcement. Sensing that this was an opportunity to become involved in a political movement that shared the same values as the civil rights movement of the early 1960s, he immediately sent a telegram pledging his support and asking what he could do to help the campaign. During Kennedy's attorney generalship, Lewis's opinion of his attitudes toward direct action and voting rights marches was generally negative. But he now "believed Kennedy had dramatically changed, that he had grown." When Kennedy spoke out against the war, and when he expressed his "concern for America's 'invisible' poor, as he called them, and [spoke] on his commitment to confront and to close the racial rifts that were turning the streets of the nation's largest cities into battlefields," Lewis concluded, "the America Bobby Kennedy envisioned sounded much like the Beloved Community I believed in."

Kennedy soon accepted Lewis's offer, and after the SRC granted him a leave, he was on his way to Indiana, the first state where the senator was competing for convention delegates. Assigned the task of bringing out the Black vote for Kennedy, he threw himself into the primary campaign, mostly in the inner-city neighborhoods of Indianapolis. Working closely with local Black leaders, he prepared the ground for Kennedy's first visit to the state, scheduled for April 4. During Lewis's first two weeks in Indianapolis, the work was progressing well, and Kennedy's campaign received a major boost when President Johnson unexpectedly dropped out of the race on March 31. The contest was now between the two antiwar candidates, though Vice President Hubert Humphrey would enter the race in late April.[6]

Kennedy's prospects of winning the nomination brightened after Johnson's withdrawal, but on April 4 a dark cloud suddenly enveloped the nation. Late that afternoon, an hour before Kennedy was scheduled to arrive in

Indianapolis, Lewis learned that King had been assassinated in Memphis. The details were sketchy, but Lewis knew that King had been in Memphis off and on for several weeks lending support to a sanitation workers' strike. To Lewis's dismay, the strikers and their supporters had lapsed into violence on several occasions, but now the great leader himself had been struck down. Lewis's immediate reaction was disbelief mixed with shock. "At that moment," he recalled, "I had no feeling. No thoughts. No words. I was obliterated, blown beyond any sensations whatsoever. I was numb. . . . I just stood there, not moving, not thinking."

The immediate problem for Lewis and the staff was what to do about the rally scheduled for later that evening in the inner-city neighborhood of Broadway—a rally that Lewis had arranged. Some of the staff wanted to cancel the event, but Lewis disagreed. "Somebody has to speak to these people," he insisted. "You can't have a crowd like this come, and something like this happen, and send them home without anything at all. Kennedy has to speak, for his own sake and for the sake of these people." Coming into town from the airport, Kennedy called from a car phone to express his sorrow. "I'm sorry," he told Lewis. "You've lost a leader. We've lost a leader."

By the time Kennedy reached the site of the rally, a crowd of more than a thousand supporters had gathered. At that point very few of them knew what had happened in Memphis two hours earlier. Ignoring the formal speaker's stage, Kennedy, looking distressed and drawn, stood on the trunk of a car as he spoke to the crowd. At first, cheers and laughter almost drowned out his words, but the sad news that he delivered—that King had been shot and killed—soon spread through the crowd "like a wave." "You could hear gasps. Shouts of 'No!'" Lewis remembered. "People broke down and wept. Some dropped to their knees." Eventually they all withdrew into silence or quiet sobbing as Kennedy spoke from the heart with no notes. "Martin Luther King dedicated his life to love and to justice between fellow human beings," he told them. "He died in the cause of that effort. In this difficult day, in this difficult time for the United States, it is perhaps well to ask what kind of a nation we are and what direction we want to move in. For those of you who are black . . . you can be filled with bitterness, and with hatred, and a desire for revenge. We can move in that direction as a country, in great polarization—black people amongst black, and white amongst whites, filled with hatred toward one another. Or we can make an effort, as Martin Luther King did, to understand and to comprehend and replace that violence, that stain of bloodshed that has spread across our land, with an effort to understand compassion and love."

He ended with a homily attributed to Aeschylus, a plea "to tame the savageness of man and to make gentle the life of the world." Just after arriving in Indiana, Lewis had told a reporter that Kennedy "is the one guy who can bring people together," and now, as the crowd headed home to a night of private grief, his judgment was confirmed. Indianapolis was one of the few large American cities that did not succumb to rioting that night, and Lewis and many others felt that Kennedy's speech was one of the reasons why. As the brother of an assassinated president, Kennedy reacted to King's death with a special sadness, which Lewis witnessed at a late-night gathering in the hotel where the candidate was staying. Surrounded by his staff, Kennedy broke down and cried, before turning to Lewis to tell him once again how sorry he was. He then phoned King's widow, Coretta, to express his condolences and ask what he could do to help. When she responded that he could "help get her husband's body back from Memphis to Atlanta as soon as possible," he promised to do what he could.[7]

Lewis flew to Atlanta the next day to prepare for the funeral and to attend an emergency SCLC board meeting. He, along with the rest of the board, was in a state of shock, saddened not only by their leader's death but also by the widespread death and destruction that had occurred across the nation the night before. But they had to press on with the selection of a new leader to replace King. The leading contenders were Ralph Abernathy, King's close friend and confidant, and the Reverend Sam Williams, who had been one of King's teachers at Morehouse College. Lewis supported Abernathy, who, after several days of deliberation, emerged as the victor on April 9, the day of King's funeral.

The night before the service at Ebenezer Baptist Church, Lewis attended a strategy meeting with Kennedy and his staff, several SCLC leaders, and Harry Belafonte. Kennedy sought their advice on how to move forward on issues related to civil rights, on the issues that had meant so much to King. After the meeting, at three in the morning, Lewis accompanied Kennedy and his wife, Ethel, to the Ebenezer sanctuary, where they spent several minutes praying next to King's casket. Those quiet moments helped Lewis to deal with the emotional crescendo of the public ceremonies held the next day. Following the service at Ebenezer, he and an estimated fifty thousand mourners walked quietly behind a wagon carrying King's casket for five miles, all the way from the church to a Morehouse chapel, where a second service was held. Later Lewis and a few others joined the King family for a private burial at South-View Cemetery, bringing a full day of reverence and grief to a close.

King's funeral brought Lewis close to the breaking point, prompting a temporary retreat from the world. Many years later, he tried to explain why he needed a few days of reflective isolation. "Now had come my time to grieve," he later wrote. "Dr. King was my friend, my brother, my leader. . . . To this day I owe more of myself to him than to anyone else I have ever known. . . . I have never believed in any man as much as I believed in Martin Luther King. When he was killed I really felt I'd lost a part of myself."[8]

*   *   *

Lewis's recovery and return to the tasks at hand, he went on to explain, grew out of his belief that Kennedy represented the nation's best hope for moral and political redemption: "Dr. King's death made it all the more important for me to put everything I had into Kennedy's campaign. I saw this as the final extension of the movement. I transferred all the loyalty I had left from Dr. King to Bobby Kennedy." In mid-April, he returned to the campaign trail, first in Indiana, where Kennedy won the primary, garnering 86 percent of the Black vote, and later in Nebraska, Oregon, and California. Kennedy won in Nebraska but lost in Oregon, making the California contest a crucial test of his ability to win the nomination.

Lewis spent nearly two weeks in California, mostly in the poorest areas of Los Angeles. Much of the time, he worked closely with Cesar Chavez, the Chicano labor leader who for several years had spearheaded the organizing efforts of the United Farm Workers. Chavez, who had become adept at employing many of the same protest methods as the civil rights movement—boycotts, marches, community organizing, and nonviolent resistance—respected Lewis and shared his enthusiasm for Kennedy's insurgent campaign. Working together to get out the vote, they made a formidable team, especially when the candidate himself was on hand for a crowd-stirring motorcade. "The outpouring of emotion as we passed through those streets was much more than mere support for Kennedy," Lewis recalled. "It was love. It was adoration. People, especially young people, just mobbed us, climbing all over the cars, trying to get close to Kennedy, to touch him. It was amazing, that Kennedy magic."

On election night, April 4, expectations were high as Lewis and other staff members, plus a number of journalists and show business celebrities, gathered around a television in a fifth-floor suite at the Hotel Ambassador in Los Angeles to watch the returns. After Kennedy became the projected winner around 9:00 p.m., jubilation broke out in the suite, and three hours later, just after the returns from the heavily Hispanic and African American precincts were announced, the smiling candidate came by the suite for a brief visit before heading downstairs to give his victory speech. Before he left, he walked over to Lewis to shake his hand and tease him about the news that the Black vote for Kennedy, though nearly 90 percent, was a little lower than the Mexican American vote. Both men laughed, of course, and then Kennedy left, promising to return after his speech.

The victory speech was gracious, as Kennedy acknowledged the efforts of his rival, Eugene McCarthy, and thanked the tireless campaign workers responsible for his triumph. He mentioned several individuals by name, including Chavez and the United Auto Workers leader Paul Schrade, but somehow he overlooked Lewis. Never one to seek public acclaim, Lewis showed no sign of disappointment. But whatever he felt during the speech was all but forgotten a few minutes later when word came that Kennedy had been shot by a lone gunman while exiting the ballroom through a kitchen hallway. "I dropped to my knees, to the carpet," Lewis remembered. "I was crying, sobbing, heaving as if something had been busted open inside. All around me the room was filled with groans and shock. . . . I sat on the floor, dazed, rocking back and forth as if I were autistic, saying one word out loud, over and over again. '*Why? Why? Why?*'"

Lewis walked back to his hotel in a daze before collapsing on his bed at three in the morning. That afternoon, he returned to Atlanta on what he later called "the loneliest, longest flight of my life." Kennedy died the next morning, and later in the day Lewis received a telegram from the Kennedy family asking him to be part of the honor guard at the public viewing at St. Patrick's Cathedral in New York. The next evening, he was at the cathedral paired with Abernathy, standing vigil over the casket for an hour as hundreds of mourners filed past. After attending a funeral mass the following day, he traveled to Washington on a twenty-one-car funeral train equipped with a special glass-walled car that allowed people beside the tracks to glimpse the senator's body. As Lewis described the scene, "All the way down, through New Jersey, Pennsylvania, Delaware, Maryland, I could look out the window and see crowds standing along the tracks, waving, holding signs, crying, 'We Love You, Bobby' and 'Goodbye Bobby'—the signs seemed so sad, so moving."

That evening, he said his final goodbye to the political leader who had given him a tantalizing glimpse of how politics could advance the search for the Beloved Community. The burial service at Arlington National Cemetery, where the two martyred Kennedy brothers now rested side by side, was profoundly sad for Lewis. This was his first visit to the cemetery, a sacred place that stirred his soul but did little to assuage his grief. It would take time for him to recover from the shocking violence of the past two months, from his sense of loss. "I sleepwalked through the next few weeks," he recalled, "wondering if I could ever put my belief and faith and trust in someone again. First Dr. King, then Bobby Kennedy, both shot dead within weeks of each other. It hurt so incredibly much when they were taken away. . . . I knew that what I was feeling was the same thing millions of Americans felt. What could we *believe* in now? How much more of this could we take?"[9]

* * *

When he returned to his work at the SRC, he felt he had changed, that he had become more wary of the ways of the world, more attuned to the tragic side of history. He also discovered there was no turning back from the politicization of his moral sensibility. In July, he attended a strategy session in Macon convened by E. T. Kehrer, the head of the AFL-CIO's civil rights division in Atlanta. Kehrer was trying to organize a challenge to the virtually all-white Georgia delegation scheduled to attend the upcoming Democratic National Convention in Chicago. Following in the footsteps of the MFDP's challenge four years earlier, the Georgia Loyal Democrats brought together a broad-based interracial coalition of sixty delegates representing civil rights groups, labor unions, and antiwar activists. Lewis helped to enlist many of the delegates, including Bond, who ended up chairing the delegation.

Lewis himself volunteered to be one of the challenge delegates, a decision that put him in harm's way for the first time since 1965. When he and the other Georgia Loyal Democrats arrived in Chicago, "the city was in a state of near war." "The parks downtown—Grant Park and Lincoln Park—were filled with thousands of antiwar protestors who had been streaming into the city all week," he observed. "These protestors, the vast majority of them young and white, a large number of them college students, many of them veterans of our civil rights movement in the South, had come from across the country to show themselves to the convention and the nation."

The sight of so many activists willing to take to the streets reminded him of the glory days in Birmingham, Selma, and other centers of struggle in the Deep South. "I was very sympathetic to those young people," he remembered. "They were trying to do exactly what we had done down south—dramatize the issue, put it in front of the politicians, put it in front of the nation, make their voices heard." Unfortunately, the reactionary force trying to stifle the protesters in Chicago was also familiar to Lewis: "Richard Daley, the bulldog-like mayor of Chicago, had responded to these kids the way Bull Connor and Jim Clark responded to us in Birmingham and Selma," unleashing "the Chicago police, who reacted swiftly and brutally and without discipline or restraint, lashing out at the slightest provocation, or even with no provocation at all."

Lewis and his Georgia colleagues had to make their way around barbed-wire fences and police barricades to enter the convention hall, and once they were inside, there were obstructions of a different kind. On the first night, there was a floor fight over the Georgia delegate challenge, and on the second night the convention approved a motion to split the delegation evenly between the regular delegates, who supported Governor Maddox, and the insurgent Georgia Loyal Democrats, giving each delegate half a vote. Lewis and his colleagues accepted the compromise, but twenty of the thirty regulars left the hall in protest.[10]

All of this controversy thrust Bond, the chairman of the Georgia delegation, into the limelight. Already something of a celebrity as the antiwar activist barred from the Georgia legislature in 1966, he now stepped forward to deliver a rousing speech seconding the presidential nomination of Eugene McCarthy. He then became involved in a clever plan to put the antiwar activist Al Lowenstein on the speaker's stand. After Bond was unexpectedly nominated for vice president, Lowenstein was chosen to second the nomination. The seconding speech had more to do with his opposition to the war than his support for Bond, who at age twenty-eight was seven years short of being eligible to accept the nomination. But the maneuver had the desired effect nonetheless, giving the antiwar delegates a brief triumph over the pro-Humphrey forces running the convention. It also greatly enhanced Bond's stature and visibility, prompting the *New York Times* to call him "the leader of the New Politics."

Lewis watched all of this with amazement. "It was an incredible experience," he later commented, "to watch my friend become a superstar. It was fun. . . . So for us, the Georgia Loyal Democrats, and for Julian, the convention was a success." For the Democratic Party and the nation, however, the nomination of Humphrey amid so much "madness and chaos" was, in Lewis's view, a "disaster."

In November, the first time he ever voted in a presidential election, Lewis chose Humphrey over Nixon, largely on the basis of the Minnesota Democrat's progressive position on civil rights. But Humphrey's refusal to oppose the war was deeply discouraging, reminding Lewis of the damage caused by Bobby Kennedy's—and Dr. King's—death. Indeed, he later concluded that the damage went well beyond the loss of an election and the perpetuation of an immoral war. "The flame of faith and hope—mine, the nation's—had been barely flickering at the beginning of that year," he noted. "By the end, it really felt as if it had gone out. Something in the civil rights movement died for good in 1966, but something died in all of America in 1968. The sense of hope, of optimism, of *possibility*, was replaced by horror, the worst of times, the feeling that maybe, just maybe, we would *not* overcome."[11]

CHAPTER 12

———

Voting Rights and the New South

THE 1968 POLICE RIOT in Chicago capped off a long summer of violence that took its toll on John Lewis's mental and spiritual health. Indeed, his weakened condition was already apparent several weeks earlier when, by his own admission, he was not his normal self. For one of the first times in his life, he felt severe fatigue and nervous exhaustion. As soon as his physician, James Palmer, took one look at Lewis in early August, he issued an order for hospitalization and several days of bed rest. Lewis's steady girlfriend, Lillian Miles, did her best to restore his strength and spirit with daily visits, bringing him his mail and a morning newspaper. But after they watched part of the reactionary Republican National Convention together, he had a relapse "which made me feel even lower than I'd been when I checked in," he claimed half-jokingly. Ironically, it was in this weak and vulnerable position that he finally mustered the courage to ask Lillian to marry him.

She said yes, and four and a half months later, on December 21, they were married at an Atlanta church filled with movement friends, including best man Don Harris. The newlyweds soon rented a house in northeast Atlanta, but within a year they managed to buy a house of their own in Venetian Hills—in Lewis's description, "a comfortable, middle-class community of established homes and rolling tree-shaded streets." They would remain there for the rest of their married life, despite an early experience with white flight. Located in a suburban area southwest of downtown, the neighborhood "was racially mixed when we moved in," Lewis noted, "but it didn't stay that way long. We were the first black family to move onto our block, and within two years we were flanked by black neighbors, both renting and buying, as the white owners began moving out."[1]

Fear of residential integration was rife among white Georgians at the time, stoked by the demagoguery of Governor Lester Maddox. Lewis faced this and other harsh realities virtually every day in his work with the SRC, but even the most liberal Georgia politicians were reluctant to deal openly and honestly with the confounding legacy of Jim Crow. "The '60s were over, but many of the problems we had confronted with the movement remained," he explained. "We had made remarkable progress, we had forced the side of segregation and discrimination to retreat on many fronts. But they did not surrender. Far from it. They simply retrenched in different, more subtle ways."

Even in a self-proclaimed New South city like Atlanta, which a decade earlier had adopted the slogan "A city too busy to hate," racial discrimination in housing, employment, and education persisted. In the recent past, the civil rights movement spearheaded by Martin Luther King Jr. and many others had pushed for fundamental change, but as a dismayed Lewis pointed out, that movement, "the massive organization and mobilization of people of conscience, Black and white together, gathered to confront racism and segregation in an aggressive, disciplined, nonviolent manner— that had all but vanished."

On a return visit to Selma in 1969, he discussed the sharp decline of the nonviolent–direct action spirit with the journalist Pat Watters and a woman who had been one of the Selma movement's foot soldiers in 1965. "Do you think, do you think, John, it will ever come back?," the woman asked plaintively. In response, Lewis tried to offer some hope, but he had no firm answer to her question. Watters's comment was even more sobering. Speaking of the nonviolent movement that had once given him so much hope, he declared: "It was there . . . in all the little churches of the movement across the South—and then it was gone. Ten years after the sit-ins started, to invoke their mood is to invite ridicule, cynical scorn." The sad reality that Lewis and Watters faced was that in the nonviolent movement's place an angry and sometimes violent array of Black nationalists and advocates of revolution had risen to prominence, mounting a frenzied and often self-destructive

challenge to the hard-edged law-and-order policies of the Nixon administration and J. Edgar Hoover's FBI.[2]

As a proponent of nonviolence and racial reconciliation, Lewis wanted
no part of this increasingly mean-spirited conflict. But he worried that his
SRC work promoting cooperatives was too modest to make a meaningful
contribution to the cause of freedom, which he still believed in with all his
heart. His options were limited to two choices: he could try to rebuild the
nonviolent movement, starting with the few remaining fragments of the
SCLC and SNCC; or he could invest his time and energy in electoral politics. Considering the tenor of the times, the first option's chance of success
seemed slim, especially after Lewis attended an impromptu SNCC reunion
held in Washington in March 1970.

The occasion was the funeral of Ralph Featherstone, who had died
when a bomb exploded in a car carrying him and William "Che" Payne to
the Bel Air, Maryland, courthouse where the riot incitement trial of H. Rap
Brown, the former SNCC chairman and minister of justice for the Black
Panther Party, was scheduled to begin the next day. At the funeral there
was talk of FBI complicity and an assassination plot, but law enforcement
officers and government officials told a different story, claiming that Featherstone and Payne had planned to blow up the courthouse. Lewis didn't
know what to believe, the conspiratorial accusations levied by the SNCC
veterans or the government claims that Featherstone had gone off the
deep end. But whatever the truth, he couldn't find much to say to any of
his former SNCC colleagues. The whole affair left him feeling empty and
dispirited.[3]

Soon thereafter, he received another jolt when Jim Bevel, who had grown
increasingly erratic and irrational since King's assassination, was expelled
from the SCLC for immoral and unethical behavior. The specific charge
was abuse of authority in a misguided effort to create a cult of personality.
At one point, after gathering a group of apostles—mostly Spelman College
women—Bevel reportedly "urinated in a glass and told them they had to
drink it to prove they were true followers." Lewis was dumbstruck that the
man he had admired since their Nashville days had sunk so low. But the
Bevel incident confirmed his suspicion that the old movement days were
gone forever.[4]

Later in the day, just minutes after Bevel's expulsion, Lewis took an important step toward active political engagement. In a meeting with Andrew Young, he tried to convince his fellow SCLC board member that it was time for Atlanta to elect a Black congressman. The previous November, Lewis had written a long letter to Julian Bond expressing his "deep interest in seeing what I call 'good men' elevated to higher positions in the political arena . . . those who are willing to inject into the body politic a degree of the honesty and morality that we witnessed in the early days of the Civil Rights Movement." The letter went on to urge his friend to run for Congress in Georgia's Fifth Congressional District, which included most of Atlanta. The celebrity and visibility that Bond had achieved in 1968 would make him a strong congressional candidate, Lewis insisted. "Let me think about it," Bond responded, but he never followed up on Lewis's suggestion, possibly because he knew no African American had been elected to Congress from a Southern state since 1898.

After six months of waiting, Lewis gave up on his first choice and handed the same letter to Young. This time the idea took hold, and within a week Young had announced his candidacy. The SNCC veteran Ivanhoe Donaldson signed on as campaign manager, and Lewis promised that he and Lillian would devote whatever spare time they had to campaigning. "Ever since I became involved in Bobby Kennedy's campaign, I'd been convinced that politics was the road that we must now take to achieve the goals we had pursued until then through direct action," he later explained. "Now that the primary purpose of those years of action—securing the right to vote—had been achieved, it was time to show black Americans in the South not only that they could select their political representatives but that it was possible to *become* those representatives." Young agreed, insisting, "There just comes a time when any social movement has to come in off the street and enter politics."[5]

The number of Black officeholders had already increased dramatically since the passage of the Voting Rights Act in 1965. By 1970 there were three Black mayors of large Northern cities—Carl Stokes of Cleveland, Richard Hatcher of Gary, and Walter Washington of Washington, D.C.—and two Black mayors of Southern towns, Carl Lee of Chapel Hill, North Carolina, and Charles Evers of Fayette, Mississippi. Even in Atlanta, Black residents had breached several political barriers: in 1968 the Black labor lawyer Maynard Jackson carried the city in a daring but unsuccessful bid to unseat Senator Herman Talmadge, and a year later he was elected vice-mayor.

Encouraged by Jackson's success, Young had reason to believe he had a legitimate shot at winning. A recent reapportionment had raised the Black proportion of the district's electorate to nearly 40 percent, and with Lewis's help he developed a promising strategy to assemble a "New South Coalition"—a mix of "black votes, liberal votes, white labor votes." This worked well in the Democratic primary, where he easily defeated the white lawyer Wyman C. Lowe. But in the general election, his coalition proved to be no match for the wide-based support won by Fletcher Thompson, a popular, two-term incumbent Republican congressman.[6]

*   *   *

Both Lewis and Young were disappointed, but neither had any thought of giving up on electoral politics. In fact, Lewis's engagement with politics had received an unexpected boost five months earlier when he replaced Vernon Jordan as the executive director of the SRC's Voter Education Project (VEP). He was elated. "The job was a perfect fit," he later noted, "a direct extension of the work I'd done during all those years with SNCC." Created in 1962, the VEP worked to expand the number of registered Black voters and candidates throughout the South, a task made much easier by the passage of the Voting Rights Act.

With a staff of thirty-eight in 1970, the VEP was a much larger operation than the Community Organization Project. Fanning out across the region, Lewis and his staff became adept at "spearheading get-out-the-vote drives, presenting seminars for young black people interested in politics, and offering technical and financial assistance to black community groups interested in political education." It was heady and rewarding work dramatized by a striking poster, commissioned by Lewis, that proclaimed, "HANDS THAT PICK COTTON NOW CAN PICK OUR ELECTED OFFICIALS." Created by a talented young Atlanta artist named Kofi Bailey, more than ten thousand copies of the poster were "distributed all through the South," where, as Lewis proudly recalled, "they wound up on the walls of beauty parlors and barbershops, schools and churches."

Lewis recruited a strong board of directors that included Bond. But sustaining the VEP's work became much more challenging after June 1, 1971, sixteen months after Lewis assumed the directorship, when the VEP became an independent organization separate from the SRC. Mandated by a provision in the 1969 U.S. Tax Reform Act, the separation severely reduced the VEP's funding, forcing Lewis to cut the staff by 75 percent. During its first nine years, the VEP relied almost exclusively on foundation funding—primarily from the Ford and Field Foundations. But the new tax law undercut this arrangement, complicating and inhibiting foundation support and forcing Lewis to devote considerable staff time to fundraising. In characteristic fashion, he made the best of a bad situation, enhancing the VEP's public profile through the use of popular media, encouraging the VEP to be more proactive, and even "expanding its services to poor and minority citizens outside the African American community." In 1974, for example, he established the Texas-based Southwest Voter Registration Education Project—essentially a "Latino-focused VEP" that greatly expanded the Latino vote during the following decade.[7]

Several of the VEP's most successful media campaigns were directed at young voters recently enfranchised by the Twenty-Sixth Amendment, which lowered the voting age to eighteen. But Lewis also reached out to older voters by organizing Voter Mobilization Tours, traveling road shows that featured Black officeholders and movement celebrities such as Coretta King, Ralph Abernathy, Fannie Lou Hamer, and Fred Gray. Lewis often traveled with them, moving across the rural and small-town landscape, giving speech after speech, or just talking to Black families in their homes or out in the fields—trying, as he put it, to persuade "people chopping cotton to vote." "I was on the go—and loving it," he remembered. "People would see me out and around so much, and they'd tease me, saying, 'John, are you *running* for something?'"

Lewis was not running for office, at least not yet. But by 1972 a number of other Black leaders were, and some were winning—notably James R. Ford, who was elected mayor of Tallahassee, Florida; Congressman Andrew Young of Atlanta; and Barbara Jordan of Texas, the first Black Southerners elected to Congress in the twentieth century. A year later, Clarence Lightner won a mayoral race in Durham, North Carolina, and to Lewis's delight, Maynard

Jackson did the same in Atlanta, moving up from vice-mayor to mayor. All of this was encouraging, even though to Lewis the state of national politics was deeply troubling during the early years of the decade. With Richard Nixon in the White House, the Republican Party on the rise, and the civil rights and antiwar movements all but stalled, American politics seemed to be going in the wrong direction.

Fortunately, there was at least a measure of hope in Georgia, where Jimmy Carter—a self-styled moderate and "peanut farmer" from the small town of Plains—replaced Maddox as governor in early 1971. After the general election, Carter would claim to be a New South Democrat who aspired to transcend the legacies of Jim Crow. During his primary campaign against ex-governor Carl Sanders, however, he had posed as a loyal segregationist, at one point allying himself with the ultraconservative White Citizens' Councils. But as soon as he took office, he reversed himself, declaring in his inaugural address that "the time for racial discrimination is over."

Lewis welcomed Carter's declaration, but at that point he didn't trust him. As Lewis later explained, he simply couldn't forget that the new governor hailed from "the region of the state where we had fought so many of our battles, mostly around Albany and Americus. Jimmy Carter was a local political leader and an influential businessman during that time, but we never heard from him. He never spoke up or spoke out about what his black neighbors were going through. Not a word."

Constrained by his new position at the VEP, a strictly nonpartisan organization, Lewis could not actively campaign during the 1970 gubernatorial race without jeopardizing the VEP's tax-exempt status. Although he strongly favored one of Carter's Democratic primary opponents, the Albany Movement attorney C. B. King, he kept his views private. Lewis faced the same situation during Young's first two congressional races, and when he attended both national party conventions in 1972, he did so as an observer who had to forgo any partisan statements.[8]

Even so, Lewis could not hide his disappointment when Nixon won a landslide reelection victory in November. He harbored a strong dislike of the Republican president, whose "Southern Strategy" appropriated many of the worst aspects of George Wallace's demagoguery. Crippled by a would-be assassin in May 1972, Wallace had little influence on national politics thereafter. But Nixon would continue to practice his relentless style of racially divisive law-and-order politics until the Watergate scandal forced him to resign in August 1974.

While it lasted, Nixon's demonization of militant Black activists and student radicals complicated the VEP's work by encouraging reactionary holdovers from the Jim Crow era to fight on. But Lewis and his staff never missed a beat, confident that federal law was still on their side. As long as the Voting Rights Act was still on the books, with its preclearance provision requiring Southern politicians to get federal approval before tampering with voting laws, the VEP felt safe. Only when the Voting Rights Act came up for renewal in 1975 did Lewis and his colleagues worry that their mission was in jeopardy. By 1972, the Voting Rights Act, with considerable help from the VEP, had radically transformed the Southern electorate and the racial profile of the region's officeholders. In eight years, voter registration among Southern Black citizens of voting age had risen by more than 1.5 million, from 43 percent to approximately 60 percent, while the number of Black officeholders in the South had risen from fewer than 20 to 873.

Clearly, Southern politics was no longer just "white folks' business." Yet as Lewis and the VEP communications director Archie Allen pointed out in an October 1972 report, Southern Black voters still had a long way to go to reach parity with Southern white voters. "To understand why approximately 2.5 million Blacks are still unregistered in 1972," Lewis and Allen explained, "it is necessary to probe beneath the sometimes illusory rhetorical image of a 'new South.' While there is some validity to the image, it would be dangerous for the black liberation struggle and for the Nation at large to conclude that, since a law has been enacted, its enforcement and full political participation of minorities will automatically follow. A climate of fear and intimidation is still far too prevalent in the South."[9]

Lewis appreciated all the praise that he and the VEP received for their efforts, especially the honor he received on January 15, 1975, on what would have been Martin Luther King Jr.'s forty-sixth birthday. In a ceremony held at the Ebenezer Baptist Church, Lewis was awarded the Martin Luther King Jr. Peace Prize, created two years earlier "to honor the philosophy and principles that Dr. King believed in." The following December, in the wake of the struggle to renew the Voting Rights Act, he received another form of recognition, this time from the editors of *Time* magazine, who lauded him as one of the world's "Messengers of Love and Hope: Living Saints." Describing him as "the young apostle of nonviolence," the cover story discussed his achievements alongside those of Mother Teresa and several other contemporary "saints." "I was embarrassed, needless to say," Lewis later confessed. "Friends took to calling me St. John. Julian teased me about it. This was during the Christmas season, and when I arrived at parties, people would straighten up and hide their drinks. Then I'd hear the little chant: 'Here comes the saint.'"[10]

* * *

Lewis had already shown his mettle, if not his actual sainthood, earlier in the year when he fought to renew and refine the Voting Rights Act. In 1970, Congress had extended the act for five years, adding one amendment that banned literacy tests and a second that reduced residency requirements for voting in presidential elections. In 1975, the stakes were even higher as Lewis and other voting rights advocates pushed for a permanent extension of the act's authority, applicability to the entire nation, and special provisions to protect the voting rights of Mexican Americans and other Hispanics, Asian Americans, and Native Americans. Working closely with Young and Texas congresswoman Jordan, Lewis testified before the House Judiciary Committee, pleading for the act's renewal and expansion. "It would be a mockery of the whole Voting Rights Act effort during the past 10 years," he told the committee, "if we leave the Voting Rights Act as it is and not cover the other minorities in this country."

In its final form, signed into law by President Gerald Ford on August 6, 1975, the tenth anniversary of the original signing, the revised Voting Rights Act included most but not all of what Lewis wanted. Extended for seven years, the act did not cover the entire nation as Lewis had hoped, but it did expand coverage to other minorities, requiring bilingual elections in 513 jurisdictions in thirty states, as well as preclearance of election law changes in 276 additional counties. Despite some disappointment, Lewis was heartened by the solid majorities for passage in both the House and Senate, even among Southern representatives and senators. As one journalist later pointed out, this was "the first time in the 20th century that a majority of southern congressmen backed civil-rights legislation."

With the new law in place, the VEP stepped up its activities, despite continuing problems with funding. During the summer of 1976, as the nation celebrated its Bicentennial, Lewis organized an ambitious banquet to raise money for the VEP's new Get Out the Vote campaign. Held at Atlanta's Hyatt Regency Hotel, the banquet featured a keynote address by former governor Carter, who had just accepted the Democratic presidential nomination at the party's national convention in New York City. This was Lewis's first opportunity to meet Carter, whom he found to be warm and personable. Carter appeared to be a different person from the moderate segregationist who had played both sides of the race issue during the 1970 campaign. During his four years as governor, he had worked hard to liberalize Georgia politics and to gain the trust of Lewis and other Black leaders, whose support he would need in his upcoming race against Ford.[11]

Although Lewis still had his doubts about Carter's commitment to civil rights and racial justice, he preferred him to Ford. Young, now in his second term as a congressman, was a strong Carter supporter who urged Lewis to give the former governor the benefit of the doubt. When Carter won in November—carrying Georgia and every other Southern state except Virginia, and winning an unprecedented 92 percent of the Black vote—Lewis justifiably celebrated the victory as a triumph of the voting rights struggle. "I cried," he recalled. "I sat in front of the television set with tears streaming down my cheeks. Lillian was shocked. She didn't know why in the world I was so emotional. I wasn't *that* crazy about Carter. But those tears weren't about him. They were about the fact that the hands that picked cotton had now picked a president."

Black voters also played a large role in the congressional campaigns of 1976, when the Democrats elected sixteen Black representatives and won a comfortable majority in both the House and Senate. A week after the election, the ascending power of the Black vote was a major topic of conversation at a SNCC reunion held in Atlanta. When Lewis and more than 150 other SNCC veterans gathered for the first time since Ralph Featherstone's funeral six years earlier, there was a lot of reminiscing and singing—and speculation about the future. "A couple of people that evening asked me a question I'd been hearing often lately," Lewis remembered. "John, when are you going to run for something? You've got to *run* for something."[12]

The idea of running for public office had been on Lewis's mind for some time, but he was uncertain about where and when to run. After six years with the VEP, he had accumulated a great deal of experience dealing with politicians and public policy, so he felt ready to move into electoral politics. Lillian was encouraging him to take the plunge, and both of them were confident their marriage was strong enough to withstand the challenges of political life. In August 1976, they had adopted a baby boy, whom they named John-Miles, ending several years of frustration trying to conceive a child. As the year drew to a close, they were still adapting to their new role as parents when an unexpected development brought them an opportunity that soon changed their lives.

In November, Young had been reelected to a third term in Congress, and the Lewises and other supporters expected him to retain this position for the foreseeable future. But less than a month after the election, he resigned his House seat to accept a position as U.S. ambassador to the United Nations. Lewis, who had no warning that Young planned to join the Carter administration, was stunned. Initially, he felt his friend had made a serious mistake, that he could do more "for the causes of social justice and progressive politics" if he remained in Congress. Young felt otherwise, explaining that his primary reason for accepting Carter's nomination was to advance the interests of the struggling African nations that had been poorly served by American foreign policy in the past. In effect, he hoped to serve humanity and justice on a broader stage by enhancing human rights and postcolonial development.[13]

Whether it was a wise move or not, Young's resignation triggered a mad scramble among Atlanta politicians interested in taking his place. The special election held in March 1977 drew twelve candidates, including state senator Paul Coverdell, Wyche Fowler, Abernathy, and Lewis, who announced his candidacy only after he was unable to convince Bond to run. The decision to enter the race involved considerable sacrifice on Lewis's part—notably, resigning his position at the VEP in January, temporarily entering the ranks of the unemployed, and spending less time with his wife and baby son. All of this, including his fear that the financially strapped VEP would go into steep decline following his departure, weighed heavily on him as he threw himself into the campaign.

Lillian supported his decision, even though they both knew from the outset that his campaign would be an uphill struggle. He had never held public office at any level and had not been a candidate for any elective position since he had run for reelection as the chairman of SNCC in 1966. And despite his exploits as a civil rights leader, he soon discovered that he had little name recognition in Atlanta, at least in comparison to several of his opponents. Lewis also had the obvious disadvantage of running in a congressional district that was 60 percent white. He calculated he would need to receive at least a third of the white vote to have any chance of winning. When an early poll indicated his support among white voters was in single digits, he was disconsolate but soldiered on in the hope that hard work and a major endorsement or two would turn things around.

Aided by two tireless campaign advisers, Lonnie King and Russ Marane, plus strong support from Lillian and Bond, Lewis eventually made some headway, especially after he received endorsements from Martin Luther King Sr., the state's popular lieutenant governor Zell Miller, and the Bipartisan Voters League, an influential Black organization spearheaded by C. A. Scott, the publisher of the *Atlanta Daily World*. Throughout February and early March, Lewis tried to distinguish himself from his opponents but was hampered by what he described as "a sea of confusion." Backed by a broad coalition of white leaders, Fowler was the obvious front-runner, forcing Lewis to campaign around the clock in an effort to catch up. "I worked my butt off," he remembered, "got up and out on the streets before dawn and was downstairs by five-thirty in the morning to pass out leaflets to black women, maids getting on the bus to go out to their jobs in the suburbs. Then I'd move to a factory and meet the 7:00 a.m. shift change at the front gate. I didn't have the money or the connections some of my opponents did. But I had energy and desire. No one was going to outwork me."

On the eve of the election, Lewis received a last-minute boost from the editorial board of the *Atlanta Journal-Constitution*. Calling him "John the Unknown," the editors observed that he seemed "to take more pride in, gain more satisfaction from, accomplishing deeds than in speaking of them," adding, "If the reverse were true, would that make him more 'known'? Perhaps. But we prefer John the Unknown, who is known by millions as a hard-working, dedicated man, sensitive to human problems, capable of helping to solve those problems."[14]

Coming from one of the South's most influential newspapers, this strong endorsement undoubtedly widened Lewis's support. But it was not nearly enough to overcome Fowler, who won 40 percent of the vote to Lewis's 29 percent. By finishing second and keeping Fowler's vote below 50 percent, Lewis forced a runoff election held three weeks later. This in itself was a moral victory of sorts, but Lewis knew his only chance of winning the runoff depended on somehow doubling the Black turnout rate, which had barely reached 25 percent in the first election. Before the runoff, Lewis and his allies—which now included Young, Abernathy, virtually all of the city's Black ministers, and even several national figures such as Senator Edward Kennedy, who came to Atlanta to speak on his behalf—pulled out all the stops to raise the Black turnout. In response, some of Fowler's white supporters, though not Fowler himself, resorted to racist appeals to beat back the "nigger" vote, which actually remained well below the 50 percent target set by the Lewis campaign.

In the April 15 runoff, Lewis lost by a wide margin, 62 to 38 percent, even though he won 90 percent of the Black vote. Disappointed but hardly surprised, an exhausted Lewis delivered a brief concession speech that tried to make the best of a bad situation. "Two months ago," he insisted, with a measure of exaggeration, "nobody knew who John Lewis was. This is only the beginning." The editors of the *Journal-Constitution* agreed, offering a postelection judgment that "even while losing his first political campaign," Lewis had "established himself as one of the few remaining serious black politicians in Atlanta." Young had gone off to New York to represent the United States on the world stage, and Georgia once again had an all-white congressional delegation. But Lewis's political debut held promise for the future.[15]

* * *

The *Journal-Constitution*'s encouraging and flattering words lifted Lewis's spirits, but the sobering reality of being an unemployed thirty-seven-year-old man brought him back to earth in short order. "I knew after the 1977 campaign that I wanted to be a congressman someday," he later explained. "But at the moment I had more immediate matters to deal with, the foremost being finding a job. The race was over. I had a campaign debt of roughly $50,000, and I was not sure which way to turn next." Although he hoped to find a meaningful position in Atlanta, his best opportunity to resume his career as a civil rights and social justice advocate seemed to lie elsewhere. Returning to his position at the VEP, now under the directorship of Vivian Malone Jones, the first Black graduate of the University of Alabama, was unfortunately not a viable option. Following Lewis's resignation, the VEP's financial situation had worsened, leaving him with feelings of guilt and his former colleagues with a sense of abandonment. Thus he felt he had no choice but to move on.

Fortunately, in the weeks following his electoral defeat, Lewis learned that the Carter administration was considering him for a position with the federal volunteer agency called ACTION, which oversaw Peace Corps volunteers serving abroad, plus Volunteers in Service to America (VISTA) and several other domestic programs. But he doubted that the ACTION job would actually be offered to him. He did not know that one of his former SNCC colleagues, Mary King, who had served as Bond's assistant in the SNCC communications department, had become the assistant director of ACTION under the directorship of Sam Brown, a former antiwar activist who had worked for Eugene McCarthy's campaign in 1968. Brown and King, who had been following Lewis's congressional campaign since January, decided that if Lewis lost the race, they would ask President Carter to appoint him as associate director of ACTION's domestic operations.

When Brown called in May 1977 to offer him the job, Lewis wasted no time in accepting. Both he and Lillian had looked forward to moving to Washington after the election, if he happened to win, and now they had found "another way of getting there." The formal nomination and confirmation process took several months, long enough for Lewis to experience a loss that he had been dreading for some time. A year earlier, his father had suffered a severe stroke, and now, on Father's Day, June 19, Eddie Lewis was dead at the age of sixty-eight. Going back to Pike County for the funeral, held at the Antioch Missionary Baptist Church, was a deeply emotional experience for John, who, unlike his brothers and sisters, had left the family fold for the wider world. In his eulogy, he spoke about his father's devotion to family and a farmer's life filled with hard work and sacrifice. Looking over at his distraught mother, he feared her death would soon follow her husband's. But she surprised him, living another twenty-six years, dying in 2003 at the age of eighty-nine.[16]

In July, Lewis's nomination for the ACTION position became official, requiring him to appear before the Senate Human Resources Committee, chaired by Alan Cranston of California. Asked to explain how he planned to advance the cause of volunteerism, Lewis promised "to tap into the spirit of the civil rights movement, to direct the agency's programs at a grassroots level, bringing our services to the disadvantaged and disabled as well as to minorities, going out into neighborhoods and communities and building a better society, a Beloved Community, literally block by block." This response impressed the committee—and its chairman, who quipped, "Mr. Lewis, it's been a long time since we heard the word 'love' used in this hallowed place. We're glad there's someone in this administration who believes in love."

An enthusiastic confirmation followed, and by November the Lewises were living in a Washington apartment on New Hampshire Avenue, just a few blocks from ACTION's Lafayette Square headquarters. Working from a tenth-floor corner office overlooking the White House, Lewis supervised a staff of 125 people, some housed in the Washington office, but most in nine regional centers located across the nation. The entire operation involved nearly five thousand full-time VISTA volunteers and a much larger number, sometimes approaching a quarter million, of part-time senior citizen volunteers affiliated with the Retired Senior Volunteer Program and the Foster Grandparent Program.

Lewis's primary job was to administer what amounted to a nationwide social work agency that reached out to a variety of marginalized people suffering from chronic poverty and neglect. In trying to implement an expanded vision of what the domestic wing of ACTION could accomplish, he traveled from one end of the nation to the other, visiting forty-two states and racking up nearly a quarter million miles of travel during his twenty-eight months with the agency. Some of the work was similar to what he had done during his early years with the SRC—organizing rural cooperatives and arranging stopgaps to alleviate substandard housing. But under his leadership, VISTA and the elderly volunteer programs became involved in a much wider range of initiatives, including the establishment and improvement of medical clinics, nursing homes, and facilities for children with special needs.

In the process, Lewis witnessed the often desperate struggles of impoverished and neglected Americans who lived well beyond the borders of the rural Black South. "Across the nation my staff and I went into the homes and communities of the poorest of the poor," he recalled, "Americans who were living in conditions that were unthinkable, obscene and largely unseen by mainstream society." In the Southwest, he encountered dispossessed Native Americans struggling to survive on isolated reservations; in Texas he visited Hispanics who were trying to overcome generations of discrimination and poverty; in Northern cities he found widespread despair among the unemployed, both Black and white; and in the coal country of West Virginia, where he spent several unnerving days in the fall of 1979, he saw enough misery and black lung disease to test his faith in the human condition.[17]

By the time Lewis visited West Virginia, nearly two years after taking the job with ACTION, he thought he had already seen the depths of American poverty. But he was mistaken. "I was so shaken by what I saw on that trip that I called a staff meeting as soon as I returned, to brief everyone on what I'd seen," he wrote. He then sent a long and impassioned letter to President Carter, urging him to tour the coal country to see the effects of severe poverty and exploitation with his own eyes. As Lewis later described the letter's admonitions, "Don't just do the ordinary, presidential things, I said. Be daring. Go to the difficult places. Make it *real*. When, I wanted to know, was the last time that an American president—not a candidate but a president—visited a Sioux reservation, or the ghettos of South Side Chicago, or a coal-mining village in eastern Kentucky?"

Carter never responded to Lewis's heartfelt plea; nor did he follow through in any meaningful way with his campaign promise to extend the war on poverty initiated by Lyndon Johnson but suspended during the Nixon and Ford administrations. The federal government's inaction on matters related to the poor was very discouraging for the millions of Americans struggling to survive in a society where economic inequality was a chronic problem. To Lewis, whose dream of creating a Beloved Community was still very much alive, this seeming lack of concern was inexcusable. The federal government, in his view, spent far too much time mired in "bureaucratic and political infighting," petty personal rivalries, and self-serving complacency.

A case in point was the stubborn resistance that stymied Sam Brown's effort to reform the Peace Corps. Instead of sending volunteers abroad to build roads, bridges, and schools, as it had done since its inception in 1961, the Peace Corps, Brown argued, should shift its focus to empowering the citizens of developing countries by teaching them the skills essential to self-government and economic sustainability. He also wanted to shorten the volunteers' foreign assignments to allow them to return to the United States with skills and experiences that could be applied to the domestic war on poverty. To Lewis, who had been helping Brown to recruit Black volunteers for the Peace Corps, this new approach made perfect sense.

Carolyn Payton, the director of the Peace Corps, disagreed and made a concerted effort to obstruct Brown's proposed reforms. The fact that Payton was a Black woman from Virginia and Brown a white man from Iowa complicated matters. When Payton turned to Lewis for support, his refusal to comply and his public agreement with Brown's position led to charges of racial and personal disloyalty. "When I didn't stand up and defend her, I was attacked for not being a 'team player,' for not being 'black' enough," Lewis painfully recalled. The controversy ended with Payton's resignation in 1978, after which Carter made the Peace Corps an autonomous agency with no formal connection to ACTION.[18]

The Payton affair was unsettling, but Lewis soon faced more serious problems. During a series of hearings held by the House Appropriations Committee, Lewis and Brown faced accusations that they had turned ACTION into an arm of the political Left. Several right-wing members of Congress mounted a red-baiting barrage against the agency and its leaders, claiming ACTION had funded several "subversive groups," including a Chicago organization associated with the late Saul Alinsky, the author of the 1971 community organizing primer *Rules for Radicals*. The attacks were clearly grounded in contempt for Brown's experiences as an antiwar activist and Lewis's involvement with SNCC, and both men were tempted to resign in disgust.

Brown decided to stick it out and remain in his post until the end of the Carter administration, but Lewis had had enough. While he hated to cut and run, he feared that sooner or later his radical past would be used to eliminate most of ACTION's budget, harming "hundreds of thousands of people who depended on our agency to give them the only help they had ever had." "After that Congressional hearing," he explained, "I said it was time for me to go. I had . . . battled over too many budgets and seen too few tangible responses to real, human, heartbreaking problems."[19]

By late November 1979, Lewis was ready to turn in his resignation, but his sobering apprenticeship in national politics was not yet complete. While attending a staff retreat in Colorado, he received a phone call from Louis Martin, one of Carter's primary Black advisers. A rumor was circulating in Washington that Lewis would soon leave the administration to join Senator Ted Kennedy's presidential campaign, and Martin and the president wanted to know if there was any truth to the rumor. Lewis denied he had any intention of actively campaigning for Kennedy or anyone else.

Later that week, Lewis was invited to meet with Carter at the White House. During the meeting, he handed the president his resignation letter but reiterated that his decision had nothing to do with the Kennedy campaign. "I simply want to return to Atlanta," he insisted. Lewis hoped this declaration would allow him to leave Washington without the president feeling he had been betrayed. But Carter's later statements condemning Lewis's disloyalty proved that even a dedicated public servant known for his integrity could fall victim to suspicion born of political ambition. To Lewis, Carter's unhealthy fixation on the politics of reelection epitomized the federal government's misplaced priorities. "Washington, unfortunately, is a city filled with ambition," he wrote, "with individuals whose first instinct when faced with a decision is to look over their shoulders and calculate how this might help or hurt *them*." This problem troubled Lewis for the rest of his life, and combatting it would become one of the hallmarks of his congressional career.[20]

CHAPTER 13

———

Sweet Home Atlanta

B Y THE TIME John Lewis had returned to Atlanta in June 1980, the Kennedy faction of the Democratic Party had indeed tried to recruit him. But he refused to join the campaign, even after Julian Bond—a strong Ted Kennedy supporter and a sharp critic of Jimmy Carter—pleaded with him to get onboard. While Lewis pledged to support the Democratic presidential nominee after the national convention made its choice, he wasn't enthusiastic enough about either Carter or Kennedy to choose one over the other during the primary season. In the meantime, he weighed his own political options. At first, after hearing that Wyche Fowler was considering resigning his congressional seat to challenge Georgia's senior senator Herman Talmadge, Lewis thought about running once again in the Fifth District. But when Fowler informed him that he had decided to remain in the House for at least one more term, Lewis began to look elsewhere for a viable political opportunity.

Maynard Jackson, Atlanta's first Black mayor, was then within a few months of completing his second and final term, and under the city's term limit law, he was prohibited from running for reelection. Several of Lewis's friends urged him to run for mayor, but Lewis had no interest in "being the chief executive officer of a city." "I prefer being a legislator," he explained, believing he would be far more effective as a member of the city council, "making laws, influencing policy." The only problem was that the next round of city council elections was scheduled for the fall of 1981. In the meantime, he needed a job to help support his family.[1]

During the summer and early fall of 1980, Lewis found temporary employment with the Field Foundation of New York, which was going through a major transition led by its new director, Richard W. Boone. The foundation hired Lewis to travel around the nation closing out several grants, some of which he had overseen during the late 1960s under Leslie Dunbar's direction. But he soon moved on to become the director of community affairs for the Atlanta regional office of the National Consumer Cooperative Bank (NCCB). Headquartered in Washington, where Lewis spent much of his time, the NCCB provided loans and technical assistance to nonprofit organizations, primarily cooperatives based in underdeveloped communities with a high proportion of low-income families. Since most of these cooperatives were staffed by and concerned with the problems of African Americans, his prior experiences were directly relevant to the bank's activities.

Lewis enjoyed his work with the NCCB but regretted that it required him to leave Atlanta and his family on a regular basis. Fortunately, by the late spring of 1981, the campaigns for city council seats were beginning, prompting him to resign to enable a run for a council seat. When he had taken the NCCB job in December, he had warned his boss that it was highly likely that he couldn't remain with the bank for more than a few months, so no one was surprised when he resigned.[2]

Lewis waited until July to make a formal announcement of his candidacy, but for several weeks before the announcement he actually campaigned for another city council candidate, Bill Campbell, a friend running for one of six at-large positions. Campbell, who would become Atlanta's third Black mayor in 1994, knew from the outset that Lewis planned to run for one of the other at-large seats. The incumbent councilman in the seat Lewis was seeking, Jack Summers, had been in office for more than two decades and was a formidable opponent. But Lewis was aware that many of Summers's constituents were beset with economic and racial problems that he largely ignored.

Lewis's platform stressed his determination to speak for "the voiceless, the dispossessed, those outside the walls of power." Since the at-large system in Atlanta required candidates to conduct a citywide campaign, even though they were competing to represent specific districts, Lewis visited the entire range of neighborhoods, from overwhelmingly white, middle- and upper-class areas to Black inner-city enclaves. "From dawn to dusk," he recalled, "I went door-to-door, not taking anything or anyone for granted. Early evenings I would attend dinners or meetings, give a speech, meet the people. Then, late at night—ten, eleven, midnight and beyond—I'd plant myself like a lamppost in front of an all-night grocery store, or a discotheque. . . . I wanted to meet people in the flesh and give them a chance to meet me."

This Herculean effort resulted in an unexpected landslide victory in October, when Lewis won 69 percent of the vote. Bill Campbell and a third Black candidate, Myrtle Davis, also won, giving the Atlanta city council its first Black majority. Some white citizens feared this new majority would invoke an unwelcome strategy of bloc voting and racialized politics, but following his official swearing-in ceremony in January 1982, Lewis announced his intention to remain independent of any faction, racial or otherwise. "I came here not being a part of any established group. I'm not part of any structure," he told the *Atlanta Journal-Constitution*. "It's not that I'm a maverick. I'm just not obligated." His primary goal was "the nurturing of an ethical, fair and just biracial community."[3]

Local white apprehensions were also fueled by Andrew Young's sweeping victory in the 1981 mayoral election. Young had returned to Atlanta after a four-year absence during which, as the U.S. ambassador to the United Nations, he had risen to the heights of the Carter administration before plummeting into disfavor and a forced resignation. In July 1979, after thirty months as ambassador, he held a secret and unauthorized meeting in New York with representatives of the Palestine Liberation Organization (PLO), violating the Carter administration's pledge to avoid any direct talks with the PLO. When the secret meeting became public in August, Carter demanded Young's resignation, provoking a firestorm of controversy, especially among the African American leaders who rushed to Young's defense.[4]

The simultaneous elections of Young and Lewis called attention to the electoral potential of former movement leaders. At that point, very few civil rights veterans were serving as elected officials, and none, with the exception of Bond, was as prominent as Young and Lewis. That they were friends living in the same city added to the drama of their political ascension. There was little doubt that the political veteran Young could adapt to the political culture and mores of Atlanta politics. But Lewis's willingness to adjust to the realities of practical politics was unclear as he began his career at city hall. Would he become a "team player" open to the collective deal-making and collaboration with business leaders that had long been acceptable practice on the city council?

It did not take long for Lewis's colleagues on the council—and for their allies in the business community—to realize that he had no intention of compromising his integrity for the purpose of making money or acquiring powerful friends. From the outset, he pressed his fellow council members to adopt rigorous ethical standards that precluded self-serving arrangements and conflicts of interest. When he proposed "legislation requiring public disclosure of sources of income of city council members," many of his colleagues, including Marvin Arrington, the powerful president of the council, balked.

The insinuation that the councillors could be bought—that they had become accustomed to accepting payoffs in one form or another—provoked cries of indignation. Clearly, Arrington and others complained, Councilman Lewis was a naïve outsider who had no respect for the rules of the game. They had dealt with righteous reformers before, of course, and in each case the zeal for reform eventually gave way to self-interest. All that was needed was a bit of pressure, and in Lewis's case they felt they could take advantage of his determination to improve the lives of his constituents. "John's approach," one councilman declared, "is not going to help him in anything else he wants to do."

The political situation in Atlanta soon tested Lewis's resolve to maintain his idealistic principles. At the beginning of Mayor Young's administration, Lewis expected his longtime movement friend to be an important ally in the struggle to clean up city politics. But he suffered a rude awakening when he and Young ended up on the opposite sides of a controversy known as the "Battle of Great Park." The point at issue was the construction of a four-lane highway that would provide access to the proposed Carter Center, a presidential library and research facility to be located near downtown Atlanta. During the 1981 campaign, most of those running for municipal offices, including Young and Lewis, had come out against the road plan, which promised to exacerbate downtown congestion and air pollution and to eliminate large parts of several historic Black neighborhoods. But after the election, many councillors—plus the mayor—reversed their positions, citing, among other arguments, the short-term benefit of added construction jobs.[5]

Lewis was one of a handful of council members who remained opposed to the road, and by the spring of 1982 they all faced heavy pressure to fall into line with the spirit of progress. The pressure took many forms, ranging from incentives to outright threats. Early on, Lewis received calls from several members of Young's staff who intimated that his campaign debt would be "taken care of" if he supported the mayor's position. A number of mutual friends, including SCLC president Joe Lowery, also chimed in, suggesting that Lewis's reputation as a loyal member of the community was at stake. One group of Black ministers distributed leaflets charging that a vote against the road was a vote against both the mayor and the Black community. At one point Lewis even had to deal with trucks with loudspeakers crisscrossing Black neighborhoods to spread the accusation that several recalcitrant council members had betrayed the mayor and the Black race.

"I had never faced anything as intense as the anger that came my way over this road," Lewis recalled. "It was in no way a racial issue, but that's what it became for many people." The week before the council vote on the issue, Young asked Lewis if he would be willing to abstain, but he refused. The pressure later escalated in a call from former president Carter himself, who teased Lewis about not loving him anymore and then pleaded with him to vote for the road. "I need your help here," Carter insisted before reminding Lewis, "I gave you a job, and you came up to Washington and took it. And then you left and went and worked for Ted Kennedy." This ill-advised recrimination, which revisited the falsehood that Lewis had betrayed Carter during the 1980 presidential race, actually stiffened Lewis's determination to hold his ground. "I'm sorry, Mr. President," he responded, "but I don't think the road is needed."

In a speech before the vote, Lewis pointed out that while Young had the right to change his mind on the Great Park road issue, the road's opponents also had the right to vote as they saw fit. In the end, Young's side prevailed, with only three council members—Lewis, Campbell, and Davis—voting no. Lewis and his allies did, however, win a partial victory in that the final bill authorized a two-lane rather than a four-lane highway. This provided him with some satisfaction and limited the physical damage to the neighborhoods surrounding the Carter Center, which opened with great fanfare in 1986. Nonetheless, the "Battle of Great Park" left a troubling legacy, opening a breach between Young and Lewis that hampered the latter's effectiveness throughout his years on the council.[6]

For the next four years, Lewis performed his duties with little cooperation from his fellow council members. His assignment to important committees was blocked by Arrington, who bitterly resented any opposition to the Great Park road. To Lewis's dismay, Arrington managed to sidestep conflict-of-interest allegations that, as the owner of a trucking company hired to haul away rubble from the site, he stood to gain considerable income from the construction of the road. Predictably, Lewis was also the only council member to be denied a leadership position as a committee chair.

In 1985, as Lewis's first term in office drew to a close, some critics claimed he was a poor fit for a position in municipal politics, that his vision was too broad and idealistic to deal effectively with down-to-earth concerns such as roads, sewers, and water systems. Perhaps, they suggested, he should bow out gracefully and refrain from running for reelection. He felt otherwise, of course, and apparently most of his constituents did as well, giving him 85 percent of the vote in the fall election. This outpouring of support was "a pretty strong mandate for my approach to the job," he later commented with some pride, and he never forgot this early vindication of his independent spirit.[7]

Despite this vote of confidence, Lewis did not have high hopes for his second term. He promised to do the best he could, but there was no indication the character of local Atlanta politics would improve anytime soon. Actually, for several years he had dreamed of switching to national politics, specifically of making another run at the Fifth District congressional seat. The only problem was that his friend Wyche Fowler had proved to be an excellent congressman. In Lewis's view, Fowler deserved to remain in Congress for as long as he wanted. However, he figured that sooner or later the congressman would try to move up to the Senate, and he was willing to wait for his opportunity. To his surprise, he didn't have to wait long.

Just before his reelection, Lewis heard a rumor that Fowler had decided to give up his House seat in 1986 to run for the Senate against Mack Mattingly, who had defeated Herman Talmadge in 1980, becoming the first Republican elected to the Senate from Georgia since Reconstruction. Fowler had promised Lewis he would be among the first to know about his plans, but it didn't take long for word of his decision to spread across the city and beyond. By mid-October there was widespread speculation about who might declare their intention to succeed him. One obvious potential candidate was Bond, but not Lewis, who at that point was not considered a serious contender for the Democratic nomination, except among his close friends. Despite winning reelection, he bore the marks of conflict with Young and of his unpopularity among most of his fellow council members. This unenviable record definitely cast a shadow over his prospects for higher office, though Lewis was undeterred.[8]

*   *   *

When Bond invited him to lunch in late October, Lewis had already begun preparing for his campaign. He was not surprised when Bond told him of his own intention to leave the state senate to run for Congress. But it saddened him that they were headed for a political collision. "What are you going to do?" Bond asked nervously. Without hesitation Lewis responded, "I'm running, too," although he would not make a formal announcement until February. The two men, born within six weeks of each other, friends who had known each other since the early days of SNCC, who had been through so much together, were now on the opposite sides of a contest that could have only one winner.

In truth, throughout much of the campaign it did not appear to be much of a contest. Almost no one believed Lewis had any chance to win. Even many of Lewis's friends warned him he was committing political suicide running against Bond. Observers as far afield as Lewis's old adversary Stokely Carmichael, with whom he had not had any contact since 1966, called to urge him to drop out of the race. Lewis suspected that Bond had convinced Carmichael, who had moved to Guinea in 1969, to make the call, which, according to Lewis, backfired, making him "more determined than ever to see this thing through."

Yet even someone as resilient as Lewis could not help but get discouraged as Bond piled up endorsement after endorsement, not only in Atlanta but from around the nation. The mayors of Los Angeles, New York, and Washington; Senator Ted Kennedy; Morris Dees, founder of the Southern Poverty Law Center; and an array of major celebrities and entertainers such as Hugh Hefner, Miles Davis, Cicely Tyson, Bill Cosby, and the Temptations—they all weighed in for Bond, some with benefit concerts that swelled his campaign fund. By contrast, Lewis limped along with meager funds and only one major local endorsement—from Ralph Abernathy. Andrew Young and Coretta King refrained from making an official endorsement, but both sent clear signals that they expected Bond to win.

All of this irked the normally unflappable Lewis. Despite their long friendship, for some time Lewis had been harboring doubts about the value of Bond's low-key approach to public service. The main problems, Lewis decided, were his talented friend's golden-boy image and lackadaisical work habits. "Julian liked being a star," he explained. "He approached his work as if it were an inconvenience. Everything had always come easily for Julian; sweating was not something he liked to do. And yet now he wanted to be a congressman. And everyone assumed he would be a shoo-in, and *that* bothered me a great deal." "I didn't like the idea of someone being anointed," he added. "That goes back to the SNCC ethos, I guess—the belief that the masses should truly decide their fate and be able to choose their representatives rather than be controlled by a chosen few. The assumption that this job was Julian's if he simply wanted it just rubbed me the wrong way."[9]

Lewis knew he lacked Bond's flair, but nonetheless he felt he deserved serious consideration as a congressional candidate. "I'd been in the arena, both in Washington, where I'd seen the workings of Congress and the federal government, and in Atlanta, where I'd learned about politics on the local level," he later pointed out. "I had worked my way up. I'd paid my dues." His biggest problem, he reasoned, was not inexperience but rather the tendency to underestimate his toughness. "With my background—the poor farmboy from the woods—and my personality—so unassuming and steady—people tended to assume I was soft, pliable, that I could be bent to meet their needs," he explained. "They were always amazed, those who didn't know me, to see me dig in and stand my ground."

If Lewis was to have any chance to overcome Bond's advantages, he would need all of that grit, and then some. Unless the situation changed dramatically during the campaign, there was no guarantee he would even finish second in the twelve-person field. To rise anywhere near the top of the field, he would have to work harder, longer, and smarter than his opponents.

Lewis's strategy was to make a biracial appeal to all elements of the district, just as he had in 1977. But this time he would have the advantage of campaigning in a revised district that was two-thirds Black rather than the white-majority district he had faced nine years earlier. He did not want to stress race, or any other social division that would compromise his goal of creating a Beloved Community. While he could not ignore the realities of racial demography, he made a concerted effort to reach out to as many cultural, social, and economic constituencies as possible. Concluding that no candidate "could get elected in this district without strong support from every segment of the community," he went after them all. "I worked harder than I ever had in my life," he recalled. "No speaking invitation was too insignificant to accept. Civic groups, firefighter units, family reunions, church picnics. . . . I planted myself at bus and factory gates and grocery store doorways, handing out leaflets and brochures describing my stand on specific issues: more resources and federal involvement in education; support for universal and single payer health care; more resources for a rapid transit system; creating jobs, of course, and protecting the environment—I said it over and over, that people have the right to know what's in the water they drink, the food they eat and the air they breathe."

In addition to pushing these pressing issues, he wisely humanized his campaign with artful storytelling that reinforced his identification with the civil rights struggle. "Whenever I had the chance, I'd tell my story, of my childhood and of the movement," he remembered, referring to his speeches in Black neighborhoods. "When you needed someone to sit in, I would say, I was there." "When you needed someone to ride," the refrain continued, "I was there. When you needed someone to march, I was there. And now, when you need someone with vision and strength to represent you in Washington, I will be there."[10]

It was all very impressive, demonstrating Lewis's political savvy. But it would have been futile had not one of his opponents, Mildred Glover, interjected a volatile issue into the race. A weak candidate whose campaign contributions failed to meet the minimum requirement for inclusion in a debate sponsored by the League of Women Voters, Glover encouraged her supporters to set up a picket line outside the auditorium where the debate was being held. And when that didn't have much effect, she turned to a more explosive means of drawing attention to her campaign. Well aware of the rumors that Bond and several members of his staff had a history of marijuana use, she challenged all of the candidates to submit to a drug test.

Most of the candidates accepted Glover's challenge, including Lewis, who nonetheless made it clear that he had long been opposed to drug testing except for the monitoring of employees such as airline pilots and others entrusted with public safety. Bond, however, refused to be tested, a decision that raised suspicions he had something to hide. As the September primary approached, the drug testing issue, which one reporter dubbed "the Jar Wars," cut into Bond's popularity, though it was widely believed he still had enough support to win more than 50 percent of the vote, the threshold needed to avoid a runoff election. Lewis fully expected Bond to receive a majority of the total vote—until Lewis received an unexpected endorsement from the *Journal-Constitution* on the eve of the election. "John Lewis is not the snappiest talker in this amazingly articulate field. He may not always be the first on the scene of a trendy new issue," the editors conceded, "but he is a thoughtful, dedicated, dead-honest man who steadily works himself toward positions that are both reasonable and, precisely because he has thought them out with care, usually durable."

Though grateful for the endorsement, Lewis did not expect this last-minute boost to be enough to put him in a runoff. But he was pleasantly surprised when, thanks in large part to a strong showing in the predominantly white precincts in north Atlanta, he finished a strong second to Bond with 35 percent of the vote. With 47 percent, Bond easily led the field, but not by enough to avoid a runoff.[11]

* * *

Lewis had three weeks to close the twelve-point gap that separated him from Bond, but nearly everyone thought it would take a miracle for him to pull it off. In trying to engineer an upset, he had to navigate the perilous cross currents of racial politics. Taking on Bond in a two-person race, unlike during the earlier free-for-all, required Lewis to criticize not only his opponent but also most of the local Black community's political establishment. Leveling such criticism risked a total break with the city council, and with former friends and allies such as Young and Coretta King. He could even be attacked as the "white folks candidate," as an "Uncle Tom," and as a traitor to the Black community.

All of these charges did indeed emerge during the runoff campaign, but Lewis soldiered on, propelled by the hope that appeals to racial solidarity would actually turn off more than a few Black voters. "Anyone who knew or learned about my past, and who met and saw and listened to me," he cautiously predicted, "would see how absurd, how ridiculous" these characterizations were. He could not be sure of anything, of course, in an unprecedented contest that had divided Black Atlantans along vaguely political lines. "Julian and I did not differ greatly on issues," Lewis explained. "Our differences were in character, leadership and attitude. During the primary I had largely left it to others—mainly the press—to point those differences out. Now it was time for me to take the offensive."

Lewis did not take this decision lightly. As he began to point out Bond's flaws, especially his "tendency to always play it safe" and his concern for image and star status at the expense of political substance, their once-warm relationship disappeared. "Any trace of our friendship was gone," Lewis lamented. "The days when Julian and Alice and Lillian and I had been inseparable . . . those days were behind us. And that hurt. It was heartbreaking. But it had to happen. This was about something beyond friendship. As painful and unfortunate as it was to cut our personal ties, this was about something bigger."[12]

Although taking Bond to task in speeches and interviews clearly had an impact on the race, Lewis feared his efforts to catch up would fall short in the end. A late infusion of campaign funds that allowed him to run a few television ads helped, but he needed something truly dramatic to eliminate his opponent's lead. That something turned out to be Bond's decision to challenge Lewis to a series of televised debates, plus one on radio. Concerned his lead was shrinking, Bond hoped to shore up his support with a demonstration of his considerable speaking skills and coolness under fire. With nothing to lose, Lewis leaped at the opportunity to present his views in front of a large audience.

Having always felt inadequate as a public speaker, he had signed up early in the campaign for a media training course. An intensive program offered by SpeakEasy, a well-known Atlanta communications firm, taught him how to behave on air, mostly how to dress and speak forcefully and convincingly without appearing to be overbearing or shrill. Later he had several additional debate-training sessions with Shawn Reed, a strong supporter and experienced media consultant. She encouraged him to be himself and not try "to out-Julian Julian." "Don't try to be anything other than who and what you are," she counseled. Be "forthright" and "look straight into the camera," expressing the confidence and sincerity of a man who believes what he is saying.

In the first debate, Bond set the tone right off the bat with an emotion-laden charge of betrayal. "We've been friends for twenty-five years," he declared. "We went to Africa together. We were in Selma together. . . . But never in those twenty-five years did I ever hear any of the things you are saying about me now. Why did I have to wait twenty-five years to find out what you really thought of me, to find out that you really don't think I amount to much?" Lewis's response, delivered with a heavy heart but a calm voice, demonstrated how far he had traveled down the road to political maturity. "Julian, my friend," he said, "this campaign is not about the past. It's not about our friendship. This is a referendum on the future of our city, on the future of our country."

Lewis more than held his own that night, and over the next two weeks Bond grew increasingly nervous about his inability to deal a knockout blow. "You could sense something close to desperation growing now," Lewis noted. "Though he was still ahead in the polls, Julian's lead was crumbling, evaporating." By the time of the third debate, held on the Friday before the election, the atmosphere was tense. Knowing he had to do something to stem the tide, Bond went on the attack, questioning Lewis's integrity by leveling allegations of conflict of interest related to improper campaign contributions. When a stunned Lewis objected, Bond doubled down with the quip, "If it looks like a duck and quacks like a duck and waddles like a duck, then it must be a duck."

Lewis—who considered the allegations to be wholly unwarranted, and who saw nothing funny in an attack on his personal integrity—wasted no time in striking back. "It's not in my nature to let my emotions rise up," he later observed. "It's not in my nature to strike out. But this was a time when it happened. This was a time when I hit back." His words cut through the air like a knife: "Mr. Bond. My friend. My brother. We were asked to take a drug test not long ago, and five of us went out and took the test. Why don't we step out and go to the men's room and take another test? It seems like *you're* the one doing the ducking." After a few moments of silence, the front-runner gathered himself and countered with an almost unintelligible joke linking *Star Wars* and "Jar Wars." When no one laughed, it was clear he was damaged goods. Almost everyone still expected Bond to win, but Lewis now had some hope that he might pull off an upset.

Lewis speculated that the September 2 election would hinge on the size of the turnout on election day; if relatively few voters went to the polls, it would probably indicate that some had stayed home because they considered Bond's triumph a foregone conclusion. Why bother to vote for Lewis if there was no chance of victory? In the early going, it appeared this might indeed be the case, though the optimists in Lewis's camp attributed the low turnout to a steady rain throughout much of the day. The vote picked up in the afternoon, but so did Bond's lead. For several hours that evening, Lewis was sure he had lost, especially after Young proclaimed in a televised interview that the election was over, adding, "If anyone was going to run against Julian, they should have started twenty years ago."[13]

Young's chastening remark hurt, but Lewis's spirits soon rebounded as the late returns began to turn the tide in his favor. At one in the morning, when Lewis left his headquarters for an interview at a downtown television station, Bond was still leading. Yet by the time Lewis rejoined his staff to monitor the returns from the last precincts, the verdict was in. To his amazement, he had won.

Ironically, for a man who had spent much of his adult life fighting for Black voting rights, Lewis owed his four-point margin over Bond, 52 to 48 percent, to the overwhelming support he received in the predominantly white precincts on the north side of the city. Postelection analysis estimated that he won more than 90 percent of the white vote but less than 40 percent of the Black vote. This anomaly suggested Lewis had a lot of work to do to shore up his standing in the Black community. But this was a problem to be addressed in the future, after he took office as one of the nation's twenty-two Black members of the House of Representatives.

In the moment of victory, he joined the joyous pandemonium at his campaign headquarters. As he remembered the scene, "People were shouting, hugging, crying, climbing on chairs and tables, leaping all over each other screaming, 'We *won!* We *won!* We *won!*'" It was 2:30 a.m., but no one was going home. Lewis had reserved a ballroom at the Westin Hotel for a victory party, in case he won, and now he and his staff headed over to the celebration. As they were leaving, one of his most enthusiastic supporters, a young limousine driver, pulled up in a long white car and opened a door, hoping Lewis and his family would join him on a victory ride to the Westin. Deciding that arriving in a limousine was not his style, Lewis politely declined and instead chose to walk the mile and a half to the Westin along with Lillian, John-Miles, and several staff members.

As they walked through the streets, Lewis later recalled with pride, "people began coming out of the darkness, seemingly from nowhere, to join us—people who had stayed up to watch the results and had now rushed downtown to be part of the jubilation. Soon there were a hundred of us. Then two hundred. Then three and four hundred, our shouts and singing and laughter echoing off the empty buildings." When the gathering throng reached the entrance to the hotel, Lewis stopped for a moment to take it all in: "I looked behind me, at the hundreds of ecstatic faces, and beyond, at the darkness out of which we had come. . . . And I thought to myself that with all the walking I had done in my life, with all the marches I had ever made, this was the sweetest. This was the best." After years of struggling to make headway against a raging tempest of racial discrimination, he was finally "walking with the wind," a telling phrase that would become the title of his 1998 "memoir of the movement."[14]

CHAPTER 14

———

Mr. Lewis Goes to Washington

I N THE GENERAL ELECTION in November 1986, John Lewis won nearly 80 percent of the vote against the Black Republican Portia Scott, the forty-three-year-old editor of the *Atlanta Daily World*. The state's Republican Party was on the rise, led by five-term congressman Newt Gingrich, but the Democrats remained in control in eight of Georgia's ten congressional districts. Nationally the Democrats retained a comfortable majority in the House, outnumbering the Republicans 258 to 177. In the Senate, with Wyche Fowler's narrow victory over the incumbent Republican Mack Mattingly, both of Georgia's senators were once again Democrats. This helped to increase the number of Democratic senators from 47 to 55, putting the party in control of the Senate for the first time since December 1980.

When Lewis arrived in Washington in early January to take the oath of office, he joined a colorful freshman class that included Bobby Kennedy's son Joe, the towering former basketball star Tom McMillen, a self-styled "half-breed Indian from Colorado" named Ben Nighthorse Campbell, and Mike Espy of Yazoo City, the first African American elected to Congress from Mississippi since Reconstruction. To Lewis, the juxtaposition of these individuals during the swearing-in ceremony had an "only in America" quality of diversity.

For the most part, he felt like he was in good company surrounded by bright and accomplished colleagues. But among the newcomers, he and Espy were the only veterans of the civil rights struggle, an obvious fact publicized by the press. Everyone in the House seemed to be aware of his background—from his many arrests and beatings to his speech at the 1963 March on Washington to the drama on the Edmund Pettus Bridge. The *New York Times* reporter Robin Toner even quipped that he was "one of the few members of Congress who must deal with the sainthood issue."[1]

Lewis never encouraged such characterizations, which he found embarrassing. But he did not shy away from his identification with the civil rights movement. "I came to Congress with a legacy to uphold," he later explained, "with a commitment to carry on the spirit, the goals and the principles of nonviolence, social action and a truly interracial democracy." He wasn't naïve; he knew it wasn't going to be easy to apply his passion for social justice and racial equality to the workings of Congress, where tradition, partisanship, and self-interest generally held sway. Yet from his first days as a congressman, he set out to remind his colleagues that the government's "first concern should be the basic needs of its citizens—not just black Americans but *all* Americans—for food, shelter, health care, education, jobs, livable incomes and the opportunity to realize their full potential as individual people." He had come to Washington to "roll up my sleeves and work."

In an era dominated by the conservative politics of President Ronald Reagan, who was entering his sixth year in the White House in 1987, the task of expanding, or even sustaining, the social and economic safety net created by Franklin Roosevelt's New Deal and Lyndon Johnson's Great Society was daunting. Lewis was out of step with a popular mood that embraced unrestrained capitalism, corporate power, the market economy, private property rights, and rigid class distinctions. The notion of fostering communal values, the social gospel, or the Beloved Community, which had been so evident during the movement's glory days in the 1960s, had given way to an acquisitive, hyperindividualistic spirit focused on personal gain. During his 1984 reelection campaign, Reagan had proclaimed, "It's morning again in America," but Lewis and other progressive thinkers saw something much darker.[2]

Clearly, Lewis and the liberal wing of the Democratic Party had their work cut out for them. The most powerful member of the House, Speaker James Wright Jr. of Texas, who had replaced the retiring Tip O'Neill of Massachusetts, was a moderate Democrat unaccustomed to taking political risks. As Lewis soon discovered, the same could be said for the rest of the party's congressional leadership, including the Senate majority leader, the former Klansman Robert C. Byrd of West Virginia. Wright, like Byrd, had a mixed record on civil rights, voting against the Civil Rights Acts of 1957 and 1964 but for the 1965 Voting Rights Act and the 1983 bill establishing Martin Luther King Jr.'s birthday as a federal holiday. Lewis was pleasantly surprised in March 1988 when the Speaker not only voted for the Civil Rights Restoration Act, which required recipients of federal funds to comply with all civil rights laws, but later led the charge to override President Reagan's veto. Six months later, in a second major victory for liberal Democrats, Congress passed and Reagan signed the Fair Housing Amendments Act, which improved Title VIII of the original 1968 act. Progress toward racial justice was possible, it seemed, even in Ronald Reagan's America.[3]

Legislation related to civil rights and other matters of social and economic justice was a special concern of the Congressional Black Caucus (CBC), which included Lewis and twenty-one others. Founded in 1971, when the House had only thirteen Black members, the CBC operated under the motto "Black people have no permanent friends, no permanent enemies, just permanent interests." After a rocky beginning—President Richard Nixon refused to meet with them, prompting a boycott of the 1971 State of the Union address—the caucus soon gained a measure of influence and visibility, issuing two controversial manifestoes in 1972: the Black Declaration of Independence and the Black Bill of Rights. The latter document included a long list of issues that the CBC planned to address, ranging from housing and education to public health and prison reform.

In 1977, the CBC extended its range of interests to the South African struggle against apartheid, nurturing TransAfrica, a fledgling Black liberation organization founded by Randall Robinson. Over the next decade, the CBC worked closely with a rising American antiapartheid movement, and in 1986, the year before Lewis's arrival in Washington, the group won its first great victory when Congress overruled President Reagan's veto of the Comprehensive Anti-apartheid Act, a law that imposed economic sanctions on South Africa.

Lewis—who had a strong interest in all of these areas, including the antiapartheid movement—became one of the CBC's most active members, though he never became chairman of the group. During his early years in Congress, two Californians, Mervyn Dymally and Ron Dellums, served as CBC chairmen, but Lewis developed his most fruitful relationships with his fellow "Southerners": Espy, Mickey Leland of Texas, Harold Ford of Tennessee, Walter Fauntroy of the District of Columbia, Kweisi Mfume of Maryland, and Alan Wheat and Bill Clay Sr. of Missouri. Together these eight men represented Black voters in Southern and border states that had not sent members of their race to Congress since the nineteenth century. For the first time in several generations, the Southern drawls heard in the House chamber came from both Black and white representatives, signaling a new departure in Democratic politics.

While no one in Congress shared the totality of his experiences in the Deep South, Lewis knew that several of his colleagues were kindred spirits who understood and valued his passions and beliefs. He was new in Washington, but he was not alone. If not quite a sacred band of brothers, Lewis and his allies in the CBC were a group of like-minded reformers who could count on each other when the chips were down. Knowing this gave him a secure sense of belonging—that he was in the right place, still working for the movement but in a new way. This was politics that mattered, part of his continuing struggle to redeem the soul of America.[4]

* * *

From the outset, Lewis threw himself into the work of the House with almost compulsive abandon. "The business at hand was no joke to me," he later wrote, "and I approached it as if the world depended on it. . . . I hit the ground running, attending every caucus meeting and every briefing session, accepting every invitation to speak, and never, not once, missing a vote during the first term." He was proud he was "one of only twelve out of the 435 members of the House to compile a perfect voting record that session." Making weekly trips to Atlanta, he was able not only to see Lillian and John-Miles, who rarely spent any time in Washington, but also to remain close to his constituents. He addressed local matters both large and small, determined to counter the suspicions voiced by his critics during his years on the city council and during the 1986 campaign—the charge that he was too idealistic "to take care of the bread-and-butter needs of my district."

During his first term, his hard work on two committees—Interior and Public Works, and Transportation—yielded hundreds of millions of dollars for the expansion of Atlanta's mass transit system, new highway construction, and the completion of several much-needed water projects.

Lewis also kept abreast of potential legislative measures related to the issues that had been important to him throughout his adult life—civil and human rights, and the amelioration of poverty—and he did all he could to publicize these issues both inside and outside the halls of Congress. During his first month as a congressman, he returned to Georgia to join Coretta King, Hosea Williams, Jesse Jackson, and more than two thousand other civil rights advocates in a "march against fear and intimidation" in Klan-infested Forsyth County, where a week earlier robed Klansmen had assaulted an interracial group holding a "walk for brotherhood" in honor of the new national holiday marking Dr. King's birthday. On the night of the holiday, Lewis appeared along with other King disciples—including Andrew Young and Julian Bond—on a national television special, *In Remembrance of Martin*. And less than a month later, on Abraham Lincoln's birthday, he and his CBC colleagues celebrated when an all-white jury awarded $7 million to the family of Michael Donald, a nineteen-year-old Black man lynched by Klansmen in Mobile, Alabama, in March 1981. This landmark judgment effectively bankrupted the United Klans of America.[5]

The civil rights struggle remained Lewis's greatest passion, but as a sitting congressman with multiple committee assignments, he spent most of his time on other matters. While some were prosaic, involving practical administrative duties, others took him far afield into problems and controversies related to military and foreign affairs, environmentalism, public health, and education. Faced with a steep learning curve, he made a concerted effort to learn all that he could about subjects with which he had little or no experience.

In early February 1987, Lewis participated in a successful effort to override President Reagan's veto of the Clean Water Act, and over the next two years he weighed in on a number of policy decisions dealing with issues that came before Congress. Many involved ongoing or potential crises abroad such as the Iran-Contra scandal related to funds transfers to anti-Sandinista rebels in Nicaragua, the repression of the antiapartheid movement in South Africa, bombings attributed to the Irish Revolutionary Army, conflict between Israel and the PLO, strikes by the Polish Solidarity movement, the Soviet military presence in Afghanistan, and East-West tensions in Germany.

The antiapartheid movement was especially important to Lewis, and in 1988 he was arrested during a protest outside the South African embassy in Washington. Later in the year, he became involved in the movement to protect human rights in the Soviet Union, traveling to Moscow "to meet with 'refuseniks'—Soviet Jews who had been denied permission to leave for Israel." Their bravery in the face of severe repression reminded him of the courageous spirit that drove the Freedom Riders and SNCC activists in the early 1960s. Inspired by what he had seen, he accepted an invitation to speak to the delegates of the Supreme Soviet on the topic of human rights. He poured all of his passion into the speech, though he realized there was little chance his words would have much effect. By the time he returned to the United States, he was exhausted but more determined than ever to combat autocracy and tyranny on a global level.

For the most part, Lewis was a sharp critic of Reagan's bellicose approach to foreign affairs, but in a few instances he supported the administration's efforts. In June 1987, he applauded Reagan's plea for German reunification: "Mr. Gorbachev, please tear down that wall." Lewis was one of the many members of Congress urging Reagan to meet with the Soviet leader to hammer out a nuclear disarmament treaty, and when Gorbachev came to Washington in December to sign an agreement eliminating medium-range nuclear missiles, Lewis was proud he had played at least a small part in the effort to deescalate the Cold War. A month later, he endorsed the administration's unexpected decision to accept up to thirty thousand Vietnamese children as immigrants.[6]

The following August, in another move to heal the wounds of the past—one that Lewis strongly favored—Congress passed the long-awaited Civil Liberties Act, which granted $20,000 reparation payments to each surviving Japanese American interned by the U.S. government during World War II. Many Republican representatives and senators opposed the act, which contained strong language tracing the internment policy to "race prejudice, war hysteria, and a failure of political leadership," and Lewis and many other Democrats were surprised when Reagan promptly signed the bill into law.[7]

To Lewis's dismay, the Civil Liberties Act was one of the few signs of progress on the domestic front, where the so-called Reagan Revolution was in full swing. Touting the libertarian influence of the market economy, "trickle-down" economics, and unrestrained capitalism, administration officials were committed to reducing government regulation, environmental and public health initiatives, and the social safety net that protected the most vulnerable members of American society. Many of the social and economic problems that Lewis and his progressive allies wanted to address—racism, poverty, homelessness, inadequate health care, the AIDS epidemic, misogyny, homophobia—were all but ignored by the Republican elite. Law and order, a draconian war against illegal drugs, the promotion of evangelical Christianity, the antiabortion crusade, and opposition to "forced busing," affirmative action, and the teaching of evolution—these were the domestic issues that consumed the energies of the Reaganites during the late 1980s.[8]

Eager to get beyond this toxic mix, Lewis looked forward to the end of the Reagan era. But he worried the presidential election of 1988 would bring another conservative Republican victory. In an effort to forestall this development, beginning in the summer of 1987 he participated in the Super Tuesday Education Project, an initiative of the Democratic Leadership Council designed to reverse a decade-long shift toward Republicanism in the white South. "You cannot have white voters flocking to the Republican Party. It's not good and it's not healthy," he insisted. "And it's not what we've been trying to bring about in the South in recent years. We've been trying to build a biracial society." In many areas of the South, Black Democrats now outnumbered white Democrats, a reality that reflected not only the rise in Black registration since the passage of the Voting Rights Act but also the sharp decline of Southern white support for the party. This unfortunate trade-off was on Lewis's mind when he spoke about the glory days of the movement at an October 1987 memorial service for Bayard Rustin, the nonviolent crusader who had famously promoted the transition from "protest to politics" in the mid-1960s.

Despite the Republican gains in the South, Lewis was confident the Democrats would retain control of both houses of Congress, and that he would be reelected in 1988. He had worked hard to stay in close touch with his constituents—to attend to the politics and needs of his district, including the sponsorship of legislation renaming a federal building in Atlanta after Dr. King as well as a special $73.1 million appropriation package that almost doubled the existing federal aid to Atlanta University and several other historically Black colleges and universities. So he didn't expect a serious challenge in either the Democratic primary or the general election.[9]

The presidential race was another matter, however. Reagan's vice president, George H. W. Bush of Texas, was an experienced and popular politician who easily defeated his rivals for the Republican nomination. On the Democratic side, the surprise nominee was Michael Dukakis, the liberal, three-term governor of Massachusetts, who defeated Joe Biden, Gary Hart, and several other Democratic senators, plus Lewis's old SCLC colleague Jesse Jackson, in the primaries. Jackson, who had sought the nomination four years earlier, had never been particularly close to Lewis, who viewed him as a grandstander. Nevertheless, Lewis recognized the importance of Jackson's emergence as only the second serious Black presidential candidate in American history, following in the footsteps of the New York congresswoman Shirley Chisholm's candidacy in 1972. When Jackson brought his campaign to Ebenezer Baptist Church in early March, on the twenty-third anniversary of Bloody Sunday, Lewis made an effort to be there and even sat in a front pew.

In the early going in the race against Bush, Dukakis appeared to be a strong candidate and built a comfortable lead in the polls, even though many Black voters were disappointed when he bypassed Jackson and selected Lloyd Bentsen, a conservative senator from Texas, as his running mate. Bush tried to take advantage of this disappointment during a speech at the NAACP's national convention, assuring Black voters, "You're going to be partners in my Presidency." These words rang hollow to Lewis, who warned, "You cannot be a tourist in the land of civil rights. You have to make it your home." Similarly, two months later, when Reagan signed a bill strengthening enforcement of the 1968 Fair Housing Act, Lewis praised the president's action but speculated it had more to do with politics than righteousness. "You don't get converted just in an election year," he counseled. "It's a continuing effort."

Despite the conservative tone of the Reagan era, Lewis remained hopeful that the spirit of the civil rights movement would reassert itself in the years to come. "I may not be typical, but I feel very . . . optimistic about the future," he told a reporter on the eve of the twenty-fifth anniversary of the March on Washington. "There are going to be some setbacks but we're going to move to the beloved community, we are going to make it as a nation and as a people."[10]

Unfortunately, Lewis and the movement soon suffered a major setback. In the final months of the campaign, the tide turned against Dukakis after Bush attacked him as a liberal do-gooder, labeling him "a card-carrying member of the ACLU" who opposed the death penalty and endorsed a Massachusetts prison furlough program open to convicted murderers. In September, a Republican political action committee ran an inflammatory ad featuring a mug shot of Willie Horton, a Black inmate convicted of murder who, after being furloughed, raped and assaulted a woman in Maryland. Bush had already mentioned the case repeatedly in his campaign speeches, leading one of his aides, Lee Atwater, to predict, "By the time we're finished, they're going to wonder whether Willie Horton is Dukakis' running mate."

Lewis, Jackson, and many other Democrats spoke out against the political exploitation of the Horton case as unprincipled racial demagoguery, but the Dukakis campaign never recovered from the attack. In November, Bush won a landslide victory, winning the electoral votes of forty states, though the Democratic Party did manage to retain control of both the House and Senate. In Georgia, where the number of Democratic representatives actually rose from eight to nine, Lewis handily defeated his Republican opponent, J. W. Tibbs Jr., a sixty-five-year-old Black pharmacist and World War II veteran. Winning 78.2 percent of the vote, Lewis increased his margin of victory by 3 percent over his 1986 showing. He interpreted this improvement as a vote of confidence in how he had conducted himself during his first term. Barring any major missteps or debacles, he could now look forward to a long career representing Georgia's Fifth District.[11]

* * *

Lewis's second term, stretching from 1989 to 1991, coincided with a volatile period in global history. In the span of twenty-four months, the world witnessed the Soviet withdrawal from Afghanistan, the dissolution of the Soviet Union, the end of the Cold War, the demolition of the Berlin Wall and the reunification of East and West Germany, violent repression of dissent in Tiananmen Square and other parts of Communist China, democratic revolutions in Eastern Europe and the Baltic states, the triumph of the Solidarity movement in Poland, the release of Nelson Mandela from a South African prison, and an Iraqi invasion of Kuwait that triggered the Persian Gulf War.

By the time Lewis ran for a third term, the geopolitics of much of the world was dramatically different from what it had been when he arrived in Washington. In the 101st Congress, domestic politics, including matters of civil rights and race, was dwarfed by sweeping changes abroad and major policy shifts in the arena of foreign affairs. Fortunately, from Lewis's perspective, most of these changes tilted toward greater freedom and democracy. For a number of years, he had made a concerted effort to broaden his vision, to adopt a more internationalist conception of the civil rights movement. In the spirit of one of Dr. King's last published essays, an evocative 1967 piece titled "The World House," he had become accustomed to the language of anticolonialism and human rights. The wisdom of this broad approach became increasingly apparent to him during his early years in Congress. A true search for the Beloved Community, he concluded, would require him to extend his moral quest beyond the United States.[12]

To Lewis, there was no bright line between domestic and foreign affairs. A case in point was the continuing saga of American involvement in the Nicaraguan civil war between the left-wing Sandinista regime and the Contra rebels. When Congress appropriated $49.7 million in aid to the Contras in April 1989, Lewis was one of ninety-nine House Democrats voting against the measure. The money would do much more good in Atlanta, he insisted, where many of his constituents lacked adequate housing, health care, and educational opportunities. He knew, of course, there were even more desperate needs abroad, especially in African countries such as Kenya and Somalia, where he would visit in 1992 and 1993 as a supporter of two United Nations humanitarian initiatives, Operation Provide Relief and Operation Restore Hope.

A second overseas crisis that, in Lewis's view, impinged on the government's ability to protect and serve its citizens was the Persian Gulf War that began in January 1991. Pitting Saddam Hussein's Iraqi regime against a coalition of thirty-five nations led by the United States, the military action to restore the independence of Kuwait was authorized by a joint congressional resolution approved by a vote of 250–183 in the House and 52–47 in the Senate. Most of those opposed to the resolution were Democrats, with Lewis being one of the most vociferous dissenters.

In an impassioned speech on the House floor, he pleaded for restraint and continued reliance on the economic sanctions imposed the previous August. Based on his commitment to nonviolence, Lewis's stirring words expressed his conviction that "death and destruction diminishes us all." At one point, he quoted a passage from the spiritual "Down by the Riverside"—"I am going to lay my burden down. . . . I ain't gonna study war no more." He went on to explain that he considered war to be "obsolete as an instrument of foreign policy." As he later recalled the gist of his argument, "Negotiation, sanctions, the way of nonviolence—these options must be exhaustively pursued before we even consider the use of weaponry. As a politician I can understand and accept the need for a certain amount of military strength as a deterrent, even though I believe as an individual that nothing, but *nothing,* justifies the use of violence between people or nations. . . . There is no excuse for the waste of the resources our nation spends on military force." Although his colleagues listened politely, a solid majority went on to endorse a war that, while brief, took the lives of thousands of soldiers and civilians.[13]

Public health was another serious concern of Lewis's that crossed international boundaries. He viewed the AIDS crisis as a worldwide phenomenon and called on Americans to share their resources and expertise with undeveloped countries in Africa and around the globe. He was adamant about the moral responsibilities of American capitalism, both at home and abroad. In the summer of 1989, he introduced a bill to encourage municipalities to replace inner-city billboard advertisements for cigarettes and alcohol with public health messages. "Every day when little children are on their way to school," he complained, "they get a message that the way to be happy and get ahead is to have a beer and smoke cigarettes."

The problem of addiction had a special resonance for Lewis. Since the mid-1980s, crack cocaine had ravaged Black communities across the nation, and several of his friends had grappled with drug habits that threatened their well-being. Marion Barry, the Nashville movement veteran who became the first chairman of SNCC and later a four-term mayor of Washington, struggled with cocaine abuse for more than a decade. Bond had less severe problems than Barry, but his recreational use of drugs cost him a seat in Congress and caused the breakup of his first marriage in 1989. Lewis's relationships with both men suffered because of their drug use, and he rarely saw them during these years—even though Barry lived a few blocks away and Bond came into the city each week for the taping of *America's Black Forum,* a television show he hosted from 1980 to 1997.[14]

During his early years in Congress, Lewis did not spend as much time with his old movement friends as he would have liked, though he occasionally ran into the former SNCC activists and Freedom Riders who lived in Washington or Atlanta. He remained in close contact with Dion Diamond and Reginald Green, two former Freedom Riders working in Washington as civil servants dealing with housing issues, and Travis and Gwen Britt, NAG veterans and former Freedom Riders active in suburban Maryland politics. When he was in Georgia, he sometimes saw old friends from his Nashville Student Movement and Freedom Rider days, especially C. T. Vivian, Charles Person, Hank Thomas, and Bill Harbour, all of whom had settled in the Atlanta area.

Many of the former Freedom Riders had maintained some contact with each other over the years, but their sense of historical connection took on new meaning after their first major reunion in 1986, a twenty-fifth anniversary commemoration held in Alabama featuring a partial re-creation of the 1961 Rides. Captured by a Canadian Broadcasting Company film crew, the reunion stirred memories of nonviolent struggle and encouraged Lewis to keep in better touch with the band of brothers and sisters who had once risked their lives for freedom and justice, many of whom were still active in various causes.

In 1990, Lewis was involved in a series of commemorative celebrations of the civil rights movement, beginning with an annual celebration of the King holiday in January, which was complicated by the recent publication of Ralph Abernathy's controversial memoir, *And the Walls Came Tumbling Down.* Abernathy's candid and scandalous revelations of King's marital infidelities drew commentary from a number of civil rights leaders, including Lewis. "He was a man, a human being, flesh and blood," Lewis acknowledged, "but he preached a message of hope and optimism that says to all of us that an individual can rise up and inspire an entire generation, an entire nation."[15]

A month later, Lewis returned to Nashville to participate in a nonviolent workshop commemorating the thirtieth anniversary of the sit-in movement, and in March he went to Selma for the second of what would become annual pilgrimages to the scene of the 1965 voting rights march. As cochair of the Selma event, he joined Coretta King, Jesse Jackson, Hosea Williams, SCLC president Joseph Lowery, and five thousand others in a re-creation of the historic march across the Edmund Pettus Bridge. When he and the other leaders gathered in front of the Brown Chapel AME Church to recall the bravery of the "foot soldiers" of the Selma movement, he was overcome with emotion. "I almost lost my life there," Lewis recalled, pointing in the direction of the bridge, "and in several ways if it wasn't for Selma in 1965, I wouldn't be in Congress today." The struggle wasn't over by any means, he told the crowd, but they had come a long way down the road to freedom.[16]

*   *   *

Seeing himself as a steward of the nonviolent civil rights movement, Lewis paid close attention to the movement's image—and its place in history. He felt that he, along with several other disciples of Dr. King, had been entrusted with the legacy of the 1960s, and his fondest hope as a congressman was that his political career would affirm and enhance the moral principles of nonviolence. Popular conceptions of Dr. King's values and beliefs were of great concern to him, and anything that besmirched King's reputation was seen as a threat to the movement's legitimacy and future prospects.

Lewis was thus crestfallen in November 1990 when an article in the *Wall Street Journal* revealed King's repeated acts of plagiarism as a graduate student at Boston University in the 1950s. Researchers at the Martin Luther King, Jr. Papers Project at Stanford University had uncovered the plagiarism three years earlier, and the *London Sunday Telegraph* had run a brief story on King's academic misdeeds in December 1989. But news of the scandal did not gain wide circulation before the *Wall Street Journal* article. Amid a flood of popular and academic criticism, some King loyalists such as Jackson and Lowery tried to minimize the importance of their mentor's transgressions.

"The youthful Martin may have sidestepped footnotes," Lowery conceded, "but thank god he stamped out greater foot prints for society later on."

Lewis, who had his own history of trying to live up to the sainthood label, empathized with King while freely acknowledging the alleged errors of omission and commission. In the end, he sided with those scholars, including Professor Clayborne Carson, the director of the King Papers Project, who concluded that most of the plagiarism stemmed from sloppiness, not outright deception. Although King clearly knew the difference between a PhD thesis and a sermon, he ran afoul of the differing standards between academic honesty and acceptable borrowing of ministerial word choices and dramatic passages. The whole affair was too painful for Lewis to say much about it in public, and there is no mention of it in his 1998 memoir. What he does mention, among other tributes to King, is a cherished memory of finding a first edition of King's first book, *Stride toward Freedom,* in an Alexandria, Virginia, bookshop in the 1970s. "Today," he assures his readers, "that book is locked in a safe in Atlanta, one of my most prized possessions." The most important reality for him was that he remained a passionate believer in King's message of hope and redemption.[17]

In July 1991, six months into his third term in Congress, Lewis—along with Jim Farmer and a dozen other former Freedom Riders, plus nearly two hundred other civil rights enthusiasts—gathered at Tougaloo College, just outside Jackson, Mississippi, for a four-day conference titled "A Look Back—a Leap Forward." Marking the thirtieth anniversary of the Rides, the conference fostered a great deal of reminiscing about the old days as well as spirited discussions of contemporary issues and controversies, including the impact of the plagiarism scandal on King's legacy, affirmative action, a nationwide antidrug war that was wreaking havoc in inner-city Black communities, and a widespread pattern of police brutality often directed at young Black men.

For many of the activists at the conference, the problem of police violence was the most pressing issue at hand, having been underscored in early March by the brutal beating of a twenty-five-year-old Black motorist named Rodney King by four Los Angeles police officers. The attack was caught on videotape and broadcast across the nation, and thirteen months later, following a long trial, the shocking acquittal of the officers led to five days of rioting that left more than fifty people dead, nearly six thousand others arrested, and hundreds of torched buildings in the predominantly Black neighborhoods of South Central Los Angeles.

Mississippi, unlike the poorest sections of Los Angeles, had obviously made significant progress since 1961, symbolized by the warm welcome that the former Riders received from a number of the state's leaders, including Jackson's Black police chief David Walker and Justice Reuben Anderson, the first Black citizen to serve on the state supreme court. While Lewis and several other Riders commented on the sharp contrast with their earlier visits to the state, he felt compelled to point out that "thirty years later, the scars and stains of racism are still deeply embedded in American society." Citing persistent discrimination and inequality and commenting on the bitter irony of President Bush's recent selection of the ultraconservative Black jurist Clarence Thomas to replace Thurgood Marshall on the Supreme Court, Lewis insisted that "we've seen the Berlin Wall tumble, but the wall of racism is still up in America."[18]

The Thomas nomination, along with the Bush administration's racially discriminatory treatment of Haitian refugees seeking asylum in America (unlike Cuban refugees, the dark-skinned Haitian "boat people" were forcibly repatriated to their native land without a hearing), confirmed Lewis's low opinion of the president's civil and human rights record. A devout Catholic, Thomas was an inveterate opponent of abortion rights and reproductive freedom—and a devoted follower of Ronald Reagan, who appointed him chairman of the Equal Employment Opportunity Commission in 1982. In 1990 President Bush nominated him to replace the conservative jurist Robert Bork on the U.S. Court of Appeals for the District of Columbia.

Lewis, along with the vast majority of the nation's civil rights leaders, strongly opposed Thomas's nomination. Like the Bork confirmation hearings four years earlier, the Thomas hearings in the Senate were highly contentious, especially after several of his former Equal Employment Opportunity Commission employees accused him of sexual harassment. Thomas's primary accuser was Anita Hill, a Black law professor at the University of Oklahoma, who delivered searing televised testimony about his inappropriate and aggressive sexualized behavior. In a highly emotional rejoinder, Thomas issued a vehement denial that he had done anything wrong, claiming he was being subjected to a "high-tech lynching for uppity Blacks." Following extensive debate, Thomas's nomination was confirmed by a vote of fifty-two to forty-eight, the narrowest margin for a successful nominee since James Buchanan's nomination of Nathan Clifford in 1857.

Lewis's opposition to Thomas was rooted in a deep respect for what the civil rights movement had accomplished since the 1950s. But as he soon discovered, some Black Americans did not seem to understand the importance of these accomplishments and the role Marshall had played in bringing them about. "My stand against Clarence Thomas," Lewis later reported, "brought an incredible amount of heat from the black community. I had turned on a 'brother,' a fellow Georgian. I had betrayed my race. I had not done 'the black thing.' That is true. I am and have always been focused on and dedicated to doing the *right* thing—which does not always mean doing the 'black' thing. This kind of attitude did not sit well back in the '60s with some of my colleagues in SNCC, and it has not sat well in the '90s with some of my black colleagues in Congress."

Lewis categorically rejected race-based criticism. "The fact that he [Thomas] is black did not matter to me," he explained in 1998. "The fact that his politics are conservative was not the issue. But like most of the black conservatives I know, he is a direct beneficiary of the civil rights movement, and the fact that he now stood poised to deny to others the kind of opportunities he enjoyed was appalling to me. Without the commitment of the federal government to equal employment opportunities, there would have been no Equal Employment Opportunity Commission for Clarence Thomas to chair—the position that catapulted him to his nomination to the Supreme Court. Without the *Brown v. Board of Education* decision, which he had come to call 'misguided,' he would not have been able to pursue the career path in law that he enjoyed, and he certainly would not ever have been considered for a seat on the Supreme Court."

Lewis went on to point out, "In fact, I have often taken the road less traveled because of the dictates of my conscience. I arrived in Washington with a commitment to addressing issues in terms of what's best for America, not in terms of what's best for this group or that group. I am a coalition builder. I will never compromise my belief in interracial democracy, and I do not ascribe to a narrow, rigid race-based orthodoxy. I don't pass my politics through the lens of race. Neither do I pass my friendships through that filter."[19]

Thomas's ascendance to the Supreme Court troubled Lewis, but two weeks after the ultraconservative Republican was sworn in as a new associate justice, the 1992 national election swept the Bush administration out of office. Bill Clinton, a liberal white Democrat from Arkansas with an impressive record on matters of race, defeated Bush by nearly six million votes, winning thirty-two states and 370 electoral votes. Campaigning in tandem with a running mate from Tennessee, Senator Al Gore, Clinton ushered in what Lewis hoped would be a new era in Southern politics. Lewis was especially enthusiastic about Gore, with whom he shared a deep interest in environmental justice; earlier in the year, in the wake of the 1991 People of Color Environmental Leadership Summit, they had cosponsored a bill designed to combat the environmental racism that often threatened the well-being of poor African Americans and other marginalized groups. Although the bill did not become law, Lewis believed that this and later efforts on behalf of environmental justice—the two men would continue to collaborate on environmental legislation during the next decade and beyond—"helped to renew the civil rights movement."

While the Democrats lost a small part of their majority in the House, they maintained their fifty-six seats in the Senate and thus retained control of both chambers. In Georgia, the Democrats gained two House seats, replacing Republican Pat Swindall with Democrat Ben Jones in the Fourth District and electing Cynthia McKinney, a thirty-seven-year-old Black state representative, in the newly created and predominantly African American Eleventh District, which stretched from Atlanta to Savannah. To Lewis's delight, McKinney's district soon became known as the "Sherman's March" district. He was ecstatic over McKinney's election, having known her father, Billy McKinney, an Atlanta policeman and a longtime civil rights activist. Lewis himself easily won a fourth term, garnering 72.1 percent of the vote against his Republican opponent, Paul Stabler. Congressman Newt Gingrich and the Georgia Republican Party had not yet given up on their effort to defeat him; their belated recognition that he was immensely popular and virtually unbeatable would come four years later when he ran unopposed.[20]

CHAPTER 15

———

Keeping the Dream Alive

I N JANUARY 1993, John Lewis welcomed the end of the George H. W. Bush presidency. While he did not consider Bush to be as dangerous as Ronald Reagan, the Texas Republican, in his view, had presided over a regime that perpetuated a political culture of complacency and white privilege. For more than a decade, the nation had been drifting with little sense of moral purpose as the persistent problems of poverty and racial discrimination were all but ignored by a Republican Party tilting to the right. This was Lewis's sobering assessment as he began his fourth term in Congress.

He had high hopes for the Clinton administration, which had received a clear mandate for change in the 1992 election. But he couldn't avoid the disturbing memory of his profound disappointment in the last Democratic administration, when Jimmy Carter had squandered an opportunity to revitalize American democracy. In many respects, Bill Clinton and Carter were cut from the same cloth. Both were well-educated men raised in the Southern Baptist church, both had served as governors of a Southern state, and, though born twenty-two years apart, both styled themselves as "New Democrats"—as political outsiders committed to challenging the reigning hierarchy of their party. The primary differences between them lay in Clinton's charisma—a quality Carter lacked—and in his considerable reputation as a wily politician. To friends and foes alike, Clinton was "Slick Willie," an artful dodger of Dickensian proportions. The only other significant difference separating them—one that was important to Lewis—was Carter's past as an avowed segregationist, an unfortunate piece of cultural baggage that Clinton had never acquired.

In the early going, Lewis was encouraged by Clinton's handling of the transition to the new administration. The chairman of the transition team was Vernon Jordan, who had preceded him as director of the VEP. Jordan would remain one of Clinton's closest advisers throughout his presidency, providing Lewis with a liaison to the highest levels of the administration. Clinton also surprised Lewis with the appointment of four African Americans to his cabinet: Mike Espy as secretary of agriculture, Ron Brown as secretary of commerce, Hazel O'Leary as secretary of energy, and Jesse Brown as secretary of veterans affairs. No prior president had ever appointed more than one African American cabinet member, including Bush, whose lone selection was Louis Sullivan as secretary of health and human services. In each case, Clinton's appointee was the first Black person to serve as secretary of his or her department, and he would appoint three more Black department heads during his second term.[1]

The new president also wasted no time in tackling some of the most difficult social issues left untended by the Reagan and Bush administrations. On January 22, two days after the inauguration and fittingly on the twentieth anniversary of the *Roe v. Wade* decision, Clinton issued an executive order lifting several restrictions on abortion put in place by his Republican predecessors. Speaking just hours after seventy-five thousand abortion rights advocates gathered outside the White House, the president revoked a five-year-old ban on fetal tissue research, a gag rule that severely limited abortion counseling at federally funded family planning clinics, and the ban against importing RU486, the French "morning after" pill. "Our vision," Clinton proclaimed, "should be of an America where abortion is safe and legal and rare."

Lewis shared this vision and looked forward to future initiatives aimed at enhancing and democratizing the nation's health-care system. During his years with the Field Foundation and the Southern Regional Council, he had witnessed the devastating effects of inadequate health care among the nation's poorest citizens, and he was determined to do what he could to establish health care as a basic human right. He was heartened when Clinton announced that universal health care was the administration's top priority and that the First Lady would head the effort to bring this about. Lewis regarded this effort as essential to the amelioration of some of the worst aspects of poverty, and he would later view Congress's failure to implement the administration's health care reforms as a tragedy.

During Clinton's first year in office, Lewis witnessed several developments confirming that the president's heart was in the right place when it came to matters of economic and social justice. In early February, Clinton signed the long-awaited Family and Medical Leave Act, and later in the month he delivered a lengthy radio address on the problem of poverty and the prospects for raising the standard of living among the nation's marginalized citizens. Later in the year, he nominated the ACLU stalwart Ruth Bader Ginsburg to the Supreme Court; awarded the Presidential Medal of Freedom to Arthur Ashe, the Black tennis star and humanitarian who had died of AIDS in February; announced a "don't ask, don't tell" policy toward gay men and women in the military; celebrated the thirtieth anniversary of the March on Washington for Jobs and Freedom with an assurance that he was still "guided by that vision of economic empowerment"; supported and signed the Brady Handgun Violence Prevention Act, which mandated federal background checks and a five-day waiting period for all gun sales; and endorsed a United Nations proposal to create a High Commissioner for Human Rights. At the end of the year, he even issued a presidential decree acknowledging the African American holiday Kwanzaa.[2]

Lewis found all of this encouraging and looked forward to at least three more years of presidential leadership on a wide variety of social and economic issues. But in 1994, with the approach of the November midterm elections, his expectations plummeted as the Clinton administration shifted noticeably to the right. Worried that the traditional midterm losses incurred by the party in power would be greater than normal, Clinton attempted to shore up the Democratic Party's support among moderate and conservative voters by taking a hard line on matters related to law and order and welfare reform.

When Clinton's health care initiative ran afoul of a conservative backlash against "socialized medicine," the administration's top legislative priority became a comprehensive anticrime bill. Fueled by a rising crime rate and the spread of crack cocaine in many inner-city neighborhoods, the pressure for enhanced law enforcement and mass incarceration provided politicians in both parties with an irresistible and exploitable issue. Introduced in October 1993, the Violent Crime Control and Law Enforcement Bill, which was signed into law in September 1994, included a wide range of anticrime provisions: an expanded federal death penalty; designation of fifty new federal offenses; funds for additional federal prisons; a mandatory "three-strikes-and-you-are-out" penalty for repeat offenders; the creation of a Community Oriented Policing Services Office authorized to add one hundred thousand police officers across the nation; registries for violent sex offenders and pedophiles; and the elimination of Pell educational grants for federal prisoners.

The act also included several liberal provisions—notably a measure to prevent and investigate violence against women and an assault weapons ban—all of which Lewis supported. But the major thrust of the act was the imposition of a heavy-handed law-and-order regime. What the NAACP called "a crime against the American people" passed the House in August by a vote of 235 to 195, gaining considerable bipartisan support. Among the House Democrats, only Lewis and 67 others voted against it.[3]

* * *

Lewis regarded the Violent Crime Act as tantamount to an attack on the nation's inner cities, an ill-advised, heavily politicized measure that might boost the popularity of his fellow Democrats but also would almost certainly exacerbate the misery and discrimination that plagued poor and marginalized Americans. He was not only disheartened by the passage of the act; he was also roundly disappointed that several of his friends and colleagues in the Congressional Black Caucus supported it. Over the past year, the CBC had fallen short of Lewis's expectations on several occasions. In September 1993, the CBC's chairman, Kweisi Mfume of Maryland, announced that the caucus planned to sign a "covenant" with the Nation of Islam leader Louis Farrakhan, a Black separatist and anti-Semite. Lewis, who wanted to avoid any association with Farrakhan's extremism, vigorously objected when Mfume later implied that the entire caucus was in favor of the proposed covenant. "I don't think it was ever an official position of the caucus," he insisted in January 1994. "I don't think a great majority of the caucus ever saw ourselves engaged in any type of partnership or covenant with Minister Farrakhan."[4]

Lewis was also deeply troubled by what he viewed as an ill-conceived Clinton administration initiative on welfare reform. During the 1992 campaign, Clinton had "vowed to end welfare as we know it," but he did not clarify what he meant by this until his second year in office, and even then he did little to advance a concrete proposal on the issue. Lewis was relieved when the president delayed the introduction of an actual welfare reform bill, but he remained worried that the administration was moving in the wrong direction. It was clear Clinton had decided to push for a new system of social welfare that instituted some form of "workfare" to replace the current Aid to Families with Dependent Children program. Although the bill that became the Personal Responsibility and Work Opportunity Reconciliation Act would not be introduced until June 1996, the warning signs were already in evidence two years earlier.[5]

The continued wrangling over the administration's national health proposal was also a serious matter of concern for Lewis. As a member of the Ways and Means Subcommittee on Health, he clashed with the ultraconservative ranking Republican on the subcommittee, Bill Thompson of California, during and after more than a month of public hearings in the winter of 1994. "Few issues grip the American people as deeply as the health care crisis," Lewis reminded Thompson and the lobbyists opposing a democratized national system. "Health care is a basic right of all individuals. It's not a privilege." He was later instrumental in defeating a Republican proposal to eliminate the mandate requiring employers to help fund the proposed system. Rejecting the Republicans' proposal as "a dagger in the heart of the bill," he insisted the mandate was essential to the guarantee of universal coverage.[6]

In the end, the forces opposed to federally mandated universal health care dealt Clinton and his liberal allies a crushing defeat that carried over into the midterm election and beyond. For the many moderate and conservative voters concerned about Clinton's attachment to big government and higher taxes, the administration's move to the right proved to be too little and too late. In a political realignment later dubbed the "Republican

Revolution," the GOP picked up ten additional governorships and won control of both houses of Congress for the first time since 1954. In the Senate, the Republicans gained 10 seats for a 53–47 majority, and in the House they gained a staggering 54 seats for a 230–204 majority, giving the party its largest edge since 1948. To Lewis's dismay, the Democratic Speaker of the House, Tom Foley of Missouri, was replaced by the Georgia Republican Newt Gingrich, and the Democratic Senate majority leader, George Mitchell of Maine, gave way to Robert Dole of Kansas.

The biggest Republican gains came in the South, where the party picked up nineteen seats in the House, establishing a GOP congressional majority in the region for the first time since Reconstruction. In Georgia, Lewis easily won reelection, defeating his Republican opponent, Dale Dixon, with nearly 70 percent of the vote. But three other Democratic congressmen lost their races, increasing the number of Republican members of Congress in Georgia from four to seven. In 1995, for the first time since 1869, the state's House delegation would have a Republican majority. Even worse, in Lewis's view, was the elevation of Gingrich from Republican minority whip to Speaker of the House.[7]

Working closely with the archconservative Heritage Foundation, Gingrich was one of a handful of Republican members of Congress who drafted the Contract with America, an innovative national campaign program that many observers later regarded as a critical factor in the Republicans' sweeping victory at the polls. With unprecedented specificity and more than a touch of demagoguery, the Contract with America promised that if Republican lawmakers gained control of Congress, the party would implement a series of reform measures designed to lower federal taxes, shrink the size of the federal government, empower entrepreneurs, and institute tort and welfare reform.

As a liberal Democrat who believed in the government's responsibility to safeguard the social welfare of all Americans, Lewis considered the Contract with America to be morally bankrupt. He was embarrassed that the man leading the charge for the Republicans represented Georgia's Sixth Congressional District, located just north of Atlanta. On matters of both personal comportment and public policy, Gingrich was Lewis's polar opposite. An aggressive, pyrotechnic type of politician, the former college history professor brought a strident, ideologically driven approach to the Speaker's position, later characterized by one historian as "burning down the house." Under Gingrich's influence, the Republican Party adopted an increasingly reactionary and illiberal stance on many issues, becoming, as Bill Clinton put it in November 1995, "very extremist" and "very negative." For a time, many Americans—especially evangelical Christians, racial conservatives, and radical libertarians—seemed to embrace this new version of Republican politics, making 1995 one of the darkest years for Democrats in living memory.[8]

Lewis, who had been battling reactionaries throughout his adult life, refused to be cowed by the Republican assault on progressive policies and values. As always, he kept the faith—and his composure—doing what he could to help the Clinton administration ride out the storm. Although most of the administration's legislative agenda was blocked during Clinton's third year in office, there were several developments on the international front that provided Lewis and other liberal Democrats with a sense of hope and accomplishment. For a six-month period in late 1994 and early 1995, Operation Uphold Democracy, a military intervention in Haiti sanctioned by the United Nations and led by the United States, dismantled a dictatorial regime that had overthrown the democratically elected government of President Jean-Bertrand Aristide in a 1991 coup d'état. As a quasi-pacifist, Lewis favored diplomatic over military actions as a means of resolving conflicts abroad, but in this case he welcomed the dispatch of American troops, which he viewed more as peacekeepers than combatants.

Another development that raised Lewis's spirits was Nelson Mandela's official visit to Washington in October 1995. The newly elected president of South Africa had long been one of his personal role models, a truth-telling freedom fighter who believed in forgiveness and racial reconciliation. Lewis could hardly contain himself when he was introduced to Mandela at a state dinner in the East Room of the White House, and later when he listened to him speak at a luncheon hosted by the CBC. Lewis lauded Mandela as "a real leader," a man who "doesn't see himself as standing out in front of the people. He sees himself as standing *beside* them, *among* them. He doesn't tell people to dig a ditch; he gets down in the ditch with them and helps dig it himself." To Lewis, Mandela was a part of the same movement, the same struggle, that had given his life meaning and purpose. To be sure, Mandela's early years with the African National Congress had involved a certain amount of armed insurrection against apartheid. But for Lewis the most salient aspect of the great South African's life was that he eventually found his way to the path of nonviolence and the power of love.[9]

Lewis also found solace in the Clinton administration's attempts to restore peace and hope in the war-torn Balkan states of Bosnia, Croatia, and Serbia. In December 1995, after more than three years of intense civil war marked by genocidal atrocities, the United States facilitated the Dayton peace accords. Within a year, several of the leaders responsible for murderous attacks on civilians were brought to trial at the International Criminal Court in the Hague, Netherlands.

Lewis applauded the administration's new emphasis on the protection of human rights, which officially extended to other parts of the world. In a November 1995 radio broadcast, Clinton talked movingly about "the American dreams of freedom, democracy and peace advancing with our support in the Middle East, Northern Ireland, in South Africa, in Haiti, and Eastern and Central Europe," a world "full of people who are making courageous efforts to escape the shackles of the past and reach their own dreams of tomorrow." While Lewis knew the nation's actual record on international human rights fell far short of this fulsome rhetoric, he now had some hope that the dream of a more peaceful and just world was still alive more than a quarter century after Dr. Martin Luther King Jr. had articulated his vision of "The World House." A global version of the Beloved Community, one world peaceful and free, remained Lewis's highest priority.

Sustaining the solidarity and moral commitment needed to advance this dream was never easy, even within the narrower confines of the American civil rights struggle. Lewis received a painful reminder of this in December 1994 when a bitter dispute over control of the King Center broke out between several members of the King family and the National Park Service. Preparing for the horde of tourists that would descend on Atlanta when it hosted the 1996 Summer Olympics, the city's leaders supported a Park Service plan to build an $11.8 million visitors' center across the street from the King Center, which had been run by the King family since 1968. When the family objected to the plan and summarily canceled a fourteen-year partnership with the Park Service, ordering the park rangers to leave the property,

Lewis offered to mediate the dispute. At a tense meeting in January 1995, he was able to work out a compromise acceptable to both sides, and the construction of the visitors' center proceeded. Even so, the public-private struggle for control of the King Center left a bitter legacy that divided Atlanta's Black community for several years.[10]

*　*　*

Wherever Lewis looked in the mid-1990s—from the sharp divide between working-class and middle-class Black citizens, to the hardening of class divisions all across the nation, to the factionalism that was plaguing the Democratic Party—the social fabric of America seemed to be fraying. He had hoped that the Clinton presidency would foster a renewed commitment to the American ideals of liberty and justice for all. But as the campaign leading up to the 1996 election unfolded, it became clear that political survival was Clinton's top priority. The things that mattered the most to Lewis—social and economic equality, the political empowerment of the nation's most vulnerable citizens, broad access to quality health care—would have to wait until after the election.

Clinton's cold-blooded pragmatism was evident in his January 1996 State of the Union address when he declared "the era of big government is over." As a self-proclaimed New Democrat, the president was committed to a centrist position on virtually every domestic issue. In foreign policy he continued to break new ground, urging the Senate to ratify the SALT II nuclear arms reduction treaty, committing the American peacekeepers in Bosnia to remain for another eighteen months, and supporting the United Nations' comprehensive nuclear testing ban. But on matters closer to home, other than vetoing a draconian late-term abortion ban in April, Clinton disappointed Lewis at almost every turn.

In August, one day after accepting a watered-down and inconsequential version of his health care bill, the president signed the Personal Responsibility and Work Opportunity Reconciliation Act, lauding the measure as a move from "welfare to workfare," a reform that offered a "hand up rather than a handout." As Lewis listened to Clinton's seemingly callous sloganeering, he was almost brought to tears thinking about all of his experiences with impoverished Americans desperate for help. Once again, the government of the wealthiest nation on earth had failed to protect and nurture the well-being of its most vulnerable citizens.[11]

Lewis knew, of course, that the Republican opposition led by Speaker Gingrich and the party's presidential candidate, Robert Dole, was far worse than Clinton and the Democrats on any number of issues. But he couldn't escape the feeling that the Democrats were squandering a golden opportunity to propel the nation toward true democracy. He was particularly upset in September when Clinton signed the Defense of Marriage Act, a blatantly homophobic measure that prohibited the federal government from sanctioning same-sex marriage. To Lewis's dismay, the bill received strong bipartisan support in both houses. In the House he was one of only sixty-seven representatives to vote against the bill. For a time in the late summer, he held out some hope that the president would veto the measure, but in the end Clinton did not dare to buck the traditionalist majority.

Clinton's strong lead over Dole in all of the early polls suggested he was actually in a position to move to the left without jeopardizing his reelection. Yet his campaign advisers did not see it that way and continued to encourage the Democratic candidate to play it safe. The Clinton campaign's primary strategy was to link Dole with Gingrich, who had grown increasingly unpopular among middle-of-the-road voters during the past two years. Clinton repeatedly warned voters that if the "Dole-Gingrich" alliance captured the presidency, the dismantling of popular programs such as Social Security and Medicare would soon follow.

This strategy, coupled with a strong economy, carried Clinton to a resounding victory, making him the first Democratic president to win reelection since Franklin Roosevelt. Winning thirty-one states with an overall popular vote margin of more than eight million, Clinton's personal triumph was complete. Many other Democrats, however, did not fare as well, and the Republicans managed to retain control of both houses of Congress. The Democratic showing was especially discouraging in the South, where Dole carried seven of eleven states, including Georgia, and where an unprecedented number of Republicans gained office. To Lewis's chagrin, the shift toward Southern Republicanism that had begun in the mid-1960s was now on the verge of creating a new "Solid South" dominated by Republicans, not Democrats. Georgia's Fifth Congressional District remained a Democratic stronghold, and Lewis won reelection without any Republican opposition. But in most of the South, the GOP was clearly on the rise.[12]

By the time Lewis began his sixth term as a congressman in January 1997, the prospects for the implementation of meaningful social legislation were dimmer than ever. He had been the Democrats' chief party whip since 1991, but he feared that maintaining party solidarity in the House had lost most of its importance. His concern was warranted; during Clinton's second term, Congress produced very few pieces of consequential legislation. Instead, the majority of the legislative body's time and energy was spent on partisan wrangling over matters such as the Whitewater real estate investment scandal and Clinton's alleged sexual indiscretions.[13]

For Lewis, the high point of Clinton's second term had little to do with public policy or what was happening in Washington. In September 1997, he had the honor of accompanying the First Lady to the state funeral of Mother Teresa, the Albanian nun and Nobel Peace Prize winner who had come to India in 1948 to found the Missionaries of Charity, an order dedicated to serving "the poorest of the poor." For many years, Lewis had dreamed of visiting the birthplace of Gandhian nonviolence, but he never expected to do so as an official emissary of the United States.

The funeral was an extraordinary event, held in Calcutta, where more than a million people lined the streets as the carriage carrying Mother Teresa's diminutive body rolled toward the site of her memorial service. The same carriage, Lewis later noted, had carried Gandhi's body to its final resting place in 1948. Sitting next to the First Lady, Lewis was deeply moved by the words of Angelo Sodano, the Vatican secretary of state who presided over the funeral mass. "The beggar, the leper, the victim of AIDS," Sodano declared in his eulogy, "do not need discussions and theories. They need love. The hungry cannot wait for the rest of the world to come up with the perfect answer." Later in the year, when Lewis wrote the final pages of his memoir *Walking with the Wind,* he repeated this call to action, reminding his readers that "Mother Teresa acted. She reached out to those who were left behind—the forsaken, the poorest of the poor, the sickest of the sick."[14]

To Lewis's disappointment, the Clinton administration proved incapable of mobilizing this kind of action on behalf of America's most marginal citizens. He saw no evidence of significant progress on pressing domestic issues, many of which received little or no attention from either the legislative or the executive branch. Virtually all of the administration's most important accomplishments involved international issues and foreign affairs, advances such as Clinton's March 1997 nuclear disarmament summit meeting with Russian president Boris Yeltsin in Helsinki, Finland, and the Senate's ratification of a chemical weapons ban treaty two months later.

Perhaps most important to Lewis, in March 1998 Clinton undertook a historic twelve-day tour of Africa, becoming the first American president to visit the continent since Jimmy Carter in 1978. Lewis had been advocating a presidential gesture of this kind for several years, and he was especially pleased that the tour's route made several stops at sites related to the transatlantic slave trade. Unfortunately, however, there was no such progress on important domestic issues such as health care, alleviation of poverty, or gun control.[15]

The disjunction between the domestic and international fronts was somewhat puzzling to Lewis, who, after a decade in Congress, began to look back on the twists and turns of his journey from protest to politics in an effort to make sense of it all. After several months of preliminary reflection in early 1996, he decided to write an autobiography, a "memoir of the movement," as he called it. He knew he needed a professional writer to help him reconstruct the details of his life and to put his thoughts in a form that would reach a broad audience, and he found a good one in Michael D'Orso, a Virginia-born author who had just published *Like Judgment Day*, a riveting book on the Rosewood, Florida, racial massacre of 1923. Working closely during two years of interviews and dialogue, D'Orso and Lewis produced one of the modern civil rights era's most valuable memoirs, *Walking with the Wind*, published by Simon and Schuster in June 1998.

Fortunately, D'Orso employed a light editorial touch that allowed Lewis's authentic voice to emerge from the book's eloquent prose. Much of the book is a straightforward narrative, but it also offers numerous philosophical and political judgments that illuminate the text and context of his life and times. In the last chapter, titled "Home," the six-term congressman tries to explain why he was so discouraged during the late 1990s, the years dominated by the "Republican Revolution" and Clinton's noticeable turn to the right. He does so, in part, by comparing the contemporary scene with the tumultuous history of the 1960s that he knew so well. "Sometimes I feel that I'm reliving that history, that I'm reliving that part of my life," he wrote. "I hear talk of 'states' rights,' of the evils of a powerful federal government, and I swear I can see George Wallace standing again in that schoolhouse door. I feel like I'm passing down a road I've walked before. The anger, the militancy, the separatism, the schism between whites and blacks and within the black community itself—it's all so familiar. It is eerie."

Lewis went on to add, "In terms of the climate in Washington, however, the situation is now worse than it was then. Back then it was essentially the states we were fighting. We could look to the federal government and the Supreme Court for redress, for hope and optimism, for justice. The response of that government was slower than it should have been, but it did come. Laws were passed. Promises were kept. Today, however, we have people in those places—in Congress and on the High Court—who are not at all sympathetic to the principles of fairness. By its actions and its statements and its votes and decisions, our government is destroying much of the hope and belief that are holding the most tenuous sections of our society together." He was particularly upset by the "backlash against affirmative action," the mean-spirited implementation of so-called welfare reform, an ill-conceived antidrug war that had led to unprecedented mass incarceration, the growing opposition to court-ordered school desegregation, and a general lack of interest in racial integration and the amelioration of poverty.[16]

One notable exception to this bleak picture on the home front—one that Lewis greeted with great enthusiasm—was Clinton's creation of a national advisory board on race in June 1997. Charged with "convening and encouraging community dialogue" and "fostering improved understanding of race relations," the board held public meetings and town halls across the country for more than a year under the direction of eighty-three-year-old John Hope Franklin, the nation's most distinguished African American historian. Lewis, who had known and admired Franklin for decades, attended several of the board's public meetings and later hailed the publication of its 1998 report, *One America in the 21st Century: Forging a New Future*, as a landmark in the history of interracial dialogue. Unfortunately, the report drew little response from the national press and the American public, both of which were preoccupied with a sensational sex scandal involving Clinton and his twenty-four-year-old White House intern Monica Lewinsky. The September 1998 release of Independent Counsel Kenneth Starr's report on the salacious Lewinsky affair received far more attention than the dissemination of the race board's report, leaving Lewis and many other civil rights advocates frustrated and bewildered.[17]

*   *   *

There were, however, two encouraging developments that lifted Lewis's spirits. The first was the publication of and subsequent acclaim for his memoir, *Walking with the Wind*, and the second was his deepening involvement with the Faith and Politics Institute (FPI), a Washington-based organization created in 1991 to "bridge racial, religious, and political divisions among elected officials, while promoting reflective and ethical leadership" and "healing, civility, and respect." Founded by the Reverend Douglas Tanner, a white Methodist minister from North Carolina, the FPI invited members of Congress, along with their staffs, to participate in experiential pilgrimages, retreats, reflection groups, and public symposia. In 1997, Tanner recruited two congressmen, John Lewis and Amo Houghton, a New York Republican, to serve as cochairs of FPI's board of directors.

Lewis soon became the organization's most active and visible member, and in March 1998, the same month that President Clinton toured Africa, he led the first FPI weekend pilgrimage to Selma. Accompanied by more than a dozen members of Congress representing both parties and a wide ideological spectrum, he revisited the site of the 1965 Selma-to-Montgomery march, leading his "pilgrims" in a commemorative march across the Edmund Pettus Bridge and singing hymns and freedom songs with them at the historic Brown Chapel AME Church. During the next two decades, more than three hundred members of Congress would visit Selma, joining Lewis in a spirit of nonpartisan fellowship and temporarily following his lead in connecting the voting rights struggle to a morality-based style of politics. The intended message, which he hoped at least some of the pilgrims would take to heart, was the importance of adopting "collaborative and visionary leadership practices" in an effort to "foster healing, civility, and respect."[18]

Unfortunately, in the months following the first pilgrimage, this effort was stymied by a rancorous partisan battle over how the Clinton-Lewinsky sex scandal should be handled. In December, Clinton's unconvincing denial of his affair led to his impeachment by the House on charges of perjury, obstruction of justice, and abuse of office. With few exceptions, the votes on four articles of impeachment followed strict party lines; Lewis and virtually all of his Democratic colleagues opposed impeachment and voted accordingly. Two articles were rejected by a majority of the House, but two others were approved and forwarded to the Senate for trial. After the Senate voted to acquit Clinton on both articles in early February 1999, Lewis was relieved and eager for the government to heal its wounds and move on. But the likelihood that congressional politics would become more civil and productive during the third year of Clinton's second term was greatly diminished by the results and consequences of the national election held the previous November.

The leaders of both parties emerged from the off-year election in a state of high anxiety and with mixed feelings. The Republicans retained control of Congress, maintaining their 55–45 majority in the Senate as well as a narrow margin in the House. But the House Democrats were pleased that they managed to add four additional seats, the first time since 1822 that a second-term president's party had gained seats in a midterm election; and they were elated when the relentlessly combative Speaker of the House Gingrich, buffeted by personal scandals and declining popularity among his Republican colleagues, resigned his leadership position less than a week after the election. Lewis and his fellow Georgia Democrats were heartened that Gingrich resigned from Congress as well—even though this did not change the partisan makeup of the state delegation. The Republicans would still hold eight of the state's eleven congressional seats when the new Congress convened in January 1999.[19]

Lewis's spirit was buoyed, however, by the Democratic Party's continuing control of the White House for at least two more years. Despite the recent turmoil over impeachment, the State of the Union address that President Clinton delivered in mid-January was full of soaring rhetoric and allusions to the administration's major accomplishments. As expected, he opened with the good news that the nation was experiencing unprecedented prosperity and the first balanced budget in a generation. "Tonight, I stand before you to report that America has created the longest peacetime economic expansion in our history," he announced, before turning to a long list of economic and social issues that the administration had either fully or partially addressed. The fiscal future of Social Security and Medicare, educational opportunity, the threat of terrorism, nuclear disarmament, conflict in Kosovo and the Middle East, fair trade, daycare and family leave, gun control, violent crime, environmental protection, immigrants' rights, campaign finance reform, the challenges and opportunities of the information age, and the crisis of the family farmer—he touched on them all with a decidedly progressive twist.

Lewis welcomed all of this, but the high point of the speech for him came when the president turned to the interconnected issues of poverty, race, and community. "We must do more to bring the spark of private enterprise to every corner of America—to build a bridge from Wall Street to Appalachia to the Mississippi Delta, to our Native American communities," Clinton insisted. "Whether our ancestors came here on the Mayflower, on slave ships, whether they came to Ellis Island or LAX in Los Angeles, whether they came yesterday or walked this land a thousand years ago—our great challenge for the 21st century is to find a way to be One America."

Citing the recent report of his Racial Advisory Board, Clinton talked about the need "to bring our people together across racial lines," before offering a brief civil rights history lesson that brought a smile to Lewis's face. "We know it's been a long journey," the president explained. "For some, it goes back to before the beginning of our Republic; for others, back since the Civil War; for others, throughout the twentieth century. But for most of us alive today, in a very real sense, this journey began 43 years ago, when a woman named Rosa Parks sat down on a bus in Alabama and wouldn't get up." He then turned to the box where his wife, Hillary, was sitting next to Rosa Parks and paid his respects.[20]

Lewis, who had been waiting to hear this kind of speech since his first days in Congress, left the Capitol that night with renewed hope for the future. The One America ideal stressed by the president sounded a lot like the Beloved Community that Lewis had been searching for most of his life. All around him that January there were echoes of his civil rights past. Two days before Clinton's address, the ABC network broadcast a television film based on a memoir by two of the youngest participants in the 1965 Selma campaign, Sheyann Webb and Rachel West, who were only eleven years old at the time of the march. Asked to comment on the film, Lewis recalled the bravery of the children who joined the Selma struggle. "There were kids who barely knew how to spell freedom," he remembered, "but they knew that it meant something."

On the eve of Clinton's speech, Lewis joined Chuck Schumer, the newly elected senator from New York, and several other distinguished speakers at a King Day celebration held at the Brooklyn Academy of Music. Speaking to a crowd of more than two thousand, Lewis talked movingly about his debt to King and—with an allusion to Clinton's recent impeachment—about the spirit of forgiveness. "If I was able to forgive Bull Connor, George Wallace, and the Ku Klux Klan, then we should be able to forgive our President," he insisted, with "his voice rising with anger," according to one reporter. At the close of his remarks, he told a story anticipating the One America theme that would be so prominent in the president's speech the following evening. Taken from his childhood, the story involved a violent windstorm that nearly destroyed his aunt's ramshackle house in rural Pike County. "We ran from corner to corner of the house trying to hold it down with our little bodies wherever it was raised up," he explained, adding, "Now, the lightning may flash, the wind may blow, the rain may beat down, but we must never leave our house. Maybe we all came to this country in different ships, but we are all in one boat together."[21]

Six weeks later, Lewis accompanied a number of his congressional colleagues on the annual FPI civil rights pilgrimage to Selma. Going back to Edmund Pettus Bridge and the scene of Bloody Sunday thirty-four years later was a highly emotional experience for Lewis, and in March 1999 he witnessed the first sign that a pilgrimage to Selma could actually transform the moral and political sensibilities of his fellow members of Congress.

Lewis always invited several conservative Republicans to join the FPI pilgrimage, and one of those who made the journey in 1999 was Michael Forbes, a three-term congressman from Long Island. A right-to-life conservative and former friend and ally of Newt Gingrich, Forbes had broken with the Speaker in December 1996 over the issues of unrelenting partisanship and campaign finance irregularities. Over the next two years, he moved to the center politically, distancing himself from Gingrich and other Republican leaders, whom he characterized as "tone-deaf extremists." At the same time, he became friendly with a number of House Democrats, including Lewis. This did not stop him from voting to impeach Clinton; nor did it stop him from resisting thoughts of switching parties. It took the pilgrimage to Selma to do that, severing his long-standing commitment to conservative Republicanism. "I captured my essence" in Selma, he later explained, and in July 1999 he changed his party affiliation to Democratic. Since he retained his antiabortion stance, not all Democrats welcomed him into the party, and in 2000 he was narrowly defeated in the Democratic primary and never held public office again. Though disappointed that Forbes was forced out of politics, Lewis considered the New York congressman's political conversion to be a redemptive moral victory—one that eventually led to a second career as a Roman Catholic priest.[22]

* * *

Political conversions of any kind were few and far between during the year following Clinton's acquittal, as self-righteous recriminations proliferated amid hardening partisan and ideological divisions. Though still popular in the public opinion polls, Clinton was a divisive figure in Washington, where he was both loved and hated. Hampered by hyperpartisanship, the wheels of government, especially in the House, seemed to be grinding more slowly than ever, and Lewis was becoming increasingly frustrated with the general failure to implement reform on important issues. There were protracted political standoffs on the federal budget, federal aid to education, school vouchers, campaign finance reform, and ratification of a comprehensive nuclear test ban treaty. Worst of all, despite the rhetoric of Clinton's State of the Union address, the pressing issues of poverty, racial discrimination, health care, immigration reform, and women's rights had dropped off the political radar altogether.

In March, Lewis was encouraged when the United States joined the NATO military intervention in Kosovo, where the Albanian and Serbian communities were locked in a bitter, sometimes genocidal civil war. The NATO intervention ended in June with the establishment of the United Nations Interim Administration Mission in Kosovo, a peacekeeping initiative that Lewis applauded. A year earlier, Lewis and other human rights advocates had hailed the creation of an international criminal court and related tribunals where crimes of genocide such as those committed in Rwanda and the former states of Yugoslavia could be adjudicated.[23]

Nevertheless, the search for justice, both at home and abroad, remained a daunting challenge, a situation complicated by indirection and hidden agendas. The villains of Jim Crow discrimination and colonialism during the 1950s and 1960s had been straightforward in their opposition to freedom and equality, but Lewis found the political world of the 1990s to be suffused with shadowy figures. Defenders of the status quo and inequality had learned to hide behind code words and in some instances to use the language of liberation to confound and neutralize the forces of change. Both inside the halls of Congress and elsewhere in the political arena, it was often difficult to distinguish between the true friends and enemies of freedom. Was a crafty politician like Bill Clinton a part of the solution or a part of the problem when it came to overcoming persistent social and economic inequities? Lewis, like most of his liberal allies, wasn't sure.

Lewis's opinion of Clinton rose somewhat in March 2000, when the president participated in the FPI event in Selma. The nation's chief executive was there among the foot soldiers of the movement and said all the right things, renewing the call for racial equality with a look back at Bloody Sunday. "Thirty-five years ago, a single day in Selma became a seminal moment in the history of our country," he declared as Lewis and thousands of others looked on. "On this bridge, America's long march to freedom met a roadblock of violent resistance. But the marchers, thank God, would not take a detour on the road to freedom." Later in the speech, he added, "Without Selma, Jimmy Carter and Bill Clinton would never have been elected president of the United States." Lewis bowed his head in embarrassment when Clinton gave him some of the credit for the victories won by liberal Southern Democrats, but he knew there was a lot of truth in the president's words.[24]

Lewis welcomed the memorable scene in Selma, but as the 2000 presidential race took center stage, the ambiguities of American political life were on full display. That it was also the first year of a new millennium was a hopeful portent of change for some, but Lewis had seen too much backing and filling and moral obtuseness to justify any real optimism. Vice President Al Gore, the Democratic presidential candidate in 2000, appeared to be a liberal with good intentions but no real commitment to fundamental change. Lewis regarded the Republican presidential candidate, George W. Bush of Texas, as wholly unqualified for higher public office, the worst national candidate since George Wallace. Far less bigoted than Wallace when it came to race, Bush was nonetheless the favored candidate of powerful and unscrupulous forces determined to forestall all challenges to white and corporate privilege. His election, Lewis feared, would prove disastrous for people of color and the poor. Gore, however flawed, was thus the best hope for the future of American democracy.

From the outset, Lewis, despite his misgivings, was one of Gore's strongest supporters in the Black community, a fact acknowledged by the vice president in early December 1999 when he chose Atlanta as the launch site of his national campaign to attract Black voters. Lewis, on hand to endorse Gore's effort, delivered a rousing speech designed to guarantee a large Black turnout in the upcoming Democratic primaries, including Georgia's primary scheduled for March 7, the thirty-fifth anniversary of Bloody Sunday. "Some of our sisters and brothers died for the right to vote," he reminded the crowd. "On March 7, we will go to the polls and we will vote like we never, ever voted before, and then in November 2000 we will come back to the polls and vote again."[25]

On Georgia's primary election day, Gore won 83.8 percent of the vote, thanks in part to a large Black turnout, and he made a similarly strong showing in most of the state primaries that followed. As expected, he went on to secure the nomination in mid-August at the Democratic National Convention held in Los Angeles, where Lewis and several other Black leaders played important supportive roles. The convention's keynote speaker was the Black congressman Harold Ford of Tennessee, the youngest member of Congress at thirty years old; and two of the featured speakers on the second and third nights of the convention were Jesse Jackson and Lewis.

"Tonight the struggle to make America better continues," Jackson proclaimed. "I know something about the tides of change. I have moved with it when the tide was coming in, and labored against it when it was flowing out. I have seen enough and done enough to know when the moment is ripe for history to be made once again. My fellow Americans, we face such a moment today. . . . A moment that we have waited for more than a generation to come our way." On the following night in a nomination speech for Gore's vice-presidential running mate, Senator Joseph Lieberman of Connecticut—the first Jew to grace a national ticket—Lewis continued in a similar vein. Realizing he would be speaking to perhaps the largest audience of his career, one that rivaled the millions of listeners who had heard his televised speech at the March on Washington in 1963, he delivered an emotional call for multicultural tolerance and inclusion. "We have come a long way from those signs that I saw in my youth that said: 'White Waiting' . . . 'Colored Waiting.' 'White Men' . . . 'Colored Men.' 'White Women' . . . 'Colored Women,'" he announced. "Looking out over this vast hall tonight I see the America I know and the nation I so deeply love. We are black and white and brown and yellow. We are Protestant and Catholic and Muslim and Jewish. We are young and old. We are straight and gay. . . . The American people see us—the Democratic Party—and they know our arms are wide open to people of every race, every creed and every religion."

Lewis's sympathetic references to Jews and other religious minorities were in keeping with beliefs he had held since his boyhood. As he noted in *Walking with the Wind,* "I've always felt an affinity with the Jewish community, ever since I was a boy growing up near Troy. As long as I could remember, I heard many white people in the South pronounce the word 'Jew' in the same way they used the term 'nigger.' They would spit the word out like a bad piece of food. There was a small department store in downtown Troy operated by a Jewish merchant. I remember how it stung me when I heard people say things about him—the same kind of things they said about us. I grew up singing songs in church such as 'Go Down Moses.' I grew up studying Bible stories about the Jewish people. I identified with those stories. I felt a kinship with the children of Israel. I could see that their struggle was very similar to ours." Lewis went on to explain that his willingness to embrace causes such as gay and women's liberation "sprang from that same affinity I felt with Jewish people, that understanding of what it means to be treated unequally, to be treated as less than, simply because you are different from the long-entrenched white Anglo-Saxon Protestant standard that defined and controlled our society for its first two hundred years."

One important sign of an emerging inclusiveness in American politics, Lewis insisted in his nominating speech, was the party's choice for vice president: "One week ago, Al Gore had the courage—the raw courage—to open the arms of our party to a Vice Presidential nominee who brings to the ticket experience, integrity and universal respect as a principled fighter for what is right, for what is fair, and for what is just. . . . After many of us had been arrested, jailed and beaten during the early days of the civil rights movement, Joe Lieberman responded to the greatest moral crisis of our time. He came to the heart of the Delta in Mississippi to help tear down the walls of segregation and racial discrimination. As a young student, he left the comfort of Connecticut and New Haven to be a foot soldier in the drive to register Black voters. And this year, right here, we will nominate for national office a person who marched with Dr. Martin Luther King, Jr. and us at the March on Washington. . . . 35 years ago some of us walked across the Edmund Pettus Bridge in Selma, Alabama. We have come a long way. But we have more bridges to cross. And we need a man like Joe Lieberman to walk with us."

On the first night of the convention, President Clinton had offered equally effusive praise of Lieberman's civil rights record, going as far as mistakenly identifying the Connecticut senator as a former "Freedom Rider, going into danger, to register Black voters in the then segregated South." This conflation of the Freedom Rides of 1961 with the later struggle for voting rights drew sharp criticism from a number of observers, including several actual Freedom Riders. And throughout the fall campaign, Republicans mocked the effort to recast a notoriously cautious middle-of-the-road Democrat—one who opposed affirmative action but supported school vouchers—as a civil rights crusader. Even some of Lieberman's strongest supporters detected a certain amount of hyperbole in both Clinton's and Lewis's speeches. But neither man apologized for what was an obvious attempt to shore up the once crucial Black-Jewish alliance that had deteriorated in recent years. Lewis, of course, privately informed the president that spending a week away from Yale working in an office in Jackson, Mississippi, did not make Lieberman a Freedom Rider, a status reserved for those who boarded the freedom buses in 1961 at the risk of their lives.

Whatever the truth of Lieberman's civil rights past, his placement on the ticket seemed a smart political move for a party worried about regional and ideological balance. From the outset, the 2000 presidential race was a highly competitive affair, with Bush maintaining a small lead over Gore in the polls.

Many observers, including Lewis, expected it to be the closest election since John F. Kennedy versus Richard Nixon in 1960, and it seemed likely that as few as a hundred thousand votes shifting from one candidate to the other might determine the outcome. Suspecting that the Black vote might be the balance of power in several key states, Lewis worked tirelessly on Gore's behalf, drumming up as many extra votes as he could around the country. Georgia, along with the rest of the South except Florida, was a lost cause for the Democrats, whose best chance of retaining the presidency lay in the cities north of the Mason-Dixon Line. So Lewis and other Black leaders concentrated their efforts there among voters in dire need of governmental assistance and a social safety net.[26]

The ideological distance between the two presidential candidates and their parties could hardly have been more stark—particularly on issues such as reproductive freedom and economic inequality—and Lewis and the Democrats shuddered at the prospect of having another Bush in the White House. On election day, Gore received 90 percent of the Black vote and won the national popular vote by 543,000. But in the Electoral College the race was a virtual dead heat, with the contested votes of Florida looming as the determining factor in the result. The rules regarding a Florida recount soon became the center of attention across the nation and in the courts, where Bush ultimately prevailed via a highly controversial five-to-four decision in the U.S. Supreme Court. Lewis, along with most Democratic leaders, roundly condemned the Court for breaching the boundary between law and politics. In the wake of *Bush v. Gore,* he was so upset that he broke with tradition and refused to attend Bush's inaugural ceremony.

The only good political news for Lewis and the Democrats was a five-seat gain in the Senate, which would be split evenly, 50–50, in the new Congress. In the House, the Republicans retained their narrow majority, 221–212, severely limiting the power of Lewis and other Democratic representatives to exercise any real authority as legislators. Now in his eighth term and nearly sixty-one years old, Lewis faced an uncertain future in a land that continued to confound his dreams.[27]

CHAPTER 16

———

Politics and Remembrance

I N JANUARY 2001, as the Clintons prepared to leave the White House—and as the new millennium entered its second year—John Lewis took stock of his life, his political career, and the state of the nation and the world. He had been in Congress for nearly a decade and a half, but what did he have to show for it? He had no complaints about his personal life; his family was reasonably healthy and happy, his bond with Lillian after thirty-two years of marriage was as strong as ever, and his son, John-Miles, now twenty-four years old, had become an accomplished musician and aspiring hip-hop artist (a career choice Lewis took some time to warm to). But he was less satisfied with his political accomplishments. Despite his sterling reputation as a hardworking and morally righteous congressman, he had been unable to affix his name to a major piece of legislation. And his prospects for doing so anytime soon seemed dim, with the Republicans now in control of both houses of Congress and the presidency. The great promise of a liberal renaissance under Bill Clinton had dissolved into a conservative backlash led by Bush and his combative vice president, Dick Cheney.

Newt Gingrich was gone, but the hyperpartisan, antiprogressive spirit that had animated his speakership was still very much alive in Washington, as well as in Georgia, where eight of the state's eleven members of Congress were ultraconservative Republicans. Lewis's party still controlled the governorship and both houses of the state legislature, and Georgia's two senators, Max Cleland and Zell Miller, were both Democrats. But the trend toward Republican dominance of the state, as throughout the rest of the South, was unmistakable and growing stronger with every election. While Georgia's Black Democrats continued to vote in large numbers, their influence on public affairs was dwindling in the face of a surging right-wing Republicanism among white voters. As in much of the nation, in Georgia—especially in rural areas and small towns beyond Atlanta—increasingly aggressive and intolerant white evangelicals associated with the so-called Christian Right were on the march, threatening to overturn the social and racial progress of the past half century.[1]

The American economy was strong, but the severe maldistribution of wealth and the popularity of the Republicans' socially destructive theory of supply-side and "trickle-down" economics persisted. Clinton's recent rhetorical flourishes promoting economic and social equality had come to nothing, and the Great Society's War on Poverty had become a distant memory. The massive incarceration fostered by a two-decade-long drug war and draconian school suspension policies had snuffed out hope in many communities, especially among young Black men who were now far more likely to go to prison than to college. To Lewis's sorrow, what would soon be known as the "school-to-prison pipeline" had become the dominant reality in much of Black America. This phenomenon would later be labeled "the New Jim Crow" by the African American law professor Michelle Alexander, whose searing 2010 volume would become one of Lewis's favorite books. The Jim Crow laws were gone and the Black middle class had expanded, but much of Black America was now crippled by an insidious form of criminalization that mimicked earlier discrimination. Combined with police brutality and continued assaults on affirmative action and social welfare measures, the carceral state left many African Americans in despair as the George W. Bush era unfolded.[2]

On the international front, a potentially explosive situation in the Middle East; the proliferation of tribalist, anti-Western jihadism among Muslims; and the rising threat of terrorist attacks by Osama bin Laden's al-Qaeda organization stood in the way of progress toward the peaceful world envisioned in Lewis's dreams for the future. The genocidal crises in the Balkans and Rwanda had subsided, but in many areas of the world the ideal of human rights seemed to be in sharp decline. Closer to home, Lewis was frightened by the harsh doctrines of the saber-rattling neoconservatives known

as "neocons"—militaristic hawks who dominated the new Bush administration's view of the world. Although Bush himself cultivated a somewhat
softer image cloaked in a folksy style, Lewis feared the president would
inevitably become an instrument of the reckless designs of Cheney and
other neocons.[3]

Lewis's despair about the poor prospects for equity and social change
during the early months of Bush's presidency led him down a nostalgic path
of recalling better days. It had been thirty-five years since his departure from
SNCC and forty years since the Freedom Rides, but his memories of the
1960s civil rights struggle were vivid and compelling. He had kept in close
touch with a number of his old movement friends and colleagues, especially
the former Freedom Riders from the Nashville Student Movement. But he
was painfully aware that they were all growing older and were now in their
sixties or seventies; and that some, like the VEP activist Joe Haas and the
SCLC "field general" Hosea Williams, had already passed, both having died
the previous fall. Haas, Lewis recalled, had "changed the lives of hundreds
of thousands of people" and "helped create an environment for nonviolent
revolution in the South." And Williams had stood shoulder to shoulder with
Lewis on Bloody Sunday in 1965 and served with him on the Atlanta City
Council twenty years later.

The loss of these and other comrades-in-arms prompted Lewis to redou-
ble his efforts to maintain and renew personal contact with movement veterans. Doing so among his former SNCC colleagues was always complicated
by the unfortunate events that led to his departure from the organization
in 1966, but there was no such ambivalence when it came to the Freedom
Riders. For Lewis, participation in the Rides was a continuing source of identity, pride, and fellowship. Bound by ties of friendship, memory, and shared
sacrifice, he and many other Freedom Riders had protected and sustained a
common legacy. Among the Riders, there were distinct subgroups—the original CORE Riders, those who survived the burning bus in Anniston, those
who spent time in Parchman prison, and so forth—each with its own set
of experiences and lore. But there was also a commonality of purpose that
bound them all together, setting them apart from everyone else, including
the rest of the movement.

Forged in the fires of nonviolent struggle, this sense of common purpose and experience persisted through the decades, despite the inevitable
physical dispersion of the Riders. During the tumultuous years of the 1960s
and 1970s, the Riders went their separate ways, passing into a wide variety
of careers and private lives. Some either became disillusioned or moved too
far to the left or right to remember the Freedom Rides without a measure
of embarrassment or regret. And, against the increasingly violent backdrop
of the Vietnam War and the Johnson and Nixon eras, many abandoned
the nonviolent philosophy that had propelled the Freedom Rides during
the relatively innocent years of the early 1960s. Some went to Vietnam as
soldiers or sailors, some became antiwar activists, and others filled both
functions, turning against a war that ultimately seemed ill-conceived and
morally unjustifiable.

Most had embraced the liberating themes of 1960s counterculture, but as
the politics of reform and revolution became darker and more complicated,
there was an inevitable divergence of opinion and belief, symbolized by
Stokely Carmichael's strident advocacy of Black Power and Jim Farmer's unexpected endorsement of Richard Nixon in the 1972 presidential campaign.
And yet, even with this divergence, a large majority continued to identify
with a broad-based struggle for human rights and social justice that drew
them into a variety of new movements from environmentalism to feminism
to gay rights. An inordinate number went on to distinguished careers as
social workers, community organizers, health care providers, labor leaders,
lawyers, jurists, writers, journalists, theologians, teachers, college professors
and administrators, entrepreneurs, local politicians, and, in two cases, members of Congress. But whatever their professional experiences or private
enthusiasms, they were still Freedom Riders, still part of a select group of
activists that had changed the course of American history.

In the immediate aftermath of the Freedom Rides and for several years
thereafter, many of the Riders maintained intermittent contact through the
natural interplay of their lives and careers, but as time went on some felt
the need to enhance the maintenance of old ties through formal reunions
and other planned gatherings. Dozens of Riders, including Lewis, attended
reunions at five-year intervals in 1981, 1986, and 1991, but as the fortieth

anniversary approached, there was widespread agreement that a commemorative meeting of a larger scale was in order. Lewis, for one, believed it
was time to renew historical and personal connections in a dramatic way.[4]

* * *

In the fall of 2000, Lewis took the lead in organizing an elaborate fortieth
anniversary reunion to be held the following May. After securing funding
from Greyhound and several other corporate sponsors, he hired a special
congressional staff liaison to mobilize a large group of Riders for a three-
day celebration and partial reenactment of the original May 1961 Freedom
Ride. He also enlisted the help of Raymond Arsenault, a historian who had
recently interviewed him for a book on the Freedom Rides, in tracking
down the addresses and contact information for many of the far-flung former Riders.

The reunion began in Washington on May 10, 2001, with a ceremony
featuring speeches by Lewis and D.C. congresswoman Eleanor Holmes Norton, the presentation of a "Greyhound Award" to each Freedom Rider in
attendance, and a Chinese buffet dinner commemorating the famous "Last
Supper" held on the eve of the original Ride's departure. Five of the thirteen original CORE Riders—Lewis, Hank Thomas, Benjamin Cox, Ed Blankenheim, and Charles Person—were on hand, as were a number of other
former Riders, many of whom lived in the Washington area; the longtime
CORE staff member Marvin Rich; the SNCC veteran and former mayor of
Washington Marion Barry; Moses Newson, one of the two Black journalists
to accompany the original Riders; and even two veterans of the 1947 Journey
of Reconciliation, George Houser and Bill Worthy.

On May 11, after an early flight south, most of the group, plus more
than a dozen other movement veterans, gathered in Atlanta for a series of
ceremonial events before boarding buses for Alabama the next morning.
Accompanied by a C-SPAN film crew, several journalists—and two civil
rights historians, Arsenault and Clayborne Carson of Stanford University,
conducting onboard interviews—the caravan of freedom buses traveled to
Anniston, Birmingham, and Montgomery, where local officials and Black
community leaders went out of their way to welcome the entourage, but
also where some of the returning Freedom Riders were visited by haunting

memories. In Anniston, where he had been beaten forty years earlier, the normally gregarious Hank Thomas, overwhelmed by memories of 1961, lost his composure and could hardly find words to express his emotions.

In Birmingham, during a stop at a historic downtown bus station and a tour of museum exhibits at the ten-year-old Civil Rights Institute, others encountered similar difficulties. "In a sense this is holy ground," Lewis told the crowd at the bus station, his voice cracking with emotion as he reminded them that this was the very place where they "planted the seeds of a mighty movement." Minutes later, upon seeing a museum replica of the burned bus where he had nearly lost his life in 1961, Ed Blankenheim, confined to a wheelchair following a disabling stroke, broke down into sobs and had to be wheeled away from the exhibit. But somehow he was later able to regain his composure, joining with his fellow Riders to sing a chorus of "Keep Your Eyes on the Prize" before leaving the museum.

Later in the day, after the group gathered for a final event at Montgomery's First Baptist Church (Colored)—the scene of the 1961 siege—there was more singing, and more reminiscing, both solemn and soulful. By the time they reboarded the buses for the return trip to Atlanta, everyone was emotionally spent, confirming to Lewis and everyone else on board that at least the dream, if not the broader reality, of the Beloved Community was still alive. And if this was not enough to prove the point, Lewis soon added a postscript to the commemoration.

Traveling to Boston with several of his closest friends on May 21, he received the first Profile in Courage Lifetime Achievement Award given by the John F. Kennedy Library Foundation. Coming forty years to the day after the siege at the First Baptist Church, the ceremony at the Kennedy Library was a fitting end to a week of renewal and remembrance. In his acceptance speech, Lewis emphasized the contributions and sacrifices of the Freedom Riders, who, he insisted, "must be looked upon as the founding mothers and fathers of a new America." He also reflected on the nature and origins of courage. "Courage is a reflection of the heart—it is a reflection of something deep within the man or woman or even a child who must resist and must defy an authority that is morally wrong," he told the gathering. "Courage makes us march on despite fear and doubt on the road toward justice. Courage is not heroic but as necessary as birds need wings to fly. Courage is not rooted in reason but rather Courage comes from a divine purpose to make things right."[5]

The ideals of interracial harmony and social justice were once again on full display six months later when an even larger group of former Freedom Riders gathered in Jackson, Mississippi. This time the organizer of the reunion was not Lewis but rather a band of California-based Freedom Riders who had kept in contact over the decades. The participants included more than sixty former Riders, many of whom had spent time in Parchman prison and other Mississippi jails in 1961. Lewis, busy with congressional business in Washington, sent his regrets; thus he missed a major milestone in Mississippi history when Governor Ronnie Musgrove, once an avowed segregationist, unveiled a plaque proclaiming November 10, 2001, as Freedom Riders Day in Mississippi. Hailing those who had taken "the long, often perilous road to end segregation," the gubernatorial proclamation saluted "the heroic efforts" of the Freedom Riders, few of whom had ever expected to live long enough to witness such a gesture by a white Mississippi politician. For those who had returned to Mississippi with mixed emotions and modest expectations, the governor's implicit apology was perhaps the most redeeming story of all.[6]

Filtered through reunions and commemorative events, the prevailing image of earlier struggles for civil rights and social justice presented a stark contrast with the political malaise enveloping progressive dissenters during the Bush era. The wheels of racial progress and social reform appeared to be going backward rather than forward, and Lewis's ideal society seemed farther away than ever. While he did not regret his decision to follow Bayard Rustin's prescribed route from protest to politics, there were moments when he wondered whether his commitment to a congressional career would ever make any real difference in the lives of ordinary Americans.

During the first six months of Bush's presidency, there was a steady stream of discouraging developments: U.S. and British bombing raids in Iraq in February; the withdrawal of American support for the 1997 Kyoto Protocol on the reduction of greenhouse gases in March; the needless police shooting of a nineteen-year-old Black man in Cincinnati that sparked three days of rioting in April; the disappointing results of a state flag referendum in Mississippi, where nearly two-thirds of the electorate voted to retain a flag emblazoned with Confederate symbolism; and in June the signing of a $1.35 billion tax cut labeled the Economic Growth and Tax Relief Reconciliation Act, an ill-conceived measure, in Lewis's view, that benefited the wealthy and exacerbated the already gross maldistribution of wealth in American society.

In the second half of 2001, the political situation grew even worse, despite an unexpected move by Republican senator Jim Jeffords of Vermont, who announced in early June that he had become an independent who would caucus with the Democrats, thus shifting control of the Senate to the Democratic Party. On August 1, Lewis watched in horror when Judge Roy Moore, the right-wing chief justice of the Alabama Supreme Court, made a mockery of the constitutional separation of church and state by installing a 2.5-ton monument inscribed with the Ten Commandments in the rotunda of the Alabama judiciary building in Montgomery. And the next day, the House, overruling the objections of Lewis and other environmentalists, sanctioned the opening of the ecologically sensitive Alaskan Arctic National Wildlife Refuge to oil exploration.[7]

In early September, just when Lewis felt the state of American politics could not get any worse, the devastating 9/11 terrorist attacks on the Twin Towers of the World Trade Center and the Pentagon in Washington unleashed an unprecedented wave of panic that demanded enhanced security through the constriction of civil liberties. Within a month, the United States had launched the Global War on Terrorism, beginning with an invasion of Afghanistan known as Operation Enduring Freedom. The urge to strike back at Osama bin Laden and al-Qaeda, the perpetrators of the 9/11 attacks that killed nearly three thousand Americans, was understandable on a human level. But Lewis nonetheless considered the Bush-led counterattack to be a self-defeating overreaction that sacrificed American values in the pursuit of revenge and bloody atonement.

In late October, when the House passed the USA PATRIOT Act by an overwhelming majority, 357–66, Lewis was one of the dissenters. In the eleven-member Georgia delegation, only Cynthia McKinney joined him in voting against an act that signaled the federal government's acceptance of enhanced security measures normally associated with authoritarian regimes. Signed into law on October 26, the PATRIOT Act gave the government unprecedented surveillance, investigation, incarceration, and prosecution powers when suspected terrorists were involved. Lewis was appalled by the act's provisions allowing government officials to run roughshod over and coerce confessions out of defendants, especially foreign-born combatants who were deemed ineligible for constitutional protection.

Despite the protestations of Lewis and other civil libertarians, in mid-November Bush extended the PATRIOT Act's powers with a draconian executive order that created special military tribunals where foreign nationals suspected of terrorism could be tried with a minimum of constitutional guarantees. Two months later, the administration opened a detention camp at Guantánamo Bay, Cuba, that soon became "a symbol of torture, rendition and indefinite detention without charge or trial," according to Amnesty International. Lewis, who agreed with this indictment of the government's policies at Guantánamo, worked ceaselessly though futilely to close down the infamous detention center that, to him, made a mockery of the humane ideals of American jurisprudence. There didn't seem to be any limit to the Bush administration's turn toward hawkish repression, and the president ended the year with an announcement withdrawing America's long-standing support of the 1972 Anti-Ballistic Missile Treaty.[8]

*   *   *

To Lewis's dismay, none of this appeared to bother the vast majority of Americans, nearly 90 percent of whom registered their approval of Bush's handling of the presidency during the months following the 9/11 attacks. The nation had succumbed to the illiberal notion of maintaining security at all costs, and for the time being there was not much that Lewis or anyone else could do about it. On January 29, Bush's State of the Union address singled out Iraq, Iran, and North Korea as major sponsors of terrorism, referring to their connections to terrorist organizations such as al-Qaeda as the "Axis of Evil." But the administration's righteous ire soon turned to Afghanistan, thought to be the staging ground for the 9/11 terrorist operatives as well as a current refuge for Osama bin Laden.

On March 1, the United States invaded the eastern Afghan province of Paktia, initiating Operation Anaconda, and within three days there was a multinational army on the ground conducting search-and-destroy missions against the Taliban forces who were protecting al-Qaeda outposts and training camps hidden deep in the nation's remote mountain ranges. The longest war in American history—a conflict that would go on for twenty years—had begun, and the armed forces of the United States and its allies would soon be entangled in a bloody and bewildering struggle that went back and forth with no clear winner or resolution.

Also alarming was the spread of suicide bombings and other acts of terror across the globe. In the span of nine weeks during the bloody spring of 2002, there were major terrorist attacks or deadly ethnic cleansing incidents in India, Israel, Tunisia, and Russia—an escalation of violence that overwhelmed the efforts of Lewis and other peace activists. During this period, Lewis found some consolation in a few developments, notably the end of the civil wars in Sierra Leone and Angola; Jimmy Carter's meeting with Fidel Castro in Havana, the first such visit by a current or former American president since 1959; and the long-awaited war crimes prosecution of the Serbian leader Slobodan Milosevic at the International Court of Justice in The Hague. But most international news was profoundly discouraging.[9]

The situation was somewhat better on the domestic front, where in April a Senate vote ended Bush's plan to open the Arctic National Wildlife Refuge to oil exploration and in May there was even a bit of good news coming out of Alabama, where a predominantly white jury convicted the Klansman Bobby Frank Cherry of murder for his role in the Sixteenth Street Baptist Church bombing in Birmingham that took the lives of four young girls in September 1963. Lewis, who sometimes quoted William Gladstone's maxim that "justice delayed is justice denied," was disappointed that it took thirty-nine years to bring Cherry to trial. But he took some solace from knowing that one of the Jim Crow South's most troubling "cold cases" had been resolved. This encouraging development was a major topic of conversation in movement circles during the summer of 2002, especially at the NAACP's annual convention held in Houston in early July, where Julian Bond delivered a stirring address on "Freedom Under Fire" and Lewis received the prestigious Joel Spingarn Medal for his meritorious service on behalf of civil rights.

Unfortunately for Lewis and the nation, such moments were all too rare as the political scene in the United States grew darker in the months leading up to the 2002 midterm election. The dominant theme driving the Republicans' popularity was the rising fear of the Islamic world, especially Iraq, where the Baathist dictator Saddam Hussein had reportedly amassed weapons of mass destruction to be used against Israel, the United States, and other globalist powers. Such fears were exacerbated on July 4 when the nation's Independence Day celebration was marred by a deadly terrorist bombing at the Los Angeles International Airport. Later in the summer, on the day after the first anniversary of the 9/11 attacks, President Bush delivered an ominous speech at the United Nations warning that the United States was prepared to use massive military force to eliminate the "grave and gathering danger of Iraq." In early October, amid renewed claims that the Baathist regime had not only stockpiled weapons of mass destruction but also conspired with Osama bin Laden before 9/11, Congress voted to authorize military intervention in Iraq. In the House, the vote in favor of the resolution was 296–133, with Lewis being one of the most vocal dissenters. Later, when it became clear that the administration's intelligence on the alleged stockpiling of weapons of mass destruction was faulty, Lewis felt justified in his opposition to the Iraqi war. But at the time of the vote and for months thereafter, he received a great deal of criticism for his stance.[10]

In the midterm election in November, Bush and the Republicans took full advantage of the popular sentiment in favor of war, regaining control of the Senate with a three-seat advantage and increasing the Republican majority in the House by eight seats. Lewis and the Democrats were devastated, realizing this was only the fourth time since the Civil War that the party in charge of the White House had gained House seats in a midterm election. Lewis was also distressed by the passing of his friend, Senator Paul Wellstone of Minnesota, who died in a plane crash the week before the election. Congress's most prominent democratic socialist, Wellstone had been Lewis's kindred spirit since entering the Senate in 1991.

Lewis and his antiwar allies missed Wellstone's powerful voice during the crisis-ridden months that followed the election. As the administration prepared for war against Saddam Hussein, Bush pushed aside all dissent, both domestic and foreign, condemning it as weak-kneed cowardice in the face of impending terrorist aggression. "Today, the gravest danger in the war on terror, the gravest danger facing America and the world," he declared in his 2003 State of the Union address, "is outlaw regimes that seek and possess, nuclear, chemical and biological weapons. . . . If Saddam Hussein does not fully disarm, we will lead a coalition to disarm him." To Lewis, as to many observers across the world, Bush was going down a dangerous path by invoking what Senate Minority Leader Robert Byrd of West Virginia called "a revolutionary doctrine—the doctrine of preemption—the idea that the United States or any other nation can legitimately attack a nation that is not imminently threatening but may be threatening in the future—a radical new twist on the traditional idea of self-defense."

After the high-tech air assault on Iraq began on March 19, Bush, in Lewis's view, added insult to injury by justifying his "shock and awe" tactics in religious terms. "The liberty we prize is not America's gift to the world," the bellicose president insisted, "it is God's gift to humanity." Five weeks later, in what turned out to be a premature proclamation of a "mission accomplished"—Bush used a biblical reference to praise America's fighting forces. Addressing a deck full of sailors aboard the aircraft carrier *Abraham Lincoln*, the president declared, "All of you—all of this generation of our military—have taken up the highest calling of history: You were defending your country and protecting the innocent from harm. And wherever you go, you carry a message of hope, a message that is ancient and ever new. In the words of the prophet Isaiah, 'To the captives, come out, and to those in darkness, be free.'" Lewis regarded Saddam as a brutal dictator who should be toppled through economic sanctions and internal and external popular pressure. But as a man of faith and as a staunch opponent of unnecessary state-sanctioned violence, he found Bush's reliance on biblical rhetoric obscene.[11]

For the remainder of 2003, the Iraq War dominated the American political scene, making it all but impossible for progressives like Lewis to advance an ambitious domestic agenda. When it came to decisions about public policy, most of the action took place in either the courts or the executive branch, not in Congress. In March, the Supreme Court issued two five-to-four decisions upholding California's "three strikes and you are out" sentencing law, a measure Lewis considered ill-advised and draconian. In May, Lewis—already deeply concerned about the federal government's inability to fund much-needed social programs—felt the nation suffered another serious blow when Bush authorized a $350 billion tax cut, the first such cut in over a decade. A month later, Lewis was pleased when one Supreme Court ruling upheld the practice of affirmative action in university admissions, and another struck down a Texas antisodomy law directed at homosexuals. But in Congress, other than among some of Lewis's colleagues in the Congressional Black Caucus, there was no sign that anyone had the will to address serious systemic problems such as economic inequality and social injustice.

The dominant tone of post-9/11 America was one of complacency punctuated by periodic paroxysms of fear related to international terrorism. The biggest stories of 2003 took place in Afghanistan and Iraq, where insurgency against American occupation was growing and where Saddam was captured in December. Nothing seemed to tilt the focus toward the issues that mattered most to Lewis and many other Black Americans, not even Bush's admission in September that there was no link between Saddam and the 9/11 terrorists. The following February, Lewis felt vindicated when the CIA finally confirmed that there were no weapons of mass destruction in Saddam's arsenal.[12]

*　*　*

These revelations had the potential to spark a Democratic resurgence in the 2004 national election, or so it seemed. But Lewis and other progressive Democrats worried about the electoral viability of their presidential ticket, Senator John Kerry of Massachusetts and his running mate, Senator John Edwards of North Carolina. For Lewis, the high point of the campaign had little to do with Kerry or Edwards; it came at the Democratic National Convention held in Boston in late July, when Barack Obama, a forty-three-year-old, first-term senator from Illinois—an African American born during the 1961 Freedom Rides—delivered a stirring keynote address. "No, people don't expect government to solve all their problems," Obama told the delegates. "But they sense, deep in their bones, that with just a change in priority, we can make sure that every child in America has a decent shot at life, and that the doors of opportunity remain open to all. They know we can do better."

Obama's speech electrified the convention, raising Lewis's hopes that the national television audience, especially in African American households, would be similarly energized by the senator's eloquence and passion. The Kerry-Edwards ticket needed to attract a large Black vote to have any chance of winning in November, and on election day the turnout among Black voters was over thirteen million, 25 percent higher than in 2000. The Democratic ticket received an estimated 88 percent of the Black vote, down slightly from the 92 percent figure of 2000. But even these impressive figures were not enough to offset Bush's strong support among white male voters, especially his overwhelming popularity among conservative white evangelicals animated by an ongoing culture war viewed as a struggle between traditional "family values" and liberal, secular humanism.

The overall results in November fell short of the Democrats' expectations, leaving Lewis and his allies profoundly discouraged. Virtually all of the pre-election polling data had predicted a tight race between Bush and Kerry, and some polls actually had Kerry in the lead, but in the end Bush eked out a narrow victory, both in the popular vote, 50.7 to 48.3 percent, and in the Electoral College, 286 to 252. The Republicans also retained control of Congress, gaining four seats in the Senate and three in the House. In Georgia, Lewis ran unopposed and won a tenth term, but the state's congressional delegation remained overwhelmingly Republican. The entire South was now solidly in the Republican camp, with progressive Democrats like Lewis fighting a rearguard action to sustain any semblance of competitive politics. The major exceptions to Republican dominance in the region were limited to a few pockets in the rural Black Belt and the predominantly Black districts in large cities such as Atlanta.[13]

As Bush entered his second term in January 2005, the prospects for liberal reform seemed darker than ever. Even though the Democrats had the support of nearly half of the electorate, the ideological trajectory of national politics was tilting to the right on many of the issues that meant the most to Lewis and other progressives. The wars in Iraq and Afghanistan were proceeding with no end in sight, consuming enormous amounts of federal funding that otherwise could have been appropriated for social services and other humane ends. A deepening culture war over issues such as abortion, gay rights, immigration, and gun control dominated much of American public life, and cultural conservatives seemed to be winning most of the battles. The federal ban on assault weapons had expired the previous September, and eleven states had banned same-sex marriage in referenda held in November. Before the election, Bush had publicly embraced a new Republican doctrine of humane politics, labeling it "compassionate conservatism," but there was no evidence of any follow-through by either the president or his party. As Lewis looked around, both inside and outside the halls of Congress, his vision of a coming Beloved Community seemed to be receding before his eyes.

Clarence Page, a Black columnist for the *Chicago Tribune*, insisted the situation was not as dire as Lewis and the progressive Democrats feared, that their problems were largely a function of pace and timing. "Most Americans eventually grow more comfortable with new frontiers of freedom and equality," he wrote in the immediate aftermath of the election, "but you can't push them too fast. So, take heart, dear Democrats, come in, come in off that ledge. . . . All is not lost. Yours is a party that once indisputably held the moral high ground in the minds of most American voters and you can seize it again."

Such comforting words helped Lewis to avoid complete despair during the first year of Bush's second term. But seizing the moral high ground from the Bush administration, the new religious Right, and the neoconservative think tanks that sustained the culture war was easier said than done. With deadly suicide bombings in Iraq, Jordan, and England; violent protests among Muslim immigrants in Paris's suburbs; and Saddam Hussein's trial in Baghdad, the political focus on the war on terrorism persisted, to the virtual exclusion of domestic issues related to social justice and economic equity.

Fortunately for Lewis's state of mind, there were a few things worth celebrating in 2005. In February the Kyoto climate protocol took effect; in March the Supreme Court struck down the death penalty for juveniles; in mid-June the Senate passed a long-overdue resolution apologizing for its role in blocking antilynching legislation in the early twentieth century, and later in the month the Klan leader Edgar Ray Killen was convicted of manslaughter for his role in the 1963 Sixteenth Street Baptist Church bombing; and in July world leaders at the G8 summit meeting in Scotland unexpectedly pledged $50 billion to combat poverty in underdeveloped countries, primarily in Africa, and also passed a resolution guaranteeing universal access to anti-HIV drugs in AIDS-ravaged Africa by 2010.[14]

Lewis welcomed all of these unexpected developments as signs of hope. But the year's most surprising development—the federal government's tragic mishandling of the Hurricane Katrina crisis—reminded him of the deep-seated and intractable nature of social and racial injustice. After the category 5 storm struck New Orleans and the Gulf Coast in late August, Lewis watched in horror as the Bush administration failed to provide any meaningful aid or relief to the hundreds of thousands of storm victims devastated by rising waters. The situation was especially desperate for the city's Black residents, many of whom lived in substandard housing in low-lying areas such as the impoverished Ninth Ward. The heartbreaking scenes of Black families clinging to half-submerged rooftops—and in more than a thousand cases perishing in the city's flooded streets—revealed a racial and class divide rooted in decades of discrimination and economic and social neglect. The city known for its charm and revelry—the Big Easy, as it was often called—had become a city of death and destruction, a new symbol of America's failure to address the dark legacy of Jim Crow.

The Bush administration's incompetence in the face of the Katrina crisis weakened the Republicans' public standing, and less than a month later the party suffered a second major blow when the House majority leader, the ultraconservative Texan Tom DeLay, was forced to step down after a grand jury indicted him for campaign finance violations and money laundering. DeLay remained in Congress until June 2006 but, shorn of his power, he could no longer terrorize the House's liberal minority. Lewis, who placed DeLay in the same category as Newt Gingrich as an autocratic opponent of democracy, breathed a sigh of relief when the Texas congressman resigned, even though DeLay's replacement as majority leader, the staunch conservative Roy Blunt of Missouri, was, in Lewis's estimation, only slightly less toxic than the Texan. Nonetheless, the shake-up in the Republican ranks provided liberal Democrats with renewed hope of reversing the partisan imbalance in Congress.[15]

The Republicans had controlled both houses of Congress since 1995, and Lewis had grown tired of waiting for a liberal Democratic resurgence. After eighteen years in office, he was not sure how many more years he had left. While some of his colleagues in the Congressional Black Caucus were still in their forties and fifties, virtually all of his movement friends had passed through middle age, and some had already passed on.

In late October 2005, the death of Rosa Parks at the age of ninety-two reinforced Lewis's awareness of the relentless and unavoidable aging of his contemporaries. Since his early years as an activist in the late 1950s, he had looked up to Parks as an inspiring role model and symbol of courage. During a memorable weekend at Highlander Folk School in 1958, he learned that her visit to Highlander three years earlier had prepared her for a seminal act of courage on a Montgomery bus. After relocating to Detroit in 1957, Parks spent little time in the South, though she did join Lewis and other voting rights activists for the final stage of the Selma-to-Montgomery march in 1965. While Lewis regretted that he never had the pleasure of working closely with her on an extended civil rights campaign, he treasured the time he spent with her at various movement gatherings, and in her capacity as a longtime staff member in Representative John Conyers's Detroit office.

Lewis was particularly fond of a striking photograph of their meeting in Atlanta in 1970, and in 1991 he was one of a handful of civil rights leaders who accompanied her to the Smithsonian Institution for the unveiling of a bust honoring her contributions to American democracy. Eight years later, he helped to spearhead a legislative effort to present her with the Congressional Gold Medal, which fell one vote short of receiving unanimous support in the House.

Parks's funeral was an elaborate affair befitting her stature as the "mother of the freedom movement." A full week of memorial services spanned three cities—Detroit, Montgomery, and Washington—and attracted tens of thousands of mourners. In Washington, her body lay in state in the Capitol Rotunda, making her the first woman and the second African American to be so honored. The ceremonies culminated in a seven-hour funeral service at the Greater Grace Temple in Detroit, as a host of celebrities, family members, and friends, including Lewis, paid tribute to her life.

In many of the eulogies, and in the press coverage before and after the funeral, Parks was characterized as a humble, "soft-spoken" woman, a dignified figure incapable of anger, a patient soul who "never raised her voice" even as she famously refused to give up her seat. One *New York Times* reporter called her "the accidental matriarch of the civil rights movement," implying that her historical significance was limited to one impulsive act born of momentary fatigue. As the historian Jeanne Theoharis later observed, Parks was widely "held up as a national heroine but stripped of her lifelong history of activism and anger at American injustice."

Lewis wisely refused to participate in this mythic recasting of Parks's role as a late-blooming activist. To him, there was nothing accidental or casual about her acts of conscience. Instead, she was part of a long tradition of women who devoted their lives to the freedom struggle, women whose many contributions to the movement had rarely been given their just due, in Lewis's view. Several of those women, he pointed out to the press, had died in recent weeks. "It seems every other day we are losing somebody," he noted on October 31, the day Parks's body lay in the Rotunda, "and we have not done enough to inform, to educate another cadre of leaders. I am thinking not only of the death of Rosa Parks, but of Constance Baker Motley, Vivian Malone Jones, C. Delores Tucker."[16]

Motley, long a stalwart attorney for the NAACP Legal Defense Fund; Jones, who had overcome George Wallace's "stand in the schoolhouse door" resistance in 1963 to become the first Black woman to attend the University of Alabama; and Tucker, a fair housing and employment activist who became the first Black secretary of the Commonwealth of Pennsylvania in 1971, would all be difficult to replace. The reactionary politics of conservative Republicans was not the only problem facing progressive advocates of social change, Lewis feared; there was also the daunting challenge of renewing the ranks and the spirit of a movement that had lost its momentum. Complacency was not an option. "We are at a crossroads," he insisted bluntly. "We can either go forward or stand still."[17]

CHAPTER 17

———

The Conscience of Congress

J
ANUARY 2006 MARKED the beginning of John Lewis's twentieth year in Congress. He was now sixty-five years old and in transition from midlife to old age. It had been nearly a half century since he arrived in Nashville in 1957 and more than four decades since he crossed the Edmund Pettus Bridge for the first time. Along the way, he had survived scores of beatings and arrests, and within the civil rights community, and to some degree in American popular culture as well, he had become a living legend. He had been instrumental in transforming the African American freedom struggle from a predominantly legal battle to a grassroots movement dedicated to nonviolent direct action. And he was one of the few civil rights leaders of the 1960s to move from activism in the streets to a career as an elected public official. Both as an activist and as a congressman, he had worked to recast America as a true democracy, as an inclusive society based on freedom, justice, and equality.

Lewis was proud of what the civil rights movement had accomplished, but he worried that many Americans failed to appreciate how much "freedom" work had been left undone. While civil society had progressed beyond many of the gross inequities of the Jim Crow era, the truly just and democratic social order of his hopes and dreams remained an unrealized vision. Part of the problem, he believed, was the prevalence of a mythic, celebratory version of movement history that placed heroic leaders and personal charisma at the center of the story. A decade earlier, he had tried to dispel this version with a memoir that paid scrupulous attention to the facts underlying the movement's ups and downs, a balanced interpretation that offered a clear-eyed acknowledgment of the importance of both leaders and foot soldiers, successes and failures, advances and limitations.

Within the limits of autobiography, Lewis accomplished most of what he set out to do, and *Walking with the Wind* established a new standard for civil rights memoirs. But he realized he could not do it alone, that no amount of personal truth-telling could replace the historical profession's responsibility to interpret the past in a meaningful and believable way by relating text and context. Civil rights historiography had come a long way during the 1980s and 1990s with the appearance of major works such as Clayborne Carson's study of SNCC, David Garrow's Pulitzer Prize–winning biography of Martin Luther King Jr., and the first two of Taylor Branch's projected three-volume history of the movement from 1954 to 1968. Major gaps in the historical literature on civil rights remained, however, including one that was particularly distressing to Lewis: the absence of a scholarly, book-length study of the Freedom Rides of 1961.[1]

A major milestone in Lewis's life, the Freedom Rides had attracted some scholarly attention over the years in the form of articles and book chapters, most notably a lengthy chapter in Branch's Pulitzer Prize–winning volume *Parting the Waters,* published in 1988, and *The Politics of Injustice,* a 2003 book-length study of the relationship between the Rides and the Kennedy administration written by the political scientist David Niven. But no one had attempted to tell the Freedom Riders' story in all of its complexity; nor had anyone researched the full range and depth of written and oral history sources capable of placing the Rides in the context of an ongoing civil rights struggle, or in the even broader context of race, politics, and social movements in American history. Despite the growing importance and sophistication of oral history research, no one had taken the time to interview the Freedom Riders themselves, nearly four hundred of whom were still alive in 2006. In the late 1990s, David Halberstam interviewed approximately a dozen Riders for *The Children,* a highly impressionistic study of the Nashville Student Movement. But as an oral historian, he barely scratched the surface of the rich vein of memory created by the Rides.

In 1998, the year both Lewis's *Walking with the Wind* and Halberstam's *The Children* were published, Raymond Arsenault, a fifty-year-old history professor at the University of South Florida, took on the challenge of remedying the historical profession's negligence toward the Freedom Rides. Agreeing to produce a volume for Oxford University Press's new Pivotal Moments in American History book series—an innovative series designed to reinvigorate historians' appreciation for both narrative history and the role of contingency in historical change—Arsenault chose the Freedom Rides as his subject, even though he warned the coeditors of the series, David Hackett Fischer and James McPherson, that civil rights historians had rarely characterized the Rides as a pivotal event.

Hoping to revise this standard view, Arsenault decided early on that the written record, as helpful as it was, needed to be supplemented with as many oral history interviews as possible. Recovering the personal perspectives and experiences of the Freedom Riders would not only provide texture and authenticity to the narrative; it would also help balance the study's research base, and in some cases provide a counterpoint to the observations of the white journalists and politicians who filled the newspapers of the time with either jaundiced or ill-informed opinions about what was transpiring during the Rides. The best way to avoid repeating this pattern of misperception was to connect history and memory by incorporating individual stories with collective experience, and this is what Arsenault set out to do.

From the outset, he suspected that Lewis's contention that the nonviolent direct action of the Freedom Rides was a much bigger and more consequential story than many contemporary observers realized—that it was indeed a pivotal movement—was correct. And with the congressman's help and the cooperation of hundreds of other former Riders, he produced a lengthy book that argued just that. Published in January 2006, *Freedom Riders: 1961 and the Struggle for Racial Justice* triggered an explosion of interest in the Rides, not only among historians and lay readers interested in civil rights history but also among documentary filmmakers; civil rights museum curators; radio, television, and print media professionals; and the Freedom Riders themselves.

Within a year, PBS's award-winning documentary series *American Experience* had begun work on a telefilm based on the book. Directed by the noted Black documentary filmmaker Stanley Nelson, the nearly two-hour-long film, *Freedom Riders,* was shown at Sundance and several other major film festivals in 2010 before being broadcast nationally on PBS in May 2011. Widely acclaimed as one of the finest and most moving civil rights documentaries ever made, *Freedom Riders* went on to win three Emmys and a George Peabody Award later in the year. During the week of the initial national broadcast—which coincided with the fiftieth anniversary of the Rides—the popular talk show host Oprah Winfrey invited all of the surviving Freedom Riders to appear on her weekly show. When the show aired on May 4, millions of Americans saw the Freedom Riders for the first time—180 Riders in the studio audience and half a dozen more, including Lewis, as featured guests.

In Lewis's segment, as noted in the preface, he shared the screen with Oprah and Elwin Wilson, one of the young Klansmen who had attacked him outside the Trailways bus station in Rock Hill, South Carolina, on May 10, 1961. In January 2009, Wilson, who had long regretted his involvement in the beating, called Lewis to apologize after seeing him on television during Obama's swearing-in ceremony on the Capitol steps. During the call, Wilson asked for and was granted forgiveness, but Lewis wouldn't let it rest there. Inviting the former Klansman to Washington for a face-to-face meeting in his office, Lewis used the power of love to move from forgiveness to friendship.

Two years later, *The Oprah Winfrey Show*'s producers decided this reconciliation and redemption story was just what they were looking for as an emotional leaven that would give the audience a sense of hope. But the segment nearly went awry when Wilson, now in his seventies and in failing health, momentarily lost his nerve as the cameras moved in for a close-up. With his voice cracking, he seemed on the verge of fleeing the stage when Lewis, sitting to his immediate left, reached out, grasped his right hand, and uttered in a voice that everyone in the studio and the television audience could hear, "He's my brother." As a startled but thankful Wilson regained his composure and began telling his story, those who had witnessed Lewis's act of kindness knew they were in the presence of a great, generous, and compassionate man. When Wilson died of heart and lung failure two years later, Lewis felt he had lost a true friend.[2]

*   *   *

Coupled with the success of the *American Experience* documentary, the Riders' dramatic appearance on *The Oprah Winfrey Show* brought a resurgence of interest in the heroics and sacrifices of 1961. Over the next decade, men and women who had once been all but forgotten by historians, the media, and the American public became celebrities. Rescued from obscurity, they were honored as heroes by colleges and universities, museums, foundations, the National Endowment for the Humanities, and President Barack Obama, who held a reception honoring Lewis and a number of other Riders and who hosted a special White House screening of the documentary. Hundreds of institutions ranging from elementary schools to the Smithsonian invited individual Riders or small groups of Riders to speak about their experiences as activists, and in several cases Riders acted as guides and commentators on university-sponsored bus tours retracing the Freedom Ride routes of 1961 and visiting sites such as Anniston, Birmingham, Montgomery, Nashville, Selma, and Jackson along the way.

Even before the public acclaim that followed the film and television appearances of 2011, Lewis—as the nation's most famous Freedom Rider—was already in frequent demand as a speaker at commemorative and celebratory events related to civil rights history. In March 2005, he presided over a Washington gala celebrating the fortieth anniversary of the Voting Rights Act, sharing the podium with a number of notable African American leaders, including Senator Obama, whom Lewis invited to deliver the keynote address. The following February, Lewis delivered a stirring tribute at the Atlanta funeral of Coretta Scott King. He had always admired her dignified bearing and loyalty to her husband, even in the face of embarrassing revelations of marital infidelity on his part. Considering her a close friend, he joined Jesse Jackson, Andrew Young, and Joseph Lowery as featured speakers at the Ebenezer Baptist Church service, after being one of the more than forty thousand mourners walking past her open casket at the Georgia State Capitol. As he witnessed this official gesture of respect, he recalled how different Atlanta's racial climate had been four decades earlier when Governor Lester Maddox had pointedly snubbed her husband's funeral.[3]

Unfortunately, Atlanta and the state of Georgia still had room for improvement when it came to racial and ethnic harmony, as Lewis discovered in April 2006 when he found himself trying to rein in the excesses of Georgia congressional colleagues from both sides of the aisle. Cynthia McKinney, the notoriously temperamental Black Democrat who had represented Georgia in

Congress since 1993, agreed with Lewis on most issues. But her fiery temper got her into one squabble after another, including an alleged "racial profiling" incident in which she struck a capitol policeman. While Lewis acknowledged the seriousness of her complaint, he told her she should get herself under control by "lowering the temperature" and that she could benefit from coming "to a nonviolent workshop." Even more troubling was the demagogic posturing of Charles Norwood, his Republican colleague from the Tenth District, who conducted a personal crusade against what he called the "theft of Medicaid benefits by illegal aliens." Norwood was the principal author of an immigration bill, signed by President George W. Bush on February 8, that banned such benefits, and Lewis and others worried that the bill's strict citizenship documentation requirements threatened the health benefits of impoverished "Blacks, American Indians and other poor people."

Lewis had become increasingly concerned about threats to the civil rights of undocumented immigrants, and in early May he joined Jackson, Julian Bond, and Lowery in hailing a series of demonstrations by Hispanic leaders "as the natural progression of their movement in the 1960s." Demanding a path to citizenship for undocumented immigrants and proclaiming the emergence of "a new civil rights movement," the demonstration organizers linked their struggle to the one headed by Martin Luther King and led their followers in chorus after chorus of "We Shall Overcome." Lewis, who loved all of this, could not help pointing out that the demonstrations coincided with the forty-fifth anniversary of the beginning of the Freedom Rides.[4]

Lewis—unlike the many Black leaders wary of allying with Hispanic immigrants, whom they regarded as rivals for employment and political power—would continue to champion the rights of undocumented and other immigrants for the remainder of his career. But in the late spring of 2006, he turned his attention to his highest legislative priority—the extension of the Voting Rights Act. Two months earlier, in late March, the *New York Times*, along with many other observers, had declared that the extension was almost a foregone conclusion. The *Times* quoted Lewis, who explained the importance of extending the act by citing the political history of his own district. Georgia's Fifth District, he argued, "would look quite different had there been no act," and "someone besides himself would have represented it for the last 20 years." Some conservative Republicans claimed the Voting

Rights Act "had outlived its usefulness" in a region that no longer practiced systematic disfranchisement, but Lewis insisted the act had become an essential bulwark of American democracy. "It's become almost like apple pie," he declared. "This act has become like America."

Subsequent events justified Lewis's optimism. In early May, the leaders of both political parties pledged their support for the extension, though a few renegade Republican members of Congress made a futile attempt to sidetrack the bill by introducing four "poison pill" amendments. On July 13, the House voted overwhelmingly for the extension, 390–33; one of the Republican representatives voting no was Lewis's ultraconservative Georgia colleague, Lynn Westmoreland, who claimed the extension meant "that states with voting problems 40 years ago can simply never be forgiven." Rising in response, Lewis gave an impassioned speech invoking the memory of Bloody Sunday. "I almost died," he reminded his Republican critics. "I gave blood; some of my colleagues gave their very lives. . . . Yes, we've made some progress; we have come a distance. The sad truth is, discrimination still exists. That's why we still need the Voting Rights Act, and we must not go back to the dark past."

Nine days later, after President Bush reiterated his support for the extension in an address to the NAACP's annual convention, the Senate followed with a unanimous 98–0 vote in favor of the bill. Once again, Lewis brought his experiences in the voting rights struggle of the 1960s to the chamber, this time as a special guest of the Senate. He was preceded by several veteran senators old enough to recount the horrors of disfranchisement during the Jim Crow era, and by the much younger junior senator Obama, who had been an infant during the Freedom Rides. Cutting across the generations, this show of support left Lewis with feelings of both pride and hope. But it did not stop several of the Republican senators who had reluctantly voted for the bill from complaining that the extension of the Voting Rights Act represented an insult to the South. "Other states with much less impressive minority programs and less impressive minority participation," Senator Saxby Chambliss of Georgia claimed, "are not covered, while Georgia still is. This seems both unfair as well as unwise."

Lewis had been around Congress long enough to know this would not be the last time an appeal for regional equity served as camouflage for an indirect assault on Black voting rights. In the years following the 2006 extension, the claim that the South had outgrown the Voting Rights Act would become a staple of Republican conservatism, and in 2013 it would undergird the landmark Supreme Court decision in *Shelby v. Holder*, which invalidated the most important sections of the act, including the "preclearance" section that required public officials covered by the act to receive approval from the federal judiciary before altering the rules regulating access to voting.[5]

* * *

In the immediate aftermath of the 2006 extension, no one, including Lewis, could have foreseen the disastrous turn of events precipitated by *Shelby v. Holder.* Indeed, it appeared that the Democrats—in addition to securing the future of voting rights—had also put themselves in position to win a landslide victory in the off-year elections. Throughout the past eighteen months, the Bush administration and the Republican Party had been rocked by one failure after another, from the mishandling of the Hurricane Katrina crisis and the Abu Ghraib and Guantánamo prison abuses to the inability to bring the Iraq War to a successful conclusion.

Liberal Democrats in the House and Senate led the charge against Bush, whose popularity had plummeted by the fall of 2006, and no member of Congress was more vocal and unsparing in his criticism of Republican mismanagement than Lewis. Some Democratic representatives and senators moved rightward during the campaign in an effort to broaden the base of the party by attracting moderate and even some conservative voters. But Lewis— unopposed for reelection and thus invulnerable—never wavered in his public commitment to the liberal causes that had animated his long political career.

Lewis was more determined than ever to preach the Beloved Community gospel, and as the national campaign drew to a close that fall, he was reminded of how long he had been part of the nonviolent movement and how far the nation and the South had come since the dark days of Jim Crow. More than four decades after being expelled from the Vanderbilt University Divinity School for his involvement in the Nashville sit-ins, James Lawson, now seventy-eight, was welcomed back to the school as a visiting distinguished university professor. His appointment to the faculty was the culmination of a string of apologies issued by the Divinity School's administration, which awarded him its first distinguished alumni award in 2005. In October 2006, Lewis was heartened by additional signs of change when the Coca-Cola corporation donated a 2.5-acre parcel of land to facilitate construction of a proposed Atlanta civil rights museum, and when he—along with Young and Jackson—was invited to speak at the Martin Luther King Jr. Memorial groundbreaking ceremony to be held on the Potomac tidal basin in Washington on November 14.[6]

The most encouraging development during the fall of 2006, however, was the Democratic off-year election victory that gave Lewis and his party new life in the halls of Congress. After twelve years of Republican dominance in the House and six years in the Senate, the Democrats won control by gaining five new senators and thirty-one new representatives. In the 110th Congress, which convened in January 2007, the Democratic majority in the Senate was razor thin, 51 to 49, but in the House the Democrats enjoyed a comfortable advantage, 233 to 202. In both houses, incumbent Democrats suddenly had greater leverage acting either as committee chairs or as senior ranking members. In Lewis's case, his role as deputy majority whip and his senior position on the powerful House Ways and Means Committee magnified his influence, opening new possibilities to advance his views and guide the legislative process.

With the liberal Californian Nancy Pelosi replacing the conservative Republican Dennis Hastert as Speaker of the House, with Senator Harry Reid of Nevada replacing William Frist of Tennessee as Senate majority leader, and with a new Congressional Black Caucus (CBC) that had swelled to a record forty-three members, the future of congressional politics suddenly seemed brighter and more hopeful for liberal Democrats like Lewis. The first six years of the Bush presidency had been a tough time for any politician intent on fostering a liberalization of American democracy. But it was an especially difficult era for someone like Lewis, who harbored expansive dreams of a new, morally awakened America dedicated to social and racial justice. Now, with the Democrats in control, there was a chance that Lewis and his liberal allies could abandon their defensive posture and go on the offensive, advocating and actually passing the bold legislation needed for progressive reform.

The "Congress with a decidedly new look," as the *New York Times* described it, got off to a slow start in January, as Washington's attention was diverted by the trial of the White House aide Scooter Libby, a drama involving betrayal, espionage, and sabotage of a CIA operative. Lewis, for one, was disgusted by Libby's politically motivated violation of national security protocols, and in June he applauded a federal judge's ruling sentencing Libby to thirty months in prison. But earlier in the year his focus was on Atlanta, where he had become embroiled in a racially tinged controversy involving a fall 2006 campaign radio advertisement attacking a Republican candidate for the Fulton County Commission.

The caustic ad, which featured statements by Atlanta's three most prominent Black political leaders—Lewis, Young, and Mayor Shirley Franklin—evoked 1960s-era images of attack dogs and fire hoses and concluded with Lewis's warning, "On November 7, we face the most dangerous situation we ever have. If you think fighting off dogs and water hoses was bad, imagine if we sit idly by and let the right-wing Republicans take control of the Fulton County Commission. . . . Your very life may depend on it." The clear implication that Atlanta Republicans planned to "turn back the clock," undoing all the good that Dr. King and other movement leaders had accomplished, led to charges that the Democrats had resorted to race-baiting demagoguery. "People were killed back then," one Republican legislator pointed out, yet despite the progress that had been made, the Black Democrats were now "saying that voting for a Republican for local office is as bad as turning water hoses on people." In response, Lewis publicly apologized for his intemperate language, but he refused to back off from his basic indictment of the Georgia Republicans' reactionary policies.[7]

Once this unfortunate local flap blew over, Lewis turned his attention back to the national scene, where most of the political excitement centered on the early stages of the races for the Democratic and Republican presidential nominations. Although the first primaries were still almost a year away, ten Democrats and twelve Republicans had already indicated their intention to run. On the Democratic side, Senator Hillary Clinton of New York was the clear front-runner, heavily favored to defeat her two major challengers, Senators Barack Obama and John Edwards. Since many observers considered Senator John McCain to be the presumptive Republican nominee, much of the press coverage and political speculation focused on the Democratic contenders.

In the early going, Hillary Clinton's substantial lead, both in the public opinion polls and in fundraising, seemed insurmountable. Lewis, like most Democrats, fully expected her to be the party's nominee in 2008, a prospect that he publicly embraced throughout the winter and spring of 2007. Part of her advantage was strong support among Black Democrats, though a number of observers speculated that Obama's rising profile as a serious contender was a potential threat to her control over the Black electorate.

Clinton's ability to retain this control rested not only on her strong record on civil rights matters but also on taking advantage of Obama's complicated racial identity. As the multiracial son of a Black Kenyan father and a white mother from Kansas—and as a man with an exotic Islamic name—Obama was hampered by claims that his status as an "African American" candidate was open to question, especially in the South, where he had virtually no cultural roots. His racial image as a Black leader, insofar as he had one, was grounded in the culture of the urban North, and even there he was often perceived as something of an outsider. "I've got nothing but love for the brother," the St. Louis–born Black journalist Debra Dickerson wrote in February, "but we don't have anything in common. His father was African. His mother was a white woman. He grew up with white grandparents. Now I'm willing to adopt him. He married Black. He acts Black. But there's a lot of distance between Black Africans and African-Americans." The Los Angeles–based Black jazz and cultural critic Stanley Crouch was even tougher on Obama, declaring, "When Black Americans refer to Obama as 'one of us,' I do not know what they are talking about."

Lewis firmly rejected this type of racial parsing, which violated his fundamental belief in social inclusivity. He had admired Obama since the young senator's spectacular appearance on the national scene in 2004, and the two men shared common views on virtually every issue, including the proper role of race in American life. Lewis had applauded Obama's famous keynote statement at the 2004 convention—"There is not a Black America and a White America and a Latino America and an Asian America. There's the *United States of America*"—welcoming his eloquence as a fresh new voice in American politics.

During the past two years, Lewis had come to regard Obama as a friend and as a man capable of unprecedented accomplishments, including an eventual run for the presidency. But he, like almost everyone else, was surprised and thrown off-balance by Obama's participation in the 2008 presidential sweepstakes. This daring and unexpected move created a difficult situation for Lewis and the many other Black politicians who had long-standing loyalties to Hillary Clinton. Reinforced by tongue-in-cheek characterizations of Hillary Clinton's husband as "the first Black President," these loyalties stood in the way of those who might otherwise have enthusiastically embraced Obama's candidacy. Even so, Lewis came close to endorsing Obama just after he announced his candidacy but decided not to after receiving a phone call from Bill Clinton. Torn between two attractive candidates, he chose to forgo any formal endorsements. "One day I lean one way, the next day I lean another way," he confessed to reporters. "Sometimes you have to have what I call an executive session with yourself, a come-to-Jesus meeting, and somehow, some way we will all have to make a decision."[8]

* * *

Lewis's dilemma was on full display in early March 2007 when Obama and both Clintons accepted invitations to attend the annual Faith and Politics Institute pilgrimage to Selma. The star-studded event exceeded Lewis's expectations. As he told reporters, "If someone had told me 42 years ago that two United States senators, leading presidential candidates, and a former president would be walking across the Edmund Pettus Bridge, I would have said that's not possible." For Lewis, however, the drama of hosting a face-to-face confrontation between two equally attractive presidential contenders was almost too stressful to handle. The situation was also uncomfortable for the candidates themselves, who, as Obama later recalled, "were scheduled to speak simultaneously at dueling church services," Obama at Brown Chapel AME and Clinton at First Baptist just down the street. While Clinton was proclaiming, "We've got to stay awake because we have a march to finish, a march towards one America," Obama was invoking his own sense of the movement's legacy. Alluding to Lewis, C. T. Vivian, and other historic figures attending the pilgrimage, he declared, "We're in the presence today of giants whose shoulders we stand on. People who battled on behalf not just of African-Americans, but on behalf of all Americans, who battled for America's soul, that shed blood, that endured taunts and torment."

Obama's words drew repeated "shouts of praise" and an explosive standing ovation when he urged the crowd to "kick off your bedroom slippers" and "put on your marching shoes." By the end of the day, he had won endorsements from Vivian and Lowery and a few other movement veterans, and when he walked across the bridge he pushed the ailing, stroke-ridden Fred Shuttlesworth's wheelchair. Lewis, by contrast, did his best to maintain his informal commitment to Clinton. As Obama later acknowledged, the hero of Bloody Sunday was in an almost impossible situation. "Our host, John Lewis, had indicated that he was inclined to endorse Hillary," he noted in his 2020 memoir. "John had become a good friend—he'd taken great pride in my election, rightly seeing it as part of his legacy—and I knew he was tortured by the decision. As I listened to him explain his reasoning over the phone, how long he had known the Clintons, how Bill's administration had supported many of his legislative priorities, I chose not to press him too hard. I could imagine the pressure this kind and gentle man was under, and I recognized that, at a time when I was asking white voters to judge me on the merits, a raw appeal to racial solidarity would feel like hypocrisy."[9]

The eventual tiebreaker for Lewis—the issue that finally put him on a path to endorsing Obama—was his discomfort with Clinton's vote to authorize the war in Iraq. Asked repeatedly to apologize for her vote, Clinton steadfastly refused, insisting "there are no do-overs in life." This stubborn defense of her part in what he considered to be a tragic mistake troubled Lewis, who was among the war's sharpest critics. In late March, moderate Democrats in the House engineered a compromise bill that allowed them to authorize an additional $124 billion to sustain funding for the war while mandating a recall of all American troops in Iraq by September 2008. Many House Democrats cheered when the bill passed by a 218–212 vote, but not Lewis. Voting no, he remained true to his long-standing antiwar beliefs. Even though he was one of the party's deputy whips in the House, he declared, "I will not and cannot vote for another dollar or another dime to support this war." Just before the vote, Speaker Pelosi, desperately seeking enough votes to put the bill over the top, asked Lewis "to pray about it." But after the bill passed over his objection, Lewis reported, "she respected my decision."[10]

Despite deeply held beliefs on a number of important moral and political issues, Lewis was an effective deputy whip who recognized the importance of being a team player. One of the reasons why he was held in such high regard by his colleagues, Democrat and Republican alike, was his willingness to listen to and debate different points of view. When he felt it was necessary to draw a line in the sand, he did so without resorting to absolutist rhetoric or self-righteous posturing. Since he sought not only social and political change but also comity and reconciliation, he tried to avoid self-indulgent recriminations that treated political differences as personal barriers. In politics, as in the civil rights struggle that framed his personal values and beliefs, the way of truth and love was the only viable way for Lewis to behave. Balancing candor and truth-telling with humility and restraint, he had no interest in crushing or silencing his political opponents.

All of Lewis's most cherished role models—from Gandhi to King to Lawson—were cut from the same cloth: leaders who moved from ideas to action without losing sight of fundamental, long-term objectives or giving in to temptations based on the notion that the end justifies the means. Like his mentors, Lewis was goal oriented and often frustrated by the slow pace of change, but he refused to sacrifice due process in the interest of getting what he wanted. Rooted in the philosophy of nonviolence, his attitude toward political conflict promoted open-ended dialogue and education, not the vanquishing of opposing points of view at all costs. As one close friend observed, he was a "gentle warrior who had both fire in his belly and kindness in his heart."

Realizing that his colleagues were well aware of his deep religious faith and clerical training, Lewis kept his political "preaching" to a minimum on the House floor. Though something less than a purist on such matters, he was a First Amendment, ACLU-style liberal when it came to the constitutionally mandated separation of church and state. He considered himself to be a close student of the liberal American democracy that had evolved over the past two centuries, and in recent years he had become increasingly aware of his responsibilities as a political leader widely regarded as a historical figure in his own right. As he grew older, he developed a consuming interest in the past—not only the history of African Americans and other Americans but also the broader history of freedom, democracy, and colonialism in the wider world. He read extensively in a variety of historical subfields, paying close attention to the dynamics of historical change and cultural and political issues of long-term consequence. He collected books on everything from African American art to African, Asian, and European history and biography, in an ongoing effort to place himself and his experiences in as broad a context as possible.[11]

The history of the civil rights movement was, of course, his greatest passion, and he could not help but notice he was one of an ever-dwindling number of individuals who had been near the center of the struggle during the 1960s. Most of his close friends from his Nashville days—Bernard LaFayette, Lawson, Diane Nash, Vivian, and others whom he saw occasionally, mostly at Freedom Rider reunions, were still around—but every month seemed to bring news of another fallen nonviolent warrior, or in some cases a white supremacist leader who had fought against the movement. During the previous fifteen years, Thurgood Marshall, Jim Farmer, Rosa Parks, Stokely Carmichael, George Wallace, Lester Maddox, and Orval Faubus had passed from the scene, and in the spring and summer of 2007 a number of others were added to the list, including Sheriff Jim Clark, David Halberstam, and even fifty-one-year-old Yolanda King, Martin and Coretta King's first-born daughter, whom Lewis had met as a child, and who had gone on to be an actress, appearing in the 1999 film *Selma, Lord, Selma*.

It had been more than a half century since Lewis's earliest involvement in the civil rights struggle, and at times it was difficult for him to recall exactly what life had been like during the Jim Crow era. This troubled him, and with the loss of so many eyewitnesses to the brutalities and humiliations of Jim Crow culture, he feared it was becoming increasingly difficult to appreciate the magnitude of change that the movement had helped to bring about. His view of the civil rights movement had always been clear-eyed and suspicious of celebratory mythic depictions of movement heroes and triumphs. Nonetheless, he worried that many Americans, especially younger Americans, failed to appreciate how far the South and the nation had come since the dark days before the national movement had emerged in the mid-1950s.[12]

* * *

In the spring of 2007, he had an opportunity to share his fears with an audience of students, family members, and professors as the commencement speaker at Adelphi University in Garden City, New York. Couching his remarks in the authority of personal experience, he offered a brief history lesson about what he had witnessed: "Sometimes I hear some young people say nothing has changed. I feel like saying, come and walk in my shoes. In 1956, at the age of 16, being so inspired by Dr. King along with some of my brothers and sisters and first cousins, we went to the little library in Pike County, Alabama, a public library in the little town of Troy trying to get library cards, trying to check out some books. And we were told by the librarian that the library was for whites only and not for coloreds. I never went back to that library until July 5, 1998. By that time I was a member of Congress, and I went there for a book signing of my book. Hundreds of black and white citizens showed up. I signed many books. In the end, they gave me a library card. It says something about the distance we've come and the progress we've made in laying down the burden of race."

Here, as in many of Lewis's speeches during his years in Congress, there was an air of optimism and an upbeat recognition of racial progress. But he was also a realist well aware of the lingering burdens of the past, from race-based economic inequality to unequal access to health care and education to continuing imputations of Black intellectual inferiority. The recent grumbling over the extension of the Voting Rights Act was indicative that progress toward political parity between Black and white citizens still had a long way to go—and even after recent gains in the House, Black representation in Congress was proportionately less than it should be.

Other than Obama, there had been no Black senator since Edward Brooke's brief tenure (1967–1979) and no Black presidential contender of any consequence since Shirley Chisholm in 1972 and Jesse Jackson in 1984 and 1988. In 1995, Colin Powell had briefly entertained the notion of running for president as a moderate Republican, but nothing came of it. Against this backdrop, Obama's candidacy for the Democratic presidential nomination loomed large among Black voters. Even Lewis, who spent months agonizing over his choice for the nomination, welcomed Obama onto the national stage as "the future of the Democratic Party," declaring in 2005, "I think the hopes and dreams and aspirations of so many of us are riding on this one man."[13]

As the campaign progressed in the closing months of 2007, the notion that Obama might actually win the nomination became increasingly credible, and by the time the first party primaries and caucuses were held in January, Black leaders faced enormous pressure to jump on the Obama bandwagon. This pressure intensified after Obama won an upset victory over Clinton in the Iowa caucuses on January 3, ran even with her in the delegate count five days later in New Hampshire, and followed later in the month with impressive victories in Nevada and South Carolina. Through all of this, Lewis's public statements gave no indication that he was considering switching his support to Obama, but in private he was mulling over his options. One factor pushing him toward a switch was a series of controversial statements by Bill Clinton diminishing Obama's overwhelming victory in South Carolina as proof that, like Jesse Jackson in the 1980s, the Illinois senator had benefited from being "the Black candidate" in the race. Lewis and many other Black leaders did not like former president Clinton's insinuation that Obama's appeal was based primarily on race, and for some this sign of desperation in the Clinton camp was the proverbial straw that broke the camel's back.

Hillary Clinton's support among Black voters continued to erode, and on Super Tuesday, February 5, when twenty-three states and territories, including Georgia, held caucuses or primaries, this trend helped Obama to win victories in thirteen of the contests. In Georgia, Obama won more than twice as many delegates as Clinton and piled up large popular majorities in predominantly Black districts, including Lewis's congressional district. Ten days later the *New York Times* published a confusing report that Lewis had told a television interviewer he was planning to cast his superdelegate vote at the Democratic National Convention for Obama, in part because he hoped to avoid a huge fight between the Clinton and Obama delegations at the convention. To confuse matters further, his staff soon issued a statement insisting his superdelegate decision did not mean that he was endorsing Obama.

Two weeks later, Lewis explained this apparent inconsistency as best he could by clarifying his responsibilities as a superdelegate. Whatever his personal preference, which he now admitted tilted toward Obama, he maintained he could "never, ever do anything to reverse the actions" of his district's voters, the vast majority of whom supported the Illinois senator. At the same time, he revealed that he was close to resolving his conflicting feelings. "Something's happening in America," he observed, "something some of us did not see coming. Barack Obama has tapped into something that is extraordinary. . . . There is a movement, there is a spirit, there is an enthusiasm in the hearts and minds of the American people that I have not seen in a long time, since the candidacy of Robert Kennedy. The people are pressing for a new day in American politics, and I think they see Senator Barack Obama as a symbol of that change." His statement ended with the declaration, "I want to be on the side of the people, on the side of the spirit of history." Considering his recent support for Clinton, these rhetorical flourishes must have left some listeners scratching their heads. But others cut through the confusion, concluding that Lewis had stopped just short of formally endorsing Obama.

Over the next three months of primaries and caucuses, Obama gained steady ground among Democrats of all races and regions—and among the all-important superdelegates like Lewis who would ultimately determine the choice of nominee. On June 3, the day of the last primary, the addition of six Obama delegates from South Dakota clinched the nomination, and two days later Clinton conceded, ending one of the most competitive presidential races in party history. Though happy for Obama and thrilled at the prospect of electing the nation's first Black president, Lewis listened to Clinton's concession speech on June 7 with mixed emotions and a certain measure of guilt. For a time, his relationship with Clinton would be strained, but somehow their friendship survived. "I understand he's been under tremendous pressure," she conceded graciously upon learning he had switched sides. "He has been my friend. He will always be my friend." She knew the risks he had taken, that his early support for her had damaged his relationship with many of Atlanta's Black leaders, including Lowery, prompting his first serious primary challenge in more than a decade.[14]

* * *

When the Democratic National Convention met in Denver in late August 2008, Lewis was on hand not only as an Obama-pledged superdelegate but also as both a proponent of party unity and a historical link to the social movement that had prepared the way for Obama's rise to greatness. On the fourth and final night of the convention, August 28—the forty-fifth anniversary of his speech at the Lincoln Memorial—Lewis addressed the convention and a national television audience as "the last remaining speaker from the March on Washington." "I was there when Dr. King delivered his historic speech before an audience of more than 250,000," he declared. "I was there when Dr. King stood up to tear down segregation and moved toward a more perfect union. His words and his examples inspired an entire generation of young and old, the rich and poor, people of all faiths, races, color, and background to believe that we have the power, we have the ability, we have the capacity to make the dream a reality tonight."

After pausing for a moment to catch his breath and to take in the extraordinary scene of more than eighty thousand people straining to hear his message of hope and deliverance, Lewis assured them, "This night is not a beginning. It is not even the end. It is the continuation of a struggle that began centuries ago, in Lexington and Concord.... We have come a long way, but we must march again on November 4. We must march in every state, in every city, in every hamlet. We must march to the ballot box. We must march like we have never marched before, to elect the next President of the United States, Senator Barack Obama. We can do it. We must do it."

Lewis's rousing convention speech, with its passionate call to march, drew thunderous applause and a chorus of amens and hallelujahs. For a few precious moments, bathed in the wild enthusiasm of the crowd, he almost felt he had gone back in time, to the glorious, spirit-filled mass meetings of the 1960s. At forty-seven, Obama, like many in the cavernous stadium that night, had no direct memory to connect him to the movement experiences of Lewis's youth. But when he thanked the congressman for his eloquent words later in the evening, embracing him as a friend and mentor, it was clear the two men shared a personal and political bond forged in the fires of common struggle. Over the next decade and beyond, until Lewis's death in 2020, the civil rights icon and the first Black president would grow even closer as they collaborated on a broad range of issues related to democracy and civil and human rights.[15]

During the general election campaign that pitted Obama and his running mate, Senator Joe Biden of Delaware, against the Republican ticket of Senator John McCain of Arizona and Governor Sarah Palin of Alaska, no one worked harder for a Democratic victory than Lewis. Returning again and again to the historic nature of the contest, he traveled across the nation to deliver the Obama-Biden campaign's message of "Yes, We Can." The ideological contrast between the Democratic and Republican standard bearers could hardly have been starker. On issues such as immigrants' rights, the war in Iraq, reproductive freedom, and gun control, the stakes were obvious and high.

All of these issues were of concern to Lewis, but one that was particularly worrisome to him was the Republican candidates' disdain for the movement against the nationwide epidemic of gun violence. In June, the Supreme Court had rendered a shocking five-to-four ruling in *District of Columbia v. Heller*, invalidating Washington's gun-control ordinance and defying decades of precedent by reinterpreting the Second Amendment as a guarantor of the individual right to bear arms. Suddenly the National Rifle Association's hard-line, libertarian doctrine in favor of virtually unrestricted gun ownership had become the law of the land. For Lewis, putting Obama in the White House held out the hope that if a vacancy on the Court emerged during the next four years, a new, more progressive justice might move the Court to the left on this and other important issues. This possibility, along with countless other potential consequences of a Democratic victory, was more than enough to fuel Lewis's passion as an Obama campaigner.

His specific task was to bring out the Black vote by emphasizing the connection between the Democratic ticket and the long-standing struggle for civil rights and racial equality. As one of the nation's most revered civil rights heroes—one closely identified with the voting rights movement—he proved indispensable to the voter turnout effort. For the first time in American history, the voter turnout among Black citizens, estimated at 76.6 percent by one prominent political scientist, exceeded the turnout, 73.6 percent, among white citizens.

Without this unprecedented level of voting among Black Americans—95 percent of whom voted for Obama—McCain, who garnered 55 percent of the white vote, might have won the election. But with strong support from the civil rights community, led by Lewis and other members of the CBC, Obama won a resounding victory, 365 to 173 in the Electoral College, and by a nearly ten-million-vote margin in the national popular vote. To Lewis's dismay, Obama lost Georgia by more than two hundred thousand votes, despite gaining overwhelming support from the state's Black electorate. But this statewide setback was no surprise, since Georgia's electoral votes had not ended up in the Democratic column since Bill Clinton had won a narrow victory in 1992. Clearly, the road to racial reconciliation still had a way to go in Georgia, but Lewis took some consolation from the fact that Obama won a significantly higher percentage of the state's vote (46.99 percent) than John Kerry had (41.37 percent) four years earlier.[16]

After the election, Lewis worked closely with the president-elect's transition team. Taking advantage of Lewis's long tenure in the House, Obama asked him for advice on various appointments and in dealing with the incoming House of Representatives, which, after a gain of 24 Democratic seats, would be firmly in Democratic control, 257–178. In the new Senate, the Democrats would have a 59–41 majority, their strongest position since 1979.

On inauguration day, Lewis experienced what he later described as one of the most joyous days of his life. As he recalled the scene, the day "was bitterly cold, one of the coldest I have ever seen in Washington. . . . But that did not stop the people. People came from all across the country, sleeping on cots and sleeping bags on the floor in the homes of families and friends some of them had not seen for years. Some started walking miles away from the National Mall in Washington to be there on time. For many, it was their first visit to the capital city and definitely the first time they ever had any desire to attend an inauguration. We all felt invested in what we had created. We felt we all had had a hand in something great, in opening a door to a new day in America."

Given a seat of honor on the Capitol dais, Lewis watched the swearing-in ceremony close at hand, sitting just one row behind Obama. A few moments after he left the podium, the new president reached out and squeezed the beaming congressman's shoulder, a gesture to the power and legacy of the movement. Observed by millions of television viewers, it would occupy a cherished place in Lewis's memory for the rest of his life.[17]

*   *   *

Caught in the afterglow of the inaugural celebration, Lewis's hopes for the future brightened during the early weeks of the new administration in 2009, when Obama enjoyed unusually high approval ratings in most public opinion polls. Despite the backdrop of a deepening economic recession, the traditional honeymoon period seemed to signal broad acceptance of the new president. Indeed, some starry-eyed observers even began to talk about the onset of a "post-racial America." But Lewis was not one of them. As an old hand, he had seen too much of the dark side of American politics to believe that a nation riven by racial and class divides had suddenly found its democratic soul. With good reason, he worried that the uglier aspects of the recent general election campaign—especially the right-wing, racist critique that Obama was a cultural outsider who lacked legitimacy as an authentic American—would resurface as soon as the new administration began to exercise executive authority and press for serious reform.

The first sign of trouble emerged the week after the inauguration when Obama's economic stimulus bill, which became the American Recovery and Reinvestment Act after its passage in February, failed to receive a single Republican vote in the House of Representatives. Over the next four months, Lewis's worst fears were confirmed as Republican obstructionism hardened into a policy of total noncooperation on legislative and executive matters. In May, Obama's nomination of Second Circuit appellate judge Sonia Sotomayor to be the Supreme Court's first Hispanic justice became enmeshed in an ongoing culture war involving the defense of white privilege and the expression of anti-immigrant impulses. In the end, Sotomayor's appointment was confirmed by the Senate 68–31, but Lewis and other progressives were disappointed that only nine Republican senators voted for confirmation.[18]

From July on, after the administration introduced its top legislative priority, the Patient Protection and Affordable Care Bill, conservative Republican opposition to Obama became even more strident and extreme.

Denigrating the bill as a subversive plot to replace traditional American free enterprise with "socialized medicine," Republican critics—including an emerging libertarian, right-wing populist group known as the Tea Party movement—condemned Obama as un-American, a characterization that often shaded into ideological and racial caricature. Mocking his multiracial identity and name, and questioning his American citizenship status—a theme that had first emerged during the 2008 election as "birtherism"—Tea Party activists led a widening political backlash infused with increasingly blatant racist overtones. All of this disturbed Lewis beyond measure, especially when he had to deal with insulting and demeaning anti-Obama rhetoric in the House chamber. Predictably, several of his Georgia colleagues were among the worst offenders, which made him even more determined to speak up on the beleaguered president's behalf.[19]

In October, Lewis's spirits lifted, at least for a time, when Obama was unexpectedly awarded the Nobel Peace Prize. Confirmation that the president's stature was greater abroad than at home, the presentation of the award to an African American president, according to Lewis, "was an indication to those familiar with our turmoil for over four hundred years that we had finally turned a corner, that we were finally willing to lay aside the vestiges of slavery and expose ourselves to the radiant sun of real freedom." "It also meant," he speculated, "that if we could do it . . . maybe even Israel and Palestine could finally admit their kinship. Maybe on every continent, in every nation, in every corner of the world people could put their longstanding grievances aside and decide to live in peace."

In offering this vision, Lewis was placing a heavy burden on Obama, casting him as a savior in the mythic "magical Negro" tradition. Lewis knew, of course, that Obama was just a man, a flesh-and-blood human being with limited power to bring about fundamental change. But in a desperate gesture of hope, he conflated his personal commitment to peace and reconciliation with the Nobel committee's supposed intention. "The Nobel committee was saying in effect," he insisted: "If the United States can move beyond the tension of hundreds of years of human slavery and the bloodshed of the Civil War, then maybe, just maybe, the world community might find a way to finally lay aside the ancient struggles of the past and move to a new level of human existence." Allowing himself a hard-earned moment of hopeful naïveté, he transferred his own feeling of euphoria to the nation at large. "At that moment," he wrote three years later, "we glimpsed a few seconds of what our future could be. We felt in this country a flash of the true joy and freedom of living in a Beloved Community, living in a society based on simple justice that values the dignity and worth of every human being."[20]

As the Obama administration moved into its second year—increasingly ensnared in racial and right-wing conspiracy theories, and more embattled than ever—Lewis's fleeting glimpse of the Beloved Community fell away, obscured by debilitating partisan and political realities. Hamstrung by a slow and uneven economic recovery—especially by a doggedly high unemployment rate that hovered between 9 and 10 percent—the Democrats faced a stiff uphill struggle in the 2010 midterm elections. The likelihood that they could hold their own against the Republicans was further diminished by *Citizens United v. Federal Election Commission,* a crushing January 2010 Supreme Court decision that removed campaign contribution limits as a violation of free speech. Opening the way for special interests, including unidentifiable corporate donors, to use "dark money" to influence elections, the ruling was hailed by conservative Republicans as a victory over intrusive government regulation. But Lewis and other Democratic leaders cried foul, deploring the decision as fundamentally antidemocratic.

Throughout the campaign, Lewis and his fellow Democrats touted the administration's strong record on a number of important issues—including the passage of the Affordable Care Act in March—and Obama barnstormed the country for six weeks in September and October defending his record on domestic and foreign affairs. But no amount of effort or rhetoric could stem the Republican tide. Suffering the worst reversal in the House since 1938, the Democrats lost 64 seats, returning control to the Republicans, 242–193. In the Senate, the Democrats lost 5 seats but remained in control by a slim majority.[21]

Becoming a minority-party representative after four years in the majority—and only two years after Obama's triumph in 2008—was devastating for Lewis, who had harbored high hopes for an extended period of liberal Democratic dominance. With this reversal of fortune, the Democratic Party's progressive agenda was reduced to a holding action, and Lewis found himself on the defensive both inside and outside the House chamber. Political discourse was growing coarser, and at one point he and other members of the CBC were spat on and called "niggers" as they walked through a crowd of Tea Party protesters on the Capitol steps. The political situation was especially bad in Georgia, where Republicans now occupied eight of thirteen congressional seats and the Democratic Party was in full retreat. It would be eight years before a newly elected Democrat would represent the state in the House. During the remainder of Obama's presidency and beyond, Lewis would be part of an overmatched minority in an increasingly conservative state that had turned sharply to the right since the 1970s.

The general situation in the 111th Congress, which convened in January 2011, was equally discouraging, but Lewis soldiered on as a strong and consistent voice for equality and tolerance. Whatever the odds of prevailing politically, he never shied away from speaking his mind on issues related to social justice and democracy. This steadfast advocacy endeared him to progressive citizens across the nation, including President Obama, who awarded him the Presidential Medal of Freedom on February 15. In a ceremony held in the East Wing of the White House, he—along with eleven other notable figures from the worlds of sports, labor, politics, and the arts—received the nation's highest civilian honor.

In awarding the coveted medal, President Obama praised his friend and ally as a man of stalwart integrity and uncommon courage. "There is a quote inscribed over the doorway in Nashville, where students first refused to leave lunch counters 51 years ago this February," the president told the gathering, "and the quote said, 'If not us, then who? If not now, then when?' It's a question John Lewis has been asking his entire life. It's what led him back to the Edmund Pettus Bridge in Selma after he had already been beaten within an inch of his life days before. It's why, time and again, he faced down death so that all of us could share equally in the joys of life. It's why all these years later he is known as the Conscience of the United States Congress, still speaking his mind on issues of justice and equality. And generations from now, when parents teach their children what is meant by courage, the story of John Lewis will come to mind—an American who knew that change could not wait for some other person or some other time; whose life is a lesson in the fierce urgency of now."

Lewis was never one to put much stock in awards or to seek formal recognition of his accomplishments; he was too busy trying to change the world. But receiving the Medal of Freedom from Obama meant a great deal to him, especially coming as it did at a low point in his political life. It helped to remind him that the struggle for freedom and justice was a long and ongoing process, a journey that would continue far beyond the discouraging political setbacks and detours of the moment. As in the past, his strong sense of history was comforting, informed by Dr. King's famous maxim that "we shall overcome, because the arc of the moral universe is long, but it bends toward justice."[22]

This sense was replenished in the spring of 2011 during the fiftieth anniversary reunion of the Freedom Riders in Chicago. This gathering of 180 former Freedom Riders meeting for several days of conference sessions devoted to reminiscing, to the history of the civil rights movement, and to the current and future prospects for social reform culminated in Lewis's emotional appearance on *The Oprah Winfrey Show* described earlier and in the public television premiere of the *American Experience* documentary *Freedom Riders*. All of this publicity heightened Lewis's national profile as a historic figure sustaining a legacy of civil rights and social justice activism, and he returned from the August recess with a renewed commitment to fighting the good fight for the ideas he had espoused for half a century.

The summer had brought a new spate of unfortunate developments in Congress: the indictment of Senator John Edwards for conspiring to avoid campaign finance laws; the "sexting" scandal that forced New York congressman Anthony Weiner's resignation; an antiunion vote in the House to limit the power of the National Labor Relations Board; continued squabbling over raising the national debt ceiling; and the Republicans' xenophobic demonization of undocumented immigrants. Regrettably, through all of this, Lewis and the House Democrats were limited to damage control, with no real power to reverse the trend toward unrelenting partisanship and political stalemate.

In September, President Obama introduced the American Jobs Bill, an economic stimulus package that Lewis strongly supported, but the bill died in the Senate thanks to unanimous Republican opposition and several Democratic defections. While the bill was still under consideration, impatient economic justice activists calling themselves the Occupy Wall Street movement resorted to picketing, marching, and other forms of non-violent direct action in an effort to call attention to wealth inequality and corrupting corporate influence on public policy. Drawing inspiration from the civil rights movement of the 1960s—especially the "Resurrection City" of tents constructed on the National Mall during the 1968 Poor People's campaign—the young Occupy activists eventually spread beyond New York City and established makeshift camps in public parks, corporate buildings, foreclosed homes, and college campuses across the nation. Although the Occupy movement eventually faded and all but disappeared after two years of spirited but often unsuccessful protests—including a mass march and general strike in New York in May 2012—Lewis took great satisfaction in watching young Americans returning to the streets for peaceful protest. While he feared the Occupy activists lacked the discipline needed to sustain a long-term nonviolent movement, he hoped that their activities, however fitful, would lead to a reinvigoration of grassroots citizen politics.

Lewis had voiced similar hopes for the Arab Spring protests that had swept across North Africa and the Middle East in 2011, protests that had drawn worldwide attention to some of the participants' claims to have been inspired by the history of nonviolent protest in the United States. The Occupy movement and Arab Spring were both on his mind when he wrote a series of philosophical essays in collaboration with his communications director, Brenda Jones. Gretchen Young, an editor at Hyperion Books who urged Lewis to write the essays as a means of extending his legacy, oversaw the publication of *Across the Bridge: A Vision for Change and the Future of America* in May 2012. When he discussed the recently published book's themes on Diane Rehm's syndicated PBS radio show, he called on "the Occupy Movement, the Arab Spring and other grassroots leaders to focus on the nonviolent principles that propelled his generation: Faith, patience, study, truth, peace and love."

In the book's final chapter, titled "Reconciliation," Lewis describes the two recent movements as links in a historical chain going back to Thoreau and Gandhi. Citing the movement anthem "This Little Light of Mine," which counsels listeners "to let it shine," he asserts his faith "that we are all a spark of the divine, and if that spark is nurtured it can become a burning flame, an eternal force of light." "Through our work, our prayer, and our successful overcoming," he explains, "we ground the light on this planet. Just as Gandhi made it easier for King, and King made it easier for Poland and Poland made it easier for Ireland and Ireland made it easier for Serbia and Serbia made it easier for the Arab Spring, and the Arab Spring made it easier for the protests in Wisconsin and Occupy Wall Street, so our actions entrench the power of the light on this planet. Every positive thought we pass between us makes room for more light. And if we do more than think, then our actions clear a path for even more light. That is why forgiveness and compassion must become more important principles in public life." The struggle for freedom and justice was all about "living as light," which for Lewis meant "putting away remedies based on fear, retribution, and revenge and acting collectively through government to respect the dignity of all humankind."[23]

*   *   *

Laying all of this out at a time when American politics looked very dark testified to Lewis's unquenchable faith in both God and humanity, and to his determination to rise above the troubles of the moment. But even if he sometimes placed his head in the clouds, he was also mindful of the immediate tasks at hand, which in 2012 centered on the reelection of Barack Obama. During the summer and fall of 2012, Lewis worked tirelessly for Obama's reelection campaign, trumpeting the president's accomplishments and rallying the Black vote. While he sometimes campaigned in other cities, he spent most of his time in Atlanta, where both his and Obama's popularity seemed to be rising. In late August, as the campaign was entering its final two months, he was honored—but undoubtedly a bit embarrassed—by the unveiling of a massive thirty-foot-high portrait of him with the word "Hero" above his head. Painted on the side of a building near a busy intersection on Auburn Avenue, just a few blocks west of Ebenezer Baptist Church, the striking mural would quickly become a symbol of his unparalleled stature in his adopted city.

After a brief speech at the mural's dedication ceremony, he was back on the campaign trail working to defeat the president's Republican adversary,

Mitt Romney, the pragmatic former governor of Massachusetts and a devout Mormon who, like Obama, claimed to represent a new departure in American politics. Lewis did not dispute the sincerity of Romney's religious faith and moralistic posturing. But in his view, the Mormon leader's disappointing record on matters related to race, class privilege, and poverty rendered him unfit for the presidency of a nation striving to live up to its professed ideals of democracy and equality of opportunity. A skilled and experienced campaigner backed by enormous financial resources, Romney posed a serious threat to Obama's presidency, and Lewis was not about to take him lightly. Fortunately for the Democrats, the campaign eventually turned on Obama's charismatic image and personality, for which his relatively bland Republican opponent had no answer.

In the end, the 2012 election results exceeded Lewis's expectations, and he found considerable solace and a measure of hope in Obama's reelection, even though the margin of victory was narrower than in 2008, with Obama winning the Electoral College 332 to 206 and the popular vote by less than 3.5 million. Lewis was disappointed with the president's showing in the South, where he carried only two states, Virginia and Florida, and where he lost Georgia by more than four hundred thousand votes, a much larger deficit than in 2008. The Democrats fared better in the Senate, however, where they gained two seats and remained in control. Lewis also took some encouragement from the House races, where his party gained eight seats—a better-than-expected result though not good enough to regain control of the chamber. The new House would have 201 Democrats versus 234 Republicans, and Lewis and his liberal colleagues would still be hamstrung by their minority status.[24]

Whether the Democratic minority in the House could do much to advance Obama's progressive agenda during his second term was questionable. But Lewis was more determined than ever to combat the Republican effort to obstruct the Democratic administration at every turn. When legislative victories eluded the outnumbered House Democrats, which occurred on a routine basis, he found himself turning to public education activities—to speaking and writing—as an alternative. Appealing for public decency and reaffirming the highest ideals of democracy and social justice, he did his best to keep these principles in the public eye. In effect, he redoubled his effort to live up to his reputation as "the conscience of Congress."

Maintaining his momentum as an idealistic, progressive advocate proved difficult during the weeks following the election, when much of Lewis's attention was focused on the rapidly declining health of Lillian, his devoted wife of forty-four years. Her death came on New Year's Eve, forty-five years to the day after their first date. She had been battling kidney disease for nearly a decade, taking early retirement from her administrative job at Clark Atlanta University in 2003. During the past year, her condition had grown steadily worse, to the point where she needed round-the-clock care from family members and nurses. A woman who had always been a strong-willed and vibrant companion had become a soft-spoken invalid dependent on her husband and those willing to help them deal with a very difficult situation. Politically astute and intellectually engaged, she had often amazed her friends with her deep knowledge of African and Caribbean culture—and her ability to quote long passages from Dr. King's speeches. Throughout Lewis's political career, she served as his most trusted adviser, in addition to being a loving partner. "She was a feisty lady," one close friend commented. "He was so sweet and gentle; he needed her to take care of his back. And she was the one to do it."

Losing Lillian was a devastating blow, even though Lewis had been preparing himself for her passing for several years. Together they had protected her privacy, revealing the seriousness of her condition only to a few close friends and family members. So when the dreaded day came, many of Lewis's congressional colleagues were caught off guard. The funeral, held at Ebenezer Baptist Church on January 7, four days after the new Congress convened in Washington, was largely a private affair, in keeping with her desire to avoid the political limelight whenever possible. Despite her deep interest in public affairs and her husband's career, she had never spent much time in Washington, preferring to stay close to her home and workplace in Atlanta. Lewis himself was perhaps the only person in Washington who knew how much he depended on her emotionally and intellectually. Without her he feared he would be lost.

Throughout the late stages of her illness, Lillian had urged her husband to concentrate on his work, and that is what he did in the weeks and months following her death. Obama's second inaugural ceremony on January 20 was a time for celebration among Democrats, and Lewis made a valiant effort to overcome his grief and participate in the launching of the president's new term. Whatever his personal trials, he knew this was no time to be missing in action. Advancing the progressive agenda was more important than ever, with ultraconservative Republicans mobilizing to thwart whatever moves the Democrats made toward a more just social, economic, and political order. Everywhere he looked, partisan fervor and political polarization seemed to be spinning out of control, threatening to destroy any semblance of common commitment to the ideals of freedom and democracy.

Even with the Democrats in control of the Senate and the White House, the pathway to the Beloved Community seemed to be blocked, lost in a fog of power politics, cynical self-interest, and racial and class privilege. At times, Lewis felt he had gone back nearly a half century, back to the carnage of Bloody Sunday and the Edmund Pettus Bridge. But for a battle-scarred veteran and nonviolent warrior like Lewis, there could be no retreat and no turning back. The road ahead might look tougher and more menacing than ever, but long odds had not deterred him in the past, and they would not do so now.[25]

Lewis was, understandably, in a bit of a daze during the early weeks of Obama's second term. He took part in the events surrounding the reconvening of Congress in early January 2013 and the president's inauguration later in the month. But he was not his old self. Adjusting to life without Lillian would take time, and he sometimes felt he was sleepwalking as he tried to carry out his congressional responsibilities. As always, he was gracious and welcoming to his colleagues, Democrats and Republicans alike, especially to the new members of the House and Senate elected in November. Wallowing in personal grief was not his style, and he refused to use Lillian's death as an excuse for his uncharacteristic lack of focus. But he was, after all, a human being susceptible to the full range of emotions and mood swings. Even "saints" have bad days, and he had plenty of them during the transition to his new life as a widower.

With Lillian gone, the rhythm and balance of his life shifted. He now spent more time in Washington and more time alone. While he still had close relationships with a wide circle of friends and family, including his thirty-six-year-old son, John-Miles, plus a devoted staff who looked after him as best they could, some of the personal leaven that had buoyed his spirits and helped him to get through the low points of life was gone. Beyond this new burden of loneliness and isolation was a worsening political situation—in the nation at large, where many of Obama's Republican critics were indulging in increasingly irresponsible attacks on the president's legitimacy, and in the House of Representatives, where Lewis and the Democrats were hopelessly outnumbered.

To Lewis's disgust, a disturbingly large number of the attacks on Obama were overtly racist in nature, and the overall tone of political rhetoric coming from the Republican side was shockingly reminiscent of the Jim Crow era. Nearly five decades had passed since the civil and voting rights victories of the mid-1960s, and he had thought he had seen the last of the blatant and unapologetic racial demagoguery that had animated reactionary politics during the century following the Civil War. But he now realized he had been too optimistic in his assessment of the changes brought about by the civil rights revolution. The fate of the struggle for American democracy was still very much in doubt, it seemed, and later in the year several unsettling developments confirmed this alarming judgment.

In early June 2013, Lewis enjoyed a moment of exhilaration when he headlined "An Evening with John Lewis," a gala held at the National Archives to celebrate the 150th anniversary of the Emancipation Proclamation. But three weeks later, Lewis and other progressive lawmakers suffered one of the most devastating setbacks of the post–civil rights era. In a stunning five-to-four decision, the conservative-leaning Supreme Court ruled in *Shelby County, Alabama v. Holder* that Section 4b, and by implication Section 5, of the 1965 Voting Rights Act was unconstitutional. Together these two sections constituted the so-called preclearance provision of the Voting Rights Act; as such they required prior judicial approval of any substantive changes in the conduct of elections in states or local precincts deemed to have a history of racial disfranchisement. For nearly half a century, preclearance had been the heart and soul of the act's enforcement power. Without it, many of the enfranchisement gains for African Americans and other minorities that had transformed American politics since the mid-1960s would be placed in jeopardy, becoming subject to the personal and political predilections of state legislators and local registrars.

In striking down the preclearance requirement, the five conservative justices validated the State of Alabama's argument that the white South no longer needed special federal supervision of voting rights. Federal intervention was only justified, the majority concluded, when there was evidence of a current effort to disfranchise voters on the basis of race—evidence independent of any historical pattern. Having experienced a measure of progress in recent decades, the white South was, in effect, off the hook. Speaking for the Court, Chief Justice John Roberts declared, "Our country has changed. While any racial discrimination in voting is too much, Congress must ensure that the legislation it passes to remedy that problem speaks to current conditions."

In a vigorous dissent, Associate Justice Ruth Bader Ginsburg lamented that an era of unprecedented federal protection of voting rights "had drawn to a close" with the *Shelby* decision. "Beyond question, the V.R.A. is no ordinary legislation," she wrote. "It is extraordinary because Congress embarked on a mission long delayed and of extraordinary importance. . . . For half a century a concerted effort has been made to end racial discrimination in voting. Thanks to the Voting Rights Act, progress once the subject of a dream has been achieved and continues to be made. The court errs egregiously by overriding Congress's decision." President Obama agreed, declaring he was "deeply disappointed" by the ruling—the irony of which several reporters pointed out: the logic of the conservative majority was based in part on Obama's election as the nation's first Black president, a milestone "cited by critics of the law as evidence that it was no longer needed."[26]

In a press conference following the ruling, Lewis and other members of the CBC did not deny that progress toward real democracy in the South had taken place, but they insisted the conclusion that federal oversight was no longer needed to guarantee Black voting rights in the South had no basis in fact. The gutting of the Voting Rights Act, Lewis feared, would allow local election officials "to go back to another period." "The purpose of the act," he insisted, "is to stop discriminatory practices from becoming law. There are more Black elected officials in Mississippi today not because attempts to discriminate against voters ceased but because the Voting Rights Act kept those attempts from becoming law." The only remedy now, in the wake of the ruling, was to pass a new voting rights bill that restored federal oversight of the electoral process. But considering the partisan bickering and gridlock that dominated the current Congress, Lewis held out little hope that such legislation was forthcoming.[27]

CHAPTER 18

Good Trouble

RESUMING A STRUGGLE that he thought had been won decades earlier—a struggle that had nearly cost him his life at the age of twenty-five—was profoundly discouraging for a man now well into his seventies. John Lewis prided himself on his perseverance, but stepping back into the voting rights fray after so many years of hard-earned satisfaction tested his mettle. He was, of course, more than willing to help draft legislation that would undo the damage that he believed the *Shelby* decision would inevitably create. But the toxic situation in the House in 2013 had already prompted him to consider alternative, nonpolitical means of reinvigorating the civil rights struggle.

For a year or more, beginning with the fiftieth anniversary of the Freedom Rides, he had played with the idea of using storytelling as a means of keeping the civil rights flame burning, of replenishing the metaphorical light of freedom that he had emphasized in his 2012 book of essays, *Across That Bridge*. While he had been pleased with the response to the philosophical musings in *Across That Bridge*, he had no illusion that a serious book of abstract notions would connect with a broad audience, especially younger readers. He had come to realize that the most effective means of sustaining the struggle that had transformed his life, and, to some extent, the character of American democracy, was to reach out to young people with words and stories of empowerment.

He remembered how the comic book *Martin Luther King and the Montgomery Story* had inspired him as an impressionable eighteen-year-old participating in James Lawson's nonviolent workshops. Lawson often passed around the King comic to dramatize the importance of commitment and solidarity in the use of nonviolence, distributing it to students in a variety of settings as part of what he called a "reconciliation tour." In Lewis's case, it helped prepare the way for his passionate involvement in the Nashville Student Movement, the Freedom Rides, and SNCC. Recalling its power a half century later, he reasoned that if he could tell his own story in a similarly dramatic way, couched in language and imagery that would appeal to teenagers, the torch might be passed to future generations of activists. As an elderly man who knew next to nothing about graphic novels, social media, or the internet, he knew he would need help to bridge the communication gap between generations. Fortunately, he found two talented and willing collaborators, twenty-four-year-old Andrew Aydin, an aspiring graphic novelist and Atlanta native who had worked in Lewis's Washington office and as an Atlanta-based campaign aide since 2007, and twenty-nine-year-old Nate Powell, an Arkansas-born comic book artist, graphic novelist, and punk rock musician.

Aydin, who had become one of Lewis's most trusted aides, began encouraging Lewis to write an autobiographical graphic novel as early as June 2008. When other members of Lewis's campaign staff ridiculed the idea and made fun of Aydin's plans to attend Dragon Con, a two-decade-old multimedia and popular culture conference held in Atlanta over Labor Day Weekend, Lewis not only told them to "stop it" but also mentioned his respect for the King comic book used by Lawson. Aydin continued to press Lewis on the graphic novel idea until mid-July, when, after Lewis blessed the project, the congressman finally agreed to a coauthorship with his young aide. In September, Lewis even accompanied Aydin to Dragon Con, where he was introduced to a world of comics, graphic arts, and modes of youth culture beyond his previous experience and imagination.

Working intermittently on the project over the next three years, Lewis and Aydin completed a text that told the story of Lewis's civil rights journey from his Alabama boyhood to the Selma-to-Montgomery march. By 2011, all they needed was a talented comic book artist to illustrate the story—and an appropriate publisher willing to produce a book designed for thirteen-to-sixteen-year-olds, the target audience Lewis was determined to reach. Unfortunately, finding the right publisher and the right artist proved far more difficult than they anticipated. With little precedent for a graphic book dealing with a serious subject such as the civil rights movement, a long line of New York–based publishers turned Aydin and Lewis away. In the end, their only option was to sign a contract with Top Shelf Productions, a small comic book and graphic novel publishing company located in Marietta, Georgia. In 2015, Top Shelf would become part of the young adult division of the publishing behemoth Penguin Random House, but when Aydin and Lewis signed their contract in 2012, the tiny company hovered near the bottom of the publishing world. They were fortunate, however, that the cofounder and publisher of Top Shelf, Chris Staros, knew a number of the nation's most talented young comic artists, including Nate Powell.

After Powell agreed to collaborate with Lewis and Aydin, it took only a few months to turn the manuscript into a graphic novel. In fact, Powell produced enough graphic material for several volumes, to be published sequentially over a three-year period under the title *March*. The drawings proved as captivating as the text, and from the moment volume 1 hit the bookstores in mid-August 2013, the dramatic way it presented Lewis's saga from childhood to the Nashville sit-ins attracted considerable attention. Before long the book gained a growing readership among teenagers and young adults, and within a few months after publication it was clear Top Shelf had a hit on its hands. Enthusiastic reviews, author tours, book signings, and eventually several major book prizes—including the Robert F. Kennedy Book Award—followed, all of which thrilled Lewis, who was suddenly having more fun as an author than as a minority-party congressman enmeshed in political gridlock.

In the midst of this burst of authorial celebrity, he attended the fiftieth-anniversary celebration of the March on Washington. Of all the speakers who held forth at the Lincoln Memorial in late August 1963, he was the only one still living. As he told the crowd that had gathered to commemorate the famous march, he was grateful not only for his longevity but also for a half century of progress toward racial equity: "Fifty years later we can ride anywhere we want to ride, we can stay anywhere we want to stay. Those signs that said 'white' and 'colored' are gone. And you won't see that anymore—except in a museum, in a book, or a video." While American society was still a long way from achieving a Beloved Community, he wanted to acknowledge the barriers that had been toppled since the era of Jim Crow.

Not everyone was old enough to remember the dark days of the past, but reading *March,* he suggested on numerous occasions, was one way to discover how far the nation had come since the 1960s. The second volume of the trilogy, *March: Book Two*—the story of the Freedom Rides—was published in January 2015, two weeks after Lewis began his fifteenth term in Congress; and *March: Book Three,* which focused on Lewis's experiences in SNCC, the voting rights campaign, and the Selma-to-Montgomery march, came out a year later. All three volumes succeeded beyond Lewis's wildest dreams, spending weeks at or near the top of the *New York Times* Best Seller List, and *Book Three* even won the prestigious National Book Award for Young People's Literature, the first "comics-style" graphic novel to do so. Along the way, Lewis and Aydin received more than two hundred invitations to speak to high school students. "*March,*" Lewis told the *Washington Post* columnist and cartoonist Michael Cavna, was designed to "get young people—another generation—to feel the hope, the dreams, the aspirations of a people that wanted to be free." Through graphic imagery and plain-speaking text, young readers would learn what it is like "to be involved" in nonviolence, "to be involved with social drama, to experience and to feel someone beating you, spitting on you, pouring hot water or hot coffee on you, to be arrested and to be jailed." Cavna, for one, got the message, concluding, "*March* was more than a storytelling, it was a torch passed."

An unexpected publishing phenomenon, *March* surpassed the King comic book on which it was modeled—in terms of both influence and intergenerational reach. Reviewing the trilogy for *Booklist,* Raina Telgemeier called it "one of the most important graphic novels ever created—an extraordinary presentation of an extraordinary life and proof that young people can change the world." A commentator for National Public Radio placed it "at the pinnacle of the comics canon," and the popular public affairs television personality Rachel Maddow termed it "an incredible accomplishment . . . a book that explains—more deeply than anything else I have ever read—the methods and moral foundations of the civil rights movement, how civil rights activists did what they did and won what they won, and how they had the strength to do it in the most difficult circumstances imaginable."[1]

Creating the *March* trilogy and using it to sustain and extend the legacy of the civil rights movement proved to be one of the most satisfying experiences of Lewis's life. Yet storytelling, even on such a broad scale, could only do so much to dull the pain of contemporary politics. Indeed, recalling the spirit and accomplishments of the 1960s was something of a double-edged sword—revealing the glories of the past on one side of the blade while highlighting the continuing frustrations of Barack Obama's second term on the other. The implicit comparison between the current state of the movement—unfocused, fragmented, and on the defensive—and the surging civil rights struggle of the 1960s at its height left Lewis with a sinking feeling. With a Black president in the White House and so much civil rights legislation enacted into law, the prospects for the future elevation of social justice and democracy should have been stronger than ever. But on the ground, in Washington and elsewhere, the dominant reality was a downward trajectory that seemed headed toward a reprise of some of the worst aspects of Jim Crow culture. The story of the journey to freedom had gone awry, the lead author of *March* feared, confounded by rising intolerance and rampant demagoguery.[2]

*   *   *

As always, Lewis regarded turning ideas into action as his primary mission, and he was willing to do just about anything short of violence to put the nation's evolving democracy back on course. While he still believed in the importance of political and legal deliberation, he began to feel it was time to widen the struggle and return to the streets. It had been many years since he had been involved in nonviolent direct action, but on October 8, 2013, he joined seven other Democratic representatives in a protest against the House's inaction on comprehensive immigration reform. Even though the Senate had already approved a bill that provided most of what Lewis and other advocates of immigrants' rights wanted, the Republican Speaker of the House, John Boehner, refused to let the bill come up for a vote on the House floor. This obstructionism prompted infuriated Democrats to stage a sit-in blocking the west entrance to the Capitol while thousands of supporters rallied nearby on the National Mall. All eight congressional protesters, along with nearly two hundred others, were promptly arrested by the Capitol police for breach of peace. It was Lewis's forty-fifth arrest, his third since entering Congress in 1987. Earlier in the day, he had told reporters, "We cannot rest, we cannot be satisfied until we have comprehensive immigration reform," and to prove his point he deliberately courted arrest.

Derided by Republican critics as a cheap publicity stunt, the "mass" arrest at the Capitol was, in fact, a limited, largely symbolic one-day action designed to dramatize the reformers' frustration with the legislative process. The next day, Lewis and the other arrestees returned to their offices and committee rooms to resume the fight for immigrants' rights in a more traditional fashion. Nonetheless, the echoes of Gandhian and Kingian nonviolence were unmistakable. Throughout the press coverage of the incident, there were frequent references to Lewis's past struggles in Selma and elsewhere—and to the phenomenon he had come to label "good trouble."[3]

Lewis had been making occasional use of the phrase "good trouble" for several years as a shorthand reference to creative disruption undertaken to promote social justice, and in the wake of his 2013 arrest the phrase became his signature motto. Before 2011, his favorite phrase along these lines had been "find a way to get in the way," but during the early collaboration on the *March* trilogy, Andrew Aydin suggested "good trouble" as an alternative and began using it as a Twitter hashtag. Lewis liked the idea and soon began using it on a limited basis. For example, in June 2014, during a commencement address at Emory University in Atlanta, he offered a lesson on "good trouble" taken from his own life. "I saw those signs that said 'white men,' 'colored men,' 'white women,' 'colored women,' 'white waiting,' 'colored waiting,'" he recalled. "I would come home and ask my mother, my father, my grandparents, my great-grandparents, 'Why?' They would say: 'That's the way it is. Don't get in the way. Don't get in trouble.'" But later, he explained, he was inspired by Rosa Parks and Martin Luther King Jr. "to get in the way, to get in trouble." "So I come here to say to you this morning on this beautiful campus," he declared, "with your great education, you must find a way to get in the way . . . to get in trouble—good trouble, necessary trouble."

Before long Lewis himself was tweeting under the hashtag "#goodtrouble," and eventually the phrase found its way onto political posters, T-shirts, and even COVID-19 facemasks. It was also the title of the first major documentary devoted to his life, a film directed by Dawn Porter and released two weeks before his death. By then, of course, most Americans already knew that Lewis's life was all about getting into "good trouble." A few weeks earlier, in March 2020, no one was surprised when he urged a crowd in Selma to "get in good trouble, necessary trouble, and redeem the soul of America."[4]

The nation was certainly in need of good trouble in the aftermath of the October 2013 arrest, when immigration reform—like virtually all of the issues that populated Lewis's political agenda—remained stalled in Congress with little hope of a breakthrough. The progressives in the House were in desperate need of reinforcement, but there was little likelihood their precarious situation would improve before the fall 2014 midterm elections. The one ray of hope, which had little bearing on their current dilemma, appeared in the Senate in late October when Cory Booker, a talented African American Rhodes Scholar who had served four terms as mayor of Newark, replaced New Jersey's recently deceased senator Frank Lautenberg. The first Black person to be elected to the Senate since Obama in 2004, Booker, accompanied by his proud mother, chose to begin his term with an early-morning visit to Lewis's office, where he paid his respects to the legendary civil rights leader. After leaving the office for his swearing-in ceremony, Booker described his meeting with Lewis as "emotional and moving." Over the next six years, the two men would develop a close friendship based on a shared belief in social justice and antipoverty initiatives.

Lewis's strong working relationship with Booker was consistent with his commitment to bridging the gap between the House and Senate. He had always been open to consultation with senators, including those with whom he had sharp political and ideological disagreements. As he often said, he could work with anyone, across the aisle or in the other chamber. Georgia's senator Sam Nunn, a moderate conservative who served from 1972 to 1997, was a case in point. While he and Lewis disagreed on a number of important issues—universal health care, school prayer, the death penalty, and gay rights, to name just a few—that did not stop them from collaborating on issues where their positions were aligned: affirmative action, reproductive freedom, immigration, gun control, and nuclear disarmament.

Lewis and Nunn remained friendly through all of the intraparty squabbles over the years, and when the former senator's eldest daughter, Michelle, the

CEO of an Atlanta-based social welfare organization, announced her decision to run against Georgia's conservative senior senator Saxby Chambliss, Lewis was one of the first Democratic leaders to lend a hand—even though one of her opponents in the Democratic primary, former state senator Steen Miles, was African American. Realizing that Michelle Nunn would need strong support from Black voters to have any chance of unseating Chambliss, Lewis not only endorsed her but stood by her side during the annual King birthday celebration in January 2014. Predictably, he received widespread criticism for supporting a white candidate running against a Black rival, but Lewis had brushed aside calls for strict racial solidarity many times during his career, and he was not about to stop now. Reaffirming and remaining true to his belief in interracial cooperation, he did what he could for her throughout the primary campaign, where she ended up with 75 percent of the vote, and during the general election campaign, which she lost by eight points to the ultraconservative Republican David Perdue.[5]

Lewis was disappointed when Nunn fell short in her Senate race, but he was hardly surprised. The conservative headwinds in Georgia, as in many areas of the nation, gained strength throughout the months leading up to the 2014 midterm elections. Especially alarming was the racially based resentment against Obama and his party that showed no sign of letting up as the election approached. This trend was deeply troubling to Lewis and other civil rights advocates. When he and dozens of other movement veterans, including Julian Bond, met with a group of scholars at Austin's Lyndon Johnson Presidential Library in April to commemorate the fiftieth anniversary of the passage of the 1964 Civil Right Act, the mood was bittersweet at best. Four presidents—Jimmy Carter, Bill Clinton, George W. Bush, and Obama—spoke to the gathering during three days of discussion, and Lewis joined Lyndon Johnson's daughter Luci and King's daughter Bernice to deliver a series of readings before Clinton's speech. The dominant themes in Lewis's prepared remarks, and in Clinton's, were the current challenge of protecting voting rights and extending the legacy of the politicians who displayed great courage when they voted for the landmark civil rights bills of the 1960s.

On the final night of the Austin conference, Lewis had the honor of introducing Obama, which gave the Georgia congressman the opportunity—both during the introduction and in a later press conference—to praise the president's recent efforts to foster a national conversation on racial tolerance and equity. Indeed, he couldn't resist encouraging Obama to exercise even more leadership along these lines in the future. "The second election and final election is behind him so he's free," Lewis exclaimed to reporters. "There's something about not having to run again that frees you. He's liberated."[6]

* * *

Liberated or not, Obama was not in an enviable position as the leader of a party facing a brutal off-year election. Factionalism was rampant throughout the party, and even the CBC was rent with conflict and dissension, often between older and younger members. Representative Charles Rangel of New York, a twenty-one-term congressman who had barely survived a 2010 ethics scandal that ended in censure, was at the center of much of the wrangling, and Lewis, as one of his oldest colleagues, found himself in the difficult position of passing judgment on a man he had known and worked with for more than a quarter century. After considerable deliberation, Lewis decided to support Rangel for renomination in 2014, joining two other veteran members of the CBC, Emanuel Cleaver of Missouri and Maxine Waters of California, in a canvass of New York City churches whose predominantly Black congregations were crucial to Rangel's political survival.

For their efforts, the three veterans were summoned to the office of the Reverend Al Sharpton, the leader of the National Action Network, for a tongue-lashing. Having his political ethics challenged was a highly unusual situation for Lewis, who had not received this kind of criticism since his race against Bond in 1986. But he held firm for Rangel, even though he obviously felt conflicted about the congressman's questionable behavior. The Democratic Party and the CBC were already dealing with so much turmoil that it didn't seem wise to add fuel to the fire in the form of Rangel's political corpse.[7]

Whether he liked it or not, Lewis had become part of the old guard in the CBC, but at the age of seventy-four he still displayed the energy and vitality normally associated with a much younger man. As the 2014 campaign progressed, he maintained a blistering pace representing and defending the Obama administration across a wide range of issues. In late June, for example, he spoke out against the same-sex marriage bans that had been imposed in a number of states, and later in the week he decried the Supreme Court's ruling against the contraception coverage mandate in the Affordable Care Act. In August, he applauded Obama for supporting and signing a bill that enhanced the quality of medical care for military veterans. As an advocate of nonviolence, Lewis found it difficult to deal with matters related to war and the military, including policies instituted to counter terrorist activity. Thus, in September, when the Obama administration authorized air strikes in Syria and announced a comprehensive plan to stop the spread of the Islamic extremist movement ISIS, Lewis tried to console himself with the belief that Obama was far less hawkish on military action than his Republican critics.[8]

In the final weeks of the campaign, the Democrats benefited from a declining unemployment rate and a resurgent economy, but this was not enough to stem the Republican tide. Resembling a political tsunami in many areas, the Republican showing on election day gave the party one of its most resounding victories in decades. The Republicans gained 13 seats in the House, where they would now enjoy their largest majority, 247–188, since 1931; and in the Senate they gained 9 seats and control of the chamber, 54–46. Senate majority leader Harry Reid, whom Lewis regarded as a loyal friend and ally, would be replaced by Senator Mitch McConnell of Kentucky, a cynical and untrustworthy man in Lewis's estimation. To make matters worse, when the South elected Tim Scott as its first Black senator since Reconstruction, the new senator from South Carolina was, ironically, a right-wing Republican with no affinity for the social justice agenda of the CBC. For Lewis, Scott's elevation to the Senate was reminiscent of the tragedy of Clarence Thomas's appointment to the Supreme Court in 1991.[9]

During the month following the election, as Lewis and the Democrats braced themselves for the seating of a Congress completely controlled by conservative Republicans, the root causes of the racial and political polarization that had animated and benefited the Republican Party were revealed in a startling way. On November 24, the failure of a Ferguson, Missouri, grand jury to indict Darren Wilson, a white police officer who had shot and killed an unarmed eighteen-year-old Black man, Michael Brown, on August 9, triggered a series of mass protests in Ferguson and several other cities. The shooting took place in front of numerous witnesses, who insisted Wilson's misconduct was tantamount to murder. Incidents of this kind had troubled Lewis for years, and he understood why the Black community in Ferguson was determined to seek justice. But he deplored the rioting and looting that accompanied the Ferguson protests.

Violence was never the answer, in Lewis's view, and he was relieved when the riots subsided. Eventually the Ferguson protests merged with the Black Lives Matter (BLM) movement, a nonviolent struggle begun a year earlier after the shocking acquittal of George Zimmerman, a vigilante who shot and killed Trayvon Martin as the seventeen-year-old Black student walked through a virtually all-white neighborhood in Sanford, Florida. By 2015, BLM had spread from Florida to Missouri and on to other parts of the nation, enlisting hundreds of thousands of outraged citizens, Black and white. Many BLM activists looked to civil rights veterans for guidance, and in March 2015, during the fiftieth anniversary of the Selma-to-Montgomery march, several dozen met with Lewis and Bernard LaFayette, who offered sage advice on nonviolent tactics and how to turn a series of protests into a sustainable movement. Discipline, patience, and rigorous adherence to the principles of nonviolence were the keys to success, the two former roommates counseled.

To Lewis's delight, BLM eventually became a major force in American society and politics. But as with past struggles against racial discrimination, miscarriages of justice—especially where young Black men were concerned—proved to be systemic and intractable. In early December 2014, a month after the Ferguson upheaval, a similar incident occurred on New York's Staten Island, where a grand jury refused to indict Daniel Pantaleo, a white police officer who had used an illegal chokehold to suffocate a forty-three-year-old Black man named Eric Garner. As he struggled to remain conscious, Garner begged Pantaleo to loosen the hold on his neck, pleading, "I can't breathe." The officer ignored him, however, and continued to bear down on the helpless man. Garner did not survive, but the haunting phrase "I can't breathe" soon became a rallying cry across the nation among citizens demanding action against police brutality.

Lewis marched in support of Garner's right to be treated with respect, just as he had earlier in support of Michael Brown. While the codified legal structure of Jim Crow "justice" was largely gone, the bitter legacy of racially prejudicial enforcement of the law remained a major problem for African Americans. Violence, it seemed, was embedded in the marrow of American life, and he and other nonviolent crusaders had not had much success in rooting it out. If Lewis had any doubts about this, his worst fears were confirmed five days after the grand jury's refusal to indict Pantaleo by the release of a five-hundred-page Senate report detailing the CIA's persistent use of torture in terrorist interrogations. Perhaps worst of all was the cavalier reaction to the report among many Republicans, who dismissed the revelations as a political stunt concocted by Democrats reeling from their recent defeat at the polls.[10]

As 2014 drew to a close, Lewis was increasingly discouraged by what he saw around him, finding few sources of consolation other than the growing support for BLM and the Obama administration's long-overdue resumption of normal diplomatic relations with Cuba. Lewis was no fan of the Castro regime, which routinely violated the civil liberties of its citizens, but he was pleased by the diplomatic normalization—and even more by the prospect of lifting the economic sanctions that had placed a heavy burden on the Cuban people, especially those mired in poverty. In his view, it was difficult to justify sanctions when the most troubling events in Cuba were taking place not in Havana but rather at the other end of the island at the American detention camp in Guantánamo Bay, where hundreds of Islamic prisoners had been languishing for years in violation of the Geneva Convention and the U.S. Constitution.

Opened in September 2001 in the aftermath of the 9/11 attacks, Guantánamo represented a serious breach of human rights, as defined by Amnesty International, and, according to many legal scholars, a clear violation of the Due Process Clause of the Fourteenth Amendment. Almost immediately after assuming office in 2009, President Obama signed an executive order banning the use of torture at Guantánamo and vowed to close the camp within a year. Obama's plan, which Lewis strongly supported, involved transferring most of the Guantánamo detainees to various federal facilities in the United States and repatriating others to their home countries. But the plan fell apart when he encountered considerable pushback from many Republican and some Democratic lawmakers, who accused him of endangering American citizens and being soft on terrorism. Despite the best efforts of the House and Senate's most vocal human rights advocates, including Lewis, Congress passed several measures between 2009 and 2012 that essentially blocked the proposed transfer and closure of the camp.

The Guantánamo detention center and the controversy surrounding it persisted into Obama's second term as a continuing source of embarrassment and concern for Lewis. In his January 2015 State of the Union address, Obama insisted that Guantánamo "is not who we are." But a year later the camp still had more than ninety prisoners, dozens of whom had never been charged with a crime. By the time Obama left office in January 2017, the number of detainees was down to forty-one, but the prospects for closure soon darkened under the policies of the Trump administration. The failure to close the camp was a great disappointment for Lewis, who now viewed human rights across the globe as an issue rivaling global warming and poverty in importance. As always, he was attentive to the pressing needs of both body and soul—and frustrated by the lack of moral progress in a world that fell far short of his cherished Beloved Community ideal.[11]

*　*　*

Lewis still held out hope that a moral transformation of the American people was possible. But he feared the state of the republic would get worse before it got better. This fear proved justified as the level of his frustration rose steadily during the final two years of Obama's presidency. As Lewis looked on in horror, the realities of American politics grew even more toxic with the escalation of a culture war pitting predominantly rural evangelical white Christians against the diverse multicultural polyglot of the nation's cities.

The cultural divide had a lot to do with race and the protection of white privilege in the face of accelerating demographic change. Many conservative white citizens—worried they would soon be buried beneath an avalanche of insurgent brown and Black bodies—were determined to resist this unwanted transformation at all costs. There was also increasingly bitter conflict over issues only tangentially related to race and ethnicity: abortion, gay rights, feminism, reproductive freedom, free speech, pornography, political correctness, and civil liberties, just to name a few. In the press and in political discourse, these disagreements were often reduced to shorthand references to a simple contest between family values and secular humanism.

But however it was represented, this polarization moved the nation farther and farther away from any sense of common purpose or community, beloved or otherwise.

Lewis placed much of the blame at the feet of Republican demagogues eager to arouse their followers with conspiratorial visions of disloyal, unpatriotic liberals and radicals affiliated with the Democratic Party. In the Republican playbook, political opponents had become enemies, and the goal now went beyond merely defeating them; their legitimacy was no longer a given, and no political rhetoric was considered too coarse or too mean-spirited if it brought about the destruction of the enemy. President Obama was the primary target of this abusive style of politics, as the "birther" movement and other attacks on his legitimacy as a national leader demonstrated. For white Americans who felt dispossessed, an almost unimaginable event— the election of a Black president—had unleashed a strain of open racial resentment that previously had been limited to fringe groups such as the Ku Klux Klan and the American Nazi Party. In the American mainstream, overt expressions of racism had become increasingly rare in recent decades. But now racial epithets that had been a vital part of Jim Crow culture were once again acceptable in certain circles, including a disturbingly large cross section of Republican voters.[12]

Lewis was disheartened by all of this coarsening of civic culture. But there were moments in 2015, the seventh year of Obama's presidency, when he detected signs that the spirit of the movement that had meant so much to him and the nation was still alive. In early March he hosted the fiftieth anniversary celebration of the Selma-to-Montgomery march. Attracting more than a hundred thousand people, including President Obama and hundreds of movement veterans, the celebration far exceeded Lewis's expectations. The ceremonial march across the Edmund Pettus Bridge brought back vivid memories of the mass mobilization of the 1960s, and Lewis was thrilled by a series of events designed to highlight the courage and contributions of the "foot soldiers" of the Selma movement. A Hollywood film released in December 2014 with the simple title *Selma* had downplayed the role of ordinary citizens in the city's voting rights struggle, so Lewis and many veteran activists welcomed a proper acknowledgment of the Selma foot soldiers' place in history.[13]

Five weeks later, on April 12, Lewis received another boost to his spirits when Hillary Clinton became the first Democrat to enter the race for the 2016 presidential nomination. His relationship with her had been a bit awkward since his shift of support to Obama during the 2008 race, but he had worked closely with her on several issues during her years as secretary of state, and he was eager to get involved in her campaign. The thought that the nation might actually elect a woman president stirred his soul and renewed his faith in American politics. From the outset, Clinton was the clear frontrunner for the nomination, and he fully expected her to succeed Obama as president. Even so, he knew she would need strong support from Black voters to ensure her victory, and he was willing to do whatever he could to bring out that vote. His strong endorsement, he hoped, would solidify her popularity in Black communities and eventually help her to carry on Obama's efforts on behalf of civil rights and racial justice. It soon became clear that she would also need all the help she could get to counter Republican efforts to demonize her as a conniving and corrupt figure. Unfortunately, this anti-Hillary barrage would prove to be far more malevolent and influential than he could imagine in the early stages of the campaign.

During the spring and summer of 2015, Lewis also found encouragement in Obama's successful effort to smooth relations with long-standing enemies such as Iran and Cuba. In the case of Iran, the United States signed a treaty designed to control the development and proliferation of nuclear weapons; and with respect to Cuba, the normalization of diplomatic relations proceeded with the removal of Cuba from the list of State Sponsors of Terrorism in April and the reopening of the U.S. embassy in Havana in July.[14]

On the domestic front, Lewis welcomed the introduction of the Voting Rights Advancement Bill, H.R. 2867, in late June. Initially sponsored by Terri Sewell, a Black Princeton graduate from Selma who was serving her third term in the House, the bill promised to restore the preclearance provision of the Voting Rights Act gutted by the *Shelby* decision two years earlier. H.R. 2867 eventually gained 179 cosponsors, including Lewis, in the House, but that did not deter Republican leaders from making sure it died in committee. Sewell would reintroduce the bill two years later with the same result.

Lewis was gratified, however, by two surprising rulings by the Supreme Court in June, one to uphold the constitutionality of the Affordable Care

Act and a second to legalize same-sex marriages. He regarded both issues—access to affordable health care and ending discrimination on the basis of sexual preference—as critically important to the promotion of fairness and equity in American life. He had long been one of Congress's most vocal advocates of universal health care, and his recent statements on behalf of same-sex marriage—which some of his devoutly religious friends found unsettling—had marked him as a forthright leader on that issue as well. Both positions, in his view, were part of a broad commitment to human rights and common decency.[15]

Much of the national and international news that summer was discouraging—right-wing extremists announcing their candidacies for the Republican presidential nomination, courts facilitating mass deportation of millions of undocumented immigrants, the Supreme Court striking down important parts of the Clean Air Act—but Lewis found some solace in even the worst developments. In mid-June, the epidemics of gun violence and racial hysteria came together in frightening fashion in Charleston, South Carolina, when Dylann Roof, a twenty-one-year-old white neo-Nazi, shot and killed nine parishioners, including the Reverend Clementa Pinckney, during a prayer meeting at the historic Emanuel AME Church.

This senseless shooting by a white gunman wearing a black jacket emblazoned with miniature flags from apartheid-era South Africa and Rhodesia triggered a wave of revulsion across the nation, sparking widespread recognition that escalating racial and extremist rhetoric can have tragic consequences. During the shooting rampage, Roof reportedly cried out, "You are raping our women and taking over our country!" It soon became clear he had strong ties to white supremacist groups such as the Missouri-based Council of Conservative Citizens, which in turn had close ties to several powerful conservative Republican politicians—including two presidential hopefuls, Senators Ted Cruz of Texas and Rand Paul of Kentucky. That Roof was also an ardent neo-Confederate further politicized the incident, though most Republican leaders joined their Democratic colleagues in roundly condemning Roof's assault, and several attended the funerals held the week after the shooting.

At Reverend Pinckney's funeral, President Obama delivered a stirring eulogy before a crowd of more than six thousand and a worldwide television audience, closing with a melodic refrain from the hymn "Amazing Grace." During his speech, the president tried to put Roof's assault on Emanuel AME in historical context. "It was an act," he reminded his listeners, "that drew on a long history of bombs and arson and shots fired at churches, not random, but as a means of control, a way to terrorize and oppress, an act that he imagined would incite fear and recrimination, violence and suspicion, an act that he presumed would deepen divisions that trace back to our nation's original sin." To the consternation of many conservative Republicans, Obama also pointed out that stricter gun control and the elimination of the painful vestiges of the Confederate defense of slavery and white supremacy—the Confederate battle flags and monuments that punctuated the Southern landscape—might have prevented the tragedy at Emanuel. "Removing the flag from this state's Capitol would not be an act of political correctness," he insisted. "It would not be an insult to the valor of Confederate soldiers. It would simply be an acknowledgment that the cause for which they fought—the cause of slavery—was wrong. The imposition of Jim Crow after the Civil War, the resistance to civil rights for all people, was wrong."[16]

Lewis had waited a long time to hear words like this from an American president; not even John Kennedy or Lyndon Johnson—or even Bill Clinton—had put the American racial dilemma in such bold and truth-telling words. Lewis broke down and wept, thankful that he had lived to see this day. But the best was yet to come. In the ensuing weeks, the nation witnessed the first widespread effort to rid itself of Confederate iconography. The courthouses and state capitols and public parks dotted with flags and monuments commemorating and honoring individuals who took up arms against the United States had long been subject to criticism, but now they became targets for reform. Within days of the Emanuel murders, Nikki Haley, the Republican governor of South Carolina, shocked many of her conservative constituents by calling for the removal of the Confederate battle flag flying on the grounds of the state capitol in Columbia. A week later, a thirty-year-old Black woman named Bree Newsome climbed up a thirty-foot flagpole outside the South Carolina capitol, ignored the commands of the capitol police, unhooked the flag, and dropped it triumphantly to the ground.

Promptly arrested, she became an inspiration to anti-Confederate activists across the region.

Some movement veterans, most notably Andrew Young, dismissed the Confederate flag controversy as too symbolic to merit sustained attention, but Lewis did not agree. He sensed the battle to remove Confederate symbols from public land could become a wedge issue that would attract younger activists to the broader civil rights struggle. As was often the case, his instincts proved reliable, and over the next five years the flow of events surrounding the removal of rebel flags—and eventually monuments to Confederate politicians and brigadiers—confirmed his hunch. The ongoing Confederate controversy became an important element of the culture war being waged between Democrats and Republicans, joining abortion, gun control, and same-sex marriage as a key issue marking the divide. It also became a political factor early in the 2016 presidential race after Hillary Clinton weighed in on the importance of removing the Confederate flag at the South Carolina capitol. Calling the flag "a symbol of our nation's racist past," she insisted, "It shouldn't fly there. It shouldn't fly anywhere." A few Republicans—including Governor Haley, who described the flag as "a deeply offensive symbol of a brutally oppressive past"—agreed with Clinton, but most of the party's presidential hopefuls lined up on the conservative side of the controversy.

By early July, the issue was being debated in Congress, and Lewis wasted no time in getting involved in the fray. Along with his close friend Representative James Clyburn of South Carolina, he led the way during a heated partisan discussion of a legislative amendment that prohibited the display of Confederate flags in national cemeteries. "There's not any room on federal property for the display of the Confederate battle flag," Lewis declared. "It represents the dark past as a symbol of separation. A symbol of division, a symbol of hate." When asked by reporters why he was so passionate about this issue, he explained that several of the Alabama policemen who had attacked him on the Edmund Pettus Bridge in 1965 had a Confederate flag painted on their helmets. He knew what the flag meant to many diehard Southern patriots, and he wanted it removed from any position of honor. As the minority party, the Democrats failed in their effort to ban the flag from the nation's more than 130 national cemeteries, but they were able to achieve a compromise in which displays of the flag were limited to Memorial Day and, in states like Georgia, Confederate Memorial Day.[17]

* * *

Legislative victories of any kind were an increasingly rare commodity during the final eighteen months of the Obama era. Most of the political activity and excitement centered on the presidential race and the coming national election. On the Democratic side, Hillary Clinton strengthened her position as the front-runner, despite a strong challenge from Bernie Sanders, an outspoken progressive senator from Vermont. But in the Republican Party the presidential race was a free-for-all among seventeen candidates, all of whom claimed to be the best choice as the conservative foil for Clinton. One of the Republican hopefuls, Ben Carson, a prominent neurosurgeon affiliated with Johns Hopkins Hospital in Baltimore, was Black, but to Lewis's dismay, he was cut from the same right-wing mold as Clarence Thomas and Tim Scott. As usual, the chance for Black Americans to elect a champion who would advance the cause of civil rights rested with the Democratic Party. The trajectory of the Republicans was trending sharply to the right, led by the unorthodox candidacy of Donald Trump, who had gained fame as a playboy and real estate mogul, and most recently as a reality TV star.

A New Yorker with a palatial mansion in Palm Beach, Florida, Trump seemed an unlikely partisan of Confederate heritage. But early on he took a strong stand against flag removal. In the past, he had generally avoided overt expressions of racial prejudice, even though he and his father had benefited from discriminatory housing practices in several of their New York properties. The one exception was his role in propagating the birther movement, an effort that began with a speech at the 2011 Conservative Political Action Conference, where he first announced that he was considering running for president. Soon he began appearing on conservative talk shows questioning Obama's claim that he was born in Hawaii and demanding to see his birth certificate. This attack on Obama's legitimacy as a "real" American citizen continued for five years, eventually taking the form of implicitly racist appeals to white nationalism. By 2015 Trump's style of right-wing populism was drawing support from a number of extremist groups, some of which he welcomed into the Republican fold.

All of this alarmed Lewis and other civil rights advocates, especially after Trump combined his thinly veiled white nationalist rhetoric with blatantly xenophobic anti-Muslim statements. In December 2015, following a terrorist shooting in San Bernardino, California, involving two Muslim immigrants, Trump called for an all-out ban on Muslim immigration to the United States. Lewis was among the many political leaders, including some Republicans, who immediately pushed back against Trump's ethnic intolerance. But the anti-Muslim ban was just the beginning of a long slide into increasingly wild and dangerous demagoguery on matters of race, ethnicity, and national identity. Trump's racialized, no-holds-barred approach to politics—which would eventually become known as "Trumpism"—reminded Lewis of the demagogic political tradition that had prevailed in the Jim Crow South. Before Trump's emergence as a popular Republican, Lewis thought this tradition had passed into history with the decline of the pyrotechnic champions of the Southern way of life—openly white supremacist figures such as Orval Faubus, Lester Maddox, and George Wallace. But he was mistaken. There were dark days ahead.[18]

As the 2016 presidential race heated up during the final months before the national political conventions, Lewis and other progressive Democrats tried to focus on the pressing issues at hand—economic recovery, immigrants' rights, gun control, bringing the war in Afghanistan to a close, and addressing the vestiges of racism at home and human rights violations abroad. For Lewis, stemming the rising tide of gun violence had become one of his top priorities, especially after a horrifying mass shooting on June 12 at Pulse, an Orlando nightclub patronized largely by gay men and women. The massacre—perpetrated by Omar Mateen, a twenty-nine-year-old American-born Afghan man wielding a semiautomatic rifle and a semiautomatic pistol—left forty-nine dead and fifty-three wounded, making it one of the deadliest mass shootings in American history.

Ten days after the shooting, Lewis launched a two-day-long sit-in to protest Republican congressional leaders' refusal to allow a stringent gun control bill to come before the full House for a vote. Within minutes, he was joined by dozens of other frustrated congressional advocates of gun control, and by the end of the first day there were 170 representatives refusing to leave the House chamber. This nonviolent ruckus infuriated the Republicans, who refused to relent on the gun control issue. But Lewis was not done. When Congress reconvened after the July 4 holiday, he told his colleagues, "We must come back here . . . more determined than ever before. The fight is not over. . . . We're going to push, to pull, to stand up, and if necessary, to sit down. So don't give up and don't give in. Keep the faith, and keep your eyes on the prize." Later in the day, he tweeted more words of encouragement: "We got in trouble. Good trouble. Necessary trouble. By sitting in, we were really standing up." The effort produced no arrests and no resolution of the problem. But Lewis derived some solace from knowing that, for at least a few hours, he had brought the spirit of the movement to Capitol Hill.[19]

Republican dominance and obstructionism would continue to frustrate Lewis throughout the remainder of Obama's second term and beyond. Even with Obama in the White House, the progressive agenda was essentially stalled, and the best Lewis and his political allies could do was to try to slow down the Republicans' momentum. The likelihood that the Democrats would regain control of either house of Congress in the coming election was slim, so their primary focus was on retaining control of the White House and the executive branch, where their prospects were much better. After a bruising contest against Senator Bernie Sanders, Hillary Clinton clinched the Democratic nomination in June, and throughout the summer and fall she enjoyed a comfortable lead in the polls over her Republican opponent, Donald Trump.

At the Democratic National Convention held in Philadelphia in late July, Clinton asked Lewis to give one of the nominating speeches, and he responded with a passionate tribute to her and their party. Welcomed with wild cheering and thunderous applause, he began with a powerful warning: "My beloved Democrats, there are forces in America that want to take us backward, they want to undo fifty years of progress this nation has made under Democratic leadership. We have come too far, we have made too much progress, and we are not going back, we are going forward! That is why we all must go to the polls in November and vote like we've never, ever voted before." Using the same rolling cadence and resonant voice that had captivated movement meetings throughout his career as a civil rights leader, he continued, "Now, eight years ago, our party, the Democratic Party, nominated and elected the first person of color to ever serve in the White House, not just for one term, but two terms. Tonight, on this night, we will shatter that glass ceiling again. We are the party of tomorrow, and we will build a true democracy in America."

After a brief pause to let the audience take in this image of a better future, Lewis went on to explain why he was so excited about Clinton's likely elevation to the presidency: "Now, I must tell you, I have known Hillary Clinton for many years. She is one of the most qualified candidates to ever run for President. She is a leader, sometimes standing against the wind, to break down barriers that divide us. . . . She could have done anything with her life, but she decided long ago that she didn't want just to do well. She wanted to do good. So she has dedicated her life to public service and building a better America for all our people where no one would be left out or left behind. . . . She will fight for us all, with her heart, her soul, and her mind."[20]

Lewis emerged from the convention with renewed hope for a Democratic victory in November, and after Trump received the Republican nomination in late August, he felt sure that, regardless of what happened in the House and Senate races, Hillary Clinton would be the next president. As the presidential race entered its final two months, he was brimming with optimism, and not just on the political front. On September 24, six weeks before the election, he experienced one of the most satisfying days of his congressional career. On the National Mall, just east of the Washington Monument, the Smithsonian's National Museum of African American History and Culture opened its doors for the first time. It had taken nearly thirty years to bring the museum project that Lewis had championed since 1987 to fruition, but now it was a reality that exceeded his wildest expectations: arguably the most beautiful building on the Mall, a striking three-tiered, metal-encased structure designed by the Tanzanian architect David Adjaye and built at a cost of $540 million.

With an extraordinary range of exhibits spanning four centuries of African American history and thirty-five hundred historical artifacts on display—including Nat Turner's Bible, Emmett Till's coffin, and a Tuskegee Airmen biplane—the museum was, in the words of President Obama's poetic remarks at the dedication ceremony, an institution dedicated to telling the African American story with all of its "suffering and delight," a story "of fear, but also of hope, of wandering in the wilderness, and then seeing, out on the horizon, a glimmer of the Promised Land." The president thanked Lewis, who was sitting nearby, for his perseverance and vision—for leading the way once again, just as he had done at the Edmund Pettus Bridge a half century earlier.[21]

Unfortunately for Lewis and other civil rights advocates, the museum opening proved to be the high point of the final weeks leading up to the election. Beginning in late August, Clinton's standing in the polls began to slip, and by the last week in October, her lead narrowed to roughly 2 to 4 percent, depending on the poll. Ten days before the election, her prospects appeared to weaken further when FBI director James Comey released an ill-advised statement informing Congress that the bureau was still investigating Clinton's alleged mishandling of emails and classified documents during her tenure as secretary of state. Lewis and other Democratic leaders immediately criticized Comey's violation of a long-standing policy prohibiting the FBI from influencing national elections, but there was no way to stop the bleeding from this "October surprise."

On election day Lewis and virtually every other political observer was still confident that Clinton would win, but it was not to be. In one of the most shocking upsets in American political history, Trump won the Electoral College, 304 to 227, despite losing the popular vote by nearly three million votes. The margin of victory was razor thin in Michigan, Wisconsin, and Pennsylvania, the three normally "blue" states that put Trump over the top. But what had been almost unimaginable earlier in the year—the election of a president who had never before held public office—had happened, and the expected election of the nation's first female president had not.[22]

The Republicans also maintained control of both the Senate and the House, though by a somewhat narrower margin than in the previous Congress. Trump, it appeared, would have the benefit of Republican dominance of all three branches of government and would thus have a good chance of advancing his conservative agenda. Lewis and the Democrats wondered exactly how this sudden reversal of fortune had come about and tried to identify the factors that had led to their defeat. Missteps by Clinton, who had been overconfident about her ability to carry parts of the Midwest, were clearly part of the story, along with race-based resentment of the incumbent president, but another probable factor that drew a lot of attention in the weeks following the election was Russian interference. On December 9, a CIA report to Congress detailed Russia's covert and systematic attempt to throw the election to Trump. Rumors of this interference had been rife for months, and there was considerable circumstantial evidence that high-level figures in the Trump campaign had colluded with Russian operatives in a sustained attempt to discredit and demonize Clinton.

Lewis, who as a member of Congress was privy to much of this information on nefarious Russian involvement in the election, was outraged. On December 29, President Obama, in one of his final acts before leaving office, imposed sanctions against the leadership of the Russian intelligence agency GRU and expelled thirty-five "diplomatic" Russian operatives from American soil. But beyond this largely symbolic response, there wasn't much anyone could do to remedy the situation. During the next four years, Russia's autocratic premier, Vladimir Putin, would have a kindred spirit in the White House, a reckless leader buoyed by a cult of personality and unencumbered by loyalty to long-standing American traditions of limited executive power.[23]

CHAPTER 19

————

Perilous Times

Most democratic leaders were shell shocked after Donald Trump's unexpected triumph in 2016, and John Lewis was no exception. Yet he had enough presence of mind to realize he had to do something to rouse his party and rekindle the fires of resistance. Accordingly, he decided to begin the Trump era with a dramatic gesture. On Martin Luther King Jr.'s birthday, January 15, five days before Trump's inauguration, he announced on the *Meet the Press* television program that he planned to boycott the coming presidential ceremony. "I believe in forgiveness, I believe in trying to work with people," he told the reporters, "but it is going to be hard, it is going to be very difficult. I don't see this President-elect as a legitimate President. I think the Russians participated in having this man get elected, and they have destroyed the candidacy of Hillary Clinton. I don't plan to attend the inauguration."

Lewis's words brought a blistering response from Trump, who tweeted a series of insults calling the Georgia congressman a man of "all talk, talk, talk, no action or results," who would be better off spending his time trying to fix his "crime infested district." Over the next few days, the conflict between the two men escalated as twenty-three other Democratic members of Congress joined the inaugural boycott and as Trump canceled a planned visit to the new National Museum of African American History and Culture.

By inauguration day a number of additional Democratic members of Congress had joined the boycott, as the president-elect continued to lash out at Lewis. House Minority Leader Nancy Pelosi, though present at the inauguration, soon followed Lewis's lead in publicly questioning the legitimacy of Trump's presidency. Legitimate or not, Trump wasted no time in aiming a wrecking ball at many of the policies and reforms enacted by the Obama administration. Issuing a series of executive orders designed to "make America great again," he ordered the Department of Homeland Security to build a massive wall on the Mexican-American border even if Congress refused to fund it; he banned refugees from seven predominantly Muslim nations from entering the United States; and he repealed the stringent clean air, clean water, and other environmental regulations put in place by Barack Obama's executive orders, reneging on the nation's commitment to abide by the 2015 Paris Climate Accords.

As Lewis and the Democrats looked on in horror, Trump also took several actions to inhibit investigations of Russian electoral interference on his behalf, including trying to circumvent probes of the mounting evidence of collusion between the Russian government and Trump campaign aides. In early May, he even fired FBI director James Comey in an apparent effort to truncate the bureau's investigation of this alleged collusion. A week later, when the Justice Department named Robert Mueller, a former FBI director, as a special counsel charged with investigating both the Russian interference and the collusion, Trump made only a minimal effort to cooperate. He became even more uncooperative in June after it became clear that Mueller was also looking into the administration's alleged obstruction of justice.[1]

During his first summer in office, Donald Trump was busy pushing Congress to repeal the Affordable Care Act ("Obamacare" in the Republican lexicon), to pass a budget that included funding for his great wall on the Mexican border, and to refrain from placing proposed sanctions on Vladimir Putin's Russian regime. All of this troubled Lewis, who helped lead the Democratic opposition in the House. But he became even more alarmed in August when an ugly incident in Charlottesville, Virginia, revealed that Trump's casual racism was rooted in an emerging political alliance with white nationalists.[2]

A Unite the Right rally—a gathering of so-called alt-right groups, including neo-Nazis, Klansmen, and other militant white nationalists—convened in Charlottesville to demonstrate their unity and power by preventing the removal of a statue of Robert E. Lee from a city park. Chanting racist and anti-Semitic slogans and carrying Confederate and Nazi flags, they clashed with liberal counterdemonstrators, leaving one woman dead and more than thirty others injured. When asked to comment on the Charlottesville riot, Trump initially issued a statement condemning "hatred, bigotry, and violence," but in subsequent statements he refused to disassociate himself from the white nationalists' grievances, implying a moral equivalency between the white supremacist marchers and those who protested against them. His comment that there were "very fine people on both sides" was roundly condemned in the mainstream media, but he steadfastly refused to alter his position.[3]

For Lewis and many others, the Charlottesville controversy was both a turning point and a wake-up call. A man whom they had judged to be an overbearing and unpleasant amateur during the 2016 presidential campaign had become a full-fledged monster. His depredations were often gratuitous, generally delivered in the form of incessant social media tweets, as in September when he interjected himself into a controversy involving professional athletes kneeling during the playing of the National Anthem in protest against police brutality against young African Americans. The dissenting athletes, he insisted, should be fired on the spot and shunned by all patriotic Americans. This aggressive defense of white America worsened later in the year when his apparent acceptance of violent white nationalists as legitimate political actors and potential members of the Republican coalition became part of a broader defense of racial and class privilege. In December, he rammed through the Tax Cuts and Jobs Act, which provided unprecedented tax relief and benefits for the wealthiest of American citizens. Ordinary Americans, especially the poor, were left to fend for themselves, and the nationwide maldistribution of wealth became more extreme than ever.[4]

*   *   *

To Lewis, Trump's regressive policies, as bad as they were, did not represent the heart of the problem. Even more disturbing was his utter lack of decorum and disregard for the moral and ethical precepts of American democracy. His professed admiration for authoritarian regimes and leaders, especially his unstinting praise for Putin, marked him as an autocrat who operated outside the boundaries of traditional American politics. Many critics charged that

Trump acted more like a mob boss than a president who respected the rule of law and the constitutional separation of powers. Lewis found this characterization to be increasingly convincing, as Trump expressed his open contempt for Democratic opponents, the press, liberal judges, Muslims, immigrants, feminists, or anyone else who got in his way. In Washington, but particularly out on the political stump, he relied on a demagogic and unrestrained style of rhetoric to energize his core supporters, his "base." This technique reminded Lewis of the no-holds-barred politics of the factional leaders who had once presided over the Jim Crow South with a litany of self-serving invective and folk wisdom dedicated to the preservation of white supremacy and the "Southern way of life." Now this cynical approach to leadership was being played out on a national scale.[5]

In January 2018, the similarity between Trump and the Southern demagogues became even more obvious when, during a bipartisan meeting of senators at the White House, the president casually referred to Haiti and several African nations as "shithole countries." Why would the United States want any immigrants from these countries? he asked. Why can't we have more immigrants from countries like Norway? United Nations human rights officials immediately condemned Trump's remarks as "shocking and shameful" and "racist," but the president refused to apologize for his statement and even doubled down in a series of tweets. When the House considered a resolution to condemn the tweets, Lewis was one of Trump's most forceful critics. The president's language was blatantly "racist," he stated on the House floor, insisting, "I know racism when I see it. I know racism when I feel it. And at the highest level of our government, there's no room for racism."[6]

This was not the last time that Lewis would speak out against Trump's xenophobia-tinged racism; in July 2019 he roundly condemned the president's insulting attack on Somalia-born Ilhan Omar and three other young Democratic congresswomen of color, who, he suggested, should "go back" to their home countries. As Lewis pointed out, two of the four congresswomen had actually been born in the United States.[7]

The most troubling aspect of Trumpism for Lewis was not Trump's personal failings, nor even his racism, but rather his toxic conquest of the Republican Party. During the first year of Trump's presidency, Lewis watched his Republican colleagues—men and women with whom he had worked for years, rarely in full agreement but always with courtesy and respect—embrace a cult of personality, jettison their personal and political principles, and accede to increasingly outrageous demands for loyalty and obedience. Indeed, as he witnessed the Republican Party's complicity in Trump's abandonment of common decency and the traditional norms and responsibilities of governance, he had the sinking feeling that American democracy itself was slipping away. In this context, his earlier hope that the Republicans—and all Americans—would eventually come to embrace his belief in liberty and justice for all seemed naïve, leaving him with the scaled-down aspiration of simply restoring the equilibrium of the flawed American political system.

Lewis had always reserved the right to criticize his own party and to point out the deficiencies of national administrations, Democratic and Republican alike. Part of his rationale for making "good trouble" was to bring the nation closer to the realization of its professed ideals. He was proud that he had participated in the renewal of democratic promise during the Clinton and Obama eras, and he had no regrets about making the transition from protest to politics. The contrast between the Democratic Party of the early twentieth century and the modern party of the post–civil rights era was dramatic and encouraging. He only wished that the Republicans had kept pace with this transformation.

The five Republican presidents elected since 1968 were, in Lewis's view, malevolent figures who promoted partisan gain at the expense of the national interest. In this sense, Trump was simply the worst of a bad lot. Lewis believed Richard Nixon had wasted his talents by surrendering to a feverish need to vanquish and punish his political enemies. He also had little respect for Ronald Reagan, whom he blamed for ushering in an era of greed and regressive policies, destroying the social safety net and immiserating the poorest of Americans in the process. To Lewis, the two Bush presidencies were not much better, though he held the father in higher regard than the son. Both father and son pandered to the reactionary views of the National Rifle Association and evangelical Christians associated with the religious Right, squandering precious resources on hawkish military adventures in the Middle East—resources desperately needed for domestic reform. For half a century the trajectory of the party had been to the hard right, pushed by a debilitating obsession with a culture war that fixated on issues such as abortion and the defense of "family values." Issues such as civil and human rights, and the problems of the poor and other marginalized Americans, had taken a back seat as the party focused on the acquisition of political power and the maintenance of a status quo sustaining white privilege and corporate dominance.

The primary difference between Trump and his Republican predecessors, Lewis came to believe, was that the new president had no loyalty to anyone or anything but himself. At the national level, there was no precedent for this political expression of extreme megalomania, and one had to look abroad or to the past for an equivalent figure. Trump's support among white nationalists and other Far Right populists had led to frequent comparisons with the totalitarian dictators of the early and mid-twentieth century—strongmen such as Hitler, Mussolini, and Stalin. But Lewis, like most observers, wasn't sure that Trump should be categorized as a fascist. During the struggles of the 1960s and 1970s, Lewis had never relished casual use of the term "fascist" as a means of identifying political enemies on the right. Even if it seemed justified in particular instances, labeling someone with such a demonic word seemed to fly in the face of the spirit of reconciliation and forgiveness that drove Lewis's moral calculus. Even Trump, he reasoned, might someday be rescued from the dark side.[8]

Unfortunately, the arc of Trump's presidency and the ongoing consolidation of his power suggested the situation would get worse before it got better. So far the nation had experienced only one year of Trump's four-year term; but who knew what horrors lay ahead? In April 2018, Lewis and the nation got an inkling of what was to come when Trump's "zero-tolerance" policy toward Hispanic refugees and migrants on the Mexican border triggered a major humanitarian crisis. For six weeks, until a massive public outcry forced a change in policy, the separation of thousands of migrant children from their parents—and the children's subsequent placement in makeshift housing resembling dog cages—drew some of the sharpest criticism of the Trump administration to date.

Virtually every major human rights group in the world condemned the administration's coldhearted treatment of the children, and one historian, Andrew Delbanco, writing in the *New York Times*, described the controversy as "the struggle for our soul." "To my ears," Delbanco wrote, "it all sounds eerily familiar. This is not the first time America has been torn apart over how to respond to people of color desperate to escape inhuman conditions. . . . I'm thinking, of course, of African-Americans who were regarded for much of American history not as human beings but as a species of animate property no different from cattle and sheep." For Delbanco, as for Lewis, it was proof that the civil rights movement of the 1950s and 1960s that had "tried to dismantle the legacy of slavery" had given way to "the age of Trump," when "rights can also be constricted and rescinded." "The question of who is considered fully human," he concluded, "has returned with a vengeance."[9]

This unexpected moral backsliding was profoundly troubling to Lewis, who had hoped the civil rights victories of his youth had permanently redirected the nation toward greater freedom and tolerance. Even so, he wasn't about to surrender to despair. Unlike many younger activists, he could remember the low points of the late 1960s when the ravages of reactionary politics rivaled those of the Trump era. His memories of 1968, the darkest time of all, were still vivid in 2018, in part because he was called on to participate in a series of events and films marking the fiftieth anniversary of the assassinations of Martin Luther King and Robert Kennedy. In late March, he appeared in a nationally broadcast documentary titled *Hope and Fury: MLK, the Movement and the Media*, and a week later, on the actual anniversary of King's death in Memphis, he was featured in *I Am MLK Jr.*, where he reflected on the meaning of his mentor's death. "He taught us how to live," Lewis insisted, "and I think he taught us how to die." In an eerie coincidence, Chuck McDew, the SNCC chairman whom Lewis had replaced in 1963, died the night before *I Am MLK Jr.* aired, giving Lewis's memory of the movement another jolt.

That same week, Lewis told David Margolick, the author of a recently published dual biography of the two martyred leaders, that the movement never fully recovered from their deaths. "When these two young men were murdered, something died in all of us," he remembered. "We were robbed of part of our future." In early June, appearing in the documentary *Bobby Kennedy for President*, Lewis described his feelings when he learned that Kennedy had been killed. "I think I cried all the way from L.A. to Atlanta," Lewis recalled. "I kept saying to myself, 'What is happening in America?' To lose

Martin Luther King, Jr. and then two months later Bobby. It was too much."
Following this confession, he apologized to the interviewer and buried his
tear-stained face in his hands.[10]

*   *   *

Lewis had a historical perspective that set him apart from most of his congressional colleagues. Whenever he spoke at public events outside the House
chamber—especially at universities such as Harvard and Cal Tech, where
he delivered commencement addresses in May and June 2018—his hosts
invariably introduced him as a civil rights "icon." A modest man, he wasn't
altogether comfortable with being termed an "icon." But he *was* pleased that
his movement days had not been forgotten.

Lewis's special status and his longevity generally enhanced his work as
a congressman, but there were times when these attributes got in the way.
Almost always in demand, he maintained an extraordinarily busy schedule
beyond his basic congressional commitments. He wouldn't have had it any
other way, but the time away from his office forced him to rely heavily on
his staff, especially on his longtime chief of staff, Michael Collins, a talented
Morehouse graduate whom he brought on board in 1999 to replace James
Williams, who had led the staff during Lewis's first decade in Congress.

Lewis took great pride in the quality of his staff, which was far and away
the youngest staff on Capitol Hill. Viewing them as a new generation of
political activists rather than as a mere workforce, he rarely hired anyone
over the age of twenty-five. As one former Lewis aide put it, "If he could
have hired every young person in politics and have them spend time with
him in Congress, he would have." Other staffers commented, "He was like a
bonus dad to me. . . . He taught me so much, including how to love the hell
out of people"; "It was like being around your grandfather." Lewis saw his
young staff as a vanguard of change and thought of himself as a "humble
mentor." This attitude extended to many of his young House colleagues,
who also benefited from his gentle style of mentoring. "There isn't a member
among us who wasn't mentored by him," California congressman Ro Khanna
insisted in 2020.[11]

This did not prevent him, however, from occasionally crossing swords
with his younger colleagues. In the summer of 2018, he became involved in

a generational spat over the congressional candidacy of Ayanna Pressley, a young Black Boston city councilwoman challenging Michael Capuano, a white, ten-term, liberal representative from Massachusetts. Trumpeting the slogan "Change can't wait" and running as a "Justice Democrat"—an insurgent group of young democratic socialists that included Alexandria Ocasio-Cortez (a.k.a. AOC) of New York—Pressley encountered stiff opposition from a number of House members who valued Capuano as a long-standing liberal colleague. Capuano received strong endorsements from several members of the CBC, including Lewis and Representative Maxine Waters of California, plus Deval Patrick, the Black ex-governor of Massachusetts. Ideologically Pressley represented just the kind of candidate that Lewis hoped would invigorate the Democratic Party, but he remained loyal to his friend. On primary election day, Pressley prevailed, thanks in large part to her strong support among Black voters, leaving Lewis and the CBC looking like members of an out-of-touch Black establishment.[12]

Both Pressley and AOC were elected in November, joining a "blue wave" of new representatives elected in opposition to Trumpism. In an off-year election that was essentially a referendum on the autocratic and antiprogressive record of the Trump administration, the Democrats gained forty-one seats in the House, gaining control of the chamber and returning Nancy Pelosi to the Speaker position. Paradoxically, the Republicans fared much better in the Senate, gaining two seats and tightening their control. But the overall results provided Lewis and the Democrats with renewed hope. The unusually large turnout among younger voters under the age of thirty, a solid majority of whom voted Democratic, was especially encouraging. Lewis, who worked tirelessly to elevate the turnout in his district and beyond, was reelected to a seventeenth term, the eleventh time without opposition.

When the new Congress convened in January 2019, the anti-Trump coalition—representing what was becoming known as "the Resistance" in American society at large—was alive and well. With his national reputation at its height, Lewis was widely acknowledged as one of the leaders of this resistance. When Ilhan Omar, a newly elected Democratic congresswoman from Minnesota, arrived in Washington for freshman orientation in December, she encountered Lewis in a House office building corridor and immediately burst into tears of joy. A Somali refugee, the second Islamic woman to serve in Congress, and the first to wear a traditional hijab covering her hair, she regained enough composure to tell Lewis how much he meant to her. "Sir, I read about you in middle school, and you're here in the flesh," she told him almost breathlessly, "and I get to be your colleague." It was an ethereal moment, she later added, when she almost wanted "to pinch" herself.[13]

With Omar and the other young Justice Democrats on board, the Democratic majority in the House was in a position to initiate congressional investigations of Trump's misdeeds. The list of affronts to democracy was long and sordid, ranging from his associations with white nationalists and his open contempt for undocumented immigrants and refugees to his refusal to release his tax returns and his general disregard for the rule of law. By the end of the year, these and other violations of democratic norms and the constitutional limits of presidential power would result in Trump's impeachment. But in early 2019, Lewis and the House Democrats were busy laying the groundwork for the resistance to come.

The first major Democratic bill introduced in the new Congress was H.R. 1, a sweeping voting rights measure labeled the For the People Bill. Broader than the Voting Rights Advancement Bill that had been languishing since 2013, the nearly six-hundred-page bill promised "to marginalize the influence of money in politics, protect American elections from foreign threats, reduce political partisanship in the electoral process, and expand voter participation." The heart of the bill, for Lewis, was the section guaranteeing almost unlimited access to the ballot. "As the foundation of our system," he declared, "it [voting rights] must be strengthened and preserved. There are forces trying to make it harder and more difficult to participate and we must drown out these forces." Predictably, Senate Majority Leader Mitch McConnell dismissed the bill as a futile exercise in "unconstitutional" overreach.[14]

Undaunted, Lewis and the House Democrats opened a second front, filing a new version of the Voting Rights Advancement legislation, now known as H.R. 4. In late February, H.R. 4 reached the House floor for a vote and passed with ease, 228–187. But McConnell made sure it never reached the Senate floor. Insisting there was currently "no threat to the voting rights law," he claimed the bill was actually a surreptitious attempt to augment the Democratic vote by federalizing state elections. The wrangling between Democratic voting rights advocates and Republican obstructionists would go on for several years, intensifying with each succeeding confrontation over the true meaning of democracy.

The long and tortuous struggle to pass the two voting rights bills saddened Lewis. He found it difficult to believe that, after all that had happened since the dawning of the civil rights era, there was much more Republican opposition to the protection of voting rights than there had been a quarter century earlier. In 2019, he had no way of knowing, of course, that he would not live long enough to see either bill enacted into law (or to see the introduction of the 2020 Voting Rights Advancement Bill renamed for him). Yet he had already seen enough hedging and prevarication to know that American democracy was in serious trouble. Many Republican representatives and senators who had once been fairly moderate conservatives had turned far to the right, marching in lockstep with Trump. Lewis was not an absolutist, and he prided himself as being genuinely tolerant of points of view that did not correspond to his own. But late in life, long after he had come up against the raging white supremacists of the Jim Crow South, the Trumpist Republicans were teaching him just how irrational and self-serving opponents of democracy could be.[15]

*   *   *

In late February, just as the congressional battle over voting rights was heating up, Lewis learned another lesson about human frailty. This time the "classroom" was, of all places, the annual Academy Awards show in Los Angeles. He was thrilled to be asked to appear onstage to introduce *Green Book*, one of the films nominated for Best Picture. Named for the historic pre–civil rights era travel guide for "Negroes," the film presented a fictionalized version of a true story from 1962—the friendship between a prominent gay, Black pianist and a blue-collar, Italian American driver that developed during a concert tour in the Deep South. According to the film's director, Peter Farrelly, "The whole story is about love. It's about loving each other despite our differences and finding the truth about who we are. We're the same people."

This was a message that Lewis was happy to endorse, and as he introduced the film he shared his memories of Bloody Sunday with the crowd, providing a stirring reminder of what the film's two protagonists were up against in

1962. But when the film unexpectedly won the Oscar for Best Picture, outpolling two other "Black" films, Spike Lee's *BlacKkKlansman* and the superhero epic *Black Panther*, Lee and many others cried foul. Why had the Academy chosen to honor a "feel-good" film written, directed, and produced by white people, instead of honoring one of the two more militant and authentically Afrocentric films? they asked. The choice was reminiscent of *Driving Miss Daisy*, which had won the Oscar for Best Picture in 1990, leading many Black critics to complain that the Academy had apparently made little progress since then. Once again Lewis found himself ensnared in an unfortunate controversy involving ideological orthodoxy and racial solidarity.[16]

A week later, Lewis was back in Washington, where he faced an even more troubling controversy that exposed the growing generational and ideological rift between the established members of the CBC and the young women of color (often referred to as "the Squad") who had joined the House at the beginning of the year. The flap erupted after Lewis's close friend Representative Elijah Cummings of Maryland asked Rashida Tlaib, a recently elected Muslim congresswoman from Michigan, to apologize for using the term "racist" to characterize the recent behavior of Mark Meadows, an ultraconservative congressman from North Carolina. Tlaib did apologize, but Ocasio-Cortez, the fiery congresswoman from New York City, complained that her friend had been mistreated by Cummings and other House leaders. "Whose emotions do we put first?" AOC asked. "We had to apologize for him getting hurt feelings over her saying and calling out a racist practice." But what about Tlaib's feelings? She, too, had "hurt" feelings, but "no apology was furnished to her."

Lewis not only agreed; he also defended Tlaib's right to speak out in plain and forceful terms. "You have to bear witness, bear witness to the truth," he insisted, praising Tlaib and the other young women of color who had no fear of getting into "good trouble." "This body is going to continue to change as more people of diverse background come," he warned. "America is changing. We all need to get on board."[17]

Lewis was right. America was, indeed, changing—but not always in ways he welcomed. While most young Americans, those under the age of thirty, seemed to be moving in the right direction—toward democratic values and wider acceptance of multicultural diversity—many of their elders were headed elsewhere. Trumpism had become embedded in roughly 40 percent of the American electorate, and there was no sign it was going to release its hold on the Republican Party in the foreseeable future. As the third year of Trump's presidency progressed, his behavior became increasingly autocratic and outrageous when judged by the normal standards of American politics, and a solid majority of Republicans, both in Congress and in the party's electorate at large, appeared willing to follow him to the extremist fringe of the spectrum.

There had been talk of impeachment since Trump's first year as president, but the idea of removing him from office finally became a realistic option during the fall and winter of 2019. Lewis was all for it, convinced Trump had forfeited his right to hold the presidency. Considering the damage that Trump was inflicting on a weekly and even daily basis, Lewis, along with many other Democratic leaders, did not want to wait until the 2020 election to bring an end to the political and social carnage. In September, Lewis urged his House colleagues to begin a formal impeachment inquiry as soon as possible, confessing, "Sometimes I am afraid to go to sleep for fear that I will wake up and our democracy will be gone and never return." Unfortunately for Lewis and Trump's other critics, with the Republicans in charge of the Senate, the chance of actually removing him from the White House in the near future was slim.

Impeachment by the House was highly likely, but getting the required sixty-seven senators to vote for conviction and removal depended on winning the support of at least twenty Republicans. For that to happen, the Democrats would need a blatant and incontrovertible violation of the law—a clear "high crime or misdemeanor"—to bring before the Senate. That is exactly what Democratic leaders thought they had when a whistleblower complaint revealed that Trump had threatened to withhold foreign aid money from Ukraine until the Ukrainian president, Volodymyr Zelensky, agreed to investigate the allegedly corrupt activities of Hunter Biden, the son of the Democrats' likely presidential candidate, Joe Biden. This blatant attempt to seek foreign involvement in the election, plus Trump's repeated attempts to obstruct investigation of his campaign's probable collusion with Russian operatives, led to the filing of two articles of impeachment, one for "abuse of power" and a second for "obstruction of Congress." Both articles were approved by a majority of the House on December 18, with no Republicans voting for impeachment on either article.

Lewis, who spoke on the House floor in favor of both articles, was disappointed by his Republican colleagues' refusal to abandon their partisan defense of a corrupt president. Before the vote, he pleaded with the House Republicans to think about the moral and historical implications of not holding Trump accountable for his transgressions. "When you see something that is not right, not just, not fair, you have a moral obligation to say something. To do something," he counseled. "Our children and their children will ask us, 'What did you do? What did you say?' For some this vote may be hard. But we have a mission and a mandate to be on the right side of history."[18]

* * *

Lewis hoped to see a far greater display of courage among Senate Republicans, but an unexpected personal challenge upstaged his concern about the coming impeachment trial. While he and the rest of the nation were waiting for the trial to begin in mid-January, his whole world suddenly turned upside down. In late December, after several days of testing and medical evaluation, he learned he had stage 4 pancreatic cancer. The dreaded disease had already spread to other organs, leaving him with a prognosis of having only two to six months to live. After attending church on Sunday, December 29, he issued a public statement disclosing his illness. "I have been in some kind of fight—for freedom, equality, basic human rights—for nearly my entire life. I have never faced a fight quite like the one I have now," he reported. Even so, he made it clear he had not given up hope that once again he might beat the odds.

"I have decided to do what I know to do and do what I have always done," he declared. "I am going to fight it and keep fighting for the Beloved Community." While conceding he might "miss a few votes over the next several weeks," he gave the distinct impression that he intended to continue to pull his weight as a congressional leader. "His tenor," a reporter for the *Atlantic* observed, "remained characteristically triumphant, even optimistic."[19]

Lewis continued to hope that during the impeachment trial enough Republican Senators would come to their senses and bring the Trump presidency to a close. But pro-Trump statements by Senate Majority Leader

McConnell, Senator Lindsey Graham of South Carolina, and other members of the Republican caucus suggested they had no intention of acting as impartial jurors. "Everything I do during this I'm coordinating with the White House counsel," McConnell revealed without a hint of shame or regret, even though his oath of office required him to judge the evidence without conscious bias. "There will be no difference between the president's position and our position as to how to handle this. . . . I'm going to take my cues from the president's lawyers." True to his word, the Senate majority leader did everything in his power to ensure an acquittal.

Lewis was disgusted by McConnell's refusal to take the trial seriously as part of his constitutional responsibilities. But there was nothing he or any other Democrat could do to rescue the prosecution. On February 5, after a three-week trial, Trump won acquittal on both articles, with only seven Republican senators joining the Democrats in voting for removal from office. To Lewis's sorrow, the Trump presidency would continue for another eleven months, led by an emboldened and increasingly autocratic leader who strayed further and further away from the tradition mainstream of American politics.[20]

As Lewis's physical condition deteriorated during the late winter and early spring of 2020, he realized there was little chance he would be alive to witness the national election in November, or even be around to attend the Democratic National Convention in August. On February 21, he celebrated his eightieth birthday in a party at the Capitol, even though the onset of the COVID-19 pandemic should have made his colleagues think twice about convening such a gathering. At that point, wearing face masks and social distancing were the exception rather than the rule, and the partygoers shared food, and even coughed into their hands, without giving it much thought. Only Representative Kim Schrier, a pediatrician from Washington State, was alarmed enough to scold her colleagues. "They did a birthday party for John Lewis with a cake," she later reported. "I pulled my friends aside and said, 'You can't do this with an 80-year-old whose immune system is already compromised.'"[21]

During the next twelve months, roughly one-tenth of the members of Congress would contract the virus, but mercifully Lewis was not one of them. He had enough to deal with without adding a second illness. As his cancer spread, he had good days and bad, but whenever he was asked about his condition, he tried to appear optimistic. "I am doing well. I am feeling good, getting stronger and stronger every day," he told a CNN reporter in early March, after attending his twentieth Faith and Politics Institute pilgrimage to Alabama and the site of Bloody Sunday. He knew this would almost certainly be his last trip to Selma and the Edmund Pettus Bridge, and he wanted to make the most of it. He couldn't manage to make the traditional commemorative walk across the bridge, but he summoned up enough strength to address the huge gathering assembled at the western end of the span. Standing near him were more than forty of his congressional colleagues, several close friends and comrades—including Bernard LaFayette, Jim Lawson, Jesse Jackson, Stacey Abrams, and Al Sharpton—and five candidates for the Democratic presidential nomination: Amy Klobuchar, Elizabeth Warren, Pete Buttigieg, Michael Bloomberg, and the frontrunner, Joe Biden, fresh from his landslide victory in the South Carolina primary the day before.

Lewis began his Selma remarks as he always did—by recounting what had happened on Bloody Sunday, March 7, 1965. "Fifty five years ago a few of God's children attempted to march from Brown Chapel across this bridge," he recalled in as loud a voice as he could muster. "We were beaten, we were tear-gassed. I thought I was going to die on this bridge. But somehow and some way, God almighty helped me here." He then gave the crowd its marching orders: "We cannot give up now. We cannot give in. We must keep the faith, keep our eyes on the prize. We must go out and vote like we never, ever voted before." "Some people gave more than a little blood. Some gave their very lives," he explained, before pausing to let the cheers roll over him. "Go out there, speak up, speak out, get in the way. Get in good trouble, necessary trouble," he counseled. "I am not going to give up, I am not going to give in. I am going to continue to fight. We need your prayers now more than ever before. Let's do it. We can do it. Selma is a different place. America is a different place. But we can make it much better. We must use the vote as a nonviolent instrument or tool to redeem the soul of America."[22]

* * *

Lewis's emotional return to Selma would be his last major public appearance. But he continued to work behind the scenes, extracting all that he could out of the limited energy left in his body. Throughout the late winter and early spring of 2020, he collaborated with Andrew Aydin and two comic book artists on a sequel to *March*. Lewis and Aydin had begun work on the sequel four years earlier and were nearing completion at the time of the congressman's death. As he explained, his goal was "to leave a civil rights 'road map' for generations to come." Titled *Run: Book One,* the fourth volume extended Lewis's story through the post–Voting Rights Act struggles of 1965 and 1966, chronicling his final year with SNCC and the divisive controversies surrounding Stokely Carmichael's advocacy of Black Power. *Run* would be published to considerable acclaim in August 2021, adding one more element to Lewis's posthumous legacy, "another monument to John Lewis," as one reviewer put it.[23]

Lewis also remained heavily involved in politics to the end, including a planned run for reelection. Though unopposed for the Democratic nomination, if he lived long enough he would face Angela Stanton-King, a former reality TV star and ultraconservative Trump loyalist in the general election. Convicted and jailed for her involvement in a car-theft ring, she had received a presidential pardon from Trump earlier in the year. An inappropriate candidate for a congressional seat or any other elective office, Stanton-King clearly posed no threat to Lewis, who was much more concerned about presidential politics than his own race.

In early April, Lewis threw his support to Joe Biden, joining a growing list of Black leaders who had endorsed the former vice president. Describing Biden as "a friend, a man of courage, a man of conscience," he promised to "travel around America to support him." But before long he realized that campaign travel on the national level was beyond him. By June he was having difficulty walking, and it was a struggle to make even occasional trips to his office. Yet he continued to speak out on a range of issues.

On several occasions he praised the ongoing efforts to remove Confederate statues from public parks, and he applauded the recent campaign—condemned by President Trump as rampant "political correctness"—to rename the ten military bases named for Confederate officers, including Georgia's Fort Benning and Fort Gordon. In June, he joined the rising chorus of Americans outraged by the brutal murder of George Floyd, a forty-six-year-old Black man choked to death by a white Minneapolis policeman on May 25. When Trump threatened to militarize the cities where Black Lives Matter activists had taken to the streets to protest Floyd's murder, Lewis warned the president that such heavy-handed efforts to quell dissent would almost certainly fail. "You cannot stop the call of history," he advised. "You may use troopers, you may use fire hoses and water, but it cannot be stopped. There cannot be any turning back. We've come too far, made too much progress, to stop now or to go back." To underscore this point, on June 7, looking gaunt and frail, he somehow mustered the strength to accompany District of Columbia mayor Muriel Bowser on a brief visit to the recently named Black Lives Matter Plaza. Featuring a massive street mural spelling out "Black Lives Matter" in thirty-five-foot-high yellow letters covering a two-block-long section of Sixteenth Street just north of Lafayette Square and the White House, the plaza was the site of a brutal June 1 incident in which President Trump ordered federal forces to disperse a peaceful gathering of BLM protesters with pepper spray and tear gas. Lewis's poignant visit six days later testified to his continued determination to take a stand against Trump's disdain for democracy and the right to engage in peaceful protest.

By this time, Lewis's political campaigning was largely limited to public statements and phone calls in support of the Fair Fight Action voter registration effort led by Stacey Abrams, a former state legislator who had lost a close race for the Georgia governorship in 2018. He also did what he could to strengthen the senatorial campaigns of Jon Ossoff, a thirty-three-year-old Jewish liberal from suburban Atlanta whom Lewis had been mentoring for four years, and of the Reverend Raphael Warnock, the fifty-year-old senior pastor of Atlanta's Ebenezer Baptist Church and the former chair of the New Georgia Project, a nonpartisan voter registration organization. A longtime friend of Lewis's, Warnock had first gained political attention as a leading activist in the campaign to expand Medicaid under the Affordable Care Act. In March 2014 he, along with several other Medicaid expansion advocates, was arrested during a sit-in at the Georgia State Capitol, drawing high praise from Lewis and other movement veterans.

After a brief career as a documentary filmmaker and investigative reporter, Ossoff lost a close race for a congressional seat in 2017, but in the process he earned a great deal of respect from Lewis and other Democratic leaders. Unfortunately, he faced an even stiffer challenge in the 2020 race, in part because he was trying to unseat a wealthy and well-connected incumbent senator, David Perdue, the first cousin of former Georgia governor and Secretary of Agriculture Sonny Perdue. Ossoff and Warnock—who was running against an even wealthier opponent, Kelly Loeffler, the co-owner of the Atlanta Dream franchise in the Women's National Basketball Association—also had to deal with the Georgia Republicans' recent legal and extralegal efforts at voter suppression. It was a steep uphill fight for both Democratic candidates, but it was one that Lewis relished.

Depending on what happened in the other 2020 Senate races, Lewis and other Democratic leaders speculated that the outcomes of the two Georgia races might determine partisan control of the Senate. He was also well aware that if Warnock won, he would become only the second African American (Senator Tim Scott of South Carolina was the first) to represent an ex-Confederate state in the Senate since Hiram Revels served as one of Mississippi's senators in 1870–1871. Lewis, who had been waiting for an opportunity like this since the passage of the Voting Rights Act in 1965, told several close friends that one of his fondest hopes was to live long enough to witness Warnock's senatorial swearing-in ceremony. Sadly, however, it was not to be. Both Warnock and Ossoff were elected to the Senate in a special runoff election held on January 5, 2021, a surprising double victory that gave the Democrats control of the Senate. But Lewis was not there to share the joy.[24]

He did live long enough to experience one more Juneteenth celebration, which saw the June 19 national premiere of the first full-length documentary film devoted to his extraordinary life. Titled *John Lewis: Good Trouble,* after his favorite phrase, the film was directed by Dawn Porter, an African American filmmaker whose best-known previous films had dealt with Black public defenders in the Deep South, anti–civil rights surveillance conducted by the Mississippi State Sovereignty Commission, and the last surviving abortion clinic in Mississippi. Dedicated to Lewis's dear friend Elijah Cummings of Maryland, the Black congressman who had died unexpectedly the previous October, the documentary featured interviews with members of the Lewis family, his congressional staff, and several of his Democratic colleagues in the House of Representatives, including James Clyburn, Nancy Pelosi, and Alexandria Ocasio-Cortez. Though not well enough to attend the premiere held in Tulsa, Oklahoma, Lewis saw the film from his hospital bed and was a bit embarrassed by its hagiographical portrayal of him as a "secular saint." Modest and humble to the very end, he preferred to focus on ideas leading to action, rather than on his own virtues or exploits.[25]

Epilogue

I̶N EARLY JULY 2020, John Lewis's condition took a turn for the worse as his cancer entered its final stage. After several months of treatment in Washington, he had returned to Atlanta, where his fellow Nashville movement activist and dear friend of more than fifty years, ninety-five-year-old C. T. Vivian, was hospitalized and in rapidly failing health. The two champions of nonviolent struggle had fought for freedom together in Nashville, Selma, and dozens of other Southern communities, and both had been awarded the coveted Presidential Medal of Freedom. So it seemed fitting that the two men approaching death were now lying in beds a few miles apart in a city where they had labored so long and hard for the same righteous cause. On Friday, July 17, both men lapsed into comas, and by nightfall they were dead. Having survived the many blows inflicted by white supremacists in Tennessee, Alabama, and Mississippi, they had succumbed to the ravages of age and disease. Their dying on the same day was an eerie coincidence that inevitably reminded some Americans of the coincidental deaths of Thomas Jefferson and John Adams on Independence Day 1826.

The passing of Vivian, whom Martin Luther King Jr. once called "the greatest preacher to ever live," set off cries of mourning throughout the civil rights community, especially among movement veterans old enough to remember the courage he had displayed at Selma and elsewhere during the voting rights struggle of the mid-1960s. But the response to Lewis's death was of a different order and magnitude and an acknowledgment of his status as a fallen national hero. The funeral services that took place over the next ten days, and the public expression of emotion surrounding them, were extraordinary by any standard—though not in keeping with Lewis's humble, self-deprecating character. Held in multiple cities and widely televised, they did not accord him the simple farewell he would have chosen for himself. His close friends, colleagues, and family members knew this, of course, but they couldn't help themselves. Losing him at a time when his deepest passion—the sacred right to vote—was under systematic assault from the president and party in power called for nothing less than an extended national display of mourning.

The outpouring of grief and the profound sense of loss that followed Lewis's death testified to his unparalleled reputation as a man of courage and conscience. No member of the House, Democrat or Republican, had been accorded such an emotional and reverential send-off in living memory. In October 2019, Elijah Cummings became the first Black member of Congress to be accorded the honor of lying in state at the Capitol, in his case in the National Statuary Hall, and now Lewis became the second in the Capitol and the first in the Rotunda. The Rotunda viewing was delayed for more than a week as House leaders dealt with concerns about spreading the COVID-19 virus among the mourners passing by his casket. But those willing to take the risk eventually prevailed. "We have to celebrate his life. Lying in state is part of the celebration of the life of a great American," argued Al Green, a CBC member from Texas who had twice joined Lewis in jail, once in 2006 after protesting genocide in the Sudan and again in 2013 after rallying for immigration reform. "He was not an ordinary person. He would not agree with me saying that, but he was not. To love the way he loved? To take what he took on the Edmund Pettus Bridge and still preach love? You're not an ordinary person."[1]

During the ten days between Lewis's death and the arrival of his body at the Capitol, there were memorial services in Troy and Selma, and an avalanche of tributes from ordinary citizens, politicians, and civil rights leaders. One of the most eloquent tributes came from Carla Hayden, the Librarian of Congress, who had grown close to Lewis during his frequent visits to the Library, including a memorable speech in November 2019, when he celebrated the arrival of the AIDS Memorial Quilt collection. "Few people that you meet truly rouse the best in you," she wrote two days after Lewis's death. "They are walking heroes, living historymakers. Their words and deeds have a thunderous impact on your soul. Congressman John Robert Lewis was such a person for me." "The world mourns," she added. "But we also celebrate a great warrior and fighter of injustice. Let us remember his story and listen to the words he passionately shared for more than half a century. Congressman John Robert Lewis embodies the best in all of us."

In Congress the tributes came from both sides of the aisle. As expected, Nancy Pelosi, the House Speaker and longtime Lewis ally, lauded her departed colleague as "a titan of the civil rights movement." Representative Hakeem Jeffries of New York spoke of Lewis as a "change agent extraordinaire" who "altered the course of history and left America a much better place"; Mike Espy of Mississippi called him "a human saint." To Senator Kamala Harris of California, Lewis was "an American hero—a giant whose shoulders upon many of us stand"; to Senator Elizabeth Warren of Massachusetts, he was "the moral compass of our nation." Even the hyperpartisan Republican stalwart and Senate majority leader Mitch McConnell issued a gracious statement recognizing the significance of Lewis's career both before and after his election to Congress. "Dr. King famously said, 'The arc of the moral universe is long, but it bends toward justice,'" the Kentucky senator recalled. "But progress is not automatic. Our great nation's history has only bent towards justice because great men like John Lewis took it upon themselves to help bend it." Brian Kemp, the conservative Republican governor of Georgia, agreed, stating the nation "will never be the same" without John Lewis.

The only major Republican officeholder to withhold praise for the man others mourned as an American hero was Donald Trump, who had never forgiven Lewis for publicly questioning the legitimacy of his presidency. Trump's acknowledgment of Lewis's death was perfunctory at best, just as it had been after the death of Senator John McCain, another vocal critic, in 2018. But many of Lewis's friends preferred it that way, urging Trump to remain respectfully silent. "Please don't comment on the life of Congressman Lewis," pleaded Karen Bass, the California congresswoman who chaired the CBC. "Your press secretary released a statement. Leave it at that. Please let us mourn in peace."

Lewis didn't need any additional vetting from the White House, Bass and others argued, when he already enjoyed the admiration and respect of four former presidents, including Barack Obama. In the past, Obama often had acknowledged his great debt to Lewis, who had served as an inspiration for his own career, and upon Lewis's death he immediately paid tribute to American democracy's fallen warrior. "He loved this country so much that he risked his life and his blood so that it might live up to its promise," Obama declared. "And through the decades, he not only gave all of himself to the cause of freedom and justice, but inspired generations that followed to try to live up to his example."[2]

On the Monday following Lewis's death, both Democrats and Republicans eulogized him on the House and Senate floors. But Democratic leaders pressed for more than rhetoric. Noting that in December Lewis had successfully shepherded a voting rights bill through the House only to have it blocked by the Republican-controlled Senate, Speaker Pelosi insisted in a morning television interview that "the appropriate way to honor John Lewis is for the Senate to take up the Voting Rights Act and name it for John Lewis. That it should be so difficult for them to take up the Voting Rights Act is really hard to comprehend, but maybe now they see a path." The hope was that the Senate Republicans would put away their objections and embrace the Lewis bill in a groundswell of emotion, perhaps in a matter of days, perhaps even before the first of Lewis's memorial services was held in Pike County on July 24. In a nation well on its way to Lewis's Beloved Community, that might have happened. But America was not that nation, as the Senate Republicans' continued opposition to voting rights legislation confirmed.[3]

The service in Pike County—held in the gymnasium of Troy University, the formerly all-white institution that had turned Lewis away in 1956 because of the color of his skin—was the beginning of a five-city pilgrimage. The crowd there included a large number of Lewis family members and former neighbors. The emphasis throughout the emotional morning service was on Lewis's enduring connection to his humble origins in rural Pike County. "This is where it all started for him," explained one of his nieces. The Reverend Darryl Caldwell, pastor of the tiny Antioch Missionary Baptist Church located in the town of Banks, just a few miles south of the Lewis farm, presided over a service that stressed Lewis's lifelong talent for getting into "good trouble." "Thank you, father of all mercy, for John," Caldwell exclaimed, "who wore the mantle of good trouble and did not flinch in the face of fear when confronted by deputized demons who intended to discourage, deny, and ultimately destroy the just course of John Robert Lewis." Other speakers pleaded with the crowd to follow in Lewis's footsteps. "If we don't carry on," the Reverend Jacquelyn Lancaster-Denson declared, "he got in good trouble for nothing."

From Troy the pilgrimage proceeded to Selma and the Brown Chapel AME Church, the starting point and staging ground for the 1965 voting rights march to Montgomery. This was hallowed ground for those who had come to admire the hero of Bloody Sunday, and a huge crowd gathered there to honor him. Charter buses from Georgia and satellite trucks connecting national news services to the wider world lined the street outside the church, as thousands of mourners stretched down the street where he had once led marchers to an uncertain fate. Family members and civil rights veterans jammed into Brown Chapel that Saturday evening to pay tribute to a man whose name had long been linked to the town where the voting rights struggle of the 1960s reached its dramatic climax.

"We in Selma were blessed to know John intimately," Congresswoman Terri Sewell reminded the mourners, and the next morning, Sunday, July 26, she and thousands of others reinforced that intimacy by standing silently nearby as a horse-drawn caisson (evoking memories of the similar caisson that had carried Martin Luther King Jr.'s casket through the streets of Atlanta in April 1968) carried Lewis's casket along the same route as the historic march of 1965, from Brown Chapel to the banks of the Alabama River, to the west end of the Edmund Pettus Bridge. As the caisson continued onto the bridge on its way to the capitol in Montgomery, where his body would lie in state, the crowd was held back, allowing Lewis's casket to cross alone, creating a poignant image of singular nobility. This time there were no state troopers blocking his path, no clouds of tear gas, and no billy clubs to knock him down and fracture his skull. This time Lewis was free to travel all the way to Montgomery.[4]

On Monday afternoon, the pilgrimage arrived in Washington for a Rotunda viewing open to members of Congress and a few other invited guests.

That evening the flag-draped casket was moved to the Capitol steps for eighteen hours of public viewing. With the pandemic in full force, Capitol officials expected a light to moderate turnout of mourners, but the long line of citizens, Black and white, who stood in the summer heat to pay their respects to Lewis testified to his extraordinary popularity and status as a beloved leader. The mourners came from near and far to say goodbye. The first person to line up for the public viewing was Rita Crosby, a sixty-eight-year-old civil rights veteran from Oklahoma. "To see how far we've come as a nation," Crosby told a reporter who asked why she was there, "to see what he has endured with dignity and with grace, and achieve what he did, it gives me much pride and joy."[5]

*   *   *

Similar testaments to Lewis's impact on ordinary citizens punctuated his memorialization in Atlanta, his adopted home and the pilgrimage's final stop. Before being interred next to Lillian at the South-View Cemetery, his body lay in state at the Georgia State Capitol, after which a final funeral service was held at Ebenezer Baptist Church, where he had attended King's funeral service more than a half century earlier. The scene at Ebenezer was reminiscent of his mentor's 1968 funeral, but Lewis, in recognition of his long and distinguished political career, was accorded the additional honor of being eulogized by three former presidents. Standing at the pulpit in front of an overflow crowd, Bill Clinton and George W. Bush expressed their admiration for one of twentieth-century America's greatest public figures, a unique moral and political leader who fought for democracy and human rights both in the streets and in the halls of Congress. Both Clinton and Bush offered eloquent and moving tributes to Lewis, but the most powerful and memorable eulogy came from Barack Obama.

The nation's first Black president delivered a stirring forty-minute speech that put Lewis's life in the context of an ongoing struggle to preserve American democracy. Without mentioning Trump by name, he contrasted the fundamentally antidemocratic character of the current administration with Lewis's glorious ideals, both in his life and as expressed through the courage of the recent Black Lives Matter movement that had given him renewed hope for the future. Calling for a series of reforms aimed at guaranteeing full access to the electoral process, preventing police brutality, and protecting the rights of nonviolent protesters, Obama invoked the history of the civil rights struggle, including Lewis's personal struggles, as a means of understanding the nation's current racial crisis. "Bull Connor may be gone, but today we witness with our own eyes kneeling on the necks of Black Americans," he told the crowd. "George Wallace may be gone, but we can witness our federal government sending agents to use tear gas and batons against peaceful demonstrators."

Reaching back to the days when white registrars concocted all sorts of tricks and tests to prevent Black voter registration, he continued, "We may no longer have to guess the number of jelly beans in a jar in order to cast a ballot, but even as we sit here there are those in power who are doing their darndest to discourage people from voting by closing polling locations, and targeting minorities and students with restrictive ID laws, and attacking our voting rights with surgical precision." He went on to advocate the creation of a national election day holiday, statehood for the District of Columbia and Puerto Rico, automatic voter registration, and elimination of the antidemocratic filibuster rule in the Senate, all measures endorsed by Lewis.

"Want to honor John?" he asked the crowd. "Let's honor him by revitalizing the law that he was willing to die for. And by the way, naming it the John Lewis Voting Rights Act, that is a fine tribute—but John wouldn't want us to stop there, just trying to get back where we already were." By this point the atmosphere in the church was electric—not unlike the spirit of the mass meetings that had drawn young John Lewis deeper and deeper into the movement.

The former president brought his eulogy to a close by warning the mourners at Ebenezer that Lewis's legacy would almost certainly be on the line in the upcoming national election. Lewis was a man of "unbreakable perseverance," he declared, but American democracy could no longer rely on his strength and his will. Lewis was gone, and the rest of his nonviolent, democratic legion would now have to step up and carry on the struggle. Paraphrasing Lewis's own words, Obama reminded the mourners that "democracy isn't automatic. It has to be nurtured; it has to be tended to; we have to work at it. If we want our children to grow up in a democracy—not just with elections, but a true democracy, a representative democracy, a bighearted, tolerant, vibrant, inclusive America—then we are going to have to be more like John."[6]

Obama's warning that the struggle for American democracy would be more difficult in the wake of Lewis's death echoed a *New York Times* editorial published a week earlier. "The passing of John Lewis deprives the United States of its foremost warrior in a battle for racial justice that stretches back into the 19th century and the passage of the 14th and 15th Amendments," the editorial declared. "Americans—and particularly his colleagues in Congress—can best honor his memory by picking up where he left off." During the week following Lewis's death, many other tributes appeared, including a proposal to strike Edmund Pettus's name from the famous Selma bridge and rename it the John R. Lewis Bridge, and another to rename a Springfield, Virginia, public school, Robert E. Lee High School, in Lewis's honor. But such symbolic gestures, as the Black diplomat Susan Rice pointed out, would not do much to advance Lewis's cherished cause. "The legacy of this current movement for racial justice must be more than merely retiring symbols of the Confederacy," she insisted. "By keeping our eyes on the prize, by embracing what the great John Lewis called 'good trouble,' by training activism and energy on the polls in November, we can make America far more fair, just and hopeful for all of its people."[7]

* * *

Many Democrats answered the clarion calls of anxious leaders such as Obama and Rice—more than enough to ensure Trump's defeat in the November 2020 election, and even enough to put two of Lewis's protégés, Ossoff and Warnock, in the Senate representing the predominantly Republican state of Georgia. Lewis's broader legacy, however, would remain in doubt for the foreseeable future. Dark days lay ahead as a number of Republican-controlled state legislatures enacted laws aimed at voter suppression or electoral suspension, and as Republican senators repeatedly used the threat of a filibuster to prevent passage of a new voting rights law that would restore the protections once guaranteed by the Voting Rights Act of 1965. More than three years after Lewis's death, the John R. Lewis Voting Rights Advancement Bill, though passed by the Democrat-controlled House in August 2021, remained moribund in the Senate.[8]

Lewis did not live to see any of this—not Joe Biden's election, not Trump's propagation of the "big lie" that the election had been stolen from him, not the violent insurrectionary attack on the Capitol on January 6, 2021, not the second impeachment trial, and not the protracted battles over voting rights legislation. But the continuing difficulties encountered by his fellow defenders of democracy would not have surprised him. Nor would they have broken his spirit. "Do not get lost in a sea of despair," he counseled three years before his death. "Be hopeful, be optimistic. Our struggle is not the struggle of a day, a month, or a year, it is the struggle of a lifetime."[9]

In the hope of advancing this lifelong struggle, Lewis did all he could to leave a legacy that would benefit future generations. Even during his cancer treatment in early 2020, when he was weak and often racked with pain, he took the time to collaborate with two of his aides, Michael Collins and Kabir Sehgal, and the editor Gretchen Young, on the writing and compilation of a book of brief essays. Titled *Carry On: Reflections for a New Generation* and published in July 2021, the book presented a treasure trove of wisdom on everything from "courage" and "justice" to "activism" and "forgiveness." In the final essay, titled "On the Future," he offered a 125-word epitaph as a vessel of hope: "We have made progress over the past many decades. Dr. King and the civil rights movement birthed a committed new generation of activists who are imagining, envisioning, and shaping the world they want to see. One hundred years from now, I would love to see that our Beloved Community, the place we call home—America—will be more at peace with itself. Let us hope and believe that there will be less turmoil, less rancor, less violence. America should be a place of respect and dignity, a beacon of light for all of our fellow human beings. I know it is within our power to make such a world exist. Be patient. Be hopeful. Be humble. Be bold. Be better. Keep the faith. Carry on."[10]

Several weeks after writing this essay, he wrote another—a final plea to those who he hoped would continue the struggle for a better world. Completed two days before his death and submitted to the *New York Times* as a parting gift to the nation he had worked so long and hard to liberate from the burdens of racism, hatred, and violence, the essay appeared on the *Times* editorial page two weeks later, on July 30. Its title, "Together, You Can Redeem the Soul of Our Nation," encapsulated Lewis's most fervent wish, and his words, simple yet eloquent, pointed the way to the Beloved Community.

"While my time here has now come to an end," he began, addressing the many caring citizens who had embraced the Black Lives Matter movement during his final years, "I want you to know that in the last hours and days of my life you inspired me. You filled me with hope about the next chapter of the great American story when you used your power to make a difference in our society. Millions of people motivated simply by human compassion laid down the burdens of division. Around the country and the world you set aside race, age, class, language and nationality to demand respect for human dignity. That is why I had to visit Black Lives Matter Plaza in Washington, though I was admitted to the hospital the following day. I just had to see and feel it for myself that, after many years of silent witness, the truth is still marching on."

Lewis closed the essay, and his life, with a moral lesson for the ages. "Though I may not be here with you," he wrote, "I urge you to answer the highest calling of your heart and stand up for what you truly believe. In my life I have done all I can to demonstrate that the way of peace, the way of love and nonviolence is the more excellent way. Now it is your turn to let freedom ring. When historians pick up their pens to write the story of the 21st century, let them say it was your generation who laid down the heavy burdens of hate at last and that peace finally triumphed over violence, aggression and war. So I say to you, walk with the wind, brothers and sisters, and let the spirit of peace and the power of everlasting love be your guide."[11]

NOTES

Abbreviations Used in the Notes

AJC	*Atlanta Journal-Constitution*
ATB	John Lewis with Brenda Jones, *Across That Bridge: A Vision for Change and the Future of America* (New York: Hachette Books, 2017)
CR	*Congressional Record*
FR	Raymond Arsenault, *Freedom Riders: 1961 and the Struggle for Racial Justice* (New York: Oxford University Press, 2006)
int.	Interview by author, unless identified otherwise
IS	Clayborne Carson, *In Struggle: SNCC and the Black Awakening of the 1960s* (Cambridge, MA: Harvard University Press, 1981)
Lewis-Blackside int.	John Lewis, interview by Henry Johnson and Judy Richardson, 1979, Blackside Productions and Washington University, St. Louis
Lewis-HM int.	John Lewis, interview by Julieanna Richardson, History Makers, April 25, 2001, https://www.thehistorymakers.org/biography/honorable-john-lewis
Lewis-HR int.	John Lewis, "The Long Struggle for Representation: Oral Histories of African Americans in Congress," interview by Matt Wasniewski, December 11, 2014, https://history.house.gov/Oral-History/People/Representative-Lewis/
Lewis-JFKL int.	John Lewis, interview by Vicki Daitch, March 19, 2004, John F. Kennedy Presidential Library
Lewis-NA int.	John Lewis, "An Evening with John Lewis, June 6, 2013," interview by Scott Simon, National Archives
Lewis-OHAS int.	John Lewis, interview by Jack Bass and Walter Devries, November 20, 1973, Oral Histories of the American South: The Civil Rights Movement, University of North Carolina, Chapel Hill
Lewis-USIA int.	John Lewis, "Assessing the Gains: Congressman John Lewis, February 7, 1990," interview, *Worldnet Today,* United States Information Agency
NYT	*New York Times*

q   Quotation
WP   *Washington Post*
WWTW   John Lewis with Michael D'Orso, *Walking with the Wind: A Memoir of the Movement* (New York: Simon and Schuster, 1998)

Preface

1. John Lewis with Michael D'Orso, *Walking with the Wind: A Memoir of the Movement* (New York: Simon and Schuster, 1998) (hereafter cited as *WWTW*). On the Roosevelt-Wilson Award for Public Service to the Discipline of History (renamed the John Lewis Award for Public Service to the Discipline of History in 2021), see "John Lewis Award for Public Service to the Discipline of History," American Historical Association, https://www.historians.org/awards-and-grants/awards-and-prizes/john-lewis-award-for-public-service-to-the-discipline-of-history (q).

2. Michael Waldman, "John Lewis Was a Hero for Democracy and Civil Rights," Brennan Center for Justice, July 18, 2020, https://www.brennancenter.org/our-work/analysis-opinion/john-lewis-was-hero-democracy-and-civil-rights. The phrase "a tugboat, not a showboat" originated in November 1992 as a self-description offered by Representative Corinne Brown of Florida. Adam Clymer, "House Democrats Proclaiming Unity," *New York Times* (hereafter cited as *NYT*), November 11, 1992. Lewis later adopted the phrase both as a self-description and as an aspiration for his followers. "Be a tugboat, not a showboat," he advised on a number of occasions.

3. David Chappell, *A Stone of Hope: Prophetic Religion and the Death of Jim Crow* (Chapel Hill: University of North Carolina Press, 2004), 75–76; Milton Viorst, *Fire in the Streets: America in the 1960's* (New York: Simon and Schuster, 1979), 95 (1st q); John Egerton, *A Mind to Stay Here: Profiles from the South* (New York: Macmillan, 1970 (2nd q); John Lewis, interview by author (hereafter cited as int.); Raymond Arsenault, "The John Lewis I Knew," *Tampa Bay Times*, July 24, 2020 (3rd q). On Elwin Wilson and the Freedom Riders' appearance on *The Oprah Winfrey Show* in May 2011, see John Lewis, *Across That Bridge: A Vision for Change and the Future of America*, with Brenda Jones (New York: Hachette Books, 2017) (hereafter cited as *ATB*), 189–194; "Oprah Honors Freedom Riders," oprah.com, May 4, 2011, https://www.oprah.com/oprahshow/oprah-honors-freedom-riders/all; Kathy Lohr, "50 Years Later, a Civil Rights Tribute . . . and Apology," NPR, April 16, 2010, https://www.npr.org/2010/04/16/126051007/50-years-later-a-civil-rights-tribute-and-apology; Alexander Abad-Santos, "What KKK Member Elwin Wilson Learned before He Died," *Atlantic*, April 1, 2013; "'His Story Must Not Be Forgotten,'" Politico, March 31, 2013, https://www.politico.com/story/2013/03/elwin-wilson-death-089498; Ray Tyler, "What John Lewis Taught Me about Forgiveness," Teaching American History, July 23, 2020, https://teachingamericanhistory.org/blog/what-john-lewis-taught-me-about-forgiveness/; *NYT*, April 2, 2013; and *Washington Post* (hereafter cited as *WP*), March 31, 2013.

Introduction

1. On Douglass, see David W. Blight, *Frederick Douglass: Prophet of Freedom* (New York: Simon and Schuster, 2018), xviii.

2. *WWTW*, 67 (1st q), 203–205 (2nd q); @repjohnlewis, The Leadership Conference@civilrightsorg, December 6, 2019; John Lewis's House speech on the Voting Rights Advancement Bill, December 6, 2019 (3rd q), available online at @repjohnlewis, The Leadership Conference on Civil and Human Rights website civilrights.org; John Egerton, *A Mind to Stay Here: Profiles from the South* (New York: Macmillan, 1970), 52 (4th q); *ATB*, 119. For profiles of the Big Six, see Jon Meacham, *His Truth Is Marching On: John Lewis and the Power of Hope* (New York: Random House, 2020); Jervis Anderson, *A. Philip Randolph: A Biographical Portrait* (New York: Harcourt Brace Jovanovich, 1973); Roy Wilkins with Tom Mathews, *Standing Fast: The Autobiography of Roy Wilkins* (New York: Viking Penguin, 1982); David J. Garrow, *Bearing the Cross: Martin Luther King, Jr., and the Southern Christian Leadership Conference* (New York: William Morrow, 1986); James Farmer, *Lay Bare the Heart: An Autobiography of the Civil Rights Movement* (New York: New American Library, 1985); and Nancy J. Weiss, *Whitney M. Young Jr. and the Struggle for Civil Rights* (Princeton, NJ: Princeton University Press, 1989).

3. *WWTW*, 456 (1st q); *Boston Globe*, July 18, 2020 (2nd q); *ATB*, 174 (3rd q); Dareh Gregorian, "Rep. John Lewis, 'Conscience of Congress,' Makes Final Trip to Capitol," NBC News, July 27, 2020, https://www.nbcnews.com/politics/congress/rep-john-lewis-conscience-congress-makes-final-trip-capitol-n1235000. The first person to use the phrase "better angels of our nature" was Abraham Lincoln in his first inaugural address, delivered on March 4, 1861. On the concept of "soul force," or *satyagraha*, see *ATB*, 136; *WWTW*, 80–97, 131, 147; Erik H. Erikson, *Gandhi's Truth: On the Origins of Militant Nonviolence* (New York: Norton, 1993), 410–428; and Joseph Kip Kosek, "Richard Gregg, Mohandas Gandhi, and the Strategy of Nonviolence," *Journal of American History* 91 (March 2005): 1318–1348.

4. *WWTW*, 53, 56, 72–78, 83–99; *ATB*, 79–80; Charles Marsh, *The Beloved Community: How Faith Shapes Social Justice from the Civil Rights Movement to Today* (New York: Basic Books, 2005), 49 (1st q), 3 (7th q); Charles Marsh and John M. Perkins, *Welcoming Justice: Movement toward Beloved Community* (Westmont, IL: IVP Books, 2018); Gary Herstein, "The Roycean Roots of the Beloved Community," *The Pluralist* 4, no. 2 (Summer 2009): 91–107; Kipton Jensen, "The Growing Edges of Beloved Community: From Royce to Thurman and King," *Transactions of the Charles S. Peirce Society* 52, no. 2 (Spring 2016): 240 (2nd and 3rd q), 242 (4th q), 244 (5th q), 255 (6th q); Kipton Jensen and Preston King, "Beloved Community: Martin Luther King, Howard Thurman, and Josiah Royce," *Amity: The Journal of Friendship Studies* 4, no. 1 (2017): 15–31; Rufus Burrow, "The Beloved Community: Martin Luther King Jr. and Josiah Royce," *Encounter* 73 (Fall 2012): 37–64; Josiah Royce, *The Problem of Christianity* (Chicago: Henry Regnery, 1968), 67–74, 81, 85, 95–99, 102, 172, 219, 251–254, 294–295, 304–308, 315–317, 352, 369; Howard Thurman, *The Search of Common Ground: An Inquiry into the Basis of Man's Experience of Community* (New York: Harper and Row, 1971); Charles Marsh, Shea Tuttle, and Daniel P. Rhodes, *Can I Get a Witness? Thirteen Peacemakers, Community Builders, and Agitators for Faith and Justice* (Grand Rapids, MI: Eerdmans, 2019), 37–57; Howard Thurman, "Desegregation, Integration, and the Beloved Community," 1966 typescript, Howard Thurman Papers Project, School of Theology, Boston University, https://www.bu.edu/htpp/files/2017/06/Desegregation-Integration-and-the-Beloved-Community.Sept_1966.pdf; Kenneth L. Smith and Ira G. Zepp Jr., *Search for the Beloved Community: The Thinking of Martin Luther King Jr.* (King of Prussia, PA: Judson, 1974); Ira G. Zepp Jr., *The Social Vision of Martin Luther King*

(New York: Carlson, 1989), 205–209; Rufus Burrow, *God and Human Dignity; The Personalism, Theology, and Ethics of Martin Luther King Jr.* (Notre Dame, IN: University of Notre Dame Press, 2006), 161ff.; James Melvin Washington, ed., *A Testament of Hope: The Essential Writings of Martin Luther King* (San Francisco: Harper, 1986), 8, 12, 20, 40, 46, 118–119, 122. On the Fellowship of Reconciliation, see Joseph Kip Kosek, *Acts of Conscience: Christian Nonviolence and Modern American Democracy* (New York: Columbia University Press, 2009); Walter Wink, ed., *Peace Is the Way: Writings on Nonviolence from the Fellowship of Reconciliation* (Ossining, NY: Orbis, 2000); Lewis Perry, *Civil Disobedience: An American Tradition* (New Haven, CT: Yale University Press, 2013), 181–206, 225–226; and Anthony C. Siracusa, *Nonviolence before King: The Politics of Being and the Black Freedom Struggle* (Chapel Hill: University of North Carolina Press, 2021). See also Casey N. Blake, *Beloved Community: The Cultural Criticism of Randolph Bourne, Van Wyck Brooks, Waldo Frank, and Lewis Mumford* (Chapel Hill: University of North Carolina Press, 1990); and Adam Russell Taylor, *A More Perfect Union: A New Vision for Building the Beloved Community* (Minneapolis: Broadleaf Books, 2021).

5. Clayborne Carson, ed., *The Papers of Martin Luther King, Jr.*, vol. 3, *Birth of a New Age* (Berkeley: University of California Press, 1997), 458 (1st q); J. Mills Thornton III, *Dividing Lines: Municipal Politics and the Struggle for Civil Rights in Montgomery, Birmingham, and Selma* (Tuscaloosa: University of Alabama Press, 2002), 576 (2nd q)–582 (3rd q).

6. Peniel Joseph, *The Sword and the Shield: The Revolutionary Lives of Malcolm X and Martin Luther King Jr.* (New York: Basic Books, 2020), 103 (1st q), 174 (2nd q); "Beloved Community," Center for Applied Nonviolence, https://nonviolencetoolkit.com/nonviolence-toolkit-way-of -life-beloved-community (3rd q).

7. *ATB*, 38–39 (q).

8. Sean Wilentz, "The Last Integrationist: John Lewis's American Odyssey," *New Republic* 215 (July 1, 1996): 19–26.

9. See Lewis's discussion of "love" and "reconciliation" in *ATB*, 179–208. On Lewis's early years as a congressman, see *WWTW*, 455–475; and Wilentz, "Last Integrationist."

10. John Lewis int.; Bernard LaFayette int. On the origins and evolution of Southern demagoguery, see Raymond Arsenault, "The Folklore of Southern Demagoguery," in *Is There a Southern Political Tradition?*, ed. Charles W. Eagles (Jackson: University Press of Mississippi, 1996), 79–132. On Southern politics between 1945 and 1976, see Jack Bass and Walter DeVries, *The Transformation of Southern Politics: Social Change and Political Consequences since 1945* (New York: Basic Books, 1976). On Lyndon Johnson's conversion to racial liberalism in the 1960s, see Nick Kotz, *Judgment Days: Lyndon Baines Johnson, Martin Luther King Jr. and the Laws That Changed America* (Boston: Houghton Mifflin, 2005); Robert A. Caro, *The Years of Lyndon Johnson: The Passage to Power* (New York: Knopf, 2012); and Julian E. Zelizer, *The Fierce Urgency of Now: Lyndon Johnson, Congress, and the Battle for the Great Society* (New York: Penguin, 2015). On Carter's emergence as a "New South" liberal, see Jonathan Alter, *His Very Best: Jimmy Carter, A Life* (New York: Simon and Schuster, 2020). On Clinton and Gore as leaders of the "New Democrats" of the 1980s and 1990s, see Bill Clinton, *My Life* (New York: Knopf, 2004); Bill Clinton, *My Life, the Presidential Years* (New York: Knopf, 2005); David Maranis, *First in His Class: A Biography of Bill Clinton* (New York: Simon and Schuster, 1995); David Maranis and Ellen Nakashima, *The Prince of Tennessee: The Rise of Al Gore* (New York:

Simon and Schuster, 2000); and Bill Turque, *Inventing Al Gore* (New York: Mariner Books, 2000). See also Alexander P. Lamis, *Southern Politics in the 1990s* (Baton Rouge: Louisiana State University Press, 1999).

11. See Barack Obama, *A Promised Land* (New York: Crown, 2020); and Julian E. Zelizer, ed., *The Presidency of Barack Obama: A First Historical Assessment* (Princeton, NJ: Princeton University Press, 2018).

12. *ATB*, 3–7. On the emergence of Trumpism as a danger to American democracy, see David Cay Johnston, *It's Even Worse Than You Think: What the Trump Administration Is Doing to America* (New York: Simon and Schuster, 2018); and Susan Hennessey and Benjamin Wittes, *Unmaking the Presidency: Donald Trump's War on the World's Most Powerful Office* (New York: Farrar, Straus and Giroux, 2020).

CHAPTER 1. "The Boy from Troy"

1. *WWTW*, 11–25 (q), 77. On the history of Pike County, see Margaret Pace Farmer, *One Hundred Fifty Years in Pike County, Alabama, 1821–1971* (Anniston, AL: Higginbotham, 1973).

2. *WWTW*, 22–28 (q); John Lewis, interview, History Makers, April 25, 2001, https://www.thehistorymakers.org/biography/honorable-john-lewis (hereafter cited as Lewis-HM int.); *1920 United States Federal Census*, MS for Gantt, Covington County, Alabama; *1930 United States Federal Census*, MS for River Road, Cross Roads, Pike County, Alabama; *1940 United States Federal Census*, MS for household 289, Street 17A, Cross Roads, Pike County, Alabama; *1950 United States Federal Census*, MS for dwelling 165, Cross Roads, Pike County, Alabama.

3. *ATB*, 7 (2nd q), 78, 105; *WWTW*, 29–30 (1st and 3rd q); Milton Viorst, *Fire in the Streets: America in the 1960's* (New York: Simon and Schuster, 1979), 96–98.

4. Jon Meacham, *His Truth Is Marching On: John Lewis and the Power of Hope* (New York: Random House, 2020), 26; *WWTW*, 19–24, 33, 34 (q), 34–36; *ATB*, 31; Lewis-HM int.; Viorst, *Fire in the Streets*, 98; Henry Lewis int.; Freddie Lewis int.; Samuel Lewis int.; Jerrick Lewis, remarks at the dedication of the John Lewis boyhood home historical marker, August 27, 2022. On slavery in Alabama, see James Benson Sellers, *Slavery in Alabama* (Tuscaloosa: University of Alabama Press, 1994); Horace Randall Williams, *Weren't No Good Times: Personal Accounts of Slavery in Alabama* (n.p.: Blair, 2004); and J. Mills Thornton III, *Politics and Power in a Slave Society: Alabama, 1800–1860* (Baton Rouge: Louisiana State University Press, 2014).

5. *WWTW*, 36 (1st and 4th q), 37 (2nd q), 38, 39 (3rd q), 40; John Egerton, *A Mind to Stay Here: Profiles from the South* (New York: Macmillan, 1970), 53 (5th q).

6. *WWTW*, 23 (3rd q), 40 (1st q), 41–42 (2nd and 4th q), 43; *ATB*, 159–161.

7. *WWTW*, 11, 30–32; Jerrick Lewis, remarks; Henry Lewis int.

8. *WWTW*, 20 (5th q), 45 (1st and 2nd q), 46 (3rd, 4th, and 6th q)–47 (7th q); *ATB*, 97–98, 157–159; Egerton, *Mind to Stay Here*, 53. On the Rosenwald Fund, see Hasia R. Diner, *Julius Rosenwald: Repairing the World* (New Haven, CT: Yale University Press, 2017), 47, 58, 61, 149, 159–175, 213–214. On the Tuskegee Institute, see Booker T. Washington, *Up from Slavery: The Autobiography of Booker T. Washington* (New York: The Outlook, 1901); Louis R. Harlan, *Booker T. Washington: The Wizard of Tuskegee, 1901–1915*, vol. 2 (New York: Oxford University

Press, 1983); and Robert J. Norrell, *Up from History: The Life of Booker T. Washington* (Cambridge, MA: Harvard University Press, 2009).

9. *WWTW*, 49 (1st–3rd q), 50 (4th q), 51 (5th–6th q).

10. *WWTW*, 51 (1st–3rd q), 52–54 (4th and 5th q).

11. *WWTW*, 54–56 (q); *ATB*, 71. On the rise of "Massive Resistance" and the White Citizens' Councils, see Numan V. Bartley, *The Rise of Massive Resistance: Race and Politics in the South during the 1950s* (Baton Rouge: Louisiana State University Press, 1969); and Neil R. McMillen, *The Citizens' Council: Organized Resistance to the Second Reconstruction, 1954–64* (Urbana: University of Illinois Press, 1971). On Rauschenbusch and the social gospel, see Christopher H. Evans, *The Social Gospel in American Religion: A History* (New York: New York University Press, 2017); and Christopher H. Evans, *The Kingdom Is Always but Coming: A Life of Walter Rauschenbusch* (Waco, TX: Baylor University Press, 2020).

12. *WWTW*, 56 (q); *ATB*, 79–80; Brian Ward, *Radio and the Struggle for Civil Rights in the South* (Gainesville: University Press of Florida, 2004), 108–109; Viorst, *Fire in the Streets*, 98. On King's early years in Montgomery, see Taylor Branch, *Parting the Waters: America in the King Years 1954–63* (New York: Simon and Schuster, 1988), 102–128.

13. *WWTW*, 57 (1st q)–58 (2nd q); *ATB*, 95–99; Lewis-HM int.; Henry Lewis int.; Freddie Lewis int.; Samuel Lewis int. Lewis remained passionately loyal and devoted to his family throughout his life. According to his chief of staff Michael Collins, "Wherever he went in the world, he took Troy and his family with him." Michael Collins int. On the nature and consequences of the *Brown* decisions of May 1954 and May 1955, see Richard Kluger, *Simple Justice: The History of "Brown v. Board of Education" and Black America's Struggle for Equality* (New York: Random House, 1975); and James T. Patterson, *"Brown v. Board of Education": A Civil Rights Milestone and Its Troubled Legacy* (New York: Oxford University Press, 2001). On the Till murder and its impact, see Stephen J. Whitfield, *A Death in the Delta: The Story of Emmett Till* (New York: Free Press, 1988); Timothy B. Tyson, *The Blood of Emmett Till* (New York: Simon and Schuster, 2017); and Elliott J. Gorn, *Let the People See: The Story of Emmett Till* (New York: Oxford University Press, 2018).

14. *WWTW*, 58 (1st q)–59 (2nd q); Lewis-HM int; Viorst, *Fire in the Streets*, 100. On the Montgomery Bus Boycott, see Martin Luther King Jr., *Stride toward Freedom: The Montgomery Story* (New York: Harper and Row, 1958); Branch, *Parting the Waters*, 143–205; and Stewart Burns, *Daybreak of Freedom: The Montgomery Bus Boycott* (Chapel Hill: University of North Carolina Press, 1997).

15. *WWTW*, 61 (1st and 2nd q)–62 (3rd q); Egerton, *Mind to Stay Here*, 53.

16. *WWTW*, 62 (1st and 2nd q)–63 (3rd q). On the NAACP's expulsion from Alabama, see Dan T. Carter, *The Politics of Rage: George Wallace, the Origins of the New Conservatism, and the Transformation of American Politics* (New York: Simon and Schuster, 1995), 92–93.

17. *WWTW*, 63. On Troy State Teachers College, see Edward M. Shackleford, *The First Fifty Years of the State Teachers College, Troy, Alabama* (London: Forgotten Books, 2019). On Alabama State, see Karl E. Westhauser, Elaine M. Smith, and Jennifer A. Fremlin, eds., *Creating Community: Life and Learning at Montgomery's Black University* (Tuscaloosa: University of Alabama Press, 2005); and Levi Watkins, *Fighting Hard: The Alabama State University Experience* (Detroit: Harlo Press, 1987).

18. *WWTW*, 63 (q); Lewis-HM int.; Cynthia Adams Wise, *The Alabama Baptist Children's Home: The First One Hundred Years* (Montgomery, AL: Brown Print Co., 1991); Bernard LaFayette int. On ABT, see American Baptist College, homepage, https://abcnash.edu/.

19. *WWTW*, 63–64 (q). On the SCLC, see Adam Fairclough, *To Redeem the Soul of America: The Southern Christian Leadership Conference and Martin Luther King, Jr.* (Athens: University of Georgia Press, 1987).

CHAPTER 2. Nashville

1. *WWTW*, 64.

2. *WWTW*, 69 (1st q), 70–71 (2nd q).

3. Bernard LaFayette int.; John Lewis int.; John Egerton, *A Mind to Stay Here: Profiles from the South* (New York: Macmillan, 1970), 54 (1st q); *WWTW*, 72–74 (2nd and 3rd q).

4. LaFayette int.; *WWTW*, 73–75 (q); Milton Viorst, *Fire in the Streets: America in the 1960's* (New York: Simon and Schuster, 1979), 101.

5. *WWTW*, 76.

6. *WWTW*, 77.

7. *WWTW*, 78 (1st and 2nd q), 79 (3rd q).

8. LaFayette int.; Harvard Sitkoff, *The Struggle for Black Equality*, 25th anniversary ed. (New York: Hill and Wang, 2008), 74 (1st q); *WWTW*, 70, 80 (2nd q), 81–82; Viorst, *Fire in the Streets*, 102–103.

9. LaFayette int.; James Lawson int.; Lewis-HM int.; *WWTW*, 83 (1st and 2nd q), 84 (3rd q); Benjamin Houston, *The Nashville Way: Racial Etiquette and the Struggle for Social Justice in a Southern City* (Athens: University of Georgia Press, 2012), 82–91; Peter Ackerman and Jack Duvall, *A Force More Powerful: A Century of Nonviolent Conflict* (New York: Palgrave, 2000), 306–333; Wesley C. Hogan, *Many Minds, One Heart: SNCC's Dream for a New America* (Chapel Hill: University of North Carolina Press, 2007), 8–26; David Halberstam, *The Children* (New York: Random House, 1998), 11–106; Cheryl Lynn Greenberg, ed., *A Circle of Trust: Remembering SNCC* (New Brunswick, NJ: Rutgers University Press, 1998), 18–23; Raymond Arsenault, *Freedom Riders: 1961 and the Struggle for Racial Justice* (New York: Oxford University Press, 2006) (hereafter cited as *FR*), 84–87; Taylor Branch, *Parting the Waters: America in the King Years 1954–63* (New York: Simon and Schuster, 1988), 204–205, 259–263, 268–269, 394; Viorst, *Fire in the Streets*, 103–117; Jeffrey A. Turner, *Sitting In and Speaking Out: Student Movements in the American South 1960–1970* (Athens: University of Georgia Press, 2010), 50–56. On Smith, see Kelly Miller Smith, "We Seek a City," in *The Pulpit Speaks on Race*, ed. Alfred T. Davies (New York: Abingdon Press, 1957), 177–183. On Lawson, see James M. Lawson Jr. with Michael K. Honey and Kent Wong, *Revolutionary Nonviolence: Organizing for Freedom* (Berkeley: University of California Press, 2022); Michael K. Honey, dir., *Love and Solidarity: James Lawson and Nonviolence in the Search for Workers' Rights* (Bullfrog Films, 2016), Prime Video; Ernest M. Limbo, "James Lawson: The Nashville Civil Rights Movement," in *The Human Tradition in the Civil Rights Movement*, ed. Susan M. Glisson (Lanham, MD: Rowman and Littlefield, 2006), 157–179; and David L. Chappell, *A Stone of Hope: Prophetic Religion and the Death of Jim Crow* (Chapel Hill:

University of North Carolina Press, 2004), 66–71. Niebuhr was among the first writers to point out the applicability of Gandhian nonviolence to the American civil rights struggle. See Reinhold Niebuhr, *Moral Man and Immoral Society: A Study in Ethics and Politics* (New York: Charles Scribner's Sons, 1932).

10. *WWTW*, 87 (q); Lewis-HM int.; LaFayette int.

11. "Highlander Folk School: Communist Training School, Monteagle, Tenn." (Athens: Georgia Commission on Education, 1957 (1st q), broadside available at dlg.usg.edu.; *WWTW*, 87, 89 (2nd q)–90 (3rd q); LaFayette int.; Houston, *Nashville Way*, 88–92; Andrew Young, *An Easy Burden: The Civil Rights Movement and the Transformation of America* (New York: HarperCollins, 1996), 125–130. On LaFayette, see Bernard LaFayette Jr. and Kathryn Lee Johnson, *In Peace and Freedom: My Journey in Selma* (Lexington: University Press of Kentucky, 2013); and Halberstam, *Children*, 64–65, 69–72, 94, 97–98, 128–129, 136–138, 412–415. On Bevel, see Halberstam, *Children*, 94–102; Branch, *Parting the Waters*, 263–264, 279–280, 482–484, 559, 753–754; *WP*, April 11–12, 2008; and *NYT*, December 23, 2008. On Highlander Folk School, see John M. Glen, *Highlander: No Ordinary School, 1932–1972* (Lexington: University Press of Kentucky, 1988); Frank C. Adams with Myles Horton, *Unearthing Seeds of Fire: The Idea of Highlander* (Durham, NC: Blair, 1975); and Myles Horton with Judith and Herbert Kohl, *The Long Haul: An Autobiography* (New York: Doubleday, 1990). On Clark, see Katherine Mellon Charron, *Freedom's Teacher: The Life of Septima Clark* (Chapel Hill: University of North Carolina Press, 2009).

12. Houston, *Nashville Way*, 1–81. See also Don Harrison Doyle, *Nashville since the 1920s* (Knoxville: University of Tennessee Press, 1985); and Tommie Morton-Young, *Nashville, Tennessee*, Black America Series (Charleston: Arcadia, 2000).

13. *WWTW*, 90–94; Houston, *Nashville Way*, 83–97 (q), 88–91; LaFayette int. On Will Campbell, see Will D. Campbell, *Brother to a Dragonfly*, 25th anniversary ed. (New York: Bloomsbury, 2000); Will D. Campbell, *Forty Acres and a Goat: A Memoir* (Atlanta: Peachtree, 1986); Thomas L. Connelly, *Will Campbell and the Soul of the South* (New York: Continuum, 1983); Merrill Hawkins, *Will D. Campbell: Radical Prophet of the South* (Macon, GA: Mercer University Press, 1997); and Halberstam, *Children*, 22, 52–56, 72, 122–123, 127, 205, 277, 713–714. On the NAACP Youth Councils, see Thomas Bynum, *"Our Fight Is for Right": The NAACP Youth Councils and College Chapters' Crusade for Civil Rights, 1936–1965* (Atlanta: Georgia State University Press, 2007); Thomas Bynum, *NAACP Youth and the Fight for Black Freedom, 1936–1965* (Knoxville: University of Tennessee Press, 2013); and Patricia Sullivan, *Lift Every Voice: The NAACP and the Making of the Civil Rights Movement* (New York: New Press, 2009), 174, 207, 223, 257. On the student activists of the 1930s, see Robert Cohen, *When the Old Left Was Young: Student Radicals and America's First Mass Student Movement, 1929–1941* (New York: Oxford University Press, 1993); and Ralph S. Brax, *The First Student Movement: Student Activism in the United States during the 1930s* (Port Washington, NY: Kennikat Press, 1981).

14. LaFayette int.; Lewis int.; Rip Patton int.; Catherine Burks-Brooks int.; Jim Zwerg int.; Matthew Walker Jr. int.; Diane Nash int.; *WTTW*, 90–91 (q), 92–96; *FR*, 87, 179–193, 537–541; Halberstam, *Children*, 51–106. On Ella Baker, see Barbara Ransby, *Ella Baker and the Black Freedom Movement: A Radical Democratic Vision* (Chapel Hill: University of North Carolina Press, 2005); and Joanne Grant, *Ella Baker: Freedom Bound* (New York: Wiley, 1998).

15. *WWTW*, 93 (1st q), 92 (2nd q), 94 (3rd q).

16. LaFayette int.; Nash int.; *WWTW*, 94 (1st and 2nd q), 95 (3rd q); Houston, *Nashville Way*, 86, 91.

17. LaFayette int.; Lewis int.; Patton int.; *WWTW*, 94–97 (q); Houston, *Nashville Way*, 9; Halberstam, *Children*, 90–92, 199.

18. LaFayette int., *WWTW*, 98–100; *FR*, 82. On the sit-in movement of the early 1960s, see William H. Chafe, *Civilities and Civil Rights: Greensboro, North Carolina, and the Black Struggle for Freedom* (New York: Oxford University Press, 1980); Miles Wolff, *Lunch at the Five and Ten: The Greensboro Sit-Ins, a Contemporary History* (New York: Stein and Day, 1970); Christopher W. Schmidt, *The Sit-Ins: Protest and Legal Changes in the Civil Rights Era* (Chicago: University of Chicago Press, 2018); Turner, *Sitting In and Speaking Out*; and Iwan Morgan and Philip Davies, eds., *From Sit-Ins to SNCC: The Student Civil Rights Movement in the 1960s* (Gainesville: University Press of Florida, 2012). On the early Nashville sit-ins, see Houston, *Nashville Way*, 82–122; Linda T. Wynn, "The Dawning of a New Day: The Nashville Sit-Ins, February 13–May 10, 1960," *Tennessee Historical Quarterly* 50 (Spring 1991): 42–54; and Aldon D. Morris, *The Origins of the Civil Rights Movement: Black Communities Organizing for Change* (New York: Collier Macmillan, 1984), 174–178, 206–211.

19. *WWTW*, 100 (1st q), 101 (2nd and 3rd q).

20. LaFayette int.; *WWTW*, 103 (q).

21. LaFayette int.; Houston, *Nashville Way*, 95 (1st q); *WWTW*, 105–106 (2nd q); Meacham, *His Truth Is Marching On*, 70.

22. *WWTW*, 106 (1st and 2nd q), 107 (3rd and 4th q).

23. *WWTW*, 73 (1st q), 108 (2nd q); Patricia Stephens Due int. On the emergence of "jail, no bail" as a civil rights movement tactic, see *FR*, 88–94; August Meier and Elliott Rudwick, *CORE: A Study in the Civil Rights Movement* (Urbana: University of Illinois Press, 1975), 104–117; and Tananarive Due and Patricia Stephens Due, *Freedom in the Family: A Mother-Daughter Memoir of the Fight for Civil Rights* (New York: Ballantine, 2003), 4, 69–82, 94–98.

24. *WWTW*, 109–110 (1st q), 111 (2nd q).

25. *WWTW*, 113 (q), 114; LaFayette int. On Marshall, see Carl Rowan, *Dream Makers, Dream Breakers: The World of Justice Thurgood Marshall* (Boston: Little, Brown, 1995); Juan Williams, *Thurgood Marshall: American Revolutionary* (New York: Times Books / Random House, 1998); Spencer R. Crew, *Thurgood Marshall: A Life in American History* (Santa Barbara, CA: ABC-CLIO, 2019); and Howard Ball, *A Defiant Life: Thurgood Marshall and the Persistence of Racism in America* (New York: Crown, 1999).

26. LaFayette int.; Lawson int.; Lewis int.; Nash int.; Clayborne Carson int.; *WWTW*, 114–115. On the founding of SNCC, see Clayborne Carson, *In Struggle: SNCC and the Black Awakening of the 1960s* (Cambridge, MA: Harvard University Press, 1981) (hereafter cited as *IS*), 19–30; and Wesley C. Hogan, *Many Minds, One Heart: SNCC's Dream for a New America* (Chapel Hill: University of North Carolina Press, 2007), 31–44. On the white delegates to the Shaw conference, see Stephen J. Whitfield, *Learning on the Left: Political Profiles of Brandeis University* (Waltham, NJ: Brandeis University Press, 2020), 259; and Debra L. Schultz, *Going South: Jewish Women in the Civil Rights Movement* (New York: New York University Press, 2001), 31–32.

27. LaFayette int.; Nash int.; C. T. Vivian int.; Lewis-HM int.; *WWTW*, 115, 116 (1st–7th q), 117; Houston, *Nashville Way*, 114, 115–116 (8th q); Halberstam, *Children*, 230–234.

CHAPTER 3. In the Movement

1. *WWTW*, 116–117 (1st q); Benjamin Houston, *The Nashville Way: Racial Etiquette and the Struggle for Social Justice in a Southern City* (Athens: University of Georgia Press, 2012), 116–117 (2nd q); Nashville *Tennessean*, April 19–21, 1960; John Egerton, *A Mind to Stay Here: Profiles from the South* (New York: Macmillan, 1970), 56 (3rd q).

2. Cleveland Sellers with Robert Terrell, *The River of No Return: The Autobiography of a Black Militant and the Life and Death of SNCC* (New York: William Morrow, 1973), 20 (1st q); *WWTW*, 120–121 (2nd q).

3. Bernard LaFayette int.; Kwame Leo Lillard int.; John Lewis, interview by Vicki Daitch, March 19, 2004, John F. Kennedy Presidential Library (hereafter cited as Lewis-JFKL int.); *WWTW*, 126–129 (q). On the 1960 presidential election, see Theodore H. White, *The Making of the President 1960* (New York: Atheneum, 1961).

4. Houston, *Nashville Way*, 33–38; *WWTW*, 121–122 (q).

5. *WWTW*, 122–123 (q), 124.

6. *IS*, 29 (q), 30; *WWTW*, 124–126.

7. *WWTW*, 124–125 (1st q); *FR*, 90 (2nd q); Taylor Branch, *Parting the Waters: America in the King Years 1954–63* (New York: Simon and Schuster, 1988), 351; Roger M. Williams, *The Bonds: An American Family* (New York: Atheneum, 1971), 178–213; Julian Bond, "The Movement We Helped to Make," in *Long Time Gone: Sixties America Then and Now,* ed. Alex Bloom (New York: Oxford University Press, 2001), 11–22. See also Julian Bond, *Race Man: Selected Works, 1960–2015,* ed. Michael Long (San Francisco: City Lights Books, 2020); and John Neary, *Julian Bond: Black Rebel* (New York: William Morrow, 1971).

8. LaFayette int.; Lewis int.; Stephen Kendrick and Paul Kendrick, *Nine Days: The Race to Save Martin Luther King Jr.'s Life and Win the 1960 Election* (New York: Farrar, Straus and Giroux, 2021), 121–235; Branch, *Parting the Waters*, 361 (q); *FR*, 91, 606n50; *WWTW*, 126.

9. *WWTW*, 129; *FR*, 90–91 (q), 92; Lewis-JFKL int. On Marian Anderson, see Raymond Arsenault, *The Sound of Freedom: Marian Anderson, the Lincoln Memorial, and the Concert That Awakened America* (New York: Bloomsbury, 2009). On John F. Kennedy and race, see Carl F. Brauer, *John F. Kennedy and the Second Reconstruction* (New York: Columbia University Press, 1977); Nick Bryant, *The Bystander: John F. Kennedy and the Struggle for Black Equality* (New York: Basic Books, 2006); David Niven, *The Politics of Injustice: The Kennedys, the Freedom Rides, and the Electoral Consequences of a Moral Compromise* (Knoxville: University of Tennessee Press, 2003); and Patricia Sullivan, *Justice Rising: Robert Kennedy's America in Black and White* (Cambridge, MA: Harvard University Press, 2021).

10. LaFayette int.; *WWTW*, 127 (1st–3rd q), 128 (4th q).

11. LaFayette int.; Rip Patton int.; *WWTW*, 48 (1st q), 129 (2nd q), 130–131 (3rd–5th q).

12. On Nash, see *WWTW*, 91 (1st q)–92 (2nd q), 93–95, 103, 110–116, 142; *FR*, 89, 94–97, 179–187, 198–200; David Halberstam, *The Children* (New York: Random House, 1998), 3–6, 9–10, 59, 62–63, 95, 133–135, 143–147; Lynne Olson, *Freedom's Daughters: The Unsung Heroines of the Civil Rights Movement from 1830 to 1970* (New York: Scribner, 2001), 150–162; and Diane Nash, "Inside the Sit-Ins and Freedom Rides: Testimony of a Southern Student," in *The New Negro,* ed. Mathew H. Ahmann (New York: Biblo and Tannen, 1969), 42–60. Howell Raines,

ed., *My Soul Is Rested: Movement Days in the Deep South Remembered* (New York: Penguin, 1983), 109–110 (3rd q); Diane Nash int.; LaFayette int.; Gordon Carey int.; Marvin Rich int.; Tom Gaither int.; Tom Gaither, field report from Rock Hill, September 29–October 1, 1960, reel 36, Congress of Racial Equality Papers, State Historical Society of Wisconsin (microfilm); Tom Gaither, "Jailed-In," February 1961, folder 3, box 8, Student Nonviolent Coordinating Committee Papers, Martin Luther King Center, Atlanta, GA; Branch, *Parting the Waters*, 391–394; Halberstam, *Children*, 267–268; August Meier and Elliott Rudwick, *CORE: A Study in the Civil Rights Movement* (Urbana: University of Illinois Press, 1975), 117–119, 136; *Rock Hill Evening Herald*, January 31–February 21, 1961; *NYT*, February 1–2, 13, 20–21, 1961.

13. LaFayette int.; *WWTW*, 132 (q), 144.

14. Houston, *Nashville Way*, 126, 129, 134; LaFayette int.; John Lewis int.; *FR*, 10–53, 93–97, 106, 114, 121–122; *WWTW*, 132 (q)–133. See also Mia Bay, *Traveling Black: A Story of Race and Resistance* (Cambridge, MA: Harvard University Press, 2021), 230–233, 249–257, 269.

15. *WWTW*, 133 (q); *FR*, 99.

16. *WWTW*, 73 (q), 133.

17. LaFayette int. (1st q); *FR*, 105–106; John R. Lewis, Freedom Rider application, March 1961, section 456, reel 44, Congress of Racial Equality Papers; *WWTW*, 133 (2nd q).

18. On the Journey of Reconciliation and its aftermath, see *FR*, 32–61.

19. *FR*, 93–94 (1st q), 95–96 (2nd q); Gaither int.; Carey int.; James Farmer, *Lay Bare the Heart: The Autobiography of the Civil Rights Movement* (New York: New American Library, 1985), 195–196.

20. Gaither int.; *FR*, 97 (q).

21. Farmer, *Lay Bare the Heart*, 195–197; Jim Peck, *Freedom Ride* (New York: Simon and Schuster, 1962); *FR*, 97–107; *WWTW*, 136–137, 146; Charles Person with Richard Rooker, *Buses Are a Comin': Memoir of a Freedom Rider* (New York: St. Martin's Press, 2021), 137–147; Carey int.; Genevieve Hughes Houghton int.; Benjamin Cox int.; Charles Person int.; Lewis int.; Hank Thomas int.; John Moody int.; Ed Blankenheim int.

CHAPTER 4. Riding to Freedom

1. *WWTW*, 136 (1st q), 138 (3rd q); James Farmer, *Lay Bare the Heart: An Autobiography of the Civil Rights Movement* (New York: New American Library, 1985), 198 (2nd q); *FR*, 106–107; Bernard LaFayette int.; Charles Person with Richard Rooker, *Buses Are a Comin': Memoir of a Freedom Rider* (New York: St. Martin's Press, 2021), 138–151.

2. Farmer, *Lay Bare the Heart*, 198 (1st and 2nd q); Benjamin Cox int. (3rd q); Gordon Carey int.; *WWTW*, 140 (4th and 5th q); *FR*, 107–108.

3. Farmer, *Lay Bare the Heart*, 198–199 (1st q); Howell Raines, ed., *My Soul Is Rested: Movement Days in the Deep South Remembered* (New York: Penguin, 1983), 111 (2nd q); *FR*, 108–109; *WWTW*, 139–140.

4. *FR*, 109–111 (q), 112; *Montgomery Advertiser*, May 5, 1961; *WWTW*, 140; John Lewis int.; Simeon Booker int.; Carey int.; Ted Gaffney int.; Moses Newson int.; Charles Person int.; Marvin Rich int.; Hank Thomas int.; Genevieve Hughes Houghton int.; Ed Blankenheim int. On Booker, see Simeon Booker, *Black Man's America* (Englewood Cliffs, NJ: Prentice-Hall, 1964);

and Simeon Booker, *Shocking the Conscience: A Reporter's Account of the Civil Rights Movement* (Jackson: University Press of Mississippi, 2013).

5. *WWTW*, 140 (1st q); *FR*, 112–117 (2nd q), 118 (3rd q); Person, *Buses Are a Comin'*, 155–178.

6. *FR*, 119 (1st q); *Greensboro Daily News*, May 7–8, 1961; *WWTW*, 141 (2nd q); Person, *Buses Are a Comin'*, 178–179.

7. Jim Peck, *Freedom Ride* (New York: Simon and Schuster, 1962), 118 (1st q); *FR*, 120 (2nd q), 121 (3rd q); Person, *Buses Are a Comin'*, 180–182.

8. *FR*, 121–124; *WWTW*, 141–142 (1st and 2nd q), 143–144; Lewis int.; Person int.; Houghton int.; Person, *Buses Are a Comin'*, 183–188.

9. *WWTW*, 142–143 (1st and 2nd q), 144 (3rd and 4th q); *FR*, 135.

10. *FR*, 135–136.

11. *FR*, 124–132; Peck, *Freedom Ride*, 123–124 (q).

12. Houghton int.; Blankenheim int.; Person int.; Thomas int.; Booker int.; Fred Shuttlesworth int.; *FR*, 132–133 (1st and 2nd q), 134–141; Farmer, *Lay Bare the Heart*, 200–201 (3rd q); Person, *Buses Are a Comin'*, 188–210.

13. Dorothy B. Kaufman, *The First Freedom Ride: The Walter Bergman Story* (Detroit: ACLU Fund Press, 1989), 154 (1st q); Simeon Booker and Ted Gaffney, "Eyewitness Report on Dixie 'Freedom Ride'—Jet Team Braves Mob Action 4 Times within 2-Day Period," *Jet*, June 1, 1961, 14–21; *FR*, 141–149 (2nd q), 150–160 (3rd q); Person, *Buses Are a Comin'*, 210–237; Taylor Branch, *Parting the Waters: America in the King Years 1954–63* (New York: Simon and Schuster, 1988), 123–124; Blankenheim int.; Person int.; Thomas int.; Houghton int.; Booker int.; Gaffney int.; Newson int.; Shuttlesworth int.

14. Andrew M. Manis, *A Fire You Can't Put Out: The Civil Rights Life of Birmingham's Reverend Fred Shuttlesworth* (Tuscaloosa: University of Alabama Press, 1999), 266–267 (1st q); *FR*, 161–164 (2nd q); Harris Wofford, *Of Kennedys and Kings: Making Sense of the Sixties* (Pittsburgh: University of Pittsburgh Press, 1992), 153.

15. *WWTW*, 144 (1st and 2nd q), 145 (3rd q), 146 (4th q); *FR*, 179–180.

16. *WWTW*, 147 (1st q); *FR*, 162–167 (2nd q), 168–170 (4th q), 171 (3rd q)–176; "Kennedy's Call to B'ham," transcript, May 15, 1961, General Correspondence, box 10, Robert Fitzgerald Kennedy Papers, John F. Kennedy Presidential Library; Manis, *Fire You Can't Put Out*, 268–269; Person, *Buses Are a Comin'*, 239–255.

17. Farmer, *Lay Bare the Heart*, 203 (1st, 3rd, and 4th q); *WWTW*, 148 (2nd q), 149 (5th q); *FR*, 177–184; Diane Nash int.; John Seigenthaler int.; Rip Patton int.; Lewis int.; LaFayette int.

18. Branch, *Parting the Waters*, 429–430 (1st–4th q); David Halberstam, *The Children* (New York: Random House, 1998), 286 (5th q); *FR*, 183–190; George Barrett int.; Nash int.; Seigenthaler int.; Lewis int.; LaFayette int.

19. *FR*, 185–189 (1st q), 190 (3rd q)–197, 537–538; *WWTW*, 149–152 (2nd q), 153 (4th and 5th q); Nash int.; Bill Harbour int.; Michael Collins int.; Jim Zwerg int.; Salynn McCollum int.; Shuttlesworth int.; Lewis int.; LaFayette int.

20. *FR*, 198 (1st–3rd and 5th q)–200; *WWTW*, 153; Catherine Burks-Brooks int. (4th q); Lewis int.; Harbour int.; Nash int.; Shuttlesworth int.

21. *WWTW*, 154 (1st and 2nd q)–155; *FR*, 199 (3rd q)–200; Kwame Leo Lillard int.; Lewis int.; Brooks int.; Nash int.; Shuttlesworth int.

22. Seigenthaler int.; *WWTW*, 155–157; *FR*, 200–201 (q), 206.

CHAPTER 5. Mississippi Bound

1. *WWTW*, 155 (1st q), 156 (3rd q); *FR*, 202 (2nd q), 203; Bernard LaFayette int.

2. *FR*, 205 (1st q), 206 (2nd q), 207–208 (3rd and 4th q); *WWTW*, 157.

3. *WWTW*, 158 (q); *FR*, 209; Catherine Burks-Brooks int.

4. *WWTW*, 158 (q); *FR*, 210–212.

5. *FR*, 212–214 (1st–3rd q); *WWTW*, 159 (4th q); Lucretia Collins int.

6. *WWTW*, 160–161 (q); *FR*, 214–220; John Seigenthaler int.

7. *FR*, 220–222 (1st q), 223–224 (2nd and 3rd q), 225–231 (5th q), 232–233 (6th q); *WWTW*, 161–162 (4th q), 163 (7th q); Lewis int.; LaFayette int.; Diane Nash int.; Fred Shuttlesworth int.

8. *FR*, 234 (1st q), 238 (3rd q); *WWTW*, 164 (2nd q).

9. *FR*, 237 (1st q)–239 (2nd q), 240; *WWTW*, 154 (3rd q).

10. *FR*, 240–248; *WWTW*, 165 (q), 166.

11. *WWTW*, 166–167 (q); *FR*, 248–251; Nash int.; Lucretia Collins int.; Lewis int.; LaFayette int.

12. *FR*, 251 (1st q), 252 (2nd q)–255 (3rd q), 256 (4th q), 257 (5th q); *WWTW*, 166–167.

13. Taylor Branch, *Parting the Waters: America in the King Years 1954–63* (New York: Simon and Schuster, 1988), 468 (1st q); *WWTW*, 167–168 (2nd q); *FR*, 254–258.

14. *FR*, 259–260 (1st q), 261 (2nd q)–262 (3rd and 4th q), 263–270; *WWTW*, 168–169.

15. *FR*, 267, 271 (1st q)–274 (5th q); James Farmer, *Lay Bare the Heart: An Autobiography of the Civil Rights Movement* (New York: New American Library, 1985), 207 (2nd q); *WWTW*, 169 (3rd and 4th q).

16. *WWTW*, 170 (q); *FR*, 274–286, 533–587.

17. *WWTW*, 170–171 (q).

18. *FR*, 325 (1st and 2nd q), 326 (3rd q); *WWTW*, 171 (4th q). On the history of Parchman, see David M. Oshinsky, *"Worse Than Slavery": Parchman Farm and the Ordeal of Jim Crow Justice* (New York: Free Press, 1996).

19. *FR*, 326 (1st q); *WWTW*, 171 (2nd q), 172 (3rd q), 173; Lewis int.

20. On Ross Barnett, see Joseph Crespino, *In Search of Another Country: Mississippi and the Conservative Counterrevolution* (Princeton, NJ: Princeton University Press, 2007); and Erle Johnston, *I Rolled with Ross: A Political Portrait* (Baton Rouge, LA: Moran, 1980).

21. *FR*, 293 (1st q), 235 (2nd q); *WWTW*, 174 (3rd–5th q); Lewis int.; Bill Harbour int. Charles Person, the youngest of the original thirteen Freedom Riders, published a memoir of the Freedom Rides with the title *Buses Are a Comin'*.

22. *WWTW*, 174–178 (1st–3rd q), 179–180; *IS*, 41; *FR*, 328–330, 396–397 (4th q); James Forman, *The Making of Black Revolutionaries: A Personal Account* (New York: Macmillan, 1972), 158–211. On Robert Williams, see Timothy B. Tyson, *Radio-Free Dixie: Robert F. Williams and the Roots of Black Power* (Chapel Hill: University of North Carolina Press, 1999); Robert F. Williams, *Negroes with Guns* (Chicago: Third World Press, 1973); and *FR*, 81–82, 404–418. On Carmichael, see Stokely Carmichael with Ekweume Michael Thelwell, *Ready for Revolution: The Life and Struggles of Stokely Carmichael (Kwame Ture)* (New York: Scribner, 2003); and Peniel E. Joseph, *Stokely: A Life* (New York: Civitas Books, 2014).

23. *WWTW*, 181 (q); *IS*, 40; Fred Powledge, *Free at Last? The Civil Rights Movement and the People Who Made It* (Boston: Little, Brown, 1991), 304–308. In Harry Belafonte with Michael

Shnayerson, *My Song, A Memoir* (New York: Knopf, 2011), 235, Belafonte discusses his complicated relationship with Lewis and SNCC: "John Lewis wasn't one of the SNCCers who came to my suite that day. For one thing, he was in jail in Mississippi with a busload of Freedom Riders. Even had he been free, though, he would have wanted no part of a meeting with Harry Belafonte, the singer who had gotten so close to the Kennedys. He feared I would try to talk the SNCCers into focusing on voter registration, and out of staging more direct actions, just as the Kennedys wanted. . . . How, John would ask angrily when he got out of jail, was registering voters an act of Gandhian nonviolence?" On Belafonte's evolution as a civil rights activist, see Judith E. Smith, *Becoming Belafonte: Black Artist, Public Radical* (Austin: University of Texas Press, 2014).

24. *FR*, 397–398 (q); *IS*, 41–42; *WWTW*, 181–182; LaFayette int.; Nash int.; Lewis int.; Forman, *Making of Black Revolutionaries*, 223–233.

25. *FR*, 386–390 (q), 391; *Jackson Daily News*, August 11, 14, 1961; *NYT*, August 13–14, 1961; Wyatt Tee Walker int.

26. *FR*, 392 (q)–394.

27. *WWTW*, 183–184; LaFayette int.; Seigenthaler int.; Lewis int.; Rip Patton int.; Harbour int.; *FR*, 430–434; Martin Luther King Jr., "The Time for Freedom Has Come," *New York Times Magazine*, September 10, 1961, 25, 118–119 (1st and 2nd q); *Birmingham News*, September 13, 1961 (3rd q).

28. *FR*, 437–439 (2nd q), 440 (1st q), 441–446; *WWTW*, 184.

29. *FR*, 446 (1st q)–448; *WWTW*, 184 (2nd q); Lewis int.; LaFayette int.

CHAPTER 6. SNCC on the March

1. *WWTW*, 185.

2. *FR*, 456–458 (1st q), 476; *WWTW*, 183–189 (2nd q), 190.

3. *WWTW*, 190 (1st q), 191–192 (2nd and 3rd q); *FR*, 487–491.

4. *WWTW*, 192 (1st and 2nd q), 193 (3rd and 4th q); John Britton, "Best City in the South for Negroes: Many Cry 'Tokenism,' but Nashville Has the Most 'Tokens,'" *Jet*, December 5, 1963, 14–21; Benjamin Houston, *The Nashville Way: Racial Etiquette and the Struggle for Social Justice in a Southern City* (Athens: University of Georgia Press, 2012), 134. On the "Battle of Oxford," see Charles W. Eagles, *The Price of Defiance: James Meredith and the Integration of Ole Miss* (Chapel Hill: University of North Carolina Press, 2009); William Doyle, *An American Insurrection: James Meredith and the Battle of Oxford, Mississippi, 1962* (New York: Doubleday, 2001); and James Meredith, *Three Years in Mississippi* (Jackson: University Press of Mississippi, 2019).

5. David J. Garrow, *Bearing the Cross: Martin Luther King, Jr., and the Southern Christian Leadership Conference* (New York: William Morrow, 1986), 226 (1st q), 228 (2nd q), 229 (3rd q); *WWTW*, 193–195 (4th and 5th q). On Wallace and his inaugural pledge, see Dan T. Carter, *The Politics of Rage: George Wallace, the Origins of the New Conservatism, and the Transformation of American Politics* (Baton Rouge: Louisiana State University Press, 2000); Marshall Frady, *Wallace* (New York: New American Library, 1976); and Carl Rowan, "A Symbol of Segregation Looks Back in Regret," *Baltimore Sun*, September 6, 1991.

6. *WWTW*, 195 (1st q), 196 (2nd and 3rd q), 197 (4th and 5th q), 198 (6th and 7th q). On the 1963 Birmingham crisis, see Taylor Branch, *Parting the Waters: America in the King Years*

1954–63 (New York: Simon and Schuster, 1988), 689–802; Glenn T. Eskew, *But for Birmingham: The Local and National Movements in the Civil Rights Struggle* (Chapel Hill: University of North Carolina Press, 1997); Diane McWhorter, *Carry Me Home: Birmingham Alabama: The Climactic Battle of the Civil Rights Revolution* (New York: Simon and Schuster, 2001); and T. K. Thorne, *Behind the Magic Curtain: Secrets, Spies, and Unsung White Allies of Birmingham's Civil Rights Days* (Montgomery: New South Books, 2021).

7. On Wallace and the 1963 "schoolhouse door" crisis, see Carter, *Politics of Rage,* 133–155; and E. Culpepper Clark, *The Schoolhouse Door: Segregation's Last Stand at the University of Alabama* (New York: Oxford University Press, 1993). On Evers's assassination, see Maryanne Vollers, *Ghosts of Mississippi: The Murder of Medgar Evers, the Trials of Byron de la Beckwith, and the Haunting of the New South* (Boston: Little, Brown, 1995); Michael Vernon Williams, *Medgar Evers: Mississippi Martyr* (Fayetteville: University of Arkansas Press, 2011); and Adam Nossiter, *Of Long Memory: Mississippi and the Murder of Medgar Evers* (Boston: Addison-Wesley, 1993).

8. *WWTW,* 199–200 (q); Lewis-HM int; James Forman, *The Making of Black Revolutionaries: A Personal Account* (New York: Macmillan, 1972), 331–332. On McDew, see *IS,* 28–30, 49–50, 54, 68, 84–85; Cheryl Lynn Greenberg, ed., *A Circle of Trust: Remembering SNCC* (New Brunswick, NJ: Rutgers University Press, 1998), 34–36, 39–40, 45–47, 68–70, 189; and Charles McDew with Beryl Gilfix, *Tell the Story: A Memoir of the Civil Rights Movement* (self-published, 2020).

9. *WWTW,* 200–203 (1st and 5th q), 205 (2nd and 3rd q)–207, 204 (4th q); *IS,* 91; Lewis-JFKL int.; Lewis-HM int. For overviews of the 1963 March on Washington, see William P. Jones, *The March on Washington: Jobs, Freedom, and the Forgotten History of Civil Rights* (New York: Norton, 2013), 163–200; Charles Euchner, *Nobody Turn Me Around: A People's History of the 1963 March on Washington* (Boston: Beacon Press, 2010); Branch, *Parting the Waters,* 846–887; and Jonathan Eig, *King: A Life* (New York: Farrar, Straus and Giroux, 2023), 319–346. On Rustin's role in the planning of the march, see John D'Emilio, *Lost Prophet: The Life and Times of Bayard Rustin* (New York: Free Press, 2003), 327–331, 335–360. On Randolph and the 1940s March on Washington movement, see David Lucander, *Winning the War for Democracy: The March on Washington Movement, 1941–1946* (Urbana: University of Illinois Press, 2014).

10. *WWTW,* 206 (1st q)–209 (3rd and 4th q); *IS,* 92 (2nd q); Lewis-JFKL int. Forman later characterized Lewis's counterparts as "a jungle of civil rights hyenas" and argued that he was not up to the task of sparring with them: "Young, inexperienced, from a small Southern town, John had fine qualities as a symbol of black resistance, but he was lost among these overpowering tricky infighters." Forman, *Making of Black Revolutionaries,* 366.

11. *WWTW,* 211 (1st q), 210 (2nd q), 213 (3rd and 4th q)–215; Bernard LaFayette int.; Zev Aelony int.; Don Harris int.; Bernard LaFayette Jr. and Kathryn Lee Johnson, *In Peace and Freedom: My Journey in Selma* (Lexington: University Press of Kentucky, 2013), 21–43; *IS,* 92 (5th q), 93 (6th q); Cleveland Sellers with Robert Terrell, *The River of No Return: The Autobiography of a Black Militant and the Life and Death of SNCC* (New York: William Morrow, 1973), 67–80; SNCC, "Americus, Georgia," press release, September 24, 1963, Civil Rights Movement Archive, https://www.crmvet.org/docs/630924_sncc_americus_insurrection-r.pdf; Don Harris, interview by Emily Stoper, 1966 or 1967, Civil Rights Movement Archive, https://www.crmvet.org/nars/harrisd.htm; "Police Smash Demonstrators, Four Face Death Penalty," *Student Voice,* October 1963, 2, https://content.wisconsinhistory.org/digital/collection/p15932coll2/id/50133.

Harris was a former football and lacrosse player at Rutgers University, where he was a prominent student activist. See Richard P. McCormick, *The Black Student Protest Movement at Rutgers* (New Brunswick, NJ: Rutgers University Press, 1990).

12. John Lewis int.; Branch, *Parting the Waters*, 874–881; Jones, *March on Washington*, 193–194; *WWTW*, 213 (1st q), 214 (2nd and 3rd q)–216 (4th and 5th q), 216–218 (q from speech text available online). This unedited written version of Lewis's speech and the revised version that he actually delivered can be accessed online: Lauren Feeney, "Two Versions of John Lewis' Speech," billmoyers .com, July 24, 2013, http://billmoyers.com/content/two-versions-of-john-lewis-speech. See also David Greenberg, "How John Lewis Saved the March on Washington," *NYT*, August 27, 2023.

13. Lewis int.; Sellers, *River of No Return*, 65–66; *WWTW*, 219 (1st–3rd q)–222 (4th and 5th q), 223 (7th–9th q); McWhorter, *Carry Me Home*, 489 (6th q); Peter J. Ling, *Martin Luther King, Jr.* (Abingdon, UK: Routledge, 2015), 147. Roy Wilkins was deeply suspicious of Lewis's motives during the March: "Lewis was going to burn Jim Crow to the ground nonviolently, taking matters into SNCC's hands and creating a source of power beyond the national structure. . . . I thought the most important point was that Lewis was denouncing the legislative process at a demonstration called in large part to back the Civil Rights Bill—that seemed like a double cross." Roy Wilkins with Tom Mathews, *Standing Fast: The Autobiography of Roy Wilkins* (New York: Viking Penguin, 1982), 292–293.

14. *WWTW*, 224 (1st–3rd q), 221 (4th q); Sellers, *River of No Return*, 66 (5th and 6th q). Lewis's speech, along with other SNCC statements and actions during the summer of 1963, led President Kennedy to condemn SNCC's leaders as "sons of bitches." Kenneth O'Reilly, *Nixon's Piano: Presidents and Racial Politics from Washington to Clinton* (New York: Free Press, 1995), 234.

15. *WWTW*, 225–226 (1st–3rd q); Lewis-HM int.; Jones, *March on Washington*, 198–205; Branch, *Parting the Waters*, 883–887; Eig, *King*, 333–342.

16. Lewis int.; LaFayette int.; *WWTW*, 227 (1st–3rd q); Lewis-JFKL int.; Lewis-HM int.

CHAPTER 7. "Bombingham" and Freedom Summer

1. *WWTW*, 227–230 (1st–3rd q), 231 (5th–8th q); Diane McWhorter, *Carry Me Home: Birmingham Alabama: The Climactic Battle of the Civil Rights Revolution* (New York: Simon and Schuster, 2001), 536–537 (4th q), 538; *WP*, September 16–19, 1963. On the tradition of racially motivated bombings in Birmingham, see T. K. Thorne, *Behind the Magic Curtain: Secrets, Spies, and Unsung White Allies of Birmingham's Civil Rights Days* (Montgomery: New South Books, 2021), 76–77, 99, 180, 194–196, 219–220, 228–236, 243–244, 256, 263–265, 268–269, 282–284. On the Sixteenth Street Baptist Church bombing and the long effort to bring the bombers to justice, see Doug Jones, *Bending toward Justice: The Birmingham Church Bombing That Changed the Course of Civil Rights* (Toronto: All Points Books, 2019); Frank Sikora, *Until Justice Rolls Down: The Birmingham Church Bombing Case* (Tuscaloosa: University of Alabama Press, 1991); T. K. Thorne, *Last Chance for Justice: How Relentless Investigators Uncovered New Evidence Convicting the Birmingham Church Bombers* (Chicago: Lawrence Hill Books, 2013); Spike Lee, dir., *Four Little Girls* (HBO Studios, 2004); and Carolyn McKinstry with Denise George, *While the World Watched: A Birmingham Bombing Survivor Comes of Age during the Civil Rights Movement* (Carol

Stream, IL: Tyndale House, 2013). See also *NYT*, September 16, 1963, April 25, 2001, June 3, 2003, and May 18, 2017; *WP*, May 18, 2017; and *Los Angeles Times*, May 18, 2017.

2. *WWTW*, 239 (1st and 2nd q), 231–232 (3rd q).

3. John Dittmer, *Local People: The Struggle for Civil Rights in Mississippi* (Urbana: University of Illinois Press, 1994), 200–207; *WWTW*, 232 (1st q)–234 (2nd–4th q), 235 (5th q); Bernard LaFayette int.; John Lewis int.; Bernard LaFayette Jr. and Kathryn Lee Johnson, *In Peace and Freedom: My Journey in Selma* (Lexington: University Press of Kentucky, 2013), 45–99; *IS*, 96–110.

4. *WWTW*, 240 (q)–241; James Forman, *The Making of Black Revolutionaries: A Personal Account* (New York: Macmillan, 1972), 221–223, 234–240, 249; Julian E. Zelizer, *The Fierce Urgency of Now: Lyndon Johnson, Congress, and the Battle for the Great Society* (New York: Penguin, 2015), 32–36, 47, 49, 62, 72–73, 82–83; Kenneth O'Reilly, *Nixon's Piano: Presidents and Racial Politics from Washington to Clinton* (New York: Free Press, 1995), 239–241. On the 1964 Freedom Summer campaign, see Dittmer, *Local People*, 208–211, 218–219, 232–234, 240–285; Doug McAdam, *Freedom Summer* (New York: Oxford University Press, 1988); Charles M. Payne, *I've Got the Light of Freedom: The Organizing Tradition and the Mississippi Freedom Struggle* (Berkeley: University of California Press, 1995); Eric Burner, *And Gently He Shall Lead Them: Robert Parris Moses and Civil Rights in Mississippi* (New York: New York University Press, 1994); Seth Cagin and Philip Dray, *We Are Not Afraid: The Story of Goodman, Schwerner, and Chaney and the Civil Rights Campaign for Mississippi* (New York: Macmillan, 1988); Bruce Watson, *Freedom Summer: The Savage Season of 1964 That Made Mississippi Burn and Made America a Democracy* (New York: Viking, 2010); Sally Belfrage, *Freedom Summer* (New York: Viking, 1965); and Michael Edmonds, ed., *Risking Everything: A Freedom Summer Reader* (Madison: Wisconsin Historical Society, 2014). The Freedom Summer Digital Collection, which encompasses several dozen collections of personal and organizational papers located at the Wisconsin Historical Society, contains 140 documents related to Lewis's activities in 1964. They are available online at "Lewis, John, 1940–2020," Civil Rights Digital Library, https://crdl.usg.edu/people/lewis_john_1940_2020.

5. *WWTW*, 242 (1st and 2nd q).

6. Dittmer, *Local People*, 219–224, 229, 237; William Sturkey, *Hattiesburg: An American City in Black and White* (Cambridge, MA: Harvard University Press, 2009), 286–289; *WWTW*, 242 (q).

7. *WWTW*, 242–243 (1st q), 244 (2nd and 3rd q)–251; *IS*, 102–103, 119. On SSOC, see Gregg L. Michel, *Struggle for a Better South: The Southern Student Organizing Committee, 1964–1969* (New York: Palgrave Macmillan, 2004).

8. *WWTW*, 246–247.

9. *WWTW*, 247–248 (1st q), 249–250 (2nd q), 251; *NYT*, June 21, 1964; Dittmer, *Local People*, 242–246.

10. *WWTW*, 255–256 (1st q), 257 (2nd and 3rd q), 258 (4th q). On the murder of Goodman, Schwerner, and Chaney, see Cagin and Dray, *We Are Not Afraid*; Dittmer, *Local People*, 252–285; and William Bradford Huie, *Three Lives for Mississippi* (Jackson: University Press of Mississippi, 2000).

11. *WWTW*, 266 (1st q), 267 (2nd–4th q), 268 (5th q). The threat of violence was so severe in Greenwood that Forman, over Lewis's objection, placed armed guards outside SNCC's

headquarters at night. Simon Wendt, *The Spirit and the Shotgun: Armed Resistance and the Struggle for Civil Rights* (Gainesville: University Press of Florida, 2007), 113. On the 1964 Civil Rights Act, see Zelizer, *Fierce Urgency of Now*, 85–130; Clay Risen, *The Bill of the Century: The Epic Battle for the Civil Rights Act* (New York: Bloomsbury, 2014); Todd S. Purdum, *An Idea Whose Time Has Come: Two Presidents, Two Parties, and the Battle for the Civil Rights Act of 1964* (New York: Henry Holt, 2014); Robert Loevy, *The Civil Rights Act of 1964: The Passage of the Law That Ended Segregation* (Albany: State University of New York Press, 1997); and Charles Whalen and Barbara Whalen, *The Longest Debate: A Legislative History of the 1964 Civil Rights Act* (New York: New American Library, 1985).

12. *WWTW*, 261 (1st and 2nd q), 259–260 (3rd q), 262–266.

13. *WWTW*, 238 (1st q), 276 (2nd q); Forman, *Making of Black Revolutionaries*, 368; Jones, *March on Washington*, 236; Mark Stern, *Calculating Visions: Kennedy, Johnson, and Civil Rights* (New Brunswick, NJ: Rutgers University Press, 1992), 197; Fred Powledge, *Free at Last? The Civil Rights Movement and the People Who Made It* (Boston: Little, Brown, 1991), 591–594; Taylor Branch, *Pillar of Fire: America in the King Years 1963–65* (New York: Simon and Schuster, 1998), 417–424; Lawrence Guyot int. On Hamer, see Kate Clifford Larson, *Walk with Me: A Biography of Fannie Lou Hamer* (New York: Oxford University Press, 2021); Kay Mills, *This Little Light of Mine: The Life of Fannie Lou Hamer* (New York: Dutton, 1993); and Chana Kai Lee, *For Freedom's Sake: The Life of Fannie Lou Hamer* (Urbana: University of Illinois Press, 1999). See also J. Todd Moye, *Let the People Decide: Black Freedom and White Resistance Movements in Sunflower County, Mississippi, 1945–1986* (Chapel Hill: University of North Carolina Press, 2004).

14. *WWTW*, 271–272. For a full account of the FBI's efforts to undercut the influence of allegedly "radical" civil rights activists during the 1960s and early 1970s, see Kenneth O'Reilly, *"Racial Matters": The FBI's Secret File on Black America, 1960–1972* (New York: Free Press, 1989); and Beverly Gage, *G-Man: J. Edgar Hoover and the Making of the American Century* (New York: Viking, 2022), 439, 455–457, 520–530, 542–553, 582–584, 588, 604–626, 643–667, 680–696, 718–719, 726–729.

15. *WWTW*, 269 (1st and 2nd q), 270 (3rd and 4th q); Cagin and Dray, *We Are Not Afraid*, 406–412. On Dennis, see David Dennis Jr., *The Movement Made Us: A Father, a Son, and the Legacy of a Freedom Ride* (New York: Harper, 2022).

CHAPTER 8. Atlantic City and Africa

1. *WWTW*, 277 (1st q), 278 (2nd–5th q); Kate Clifford Larson, *Walk with Me: A Biography of Fannie Lou Hamer* (New York: Oxford University Press, 2021), 161–178; Taylor Branch, *Pillar of Fire: America in the King Years 1963–65* (New York: Simon and Schuster, 1998), 438–457.

2. *WWTW*, 279 (1st–3rd q), 280 (4th q); Larson, *Walk with Me*, 178–179; Branch, *Pillar of Fire*, 458–462.

3. *WWTW*, 280 (1st q), 281 (2nd and 3rd q), 282 (4th q); Larson, *Walk with Me*, 179–185; John Dittmer, *Local People: The Struggle for Civil Rights in Mississippi* (Urbana: University of Illinois Press, 1994), 285–302; Branch, *Pillar of Fire*, 463–476; John C. Skipper, *Showdown at the 1964 Democratic Convention: Lyndon Johnson, Mississippi, and Civil Rights* (New York: McFarland, 2012); Julian E. Zelizer, *The Fierce Urgency of Now: Lyndon Johnson, Congress, and the Battle for*

the *Great Society* (New York: Penguin, 2015), 152–154; Cleveland Sellers with Robert Terrell, *The River of No Return: The Autobiography of a Black Militant and the Life and Death of SNCC* (New York: William Morrow, 1973), 109; Fred Powledge, *Free at Last? The Civil Rights Movement and the People Who Made It* (Boston: Little, Brown, 1991), 594–600.

4. Dittmer, *Local People*, 320–327; Larson, *Walk with Me*, 186–188; *IS*, 128–129, 133–134; Branch, *Pillar of Fire*, 479–480, 483–523; *WWTW*, 282 (1st and 2nd q), 283 (3rd–5th q); Powledge, *Free At Last?*, 600–604, 607–608.

5. Bernard LaFayette int.; *WWTW*, 273 (q).

6. Harry Belafonte with Michael Shnayerson, *My Song: A Memoir* (New York: Knopf, 2011), 291–294; *WWTW*, 284 (1st q), 285 (2nd q), 286 (3rd and 4th q); *IS*, 134–136; Larson, *Walk with Me*, 187–191; Don Harris int.; Branch, *Pillar of Fire*, 480–482.

7. John Lewis and Don Harris, "The Trip," report to SNCC staff, December 14, 1964, Student Nonviolent Coordinating Committee Papers, Martin Luther King Center, Atlanta, GA; Harris int.; John Lewis int.; "Don Harris," SNCC Digital Gateway, https://snccdigital.org/people/don-harris/; *WWTW*, 286–289 (q), 290; *WP*, November 23, 1964; Branch, *Pillar of Fire*, 482; James Forman, *The Making of Black Revolutionaries: A Personal Account* (New York: Macmillan, 1972), 407–411; Belafonte, *My Song*, 292–294. On Mayfield, see *NYT*, October 23, 1984. On the last few months and assassination of Malcolm X, see Manning Marable, *Malcolm X: A Life of Reinvention* (New York: Viking, 2011), 297–458; Les Payne and Tamara Payne, *The Dead Are Arising: The Life of Malcolm X* (New York: Liveright, 2020), 421–515; Peniel Joseph, *The Sword and the Shield: The Revolutionary Lives of Malcolm X and Martin Luther King Jr.* (New York: Basic Books, 2020), 208–234; and George Breitman, *The Last Year of Malcolm X: The Evolution of a Black Revolutionary* (New York: Schocken Books, 1968). On David Graham Du Bois, see *Los Angeles Times*, February 10, 2005 (obit.).

8. *WWTW*, 291 (1st and 2nd q), 292 (3rd and 4th q); *IS*, 136–140.

9. Howard Zinn, *SNCC: The New Abolitionists* (Boston: Beacon Press, 1965), 267–275; *IS*, 137–140; *WWTW*, 292 (1st q)–294 (6th q), 295 (8th q)–296 (7th q), 297 (2nd q); Harris Wofford, *Of Kennedys and Kings: Making Sense of the Sixties* (Pittsburgh: University of Pittsburgh Press, 1992), 187 (3rd and 4th q); Forman, *Making of Black Revolutionaries*, 412–432; 437 (5th q); Pat Watters, *Down to Now: Reflections on the Southern Civil Rights Movement* (New York: Pantheon, 1971), 348–349 (6th q).

10. Wesley C. Hogan, *Many Minds, One Heart: SNCC's Dream for a New America* (Chapel Hill: University of North Carolina Press, 2007), 197–225; *IS*, 140–149; Forman, *Making of Black Revolutionaries*, 433–439; *WWTW*, 298 (1st and 2nd q). For the papers and other documents produced at the Waveland Retreat, see folder 23, Charles Sherrod Papers, Civil Rights Collection, State Historical Society of Wisconsin. On the rise of feminist consciousness in SNCC, see Sara Evans, *Personal Politics: The Roots of Women's Liberation in the Civil Rights Movement and the New Left* (New York: Knopf, 1979); Mary King, *Freedom Song: A Personal Story of the 1960s Civil Rights Movement* (New York: William Morrow, 1987); Faith S. Holsaert et al., eds., *Hands on the Freedom Plow: Personal Accounts by Women in SNCC* (Urbana: University of Illinois Press, 2010); and Constance Curry et al., *Deep in Our Hearts: White Women in the Freedom Movement* (Athens: University of Georgia Press, 2000).

11. *WWTW*, 298 (1st q), 299 (2nd q).

12. *WWTW*, 300. The entire letter, addressed "From John Lewis to All SNCC Staff," is reprinted in *WWTW*, 300–301.

13. *WWTW*, 301 (1st–3rd q).

CHAPTER 9. Selma and Bloody Sunday

1. Bernard LaFayette int.; John Lewis, interview by Jack Bass and Walter Devries, November 20, 1973, Oral Histories of the American South: The Civil Rights Movement, University of North Carolina, Chapel Hill (hereafter cited as Lewis-OHAS int.); Bernard LaFayette Jr. and Kathryn Lee Johnson, *In Peace and Freedom: My Journey in Selma* (Lexington: University Press of Kentucky, 2013), 1–90; Taylor Branch, *Pillar of Fire: America in the King Years 1963–65* (New York: Simon and Schuster, 1998), 63–66, 321–351, 552–555; David Colburn, *Racial Change and Community Crisis: St. Augustine, 1877–1980* (Gainesville: University Press of Florida, 1991); *WWTW*, 190, 301–302; David Garrow, *Protest at Selma: Martin Luther King, Jr., and the Voting Rights Act of 1965* (New Haven, CT: Yale University Press, 1978), 39; Pat Watters, *Down to Now: Reflections on the Southern Civil Rights Movement* (New York: Pantheon, 1971), 322–329; *FR*, 468–474; J. Mills Thornton III, *Dividing Lines: Municipal Politics and the Struggle for Civil Rights in Montgomery, Birmingham, and Selma* (Tuscaloosa: University of Alabama Press, 2002), 380–499. See also Charles E. Fager, *Selma 1965: The March That Changed the South* (Boston: Beacon, 1985).

2. *WWTW*, 303–306 (1st and 2nd q), 307 (3rd and 5th q), 308 (4th q).

3. *WWTW*, 308–310 (q); *NYT*, January 20, 1965; David J. Garrow, *Bearing the Cross: Martin Luther King, Jr., and the Southern Christian Leadership Conference* (New York: William Morrow, 1986), 379.

4. *WWTW*, 311–312 (1st q), 313–316; Garrow, *Protest at Selma*, 47 (2nd q).

5. LaFayette and Johnson, *In Peace and Freedom*, 112–118; Branch, *Pillar of Fire*, 578–579; *WWTW*, 313 (1st and 2nd q)–314; Garrow, *Protest at Selma*, 51 (3rd and 4th q), 52; *NYT*, February 5, 1965; Peniel Joseph, *The Sword and the Shield: The Revolutionary Lives of Malcolm X and Martin Luther King Jr.* (New York: Basic Books, 2020), 225–226.

6. *WWTW*, 313–314 (1st and 2nd q), 315 (3rd q); Branch, *Pillar of Fire*, 580–587.

7. Branch, *Pillar of Fire*, 586–600; C. T. Vivian int.; Garrow, *Protest at Selma*, 60–66; *WWTW*, 315 (q).

8. *WWTW*, 316 (1st q), 317 (2nd q), 318 (3rd and 4th q); Taylor Branch, *At Canaan's Edge: America in the King Years 1965–68* (New York: Simon and Schuster, 2006), 8–22, 42; Garrow, *Protest at Selma*, 70–72.

9. *WWTW*, 320 (1st q), 321 (2nd q).

10. Garrow, *Protest at Selma*, 73–77; Branch, *At Canaan's Edge*, 42–57; *WWTW*, 324 (1st q)–326 (2nd q), 327 (3rd–6th q), 328 (7th q); Robert A. Pratt, *Selma's Bloody Sunday: Protest, Voting Rights, and the Struggle for Racial Equality* (Baltimore: Johns Hopkins University Press, 2017), 58–65.

11. *NYT*, March 8, 1965 (1st q); *WWTW*, 328 (2nd q), 329 (3rd q), 330 (4th–6th q), 331 (7th and 8th q); *NYT*, March 8, 1965; Garrow, *Protest at Selma*, 78–83; Pratt, *Selma's Bloody Sunday*, 65–67; Cleveland Sellers with Robert Terrell, *The River of No Return: The Autobiography of a Black Militant and the Life and Death of SNCC* (New York: William Morrow, 1973), 119–122.

12. John Lewis int.; LaFayette int.; Lewis-OHAS int.; *WWTW*, 331–333 (q); Branch, *At Canaan's Edge*, 58–82; Garrow, *Protest at Selma*, 83–87; Pratt, *Selma's Bloody Sunday*, 67–71. On Judge Frank Johnson's hearings and deliberations during the Selma crisis, see Jack Bass, *Taming the Storm: The Life and Times of Frank M. Johnson and the South's Fight over Civil Rights* (New York: Doubleday, 1992), 236–253; and Frank Sikora, *The Judge: The Life and Opinions of Alabama's Frank M. Johnson, Jr.* (Montgomery: Black Belt, 1992), 182–225.

13. LaFayette int.; Lewis-OHAS int.; *WWTW*, 334 (1st q), 335 (2nd and 3rd q); Branch, *At Canaan's Edge*, 71–79; Garrow, *Bearing the Cross*, 402–404; Pratt, *Selma's Bloody Sunday*, 72–76; James Forman, *The Making of Black Revolutionaries: A Personal Account* (New York: Macmillan, 1972), 441–442.

14. *WWTW*, 336 (1st and 2nd q), 337 (3rd and 4th q); Garrow, *Protest at Selma*, 90–99; Branch, *At Canaan's Edge*, 81–93; Pratt, *Selma's Bloody Sunday*, 74–78.

15. *NYT*, March 14, 1965 (1st q); Garrow, *Protest at Selma*, 99–106; Branch, *At Canaan's Edge*, 94–101, 104–110; Pratt, *Selma's Bloody Sunday*, 79–81; *WWTW*, 338 (2nd q), 339 (3rd q); Doris Kearns, *Lyndon Johnson and the American Dream* (New York: Harper and Row, 1976), 228, quotes Wallace: "If I hadn't left when I did, he'd have had me coming out *for* civil rights."

16. Lyndon Johnson, "The American Promise," March 15, 1965, in *Public Papers of the Presidents of the United States, 1965* (Washington, DC: Government Printing Office, 1965), 281 (3rd q); Kearns, *Lyndon Johnson*, 229; Branch, *At Canaan's Edge*, 110–115; Pratt, *Selma's Bloody Sunday*, 82–84; *WWTW*, 339 (1st, 2nd, and 4th q); Garrow, *Protest at Selma*, 107; *NYT*, March 16, 1965.

17. *WWTW*, 340 (1st–4th q), 341 (5th–7th q); Bass, *Taming the Storm*, 249–253; Branch, *At Canaan's Edge*, 116–139; Garrow, *Protest at Selma*, 111; Pratt, *Selma's Bloody Sunday*, 84–85.

18. Garrow, *Protest at Selma*, 108 (q), 113–114.

19. LaFayette int.; Lewis-OHAS int.; *WWTW*, 342–343 (1st and 2nd q), 344 (3rd q); LaFayette and Johnson, *In Peace and Freedom*, 131–135; Branch, *At Canaan's Edge*, 136–150, 153–154, 159; Pratt, *Selma's Bloody Sunday*, 86–91.

20. *WWTW*, 344 (1st q)–345 (3rd–5th q); Garrow, *Protest at Selma*, 116; *NYT*, March 25, 1965 (2nd q); LaFayette and Johnson, *In Peace and Freedom*, 136–138; LaFayette int.; Branch, *At Canaan's Edge*, 157–159; Pratt, *Selma's Bloody Sunday*, 91–93.

21. *WWTW*, 345 (1st q), 346; Branch, *At Canaan's Edge*, 159–170 (2nd q); *NYT*, March 25, 1965; LaFayette and Johnson, *In Peace and Freedom*, 138–140; LaFayette int.; Lewis-OHAS int.; Branch, *At Canaan's Edge*, 159–170; Garrow, *Protest at Selma*, 117; Pratt, *Selma's Bloody Sunday*, 93, 95, 97.

22. Mary Stanton, *From Selma to Sorrow: The Life and Death of Viola Liuzzo* (Athens: University of Georgia Press, 1998); Branch, *At Canaan's Edge*, 171–181, 185, 188, 191–194; Garrow, *Protest at Selma*, 117–119; Pratt, *Selma's Bloody Sunday*, 99–104; Beverly Gage, *G-Man: J. Edgar Hoover and the Making of the American Century* (New York: Viking, 2022), 623–625; LaFayette and Johnson, *In Peace and Freedom*, 140–142; Lyn Tornabene, "Murder in Alabama," *Ladies' Home Journal*, July 1965, 42–44; Gary Thomas Rowe Jr., *My Undercover Years with the Ku Klux Klan* (New York: Bantam, 1976); Sikora, *Judge*, 228–260; *WWTW*, 347; LaFayette int.; Lewis int.; Howard Simon int.; Mary Liuzzo Lilliboe int. See also Kenneth O'Reilly, *"Racial Matters": The FBI's Secret File on Black America, 1960–1972* (New York: Free Press, 1989), 84–88, 112,

195–198, 216–222, 226–227. Two days before Liuzzo's murder, Lewis commented on the civil rights whore stereotype being perpetrated by several ultrasegregationist Alabama newspapers, telling a *New York Times* reporter: "Segregationists are preoccupied with interracial sex. Which is why you see so many shades of brown on this march." *NYT*, March 24, 1965; Branch, *At Canaan's Edge*, 153.

CHAPTER 10. Leaving SNCC

1. *WWTW*, 352 (q); *IS*, 169–170; Bernard LaFayette int.

2. *WWTW*, 346 (1st, 2nd, and 4th q), 347 (3rd q), 352 (5th q); Taylor Branch, *At Canaan's Edge: America in the King Years 1965–68* (New York: Simon and Schuster, 2006), 215, 224, 230–231, 252–254, 260, 270–278; David Garrow, *Protest at Selma: Martin Luther King, Jr., and the Voting Rights Act of 1965* (New Haven, CT: Yale University Press, 1978), 123–178; Robert A. Pratt, *Selma's Bloody Sunday: Protest, Voting Rights, and the Struggle for Racial Equality* (Baltimore: Johns Hopkins University Press, 2017), 104–110; Steven F. Lawson, *Black Ballots: Voting Rights in the South, 1944–1969* (New York: Columbia University Press, 1976), 307–321; Bernard LaFayette Jr. and Kathryn Lee Johnson, *In Peace and Freedom: My Journey in Selma* (Lexington: University Press of Kentucky, 2013), 143–144; LaFayette int. For more general treatments of disfranchisement and the voting rights struggle, see Alex Keyssar, *The Right to Vote: The Contested History of Democracy in the United States* (New York: Basic Books, 2000); Michael Waldman, *The Fight to Vote* (New York: Simon and Schuster, 2016); Gary May, *Bending toward Justice: The Voting Rights Act and the Transformation of American Democracy* (Durham, NC: Duke University Press, 2015); Charles S. Bullock III, Ronald Keith Gaddie, and Justin J. Wert, *The Rise and Fall of the Voting Rights Act* (Norman: University of Oklahoma Press, 2016); Carol Anderson, *One Person, No Vote: How Voter Suppression Is Destroying Our Democracy* (New York: Bloomsbury, 2018); and Ari Berman, *Give Us the Ballot: The Modern Struggle for Voting Rights in America* (New York: Farrar, Straus and Giroux, 2015).

3. *WWTW*, 348–349 (q); LaFayette int. On the Watts crisis, see Robert E. Conot, *Rivers of Blood, Years of Darkness* (New York: Bantam, 1967); and Gerald Horne, *Fire This Time: The Watts Uprising and the 1960s* (Charlottesville: University of Virginia Press, 1995).

4. *IS*, 162–166; *WWTW*, 294, 351–353 (1st and 5th q); Jon Meacham, *His Truth Is Marching On: John Lewis and the Power of Hope* (New York: Random House, 2020), 217 (2nd q); Milton Viorst, *Fire in the Streets: America in the 1960's* (New York: Simon and Schuster, 1979), 354 (3rd q), 368 (4th q); Charles W. Eagles, *Outside Agitator: Jon Daniels and the Civil Rights Movement in Alabama* (Chapel Hill: University of North Carolina Press, 1993), 89–184; Hasan Kwame Jeffries, *Bloody Lowndes: Civil Rights and Black Power in Alabama's Black Belt* (New York: New York University Press, 2009); Charles E. Fager, *Selma 1965: The March That Changed the South* (Boston: Beacon, 1985), 80–84, 87, 142, 153–154, 158, 163, 172, 205; LaFayette int. On the full history of the Black Panther Party, see Joshua Bloom and Waldo E. Martin Jr., *Black against Empire: The History and Politics of the Black Panther Party* (Berkeley: University of California Press, 2013). On the growing dissension in SNCC, see Cheryl Lynn Greenberg, ed., *A Circle of Trust: Remembering SNCC* (New Brunswick, NJ: Rutgers University Press, 1998), 87–109, 127–219; James Forman, *The Making of Black Revolutionaries: A Personal Account* (New York:

Macmillan, 1972), 411–459; and Sharon Monteith, *SNCC's Stories: The African American Freedom Movement in the Civil Rights South* (Athens: University of Georgia Press, 2020), 171–251.

5. *WWTW*, 355 (1st q), 356 (2nd q), 358–359 (3rd, 4th, 6th, and 7th q); Meacham, *His Truth Is Marching On*, 181 (5th q); Branch, *At Canaan's Edge*, 221–224, 263–264, 277–279, 286, 579–604; *IS*, 174, 176, 183–189, 220–221, 246, 260, 265; Wesley C. Hogan, *Many Minds, One Heart: SNCC's Dream for a New America* (Chapel Hill: University of North Carolina Press, 2007), 291–292.

6. Bayard Rustin, "From Protest to Politics: The Future of the Civil Rights Movement," *Commentary*, February 1965, reprinted in Bayard Rustin, *Down the Line: The Collected Writings of Bayard Rustin* (Chicago: Quadrangle, 1971), 111–122; *WWTW*, 360 (1st and 2nd q), 361 (3rd q); Branch, *At Canaan's Edge*, 408–413, 419, 430–431, 440, 456; *IS*, 189–190.

7. *WWTW*, 352 (1st q), 347 (2nd q), 362 (3rd q)–363, 373 (4th q), 349 (6th q); Robert Weisbrot, *Freedom Bound: A History of America's Civil Rights Movement* (New York: Norton, 1990), 191, 195–196 (5th q); *IS*, 187; Viorst, *Fire in the Streets*, 370 (7th q).

8. Branch, *At Canaan's Edge*, 456; *WWTW*, 363.

9. Forman, *Making of Black Revolutionaries*, 447–456, 519; *WWTW*, 363–365 (1st–3rd q), 369 (5th q), 366–368 (7th q); Viorst, *Fire in the Streets*, 370 (4th q); Pat Watters, *Down to Now: Reflections on the Southern Civil Rights Movement* (New York: Pantheon, 1971), 351 (6th q); *IS*, 191–205, 244, 252–260, 278–285, 292–297, 306; Stokely Carmichael with Ekwueme Michael Thelwell, *Ready for Revolution: The Life and Struggles of Stokely Carmichael (Kwame Ture)* (New York: Scribner, 2003), 455, 477–483; Peniel E. Joseph, *Stokely: A Life* (New York: Civitas Books, 2014), 5–99; John Lewis et al., *Run: Book One* (New York: Abrams ComicArts, 2021), 84–102; Mark Whitaker, *Saying It Loud: 1966—the Year Black Power Challenged the Civil Rights Movement* (New York: Simon and Schuster, 2023), 100–121.

10. *WWTW*, 369 (q); Whitaker, *Saying It Loud*, 121.

11. Adam Goudsouzian, *Down to the Crossroads: Civil Rights, Black Power, and the Meredith March against Fear* (New York: Farrar, Straus and Giroux, 2014), 3–62, 137–247; David J. Garrow, *Bearing the Cross: Martin Luther King, Jr., and the Southern Christian Leadership Conference* (New York: William Morrow, 1986), 484–487 (1st q); Jonathan Eig, *King, A Life* (New York: Farrar, Straus and Giroux, 2023), 483–494; Joseph, *Stokely*, 101–117, 123–147; Branch, *At Canaan's Edge*, 475–495; Adam Fairclough, *To Redeem the Soul of America: The Southern Christian Leadership Conference and Martin Luther King, Jr.* (Athens: University of Georgia Press, 1987), 308–322; Forman, *Making of Black Revolutionaries*, 456–460; *WWTW*, 370 (2nd q)–372 (3rd–5th q); Paul Good, "Odyssey of a Man—and a Movement," *NYT Magazine*, June 25, 1967; Lewis et al., *Run*, 103–108; Whitaker, *Saying It Loud*, 121–185. On the Black Power movement, see William I. Van Deburg, *New Day in Babylon: The Black Power Movement and American Culture, 1965–1975* (Chicago: University of Chicago Press, 1992); Peniel Joseph, *Waiting 'til the Midnight Hour: A Narrative History of Black Power in America* (New York: Henry Holt, 2006); and Stokely Carmichael and Charles V. Hamilton, *Black Power: The Politics of Liberation* (New York: Random House, 1967).

12. *WWTW*, 373 (q), 374; Lewis et al., *Run*, 108–115; Leslie Dunbar int.; LaFayette int. On the Field Foundation, created by the Chicago merchant and philanthropist Marshall Field III in 1940, see "Our History," Field Foundation of Illinois, https://fieldfoundation.org/about/history/. On the SRC, see John Egerton, *Speak Now Against the Day: The Generation before the*

Civil Rights Movement in the South (New York: Knopf, 1994), 48, 210, 285, 311–316, 325, 355, 377, 385, 414–417, 432–434, 439–442, 446–448, 481–485, 526–527, 555, 562, 615–617. On Dunbar, see Leslie Dunbar, *The Shame of Southern Politics: Essays and Speeches* (n.p.: Generic, 2002); Leslie W. Dunbar, *Reclaiming Liberalism* (New York: Norton, 1991); Anthony Dunbar, ed., *Leslie W. Dunbar: Reflections by Friends* (Montgomery: New South Books, 2016), which includes remarks by John Lewis; and *NYT*, January 12, 2017 (obit.).

CHAPTER 11. Transition and Tragedy

1. *WWTW*, 375 (q)–378; Don Harris int.

2. *IS*, 241–269; Harris int.; *WWTW*, 376–379 (q). On Kenneth Clark, see Kenneth B. Clark, *Toward Humanity and Justice: The Writings of Kenneth B. Clark, Scholar of the 1954 "Brown v. Board of Education" Decision*, ed. Woody Klein (New York: Praeger, 2004); Kenneth B. Clark, *Dark Ghetto: Dilemmas of Social Power* (New York: Harper and Row, 1965); and Ben Keppel, *The Work of Democracy: Ralph Bunche, Kenneth B. Clark, Lorraine Hansberry, and the Cultural Politics of Race* (Cambridge, MA: Harvard University Press, 1995).

3. Jon Meacham, *His Truth Is Marching On: John Lewis and the Power of Hope* (New York: Random House, 2020), 224 (1st q); *WWTW*, 377 (2nd–4th q), 379 (5th q), 380 (6th q); John Lewis int. Both King and Lewis placed a high priority on eliminating poverty as an element of the civil rights struggle. See Thomas F. Jackson, *From Civil Rights to Human Rights: Martin Luther King, Jr., and the Struggle for Economic Justice* (Philadelphia: University of Pennsylvania Press, 2007); Michael K. Honey, *To the Promised Land: Martin Luther King and the Fight for Economic Justice* (New York: Norton, 2018); Gerald D. McKnight, *The Last Crusade: Martin Luther King, Jr., the FBI, and the Poor People's Campaign* (Boulder, CO: Westview Press, 1998); Sylvie Laurent, *King and the Other America: The Poor People's Campaign and the Quest for Economic Equality* (Berkeley: University of California Press, 2018), 100–101, 106, 120, 173–174; and Pat Watters, "Keep On a'Walkin', Children," in *New American Review*, ed. Theodore Solotaroff (New York: New American Library, 1969), reprinted in Jon Meacham, ed., *Voices in Our Blood: America's Best on the Civil Rights Movement* (New York: Random House, 2001), 413–449.

4. On Maddox, see Bruce Galphin, *The Riddle of Lester Maddox* (Atlanta: Camelot, 1968); and Robert Sherrill, *Gothic Politics in the Deep South: Stars of the New Confederacy*, rev. ed. (New York: Ballantine, 1969), 277–301. *WWTW*, 380 (1st q)–381 (2nd and 3rd q); Pat Watters, *Down to Now: Reflections on the Southern Civil Rights Movement* (New York: Pantheon, 1971), 24 (4th q). Ulmer served as SRC director Paul Anthony's assistant from 1964 to 1967, and in 1965 he became the director of organization planning. See his correspondence, reports, and other documents related to the Community Organization Project in Series 14, Reels 214–215, Southern Regional Council Papers (microfilm), Atlanta University Center, Robert W. Woodruff Library, Archives and Special Collections.

5. *WWTW*, 382–383, 405; Julian Bond int.; Harris int.; Bernard LaFayette int.

6. *WWTW*, 384 (1st–3rd q)–385; Lewis-JFKL int. On Robert Kennedy's 1968 campaign, see Arthur M. Schlesinger Jr., *Robert Kennedy and His Times* (Boston: Houghton Mifflin, 1978), 842–916; Evan Thomas, *Robert Kennedy: His Life* (New York: Simon and Schuster, 2000), 348–394; Chris Matthews, *Bobby Kennedy: A Raging Spirit* (New York: Simon and Schuster, 2017), 309–342;

and Patricia Sullivan, *Justice Rising: Robert Kennedy's America in Black and White* (Cambridge, MA: Harvard University Press, 2021), 386–442. For an enlightening comparison of Kennedy and King, see David Margolick, *The Promise and the Dream: The Untold Story of Martin Luther King Jr. and Robert F. Kennedy* (New York: Rosetta Books, 2018).

7. Lewis-JFKL int.; Taylor Branch, *At Canaan's Edge: America in the King Years 1965–68* (New York: Simon and Schuster, 2006), 683–759; Watters, "Keep On a'Walkin', Children,", 28, 54; *WWTW*, 385–386 (1st–3rd q), 387 (4th and 5th q), 384 (8th q), 388 (9th q); Matthews, *Bobby Kennedy*, 325 (6th q), 326 (7th q); Schlesinger, *Robert Kennedy*, 873–875; Sullivan, *Justice Rising*, 412–415; Lewis int. On the King assassination, see Gerald Posner, *Killing the Dream: James Earl Ray and the Assassination of Martin Luther King, Jr.* (New York: Random House, 1998). On the aftermath of King's death, see Clay Risen, *A Nation on Fire: America in the Wake of the King Assassination* (New York: Wiley, 2009).

8. *WWTW*, 388–392 (q), 393; Ralph Abernathy, *And the Walls Came Tumbling Down* (New York: Harper and Row, 1989), 412–466, 478.

9. *WWTW*, 393 (1st q), 394 (2nd q), 395 (3rd q), 396 (4th and 5th q), 397 (6th q); Lewis-JFKL int. On Robert Kennedy's assassination, see Sullivan, *Justice Rising*, 438–447; and William Turner and John Christian, *The Assassination of Robert F. Kennedy: The Conspiracy and Coverup* (New York: Basic Books, 2006).

10. *WWTW*, 398 (1st–3rd q)–399; Lewis int.; Bond int. On the controversies surrounding the 1968 Democratic National Convention in Chicago, see Lewis Chester, Godfrey Hodgson, and Bruce Page, *An American Melodrama: The Presidential Campaign of 1968* (New York: Viking, 1969), 503–591; David Farber, *Chicago '68* (Chicago: University of Chicago Press, 1988); Norman Mailer, *Miami and the Siege of Chicago: An Informal History of the Republican and Democratic Conventions of 1968* (New York: Penguin, 2018); John Schultz, *No One Was Killed: The Democratic National Convention, August 1968* (Chicago: University of Chicago Press, 2009); and Nicholas W. Proctor, *Chicago, 1968: Policy and Protest at the Democratic National Convention* (New York: Norton, 2020). On Bond and the Georgia challenge delegation, see Roger M. Williams, *The Bonds: An American Family* (New York: Atheneum, 1971), 242–256.

11. *WWTW*, 400 (1st and 2nd q), 401 (3rd q); Lewis-JFKL int.; Williams, *Bonds*, 252–256.

CHAPTER 12. Voting Rights and the New South

1. *WWTW*, 405 (1st q), 406 (2nd and 3rd q); Don Harris int.

2. *WWTW*, 406 (1st q). Mayor William Hartsfield coined the phrase "A city too busy to hate" in 1960, and many other Atlantans soon adopted it as the city's favorite slogan. Louis Williams, "William B. Hartsfield," *New Georgia Encyclopedia*, last modified July 15, 2020. https://www.georgiaencyclopedia.org/articles/government/politics/william-b-hartsfield-1890-1971/; Pat Watters, *Down to Now: Reflections on the Southern Civil Rights Movement* (New York: Pantheon, 1971, 376 (2nd q), 377 (3rd q). On the evolution of race relations and the civil rights struggle in Atlanta, see Tomiko Brown-Nagin, *Courage to Dissent: Atlanta and the Long History of the Civil Rights Movement* (New York: Oxford University Press, 2011); Kevin M. Kruse, *White Flight: Atlanta and the Making of Modern Conservatism* (Princeton, NJ: Princeton University Press, 2005); and Ronald H. Bayor, *Race and the Shaping of Twentieth-Century Atlanta* (Chapel

Hill: University of North Carolina Press, 1996). See also Stephen G. N. Tuck, *Beyond Atlanta: The Struggle for Racial Equality in Georgia, 1940–1980* (Athens: University of Georgia Press, 2001).

3. *WWTW*, 406–407; *IS*, 297–298.

4. Bernard LaFayette int.; Diane Nash int.; Rip Patton int.; *WWTW*, 408 (q); Andrew Young, *An Easy Burden: The Civil Rights Movement and the Transformation of America* (New York: HarperCollins, 1996), 503–504.

5. Andrew Young int.; Young, *Easy Burden*, 504–511; *WWTW*, 408 (3rd q), 410 (1st q)–412 (2nd q); Hamilton Bims, "A Southern Activist Goes to the House," *Ebony*, February 1973, 84 (4th q).

6. Bims, "Southern Activist," 84; *WWTW*, 412–413; Young int. On the Black mayors and vice-mayors elected during the late 1960s and early 1970s, see Leonard M. Moore, *Carl B. Stokes and the Rise of Black Political Power* (Urbana: University of Illinois Press, 2002); David Stradling and Richard Stradling, *Where the River Burned: Carl Stokes and the Struggle to Save Cleveland* (Ithaca, NY: Cornell University Press, 2015); Alex Poinsett, *Black Power, Gary Style: The Making of Mayor Richard Gordon Hatcher* (Chicago: Johnson, 1970); Charles Evers and Andrew Szanton, *Have No Fear: The Charles Evers Story* (New York: Wiley, 1998); and Robert A. Holmes, *Maynard Jackson: A Biography* (Miami: Barnhardt and Ashe, 2009).

7. *WWTW*, 413 (1st–4th q), 414; Archie E. Allen, "John Lewis: Keeper of the Dream," *New South* 26 (Spring 1971): 15–25; *NYT*, August 6, December 31, 1969; *Chicago Daily Defender*, August 16, 1969; *WP*, October 18, 1969; *Atlanta Journal-Constitution* (hereafter cited as *AJC*), December 9, 1974; David Sanford, "Rocking the Foundations: A Tax Reform that Clubs Reform," *New Republic* (November 29, 1969): 17–20; Courtney E. Chartier, "Voter Education Project," *New Georgia Encyclopedia*, last edited August 30, 2013, https://www .georgiaencyclopedia.org/articles/history-archaeology/voter-education-project/ (5th q); Evan Faulkenbury, *Poll Power: The Voter Education Project and the Movement for the Ballot in the American South* (Chapel Hill: University of North Carolina Press, 2019), 125–131 (6th q), 132–134. Lewis's activities as the director of the VEP are fully documented in the Voter Education Project Organizational Records located in the Archives Research Center at the Atlanta University Center, Robert W. Woodruff Library. Among the collection's 190 boxes are several containing the correspondence of Lewis as the executive director, his reports, material on various VEP projects and elections, posters, brochures, and flyers. See also Series 6, Voter Education Project, 1954–1971, Southern Regional Council Papers (microfilm), Atlanta University Center, Robert W. Woodruff Library, Archives and Special Collections.

8. *WWTW*, 414 (1st and 2nd q), 415; *AJC*, August–November 1970, January 13, 1971 (3rd q); Faulkenbury, *Poll Power*, 129–133; Kay Mills, *This Little Light of Mine: The Life of Fannie Lou Hamer* (New York: Plume, 1994), 299–300; *NYT*, January 13, 17, 1971; Jonathan Alter, "When Jimmy Carter Was Silent on Civil Rights," *Wall Street Journal*, September 18, 2020; Jonathan Alter, *His Very Best: Jimmy Carter, a Life* (New York: Simon and Schuster, 2020), 148–169. On Barbara Jordan, see Mary Beth Rogers, *Barbara Jordan, American Hero* (New York: Bantam, 2000).

9. John Lewis and Archie Allen, "Black Voter Registration Efforts in the South," *Notre Dame Law Review* 48 (1972): 121 (1st q), 119 (2nd q); *WWTW*, 415; Faulkenbury, *Poll Power*,

129–134. See also Charlayne Hunter-Gault, "Black Activist Sees New South: Lewis Seeks Funds to Help Enroll More Voters," *NYT*, November 18, 1973, reprinted in Charlayne Hunter-Gault, *My People: Five Decades of Writing about Black Lives* (New York: Harper, 2022), 12–14. On the 1972 presidential election, see Theodore H. White, *The Making of the President, 1972* (New York: Atheneum, 1973).

10. *WWTW*, 415 (1st q), 416 (2nd and 3rd q); "Living Saints," *Time*, December 29, 1975.

11. Ari Berman, "The Lost Promise of the Voting Rights Act," *Atlantic*, August 5, 2015 (q); David H. Hunter, "The 1975 Voting Rights Act and Language Minorities," *Catholic University Law Review* 25 (1976): 250–270; *WWTW*, 415, 417; Steven F. Lawson, *In Pursuit of Power: Southern Blacks and Electoral Politics, 1965–1982* (New York: Columbia University Press, 1985), 224–253; Faulkenbury, *Poll Power*, 129–133; Alter, *His Very Best*, 166–215; *NYT*, December 13–14, 1974; Janet Wells, "Voting Rights in 1975: Why Minorities Still Need Federal Protection," *Civil Rights Digest* 70 (Summer 1975): 13–19.

12. *WWTW*, 417 (1st q), 418 (2nd q); Chuck Stone, "Black Political Power in the Carter Era," *The Black Scholar* 8, no. 4 (January/February 1977): 6–15; Alter, *His Very Best*, 247–281. On the 1976 presidential election, see Daniel K. Williams, *The Election of the Evangelical: Jimmy Carter, Gerald Ford, and the Presidential Contest of 1976* (Lawrence: University Press of Kansas, 2020); and U.S. Congress, *1976 Congressional and Federal Election Statistics* (Washington, DC: Qontro Election Publications, 2009). The results of the 1976 election were not the only signs that a new day was dawning in the New South. Eighteen months earlier, Lewis had been heartened by the response to his call for a march commemorating the tenth anniversary of Bloody Sunday and the 1965 march to Montgomery. More than five thousand marchers joined Lewis in a ceremonial walk across the Edmund Pettus Bridge, and this time, instead of being blocked and beaten at the east end of the bridge, the marchers were escorted by several patrol cars driven by Alabama state troopers. Three years later, he received further confirmation that the racial divide in Alabama was softening when a repentant George Wallace, the governor largely responsible for Bloody Sunday, requested a meeting with Lewis to ask for his "foreignness for anything I've done to wrong you." Meeting in Willie Mae Lewis's living room in Pike County, the former adversaries "grasped hands and prayed together." As Lewis later described the scene, "It was almost like someone confessing to a priest." Stephen A. Smith, *Myth, Media and the Southern Mind* (Fayetteville: University of Arkansas Press, 1986), 83, 92; Dan T. Carter, *The Politics of Rage: George Wallace, the Origins of the New Conservatism, and the Transformation of American Politics* (Baton Rouge: Louisiana State University Press, 2000), 460–461 (q); Lawson, *In Pursuit of Power*, 224–225; Jason Sokol, *There Goes My Everything: White Southerners in the Age of Civil Rights, 1945–1975* (New York: Knopf, 2006), 251; Frye Gaillard, *Cradle of Freedom: Alabama and the Movement That Changed America* (Tuscaloosa: University of Alabama Press, 2004), 343.

13. *WWTW*, 416–418 (q); Young int.; Alter, *His Very Best*, 115, 364–365.

14. *WWTW*, 418–420 (1st q), 421 (2nd and 3rd q); *AJC*, March 14, 1977; Ralph Abernathy, *And the Walls Came Tumbling Down* (New York: Harper and Row, 1989), 584–585.

15. *WWTW*, 420–422 (1st q), 423 (2nd and 3rd q), 424; *AJC*, March 15–April 6, 1977.

16. Within two years the VEP would be $55,000 in debt, under investigation for financial irregularities, and in total disarray, and it would continue to struggle until its dissolution in

1992. *WWTW,* 424 (1st q), 425 (2nd q); Faulkenbury, *Poll Power,* 133–136. Kenneth O'Reilly, *Nixon's Piano: Presidents and Racial Politics from Washington to Clinton* (New York: Free Press, 1995), 341–342, notes that Carter appointed a number of African Americans and civil rights movement veterans—notably Lewis, Andrew Young, Eleanor Holmes Norton, Patricia Harris, Mary King, Wade McCree, and Drew Days—to important positions in his administration. On Mary King, see Mary King, *Freedom Song: A Personal Story of the 1960s Civil Rights Movement* (New York: William Morrow, 1987). On Sam W. Brown Jr., see Sam Brown, "The Legacy of Choices," in *The Wounded Generation: America after Vietnam,* ed. A. D. Horne (New York: Prentice-Hall, 1981), 183–192; Sam Brown, *Storefront Organizing: A Mornin' Glories Manual* (London: Pyramid Books, 1972); and Gordon Chaplin, "Action's Where the Peace Corps Is," *WP,* February 5, 1978. See also Elizabeth Cobbs Hoffman, *All You Need Is Love: The Peace Corps and the Spirit of the 1960s* (Cambridge, MA: Harvard University Press, 1998); and Tom Wells, *The War Within: America's Battle over Vietnam* (Berkeley: University of California Press, 1994). ACTION became the Commission for National and Community Service in 1993 following the implementation of the National and Community Service Trust Act. On the creation of the ACTION agency, see "Action Agency: Peace Corps, Vista Merged in New Unit," in *Congressional Quarterly Almanac 1971,* 27th ed. (Washington, DC: Congressional Quarterly, 1972). On Eddie Lewis, see the obituary in *Troy Messenger,* September 15, 1977; "Willie Mae Lewis (Carter)," Geni, https://www.geni.com/people/Willie-Lewis/6000000040495864871; John Lewis int.; Lewis-HM int.

17. *WWTW,* 425 (1st and 2nd q), 426 (3rd q).

18. *WWTW,* 426–427 (1st–3rd q), 428 (4th q). On Carolyn Payton and the Peace Corps controversy of 1978, see her obituary in *WP,* April 12, 2001; and "Dissatisfaction with ACTION Head Sam Brown Erupted into Public View When He Fired the Peace Corps Director, Dr. Payton," Peace Corps Online, July 14, 2001, http://peacecorpsonline.org/messages/messages/2629/4208.html.

19. *WWTW,* 428 (q); LaFayette int. On Alinsky, see Saul D. Alinsky, *Reveille for Radicals* (Chicago: University of Chicago Press, 1946); Saul D. Alinsky, *Rules for Radicals: A Practical Primer for Realistic Radicals* (New York: Random House, 1971); Sanford D. Horwitt, *Let Them Call Me Rebel: Saul Alinsky, His Life and Legacy* (New York: Vintage, 1992); and Nicholas von Hoffman, *Radical: A Portrait of Saul Alinsky* (London: Nation Books, 2010).

20. *WWTW,* 428–429 (q), 430. On the Carter–Kennedy contest of 1980, see Jon Ward, *Camelot's End: Kennedy vs. Carter and the Fight That Broke the Democratic Party* (New York: Twelve, 2019).

CHAPTER 13. Sweet Home Atlanta

1. *WWTW,* 430 (q); John Lewis, "The Long Struggle for Representation: Oral Histories of African Americans in Congress," interview by Matt Wasniewski, December 11, 2014, https://history.house.gov/Oral-History/People/Representative-Lewis/ (hereafter cited as Lewis-HR int.).

2. *WWTW,* 431–432. The NCCB was created by the National Consumer Cooperative Bank Act of 1978. See John Curl, *For All the People: Uncovering the Hidden History of Cooperation, Cooperative Movements, and Communalism in America* (Oakland, CA: PM Press, 2012); Steve Dubb,

"Historic Federal Law Gives Employee-Owned Businesses Access to SBA Loans," *Nonprofit Quarterly*, August 14, 2018; and National Cooperative Bank, homepage, https://www.ncb.coop.

3. *WWTW*, 432 (1st and 3rd q), 433 (2nd q); Ernie Suggs, "Years in Atlanta City Hall Tested Lewis' Mettle," *AJC*, July 17, 2020 (4th q).

4. *NYT*, August 19, 1979; *WP*, August 15, 19, 1979; *Los Angeles Times*, September 12, 1993; Michael R. Fischbach, "Andrew Young, Marc Lamont Hill, and Palestine," *Stanford University Press Blog*, December 20, 2018, https://stanfordpress.typepad.com/blog/2018/12/andrew-young -marc-lamont-hill-and-palestine.html; Michael R. Fischbach, *Black Power: Transnational Countries of Color* (Palo Alto, CA: Stanford University Press, 2018); *WWTW*, 418–419.

5. *WWTW*, 433–434 (q); Lewis-HR int.

6. Andrew Young int.; John Lewis int.; *WWTW*, 435 (1st and 2nd q), 436 (3rd q).

7. *WWTW*, 436–437 (q).

8. *WWTW*, 437; *NYT*, February 6–7, 1985; *WP*, February 7, 1985. On Mattingly and Talmadge, see Timothy J. Minchin, "'An Historic Upset': Herman Talmadge's 1980 Senate Defeat and the End of a Political Dynasty," *Georgia Historical Quarterly* 99 (2015): 156–197; and Herman E. Talmadge, *Talmadge: A Political Legacy, a Politician's Life: A Memoir* (Atlanta: Peachtree, 1987).

9. Lewis int.; Julian Bond int.; *AJC*, October 15–November 1, 1985; *WWTW*, 438 (1st q), 439–440 (2nd q), 437 (3rd and 4th q). On Bond's long-standing "golden boy" image and nonchalant personal style, see Roger M. Williams, *The Bonds: An American Family* (New York: Atheneum, 1971), 181–218, 254–282.

10. Lewis int.; *WWTW*, 437 (1st q)–441 (2nd q), 442 (3rd q), 443 (4th and 5th q)–444 (6th q).

11. *WWTW*, 445 (q); *NYT*, September 3, 1986; *AJC*, September 2–3, 1986; Bernard LaFayette int. See Art Harris, "Legends in the Cross Fire," *WP*, July 21, 1986; Adolph Alzuphar, "Julian Bond vs. John Lewis: An Unforgettable Fight for Atlanta's Fifth Congressional District," Blavity, July 3, 2017, https://blavity.com/julian-bond-vs-john-lewis-an-unforgettable-fight-for-atlantas -fifth-congressional-district?category1=black-history&category2=community-submitted; Vincent Coppola, "The Parable of Julian Bond and John Lewis," *Atlanta Magazine*, March 1, 1990; and John Beifuss, "Meet the Memphis Man Who Helped John Lewis Get to Congress," *Memphis Commercial Appeal*, July 26, 2020. The Memphis man, Love Collins, claimed he came up with the idea of urging the candidates to take a drug test.

12. Lewis int.; LaFayette int.; Bond int.; *WWTW*, 446–447 (1st–3rd q), 448 (4th q); *AJC*, August 1–14, 1986.

13. Lewis int.; LaFayette int.; *WWTW*, 449–450 (1st–4th q), 451 (5th and 6th q), 452 (7th–10th q); *AJC*, August 15–September 2, 1986.

14. Lewis int.; LaFayette int.; Lewis-HR int.; *WWTW*, 453 (1st–3rd q), 454 (4th q).

CHAPTER 14. Mr. Lewis Goes to Washington

1. *NYT*, November 7, 1986; R. W. Apple Jr., "Delivering the South," *NYT Magazine*, November 30, 1986; *WWTW*, 456 (q); Robin Toner, "A Long Way, Tear Gas to Tax Law," *NYT*, December 12, 1986; Lewis-HR int.; *Congressional Record* (hereafter cited as *CR*), vol. 133, January 6–16, 1987.

2. *WWTW*, 456 (1st and 2nd q); Toner, "Long Way" (3rd q). On the rhetoric of the 1984 presidential candidates, see Jack W. Germond, *Wake Me When It's Over: Presidential Politics of 1984* (New York: Macmillan, 1985). "It is morning in America, again" was the opening line of one of Reagan's most influential television advertisements. On the politics of the Reagan era, see Garry Wills, *Reagan's America: Innocents at Home* (Portsmouth, NH: Heinemann, 1988); Gil Troy, *Morning in America: How Ronald Reagan Invented the 1980s* (Princeton, NJ: Princeton University Press, 2005); Haynes Johnson, *Sleepwalking through History: America in the Reagan Years* (New York: Norton, 1991); Sean Wilentz, *The Age of Reagan: A History, 1974–2008* (New York: Harper, 2008); and Rick Perlstein, *Reaganland: America's Right Turn, 1976–1980* (New York: Simon and Schuster, 2020).

3. *NYT*, January 3–31, 1987; *WP*, January 1–25, 1987; Lewis-HR int. On Wright, see J. Brooks Flippen, *Speaker Jim Wright: Power, Scandal, and the Birth of Modern Politics* (Chicago: University of Chicago Press, 2018). On Byrd, see Robert C. Byrd, *Robert C. Byrd: Child of the Appalachian Coal Fields* (Morgantown: West Virginia University Press, 2005); and David A. Corbin, *The Last Great Senator: Robert C. Byrd's Encounters with Eleven U.S. Presidents* (Washington, DC: Potomac Books, 2012). On the Fair Housing Amendments Act, see *WP*, September 14, 1988; Fair Housing Amendments Act of 1988, Pub. L. No. 100–430, 102 Stat. 1619 (1988), https://www.govinfo.gov /content/pkg/STATUTE-102/pdf/STATUTE-102-Pg1619.pdf#page=1; *CR*, vol. 134, March 3–30, 1988; and *CR*, vol. 134, September 7–14, 1988.

4. *WWTW*, 455–456, 469; John Lewis int. On the history of the CBC, see "About the CBC," cbc.house.gov (q); Sherice Janaye Nelson, *The Congressional Black Caucus: Fifty Years of Fighting for Equality* (New York: Archway, 2021); Robert Singh, *The Congressional Black Caucus: Racial Politics in the US Congress* (New York: Sage, 1997); Major Owens, *The Peacock Elite: A Case Study of the Congressional Black Caucus* (Geneva, IL: Granthouse, 2011); and Christina R. Rivers, *The Congressional Black Caucus, Minority Voting Rights, and the U.S. Supreme Court* (Ann Arbor: University of Michigan Press, 2012). On the American antiapartheid movement, see David L. Hostetter, *Movement Matters: American Antiapartheid Activism and the Rise of Multicultural Politics* (Abingdon, UK: Routledge, 2005).

5. *WWTW*, 456 (1st and 2nd q); *NYT*, January 15, 23, 1987 (3rd and 4th q); Randall Williams int.; Lewis-HR int. On the 1981 murder of Michael Donald and its legal aftermath, see *"The People vs. the Klan": A Mother's Courage to Pursue Justice*, CNN, produced by Blumhouse Television, 2021; Laurence Leamer, *The Lynching: The Epic Courtroom Battle That Brought Down the Klan* (New York: William Morrow, 2016); and *NYT*, February 12, 1987.

6. Lewis int.; Bernard LaFayette int.; Patrick Phillips, *Blood at the Root: A Racial Cleansing in America* (New York: Norton, 2017), 207–223; *WWTW*, 457 (1st q); *NYT*, June 12, 1987 (2nd q). Congressional activity related to all of these issues is covered extensively in the *NYT*, 1986–1988. On Reagan's veto of the Clean Water Act and the veto's subsequent override, see *NYT*, February 4–5, 1987; and *CR*, vol. 133, February 5, 1987.

7. Sharon Yamato, "Civil Liberties Act of 1988," *Densho Encyclopedia*, last updated August 24, 2020, https://encyclopedia.densho.org/Civil_Liberties_Act_of_1988/ (q); Michael Isikoff, "Delayed Reparations and an Apology," *WP*, October 10, 1990; *NYT*, August 10, 1988; *CR*, vol. 134, August 10–11, 1988.

8. On the second Reagan administration's conservative agenda, see Johnson, *Sleepwalking through History*; Troy, *Morning in America*; and Wills, *Reagan's America*.

9. *NYT*, June 24, 1987 (q), January 6, June 22, 1988; John D'Emilio, *Lost Prophet: The Life and Times of Bayard Rustin* (New York: Free Press, 2003), 493.

10. *NYT*, February 28, March 7, May 11, July 13 (1st and 2nd q), August 26 (4th q), September 2, 14 (3rd q), 1988. On Shirley Chisholm and the 1972 campaign, see Shola Lynch, dir., *Chisholm '72: Unbought and Unbossed* (Prime Video, 2004); and Anastasia C. Kerwood, *Shirley Chisholm: Champion of Black Feminist Power Politics* (Chapel Hill: University of North Carolina Press, 2023). On the 1988 presidential campaign, see Richard Ben Cramer, *What It Takes: The Way to the White House* (New York: Random House, 1992).

11. Richard Cohen, "Another 'Card-Carrying Member of the ACLU,'" *WP*, September 22, 1988 (1st q). Bush first leveled the charge on August 26, 1988. Roger Simon, "How a Murderer and Rapist Became the Bush Campaign's Most Valuable Player," *Baltimore Sun*, November 11, 1990 (2nd q); *AJC*, October 15–November 10, 1988; *NYT*, November 2–12, 1988; David C. Anderson, *Crime and the Politics of Hysteria: How the Willie Horton Story Changed American Justice* (New York: Crown, 1995).

12. Lewis int.; LaFayette int.; *NYT*, February 15, April 27–June 4, August 19, 23, October 19, November 4, 11, December 3, 20, 1989, January 3, February 7, 11, August 2, 1990; Martin Luther King Jr., "The World House," in *Where Do We Go from Here: Chaos or Community?* (Boston: Beacon, 1967), 167–191; *ATB*, 174–175, 194–196, 204.

13. *WWTW*, 457 (q); *NYT*, April 14, 1989, January 10–13, 1991; *CR*, vol. 135, April 14–15, 1989; James M. Lindsay, "TWE Remembers: Congress's Vote to Authorize the Gulf War," *Council on Foreign Relations blog*, January 12, 2011, https://www.cfr.org/blog/twe-remembers -congresss-vote-authorize-gulf-war; Andrew Glass, "House Approves Military Action against Iraq, Jan. 12, 1991," Politico, January 12, 2017, https://www.politico.com/story/2017/01/house -approves-military-action-against-iraq-jan-12-1991-233336; *CR*, vol. 137, January 12, 1991. On Operation Provide Relief and Operation Restore Hope, see UN Security Council Resolution 794, April 24, 1992; and Kenneth Allard, *Somalia Operations: Lessons Learned* (Washington, DC: National Defense University Press, 1995). On the Persian Gulf War, see Alastair Finlan, *The Gulf War 1991* (Oxford: Osprey Books, 2003); and Rick Atkinson, *Crusade: The Untold Story of the Persian Gulf War* (Boston: Houghton Mifflin, 1993).

14. Lewis int.; LaFayette int.; *NYT*, December 28, 1988, January 20, May 1 (q), 5, 1989, January 18–20, October 27, 1990; *CR*, vol. 135, May 1, 1989. On Barry, see Jonetta Rose Barras, *The Last of the Black Emperors: The Hollow Comeback of Marion Barry in a New Age of Black Leaders* (Baltimore: Bancroft, 1998); Marion Barry Jr. and Omar Tyree, *Mayor for Life: The Incredible Story of Marion Barry, Jr.* (New York: Strebor, 2014); and *NYT*, November 23, 2014 (obit.).

15. Lewis int.; LaFayette int.; Dion Diamond int.; Reginald Green int.; C. T. Vivian int.; Charles Person int.; Hank Thomas int.; Bill Harbour int.; *FR*, 515–518; *NYT*, January 14, 1990 (q); *CR*, vol. 137, September 19–20, 1991; Congressional Black Caucus Foundation, "In Opposition to Clarence Thomas: Where We Must Stand and Why," *The Black Scholar* 22, no. 1–2 (1992): 126–137. See also John Lewis, "Assessing the Gains: Congressman John Lewis, February 7, 1990," interview, *Worldnet Today*, United States Information Agency (hereafter cited as

Lewis-USIA int.); and the video of Lewis's address "Assessing the Gains: Congressman John Lewis, February 7, 1990," broadcast on the USIA program *Worldnet Today,* National Archives Catalog ID# 95112911. On the King infidelity controversy and the FBI's campaign to ruin him by exposing his private life, see David L. Chappell, *Waking from the Dream: The Struggle for Civil Rights in the Shadow of Martin Luther King, Jr.* (New York: Random House, 2014), 149–160, 228–230; Ralph Abernathy, *And the Walls Came Tumbling Down* (New York: Harper and Row, 1989), 470–475; and David J. Garrow, *Bearing the Cross: Martin Luther King, Jr., and the Southern Christian Leadership Conference* (New York: William Morrow, 1986), 281, 303–304, 310–313, 318–319, 323, 340, 360–37, 371–377, 425. See also David J. Garrow, *The FBI and Martin Luther King: From "SOLO" to Memphis* (New York: Norton, 1981).

16. *NYT,* March 5, 1990 (q); *FR,* 518–519. In 1985, Lewis, LaFayette, Jesse Jackson, and other civil rights leaders met in Selma to celebrate the twentieth anniversary of the Selma-to-Montgomery march, and thirteen years later the 1998 Selma visit initiated a series of annual pilgrimages commemorating the March 7 anniversary of Bloody Sunday; the sponsor was the Faith and Politics Institute (FPI), with Lewis serving as chair of the organization's board of directors beginning in 1997. See faithandpolitics.org. Since 1998, more than three hundred members of Congress have participated in the annual March pilgrimages to Alabama. Following Lewis's death, the organization created the John Robert Lewis Scholars and Fellows Program, designed to attract college-age students to the FPI's pilgrimages and other activities.

17. Clayborne Carson int. On the King plagiarism controversy, see Chappell, *Waking from the Dream,* 160–174, 164 (1st q); *WWTW,* 458–459 (2nd q).

18. *FR,* 518–519 (1st and 2nd q). On the Rodney King incident and the ensuing crisis, see Lou Cannon, *Official Negligence: How Rodney King and the Riots Changed Los Angeles and the LAPD* (New York: Times Books/Random House, 1998); Rodney King, *The Riot Within: My Journey from Rebellion to Redemption* (New York: HarperOne, 2013); and *Los Angeles Times, Understanding the Riots: Los Angeles before and after the Rodney King Case* (Los Angeles: Los Angeles Times Syndicate, 1996).

19. Lewis int.; LaFayette int.; *NYT,* October 12, 1991 (1st q); *WWTW,* 469 (2nd q), 468 (3rd q). On George H. W. Bush's discriminatory policies toward Haitian refugees, see *NYT,* May 24–25, 29, 1992; *WP,* May 29, 1992; "History Lesson 9: Refugees from the Caribbean: Cuba and Haiti 'Boat People,'" Constitutional Rights Foundation, http://www.crfimmigrationed.org/lessons-for-teachers/148-hl9; and David W. Haine, *Refugees in America in the 1990s: A Research Handbook* (Westport, CT: Greenwood, 1996). On Clarence Thomas and the Anita Hill hearings, see Jane Mayer and Jill Abramson, *Strange Justice: The Selling of Clarence Thomas* (Boston: Houghton Mifflin, 1994); Timothy M. Phelps and Helen Winternitz, *Capitol Games: Clarence Thomas, Anita Hill, and the Story of a Supreme Court Nomination* (New York: Hyperion, 1992); Anita Hill, *Speaking Truth to Power* (New York: Doubleday, 1997); Toni Morrison, ed., *Race-ing Justice, En-gendering Power: Essays on Anita Hill, Clarence Thomas, and the Construction of Social Reality* (New York: Pantheon, 1992); and Victoria M. Massie, "How Racism and Sexism Shaped the Clarence Thomas/Anita Hill Hearing," Vox, April 16, 2016, https://www.vox.com/2016/4/16/11408576/anita-hill-clarence-thomas-confirmation.

20. Lewis-HR int.; *NYT,* November 1–10, 1992; *AJC,* November 2–9, 1992; "Party Divisions of the House of Representatives, 1789 to Present," History, Art, and Archives, United

States House of Representatives, https://history.house.gov/Institution/Party-Divisions/Party
-Divisions/; "U.S. Senate: Party Division," United States Senate, https://www.senate.gov
/history/partydiv.htm. On the 1992 presidential election and the ascendancy of Bill Clinton,
see John Hohenberg, *The Bill Clinton Story: Winning the Presidency* (Syracuse, NY: Syracuse
University Press, 1994); James Ceaser and Andrew Busch, *Upside Down and Inside Out: The
1992 Elections and American Politics* (Lanham, MD: Rowman and Littlefield, 1993); and Peter
Goldman et al., *Quest for the Presidency, 1992* (College Station: Texas A&M University Press,
1994). On the environmentalist collaboration between Lewis and Gore, see Stephen Tuck, *We
Ain't What We Ought to Be: The Black Freedom Struggle from Emancipation to Obama* (Cambridge,
MA: Harvard University Press, 2010), 383–385 (1st q). On the environmental justice movement, see Luke W. Cole and Sheila R. Foster, *From the Ground Up: Environmental Racism and
the Rise of the Environmental Justice Movement* (New York: New York University Press, 2000).
On McKinney, see Cynthia Mckinney, *Ain't Nothing Like Freedom* (Atlanta: Clarity Press,
2013); Lynne E. Ford, "Cynthia McKinney," in *Encyclopedia of Women and American Politics*,
ed. Lynne E. Ford (New York: Infobase, 2008), 306 (2nd q), available online at https://www
.infobadepublishingh.com; and Karen Foerstel, *Biographical Directory of Congressional Women*
(Westport, CT: Greenwood, 1999), 181.

CHAPTER 15. Keeping the Dream Alive

1. On the "New Democrats," see Al From, *The New Democrats and the Return to Power*
(New York: St. Martin's, 2013). On the "Slick Willie" characterization, see Floyd G. Brown,
"Slick Willie": Why America Cannot Trust Bill Clinton (Annapolis: Annapolis-Washington, 1992).
On Jordan, see Vernon E. Jordan Jr. with Annette Gordon-Reed, *Vernon Can Read: A Memoir*
(New York: Public Affairs, 2001); and Vernon Jordan Jr., *Make It Plain: Standing Up and Speak-
ing Out* (New York: Public Affairs, 2008). For profiles of Lewis's congressional colleagues in
1993, see *Congressional Quarterly Almanac, 103rd Congress* (Washington, DC: Congress at Your
Fingertips, 1994).

2. *NYT*, January 21, 22 (1st q), February 6, June 14, July 19 (2nd q), August 28 (3rd q),
November 30, December 20, 29, 1993; *CR*, vol. 139, November 26, 1993; Raymond Arsenault,
Arthur Ashe: A Life (New York: Simon and Schuster, 2018), 613–614. On Ginsburg, see Jane
Sherron De Hart, *Ruth Bader Ginsburg: A Life* (New York: Knopf, 2018).

3. *NYT*, July 21, 1994 (2nd q); *WWTW*, 457; "The Violent Crime Control and Law Enforcement Act of 1994," History, Art, and Archives, United States House of Representatives,
August 21, 1994 (1st q), https://history.house.gov/Historical-Highlights/1951-2000/The-Violent
-Crime-Control-and-Law-Enforcement-Act-of-1994/; *CR*, vol. 139, October 26, November 3,
19, 1993; *CR*, vol. 140, August 21, September 13, 1994; Carrie Johnson, "20 Years Later, Parts
of Major Crime Bill Viewed as Terrible Mistake," *Morning Edition*, NPR, September 12, 2014,
https://www.npr.org/2014/09/12/347736999/20-years-later-major-crime-bill-viewed-as-terrible
-mistake; Jill Lepore, *These Truths: A History of the United States* (New York: Norton, 2018),
698–699 (3rd q). On the promotion and defeat of the Clinton health care reform effort, see
Paul Starr, *Remedy and Reaction: The Peculiar American Struggle over Health Care Reform* (New
Haven, CT: Yale University Press, 2013); and Mark E. Rushefsky and Kant Patel, *Politics, Power*

and Policy Making: The Case of Health Care Reform in the 1990s (New York: Routledge, 2013). For an excellent overview of the racial dimension of the anticrime movement of the 1980s and 1990s, see Michelle Alexander, *The New Jim Crow: Mass Incarceration in the Age of Colorblindness* (New York: New Press, 2020).

4. *NYT*, October 31, 1993 (1st q), January 25, 1994 (2nd q); *WWTW*, 469–470. Lewis was very pleased, however, when the CBC rallied behind the 1994 King Holiday and Service Bill, initiated by him as a means of transforming the King holiday from "a day off to a day on." Lewis thought the best way to honor King was to make the holiday "a day of community service and action rather than just a day off from work. . . . We could honor his memory best by making this a day of sharing and caring on the principle of community and connection." *WWTW*, 459.

5. Jason DeParle, "Clinton Puzzle; How to Delay Welfare Reform Yet Seem to Pursue It," *NYT*, January 5, 1994 (q); *CR*, vol. 142, June 22, July 18–21, 1996; Brendon O'Connor, "The Protagonists and Ideas behind the Personal Responsibility and Work Opportunity Reconciliation Act of 1996: The Enactment of a Conservative Welfare System," *Social Justice* 28, no. 4 (2001): 4–32. See also Steven Gillon, *The Pact: Bill Clinton, Newt Gingrich, and the Rivalry That Defined a Nation* (New York: Oxford University Press, 2008).

6. *NYT*, March 9 (1st q) and 16 (2nd q), 1994; *CR*, vol. 140, March 9, 16, 1994.

7. *WWTW*, 465 (q); *NYT*, November 4–9, 1994; *AJC*, November 4–10, 1994; U.S. Congress, *1994 Congressional and Federal Election Statistics* (Washington, DC: Qonto, 2019); Steven S. Smith, *The American Congress after the 1994 Election* (Boston: Houghton Mifflin, 1995); Philip A. Klinkner, ed., *Midterm: The Elections of 1994 in Context* (New York: Routledge, 2019).

8. Newt Gingrich et al., eds., *Contract with America: The Bold Plan by Rep. Newt Gingrich, Rep. Dick Armey, and the House Republicans to Change the Nation* (New York: Times Books, 1994); Nicholas Hemmer, *Partisans: The Conservative Republicans Who Remade American Politics in the 1990s* (New York: Basic Books, 2022); Julian E. Zelizer, *Burning Down the House: Newt Gingrich, the Fall of a Speaker, and the Rise of a New Republican Party* (New York: Penguin, 2020) (1st q); *NYT*, November 1–2, 1995 (2nd q); *WWTW*, 465–468; Bernard LaFayette int. On the political and racial roots of the "new conservatism" of the 1980s and 1990s, see Dan T. Carter, *The Politics of Rage: George Wallace, the Origins of the New Conservatism, and the Transformation of American Politics* (Baton Rouge: Louisiana State University Press, 2000); and Dan T. Carter, *From George Wallace to Newt Gingrich: Race in the Conservative Counterrevolution, 1963–1994* (Baton Rouge: Louisiana State University Press, 1996).

9. On the 1994 Haitian intervention, see Philippe R. Girard, *Clinton in Haiti: The 1994 US Invasion of Haiti* (New York: Palgrave Macmillan, 2004). *WWTW*, 472 (q); *NYT*, October 4–5, 1995; *WP*, October 4–5, 1995; *CR*, vol. 141, October 4–5, 1995. On Mandela, see Nelson Mandela, *Long Walk to Freedom* (Boston: Little, Brown, 1994); Anthony Sampson, *Mandela: The Authorised Biography* (London: HarperCollins, 1999); and Tom Lodge, *Mandela: A Critical Life* (New York: Oxford University Press, 2006).

10. John Lewis int.; LaFayette int.; *WWTW*, 458; *NYT*, December 23, 29, 1994, November 22–26 (q), December 31, 1995, May 15, 1996. On the Dayton peace accords, see D. Chollet, *The Road to the Dayton Accords: A Study of American Statecraft* (New York: Palgrave Macmillan, 2007); and Elizabeth M. Cousens, *Toward Peace in Bosnia: Implementing the Dayton Accords* (Boulder, CO: Lynne Rienner, 2001). Martin Luther King Jr., "The World House," in *Where Do We Go from Here: Chaos or Community?* (Boston: Beacon, 1967), 167–191; Steve Glasser, "King Center De-

fends Park Service Eviction," UPI, December 29, 1994, https://www.upi.com/Archives/1994/12/29/King-Center-defends-park-service-eviction/5267788677200/; *AJC*, December 23–29, 1994, January 15–18, 1995; *Los Angeles Times*, December 29, 1994.

11. *WWTW*, 466–473; *NYT*, January 22 (1st q) and 26, April 10, August 21–22 (2nd q), September 24, 1996. On Clinton and welfare reform, see Patrick J. Maney, *Bill Clinton: New Gilded Age President* (Lawrence: University Press of Kansas, 2016); and Marisa Chappell, *The War on Welfare: Family, Poverty, and Politics in Modern America* (Philadelphia: University of Pennsylvania Press, 2009).

12. *NYT*, July 12–13, September 10, 21, October 15–November 7, 1996. On the legislative history of the Defense of Marriage Act, see U.S. Congress, *Defense of Marriage Act: Hearing before the Subcommittee on the Constitution of the Committee on the Judiciary, House of Representatives, One Hundred Fourth Congress, Second Session, on H.R. 3396, Defense of Marriage Act, May 15, 1996* (n.p.: Palala Press, 2015). See also Mark E. Brandon, *States of Union: Family and Change in the American Constitutional Order* (Lawrence: University Press of Kansas, 2013); "Election Special: The Remaking of a President," *Time*, November 18, 1996; Michael Nelson, *Clinton's Elections: 1992, 1996, and the Birth of a New Era of Governance* (Lawrence: University Press of Kansas, 2020); and Paul R. Abramson, John H. Aldrich, and David W. Rohde, *Change and Continuity in the 1996 and 1998 Elections* (Washington, DC: CQ Press, 1999).

13. On the aftermath of the 1996 election, see Harvey L. Schantz, *Politics in an Era of Divided Government: The Election of 1996 and Its Aftermath* (New York: Routledge, 2001); Gerald M. Pomper et al., *The Election of 1996: Reports and Interpretations* (London: Chatham House, 1997); Zelizer, *Burning Down the House*; and Abramson, Aldrich, and Rohde, *Change and Continuity*.

14. *WWTW*, 473–474 (q). On Mother Teresa, see Kathryn Spink, *Mother Teresa: An Authorized Biography* (New York: HarperCollins, 1997); and Aroup Chatterjee, *Mother Teresa: The Untold Story* (New Delhi: Prakash Books, 2016). In 2009, Lewis returned to India as part of a congressional delegation commemorating the fiftieth anniversary of Martin Luther King Jr.'s 1959 visit to Gandhi's homeland. Clayborne Carson, *Martin's Dream* (New York: Palgrave Macmillan, 2013), 79.

15. Lewis int.; *NYT*, March 21, April 24, 1997, March 21–April 2, 1998; *WP*, March 29–April 2, 1998; "Clinton Africa Trip, March 1998," Human Rights Watch, March 30, 1998, https://www.hrw.org/report/1998/03/30/clinton-africa-trip-march-1998.

16. Lewis int.; *WWTW*, 405–465 (1st and 2nd q), 466 (3rd q), 467–475. The book's editor at Simon and Schuster was the legendary Alice Mayhew.

17. John Hope Franklin int. (q); Steven F. Lawson, ed., *One America in the 21st Century: The Report of President Bill Clinton's Initiative on Race* (New Haven, CT: Yale University Press, 2008); President's Initiative on Race, *One America in the 21st Century: Forging a New Future* (n.p., 1998). On the Lewinsky scandal, see Andrew W. Morton, *Monica's Story* (New York: St. Martin's, 1999); and Starr Commission, *The Starr Report: The Official Report of the Independent Counsel's Investigation of the President* (Toronto: Prima Lifestyles, 1998).

18. In addition to being a best seller, *Walking with the Wind* won several major book prizes, including the Robert F. Kennedy Book Award, the Ainsfield-Wolf Book Award, the Christopher Award, and the Lillian Smith Book Award. The *New York Times* selected it as a Notable Book of the Year for 1998, and the American Library Association chose it as the Nonfiction Book of the Year. In 2009, more than a decade after its publication, *Newsweek* magazine listed it as

one of the "50 Books for Our Times." Mary McCrory, "A Man of Consequence," *WP*, June 14, 1998; "Editors' Choice: The Best Books of 1998," *NYT*, December 6, 1998; Chantale Wong int.; Lewis int.; LaFayette int.; *Baltimore Sun*, April 8, 1994. On the FPI, see its homepage, https://www.faithandpolitics.org (1st and 2nd q).

19. *NYT*, November 2–12, 1998, January 17, February 12, 1999; *WP*, November 2–12, 1998; *AJC*, November 1–11, 1998. On the 1998 election, see Abramson, Aldrich, and Rohde, *Change and Continuity*; Wilson Carey McWilliams, *Beyond the Politics of Disappointment: American Elections, 1980–1998* (Washington, DC: CQ Press, 1999); and John Clifford Green, Mark J. Rozell, and Clyde Wilcox, eds., *Prayers in the Precincts: The Christian Right in the 1998 Elections* (Washington, DC: Georgetown University Press, 2000). On the Clinton impeachment, see Peter Baker, *Inside the Impeachment and Trial of William Jefferson Clinton* (New York: Simon and Schuster, 2012); and Richard A. Posner, *An Affair of State: The Investigation, Impeachment, and Trial of President Clinton* (Cambridge, MA: Harvard University Press, 1999).

20. "President William Jefferson Clinton, State of the Union Address, January 19, 1999," Office of the Press Secretary, White House (1st and 2nd q), https://clintonwhitehouse4.archives.gov/WH/New/html/19990119-2656.html; *NYT*, January 20–21, 1999. On the impact of the impeachment on Clinton, see John F. Harris, *The Survivor: Bill Clinton in the White House* (New York: Random House, 2005).

21. *NYT*, January 17 (1st q), 19 (2nd q), 1999.

22. Lewis int.; *NYT*, July 19, 1999; Karl Grossman, "From Congress to Catholic Deacon: Mike Forbes Reinvents Himself, Again," *Suffolk Closeup*, April 14, 2016.

23. *NYT*, March 12, 24, May 6, June 10, 22 (1st and 2nd q), 1999; McWilliams, *Beyond the Politics of Disappointment*. On the Kosovo crisis and NATO's intervention, see Dag Henriksen, *NATO's Gamble: Combining Diplomacy and Airpower in the Kosovo Crisis, 1998–1999* (Annapolis, MD: Naval Institute Press, 2007); and Martin A. Smith and Paul Latawski, eds., *The Kosovo Crisis and the Evolution of Post–Cold War European Security* (Manchester: Manchester University Press, 2003).

24. *NYT*, March 6, 2000 (q); Lewis int.; LaFayette int. On Lewis's complicated relationship with Clinton, see Teresa Carpenter, "John Lewis," in *Profiles in Courage for Our Time*, ed. Caroline Kennedy (New York: Hyperion, 2002), 341–342.

25. Lewis int.; LaFayette int.; *NYT*, December 12, 1999 (q). On Gore, see David Maranniss and Ellen Nakashima, *The Prince of Tennessee: The Rise of Al Gore* (New York: Simon and Schuster, 2000); and Bill Turque, *Inventing Al Gore* (New York: Mariner Books, 2000). On George W. Bush, see Jean Edward Smith, *Bush* (New York: Simon and Schuster, 2016). On Bradley, see Bill Bradley, *Time Present, Time Past: A Memoir* (New York: Vintage, 1997). See also Rhodes Cook, *Race for the Presidency: Winning the 2000 Nomination* (Washington, DC: CQ Press, 1999).

26. Lewis int.; LaFayette int.; "2000 Presidential Democratic Primary Election Results," Dave Liep's Atlas of U.S. Presidential Elections, https://uselectionatlas.org/RESULTS/national.php?year=2000&f=0&off=0&elect=1; *NYT*, August 8, 14–16 (1st q), 17–18, 2000; "2000 Democratic Convention: Rep. John Lewis," Online NewsHour, August 16, 2000 (2nd and 5th q), https://www.pbs.org/newshour/spc/election2000/demconvention/lewis.html; *WWTW*, 442–443 (3rd and 4th q); "President Clinton: Remarks to the Democratic Party National Convention," August 14, 2000, The American Presidency Project, https://www.presidency.ucsb.edu/documents/remarks

-the-democratic-national-convention-los-angeles-california; (6th q); *FR*, 514. pbs.org. On Lieberman, see "Joseph Lieberman: The Historic Choice," *Hartford Courant*, August 8, 2000; Kevin Sack, "Trip South in '63 Gave Lieberman a Footnote, and Hold, in History," *NYT*, September 26, 2000; Joseph I. Lieberman and Hadassah Lieberman, *An Amazing Adventure: Joe and Hadassah's Personal Notes on the 2000 Campaign* (New York: Simon and Schuster, 2003); and Joe Lieberman, *The Centrist Solution: How We Made Government Work and Can Make It Work Again* (New York: Diversion Books, 2021).

27. Lewis int.; David M. Jackson, "Attacked by Trump, Lewis Acknowledges He Boycotted Bush Inauguration, Too," *USA Today*, January 17, 2017. On the contested 2000 presidential election, see Jeffrey Toobin, *Too Close to Call: The Thirty-Six-Day Battle to Decide the 2000 Election* (New York: Random House, 2001); Jack N. Rakove, ed., *The Unfinished Election of 2000: Leading Scholars Examine America's Strangest Election* (New York: Basic Books, 2001); and Correspondents of the *New York Times, 36 Days: The Complete Chronicle of the 2000 Presidential Election Crisis* (New York: Times Books, 2001).

CHAPTER 16. Politics and Remembrance

1. On John-Miles's interest in hip-hop music and his feelings about the violent attacks against his father during the 1960s, see Daniel Aldridge, "From Civil Rights to Hip-Hop: Toward a Nexus of Ideas," *Journal of African American History* 90 (Summer 2005): 232; and Stephen Tuck, *We Ain't What We Ought to Be: The Black Freedom Struggle from Emancipation to Obama* (Cambridge, MA: Harvard University Press, 2010), 375. John Lewis int.; Jean Edward Smith, *Bush* (New York: Simon and Schuster, 2016), 148–203. Andrew B. Lewis, *The Shadows of Youth: The Remarkable Journey of the Civil Rights Generation* (New York: Hill and Wang, 2009), 295–298, argues that the time Lewis devoted to nostalgic commemoration of civil rights milestones limited his effectiveness as a legislator. On the new Christian Right, see Michelle Goldberg, *Kingdom Coming: The Rise of Christian Nationalism* (New York: Norton, 2006); Christian Hedges, *American Fascists: The Christian Right and the War on America* (New York: Free Press, 2008); and Daniel K. Williams, *God's Own Party: The Making of the Christian Right* (New York: Oxford University Press, 2012). See also the fascinating case study of the emergence of conservative, evangelical politics among Southern migrants to California: Darren Dochuk, *From Bible Belt to Sun Belt: Plain-folk Religion, Conservative Politics, and the Rise of Evangelical Conservatism* (New York: Norton, 2011).

2. For interpretations of supply-side economics and its effects on economic growth and wealth distribution in the United States, see Brian Domitrovic, ed., *The Pillars of Reaganomics: A Generation of Wisdom from Arthur Laffer and the Supply-Side Revolutionaries* (San Francisco: Pacific Research Institute, 2014); Robert D. Atkinson, *Supply-Side Follies: Why Conservative Economics Fails, Liberal Economics Falters, and Innovation Economics Is the Answer* (Lanham, MD: Rowman and Littlefield, 2006); and Kurt Andersen, *Evil Geniuses: The Unmaking of America: A Recent History* (New York: Random House, 2020). On the "school-to-prison pipeline," see Nancy A. Heitzeg, "Education or Incarceration: Zero Tolerance Policies and the School to Prison Pipeline," *Forum on Public Policy Online* 2009, no. 2 (2009); Richard Mora and Mary Christianakis, "Feeding the School-to-Prison Pipeline: The Convergence of Neoliberalism,

Conservatism, and Penal Populism," *Journal of Educational Controversy* 7 (2013): article 5; and Michelle Alexander, *The New Jim Crow: Mass Incarceration in the Age of Colorblindness* (New York: New Press, 2020).

3. Justin Vaisse, *Neoconservatism: The Biography of a Movement* (Cambridge, MA: Harvard University Press, 2010). On Cheney, see Dick Cheney, *In My Time* (New York: Threshold, 2011); Peter Baker, *Days of Fire: Bush and Cheney in the White House* (New York: Doubleday, 2013); Lou Dubose and Jake Bernstein, *Vice: Dick Cheney and the Hijacking of the American Presidency* (New York: Random House, 2006); and Barton Gellman, *Angler: The Cheney Vice Presidency* (New York: Penguin, 2008).

4. Lewis int.; Bernard LaFayette int.; Bill Harbour int.; *NYT*, October 8 (q), November 17, 2000; *FR*, 507–522. On Williams, see Rolundus R. Rice, *Hosea Williams: A Life of Defiance and Protest* (Columbia: University of South Carolina Press, 2022).

5. Lewis int.; Hank Thomas int.; Benjamin Cox int.; Ed Blankenheim int.; Charles Person int.; Jim Zwerg int.; Marvin Rich int.; Moses Newson int.; George Houser int.; Clayborne Carson int.; John Moody int.; Catherine Burks Brooks int.; Glenda Gaither Davis int.; Jim Davis int.; Kwame Leo Lillard int.; Dion Diamond int.; Rip Patton int.; *FR*, 522–523 (1st q); *AJC*, May 10, 2001; *Boston Globe*, May 22, 2001; "John Lewis," John F. Kennedy Presidential Library and Museum, 2001, https://www.jfklibrary.org/events-and-awards/profile-in-courage-award /award-recipients/john-lewis-2001 (2nd q).

6. Larry Copeland, "Freedom Riders Go South Again," *USA Today*, November 8, 2001; Steve Green, "Freedom Rider Diary—Forty Years Later" (unpublished manuscript in author's possession, 2001); "Governor Musgrove Declares Freedom Riders Day in Mississippi," *Newsletter of the Freedom Riders' 40th Reunion*, November 10, 2001 (q); Carol Ruth Silver int.; Tom Gaither int.; Israel Dresner int.; Martin Freedman int.; Steve Green int.; John Maguire int.; Claire O'Connor int.; Bob Singleton int.; Helen Singleton int.; *FR*, 525. On Carol Ruth Silver, the primary organizer of the Jackson reunion, see Carol Ruth Silver, *Freedom Rider Diary: Smuggled Notes from Parchman Prison* (Jackson: University Press of Mississippi, 2014).

7. Lewis int.; *NYT*, February 16, March 28, April 7, 17, June 5, 7, August 1–2, 2001; *CR*, vol. 147, May 15–16, 23, August 1–2, 2001. See also Roy Moore, *So Help Me God: The Ten Commandments, Judicial Tyranny, and the Battle for Religious Freedom*, with John Perry (Nashville: Broadman and Holman, 2005).

8. Lewis int.; Mitchell Zuckoff, *Fall and Rise: The Story of 9/11* (New York: Harper, 2019); Peter L. Bergen, *Manhunt: The Ten-Year Search for Bin Laden from 9/11 to Abbottabad* (New York: Crown, 2012); Seth G. Jones, *Hunting in the Shadows: The Pursuit of Al Qa'ida Since 9/11* (New York: Norton, 2012); "HR 3162—USA Patriot Act of 2001—Voting Record," October 25, 2001, https://justfacts.votesmart.org/bill/votes/7877; *NYT*, September 11–18, October 7, 26, November 13, December 11–13, 2001; *CR*, vol. 147, October 23–26, 2001; "Guantánamo Bay: 14 Years of Injustice," May 18, 2020, Amnesty International UK (q), https://www.amnesty.org.uk/guantanamo-bay-human-rights.

9. Gary Langer, "Poll: Bush Approval Rating 92 percent," ABC News, October 1, 2001; Smith, *Bush*, 277–280; *NYT*, January 18, 30 (q), May 12, 2002, March–June 2002. See Bergen, *Manhunt*; and Seth G. Jones, *In the Graveyard of Empires: America's War in Afghanistan* (New York: Norton, 2009).

10. Lewis int. (1st q); Smith, *Bush*, 279–329; *NYT*, April 19, May 22, July 4, 8, September 13 (2nd q), 2002; Doug Jones, *Bending toward Justice: The Birmingham Church Bombing That Changed the Course of Civil Rights* (Toronto: All Points Books, 2019); *NYT*, October 10, 2002; *CR*, vol. 148, October 2, 10–11, 16, 2002; Julian Bond, "Freedom under Fire," *Black Scholar* 32 (Summer 2002): 2–9. Seven years later, in 2009, on the hundredth anniversary of the NAACP, Bond joined Lewis as a Spingarn Award winner. Anne E. Bromley, "Bond Receives NAACP's Highest Award on Its 100th Anniversary," *UVAToday*, July 17, 2009, https://news.virginia.edu.

11. John Lewis int.; LaFayette int.; Smith, *Bush*, 329–330, 342 (1st q)–346 (2nd q), 356–357 (3rd q), 359 (4th q), 364–367 (5th q); *NYT*, May 1, 2003. On Wellstone, see Bill Lofty, *Paul Wellstone: The Life of a Passionate Progressive* (Ann Arbor: University of Michigan Press, 2005).

12. *NYT*, March 5 (q), May 28, June 23, 26, September 7, 17, November 20, December 13, 2003; Smith, *Bush*, 370–380; John Lewis int.; LaFayette int.

13. On Kerry, see John Kerry, *Every Day Is Extra* (New York: Simon and Schuster, 2018); Douglas Brinkley, *Tour of Duty: John Kerry and the Vietnam War* (New York: William Morrow, 2004); and John F. Kerry and John Edwards, *Our Plan for America: Stronger at Home, Respected in the World* (New York: Public Affairs, 2004). On Edwards, see John Edwards, *Four Trials*, with John Auchard (New York: Simon and Schuster, 2003). Barack Obama, *A Promised Land* (New York: Crown, 2020), 50–53, 87; *NYT*, July 27–28 (q), 2004; *WP*, July 28, 2004; Clarence Page, "Bush's 'Values' Got More Black Voters in His Camp Than in 2000, but All Is Not Lost for Democrats," *Chicago Tribune*, November 7, 2004; Smith, *Bush*, 413–415. On the 2004 presidential election, see William J. Crotty, *A Defining Moment: The Presidential Election of 2004* (New York: Routledge, 2005); and Larry J. Sabato, *Divided States of America: The Slash and Burn Politics of the 2004 Presidential Election* (London: Longman, 2005).

14. *NYT*, January 6, 30, February 16, 28, March 1, 7, April 1, 13, 20, June 13, 27, July 7–8, 19, September 5–6, 15, 29, November 7, 2004; Smith, *Bush*, 229, 390 (1st q), 394–395, 427–429, 444–451; Page, "Bush's 'Values'" (2nd q); Doug Jones, *Bending toward Justice*. On the conservative trend on the Supreme Court during the Bush years, see Jeffrey Toobin, *The Nine: Inside the Secret World of the Supreme Court* (New York: Doubleday, 2007). On the G8, see Nicholas Bayne, *Staying Together: The G8 Summit Confronts the 21st Century* (Aldershot, U.K.: Ashgate, 2005).

15. On the Katrina crisis and its exposure of racial inequality in New Orleans and the Louisiana and Mississippi Gulf Coast region, see Douglas Brinkley, *The Great Deluge: Hurricane Katrina, New Orleans, and the Mississippi Gulf Coast* (New York: William Morrow, 2006); Andy Horowitz, *Katrina: A History, 1915–2015* (Cambridge, MA: Harvard University Press, 2020); Michael Eric Dyson, *Come Hell or High Water: Hurricane Katrina and the Color of Disaster* (New York: Civitas, 2006); and Chester Hartman and Gregory Squires, eds., *There Is No Such Thing as a Natural Disaster: Race, Class, and Hurricane Katrina* (New York: Routledge, 2006). On DeLay's legal issues and resignation, see *Chicago Tribune*, September 29, 2005; *NYT*, September 29, 2005, November 24, 2010; *WP*, April 4, 16, September 10, 2006, January 9, 2007; Jim Drinkard, "DeLay's Hardball Tactics Coming Back on Him," *USA Today*, April 29, 2006; and *The Big Buy: Tom DeLay's Stolen Congress* (Brainstorm Media, 2006), DVD.

16. The characterization of Parks as the "mother of the freedom movement" (1st q) appears in the text of Public Law 106–26, enacted by the 106th Congress in May 1999 "to authorize the President to award a gold medal on behalf of the Congress to Rosa Parks in recognition

of her contributions to the nation." There have also been numerous public references, in the press, Congress, and elsewhere, to Parks as the "mother of the civil rights movement" and "the first lady of civil rights." See Public Law 106–26, May 4, 1999, https://govinfo.gov. Jeanne Theoharis, *The Rebellious Life of Mrs. Rosa Parks* (Boston: Beacon, 2013), xxi–xxiii (2nd and 3rd q), xxiv, 165–239; *NYT*, October 31, 2005 (4th q); *WWTW*, 88; Lewis int.; C. T. Vivian int.; Sheldon Hackney int. On the Parks photo, see "Rosa Parks and John Lewis," circa 1970, photo by Boyd Lewis, Digital Resources of the Kenan Research Center, Atlanta History Center, https://album.atlantahistorycenter.com/digital/collection/byd/id/85/rec/2. On December 4, 2019, Lewis spoke at the opening of the Library of Congress exhibit "Rosa Parks in Her Own Words." See Carla D. Hayden, "Remembering John Lewis: The Power of 'Good Trouble,'" *Timeless: Stories from the Library of Congress* (blog), July 19, 2020, https://blogs.loc.gov/loc/2020/07/remembering-john-lewis-the-power-of-good-trouble/.

17. Dan T. Carter, *The Politics of Rage: George Wallace, the Origins of the New Conservatism, and the Transformation of American Politics* (Baton Rouge: Louisiana State University Press, 2000); 136–142 (1st q), 143–151; E. Culpepper Clark, *The Schoolhouse Door: Segregation's Last Stand at the University of Alabama* (New York: Oxford University Press, 1993); *NYT*, September 28, October 12–13, 31 (2nd q), 2005. On Motley's brilliant and groundbreaking career as a civil rights attorney, see Constance Motley, *Equal Justice under Law* (New York: Farrar, Straus and Giroux, 1998); Gary L. Ford Jr., *Constance Baker Motley: One Woman's Fight for Civil Rights and Equal Justice under Law* (Tuscaloosa: University of Alabama Press, 2017); and Tomiko Brown-Nagin, *Civil Rights Queen: Constance Baker Motley and the Struggle for Equality* (New York: Pantheon, 2022).

CHAPTER 17. The Conscience of Congress

1. John Lewis int. On civil rights historiography, see Adam Fairclough, "Historians and the Civil Rights Movement," *Journal of American Studies* 24 (1990): 387–398; Steven Lawson, "Freedom Then, Freedom Now: The Historiography of the Civil Rights Movement," *American Historical Review* 96 (March 1991): 456–471; Charles W. Eagles, "Toward New Histories of the Civil Rights Era," *Journal of Southern History* 66 (November 2000): 815–848; Kevin Gaines, "Historiography and the Struggle for Black Equality Since 1945," in *A Companion to Post-1945 America*, ed. Jean Agnew and Roy Rosenzweig (Malden, MA: Blackwell, 2002): 211–234; Jacquelyn Dowd Hall, "The Long Civil Rights Movement and the Political Uses of the Past," *Journal of American History* 91 (March 2005): 1233–1250; Danielle McGuire and John Dittmer, eds., *Freedom Rights: New Perspectives on the Civil Rights Movement* (Lexington: University Press of Kentucky, 2011); and Jeanne Theoharis, *A More Beautiful and Terrible Story: The Uses and Misuses of Civil Rights History* (Boston: Beacon, 2018).

2. Lewis int.; Taylor Branch, *Parting the Waters: America in the King Years 1954–63* (New York: Simon and Schuster, 1988), 412–491; David Niven, *The Politics of Injustice: The Kennedys, the Freedom Rides, and the Electoral Consequences of a Moral Compromise* (Knoxville: University of Tennessee Press, 2003); David Halberstam, *The Children* (New York: Random House, 1998); David Halberstam, "The Kids Take Over," *Reporter*, June 22, 1961, 22–23. See also Derek Catsam, *Freedom's Main Line: The Journey of Reconciliation and the Freedom Rides* (Lexington: University

Press of Kentucky, 2008). *Freedom Riders: 1961 and the Struggle for Racial Justice,* by Raymond Arsenault, was published in January 2006, and an abridged version was published in 2011 as a companion volume to the PBS *American Experience* documentary *Freedom Riders,* which premiered at the Sundance Film Festival in January 2010, sixteen months before being broadcast nationally on public television in May 2011. The book won the 2007 Owsley Prize, awarded to the best book in Southern history published during the preceding year, and the documentary won three Emmy Awards—for writing, editing, and best documentary—in 2011. The film later won a George Peabody Award. On Elwin Wilson and the Freedom Riders' appearance on the *Oprah Winfrey Show* in May 2011, see the preface to the present book.

3. Lewis int.; Bernard LaFayette int.; Rip Patton int.; David Myers int.; Winonah Beamer Myers int.; Benjamin Cox int.; Charles Person int.; Bill Harbour int.; Hank Thomas int.; Carol Ruth Silver int.; Diane Nash int.; Catherine Burks-Brooks int.; Jim Zwerg int.; John Seigenthaler int.; Lauren Prestileo int.; Laurens Grant int.; Stanley Nelson int.; *NYT,* February 7, 2006, March 14, 2007. See also "Freedom Riders," PBS, https://www.pbs.org/wgbh/americanexperience/films/freedomriders/.

4. Lewis int.; Lewis-HR int.; *NYT,* April 7, 9 (1st q), 16 (2nd and 3rd q), May 4 (4th q), 2006; *AJC,* April 7–9, 2006.

5. *NYT,* March 29 (1st q), July 13 (2nd and 3rd q), 21 (4th q), 2006; *CR,* vol. 152, July 13, 21–22, 2006; Carol Anderson, *One Person, No Vote: How Voter Suppression Is Destroying Our Democracy* (New York: Bloomsbury, 2018), 25–30; Lewis-HR int.

6. Lewis int.; James Lawson int.; Lewis-HR int.; *NYT,* July 31, August 27, October 4, 14, 23, 30, November 14, 2006; Jean Edward Smith, *Bush* (New York: Simon and Schuster, 2016), 416–520.

7. On the 2006 midterm election, see Karen O'Connor and Larry Sabato, *Essentials of American Government: Continuity and Change: 2006 Edition* (London: Longman, 2006); Rhodes Cook, Alice McGillivray, and Richard Scammon, *America Votes 2005–2006: Election Returns by State* (Washington, DC: CQ Press, 2007); Gary C. Jacobson, *A Divider, Not a Uniter: George W. Bush and the American People* (London: Longman, 2007); Smith, *Bush,* 499–548; and *NYT,* November 2–9, 2006, January 17, 22 (2nd and 3rd q), 23 (1st q), June 5, 2007. On Pelosi, see Susan Page, *Madam Speaker: Nancy Pelosi and the Lessons of Power* (New York: Twelve, 2021); and Molly Ball, *Pelosi* (New York: Henry Holt, 2020).

8. Lewis int.; LaFayette int.; Barack Obama, *A Promised Land* (New York: Crown, 2020), 65–100; *NYT,* February 2 (1st and 2nd q), March 4 (4th and 5th q), 2007. Obama often repeated the line ending with "There is only the United States of America," a line he spoke first in his 2004 Democratic National Convention keynote address. For a discussion of its significance, see Jim Gilmore's interview with David Remnick on *Frontline,* "The Promise of Obama," August 19, 2019 (3rd q), https://www.pbs.org/wgbh/frontline/interview/ben-rhodes/. On Giuliani, see Andrew Kirtzman, *Giuliani: The Rise and Tragic Fall of America's Mayor* (New York: Simon and Schuster, 2022).

9. *NYT,* March 4, 2007 (1st–4th q); Obama, *Promised Land,* 122–123 (5th q).

10. Ron Fournier, "No Do-Overs, Hillary? You'll Need Them in '08," NBC News, February 2, 2007, https://www.nbcnews.com/id/wbna16930958; Roger Simon, "Hillary Pushes Personality, Ducks Iraq," Politico, January 27, 2007, https://www.politico.com/story/2007/01

/hillary-pushes-personality-ducks-iraq-002493; *NYT*, March 6 (1st q), 21 (2nd q), 23 (3rd q), 2007; *CR*, vol. 153, March 21–23, 2007. Hillary Clinton made the "no do-overs" statement while campaigning in Iowa on January 27, 2007.

11. Lewis int.; LaFayette int. (q); Lewis-HR int. The best source on Lewis's philosophies of life and leadership is John Lewis with Kabir Sehgal, *Carry On: Reflections for a New Generation* (New York: Grand Central, 2021).

12. Lewis int.; LaFayette int.; Lawson int.; Nash int.; C. T. Vivian int.; *NYT*, May 17, June 7, 13, 2007 (obits.); Charles Burnett, dir., *Selma, Lord, Selma* (Walt Disney Pictures, 1999). Yolanda King played Miss Bright in the film.

13. *NYT*, March 4 (2nd q), June 10 (1st q), 2007. On Brooke, see Edward Brooke, *Bridging the Divide: My Life* (New Brunswick, NJ: Rutgers University Press, 2006); and Leah Wright Rigueur, *The Loneliness of the Black Republican: Pragmatic Politics and the Pursuit of Power* (New York: Oxford University Press, 2014). On Powell, see Colin Powell, *My American Journey: An Autobiography* (New York: Random House, 1995); Jeffrey J. Matthews, *Colin Powell: Imperfect Patriot* (Notre Dame, IN: University of Notre Dame Press, 2019); and James Mann, *The Great Rift: Dick Cheney, Colin Powell, and the Broken Friendship That Defined an Era* (New York: Henry Holt, 2020).

14. Michael Tackett, "Next Stop on Campaign Trail: Bizarro World," *Anderson Herald Bulletin*, January 23, 2008 (1st q); *NYT*, January 24, February 18 (2nd q), 28, 2008; *Los Angeles Times*, February 28, 2008; Obama, *Promised Land*, 125–126; Jon Meacham, *His Truth Is Marching On: John Lewis and the Power of Hope* (New York: Random House, 2020), 240 (3rd and 4th q); LaFayette int.; Andrew Aydin int. See the extensive coverage of the 2008 Democratic primaries in the *NYT* and the *WP*, February–June 2008. See especially *NYT*, January 3, February 5, 15, June 3–6, 2008. On Lewis's primary campaign against the Reverend Markel Hutchins and Georgia state representative Mabel "Able" Thomas, see *AJC*, July–August 2008; and Greg Bluestein, "Several Prominent Democrats Line Up to Succeed John Lewis in Congress," *AJC*, August 6, 2020.

15. Lewis int.; LaFayette int.; Obama, *Promised Land*, 122–123, 165–168, 349; 2008 Democratic Convention, Day 4 coverage, C-SPAN.org, August 28, 2008 (1st and 2nd q), https://www.c-span .org; "Transcript: John Lewis Introduces Tribute to King," NPR News Democratic National Convention coverage, August 28, 2008, https://npr.org; *NYT*, August 24–29; *Denver Post, Democratic National Convention 2008: Obama's Mile High Moment* (Denver: Fulcrum, 2008); Connie Corcoran Wilson, *Obama's Odyssey*, vol. 2, *Convention to Inauguration* (Moline, IL: Quad City Press, 2015).

16. *NYT*, September 1–November 10, 2008; Obama, *Promised Land*, 139–202; Tasha S. Philpot, Daron R. Shaw, and Ernest B. McGowen, "Winning the Race: Black Voter Turnout in the 2008 Presidential Election," *Public Opinion Quarterly* 73, no. 5 (2009): 995–1022; Rachel Weiner, "Black Voters Turned Out at Higher Rate Than White Voters in 2012 and 2008," *WP*, April 29, 2013, https://www.washingtonpost.com/news/the-fix/wp/2013/04/29/black-turnout -was-higher-than-white-turnout-in-2012-and-2008/ (the scholar was Michael McDonald of George Mason University); "How Groups Voted in 2008," Roper Center, https://ropercenter .cornell.edu/how-groups-voted-2008. On the 2008 presidential election, see Chuck Todd, *How Barack Obama Won: A State-by-State Guide to the Historic 2008 Presidential Election* (New York: Vintage, 2012); Dewey M. Clayton, *The Presidential Campaign of Barack Obama: A Critical*

Analysis of a Racially Transcendent Strategy (New York: Routledge, 2010); and Evan Thomas and the *Newsweek* Staff, *Long Time Coming: The Inspiring, Combative 2008 Campaign and the Historic Election of Barack Obama* (Washington, DC: Public Affairs, 2009). On the *Heller* decision, see U.S. Supreme Court, *U.S. Supreme Court Decision on District of Columbia, et al. v. Heller* (n.p.: Policy Reference Press, 2012); and Burton Boyd, *The Second Amendment and the Heller Decision: A Critique* (n.p.: CreateSpace, 2018).

17. *NYT*, November 2–9, 2008, December 1, 2008–January 20, 2009; Lewis int.; *ATB*, 171, 172–173 (q); Obama, *Promised Land*, 206–234; John P. Burke, "The Obama Presidential Transition: An Early Assessment," *Presidential Studies Quarterly* 39, no. 3 (September 2009): 574–604.

18. Lewis int.; Obama, *Promised Land*, 233–391; *CR*, vol. 155, January 26–28, February 10, 12–13, 2009. On the concept and likelihood of a "post-racial society" during and after the Obama years, see *ATB*, 3; Daniel Schorr, "A New, 'Post-racial' Political Era in America," *All Things Considered*, NPR, January 28, 2008, https://www.npr.org/templates/story/story.php?storyId=18489466; David A. Hollinger, "The Concept of Post-racial: How Its Easy Dismissal Obscures Important Questions," *Daedalus* 140, no. 1 (Winter 2011): 174–182; Dewey Clayton and Sean Welch, "Post-racial America and the Presidency of Barack Obama," *Endarch: Journal of Black Political Research* 2017, no. 1 (Spring 2017): 6–47; https://radar.auctr.edu/islandora/object/endarch%3Afall_2017 .003; Richard H. King, "Becoming Black, Becoming President," Peter Kuryla, "Barack Obama and the American Island of the Colour Blind," and Jonathan Y. Okamura, "Barack Obama as the Post-racial Candidate for a Post-racial America: Perspectives from Asian America and Hawai'i," in "Obama and Race: History, Culture, and Politics," ed. Richard H. King, special issue, *Patterns of Prejudice* 45, nos. 1–2 (February–May 2011): 62–85, 119–132, 133–154. On Sotomayor, see Sonia Sotomayor, *My Beloved World* (New York: Knopf, 2013); and Antonia Felix, *Sonia Sotomayor: The True American Dream* (London: Berkley, 2010).

19. Obama, *Promised Land*, 375–426, 672–675, 683–685. On the legislative history of the Patient Protection and Affordable Care Act, see *CR*, vol. 155, September 17, November 7, December 24, 2009; and *CR*, vol. 156, March 21, 2010. On the Tea Party movement, see Nella Van Dyke, *Understanding the Tea Party Movement* (New York: Routledge, 2014); and Theda Skocpol and Vanessa Williamson, *The Tea Party and the Remaking of Republican Conservatism* (New York: Oxford University Press, 2012). For an inside look at the origins of the "birther" campaign against Obama, see Jeff Lichter, *Barack Obama's Birth Certificate: Questions Raised by Donald Trump, Joe Arpaio, and a Tea Party Group* (self-published, 2018). See also Anna Merlan, *Republic of Lies: American Conspiracy Theorists and Their Surprising Rise to Power* (New York: Metropolitan Books, 2019).

20. *ATB*, 174 (1st, 2nd, 4th, and 5th q), 175; Obama, *Promised Land*, 439–440, 445–446; Jamil Smith, "A Black President Is Not a Magical Negro," *New Republic*, October 9, 2015 (3rd q); Dawn Mendez, "The 'Magic Negro,'" *Forbes*, January 23, 2009. In 2008, Chip Saltsman, the chairman of the Republican National Committee, sent a special Christmas gift to friends: a CD that included a song satirizing Obama as a "magic Negro," a tradition dating back to the "Uncle Remus" folk tales of Joel Chandler Harris in the 1880s. In 2007, eighteen months before Saltsman's controversial gesture, the right-wing radio talk show host Rush Limbaugh aired a parody song, "Barack, the Magic Negro," in an effort to ridicule Obama. Christi Parsons, "Limbaugh Draws Fire on Obama Parody," *Seattle Times*, May 6, 2007. See also "Satire, Race

and the 'Magic Negro,'" *Talk of the Nation*, NPR, December 30, 2008, https://www.npr.org/templates/story/story.php?storyId=98828353; and Jason DeParle, "G.O.P. Receives Obama Parody to Mixed Reviews," *NYT*, December 27, 2008.

21. On the *Citizens United* decision, see Melvin I. Urofsky, *The Campaign Finance Cases: "Buckley," "McConnell," "Citizens United," and "McCutcheon"* (Lawrence: University Press of Kansas, 2020); Zephyr Teachout, *Corruption in America: From Benjamin Franklin's Snuff Box to "Citizens United"* (Cambridge, MA: Harvard University Press, 2014); and Jane Mayer, *Dark Money: The Hidden History of the Billionaires behind the Rise of the Radical Right* (New York: Doubleday, 2016). On the 2010 midterm election, see Gregory Giroux, *Midterm Mayhem: What's Next for Obama and the Republicans?* (Washington, DC: CQ Press, 2010); and the special midterm election issue of *Time*, November 15, 2010. Obama, *Promised Land*, 424–426, 519–592; *NYT*, January 21, March 21, November 1–8, 2010.

22. Lewis-HR int.; *AJC*, November 1–3, 2010, January 3, 2011. The right-wing Breitbart report later claimed the Tea Party protesters' racist behavior on the Capitol steps was a fabrication. See Joel B. Pollak, "Six False Accusations by John Lewis, Hero-Turned-Hack," *Breitbart News*, January 15, 2017, https://www.breitbart.com/politics/2017/01/15/john-lewis-false-racism-hero-partisan/. Joshua Bote, "Rep. John Lewis Received the Presidential Medal of Freedom in 2011. This Is What Barack Obama Said about Him," *USA Today*, July 18, 2020 (1st q). See the inscription on the King Memorial, Washington, DC (2nd q), excerpted from King's March 31, 1968, speech at the National Cathedral, "Remaining Awake through a Great Revolution," https://cathedral.org/MLK50/. An earlier version of the same speech was delivered at Morehouse College in June 1959. Martin Luther King Jr., *The Papers of Martin Luther King, Jr.*, vol. 5, *Threshold of a New Decade, January 1959–December 1960*, ed. Clayborne Carson et al. (Berkeley: University of California Press, 2005), 219–226. See also the op-ed by Paul Caron, "Martin Luther King Jr.'s Last Sunday Sermon 'Remaining Awake through a Great Revolution,'" *NYT*, January 16, 2023.

23. Lewis int.; *NYT*, June 3, 6, August 4–10, 19, September 8, 16–24, October 11, 2011. On Resurrection City and the Poor People's Campaign, see Sylvie Laurent, *King and the Other America: The Poor People's Campaign and the Quest for Economic Equality* (Berkeley: University of California Press, 2018); and Michael K. Honey, *To the Promised Land: Martin Luther King and the Fight for Economic Justice* (New York: Norton, 2018), 120–132, 171–172, 183–185. On the ups and downs of the effort to pass the American Jobs Bill, see *CR*, vol. 157, September 8–9, October 11, 17, 20, November 7, 2011. On the Occupy movement, see Todd Gitlin, *Occupy Nation: The Roots, the Spirit, and the Promise of Occupy Wall Street* (New York: It Books, 2012). On the Arab Spring, see Asef Bayat, *Revolution without Revolutionaries: Making Sense of the Arab Spring* (Palo Alto, CA: Stanford University Press, 2017); and Mark L. Haas and David W. Lesch, eds., *The Arab Spring: The Hope and Reality of the Uprisings*, 2nd ed. (New York: Routledge, 2019). "John Lewis: 'Across That Bridge: Life Lessons and a Vision for Change,'" *The Diane Rehm Show*, May 30, 2012 (1st q), https://wamu.org/story/12/05/30/john-lewis-across-bridge-life-lessons-and-vision-change/; *ATB*, 197–199 (2nd q), 200–206 (3rd q), 207 (4th q), 209–210.

24. Rebecca Burns, "Dedication of a New Downtown Mural Honoring John Lewis, Civil Rights Hero," *Atlanta Magazine*, August 27, 2012, https://www.atlantamagazine.com/civilrights/dedication-of-new-downtown-mural-honoring-joh/. Painted by Sean Schwab, the mural would

soon become a notable Atlanta landmark visited by curious tourists as well as proud residents of the Auburn Avenue neighborhood. *NYT*, November 2–12, 2012; *AJC*, November 6–9, 2012. On the 2012 presidential election, see Jane W. Ceaser, Andrew E. Busch, and John J. Pitney Jr., *After Hope and Change: The 2012 Election and American Politics* (Lanham, MD: Rowman and Littlefield, 2013); and John Sides and Lynn Vavreck, *The Gamble: Choice and Chance in the 2012 Presidential Election* (Princeton, NJ: Princeton University Press, 2013). On Romney, see Michael Kranish and Scott Helman, *The Real Romney* (New York: Harper, 2012).

25. John Lewis int.; John-Miles Lewis int.; LaFayette int.; Jim Galloway, "A Way to Keep the late John Lewis as the 'Conscience of Congress,'" *AJC*, July 18, 2020 (1st q); Renee Graham, "John Lewis—the 'Conscience of Congress,' the Conscience of America," *Boston Globe*, July 18, 2020; *AJC*, December 31, 2012 (2nd q).

26. LaFayette int.; Michael Collins int.; John-Miles Lewis int.; John Lewis, "An Evening with John Lewis, June 6, 2013," interview by Scott Simon, National Archives (hereafter cited as Lewis-NA int.). The Emancipation Proclamation gala audience received a companion booklet with an introduction by Lewis. archives.gov. On the *Shelby* decision, see *Shelby County, Alabama v. Holder*, 570 U.S. 529 (2013); *NYT*, June 25–26, 2013 (1st and 2nd q); Anderson, *One Person, No Vote*, 25–26, 37–42, 63–69, 104, 113, 123–127; Joyce White Vance, "Ruth Bader Ginsburg Lost Her Battle to Save Voting Rights. Here's How We Can Take Up the Fight and Honor Her Legacy," *Time*, September 21, 2020, https://time.com; Committee on the Judiciary, United States Senate, *From Selma to Shelby: Working Together to Restore the Protections of the Voting Rights Act* (Washington, DC: Government Printing Office, 2015); and Joe Street and Henry Knight Lozano, eds., *The Shadow of Selma* (Gainesville: University Press of Florida, 2018).

27. *WP*, June 25, 2013 (q); Lewis int.; LaFayette int.; Lewis-HR int. Eighteen months after the *Shelby* decision, Lewis reminded Americans of what they had lost in a December 25, 2014, *Time* essay titled "An Oral History: History of Selma and the Struggle for the Voting Rights Act."

CHAPTER 18. Good Trouble

1. *ATB*, 207; Andrew Aydin int. (1st and 2nd q); John-Miles Lewis int.; *WWTW*, 83; Andrew Aydin, "The Comic Book That Changed the World," *Creative Loafing*, August 1, 2013, https:// creativeloafing.com. Powell was the first cartoonist to win a National Book Award. *WP*, August 12, 28 (3rd q), 2013, March 7, 2016; Todd S. Purdum, *An Idea Whose Time Has Come: Two Presidents, Two Parties, and the Battle for the Civil Rights Act of 1964* (New York: Henry Holt, 2014), 332: Greg Herbowy, "Q + A: Congressman John Lewis, Andrew Aydin, and Nate Powell," *Visual Arts Journal*, November 17, 2016, 48–51; Heidi MacDonald, "March Book One Is First Graphic Novel to Win the RFK Book Award," *Comics Beat*, May 21, 2014; Erin Blakemore, "Civil Rights Legend John Lewis Won a Prestigious Comic Book Award," *Smithsonian Magazine*, July 26, 2016; Michael Cavna, "Rep. John Lewis's National Book Award Win Is a Milestone Moment for Graphic Novels," *WP*, November 17, 2016; Michael Cavna, "How John Lewis' Masterful Illustrated Memoir Is a Shining Torch for the Next Generation," *WP*, August 1, 2020 (4th and 5th q); Amazon listing for *March: Book One*, by John Lewis, Andrew Aydin, and Nate Powell (6th–9th q), https://www.amazon.com/March-Book-One-John-Lewis/dp/1603093001;

Mikaela Lefrak, "He's a Hill Staffer for Rep. John Lewis by Day—and an Award-Winning Graphic Novelist by Night," *WP*, October 15, 2019. The Fellowship of Reconciliation's *Martin Luther King and the Montgomery Story* was published in December 1957.

2. On the frustrating state of affairs during the early months of Obama's second term, see Kenneth W. Jost, *Obama's Agenda: The Challenges of a Second Term* (Washington, DC: CQ Press, 2013).

3. NBCNews.com, Andrew Rafferty, reporter, October 8, 2013; *PBS NewsHour*, October 8, 2013; *CR*, vol. 159, October 7–9, 2013. The arrested members of Congress were Lewis, Keith Ellison, Joe Crowley, Raul Grijalva, Jan Schakowsky, Al Green, Charles Rangel, and John Conyers. Erin Blakemore, "John Lewis' Arrest Records Are Finally Uncovered," *Smithsonian Magazine*, December 1, 2016 (1st q), https://www.smithsonianmag.com/smart-news/john-lewis -arrest-records-are-finally-uncovered-180961255/; Becky Little, "'Good Trouble': How John Lewis and Other Civil Rights Crusaders Expected Arrests," History, July 20, 2020, https://www .history.com/news/john-lewis-civil-rights-arrests; Sophie Lewis, "Remembering John Lewis," CBS News, July 18, 2020, https://www.cbsnews.com/pictures/remembering-john-lewis-dead-at -80/; *NYT*, October 8, 2013 (2nd q). Lewis's last previous arrest had come in late April 2009, when he took part in a demonstration outside the Sudanese embassy to call attention to the genocidal warfare in the Darfur region of western Sudan. *WP*, April 28, 2009.

4. *NYT*, June 15, 2014 (1st q); Bernard LaFayette int.; Aydin int.; Rashawn Ray, "Five Things John Lewis Taught Us about Getting in 'Good Trouble,'" Brookings, July 23, 2020 (2nd q), https://www.brookings.edu/blog/how-we-rise/2020/07/23/five-things-john-lewis-taught-us -about-getting-in-good-trouble/; Alex B. Johnson, "Good Trouble: John Lewis and Andrew Aydin: Two Southerners in Action," *The Bitter Southerner*, July 4, 2017, https://bittersoutherner .com/good-trouble-john-lewis-andrew-aydin-march; "Can the South Be Redeemed?," *The Bitter Southerner Podcast*, season 2, episode 8, https://bittersoutherner.com/podcast/season -two-episode-eight/can-the-south-be-redeemed-john-lewis; John Lewis, "The Future of Non-violence," *Creative Loafing*, special John Lewis issue, August 1, 2013; John Lewis, "Why Getting into Trouble Is Necessary to Make Change," *Time*, January 4, 2018.

5. *NYT*, November 1 (q), December 15, 2013, January 25, 2014; *AJC*, July 22, November 4, 2014. On the significance of Cory Booker and his election to the Senate, see Andra Gillespie, *The New Black Politician: Cory Booker, Newark, and Post-racial America* (New York: New York University Press, 2012); Jonathan Wharton, *A Post-racial Change Is Gonna Come: Newark, Cory Booker, and the Transformation of Urban America* (New York: Palgrave Macmillan, 2013); and Cory Booker, *United: Thoughts on Finding Common Ground and Advancing the Common Good* (New York: Ballantine, 2016). On Sam Nunn, see Frank Leith Jones, *Sam Nunn: Statesman of the Nuclear Age* (Lawrence: University Press of Kansas, 2020).

6. *NYT*, April 10–11 (q), 2014.

7. *NYT*, June 17, 2014. On Rangel and the charges of corruption that led to his censure, see Jack R. Van der Slik, *Disgrace in the U.S. House: A Political Biography of Harlem's Charlie Rangel* (n.p.: CreateSpace, 2013). See also Katherine Tate, *Concordance: Black Lawmaking in the U.S. Congress from Carter to Obama* (Ann Arbor: University of Michigan Press, 2014); and Michael D. Minta, *Oversight: Representing the Interests of Blacks and Latinos in Congress* (New York: Oxford University Press, 2011).

8. *NYT,* June 25, 30, August 7, September 10, 22, 2014.

9. On the 2014 midterm election, see Ed Kilgore, *Election 2014: Why the Republicans Swept the Midterms* (Philadelphia: University of Pennsylvania Press, 2015); and Christopher J. Galdieri, Tauna Sisco, and Jennifer Lucas, eds., *Races, Reforms, and Policy: Implications of the 2014 Midterm Elections* (Akron: University of Akron Press, 2017). See also The Wall Street Journal, *The Right Way? Republicans Rethink, Reload for 2014* (New York: Wall Street Journal, 2014); *NYT,* November 2–12, 2014; and *WP,* November 2–10, 2014. On McConnell, see Alec MacGillis, *The Cynic: The Political Education of Mitch McConnell* (New York: Simon and Schuster, 2014); Mitch McConnell, *The Long Game: A Memoir* (New York: Sentinel, 2016); and Ira Shapiro, *The Betrayal: How Mitch McConnell and the Senate Republicans Abandoned America* (Lanham, MD: Rowman and Littlefield, 2022). On Scott, see Tim Scott and Trey Gowdy, *Unified: How Our Unlikely Friendship Gives Us Hope in a Divided Country* (Carol Stream, IL: Tyndale Momentum, 2018); and Tim Scott, *Opportunity Knocks: How Hard Work, Community, and Business Can Improve Lives and End Poverty* (Nashville: Center Street, 2020).

10. *NYT,* November 24, December 4, 9, 2014; U.S. Department of Justice, *The Ferguson Report* (n.p.: CreateSpace, 2015). On the evolution of BLM, see Christopher J. Lebron, *The Making of Black Lives Matter: A Brief History of an Idea* (New York: Oxford University Press, 2017); Barbara Ransby, *Making All Black Lives Matter: Reimagining Freedom in the 21st Century* (Berkeley: University of California Press, 2018); Keeanga-Yamahtta Taylor, *From #Black Lives Matter to Black Liberation* (Chicago: Haymarket Books, 2021); Peniel Joseph, *The Third Reconstruction: America's Struggle for Racial Justice in the Twenty-First Century* (New York: Basic Books, 2022); Jelani Cobb and David Remnick, *The Matter of Black Lives: Writing from the "New Yorker"* (New York: Ecco, 2021); and Curtis Bunn, Michael H. Cottman, and Patrice Gaines, *Say Their Names: How Black Lives Came to Matter in America* (New York: Grand Central, 2021).

11. *NYT,* January 20, 2015 (q); Barack Obama, *A Promised Land* (New York: Crown, 2020), 233, 355–356, 520, 580–587; Carol Rosenberg, "Obama to Leave with 41 Captives Still at Guantánamo, Blames Politics," *Miami Herald,* January 19, 2017. On the continuing controversy surrounding the Guantánamo Bay detention facility, see Carol Rosenberg, *Guantánamo Bay: The Pentagon's Alcatraz of the Caribbean* (Miami: Herald Books, 2016); and Jonathan Hafetz, ed., *Obama's Guantánamo: Stories from an Enduring Prison* (New York: New York University Press, 2016). See also Jonathan M. Hansen, *Guantánamo: An American History* (New York: Hill and Wang, 2011); and Jana K. Lipman, *Guantánamo: A Working-Class History between Empire and Revolution* (Berkeley: University of California Press, 2008).

12. On the notion and evolution of the American culture war, see James Davison Hunter, *Culture Wars: The Struggle to Define America* (New York: Basic Books, 1991); Morris P. Fiorina with Samuel J. Abrams and Jeremy Pope, *Culture Wars? The Myth of a Polarized America* (London: Longman, 2010); Robert O. Self, *All in the Family: The Realignment of American Democracy since the 1960s* (New York: Hill and Wang, 2012); Andrew Hartman, *A War for the Soul of America: A History of the Culture Wars* (Chicago: University of Chicago Press, 2016); and Jonathan Zimmerman, *Whose America? Culture Wars in the Public Schools* (Chicago: University of Chicago Press, 2022).

13. John Lewis int.; LaFayette int.; *NYT,* December 25, 2014, March 2–8, 2015. The film *Selma,* released on December 25, 2014, was directed by Ava DuVernay and produced by

Paramount Pictures. It won the 2015 NAACP Image Award for Outstanding Motion Picture. Somewhat critical of the film, Lewis felt more positive toward the National Archives photo exhibit, "On Exhibit: Bloody Sunday," that opened on July 30, 2015, in the East Rotunda Gallery. Jessie Kratz, "On Exhibit: Bloody Sunday," *Pieces of History* (blog), National Archives, July 30, 2015, https://prologue.blogs.archives.gov/2015/07/30/on-exhibit-bloody-sunday/.

14. John Lewis int.; *NYT*, December 17, 25, 2014, March 2, 9, April 11–12, 14, May 29, 2015. On the effort to derail Hillary Clinton's political career, see Michael D'Antonio, *The Hunting of Hillary: The 40-Year Campaign to Destroy Hillary Clinton* (New York: Thomas Dunne, 2020).

15. John Lewis int.; LaFayette int.; Terri Sewell int.; *NYT*, June 24–26, 2015; "114th Congress (2015–2016): Voting Rights Advancement Act of 2015," Congress.gov, introduced in House June 24, 2015, https://www.congress.gov/bill/114th-congress/house-bill/2867/text; "Bill Summary: Voting Rights Advancement Act of 2015," Leadership Conference, July 17, 2015, https://civilrightsdocs.info/pdf/voting/2015-07-17%20VR%20Advancement%20Act%20Bill%20Summary_c4.pdf; Ari Berman, "Congressional Democrats Introduce Ambitious New Bill to Restore the Voting Rights Act," *Nation*, June 24, 2015, https://www.thenation.com/article/archive/congressional-democrats-introduce-ambitious-new-bill-to-restore-the-voting-rights-act/; *CR*, vol. 161, June 24, 2015. On Sewell, see "The Honorable Terri A. Sewell's Biography," interview by History Makers, May 15, 2017, https://www.thehistorymakers.org/biography/honorable-terri-sewell; Krissah Thompson, "Rep. Terri Sewell, a Daughter of Selma, Rues Her City's Lost Promise," *WP*, March 1, 2015; and Ed Pilkington, "'We Should Be Outraged': Alabama Congresswoman Tackles Voter Suppression," *Guardian*, December 24, 2019.

16. *NYT*, March 23, 25, April 7, May 4–5, June 4, 15–16, 18–19 (1st q), 22, 26 (2nd and 3rd q), 29, July 3, 2015; *WP*, June 17–18, 2015. On the Emanuel AME massacre, see Greg Grandin, "The Charleston Massacre and the Cunning of White Supremacy," *Nation*, June 18, 2015; Michelle Goldberg, "The 2 Degrees of Separation Between Dylann Roof and the Republican Party," *Nation*, June 22, 2015; Don Gonyea and Domenico Montanaro, "Predictably, Democrats, Republicans Don't Agree on Charleston Causes, Solutions," *All Things Considered*, NPR, June 19, 2015, https://www.npr.org/sections/itsallpolitics/2015/06/19/415747034/predictably-democrats-republicans-dont-agree-on-charleston-causes-solutions; and Jennifer Berry Hawes, *Grace Will Lead Us Home: The Charleston Church Massacre and the Hard, Inspiring Journey to Forgiveness* (New York: St. Martin's, 2019).

17. *NYT*, May 19, June 23 (1st and 2nd q), June 27, July 10 (3rd q), 13, August 23, 31, 2015; *CR*, vol. 161, June 23, July 10, 2015; Andrew Young int.; Karen L. Cox, *No Common Ground: Confederate Monuments and the Ongoing Fight for Racial Justice* (Chapel Hill: University of North Carolina Press, 2021); Roger C. Hartley, *Monumental Harm: Reckoning with Jim Crow Era Confederate Monuments* (Columbia: University of South Carolina Press, 2021); W. Fitzhugh Brundage et al., *Confederate Statues and Memorialization,* ed. Catherine Clinton (Athens: University of Georgia Press, 2019); J. Michael Martinez, William D. Richardson, and Ronald M. McNinch-Su, eds., *Confederate Symbols in the Contemporary South* (Gainesville: University Press of Florida, 2001); W. Fitzhugh Brundage, *The Southern Past: A Clash of Race and Memory* (Cambridge, MA: Harvard University Press, 2005).

18. Alana Abramson, "How Donald Trump Perpetuated the 'Birther' Movement for Years," ABC News, September 16, 2016, https://abcnews.go.com/Politics/donald-trump-perpetuated-birther-movement-years/story?id=42138176; *NYT*, December 7, 2015. On the 2016 presidential

election, see Larry Sabato, *Trumped: The 2016 Election That Broke All the Rules* (Lanham, MD: Rowman and Littlefield, 2017); Joshua Green, *Devil's Bargain: Steve Bannon, Donald Trump, and the Storming of the Presidency* (New York: Penguin, 2017); John Sides, Michael Tesler, and Lynn Vavreck, *Identity Crisis: The 2016 Presidential Election and the Battle for the Meaning of America* (Princeton, NJ: Princeton University Press, 2018); Maggie Haberman, *Confidence Man: The Making of Donald Trump and the Breaking of America* (New York: Penguin, 2022); Jonathan Allen and Amie Parnes, *Shattered: Inside Hillary Clinton's Doomed Campaign* (New York: Crown, 2017); Susan Bordo, *The Destruction of Hillary Clinton* (New York: Melville House, 2017); Rachel Bitecofer, *The Unprecedented 2016 Presidential Election* (New York: Palgrave Macmillan, 2018); and John Aldrich, Jamie L. Carson, and Brad T. Gomez, *Change and Continuity in the 2016 Elections* (Washington, DC: CQ Press, 2018). On Trumpism's roots in the traditions of Southern demagoguery, see Andrew E. Stoner, *Fear, Hate, and Victimhood: How George Wallace Wrote the Donald Trump Playbook* (Jackson: University Press of Mississippi, 2022).

19. *NYT*, June 12–13, 22, 2016; *Miami Herald*, June 15, 2016; *Orlando Sentinel*, June 13, 2016; Deirdre Walsh et al., "Democrats End House Sit-In Protest over Gun Control," CNN, June 24, 2016 (q), https://www.cnn.com/2016/06/22/politics/john-lewis-sit-in-gun-violence/index.html; *WP*, June 22–24, 2016; *CR*, vol. 162, June 22–24, 2016. On the Pulse nightclub shooting and similar acts of mass violence, see Jaclyn Schildkraut, ed., *Mass Shootings in America: Understanding the Debates, Causes, and Responses* (Santa Barbara, CA: ABC-CLIO, 2018).

20. *NYT*, June 10, 2016; Democratic National Convention, "Representative John Lewis at DNC 2016," YouTube video, 4:48, posted July 26, 2016 (1st and 2nd q), https://www.youtube.com/watch?v=iDbDH79Kpd8. On the Clinton–Sanders race for the Democratic presidential nomination, see "The Split," *New Republic*, July/August 2016.

21. Lonnie Bunch int.; Lois Horton int.; James Horton int.; LaFayette int.; *NYT*, September 25, 2016 (q); Tamar Hallerman and Erica Fernandez, "Another Historic Crusade for John Lewis," *AJC*, September 24, 2016, http://specials.myajc.com/african-american-history-museum/; *WWTW*, 458. On the origins and building of the National Museum of African American History and Culture, see Mabel O. Wilson, *Begin with the Past: Building the National Museum of African American History and Culture* (Washington, DC: Smithsonian Books, 2016); and National Museum of African American History and Culture and Kathleen M. Kendrick, *Official Guide to the Smithsonian National Museum of African American History and Culture* (Washington, DC: Smithsonian Books, 2017). The museum was officially established in 2003, and the site was selected in 2006, but it did not open until September 2016. In 1988 and 1989, Lewis coauthored two national Black history museum bills with Representative Mickey Leland of Texas, but Congress failed to pass either bill; many representatives and senators regarded the proposed museum as too costly. Leland, the onetime chair of the CBC, died in 1989 at the age of forty-four while visiting Ethiopia. Leland's passing placed a heavier legislative burden on Lewis, but the Georgia congressman never wavered in his determination to see the project to completion.

22. John Cassidy, "James Comey's October Surprise," *New Yorker*, October 28, 2016; *NYT*, July 8, October 28–November 15, 2016. Comey explains and defends his actions in James Comey, *A Higher Loyalty: Truth, Lies, and Leadership* (New York: Flatiron Books, 2018).

23. On Russian interference in the 2016 national election, see Michael Isikoff and David Corn, *Russian Roulette: The Inside Story of Putin's War on America and the Election of Donald Trump* (New York: Twelve, 2018); Robert S. Mueller III and Special Counsel's Office, Department of Justice, *The Mueller Report: Report on the Investigation into Russian Interference in the 2016 Presidential Election* (New York: Melville House, 2019); and *NYT*, December 9, 29, 2016.

CHAPTER 19. Perilous Times

1. "Civil Rights Hero John Lewis Challenges Legitimacy of Donald Trump's Election Win," *Guardian*, January 15, 2017 (q), https://www.theguardian.com/us-news/video/2017/jan/15/civil-rights-hero-john-lewis-challenges-legitimacy-trumps-election-win-video; Alexander Mallin, "President-Elect Trump Attacks Civil Rights Icon Who Said His Presidency Not 'Legitimate,'" ABC News, January 14, 2017, https://www.abcnews.go.com; "Congress Members Join John Lewis in Boycott of Trump's Inauguration," ABC News, January 15, 2017, https://www.abcnews.go.com; *NYT*, January 10, 15–21, 25, 27, March 28, May 9, 16–17, 25, June 1, 8, 14, July 9, 11, 2017. The 2017 inauguration marked the second time that Lewis boycotted an inaugural ceremony; in 2001, he chose not to attend the inauguration of George W. Bush.

2. *NYT*, July 9, 11, 18, 26–28, 2017.

3. *NYT*, September 12–15, 2017. See Louis P. Nelson and Claudrena N. Harold, eds., *Charlottesville 2017: The Legacy of Race and Inequity* (Charlottesville: University of Virginia Press, 2018); and Hawes Spencer, *Summer of Hate: Charlottesville USA* (Charlottesville: University of Virginia Press, 2018).

4. Bryan Armen Graham, "Donald Trump Blasts NFL Anthem Protestors: 'Get That Son of a Bitch off the Field,'" *Guardian*, September 23, 2017; *Guardian*, September 24, 2017; "Trump: NFL Kneelers 'Maybe Shouldn't Be in Country,'" BBC, May 24, 2018, https://www.bbc.com/news/world-us-canada-44232979; Jemele Hill, "The War on Black Athletes," *Atlantic*, January 13, 2019. On the Tax Cuts and Jobs Act, see *NYT*, December 16, 20–23, 2017; David Frum, "Republicans Extract Their Revenge through a Tax Bill," *Atlantic*, December 21, 2017; and *CR*, vol. 163, November 2, 9, 2017, vol. 164, December 2, 19–22, 2018.

5. See Jamelle Bouie, "John Lewis Was the Anti-Trump," *NYT*, July 31, 2020; Bob Woodward, *Fear: Trump in the White House* (New York: Simon and Schuster, 2018); Michael Wolff, *Fire and Fury: Inside the Trump White House* (New York: Henry Holt, 2018); and Maggie Haberman, *Confidence Man: The Making of Donald Trump and the Breaking of America* (New York: Penguin, 2022).

6. Ali Vitali, Kasie Hunt, and Frank Thorp V, "Trump Referred to Haiti and African Nations as 'Shithole' Countries," NBC News, January 11, 2018 (q), https://www.nbcnews.com/politics/white-house/trump-referred-haiti-african-countries-shithole-nations-n836946; Woodward, *Fear*, 320–321; *NYT*, July 18, 2020 (Lewis q); *CR*, vol. 164, January 11–12, 2018.

7. *NYT*, July 14, 2019.

8. Bernard LaFayette int.; John Lewis int. See Haberman, *Confidence Man*; David Frum, *Trumpocracy: The Corruption of the American Republic* (New York: Harper, 2018); David Frum, *Trumpocalypse: Restoring American Democracy* (New York: Harper, 2020); Philip Rucker

and Carol Leonnig, *A Very Stable Genius: Donald J. Trump's Testing of America* (New York: Penguin, 2020); Bob Woodward, *Rage* (New York: Simon and Schuster, 2020); Stuart Stevens, *It Was All a Lie: How the Republican Party Became Donald Trump* (New York: Knopf, 2020); Brian Stelter, *Hoax: Donald Trump, Fox News, and the Destructive Distortion of the Truth* (New York: Atria, One Signal, 2020); John W. Dean and Bob Altemeyer, *Authoritarian Nightmare: Trump and His Followers* (New York: Melville House, 2020); and Richard W. Painter and Peter Golenbock, *American Nero: The History of the Destruction of the Rule of Law, and Why Trump Is the Worst Offender* (Dallas: BenBella, 2020).

9. *NYT*, April–June, September 12, 2018; *Guardian*, June 17, 2018; "Trump Migrant Separation Policy: Children 'in Cages' in Texas," BBC, June 18, 2018, https://www.bbc.com/news/world-us-canada-44518942; Karl Vick, "A Reckoning after Trump's Border Separation Policy: What Kind of Country Are We?," *Time*, June 21, 2018; Jacob Soboroff, "Kids in Cages and Other Scenes from Trump's 'Zero-Tolerance' Border," *Vanity Fair*, June 22, 2018, https://www.vanityfair.com/news/2018/06/scenes-from-trumps-zero-tolerance-border; Alice Driver, "13,000 Migrant Children in Detention: America's Horrifying Reality," CNN, October 1, 2018, https://www.cnn.com/2018/10/01/opinions/13000-migrant-children-horrifying-reality-driver/index.html; Andrew Delbanco, "The Struggle for Our Soul," *NYT*, November 3, 2018 (q).

10. *NYT*, April 2–4 (1st q), 6 (2nd q), June 2 (3rd q), 2018.

11. Andrew Aydin int.; Sydnie Cobb, "Former Chief of Staff to Rep. Lewis Reflects on Life, Legacy of His Colleague and Friend," ABC News, July 13, 2021, https://abcnews.go.com/Politics/chief-staff-rep-john-lewis-reflects-life-legacy/story?id=78710431; Michael Collins int.; Curtis Bunn, "'We Are the Legacy': John Lewis Lives on in the Generations of Young Staffers He Empowered," NBC News, July 28, 2020 (1st–3rd q), https://www.nbcnews.com/news/nbcblk/we-are-legacy-john-lewis-lives-generations-young-staffers-he-n1235038; Katherine Tully-McManus and Lindsey McPherson, "Colleagues and Leaders Remember John Lewis as a Humble Mentor," *Roll Call*, July 18, 2020 (4th and 5th q), https://rollcall.com/2020/07/18/colleagues-and-leaders-remember-john-lewis-as-a-humble-mentor-in-addition-to-an-icon/.

12. *NYT*, September 1, 5, 9, 2018; *Boston Globe*, September 5, 2018. On Pressley, see Kayla Epstein, "For Ayanna Pressley, the Beauty of Unexpected Wins Led to Congress and a Historic Office," *WP*, January 16, 2019. On Ocasio-Cortez, see Lynda Lopez, *AOC: The Fearless Rise and Powerful Resonance of Alexandria Ocasio-Cortez* (New York: St. Martin's, 2020). See also Maurice Isserman, "Socialists in the House: A 100-Year History from Victor Berger to Alexandria Ocasio-Cortez," *In These Times*, November 8, 2018.

13. *NYT*, September 23 (1st q), November 10, 17, December 31 (2nd q), 2018; Robert Draper, "Nancy Pelosi's Last Battle," *NYT Magazine*, November 25, 2018; John H. Aldrich et al., *Change and Continuity in the 2016 and 2018 Elections* (Washington, DC: CQ Press, 2019); Elizabeth Theiss-Morse and Michael W. Wagner, *2018 Congressional Elections* (Washington, DC: CQ Press, 2018).

14. *NYT*, January 5, 2019 (q).

15. Vann R. Newkirk III, "Voter Suppression Is Warping Democracy," *Atlantic*, July 17, 2018; Ella Nilsen, "The House Has Passed a Bill to Restore Key Parts of the Voting Rights Act," Vox, December 7, 2019, https://www.vox.com/2019/12/6/20998953/house-bill-voting

-rights-advancement-act; *CR*, vol. 165, February 26, December 6–7, 2019. See also Timothy R. Homan, "McConnell: John Lewis Voting Rights Bill 'Unnecessary,'" *The Hill*, June 8, 2021 (q).

16. *NYT*, February 25, 26 (q), 2019; *Boston Globe*, February 25, 2019; Andrew R. Chow, "What to Know about the Controversy Surrounding the Movie *Green Book*," *Time*, February 13, 2019, updated February 24, 2019, https://time.com/5527806/green-book-movie-controversy/. For a sharp criticism of *Green Book*, see Austin Collins, "The Truth about *Green Book*," *Vanity Fair*, December 11, 2018; and Gabrielle Bruney, "The Problems with *Green Book* Start with Its Title and Don't Stop Coming," *Esquire*, February 23, 2019.

17. *NYT*, March 1, 2019 (1st and 2nd q). On Tlaib, see Todd Spangler, "How Detroit's Rashida Tlaib Will Make History in Washington," *Detroit Free Press*, September 9, 2018.

18. *AJC*, September 25, 2019 (1st q), quoted in Jon Meacham, *His Truth Is Marching On: John Lewis and the Power of Hope* (New York: Random House, 2020), 238; *NYT*, July 18, 2020 (2nd q); House Intelligence Committee, *The Impeachment Report: The House Intelligence Committee's Report on Its Investigation into Donald Trump and Ukraine* (New York: Crown, 2019); House Permanent Select Committee on Intelligence, *The Trump-Ukraine Impeachment Inquiry Report* (New York: Melville House, 2019); Michael D'Antonio and Peter Eisner, *High Crimes: The Corruption, Impunity, and Impeachment of Donald Trump* (New York: Thomas Dunne, 2020); Eric Swalwell, *Endgame: Inside the Impeachments of Donald J. Trump* (New York: Abrams, 2020); "The Impeachment of Donald Trump," special issue, *Time*, November 18, 2019; *CR*, vol. 165, December 18–19, 2019. See also Julian E. Zelizer, ed., *The Presidency of Donald J. Trump: A First Historical Assessment* (Princeton, NJ: Princeton University Press, 2022).

19. John Hamblin, "John Lewis and the Fight That Can't Be Won," *Atlantic*, December 31, 2019 (q); *NYT*, December 29, 2019; Margaret Renkl, "An Open Letter to John Lewis," *NYT*, January 6, 2020; Chantale Wong int.

20. Aaron Blake, "McConnell Indicates He'll Let Trump's Lawyers Dictate Trump's Impeachment Trial," *WP*, December 14, 2019; Jordan Carney, "McConnell Says He Will Be in Total Coordination with White House on Impeachment Trial Strategy," *The Hill*, December 12, 2019; *NYT*, January 16–February 6, 2020.

21. *NYT*, April 5, 2020. The day before his eightieth birthday, Lewis published a passionate essay, "'We Have to Redeem the Soul of America': What's Changed and What Hasn't since the March on Washington," in the February 20, 2020, issue of *Time*.

22. Lindsey McPherson and Chris Cioffi, "One-Tenth of Congress Had COVID-19, but Cases Halted Soon after Vaccinations," *Roll Call*, March 11, 2021, https://rollcall.com/2021 /03/11/one-tenth-of-congress-had-covid-19-but-cases-halted-soon-after-vaccinations/; "John Lewis Returns to Selma on 55th Anniversary of March," CNN, March 2, 2020, https://www .cnn.com/videos/us/2020/03/01/john-lewis-returns-to-selma-anniversary-nr-vpx.cnn,video on YouTube, https://www.youtube.com/watch?v=JFsOoA8v2HY (1st and 2nd q); *NYT*, March 2, 2020; Wong int.

23. Aydin int.; John Lewis et al., *Run: Book One* (New York: Abrams ComicArts, 2021). The publication date was August 3, 2021. Heidi MacDonald, "'Run,' Rep. John Lewis's Posthumous Memoir, Is Coming Out in August," Comics Beat, March 30, 2021, https://www.comicsbeat.com /run-rep-john-lewiss-posthumous-memoir-is-coming-out-in-august/; Michael Cavna, "John Lewis Finished the Graphic Memoir as He Died. He Wanted to Leave a Civil Rights 'Road Map'

NOTES TO PAGES 444–449

for Generations to Come," *WP*, August 2, 2021 (q). The quoted review is the customer review for *Run* posted by "Confessed Movie Junky," Amazon.com, August 25, 2021, https://www.amazon.com/Run-John-Lewis/dp/141973069X.

24. *NYT*, April 8 (1st q), July 18 (2nd q), 2020, January 6, 2021; *WP*, June 1–8, 2020. On Warnock, see Raphael G. Warnock, *The Divided Mind of the Black Church: Theology, Piety, and Public Witness* (New York: New York University Press, 2013); and Raphael G. Warnock, *A Way out of No Way: A Memoir of Truth, Transformation, and the New American Story* (New York: Penguin, 2022). On Ossoff, see Charles Bethea, "Can This Democrat Win the Georgia Sixth?," *New Yorker*, March 3, 2017; and Jill Nolen, "Ossoff Aims to Connect John Lewis Legacy with a New Generation," *Georgia Recorder*, December 21, 2020.

25. *NYT*, July 3–4, 2020; Dawn Porter, dir., *John Lewis: Good Trouble* (CNN Films, 2020). The film's CNN television premiere was on September 27, 2020.

Epilogue

1. *NYT*, March 4, 2007 (1st q), July 3, 17–19 (2nd q), 2020; "John Lewis Risked His Life for Justice," *NYT*, July 17, 2020 (editorial); Tina Ligon, "In the Long Tradition of Civil Rights: Tribute to C. T. Vivian and John Lewis," *Rediscovering Black History* (blog), National Archives, July 27, 2020, https://rediscovering-black-history.blogs.archives.gov/2020/07/27/in-the-long-tradition-of-civil-rights-tribute-to-c-t-vivian-and-john-lewis/. Vivian received the Presidential Medal of Freedom in 2013, two years after Lewis.

2. Carla D. Hayden, "Remembering John Lewis: The Power of 'Good Trouble,'" *Timeless: Stories from the Library of Congress* (blog), July 19, 2020 (1st q), https://blogs.loc.gov/loc/2020/07/remembering-john-lewis-the-power-of-good-trouble/; *NYT*, July 18 (2nd–9th, and 11th q), 19 (10th). For an especially poignant tribute to Lewis and his legacy, see Charlayne Hunter-Gault, *My People: Five Decades of Writing about Black Lives* (New York: Harper, 2022), 312–315. Many of Lewis's House colleagues offered moving eulogies in the days after his death. See *CR*, 116th Congress, vols. 127–136, July 20–31, 2020. On August 3, 2020, *Time* magazine published a special issue honoring Lewis.

3. *NYT*, July 21, 2020; *CR*, vol. 166, July 20–24, 27, 2020. During the two years following Lewis's death, his Democratic colleagues in the House continued to offer tributes to him, both on the House floor and in extended remarks placed in the *Congressional Record*. See *CR*, vol. 167, March 1, 8, 9, 12, 21, June 14, and August 10, 24, 2021; vol. 168, February 1, 17, 2022. There were also numerous material tributes to Lewis during this period. In November 2021, the Obama Foundation received a $100 million gift in Lewis's name from Jeff Bezos, the founder of Amazon. Under the terms of the gift, a plaza at the future Obama Presidential Center in Chicago would be named for Lewis, and programs would be established to recruit young leaders to carry on his legacy. Other tributes included a massive "good trouble" mural in Nashville and a wooden sculpture series titled "SEEINJUSTICE" (featuring three busts honoring Lewis and two victims of police violence, George Floyd and Breonna Taylor) that was installed in Union Square Park in Lower Manhattan in late September 2021, where it remained for a month. *NYT*, October 2, November 2, and November 22, 2021. On July 21, 2023, the United States Postal Service issued a commemorative stamp that "celebrated the life and legacy of civil

509

rights leader and congressman John Lewis (1940–2020), an American hero and key figure in some of the most pivotal moments of the Civil Rights Movement." At the stamp dedication ceremony held at Morehouse College, Lewis's former chief of staff Michael Collins noted: "As an avid collector, stamps were important to Congressman John Lewis who always made sure he purchased stamps on their first day of issue." about ups.com, July 21, 2023.

4. *NYT*, July 25, 26 (q), 2020. Following Lewis's death, the Lewis family created the John R. Lewis Legacy Institute, headquartered in Pike County, Alabama. Lewis's nephew Jerrick Lewis was named executive director of this family-centered foundation. In August 2022, the foundation convened a major celebration to honor Lewis with a historical marker placed at the site of his boyhood home. Part of the celebration was held at Troy University, which in 2021 had named one of its principal buildings John Robert Lewis Hall. See the John R. Lewis Legacy Institute homepage, https://www.johnrlewisinstitute.org. A second foundation, the John and Lillian Miles Lewis Foundation, was founded in Atlanta in 2020 by John Lewis, with the hope of sustaining his legacy of making "good trouble." Its board of directors included several prominent Atlanta business leaders and Lewis's chief of staff, Michael Collins. The foundation's inaugural gala and fund raiser was held in Washington, D.C., on May 17, 2022, the sixty-eighth anniversary of the *Brown v. Board of Education* school desegregation ruling. See the John and Lillian Miles Lewis Foundation homepage, https://www.johnandlillian mileslewisfoundation.org/.

5. *NYT*, July 27, 29 (q), 2020; *CR*, vol. 166, July 27–28, 2020.

6. *NYT*, July 30, 2020 (q).

7. *NYT*, July 21(q)–24, 2020.

8. Andrew E. Busch and John J. Pitney Jr., *Divided We Stand: The 2020 Elections and American Politics* (Lanham, MD: Rowman and Littlefield, 2022); Larry J. Sabato, Kyle Kondik, and J. Miles Coleman, eds., *A Return to Normalcy? The 2020 Election That (Almost) Broke America* (Lanham, MD: Rowman and Littlefield, 2021).

9. *NYT*, July 19 (q), 2020; Julian E. Zelizer, ed., *The Presidency of Donald J. Trump: A First Historical Assessment* (Princeton, NJ: Princeton University Press, 2022); Michael Wolff, *Landslide: The Final Days of the Trump Presidency* (New York: Henry Holt, 2021); Carol Leonnig and Philip Rucker, *I Alone Can Fix It: Donald J. Trump's Catastrophic Final Year* (New York: Penguin, 2021); Jonathan Karl, *Betrayal: The Final Act of the Trump Show* (New York: Dutton, 2021); Jeremy W. Peters, *Insurgency: How Republicans Lost Their Party and Got Everything They Ever Wanted* (New York: Dutton, 2021); Adam Schiff, *Midnight in Washington: How We Almost Lost Our Democracy and Still Could* (New York: Random House, 2021); Bob Woodward and Robert Costa, *Peril* (New York: Simon and Schuster, 2021); William Crotty, ed., *The Presidential Election of 2020: Donald Trump and the Crisis of Democracy* (Lanham, MD: Lexington Books, 2021).

10. John Lewis with Kabir Sehgal, *Carry On: Reflections for a New Generation* (New York: Grand Central, 2021), 203 (q); John Lewis int.; Bernard LaFayette int.

11. *NYT*, July 30, 2020 (q). Accompanied by the District of Columbia's mayor Muriel Bowser, Lewis visited the Black Lives Matter Plaza north of the White House on June 7, 20220, six weeks before his death.

NOTE ON SOURCES

The primary sources related to John Lewis's life are extensive, even though currently there is no organized collection of his personal papers available to researchers—no letters, diaries, or logs that might shed light on his daily activities, public or private. In the absence of personal papers, Lewis's published writings constitute the most important source of information on his life. I have relied heavily on his 1998 memoir, *Walking with the Wind: A Memoir of the Movement;* his 2017 book of essays, *Across That Bridge: A Vision for Change and the Future of America;* his 2021 posthumously published *Carry On: Reflections for a New Generation;* and the four volumes of his acclaimed graphic novel series, *March* (vols. 1–3, 2013–2016) and *Run* (vol. 1, 2021).

Beyond Lewis's writings, there are several memoirs that provide revealing information and reflections on his career as a civil rights activist. See especially Jim Peck, *Freedom Ride* (1962); James Forman, *The Making of Black Revolutionaries* (1972); Cleveland Sellers, *The River of No Return* (1973); James Farmer, *Lay Bare the Heart* (1985); Ralph Abernathy, *And the Walls Came Tumbling Down* (1989); Andrew Young, *An Easy Burden* (1996); Stokely Carmichael, *Ready for Revolution* (2003); Bob Zellner, *The Wrong Side of Murder Creek* (2008); Bernard LaFayette Jr. and Kathryn Lee Johnson, *In Peace and Freedom* (2013); Carol Ruth Silver, *Freedom Rider Diary* (2014); and Charles Person, *Buses Are a Comin'* (2021). See also Cheryl Lynn Greenberg, ed., *A Circle of Trust: Remembering SNCC* (1998).

There are also a number of archival collections that contain significant information on various aspects of Lewis's public life: the Centers of the Southern Struggle FBI files at the Birmingham Public Library; the A. Philip Randolph Collection at the Library of Congress; the Martin Luther King Jr. Papers, the Student Nonviolent Coordinating Committee Papers, and the Southern Christian Leadership Conference Records at the Martin Luther King Jr. Center for Nonviolent Social Change; the Martin Luther King Jr. Papers at the Mugar Memorial Library, Boston University; the Southern Regional Council Papers (microfilm); the Congress of Racial Equality Papers (microfilm); the Voter Education Project Organizational Records at the Robert W. Woodruff Library, Atlanta University Center; the U.S. Department of Justice, Civil Rights Division, Records at the U.S. National Archives; and the Robert F. Kennedy Papers at the John F. Kennedy Presidential Library.

In addition, Lewis-related materials in digital form are available online from the follow-ing sites: Duke University's Civil Rights Movement Archive at https://www.crmvet.org/about.htm; the SNCC Digital Gateway at https://snccdigital.org/; and the Civil Rights Digital Library (CRDL) at https://crdl.usg.edu/. The CRDL holdings are especially useful for tracking Lewis's activities during his years as chairman of SNCC (1963–1966), providing digitized documents from several dozen civil rights–related collections located in the Library and Archives of the Wisconsin Historical Society. Many of these collections can be accessed as part of CRDL's Freedom Summer Digital Collection.

Lewis's early career as an activist in Nashville is well documented in a wide range of materials held in the Civil Rights Collection at the Nashville Public Library; these materials include local press clippings from the *Nashville Tennessean* and *Nashville Banner*, documentary films, and interviews conducted with members of the Nashville Student Movement and the Nashville Christian Leadership Council.

Newspapers and magazines are another essential primary source of information on Lew-is's activities. He received extensive coverage in the national and regional press during the Freedom Rides, his SNCC years, and after he became a congressman—especially in the *New York Times*, the *Washington Post*, the *Atlanta Journal-Constitution*, and *Time* magazine. The Black press—notably the *Atlanta Daily World*, the *Chicago Defender*, the *Baltimore Afro-American*, and *Jet* and *Ebony* magazines—also closely followed Lewis after he became a public figure in the early 1960s, often offering a different perspective from the overwhelmingly white mainstream press. Also useful is Clayborne Carson, ed., *The Student Voice, 1960–1965: Periodical of the Stu-dent Nonviolent Coordinating Committee* (1990). Complementing these journalistic sources, the *Congressional Record* is an extremely valuable source of information on Lewis's congressional career, chronicling his participation in the daily activities of the House of Representatives from 1987 to 2020.

Beyond these written accounts, oral history testimony provides a wide range of informa-tion and perspectives on Lewis's life from childhood to old age. When a biographer cannot rely on personal papers, oral sources take on added importance, often revealing biographical and historical details unavailable anywhere else. Fortunately, over a span of five decades, Lewis participated in a number of lengthy interview sessions that explored the origins and evolution of his career as a civil rights activist. For my purposes as a Lewis biographer, the most useful of these interviews were Oral Histories of the American South: The Civil Rights Movement, University of North Carolina, Chapel Hill, interview by Jack Bass and Walter Devries, Novem-ber 20, 1973; Blackside Productions and Washington University, St. Louis, interview by Henry Johnson and Judy Richardson, 1979; *Worldnet Today*, United States Information Agency series, "Assessing the Gains: Congressman John Lewis, February 7, 1990"; History Makers, interview by Julieanna Richardson, April 25, 2001; John F. Kennedy Presidential Library, interview by Vicki Daitch, March 19, 2004; National Archives, "An Evening with John Lewis, June 6, 2013," interview by Scott Simon; and House of Representatives, "The Long Struggle for Represen-tation: Oral Histories of African Americans in Congress," interview by Matt Wasniewski, De-cember 11, 2014.

In addition to these institution-based Lewis interviews, this book draws on more than two hundred other interviews that I conducted over the past twenty-five years. The interviewees include Lewis himself; his close movement friends such as Bernard LaFayette, Diane Nash, Julian Bond, C. T. Vivian, James Lawson, Andrew Young, and Don Harris; former Freedom Riders, SNCC activists, and other movement colleagues who witnessed his development as a leader during the 1960s; journalists; public officials; members of his congressional staff; Lewis family members, including his son, John-Miles, and his brothers Henry, Samuel, and Eddie Lewis; and numerous others. The list of interviewees is too long to mention each by name here, but many of them are cited in the endnotes in both this book and *Freedom Riders*, and also thanked in the acknowledgments.

My interviews were conducted both by phone and in person; their length and character ranged from lengthy formal interview sessions to casual conversations; and in many cases the initial discussion of Lewis fostered a continuing relationship and additional conversations. Whatever their length or degree of formality, each interview and conversation enriched my understanding of Lewis and the movement. Most took place between 2000 and 2013, as research for my 2006 book *Freedom Riders* or in follow-up interviews following the book's publication and transformation into the 2011 PBS *American Experience* documentary *Freedom Riders*. More recently, I conducted a number of interviews expressly for use in my Lewis biography.

*   *   *

The secondary literature on Lewis, though substantial, is not as extensive as one might expect for a public figure of his prominence and longevity. While many monographs dealing with the civil rights movement of the 1960s touch on the major episodes of Lewis's early career—especially his role in the Nashville Student Movement, the Freedom Rides, SNCC, the March on Washington, Freedom Summer, and the Selma voting rights campaign—he has rarely been a subject of extended analysis. His career has received surprisingly little attention in scholarly journals, and the most notable article-length profiles of him appear elsewhere, either in popular magazines or journalistic anthologies. The most informative profiles include a chapter in the journalist John Egerton's 1970 book on progressive Southerners, *A Mind to Stay Here*; Sean Wilentz's 1996 *New Republic* essay "The Last Integrationist: John Lewis's American Odyssey"; Teresa Carpenter's essay in Caroline Kennedy's 2002 edited anthology *Profiles in Courage for Our Time*; and the August 3–10, 2020, issue of *Time* magazine, much of which is devoted to Lewis.

Also surprising is the dearth of books on Lewis's life. To date, other than a handful of children's and young adult books—see especially Ann Bausum, *Freedom Riders: John Lewis and Jim Zwerg on the Front Lines of the Civil Rights Movement* (2005) and Jim Haskins and Kathleen Benson, *John Lewis in the Lead* (2011)—only one book-length study of Lewis, Jon Meacham's *His Truth Is Marching On: John Lewis and the Power of Hope*, has been written. Published in 2020, five weeks after Lewis's death, this book represents a creditable and beautifully written effort to explore Lewis's contributions to the civil rights struggle. But Meacham chose to end his detailed narrative in 1968, well before the onset of Lewis's long political career. He covers the remainder of Lewis's life in a brief thirteen-page epilogue, which is unfortunate because other than contemporary commentary by journalists, there are very few extant secondary sources on the last fifty-two years of Lewis's life. His term as director of the Voter Education Project is discussed in Evan Faulkenbury, *Poll Power* (2019), and several other books mention his efforts to extend the Voting Rights Act. But the other parts of his post-1968 career—his work with the Field Foundation and the Southern Regional Council, as a federal official with the ACTION agency, as an Atlanta city councilman, and later as a seventeen-term congressman—have received negligible attention from historians.

The secondary literature on Lewis thus deals almost exclusively with his civil rights activism during the 1960s. His exploits as a Nashville Student Movement leader, Freedom Rider, and SNCC chairman during the March on Washington, Freedom Summer, and the Selma crisis are discussed in virtually all of the standard works on the modern civil rights struggle. Indeed, many historians have enlivened their narratives with stories of Lewis's courage, highlighting his role in several of the decade's most dramatic confrontations with Jim Crow. Though generally limited to a few sentences or paragraphs, carefully rendered treatments of Lewis can be found in a wide range of books. See especially Howard Zinn, *SNCC: The New Abolitionists* (1965); Pat Watters, *Down to Now* (1971); David J. Garrow, *Protest at Selma* (1978) and *Bearing the Cross* (1986); Milton Viorst, *Fire in the Streets* (1979); Clayborne Carson, *In Struggle* (1981); Harvard Sitkoff, *The Struggle for Black Equality* (1983); Taylor Branch, *Parting the Waters* (1988), *Pillar of Fire* (1998), and *At Canaan's Edge* (2006); Fred Powledge, *Free at Last?* (1991); David Halberstam, *The Children* (1998); J. Mills Thornton III, *Dividing Lines* (2002); David Chappell, *A Stone of Hope* (2004); Charles Marsh, *The Beloved Community* (2005); Raymond Arsenault, *Freedom Riders* (2006); Wesley C. Hogan, *Many Minds, One Heart* (2007); Derek Catsam, *Freedom's Main Line* (2008); Benjamin Houston, *The Nashville Way* (2012); William P. Jones, *The March on Washington* (2013); Robert A. Pratt, *Selma's Bloody Sunday* (2017); Thomas C. Holt, *The Movement* (2021); Kate Clifford Larson, *Walk with Me* (2021); Peniel E. Joseph, *The Third Reconstruction* (2022); and Mark Whitaker, *Saying It Loud* (2023).

Collectively, these and other secondary historical accounts confirm Lewis's status as one of the nonviolent movement's most important leaders, providing a starting point for deeper inquiry into his life story. It is my hope that the inclusion of a Lewis biography in the Black Lives series will encourage others to engage in such inquiry. Surely his remarkable life merits as much scholarly attention, critical analysis, and creative storytelling as the historical profession can muster.

ACKNOWLEDGMENTS

───────

Writing a biography of John Lewis has been a labor of love from start to finish. But it has also been a daunting challenge. How could I—or any other biographer—do full justice to Lewis's extraordinary life? I wanted to write a book that captured his unique set of gifts and accomplishments but that also avoided hagiography. I wanted to express my admiration for him while acknowledging his frailties and limitations. This is a difficult balance to strike, but fortunately I have not had to shoulder this burden alone. Over the past several years, many individuals have stepped up to offer me encouragement and advice as I dealt with the nuances and complexities of Lewis's eighty years of experience. There are many people to thank, too many to mention each of them by name. But I am grateful to all of them for their friendship, generosity, and uplifting collegial spirit.

I want to begin by thanking the editors of Yale University Press's Black Lives series—David Blight, Henry Louis Gates Jr., and Jacquelyn Goldsby—for inviting me to contribute a volume to this important new series. I feel privileged to be part of this effort to recognize the historical importance of a wide range of Black leaders in American and world history, and I hope that my contribution to this effort justifies the series editors' faith in me. Special thanks to David Blight, a good friend for more than thirty years, who took the lead in making my work a part of this series. I would also like to acknowledge the professionalism and patience of the Yale University Press staff—especially the expert editorial work of Seth Ditchik, Josh Panos, Amanda Gerstenfeld, and Joyce Ippolito, who oversaw the production of the book. At the copyediting stage, John Donohue and Ashley Moore of Westchester Publishing Services provided exceptional expertise that greatly improved the manuscript.

I also want to express my gratitude to Oxford University Press, the publisher of my 2006 book *Freedom Riders: 1961 and the Struggle for Racial Justice*. To a large extent, my biography of Lewis grew out of the many years that I devoted to the Freedom Rider saga. By facilitating my relationship with Lewis, and deepening my curiosity about his life, *Freedom Riders* paved the way for the creation of a volume in the Black Lives series; and I am also deeply appreciative that Oxford University Press has graciously permitted me to republish and adapt passages from *Freedom Riders* for use in chapters 3, 4, and 5 of this book. Special thanks to Oxford

ACKNOWLEDGMENTS

University Press editors Tim Bent, Nancy Toff, and Susan Ferber—and to Peter Ginna, my original editor at Oxford University Press, who remains a good friend and trusted adviser.

I also want to thank the editors and staff of Simon and Schuster, the publisher of my 2018 biography of Arthur Ashe, for their earlier publication of Lewis's 1998 memoir, *Walking with the Wind.* The captivating autobiography they helped to craft has become one of the essential works in the canon of civil rights literature, and without it I could not have given full voice to Lewis in my contribution to the Black Lives series.

As in the past, I have also relied heavily on my wonderful agent Wendy Strothman, who was always there when I needed her, encouraging and supporting me through the inevitable ups and downs of bringing this project to completion. Thanks also to her talented associate Lauren MacLeod. I am also deeply appreciative of the advice and legal counsel provided by Alison Steele, one of Florida's finest media law specialists.

Throughout my career, I have been able to draw on the talents and support of a wide circle of friends and colleagues. Some of these relationships go back to my days as a student at Princeton and Brandeis, or to my time on the faculty of the University of Minnesota; others began later, during my long tenure at the University of South Florida. But I greatly appreciate the generosity and wisdom that all of these individuals have displayed over the years. I am particularly grateful to Steve Whitfield, whose brilliant scholarship and consummate friendship are recognized by all who know him. Steve took time out of his hard-earned retirement from the American Studies program at Brandeis to read and critique the entire Lewis manuscript, offering indispensable sage advice on matters both intellectual and editorial. I can never repay his many kindnesses.

Several other friends provided timely and valuable help and encouragement during my work on this book. Special thanks to Paul and Eileen Arsenault, Reba Beeson, Susan Bellows, Peter Belmont, John Belohlavek, Susan and Peter Betzer, Frank and Leeanne Biafora, Jim Bledsoe, Blaine and Mardi Brownell, Granville Burgess, Vernon Burton, Rita Coburn, Jack Day, Charles Dew, Rebecca Falkenberry, Peter Golenbock, Wendy Grassi, David Greenberg, Jim Grossman, Ted and Nan Hammett, Jeff Harper, Mike Honey, Lois Horton, Jim Howell, Fred Hoxie, Jackie Hubbard, Allen and Bobbie Isaacman, Carolyn Johnston, Bob Devin Jones, CeCe Keeton, Richard King, Susan King, Kelly Kirschner, Jeff Klinkenberg, Laurie MacDonald, Erin Mauldin, Peter and Jeanne Meinke, Randall Miller, Gary and Lynne Mormino, Bridget Nickens, Marty Normile, Adrian O'Connor, John Ogden, David and Molly Raymond, Mimi Rice, Terri Lifsey Scott, Howard Simon, John David Smith, Thomas Smith, Mitchell and Liz Snay, Wendy Snyder, Jay Sokolovsky, Susan Steger, Ted Steger, Bill Stokes, Mills Thornton, Sudsy Tschiderer, Susan Turner, Jim Verhulst, Maria Vesperi, Sally Wallace, and Lee Whitfield.

A number of my former students also deserve thanks for their unflagging support and keen interest in the Lewis book. Thank you to Ellen Babb, Theresa Collington, Jack Davis, Woody Hanson, Lee Irby, Judy Jesiolowski, Peyton Jones, Monica and Jon Kile, Deelynn Rivinius, Melissa Seixas, David Shedden, David Starr, Jonathan Tallon, Chris Warren, and many others for continuing to be a part of my life and work after my retirement from teaching in December 2020.

I also relied on the generosity and knowledge of a number of librarians, archivists, and civil rights museum professionals. David Shedden, a former student who serves as the special collections librarian at the Nelson Poynter Memorial Library at the University of South

Florida, St. Petersburg, deserves special mention here, as do Dorothy Walker of the Freedom Rides Museum in Montgomery, Alabama; Meredith McDonough of the Alabama Department of Archives and History; and my longtime friend and colleague Jerry Eisterhold, one of the nation's premier civil rights museum designers. I would also like to thank executive director Terri Lipsey Scott and my fellow members of the board of directors of the Carter G. Woodson African American Museum of Florida for encouraging me—and for tolerating my absences from board meetings.

I could not have written this book without the cooperation of the large number of individuals who shared their perspective on and memories of Lewis. Over the past twenty-five years, my many conversations with these individuals have helped to shape my evolving understanding of Lewis's life and legacy. I am very grateful for the cooperation and support of Zev Aelony, Andrew Aydin, George Barrett, Ed Blankenheim, Julian Bond, Simeon Booker, Joan Browning, Lonnie Bunch, Catherine Burks-Brooks, Gordon Carey, Clayborne Carson, Kathy Castor, Lucretia Collins, Michael Collins, Benjamin Elton Cox, Glenda Gaither Davis, Jim Davis, Dion Diamond, Israel Dresner, Patricia Stephens Due, Leslie Dunbar, John Hope Franklin, Martin Freedman, Ted Gaffney, Tom Gaither, Laurens Grant, Reginald Green, Steve Green, Lawrence Guyot, Sheldon Hackney, Bill Harbour, Don Harris, James Horton, Lois Horton, Genevieve Hughes Houghton, George Houser, Larry Hunter, Pauline Knight, Bernard LaFayette, James Lawson, Fred Leonard, Joy Leonard, Freddie Lewis, Henry Grant Lewis, Jerrick Lewis, John-Miles Lewis, John Robert Lewis, Samuel Lewis, Kwame Leo Lillard, Mary Liuzzo Lilliboe, John Maguire, Salynn McCollum, John Moody, Joan Trumpauer Mulholland, David and Winonah Beamer Myers, Diane Nash, Stanley Nelson, Moses Newson, Claire O'Connor, Rip Patton, Charles Person, Kredelle Petway, Lauren Prestileo, Marvin Rich, John Seigenthaler, Terri Sewell, Fred Shuttlesworth, Carol Ruth Silver, Howard Simon, Bob and Helen Singleton, Hank Thomas, C. T. Vivian, Matthew Walker Jr., Angela Lewis Warren, Susan Wilbur, Randall Williams, Chantale Wong, Andrew Young, and Jim Zwerg.

Several of the individuals listed above provided critically important information during the final stages of my research. Special thanks to Andrew Aydin, the coauthor of Lewis's graphic novels *March* and *Run;* to Michael Collins, Lewis's chief of staff from 1999 to 2020; to Lewis's close friend and SNCC colleague Don Harris; to Lewis's photographer Chantale Wong; and to Henry "Grant" Lewis, his son Jerrick, and other members of the Lewis family who invited me to the August 2021 historical marker ceremony at the Lewis homestead in Pike County, Alabama. Meeting three of John Lewis's brothers, his son John-Miles, and several nieces and nephews gave me greater understanding of the family that nurtured his character, moral sensitivity, and courage. The Lewis family also graciously allowed me to include a family photo of eleven-year-old John Lewis in this book.

My most important oral source was Bernard LaFayette, Lewis's dear friend, onetime college roommate, and fellow champion of nonviolent direct action. I have known Bernard since 2001, when we met at a Freedom Rider symposium at Tulane University in New Orleans, and over the last two decades we have forged a treasured friendship that has provided me with a window through which I have gained invaluable information on Lewis and the civil rights movement. In scores of conversations in a wide variety of settings, Bernard has talked with me about virtually every aspect of his and Lewis's experiences over the course of a six-decade-long collaboration and friendship. When Lewis died unexpectedly in July 2020 and I was unable to follow through with my plan to conduct several additional interviews with him, Bernard agreed to fill in as many gaps as he could during a marathon interview at his home in Tuskegee. I will be eternally grateful to Bernard and his wife, Kate, for interrupting their busy lives to turn their attention to my lingering questions about Lewis and the movement. For this, for the uncommon decency and courage that has marked his life, and for all of the many kindnesses that he has shown me during our long friendship, I dedicate this book to him. As one of the world's most prominent advocates of nonviolence, the man once known as "Little Gandhi" richly deserves his own biography, which I hope this small gesture of dedication will help bring about.

I also owe a great debt to my loving family for being so generous and gracious in their efforts to boost my spirits and lend a hand in countless ways during the writing of this book. To my wife, Kathy; my daughters Amelia and Anne; my son-in-law Shawn; and my grandchildren Lincoln and Poppy, thank you for providing more love and support than I deserve. Mercifully for them, this is likely to be my last book. But whether it is or not, I have taken this opportunity to add the names of my two beloved grandchildren to the dedication page. For me, Lincoln and Poppy, with their bright smiles and even brighter hopes and dreams, represent the best of humanity, and I want to leave them with a close and meaningful connection to John Lewis and his legacy.

Other members of my family already have that connection, having met and talked with Lewis on several occasions, including during the taping of a memorable episode of *The Oprah Winfrey Show* in 2011. That day they witnessed the stunning act of compassion that Lewis tendered to a repentant former Klansman who had assaulted him in 1961, grabbing the man's hand and calling him "my brother." Who knows how many more ennobling acts of forgiveness and reconciliation will grace our common future, now that Lewis is no longer around to set an example. We can only hope that his legacy will persist and perhaps eventually bring us closer to the Beloved Community. It will, of course, be up to Lincoln and Poppy's generation, and the generations that follow, to continue the search for equity and justice that meant so much to Lewis—and to all those inspired by the nonviolent struggle that graced his life.

INDEX

199; "Letter from a Selma, Alabama, Jail" in, 226; on Lewis joining House of Representatives, 311; Lewis on extension of Voting Rights Act in, 373; Lewis's final essay published in, 454–455; on Lewis's superdelegate vote, 384; reports on Bloody Sunday in, 232, 233; on Rosa Parks, 366; on Selma-to-Montgomery march, 244; on Trump's treatment of immigrants, 431; *Walking with the Wind* as Notable Book of the Year, 491n18

New York Times Best Seller List, 405

New York Times Magazine, 147, 262

Niagara Falls, Lewis's visit to, 21

Nicaranguan civil war, Lewis's opposition to American involvement in, 319

Niebuhr, Reinhold, 41, 43, 463–464n9

Niven, David, 369

Nixon, Richard, 277; CBC and, 312; Farmer and, 353; King arrest and, 68, 69; Lewis on, 430; presidential election of 1960, 63, 64; reelection of, 284

Nkrumah, Kwame, 211

Nobel Peace Prize: awarded to King, 218; Lewis's reaction to Obama award of, 390–391

nonviolence: eulogies at slain civil rights workers' funerals and, 200–201; Freedom Rides and emphasis on, 87; King urging commitment to, 62; Lewis on problem of fear and deprivation as challenge to nonviolent struggle, 250; Lewis's commitment to, 224, 257; Lewis's speech at the March on Washington and principle of, 173–174; Montgomery Bus Boycott and Lewis's predisposition toward, 28; Nash's commitment to, 75; SNCC and challenges to, 142, 154–155, 239, 241; teaching Birmingham children the techniques of, 160

Nonviolent Action Group (NAG), 84

nonviolent activism: demonstrated by Freedom Riders, 137; Lawson's instruction in, 41; Lewis on decline of, 279–280; stand-ins and, 73

the North (United States), Lewis's childhood fascination with, 20–21

North Carolina A&T College, student sit-in, 50–51

Norton, Eleanor Holmes, 354, 484n16

Norvell, Aubrey James, 260

Norwood, Charles, 373

Nunn, Michelle, criticism of Lewis for supporting her, 408–409

Nunn, Sam, Lewis and, 408–409

Obama, Barack, 497n8; acknowledging debt to Lewis, 449; awarded Nobel Peace Prize, 390–391; awarding Lewis Presidential Medal of Freedom, 392–393; "Barack, the Magic Negro" song and, 499n20; birtherism and, 390, 415, 420; at commemoration of passage of Civil Rights Act, 409–410; dedication of National Museum of African American History and Culture and, 423–424; eulogy for Lewis, 451–453; eulogy for Pinckney, 417–418; Guantánamo Bay and, 413–414; inauguration of 2008, 388–389; keynote address at 2004 Democratic National Convention, 362–363; Lewis and 2008 presidential campaign of, 379–381; Lewis and election of, 8; Lewis and reelection of, 395–396; Lewis casting him as "savior," 390; Lewis's admiration for, 378–379; at NAACP convention, 374; pilgrimage to Selma, 379–380; presidential campaign of 2008, 383–388; racial identity of, 378; racially based resentment of, 409; racist attacks on, 389, 399; reaction among many whites to election of, 8; reception for Freedom Riders at White House, 372; relationship with Lewis,